Fundamentals of
Individual Appraisal

Fundamentals of Individual Appraisal

Assessment Techniques for Counselors

Bruce Shertzer
Purdue University

James D. Linden
Purdue University

Houghton Mifflin Company   Boston
Dallas   Geneva, Ill.   Hopewell, N.J.   Palo Alto   London

Library of Congress Catalog Card Number: 78-69542
ISBN: 0-395-26536-3

Contents

Preface

Fundamentals of Individual Appraisal has been written for use in courses variously entitled Techniques of Individual Appraisal, Individual Analysis, Educational Assessment, Educational Tests and Measurements, and Mental Measurement. Almost all institutions that train counselors require students to take such a course. Too frequently, however, the required course has been designed primarily for teachers, school administrators, curricular and supervisory personnel, and educational specialists other than counselors. Consequently, emphasis is placed on standardized achievement measures and the construction of classroom tests.

This book represents a departure from that emphasis. Its content treats all kinds of assessment measures, as well as the principles and appraisal techniques used by counselors. Part One outlines the historical background of individual appraisal. Part Two takes up the major technical considerations governing assessment. Parts Three and Four survey measurement devices in the cognitive and affective domains. Part Five presents a variety of nonstandardized appraisal tools, and Part Six closes the book by emphasizing the responsible use of test data and exploring future developments in the field. The interpretation and responsible use of ability, aptitude, interest, personality, and career-development measures are stressed.

Counselors make use of assessment data not only in counseling but also in a variety of relationships with teachers, parents, administrators, and others. Appropriate and responsible use of appraisal data in these situations would do much to reduce the criticisms currently leveled against tests and test practices. We note, and with considerable concern, that these criticisms have intensified in recent years. Despite this increased controversy, required course work in measurement for future counselors has declined.

We do not anticipate that this book alone will reverse that trend. Rather our hope is more modest. It is that the content of this book, directed toward representative coverage of assessment tools, practices, issues, and ethics, will equip counselors with the fundamentals necessary to engage in individual appraisal. Such an outcome could reduce the criticisms confronted by counselors; but more important, counselors will better serve their publics.

Seven specific objectives of the book are stated in Chapter One. Given these objectives, we have tried to present a balanced account of the major assessment measures used by counselors, and to provide a firm foundation for students who wish to pursue more advanced measurement courses or who would prefer to study on their own.

We gratefully acknowledge the help of many people in the preparation of this book: colleagues on whose research we have drawn, and students in a variety of courses who have responded to successive versions of the ideas in this book. Thanks are due Linda Layton, Gloria Brown, and Barbara Krause, who typed and retyped the manuscript. The special contribution of Kathryn Linden, who wrote Chapters 11, 12, 13, and 14, is particularly appreciated. Finally, Donald Biggs, Roger W. Cummings, and Donald Zytowski read, criticized, and offered suggestions for improving the text. Their help was invaluable in reducing error, closing gaps, and pruning overlap.

B. E. S.
J. D. L.

Fundamentals of
Individual Appraisal

Part *1*

Foundations of Individual Analysis

IN THIS SECTION, WE SHALL DISCUSS THE PRINCIPLES THAT WE BELIEVE to be essential in developing and maintaining effective assessment practices. We also shall present enough historical background to give the reader an accurate perspective on current appraisal procedures. The principles and purposes set forth in Chapter 1 establish the theme of the book. They are basic to the work of the counselor and are referred to repeatedly in subsequent chapters.

The foundations of individual analysis lie in a complex of social, economic, political, psychological, and educational factors and forces, both past and current. Understanding the history of assessment (Chapter 2) is essential to understanding current practices and future developments. It also helps explain the rationale underlying the principles given in Chapter 1. The reasons for basing a counseling practice on these principles emerge clearly from this historical perspective.

Chapter 1

Principles and Purposes of Assessment and Appraisal

What are the theme and objectives of this book?

What philosophy underlies individual appraisal?

What are the major purposes of appraisal?

What is the meaning of assessment, appraisal, and other terms?

What principles characterize the processes of individual appraisal?

Where can information about assessment devices be obtained?

THEME AND OBJECTIVES

This book has been written especially for counselors, both those in preparation and those in practice. It may be of value to professional educators and many helping professionals as well. We have sought to provide a body of knowledge that we believe to be central to the counselor's work of helping students, parents, teachers, administrators, and other professionals. Basic to any intervention by counselors is an understanding of an individual. Hypotheses about a person can be derived quickly and economically from assessment devices and appraisal techniques. Thus, assessment outcomes are the means that lead to such understanding.

Understanding, while necessary, is not all a counselor must do to assist most people. In one way or another, counselors and their clients need to make predictions about future behavior. Predictions emerge when the counselor has established an appropriate data base about a person. Assessment devices and techniques are the primary source of any data base. The power of a prediction is dependent on the relevance, the scope, and the precision of the data, which depend in turn on the counselor's ability to select appraisal devices and techniques and to interpret, to apply, and to communicate the understandings he or she derives from them.

Our objective is to promote counselors' knowledge of and skills in assessment and appraisal, enabling them to make an informed selection and a judicious use of appraisal tools. We believe that the ability to assess an individual is a basic skill required of all counselors regardless of the setting in which they practice. Accordingly, we hope:

1. to familiarize counselors with the major assessment tools and techniques, their purposes, make-up, strengths, and weaknesses by providing commentary on representative examples and suggesting references to other sources of information
2. to provide counselors with guidelines for selecting assessment measures and for applying, interpreting, and reporting assessment data
3. to present the minimal necessary technical considerations essential for informed selection and use of any measure of behavior
4. to help students acquire a perspective of assessment measures by presenting historical highlights of their development and use
5. to foster awareness among students of the technical, legal, ethical, and social issues associated with assessment practices
6. to acquaint students with current and possible future trends in measurement devices and practices
7. to encourage counselors to develop an understanding of the field of measurement, its contributions to their practice, its aspirations, and its problems

PHILOSOPHY
UNDERLYING APPRAISAL

A fundamental premise of appraisal is that individuals are alike in some ways and different in others. This premise was stated by Clyde Kluckhohn and his associates in these words: "Every man is, in certain respects, like all other men, like some other men, like no other man."[1] Each person is like all others, because all people belong to the same species. They have, therefore, similar biological endowments. Each person is similar to some other people, because he or she is a member of an organized and intergenerational group,

---

[1] Clyde Kluckhohn, Henry A. Murray, and David Schneider, *Personality in Nature, Society, and Culture* (New York: Knopf, 1964), p. 12.

or society, and so shares behavior with others in it. Each individual is like no other person, because each person is unique. If each person were only like all other people there would be no need for appraisal; if like no other person, appraisal would be impossible. The fact, however, that every individual is like some other people suggests why appraisal is necessary and useful.

The total complex of attitudes, abilities, and behavioral tendencies that make up a single personality is unique. Yet, most of the literature of human behavior is concerned with comparing individuals. Frequently, comparisons between individuals are made for such purposes as selecting candidates for a scholarship or a job. Similarly, in teaching and counseling, an individual's current performance is often compared with previous performances. But most comparisons are interpersonal.

A cardinal philosophical principle of American society is a belief in the worth and dignity of the individual. People everywhere proclaim a generalized acceptance of this principle, but many of these people are so entangled in the loves and hates stemming from particular ideologies and their own self-interest that they are unable to practice what they espouse. Appraisal practices must be consistent with this belief in the worth and dignity of the individual. This means, first, that the major purpose of appraisal is to help the individual, and second, that appraisal should be done with rather than to an individual. That is, an individual must consent to data collection and must be willingly and actively involved in the undertaking.

Another tenet of American democracy is that each person should develop his or her potential. Fullest development of the individual requires recognition of his or her essential individuality. Recognizing one's talents and individuality is accomplished by means of rational appraisal by oneself and others. Without question, the judgments required in appraising an individual's potential are complex in their composition, difficult to make, and filled with error. Error in appraisal can be reduced but never eliminated entirely; hence, no appraisal may ever be considered final or absolute.

Lee J. Cronbach has identified two philosophies of testing that emerge from different historical roots and foster different types of appraisal procedures and interpretation.[2] The *psychometric approach*, chiefly American in origin, obtains a numerical estimate of a single aspect of performance. It is based on Edward L. Thorndike's

---

[2] Lee J. Cronbach, *Essentials of Psychological Testing,* 3rd ed. (New York: Harper and Row, 1970), pp. 29–30.

dicta that, "If a thing exists, it exists in some amount," and, "If it exists in some amount, it can be measured." Individuals are considered to have the same traits, such as intelligence or mechanical dexterity, but in different amounts. The psychometric approach considers how much of a trait is present and looks at the relationship between and among traits.

The second approach, called *impressionistic,* seeks to develop a comprehensive picture of an individual by examining any cue by any available means. This approach, mainly German in origin, gives minimal consideration to how much of a characteristic is present, seeking instead to understand how and why the individual expresses his or her abilities, interests, and so on.

Both approaches have merit as well as shortcomings. The psychometric approach is definite and structured, while the impressionistic relies on observation, descriptive data, and self-report. Differences between the two approaches, according to Cronbach, may be found in the (1) definiteness of tasks employed, (2) control of response, (3) recording of basic data, (4) scoring, and (5) interpretation. Counselors commonly employ both approaches in their efforts to appraise, understand, and assist individuals.

Recently, there has been an increasing emphasis on the use by both teachers and counselors of impressionistic measures to assess the behavior of children in school. In Parts 5 and 6, we discuss this orientation, while in Parts 3 and 4 as well as sections of Part 6, we deal with aspects of the psychometric approach to assessment.

Classic *trait and factor counseling* was based on the extensive use of tests in the belief that human behavior can be measured and categorized by specific traits, such as abilities, interests, and personality characteristics. These characteristics, in turn, were thought to relate systematically to each other, thus forming families of traits known as *factors* of behaviors. Test data were used to help people understand their strengths and limitations, in accordance with their profile of measured traits and factors, and to make predictions of future behavior based on these factors.

This kind of counseling has been criticized for being mechanistic and impersonal. Client-centered counseling, which emerged during the 1950s, is thought to be a contrast to the trait and factor approach because it relies on impressionistic approaches to assessment, and it questions the use of structured tests to appraise individuals. Client-centered counseling has in turn been criticized for its failure to obtain a rigorous and objective data base about a person. Client-centered counselors can become too dependent on subjective impressions in assisting individuals. Many, if not most, counseling practitioners now effectively combine methodologies and concepts from both approaches.

While we support the emphasis placed on the individual in the client-centered orientation, we also believe that objective and systematic appraisal data are crucial to counseling. The application, interpretation, and use of such data in counseling increase rather than diminish the focus on the individual, his or her opportunities for decision-making and planning, and the counselor's efforts to help.

A consideration with both philosophical and legal aspects underlying appraisal is the right to privacy: the right to be left alone, to have one's papers, records, thoughts, and behavior exempt from the scrutiny of others. Invasion of privacy is the intrusion into or compulsory exposure of one's private affairs and/or papers. The essence of privacy is that an individual has the freedom to select the time and circumstances under which and, most importantly, the extent to which, his or her attitudes, beliefs, behavior, and opinions are to be shared with or withheld from others. Appraisal practices consistent with the right of privacy require that the individual give informed consent to the use of assessment tools and uphold the right of the person to know what information about him or her exists, the right to have access to this information, and the right to challenge its accuracy. Obviously, counselors are obliged to maintain the confidentiality of all information entrusted to them and to provide sufficient security. Adherence to privacy and confidentiality can do much to insure that appraisal data are employed to the advantage of the individual.

PURPOSES OF APPRAISAL

Appraisal of an individual is undertaken for two purposes. First, information is collected to gain an understanding of a person in order to provide assistance. We do not mean to suggest that an individual is a "case" that must be solved. Collecting and appraising the best obtainable information in a systematic manner need not require a cold, aloof, "professional" attitude. A client is a warm, flesh-and-blood person, a complex pattern of hopes and enthusiasms, strengths, fears, inconsistencies, repressions, and weaknesses. Appraisal is necessary if the counselor is to select those procedures and practices out of a variety available that will best benefit an individual.

One purpose of engaging in appraisal, then, is to understand a person; but even more important, it is necessary to foster an individual's understanding of himself or herself. Individuals who understand themselves can engage in realistic planning and problem-solving, leading to better decision-making. Leo Goldman states:

> In most of the uses of tests, *information* is collected for the purpose of improving the nature of decisions, plans and adjustments. This is as true of the decisions regarding a pupil's grade placement as it is of the decision regarding an adolescent's vocational plans. There is always an assumption, whether stated or not, that the test results provide information which is *valid* for the action in question.[3]

GENERAL PURPOSES

The general reasons for which tests are given have been described in detail by Lee Cronbach.[4] The four purposes he explains in detail can be summarized as:

1. *Prediction.* Tests are given to obtain a measure of ability, achievement, and/or other characteristics that provide a solid basis on which predictions can be made as to what individuals will do at a later time. Prediction based on quantitative data is more likely to be reliable and accurate and provide a balance against wishful thinking than prediction based on clinical observation or subjective judgment.
2. *Selection.* Tests are used by institutions and organizations (such as colleges or employers) in accepting some individuals and rejecting others. The decision to hire or admit an applicant is a selection decision.
3. *Classification.* Classification is an arrangement according to a systematic division into categories or groups. Classification involves deciding which treatment to use or to which group a person should be assigned. Examples of classification include diagnosing emotionally disturbed patients, choosing a school or college curriculum, or assigning a person to a military occupational specialty. Placement should not be confused with classification. *Placement* tests (used in assigning individuals to different levels of work within a type of work) differ from classification tests (used in assigning people to different types

---

[3] Leo Goldman, *Using Tests in Counseling,* 2nd ed. (New York: Appleton-Century-Crofts, 1969), p. 17.
[4] Cronbach, *Essentials of Testing.*

of work) in terms of the kind of validity data available and in terms of providing individualized descriptions.
4. *Evaluation.* Tests are used to assess and to evaluate programs, methods, treatments, and so on.[5]

The specific purposes for which appraisal data are used may be seen more clearly by considering separately their use by teachers, administrators, and counselors. It should be noted, however, that overlap is to be expected.

TEACHERS' USE OF DATA

Teachers, like counselors, use appraisal data to gain an understanding of students, especially behaviors associated with learning. They use both test and non-test data to determine the relationships among ability, educational practices, and changes in pupil behavior to better predict and control teaching and learning. Some time ago, Henry Chauncy and John E. Dobbin summarized concisely the particular uses of data by teachers. They stated that appraisal data, particularly testing data, were used to judge capacity to learn, to guide teaching, to check learning progress, to discover learning difficulties, to improve teaching techniques, and to assess teaching effectiveness.[6]

ADMINISTRATORS' USE OF DATA

The central purpose of educational administration is to provide conditions that facilitate the learning process. Appraisal data are useful, therefore, in determining how well an educational program is functioning. Administrators can use data in making decisions about overall educational planning, in determining an instructional program's strengths and weaknesses, in making decisions about grouping students for instructional purposes, in identifying areas in which supervision is needed, and in determining how well a school achieves its objectives.

---

[5] Cronbach, *Essentials of Testing,* pp. 22–24.
[6] Henry Chauncy and John E. Dobbin, *Testing: Its Place in Education Today* (New York: Harper and Row, 1963), pp. 82–107.

COUNSELORS' USE OF DATA

Among the several skills demanded of counselors is that they be sophisticated in the general field of measurement and understand thoroughly the strengths and weaknesses of the appraisal data collected and used most frequently in their work. A counselor well versed in test theory and practice can use test scores to support the clinical aspects of his or her work.

Counselors engage continuously in individual appraisal in their relationships with individuals. Their reasons for studying an individual may change as counseling proceeds. For example, a student who is referred to a high school counselor because of vocational indecision may at first need special information about educational and vocational opportunities or about the availability of financial aid, assistance with a problem of home adjustment, tutoring in social skills, or help in solving any of the many problems that adolescents experience. Although the kind and quantity of data needed to help each counselee will vary from situation to situation, certain basic information must be collected in addition to that suggested by the counselee's presenting problem or the information submitted from the source of referral. Some information, such as age, is required largely for legal purposes and does not substantially increase the counselor's knowledge of his or her client. Other appraisal data are fundamental to gaining an understanding of the client. Examples are:

1. evidence about an individual's usual behavior and significant variations from it (his or her personality); this includes values, interests, habitual methods of solving personal problems, and patterns of relating to others
2. information about a counselee's environmental background and experiences
3. information about a counselee's physical health and health history
4. history of an individual's educational and work experiences
5. performance on tests designed to assess achievement, ability, and so on
6. records of academic performance and education levels

These data are the minimum required in extending counseling to an individual. They frequently require supplementation, but rarely can they be diminished.

Goldman has pointed out that, "Although a perfect separation of counseling and other uses of tests . . . is not possible, one characteristic distinguishes the counseling uses of tests: in counseling an individual is under study, and *his* (or *her*) values, goals, and decisions are the beginning and ending points of this process."[7] The use of data most appropriate to the counselor's work may be outlined as follows:

1. Counselors use test and other data to estimate each counselee's abilities, aptitudes, interests, and personal characteristics in order to help the counselee gain self-understanding. Some time ago, James Lister and Merle Ohlsen, investigating the extent to which test interpretation improved the self-understanding of pupils in grades 5, 7, 9, and 11, reported that at all grade levels, interpretation was associated with increasing accuracy of self-estimates of achievement, intelligence, and interests.[8]

By securing test and other data on a counselee's characteristics, a counselor can provide descriptive statements about the person's behavior useful to both counselor and client in planning and decision-making. Objective comparisons of the individual's characteristics appraised across time and matched with the performance of others can contribute to self-understanding and improved decision-making by both counselor and counselee. Sections of Parts 3, 4, and 5 of this book discuss this process.

2. Counselors use data to help predict future performance at college, at work, and so on. Test data in particular provide a good basis for predicting success in those activities in which prospective performance can be estimated. (See especially Chapters 4 and 15.)

3. Counselors use appraisal data to assist in educational and vocational planning. As counselors work with clients on such matters as selecting a curriculum, selecting courses within a curriculum, planning further education, and making career decisions and plans, data that reflect the client's aptitudes, achievement, interests, and personal characteristics are identified and brought into consideration. When a high school student is facing a difficult problem of vocational choice or planning, he or she may reach a better decision by examining psychological test data that provide some basis for assessing and appraising his or her potential in relation to the requirements of an occupation. Such data may furnish information

---

[7] Goldman, *Using Tests*, p. 1.
[8] James L. Lister and Merle M. Ohlsen, "The Improvement of Self-Understanding Through Test Interpretation," *Personnel and Guidance Journal* 43 (April 1965): 804–810.

regarding limitations of ability, unknown assets, or inappropriate interests or aptitudes, the knowledge of which is useful and relevant to counseling. The counselor can interpret such information to help the counselee develop insight into his or her assets and liabilities regarding various educational and vocational ventures. Chapter 9 deals specifically with these considerations, although other chapters contribute as well.

4.   Counselors use appraisal data to diagnose student problems. Such problems as reading disabilities, study skill deficits, or difficulty in relating to other people may be identified more precisely and solutions determined with the use of test data. Accurate diagnosis involves understanding not only the indications of maladjustment but also the probable underlying factors related to the maladjustment. Chapter 7 elaborates on this topic.

5.   Counselors use data in evaluating the outcome of counseling. In attempting to assess the worth of counseling programs, many counselors have turned to test and non-test data. The usual approach to such efforts involves data collection before and after counseling with the use of appropriate control groups. Psychological test measures that have been employed include tests in the areas of achievement, interests, social and emotional adjustment, and social attitudes. Chapter 15 and Appendixes B and E are useful in this process.

THE MEANING
OF ASSESSMENT AND APPRAISAL

Counselors work intimately with individuals. In doing so, they bring particularized knowledge derived from observations, interviews, records, and tests to bear on an individual's questions, choices, or dilemmas. A fundamental skill of counselors, then, is appraising human behavior. Measures of behavior are collected, collated, and interpreted to the individual so that he or she can solve problems, determine goals, or resolve conflicts. Appraisal is all too frequently conceived of in a very limited sense, that of telling what someone is like from test scores. It is better viewed as a process of arriving at a systematic understanding of an individual's characteristics and situation within the context of his or her life pattern.

Appraisal involves collecting, organizing, and interpreting data. These are fundamental skills demanded in counseling. They involve the ability to interpret information accurately. They might be called skills of analysis and skills of synthesis. For example, a good deal must be known about rating scales before one is able to interpret an individual's ratings. Interpreting the place and significance of such information in the total pattern of data requires skills and insights of a higher order—that of diagnosis and integration. A whole body of skills and technical knowledge is essential for the correct interpretation of test data, whereas a different set of understandings is essential for an interpretation of information from interview sources.

We have used the terms *analysis, measurement, evaluation, assessment, appraisal,* and *interpretation.* Here are the meanings of the terms.

INDIVIDUAL ANALYSIS

This term refers to the process of observing, studying, and interpreting the behavior of an individual. Behaviors are viewed separately as component parts or elements that form a functioning whole. Frequently, use of the term specifically suggests an intent to discover or uncover qualities, causes, effects, motives, or possibilities as a basis for action, judgment, or decision-making. An analysis of an individual is a description of his or her behavior, usually with emphasis on his or her assets and liabilities.

MEASUREMENT

In common usage, *measurement* is the act or process of determining the extent or the dimensions of an object, attribute, or trait. A measure estimates how much of something an individual displays or possesses. The fundamental question it responds to is: "What is the amount of that something?" An exact and quantitative number is assigned to an object—such as 4 pounds, 1 mile, 44 words per minute—according to a standard or set of rules established for representing the amount of an attribute possessed by that object. Dale P. Scannell and D. B. Tracy point out that when an attribute cannot be measured directly but must be inferred from outward behavior or performance, the measurement is *indirect.*[9] Virtually all educa-

---

[9] Dale P. Scannell and D. B. Tracy, *Testing and Measurement in the Classroom* (Boston: Houghton Mifflin, 1975), p. 14.

14

school counselor may make observations on the
haviors of certain fifth-graders for the purpose
dents in different counseling groups. The ob
classified as assessment, and yet they may f
process. Assessment tools include obs
tests, and non-test techniques of c
individuals.

Appraisal is used interch
ation. Appraising, ther
the presence and ex
also calls for a ju

Interpr
beha
th

acceptable

ASSESSMENT

Assessment refers to the procedures and processes employed in
collecting information about or evidence of human behavior. The
measure of certain dimensions or characteristics of human beings
is obtained through assessment instruments such as educational
and psychological tests and inventories. The preferred practice in
education and psychology is to use the term *assessment* to refer to
methods and measures employed to determine an individual's
status or behavior, and the terms *appraisal* or *evaluation* when
making value judgments concerning goodness or usefulness about
a person's behavior. While the preferred use of the two terms expresses a good intention, it is difficult to carry out completely in
practice, because a program of assessment is often related to a total
appraisal process that involves a value judgment. For example, a

characteristic be-
of placing the stu-
servations should be
rm part of the appraisal
rvations, interview data,
llecting information about

PPRAISAL

angeably with or as a synonym for *evalu-*
fore, is not merely the practice of measuring
tent of human attributes or characteristics; it
gment of their strength, desirability, or utility.

INTERPRETATION

etation refers to explaining the meaning or usefulness of
vioral data. It may consist of explaining the circumstances or
context that gives meaning to such data or describing possibil-
ties that seem warranted and the probabilities associated with each
possibility. Interpreting an IQ (Intelligence Quotient) score, for example, involves clarifying the meaning of the score, representing
the inferences drawn about behavior by this measure of ability, and
conceptualizing and translating its implications for current or future endeavors.

PRINCIPLES OF APPRAISAL

A *principle* is usually defined as a basic truth, law, or assumption.
Here are some principles that describe the nature of appraisal, its
characteristics, and the boundaries of the field. These sixteen principles provide an overview of standards of counselor practice that
we shall refer to in subsequent chapters. The substance of these
principles is the theme of Chapter 15, Responsible Use of Data, and
Chapter 16, Trends in Assessment and Appraisal. Essentially, these
principles summarize the book's major topic: responsible counselor
selection and use of appraisal tools and techniques for the benefit
of the individual.

1. *Appraisal is the systematic process of arriving at an accurate understanding of an individual within the context of his or her life pattern.* The individual's characteristics, abilities, personality needs, goals, and ways of behaving are the object of appraisal. Appraisal involves understanding a dynamic (changing) personality; therefore, it is best viewed as an understanding of the person at a given moment. To aim for complete understanding of an individual is both futile and foolish. Rather, appraisal is viewed best as the development of an accurate working understanding of a person.

Human characteristics are dynamic in varying degree and should not be assumed without verification to be constant. In many ways, an appraisal of an individual may be likened to a series of snapshots of a person. Many such snapshots are needed to be sure of consistency.

Any fact about an individual—a test score, a course grade, a statement about himself or herself—must be interpreted within the context of all other available information about the person. A test score may be a fact, but its meaning depends on a variety of supporting and contradictory information regarding other facets of the same person.

2. *In any appraisal, three major aspects of behavior must be considered singly and in relation to each other: capacity, motivation, and control of expression.* In a simple analogy, *capacity* might be likened to the size and shape of the nozzle on a lawn hose, *motivation* to the force and constancy of the pressure behind the water, and *control* to the skill and steadiness of the person who holds the hose. The physical and psychological capacity of an individual can be measured with some explicitness. A fair estimate can be made of emotional control and of the presence of conflict that might affect efficient use of capacity. But measuring the magnitude and strength of the motivations involved can be little more than a guess. Yet, in a practical sense, an estimate of one aspect of behavior is meaningless without knowledge of the other two.

3. *Two kinds of data are used in almost every appraisal: information that derives its meaning from comparing the individual with others (normative data) and information the meaning of which lies within that person's life pattern (idiographic or individualized information).* An individual's scores on the *Strong-Campbell Interest Inventory*, for example, are of significance only when his or her pattern of interests is compared with the pattern of interests of people in each of certain occupations or other appropriate reference groups. This is a *normative* datum. On the other

hand, the information about an individual's social pattern—working in a gas station, participating in school athletics, living in an apartment with two other people—must be assessed within the pattern of the individual's life. What other people have done or might do in these activities is of little importance here, because an individual's organization of these experiences is unique to that person. The meaning of these items of information about a person must be seen within the boundaries of that individual's own life. Neither kind of information, the objectively interpreted or the subjectively interpreted, is inherently superior to the other. Both are useful in appraising an individual's behavior.

4. *Selecting assessment measures and procedures to be used in appraisal is based on the client's situation, the appraisal skills of the professional, and the demands of the situation.* There is no single best appraisal method or procedure to be recommended universally. Numerous assessment tools and procedures are available, and the situation surrounding the appraisal must determine which procedures are used. The *law of parsimony,* which calls for collecting the most obvious and the most elementary data first, should be observed in appraisal. While the law of parsimony may seem to conflict with the notion of multiple causation of behavior, they actually are complementary. This principle merely states that obvious and easily available data should be collected and examined first. For example, data about an individual's physical condition should be obtained before more complex personality data. If a student complains of lethargy or exhibits a "don't care" attitude toward school work, a counselor ought to collect and examine data about his or her physical health before spending great amounts of time collecting data regarding possible emotional conflict or frustrated motivations. If a student's grades are low, a counselor must first consider his or her scholastic ability. But he or she should not stop there. Doubtless other factors are present that have arisen out of the major or first cause and that contribute equally. Most major causes of behavior have supporting factors that also influence an individual's behavior.

5. *Inductive and deductive methods of reasoning are used reciprocally in the appraisal process.* Perhaps the only reason for stating this principle is that it is often overlooked or ignored, breaking the law of parsimony. A professional may gather evidence before drawing conclusions about an individual's behavior. Conversely, he or she may propose a hypothesis and then collect information that relates to it. Support for the hypothesis helps explain the person's

behavior. Or, in appraising a given kind of information, one can refer to an already demonstrated principle or relationship—the positive relationship between measures of intellectual ability and scholastic achievement, for example. Of course, it is necessary to look at other factors besides that of inferred capacity, which assumes a perfect relationship between ability and achievement. Other data must be gathered and used inductively. This practice keeps the counselor from making incomplete or inappropriate use of data because of inflexibility of approach toward interpretation. It is easy to fall into an unfortunate habit of overemphasizing normative data, forgetting that intra-individual differences and characteristics are always necessary in making up a psychological profile.

6. *Any information about an individual that contributes to understanding his or her behavior must be given consideration.* No evidence of competence, skill, talent, weakness, limitation, or idiosyncracy can be ignored or overlooked, wherever and whenever it appears. The value of data is not linked necessarily to their proportion or frequency of appearance in society. All too often, frequency of occurrence has been used as the criterion for including information about an individual in describing his or her functioning in school or at home, or his or her emotional well-being. Recognizing that unique or very special motives, characteristics, or factors operate in the life of an individual may lead to success in helping that person.

For example, Margaret was the only girl in school who always wore loose coveralls. She did this not because she had no other clothes but because she was sensitive about certain pubescent changes in the shape of her body. Charles, a brilliant student, received a *C* in physics because he spent all his spare time building a rocket and never completed his assignments. These examples of the influence of special conditions and situations on behavior are frequently ignored when helping professionals rely on data collected by group procedures and when they fail to realize that any datum about an individual that assists in understanding his or her behavior cannot be ignored.

7. *Any personality attribute, or any information about such an attribute, can be understood only in relation to the personality as a dynamic whole.* No matter how reliable the datum or how accurate the measurement, its importance and meaning are apparent only when it is understood as a part of a functioning whole—a person. The individual is the reality, and no fact is more important than the fact of his or her existence. Visualizing a flesh-and-blood

person from a body of data is the task of appraisal. Appraisers must use data that describe parts of an individual in relation to the whole, though such parts rarely add up to the whole. Of necessity, gaps must be filled through the use of clinical observation and professional judgment. Systematic appraisal makes use of each item of information, estimates its reliability (accuracy), determines its significance and context, and draws conclusions regarding the meaning of the behavior of the person being evaluated. Judgments regarding the whole put flesh on the skeleton of the bare facts and help to arrive at a better understanding of the behavior being appraised.

8. *Appraisal is based on a pattern of information and not drawn from a single datum, no matter how striking.* A fundamental principle of appraisal is that it is based on a pattern of information. For example, limited academic preparation may be one reason for experiencing difficulty in school, but it is seldom the sole factor. Behind poor study habits may lie attitudes and reasons that require careful consideration and analysis. An adequate pattern of information about an individual is as close an approximation to a picture of a total individual as it is possible to obtain. Assistance is required by the total functioning person, not by any limited aspect of that person's life, such as his or her intellectual life or social relationships. True, an individual's academic performance may be the immediate concern, but this performance is affected by social adjustment, self-confidence, health, and intellectual ability. A single datum, while considered by necessity (see principle 6), is therefore relatively useless unless it is viewed in relation to all other available information. It, in turn, contributes to the meaning of that information. The datum, "The father died when the student was twelve years old," is meaningful only when the student's school progress, social adjustment, and health at that time, earlier, and later are examined.

9. *An individual's environment must be taken into account.* An appraisal is made of the person-in-situation, never just the person. Social scientists, particularly sociologists, have pointed out that social mores may exercise tyrannical influence over a person and determine, within limits that are seldom passed, the possibilities of action. Counselors sometimes act as though an individual can be understood simply through personal analysis. But understanding is always the product of an analysis of the person's environment as well. The pressures and demands of both the larger social culture and those of the immediate environment of home, friends, school, and town must be understood in relation to the individual. The failure to consider the culture in which the individual functions

may lead to appraisals of behavior based on simple, direct relationships, which, while tempting in their seeming clarity, are inadequate in illuminating behavior. The counselor who takes the environment of the individual into account will not, for example, be satisfied with simple statements such as those that attribute certain kinds of behavior only to the presence of certain physical characteristics. Rather, the counselor will want to know the conditions under which the behavior appeared.

However, as we shall see, the instruments for obtaining data about environmental factors are few, and none is outstanding. Consider the difficulty, for example, of getting a good measure of a student's home environment or the psychological adequacy of a classroom. If the person-in-situation is to be studied, better tools must be developed. This suggests that relevancy in appraisal has to be observed. For all of the many factors in the individual and environment, only those that pertain to the immediate problems or needs of the individual ought to be considered.

10. *Acute episodes in the life of an individual may be less significant than continuing trends.* Counselors unskilled in appraising behavior often magnify some striking act in the life of an individual—an unusual breach of the social code, an act of rudeness, a stupid answer to a question, an incomprehensible act. Such episodes may be the result of a short-term condition or a disturbing experience that has resulted in temporarily uncontrolled or preoccupied behavior. The effect of such an episode on later behavior depends on its meaning to that person, not its significance to others. Such behavior must also be considered episodic and without much significance unless it is viewed as consistent with a pattern of behavior over a longer time.

11. *Longitudinal data should be considered in any appraisal of an individual.* The life of a person is, and should be viewed as, a single connected whole. Events that precipitate appraisal of an individual must be placed in context and sequence. This principle suggests that, in reality, there is no sudden delinquency of the model child, no sudden failure or success, no sudden emotional breakdown, no sudden attainment of readiness, and perhaps not even sudden insight. All such seemingly sudden changes have seriation and chronological order. Though this order may be difficult to draw out, it must be identified if there is to be real understanding of current behavior and accurate prediction of future activity.

Longitudinal data collected on a person over a period of time may have validity, reliability, and meaning unmatched by merely current data. Longitudinal data collections have never been popular or plentiful because they demand time, effort, and money. Many case materials contain longitudinal data, but they frequently are incomplete and are collected after the fact. Often, intentional or unconscious bias and faulty memory reduce their validity.

Study of an individual's development over a long period of time frequently reveals that current modes of behavior may be stimulated by past events. Indeed, some psychologists argue that all stimuli might be found in the individual's past if sufficient data were available. Even though an individual's current behavior appears to be related primarily to a current circumstance, it is unlikely that any reaction or response to a situation can be divorced completely from experiences in situations that have preceded it. It must also be acknowledged that, as one goes further back into a person's past, some data lose their efficiency in forecasting behavior. However, the omission of any event in the life history of an individual may result in the failure to evaluate certain factors that could explain his or her behavior.

Some counselors assert that there is no reason to study the past because it seems obvious that an individual's problems arise from inappropriate handling of a current situation. For example, a student's problem is caused by a sudden personality clash with a particular teacher. That explanation overlooks the fact that the student may have met similar personalities before and may meet them again. Thus, the simple remedy of removing the student from that teacher's classroom may not be an effective means of preparing the student for later meetings with other teachers, supervisors, employers, or even a marriage partner.

The influence of the individual's comparison of present to previous performances and the expectation for performance that these comparisons arouse cannot be ignored at any stage in the appraisal process. The very fact of consistency of performance (or the lack of it) may be as important as the complete description of any single event, for the discovery of cyclic behavior may predict the next action if the current position in the cycle can be determined accurately. Any explanation of that discovery should note that specific environmental forces may exert differential effects on the developing individual.

We believe that counselors would do well to refrain from aligning themselves with any school of thought that asserts that certain stages of growth are more vital than others in determining behavior. Few who have observed changes in behavior patterns during adolescence would assert that patterns are always set permanently in early infancy. Any change in behavior during adulthood suggests that adolescent trends may vary significantly as growth proceeds.

Old dogs do learn new tricks. But even when marked changes do occur, it is more likely that the performance of an individual will be understood better and better predictions of future behavior will be made if the counselor obtains longitudinal data rather than relying completely on current information.

12. *Any information about an individual that is to be used in appraisal must be assessed accurately, fully, and economically.* The multiplicity of assessment instruments and procedures used in appraisal and the wide variations that exist in their dependability and cost require that this principle be employed. If all measurements, all descriptions, all appraisals of individuals or situations were wholly valid and reliable, or if the use of several techniques of appraisal required the same expenditure of time, money, and effort, this principle would not be needed. Unfortunately, this is not the case. Many appraisals are uneconomical because those who conduct them stop short of what might be accomplished if slightly more effort were spent to bring them to fruition. Fragmentary data about individuals limit the usefulness of many appraisal efforts. Although testing may seem to be the most accurate and economical way of collecting data, because large groups can be tested simultaneously, the procedure can be very expensive when it results, as it frequently does, in the accumulation of large masses of unused and uninterpreted data.

Though we shall discuss this principle more fully in the study of specific instruments, we want to point out here that, to a greater or lesser degree, all instruments measure inaccurately and that the extent of error must be determined and considered when interpreting data. Predictions of a person's performance must be stated in terms of probability, and some estimate of the likelihood of continued occurrence or change must be made. The accuracy of measurement and the probability of successful prediction depend on the acuity of instruments, the length of time available to obtain data, and the appraiser's skill in their use. The counselor who has realized the complexity of the human being and the fallibility of instruments is properly modest when making predictions of human performance. Those whose work depends on appraisal must be aware of these limitations. In that awareness lies not only the hope of improving appraisal procedures but also the reawareness of the dignity of the individual being evaluated.

13. *An individual's behavior must be considered consistent and understandable in terms of his or her motives and values.* People tend to consider a person's behavior inconsistent when he or she does not behave as others believe he or she ought to. Such behavior

is inconsistent from the observer's point of view, not from that of the individual. In appraisal, the professional must search for cues to purposes and motives, perhaps reflected through a study of previous experiences, that will make an individual's behavior appear consistent. A person's life as a whole, including all forms of behavior that may seem odd to the observer, is consistent, and the purpose of those who appraise it is to find the motives and mechanisms that make it so.

To understand a person, one must see that individual in his or her personal frame of reference, in his or her world that is composed of the self and all in the world that is related to the person. Appraisal rests on comprehending the *phenomenal field* of the individual, the individual's personal universe, including self-concept at the time of action. While the appraiser can never fully enter this phenomenal field, it can be reconstructed, within limits, by observing the individual's behavior. This field is reality for the individual and it must become so for the appraiser.

14. *It is as essential in appraisal to understand subtleties and the implicit in behavior as it is to assess correctly the objective and the obvious.* This principle suggests a function that is difficult to communicate easily. Those responsible for the training of teachers, counselors, psychologists, special education specialists, and social workers run headlong into the problem of transmitting to others what they have absorbed as a fact of life. To put it succinctly, there is no substitute for the use of the senses and experience.

The evidence gathered by the counselor's eyes and ears can be secured in no other way. The clinical signs that form so invaluable a supplement to recorded data can be ascertained only in observing an individual. Cues from facial expressions, mannerisms, tone of voice, hesitations, and responses to questions or other stimuli, and the impressions gained of the total person, are perceived only by careful, systematic observation.

Recognizing subtleties is a major step toward reconciling the whole approach to partial approaches to psychological understanding. When objective data and clinical cues are related to each other, there emerges the first vague outline of the whole person. Then enters the third element: the counselor's experience with others. Comparing characteristics of the individual being appraised to those of other known personalities adds flesh to the skeleton of recorded specifics.

15. *Conceptualization of an individual must be continuous as each separately evaluated datum is added to the study of the person.* The counselor begins to get a sense of what an individual

is like at the first contact with the person or data about him or her. Hypotheses about the individual's strengths and weaknesses emerge. Patterns in the counselor's thoughts and actions come into prominence, and, although they may appear later to have been entirely false initial impressions, they provide preliminary concepts about the individual and suggest areas for exploration. This principle suggests that one danger lies in too early generalization about a person and another danger lies in the possibility that action may be delayed too long in the search for more data. The possibility of error exists in either alternative.

As more data are collected, preliminary conceptualizations of the individual tend to be confirmed or rejected or remain uncertain. All conceptualizations of the individual should be viewed as tentative estimates, if for no other reasons than the limited validity of assessment instruments and the immense complexity of human behavior. The major point here is that in very few cases is conceptualization of the individual so complete that what is to be undertaken is seen clearly by the counselor. For example, in most evaluations of emotional components of behavior, preliminary conceptualizations of cause-and-effect relationships seldom are sufficient for later actions or treatment.

Refinements in conceptualizing the individual as more data are secured enable a counselor to take effective action. There are pitfalls in each step of the process of organizing data about, and conceptualizing, the individual. One of the most difficult to overcome is that of bias in point of view. Success with one procedure too often leads to its use in all subsequent cases, until one is in danger of becoming a zealot for a technique, administering the same instrument to all people and for all purposes. Counselors must frequently remind themselves that every case provides its own unique combination of data. Labels have no meaning if they are attached to people without this individualizing process. Some newly discovered information that eluded the counselor when he or she first began to work with an individual may change the picture. Conceptualization is a continuous process, not an event. The person does not remain the same, especially if counseling is successful. Equally true, conceptualization of the individual, or even a faltering attempt to understand the person, has little practical value unless it leads to assistance.

16. *The prediction of future behavior should always be stated in terms of probability, supported whenver possible by actuarial evidence.* In the last analysis, the prediction of behavior is a major goal of appraisal processes. Prediction as an outcome of appraisal

should be stated in terms of probabilities, not absolutes. Human behavior is too complex to permit consideration of more than a fraction of the factors that enter into a conclusive prediction of behavior. No prediction of behavior can be guaranteed. Statements of probability favor the outcomes for which there is actuarial evidence of higher incidence. Whenever possible, the statement of probability should be based upon actuarial evidence as in cases of probable academic success in college. The chances are better that an individual will behave in a manner consistent with the highest known incidence of behavior where similar factors are concerned than that he or she will behave in any other way. If there is no statistical evidence, prediction must then be stated in probability terms based on clinical judgment. Such judgment is based on the evidence of experience, though not necessarily evidence that has been subjected to statistical analysis.

SOURCES
OF APPRAISAL INFORMATION

Counselors have an obligation to keep up to date with new developments in the field. That is increasingly difficult, particularly in testing, given its increasing proliferation and the frequent revision of its products. Many sources of information have been developed for those interested in tests, but far fewer sources exist for non-test appraisal devices. Familiarity with these sources is a necessity for counselors.

THE BUROS' PUBLICATIONS

Much important information about tests can be found in several monumental works by Oscar K. Buros. Prominent among those works are the mental measurements yearbooks. Seven yearbooks have been published to date; each one is unique, supplementing rather than supplanting previous works. The latest yearbook, for example, presents information on 1,157 tests, gives 798 original test reviews and excerpts of 181 published reviews of tests, and provides numerous references on the construction, use, and validity of specific tests.[10] The third through seventh yearbooks include critical

---

[10] Oscar K. Buros, ed., *The Seventh Mental Measurements Yearbook*, 2 vols. (Highland Park, N.J.: Gryphon Press, 1972).

reviews by test experts of most of the tests. In addition, each yearbook lists the publisher, date of publication, price, forms, age levels, and other pertinent data.

Another publication edited by Buros is the two-volume set of *Tests in Print*, which presents a comprehensive bibliography of tests and serves as a classified index and supplement to the seven editions of the *Mental Measurement Yearbook*.[11] It contains a comprehensive listing of tests available up to that time (1974) and also lists out-of-print tests. It does not, however, contain reviews of the tests. Some of its listings have undergone revisions and restandardizations.

A monograph series edited by Buros presents information about tests in particular areas such as reading, intelligence, personality, and vocational testing.[12] Each volume, abstracted from the *Mental Measurement Yearbook* series, presents entries for all standardized tests in that area as well as reviews of the tests.

PUBLISHERS'
CATALOGUES AND MANUALS

Additional information about tests may be found in the catalogues and manuals provided by test publishers. Certainly, each test manual should detail all the information required for administering, scoring, interpreting, and evaluating a test. Data on norms, validity, and reliability should be reported. It should be kept in mind that some test manuals fall short of this desired goal, but more and more reputable test publishers are giving careful attention to this important means of providing information about their products.

JOURNALS

Other sources of information for those who use tests are the reviews of newly published tests in educational and psychological journals. Among the journals that either contain a special section on tests or give some attention to tests are *Psychological Abstracts*, *Educational and Psychological Measurement*, *Measurement and Evaluation in Guidance*, *Journal of Consulting Psychology*, and *Journal*

---

[11] See Oscar K. Buros, ed., *Tests in Print* (Highland Park, N.J.: The Gryphon Press, 1961) and *Tests in Print II* (Highland Park, N.J.: Gryphon Press, 1974).

[12] See for example Oscar K. Buros, ed., *Personality Tests and Reviews II* (Highland Park, N.J.: Gryphon Press, 1975).

of Counseling Psychology. A comprehensive critical survey of all types of psychological and educational tests is published every three years in the February issue of the *Review of Educational Research.*

NON-TEST SOURCES

Information about non-test appraisal devices and practices can be found in various professional journals and texts that treat the method or practice. An example of the latter is *The Sociometry Reader.* [13] The paucity of regularly published information about non-test appraisal devices and methods reflects the limited degree to which these procedures have been employed. Criticism and controversy associated with tests as a source of appraisal information promise to stimulate greater use of non-test measures, which should produce more literature.

ETHICAL GUIDES

Individual appraisal requires its practitioners to exercise informed judgment in the selection, use, and security of appraisal data, assessment tools, and practices. Changes in assessment devices, marked advances in the technology supporting appraisal, and increasing public awareness of and concern for protecting individual rights all serve to mandate that those who engage in appraisal services know and observe certain ethical and legal standards in their work. Ethical standards are codified or systematic statements of practices that have evolved out of the experiences of the practitioner. They define certain ways of behaving that have stood the test of time. When situations of conflict arise, ethical standards enable practitioners to determine what should be done. Ethical codes clarify the practitioner's responsibilities to the client and give society some guarantee that the practitioner will demonstrate a sensible regard for the social and moral expectations of the community.

In 1971, the American Psychological Association, the American Educational Research Association, and the National Council on Measurement in Education formed a joint committee that updated standards applying to assessment devices and procedures in general

---

[13] J. Moreno et al., *The Sociometry Reader* (Glencoe, Ill.: The Free Press, 1960).

and to tests in particular.[14] These standards were grouped into three levels: essential, very desirable, and desirable. Statements of essential standards are thought to represent the consensus of present-day thinking and practice. Standards labeled very desirable convey information or practices that foster understanding of, and competence in, assessment; the desirable category suggests information and practices that are helpful but not essential. The standards set forth ethical principles to be observed in disseminating test data; in interpreting test results; in administering and scoring tests; in using norms and scales; in assessing validity and reliability estimates; in determining measurement error; and in setting forth qualifications and concerns of test users.

The reader is urged to examine the standards carefully (an abstract is included in Appendix B) as well as the principles governing appraisal contained in the ethical codes of the American Psychological Association[15] and the American Personnel and Guidance Association.[16] Chapter 15 includes further treatment of this topic. Certainly, knowledge of and adherence to ethical principles would go far in reducing much criticism of appraisal, and it would promote the professional development of practitioners and the personal development of their clients.

ISSUES

The issues—matters of disagreement to be resolved—set forth in this chapter (and in the chapters that follow) are presented here to furnish students with a way to organize and analyze their opinions on these matters. In discussing these issues, we offer an identification or statement of each issue, a summary statement of the pros and cons of each issue, and some discussion pertinent to the issue that reflects our own biases and thinking.

The major purpose of presenting these issues is to encourage active discussion among students about these matters so that they will gain an understanding of where they stand and why. Resolution of issues comes only through analysis, discussion, understanding,

[14] American Psychological Association, *Standards for Educational and Psychological Tests* (Washington, D.C.: The Association, 1974).

[15] American Psychological Association, *Ethical Standards of Psychologists* (Washington, D.C.: The Association, 1977).

[16] American Personnel and Guidance Association, *Ethical Standards* (Washington, D. C.: The Association, 1974).

and choice. It is doubtful that final resolution of many issues is possible. Certainly it would not be healthy for the field if premature solutions were reached.

1. *Only objective data are useful in individual appraisal*
   Yes, because:
   1. Objective data about the individual can be counted and verified.
   2. Subjective data, either that reported by the individual or that derived by the counselor, are unreliable and inefficient for prediction or control.
   3. Use of subjective data is akin to including the experimenter in the experiment and contaminating the results.

   No, because:
   1. Subjective data report the individual's experience of living through an event or events and are, therefore, useful in understanding that person's functioning.
   2. Objective data are public or external data and fail to convey the essence of the individual.

   Discussion:
   Many regard objective data and the experimental approach as the antithesis of subjective data and the clinical approach. This long-standing issue arose at the end of the nineteenth century, when psychology was separating itself from philosophy and attempting to establish itself as a science. In order to be accepted as true scientists, its leaders did their best to employ the same methods that had won prestige for the older and more advanced science of physics. Taking the physicist's atom, the most elementary unit of matter, as a model, psychologists sought to identify "atoms" of behavior—that is, irreducible elements of human behavior that might serve as building blocks for more complicated reactions. They sought to do this by employing experimental analysis as similar as possible to that used in physics. By current standards, these early efforts were crude; but, despite increased sophistication, many helping professionals still tend to be conservative about selecting and using behavioral data. They suggest that collecting data not at once countable or measurable by techniques already at hand is of little or no value in helping an individual.

   Other professionals advance the idea that they, unlike the experimenter in the laboratory, are forced to deal in some fashion with the full complexity of human behavior. The urgency of their cases, centered as they are on emotional crisis, requires professionals to play hunches and to formulate hypotheses about an individual's behavior based on keen insight and speculation. Moreover, they suggest that objective or external data have no significance except as counterparts of implied internal data. Finally, they believe that total reliance on objective data is an attempt to deal with people as if they were inanimate and reduces the counselor to nothing more than a disembodied eye that studies individuals. While the eye views the individual as a source of activity, and while it finds activity that regulates other activity, it finds nothing more. Both overt and covert behavioral data are useful in gaining an understanding of the individual.

2. *Appraisal is inimical to helping relationships*
   Yes, because:
   1. Appraisal places the burden of evaluation on the expert and increases clients' dependent tendencies, making them hope that their situations will be improved by the expert rather than by themselves.
   2. Engaging in appraisal activities discourages clients and suggests that because someone else is conducting the assessment, they can never know themselves.
   3. Appraisal practices lead to control of persons, their values, and goals by professionals who have selected themselves to do the controlling.

   No, because:
   1. Systematic assistance cannot be planned and conducted without appraising the individual and his or her situation.
   2. The principal purpose of appraisal is to collect and interpret information that enables clients to understand themselves and their possibilities.
   3. Judgments and decisions based on systematic, objective data are better than those based on whim, prejudice, or other subjective factors.

   Discussion:
   This issue, long debated in the counseling professions, depends, at least in part, on how appraisal is defined, conceptualized, and conducted. Advocates of client-centered therapy in particular have argued that testing and diagnosis are evaluative functions

that short-change clients and inhibit them from taking responsibility for what takes place in helping relationships. Using tests to collect data, they suggest, reinforces the idea that the counselor is an authority figure who solves the client's problem without much investment from the client in the helping process. Appraisal, in their view, consists of assessment devices and practices applied to individuals (is something done to them) rather than for and with them. The outcome is that collecting appraisal data means that the counselor becomes preoccupied with data and neglects the individual's current attitudes and behavior. As such, the counselor is evaluative and judgmental rather than consultative and helpful.

Other counselors believe that appraisal should be thought of as the means of obtaining a comprehensive picture of the individual. They hold that from the first moment of contact, counselors collect, process, and assess data about their clients and begin forming working images of them. Assessments of clients' development to date, of the nature of their interpersonal relationships, of their work all enter into this picture. Moreover, the outcome of tests, interviews, observations, and other assessment devices enriches and enlarges the picture of the individual and sensitizes counselors, enabling them to plan and conduct intelligent, informed intervention.

ANNOTATED REFERENCES

Bauernfeind, Robert H. *Building a School Testing Program.* 2nd ed. Boston: Houghton Mifflin, 1969.

Bauernfeind presents a verbatim account of the reasoning that lies behind the selection and use of aptitude, achievement, and interest tests in an actual school (pp. 15–21). He subsequently recommends improvements in the program (pp. 271–279).

Goldman, Leo. *Using Tests in Counseling.* 2nd ed. New York: Appleton-Century-Crofts, 1971, 483 pp.

A good illustration is given of the effective use of tests in counseling a college student (Kathy Musgrove) about her vocational choices (pp. 246–254). Measures of ability, interest, and personality were administered and interpreted to the student. Goldman points out that the tests did not solve the student's problem but did help to raise fundamental questions about her plans, which she discussed with her counselor.

Scannell, Dale P., and Tracy, D. B. *Testing and Measurement in the Classroom.* Boston: Houghton Mifflin, 1975, 288 pp.

The authors define measurement and evaluation and illustrate the definitions. They describe the functions of classroom measurements and give five principles for establishing classroom measurements.

SELECTED REFERENCES

Bradley, Richard W. "Person-Referenced Test Interpretation: A Learning Process." *Measurement and Evaluation in Guidance* 10 (January 1978): 201–210.

Clark, Alice T. "Follow-Up on Follow Through." *Measurement and Evaluation in Guidance* 7 (January 1975): 234–238.

Cleary, T. Anne; Humphreys, Lloyd G.; Kendrick, S. A.; Wesman, Alexander. "Educational Uses of Tests with Disadvantaged Students." *American Psychologist* 30 (January 1975): 15–41.

Hopper, Gordan. "Parental Understanding of Their Child's Test Results as Interpreted by Elementary School Teachers." *Measurement and Evaluation in Guidance* 10 (July 1977): 84–89.

Kopp, Richard Royal, and Dinkmeyer, Don. "Early Recollections in Life Style Assessment and Counseling." *The School Counselor* 23 (September 1975): 22–27.

Loesch, Larry C. "Flow Chart Models for Using Tests." *Measurement and Evaluation in Guidance* 10 (April 1977): 18–23.

McNemar, Quinn. "On So-Called Test Bias." *American Psychologist* 30 (August 1975): 848–851.

Messick, Samuel. "The Standard Problem: Meaning and Values in Measurement and Evaluation." *American Psychologist* 30 (October 1975): 955–966.

Pearson, Henry G. "Self Identification of Talents: First Step to Finding Career Decisions." *Vocational Guidance Quarterly* 24 (September 1975): 20–26.

Singer, Jerome L. "Navigating the Stream of Consciousness: Research in Daydreaming and Related Inner Experience." *American Psychologist* 30 (July 1975): 727–738.

"Tracks and Trails from The Measuring Worm." *Measurement and Evaluation in Guidance* 7 (October 1974): 169–170.

Van Riper, B. W. "From a Clinical to a Counseling Process: Rehearsing the Test Appraisal Process." *Measurement and Evaluation in Guidance* 7 (April 1974): 24–31.

Chapter 2

The Origins and Development of Assessment

What major events mark the development of assessment?

What factors have influenced the development of assessment techniques?

What criticisms are made of assessment?

What is the value of assessment?

A BRIEF HISTORY

Lewis Carroll, speaking through his most famous character, Alice, once said that the best place to start is at the beginning. As appropriate and as intuitively satisfying as that advice is, it is of little help here, for in truth, the origin of mental measurement is lost in antiquity. Throughout the ages, human beings have assessed their own actions and those of others with the aim of understanding and predicting behavior. They have sought to measure human behavior, seeking thus to reduce it so that it could be processed, understood, and managed.

A complete account of the origin and development of mental measurement would be a chronicle of human behavior in all of its bewildering developments. It would involve demonstrating what people have learned about themselves and the individual in relationship to others over hundreds of thousands of years. The history of mental measurement is a record that is being enlarged continuously. This record is subject to various interpretations. Assessment tools that appear stable and enduring at present may, in the future, be swept suddenly into oblivion by a tide of forces as yet dimly perceived.

Many great philosophers, including Plato and Aristotle, speculated about human nature and proposed theories about it, some of which persisted until modern times. Formal mental measurement is of fairly recent origin. While the careful and systematic assessment of human behavior has but a brief history, it incorporates a broad area. The pioneer work of German physiologists such as Gustav Theodor Fechner, Herman Von Helmholtz, and others established that human behavior was related closely to bodily functions. While research on eye, ear, and brain functions is linked to physiology and neurology, the study of attitudes, opinions, and propaganda, on the other hand, is akin to sociology. Between these extremes, social scientists and educators work at measuring and understanding the abilities, interests, motives, and personalities of children, adolescents, and adults, both normal and atypical.

Robert L. Thorndike and Elizabeth Hagen have sorted the history of measurement into four parts covering the years 1900-1960. They saw the period from 1900-1915 as the *pioneering* phase, for those years marked the origin, development, and expansion of many measurement methods. The years from 1915-1930 were classified as the "boom" period in test development, because standardized tests of ability, achievement, personality, and interests proliferated and were used widely and indiscriminately. The third period, from about 1930-1945, they called a time of critical appraisal, during which attention shifted from measuring a limited range of academic skills to evaluating achievement of the range of educational objectives. The years from 1945-1960 were characterized as a period of test batteries and testing programs, because integrated aptitude batteries for educational and personnel use multiplied during this phase, and large-scale testing programs expanded in size and number at an unparalleled rate.[1]

We would extend their classification by suggesting that the years from 1960-present may best be viewed as a time of public controversy. Issues derived from test use were taken to court for settlement. Professional associations, test publishers, and testing practitioners engaged in serious public examination and discussion of the merits, limitations, benefits, and adverse consequences of tests and testing.

We shall not attempt to provide a comprehensive treatment of the history of individual appraisal. Rather, we have identified and presented in Table 2.1 the major milestones that have marked the origin and development of assessment techniques. Highly readable

[1] Robert L. Thorndike and Elizabeth Hagen, *Measurement and Evaluation in Psychology and Education*, 3rd ed. (New York: John Wiley and Sons, 1969), pp. 5-7.

TABLE 2.1
SUMMARY OF SELECTED HISTORICAL EVENTS
IN ASSESSMENT PRACTICES

DATE	LEADER	CONTRIBUTION
202 B.C.	Han dynasty (China)	Competitive civil service examination
1200 A.D.	University of Bologna	Oral doctoral examination
1599	Society of Jesus	Rules for administering written examinations
1809	Carl Frederick Gauss	Measurement error
1816	Johann Friedrich Herbart	First psychology textbook
1848	Edouard Seguin	Forerunner of performance test to screen feeble-minded children
1865	Regents of New York State	State testing programs
1869	Francis Galton	Publication of *Hereditary Genius*
1879	Wilhelm Wundt	Psychological laboratory
1889	James McKeen Cattell	Measures of mental abilities
1894	Joseph M. Rice	Examiner influence on spelling test performance
1897	Hermann Ebbinghaus	Completion test for investigating learning and retention rates
1899	Charles W. Eliot	College Entrance Examination Board
1901	Karl Pearson	Theory of correlation
1903	Edward L. Thorndike	First textbook in educational psychology
1904	Charles Spearman	Measurement reliability, correction for attenuation, standard error
1905	Alfred Binet	First practical intelligence test
1908	Edward L. Thorndike	Handwriting scale
1912	Wilhelm Stern	Suggestion for use of mental quotient
1914	Charles Spearman	Factors of intelligence
1915	John L. Stenquist	Test of mechanical ability

TABLE 2.1 (*cont.*)
SUMMARY OF SELECTED HISTORICAL EVENTS
IN ASSESSMENT PRACTICES

DATE	LEADER	CONTRIBUTION
1915	Stanley D. Porteus	Maze test to diagnose retardation
1916	Lewis M. Terman	Standardized and validated Binet test
1917	Arthur Otis	Items for *Army Alpha*, first group-administered intelligence test
1918	Robert S. Woodward	First personality inventory
1918	Carl Seashore	Musical aptitude test
1921	Hermann Rorschach	*Psycholodiagnostik*, inkblot projective test
1922	Lewis M. Terman	Survey of gifted children
1923	Hugh Gordon	Environmental influence on intelligence of canal boat and gypsy children
1923	T. L. Kelley et al.	*Stanford Achievement Test Battery*
1925	E. K. Strong, Jr.	Vocational interest inventory
1926	H. C. Morrison	School mastery tests
1926	Florence L. Goodenough	Draw-a-man test
1929	Louis L. Thurstone	Attitude measurement scales
1931	Louis L. Thurstone	Multiple factor analysis
1933	American Psychiatric Association	Adoption of classification of emotional disorders
1934	J. L. Moreno	Sociometric technique
1934	G. F. Kuder	*Kuder Preference Record*
1935	Reynold B. Johnson	Test scoring machine
1936	Edward F. Lindquist	*Iowa Every-Pupil Test*
1938	Louis L. Thurstone	Primary mental abilities
1938	Oscar K. Buros	First *Mental Measurement Yearbook*
1938	Loretta Bender	Bender-Gestalt test
1939	David Wechsler	Individual intelligence scale

TABLE 2.1 (*cont.*)
SUMMARY OF SELECTED HISTORICAL EVENTS
IN ASSESSMENT PRACTICES

DATE	LEADER	CONTRIBUTION
1940	Stark Hathaway and Fred McKinley	*Minnesota Multiphasic Personality Inventory*
1947	U.S. Employment Service	*General Aptitude Test Battery*
1949	David Wechsler	Individual intelligence scale for children
1953	Edward F. Lindquist	Electronic test processing
1953	William Stephenson	*Q*-sort
1954	American Psychological Association, AERA, NCME	Technical recommendations for tests
1956	Benjamin S. Bloom	Taxonomy of educational objectives
1957	Ronald Frederikson	In-basket assessment technique
1957	C. E. Osgood	Semantic differential
1960	John C. Flanagan	Project Talent
1964	Ralph Tyler	National assessment of education
1965	Education Testing Service	Commercial service of criterion-referenced tests
1968	Joe Kamiya	Biofeedback
1972	Association for Measurement and Evaluation in Guidance	Position paper on test moratorium
1974	American Psychological Association, AERA, NCME	Revised standards for tests
1974	James F. Buckley	Family Educational Rights and Privacy Act

and comprehensive treatments of the events cited in this table are to be found in the monograph by Kathryn W. Linden and James D. Linden[2] and the small volume by Phillip H. DuBois.[3]

[2] Kathryn W. Linden and James D. Linden, *Modern Mental Measurement: A Historical Perspective* (Boston: Houghton Mifflin, 1968).

[3] Phillip H. DuBois, *A History of Psychological Testing* (Boston: Allyn and Bacon, 1970).

MAJOR FORCES IN THE
DEVELOPMENT OF ASSESSMENT

Concentrating on the significant events that highlight the history of assessment overlooks and ignores an ingredient useful in understanding and illuminating its progress: the factors and forces that produced these events. Not even a brief outline of the history of mental measurement can afford to limit itself to a bare narration of events. It is also necessary to provide some interpretation of how and why these events occurred. Indeed, understanding the relationships between an event and the economic, social, and political forces surrounding it is imperative for a comprehensive grasp of the past as well as for forecasting future directions.

PSYCHOLOGICAL THOUGHT

Certain forces operating within the field of psychology have influenced the development of assessment practices, and certain schools of thought have been dominant for a period of time. Advocates of these viewpoints advance what they regard as the proper subjects of study and how those subjects are to be assessed.

STRUCTURALISM During the late 1800s and early 1900s, this viewpoint became prominent in psychology and influenced measurement endeavors. Wilhelm Wundt (a German who in 1879 established the first psychological laboratory) and Edward B. Titchener (an Englishman who came to America to head the psychology department at Cornell University) were leaders in suggesting that mental images, thoughts, and feelings should be investigated in order to understand human behavior. These three elements form the structure of consciousness, which can be investigated by introspection, interviews, questionnaires, and other non-test appraisal devices. Concentrating on structuralism rules out atttending to learning, intelligence, motivation, and abnormal behavior. Assessment focuses upon perceiving, thinking, and using imagery.

FUNCTIONALISM An American, William James, as well as other psychologists emphasized the changing nature of mental activities and questioned whether mental behavior could be analyzed into structural elements. Shortly after 1900, John Dewey and James Rowland Angell at the University of Chicago began to stress the ways in which an organism adjusts to the environment. Their objective in studying behavior was to discover how thinking, feeling emotion, and other processes fulfill an individual's needs. They employed trained observers and interviewers in their assessment of behavior. The views of the functionalists helped to align psychology with biology and brought about a genetic approach to psychological problems.

BEHAVIORISM   This approach was founded about 1914 by John B. Watson, then a psychologist at Johns Hopkins University. He too was impatient with the narrowness of structuralism, but he did not believe that the functionalists went far enough in their criticism. Watson objected particularly to introspection as a means of measuring behavior, considering it unscientific. The main objective, he said, was to study action, not consciousness. His technique was to expose an animal or a human being to a stimulus, measure the responses, and record this behavior objectively so as to provide real scientific evidence. Watson and other behaviorists experimented on learning, motivation, emotion, and individual development. The rise of behaviorism brought about a decline in the use of self-report measurement devices and an upsurge in the use of psychometric approaches. The behaviorists employed quantifiable assessments that yielded estimates of how much and to what extent certain behaviors were emitted. The present-day behaviorist continues to stress action and urges that psychology rid itself of mentalistic terms.

GESTALTISM   During the early 1930s, Wolfgang Kohler and Kurt Koffka maintained that experience and behavior could not be analyzed into elements of consciousness, as claimed by the structuralists, nor could they be broken down into stimulus-response units, as the behaviorists suggest. Gestaltists believe that behavior and experience are unanalyzable wholes, though certain relationships between the whole and its parts can be discerned. Studying one element at a time is, in their view, no substitute for considering a person as a whole. More important to the gestaltist than knowing how much of some attribute a person has is knowing how it is expressed and why. They emphasize *impressionistic* approaches (see Chapter 1), in that they conduct appraisal by looking for significant cues of behavior by any available means. The appraiser then integrates these cues to form a total impression of the individual.

HUMANISTIC PSYCHOLOGY   Drawing heavily on such existential and phenomenological ideas and societal forces as the civil rights movement, student protests, and university reforms, this approach became prominent during the 1960s. Humanistic psychologists stress the humanness of the individual and reject any form of inhumanity. They called for recognition that the supposedly objective approaches are in fact dependent on or based on other ideas and approaches that are clearly subjective. In their view, the goal of assessment is to describe what it means to be alive. This calls for taking an inventory of an individual's potentialities, including feelings, thoughts, actions, growth, interactions with environmental conditions, the range and variety of experiences available to the person, and his or her meaningful place in the environment. They have sought to develop methods to assess conceptual thinking, vicarious experience, imagination, mystical concerns, and artistic creation.

ADVANCES
IN STATISTICAL METHODOLOGY

The development of individual appraisal techniques is linked closely to the advances made in statistical methodology. Tests are scored in points. Learning is judged by the number of units mastered in a given time and problem-solving ability by the amount of time required to get an answer. Statistical techniques are essential in interpreting the results, particularly when many subjects are used. Many statistical concepts stem from the works of Karl Pearson and Charles Spearman. While Pearson gave credit to Sir Francis Galton for originating the concept of correlation (relationship), in 1901, Pearson devised the product-moment formula for computing correlation (see Chapter 4) as well as other contributions such as multiple correlation, correction of correlations for changes in range, and the chi-square test for goodness of fit. In 1904, Charles Spearman extended the concept of reliability, including corrections for attenuation, the standard error of measurement, split-half reliability, and other statistics. Their statistical contributions are still used routinely in test development and assessment practices. Application of statistical methods to such matters as validity, reliability, homogeneity, item efficiency, differential factors, and so on has brought about progress in assessment practices.

PROFESSIONAL ORGANIZATIONS

Several professional organizations have been instrumental in the development of mental measurement through their publications and national meetings. The Psychometric Society was founded in 1935 and began conducting conferences to present test methods, developments, and research. Division 5, Evaluation and Measurement, was created by the American Psychological Association (APA) when it reorganized in 1949. Other APA divisions, covering clinical psychology, industrial psychology, educational psychology, and counseling psychology, discuss test use and assessment practices at their national and regional conventions and in their publications. The Association for Measurement and Evaluation of Guidance, a division of the American Personnel and Guidance Association, was organized in 1966 to advance counselors' measurement and assessment practices. Other professional organizations, including the American Educational Research Association, the National Council on Measurement in Education, and the Invitational Conference on Testing Problems, sponsored annually by the Educational Testing Service, have contributed greatly to test developments, psychometric theory, and assessment practices.

SOCIAL CHANGES

The impact of two world wars, unemployment, depression, technological advances, and compulsory school attendance has influenced the development of assessment tools and practices. During wartime, marked advances were made in assessment, because critical labor power shortages demanded the careful screening and allocation of people to both military and civilian work forces. Compulsory school attendance brought into schools thousands of young people who had no marked desire to be there and few clear ideas about why they were there or what they wanted. It was soon apparent that increased personal assistance was needed to help these students marshal their assets to find their way through school and the complex environment outside school. Tests and other assessment tools were developed to collect information about people. They were used to sort out students who should move quickly, those who should move slowly, those who could go to college, and those who could not. Test data were used as criteria for ability grouping as well as for extending assistance that was personal, systematic, and useful.

More recently, technological advances in data gathering have generated public demand for controlling abuse of personal information files maintained by school, government, and commercial organizations. The Family Educational Rights and Privacy Act of 1974 (section 438), sponsored by former Senator James F. Buckley of New York, gave parents access to their children's school records; required parental consent for students to undergo medical, psychological, or psychiatric examination, testing, or treatment; and prohibited educational institutions from releasing a student's record to any person other than other school officials without parental consent.

MAJOR CRITICISMS
OF ASSESSMENT

Any examination of the history of assessment would be remiss if it failed to note the criticisms of and controversy over standardized testing. Earlier in this chapter, we noted that the current stage in the history of assessment is one marked by public controversy. Moreover, the changing social forces that we have described have accentuated the stormy debates surrounding the development and use of assessment measures. Lee J. Cronbach has discussed criticisms of testing that began as early as the 1920s and continued during the next five decades.[4] Until the late 1950s, these came for the most part from within the measurement profession. Recently, the major sources of criticism have been external to the profession. These are some of the frequent criticisms of tests and testing.

CRITICISM:
TESTS LABEL AND PREDETERMINE

A major and long-standing criticism is that classification by ability test measures categorize an individual early in his or her school career and thus predetermine that person's success and status in school and as an adult. The charge is that classification labels—bright, average, inferior—are applied to individuals based on measured intelligence and that these labels follow people throughout school and career. Cronbach puts the charge in these words:

---

[4] Lee J. Cronbach, "Five Decades of Public Controversy over Mental Testing," *American Psychologist* 30 (January 1975): 1–14.

William James had warned psychologists that to understand man was not to write his biography in advance, but the testers came very close, in their estimate as to how much education a man could use and what careers he could thrive in. More serious, when the tests determined who would enter the college preparatory program and before that determined who would go into the "fast" section of an early grade, the tests began to determine fates. The testers' sorting process was to shield the child destined to be a worker from the rigors of an academic curriculum. Such a plan would reduce distaste for schooling, prevent failure, and retain him in school longer. Testers said that the IQ was constant; hence, to make decisions early was merciful and just.[5]

Critics assert that these labels establish expectations in the minds of teachers and so become self-fulfilling prophecies. This criticism has been particularly strong since 1968, when Robert Rosenthal and Lenore Jacobsen reported that a teacher's expectation of how a student will perform influences the pupil's actual performance.[6] Teachers in a California school were given a list of pupils who had supposedly shown exceptional promise on a test but who had, in fact, been picked at random. Months later, according to Rosenthal and Jacobson, these children had progressed more than had their unheralded classmates. Since that time, more than 200 studies have tested that hypothesis, and Rosenthal states that the results have been mixed.[7] The labels and the expectations associated with them, critics charge, do irreparable harm to the individual's self-esteem and to his or her educational and career motivations:

> The strangling and starvation go on in schools, hospitals, clinics, families—wherever we freeze our expectations of a child in terms of the belief that tests are the truth, the whole truth and the final permanent truth about a child's potentialities. Judgments are too often weighted on the negative side.[8]

CRITICISM: TESTS ARE IMPERFECT

The validity and reliability of standardized tests have been subjected to much criticism. Simply defined, *validity* refers to the degree of

---

[5] Cronbach, "Five Decades of Controversy," p. 11.

[6] Robert Rosenthal and Leonore Jacobsen, *Pygmalion in the Classroom* (New York: Holt, Rinehart and Winston, 1968).

[7] Robert Rosenthal, "The Pygmalion Effect Lives," *Psychology Today* 7 (September 1973).

[8] Lois B. Murphy, "The Stranglehold of Norms on the Individual Child," *Childhood Education* 49 (April 1973).

relationship between what the test measures and what it is designed to measure; *reliability* refers to the consistency and thus the accuracy of test scores. Criticisms of the validity and reliability of standardized tests strike at the very heart of testing, for if tests do not measure what they purport to measure or fail to measure accurately, then little confidence can be placed in their results, and there is little use in administering them.

Standardized personality inventories have been criticized repeatedly as invalid measures. Critics' questioning the validity of standardized group intelligence tests led the New York City public school system, the largest in America, to discontinue their use in 1964 and to substitute an extensive achievement test program. Other large city school districts, including those of Washington, D.C., and Los Angeles, also discontinued group intelligence testing. The struggle over validity and reliability has been carried to the courts. The U.S. Supreme Court ruled, in 1971, in *Griggs et al.* v. *Duke Power Company*, that thirteen black employees had been excluded wrongly from getting better jobs through the use of a general intelligence test. Any test is illegal, the Court decided, unless it clearly measures the skills needed for a specific job (is valid).

Test validity and reliability are highly technical components of tests, and when criticisms of this nature are made by those who are expert in testing and measurement, they are particularly serious. We should point out that there are different forms of validity and reliability for different tests, based on the purposes for which the tests are designed (see Chapter 4). No test measure is exact. Some tests are more valid and reliable than are others, but none is perfect in every respect. The charge of imprecision applies equally to other measurements that are important in our daily lives. Yet no one argues that these measures—temperature, mileage, and so on—should be abandoned because they are inexact.

CRITICISM: TESTS ARE BIASED

Many critics have asserted that standardized tests of ability and achievement are biased toward white middle-class experience, achievement, and school success. In consequence, children born and reared in impoverished environments or those who are culturally different are penalized because their experience limits their performance on tests. Critics argue that the questions, activities, and objects used in intelligence and achievement tests tend to be drawn from middle-class culture. Consequently, a student who is a member of middle-class culture has a better chance of scoring well than a student from a lower-class home because the former is generally encouraged to develop verbal abilities and to reason critically. Scholastic aptitude tests used in selecting students for college have often been a target of such criticism. Robert L. Williams argues:

> The primary issues in the great black–white I.Q. controversy are not those of cultural test bias, the nature of intelligence, or the heritability of I.Q. The issue is admittance to America's mainstream. . . . University admission policies have required standardized psychological tests such as the Scholastic Aptitude Test (SAT) or the Graduate Record Examination (GRE) as a criterion for admission to colleges, graduate schools, medical or law schools and other professional schools. For blacks, these tests more often mean exclusion.[9]

The charge of sex bias has been leveled at standardized personality and interest measures. The Association for Measurement and Evaluation in Guidance (AMEG) defined sex bias as "that condition or provision which influences a person to limit his or her consideration of career opportunities solely on the basis of that person's sex."[10] They believe that vocational interest inventories have tended to limit women's choices to stereotypical women's careers.

Some years ago, Benjamin S. Bloom estimated that insecurity and an impoverished environment can cut 10 IQ points from a child's score by age 4 and another 10 by age 17.[11] Conversely, many studies have shown that the intelligence scores of underprivileged students have climbed—sometimes by as much as 18 points in 18 months—when they received special help, tutoring, or improved schooling. Some students' ability test scores have varied as much as 40 points from one period of their lives to another. Richard Herrnstein observed:

> The correlation between I.Q. and social class (usually defined in terms of occupation, income, and patterns of personal association) is undeniable, substantial, and worth noting. A cautious conclusion, based on a survey of the scientific literature, is that the upper

---

[9] Robert L. Williams, "The Silent Mugging of the Black Community," *Psychology Today* 7 (May 1974): 34.

[10] AMEG Commission of Sex Bias in Measurement, "AMEG Commission Report on Sex Bias in Interest Measurement," *Measurement and Evaluation in Guidance* 6 (October 1973): 171–177.

[11] Benjamin S. Bloom, *Stability and Change in Human Characteristics* (New York: John Wiley and Sons, 1964), p. 77.

class scores about thirty I.Q. points above the lower class. A typical member of the upper class gets a score that certifies him as intellectually "Superior," while a typical member of the lower class is a shade below average (that is, below I.Q. 100).[12]

Most test experts admit that students from impoverished backgrounds do poorly on standardized tests. However, they do not advocate that testing be abandoned but rather that conditions be improved for such children, both at home and at school. They suggest that discarding tests would be like whipping the bearer of bad news. They argue that standardized tests are an objective, fair, and democratic means by which able students receive due recognition, no matter what their race or social class. Finally, they urge that extreme care be used in interpreting them and that greater effort be undertaken in developing more culturally fair tests.

CRITICISM:
TESTS OBSCURE TALENTS

Testing fosters limited conceptions of ability, achievement, and personality: this is another frequent criticism. Critics aver that tests used in schools are based heavily on verbal and quantitative skills that do not exhaust all types of achievement needed in American society. They point out that the prominence given these skills by testing throughout the schooling period tends to discourage the development of other qualities—such as social ability, creativity, artistic abilities, honesty—and serves to reduce the diversity of skills and talents needed in and available to society.

CRITICISM:
TESTS INVADE PRIVACY

A charge often made is that testing is an invasion of an individual's privacy. The right to privacy is a fundamental right that is increasingly being given protection by state and federal laws. Many individuals are concerned not only that administering a test violates a person's right to privacy but that test results are entered on a cumulative record that follows an individual through school and on to work. They are concerned about access to test data in this record.

---

[12] Richard Herrnstein, "I.Q.," *The Atlantic* 228 (September 1971): 50.

The criticism of invasion of privacy is most often leveled against standardized inventories of personality, values, beliefs, and attitudes than other assessment devices. Cronbach has pointed out that

> any test is an invasion of privacy for the subject who does not wish to reveal himself. . . . Virtually all measures of personality seek information in areas that the subject has every reason to regard as private, in normal social intercourse. He is willing to admit the psychologist into those private areas only if he sees the relevance of the questions to the attainment of his goals in working with the psychologist. The psychologist is not "invading privacy" when he is freely admitted and when he has a genuine need for the information obtained.[13]

Cronbach's criteria for justifying testing are that the individual must consent to the administration of the personality inventory and the psychologist must need the information. School personnel justify the administration of ability and achievement tests on the grounds that they have a genuine need to know the information obtained in order to provide appropriate instruction and other forms of assistance to the student.

CRITICISM:
TESTS ARE NOT INTERPRETED

Another charge against testing is that feedback about test results is not given to the person who was tested. This charge stems from the practice of testing an individual and withholding from that person the outcome of the test. The practice was initiated and continued because it was believed that those who did poorly would find the results disturbing and inhibiting. Also, it was believed that too many students and their parents would misunderstand test interpretations and use such data in harmful ways. While test results circulate freely among counselors, teachers, and administrators, all too often the examinee never learns what they reveal about him or her. At best, the individual goes through a brief session at which a teacher or counselor reads from a hidden sheet and draws some conclusions never fully explained. Certainly, it would seem that if individuals take tests, they have a legitimate interest in and

---

[13] Lee J. Cronbach, *Essentials of Psychological Testing*, 3rd ed. (New York: Harper and Row, 1970), pp. 509–510. Copyright, 1949 by Harper & Row, Publishers, Inc. Copyright © 1960, 1970 by Lee J. Cronbach. By permission of the publisher.

a right to all information yielded by the test. According to the American Civil Liberties Union, nobody owns test information except the person who takes the test.

CRITICISM:
TESTS CONTROL SCHOOLS

A long-standing criticism is that test publishers influence educational decisions by exercising control over what is taught and valued in the classroom. This charge stems from the practice of using achievement tests at the end of the year to evaluate students' gains and losses. Critics argue that it is the test publisher—not the classroom teacher—who selects test items and who, therefore, determines what is taught in the classroom. In response, test publishers argue that they do not design standardized achievement tests for individual schools and that any teacher exercises judgment as to what material is selected and presented to a class.

Robert L. Ebel has pointed out:

> Those who know well how tests are made and used in American education know that the tests more often lag than lead curricular change, and that while tests may affect particular episodes in a student's experience, they can hardly ever be said to determine a student's destiny. American education is, after all, a manifold, decentralized, loosely organized enterprise. Whether it restricts student freedom too much or too little is a subject for lively debate. But it does not even come close to determining any student's destiny, not nearly as close as the examination systems in some other countries, ancient and modern.[14]

CRITICISM:
TESTS MEASURE IRRELEVANT SKILLS

Another criticism is that testing provides incentives to students to develop specious test-taking skills rather than develop skills that facilitate true learning. According to this charge, students learn for the sake of passing tests rather than understanding the content. Learning how to master tests becomes overly important to students,

---

[14] Robert L. Ebel, "The Social Consequences of Educational Testing," in *Introduction to Guidance: Selected Readings*, ed. Bruce Shertzer and Shelley C. Stone (Boston: Houghton Mifflin, 1970), p. 231.

according to this criticism, and they process course material with a view to how it will appear and how it must be dealt with on a test. A persistent critic of multiple-choice questions, Banesh Hoffman, has said that "multiple-choice tests penalize the deep student, dampen creativity, foster intellectual dishonesty, and undermine the very foundations of education."[15]

CRITICISM: TESTS FOSTER
MECHANISTIC DECISION-MAKING

Traditionally, testing has been designed to measure the progress and attainments of students. However, critics charge that too often these data are used mechanistically, without regard to other factors, to make decisions about an individual. Without question, test scores are often used by an individual to help make decisions and by others to make decisions about him or her. Included in this charge is that the individual disappears or is submerged when test data about him or her are accumulated to make an institutional decision. One becomes more and more a manipulated being, caught in the grip of computer-processed data that mechanistically indicate whether one is to be accepted or rejected.

An illustration of this charge is that school administrators have used end-of-year achievement test data to evaluate teachers and to determine whether to continue their assignments. Those nontenured teachers whose classes do not exhibit sufficient achievement are released from their contracts without any consideration given to the experience and previous background of students in their classes. Such ill-advised, mechanistic decision-making practices, of course, are condemned by all knowledgeable educators.

CRITICISM:
TESTS ENCOURAGE COMPETITION

The final criticism is that testing stresses competition and success rather than cooperation. Too much emphasis, critics say, is placed on doing better than fellow students when what should be encouraged is teamwork. S. L. Washburn put it in these words:

---

[15] See Paul L. Houts, "A Conversation with Banesh Hoffman," *The National Elementary Principal* 43 (July–August 1975): 33.

The desire to grade a paper (how will we know who did the work?) forces immediate and trivial emphasis on individual work, which, in effect, discourages learning the complex personal and intellectual complications of cooperation. Yet performance in cooperative projects that lead toward problem solution is probably a far more useful measure of ability than the usual tests.[16]

THE VALUES OF ASSESSMENT

Criticisms of assessment reflect the dissatisfaction of many adults and students. For example, Orville G. Brim, Jr., reported that of a representative group of Americans over 18, many were opposed to using tests to help decide on admitting students to college (41 percent); using tests to help in job selection (37 percent); using tests to help determine job promotions (50 percent); and using intelligence tests to help establish special classes in school (25 percent). High school students were even more opposed to the use of intelligence tests: 50 percent were against their use in job hiring; 60 percent were against their use in promotion decisions; 54 percent were against using them to help select students for college; and 50 percent were against their use to help establish special classes in schools.[17]

Despite intense criticism and dissatisfaction, test usage has not decreased, nor has testing been abandoned. However, during the late 1960s and early 1970s, some professional organizations considered or adopted resolutions that called either for abandoning testing or declaring a moratorium on testing and the use of test data. Position papers and policy statements on testing have been issued by many associations. For example, in 1972, the American Personnel and Guidance Association (APGA) adopted the position that abandoning testing would not be wise, for the information obtained from tests is essential to the realistic handling of educational and personnel problems. It argued against banning tests on the grounds that "the role of measurement is too central, too fundamental to the conduct and improvement of education and to sound personnel

---

[16] S. L. Washburn, "Evolution and Learning: A Context for Evaluation," *The National Elementary Principal* 54 (July–August 1975): 10.

[17] Orville G. Brim, Jr., "American Attitudes Toward Intelligence Testing," in *Introduction to Guidance: Selected Readings*, ed. Bruce Shertzer and Shelley C. Stone (Boston: Houghton Mifflin, 1970), pp. 234–235.

practices in business and industry for this to be a realistic alternative."[18] The APGA position paper suggested that a better choice is to provide procedures for the review and remedy of ills through professional associations, the law, and the courts.

The purposes for which assessment is conducted have been described in Chapter 1. The value of tests lies in these purposes; information is needed if prediction, selection, classification, and evaluation are to be conducted systematically, fairly, and humanely. Ebel has stated that if test usage were abandoned,

> encouragement and reward of individual efforts to learn would be made more difficult. Excellence in programs of education would become less tangible as a goal and less demonstrable as an attainment. Educational opportunities would be extended less on the basis of aptitude and merit and more on the basis of ancestry and influence; social class barriers would become less permeable. Decisions on important issues of curriculum and method would be made less on the basis of solid evidence and more on the basis of prejudice or caprice.[19]

T. Anne Cleary and her colleagues point out that alternatives to testing—lotteries, use of prior experience, quotas, interviewing, academic grades—have shortcomings equal to, if not greater than, the failings associated with test data. Abandoning testing techniques that encourage evenhanded appraisal would make the costs of education prohibitive and outside the reach of prospective applicants and educational institutions.[20]

Examination of the criticisms of test appraisal tools reveals that most are based on the abuse of test data. While the technical shortcomings (validity and reliability) of some standardized tests and inventories cannot be ignored, the most serious limitation, at present, is the way in which test data are viewed, interpreted, and used. Errors in interpretation and use are undoubtedly more common when test users deal with the underprivileged, but privilege provides little insurance against either of these hazards. Cameron Fincher has written:

[18] American Personnel and Guidance Association, "The Responsible Use of Tests: A Position Paper of AMEG, APGA and NCME," *Measurement and Evaluation in Guidance* 5 (July 1972): 388.

[19] Robert L. Ebel, "The Social Consequences of Educational Testing," p. 231.

[20] T. Anne Cleary, Lloyd G. Humphrey, S. A. Kendrick, and Alexander Wesman, "Educational Uses of Tests with Disadvantaged Students," *The American Psychologist* 30 (January 1975): 35.

There remains a great need for better education and understanding concerning the uses and applications of all psychological tests. Because tests have been identified with abusive practices in the employment area, they are often rejected for the wrong reasons in other areas. They are regarded too frequently as intrinsically discriminatory and ipso facto, morally reprehensible. That tests have served other social needs in a most valuable way at other times is not fully appreciated.[21]

Without question, teachers and counselors need extended pre- and in-service training in the appropriate interpretation and use of test appraisal data. Because counselors are often the personnel in the schools most qualified to use appraisal practices, they have a responsibility to exercise leadership in initiating and implementing sound practices of test administration, interpretation, use, and reporting. That will not be achieved through innocence but only by being well-informed on appraisal practices.

ISSUES

1. *The use of standardized tests and inventories should be abandoned.*

   Yes, because:
   1. The bias, gross limitations, and imprecision inherent in data obtained from standardized tests and inventories render them ineffective and useless in performing their intended functions.
   2. Misuse and misinterpretation of test data result in harmful consequences for both the individual and society.

   No, because:
   1. The alternatives to standardized tests and inventories have equal, if not greater, limitations.
   2. The misuse and misinterpretation of test data are a function of faulty professional practices that can be corrected through systematic preservice and in-service educational programs for professionals.

---

[21] Cameron Fincher, "Personnel Testing and Public Policy" *The American Psychologist* 28 (June 1973): p. 496.

Discussion:

Increasing demands have been made during the past few years that standardized testing be abandoned or that a moratorium be placed on the use of test data for the purposes of selecting, classifying, or evaluating people. Minority group members, particularly blacks and women, have been prominent in calling attention to test bias and abuses in the use of test data. By doing so, they have performed a valuable service to all who are associated in any way with tests and testing.

The variables involved in this issue are too numerous and complex to be detailed here and described fully. We have made previous reference to an article by Cronbach, which we recommend highly for its grasp of the issue.[22] Equally important are the comments by George D. Jackson, Ernest M. Bernal, Jr., Lloyd G. Humphreys, and Julia Vane in the January 1975 issue of the *American Psychologist* (pp. 88–96).

While we recognize that abuses of tests have occurred and no doubt will continue, we do not believe that the use of standardized tests and inventories should be abandoned. Alternative appraisal devices and screening procedures appear to be subject to even greater bias, whim, and caprice than test appraisals. Certainly, tests are useful in providing information helpful to clients in making decisions and plans for the future. Test data have proved to be valuable in identifying possible courses of action, evaluating alternatives, and clarifying the suitability of an individual's plans.

2. *Test results should be interpreted to students and/or their parents.*

    Yes, because:

    1. Knowledge of test scores is vital to sound educational and vocational planning, since test results supply valuable estimates of probable success.
    2. There is no use in trying to conceal from pupils the facts concerning their capabilities, however limited or promising. If they show strengths or limitations in one area or in a variety of areas, the counselor's responsibility is to make these conditions known to them and to help pupils cope with them effectively.

---

[22] Cronbach, "Five Decades of Public Controversy."

3. Testing is not conducted just because it is the thing to do; it is conducted to yield information that can contribute to wise decision-making, and students should enter into such decision-making.
4. Taking a test requires an individual to invest part of himself or herself in a situation. Therefore, he or she has a right to know the outcome.
5. Not informing pupils of their strengths and limitations is contrary to democratic principles, which emphasize individuality, self-reliance, and individual attainment.

No, because:
1. Interpretation develops class consciousness, thereby increasing snobbishness among highly able students and feelings of inferiority among less capable students.
2. Interpretation and reporting of test scores lead to labeling and rating students as slow, fast, or average. Test results often are used against students like clubs by teachers and parents.
3. Test interpretation takes too much time and effort.
4. Test data are complex. Limitations in validity, reliability, and so on may lead to misunderstanding and subsequent misuse of data by students and others.
5. A fully satisfactory way of reporting test results that will ensure understanding by all has yet to be worked out.

Discussion:
This issue revolves around the social implications of testing and the accurate understanding of results reported to individuals. We shall restrict our discussion, however, to the kind and amount of test information provided individuals, though we recognize that this facet of the problem is not entirely free from social implications. This is in itself an extremely important topic. Some states have legislative regulations regarding the kinds of tests that may be used, and many school districts have an established administrative policy regarding test use and interpretation. However, most states and school districts, either by design or omission, permit counselors full latitude in test use and interpretation.

The counselor's responsibility for accurate, thorough, and meaningful interpretation is always subject to counteraction by what the counselee perceives and the way in which that individual may act upon the information given. It is perfectly clear that merely reporting scores without offering relatively extensive counseling is inappropriate. It is only through patient, detailed interpretation, coupled with extensive discussion of the individual's reactions, that truly meaningful use can be made of test results.

ANNOTATED REFERENCES

Aiken, Lewis R., Jr., ed. *Readings in Psychological and Educational Testing.* Boston: Houghton Mifflin, 1973, 447 pp.
The content of Section VIII (pp. 325–370) is devoted to ethical issues and the social impact of testing. Several criticisms are analyzed and examined by noted authors.

DuBois, Philip A. *A History of Psychological Testing.* Boston: Allyn and Bacon, 1970, 173 pp.
This book offers a short but systematic history of psychological testing that is informative and readable. The major contributors who developed tests are identified, and portraits of many of these individuals are included.

Ingenkamps, Karlheinz, ed. *Developments in Educational Testing.* Vol. 1. New York: Gordon and Breech Science Publishers, 1969, 446 pp.
The volume is essentially a report of an international conference on educational measurement. Examination of the work reveals that standardized testing is becoming increasingly prevalent throughout the world. Americans who contributed articles include Eric F. Garner, Henry Chauncy, and E. F. Lindquist.

Linden, Kathryn W., and Linden, James D. *Modern Mental Measurement: A Historical Perspective.* Boston: Houghton Mifflin, 1968, 114 pp.
This monograph presents a comprehensive account of the history of mental measurement. The volume features the individuals whose works markedly influenced modern appraisal practices. Events and contributions are examined carefully and systematically.

SELECTED REFERENCES

Bailey, Roger L. "The Test of Standard Written English: Another Look." *Measurement and Evaluation in Guidance* 10 (July 1977):70–74.

Bardo, Harold R., and Cody, John J. "Minimizing Measurement Concerns in Guidance Evaluations." *Measurement and Evaluation in Guidance* 8 (October 1975): 175–179.

Cleary, T. Anne; Humphrey, Lloyd G.; Kendrick, S. A.; and Wesman, Alexander. "Educational Uses of Tests with Disadvantaged Students." *American Psychologist* 30 (January 1975): 15–41.

Cormany, Robert B. "Faculty Attitudes Toward Standardized Testing." *Measurement and Evaluation in Guidance* 7 (October 1974): 188–194.

Cronbach, Lee J. "Five Decades of Public Controversy Over Mental Testing." *American Psychologist* 30 (January 1975): 1–14.

Hodgson, Mary L., and Cramer, Stanley H. "The Relationship Between Selected Self-Estimated and Measured Abilities in Adolescents. *Measurement and Evaluation in Guidance* 10 (July 1977): 98–105.

Jackson, George D. "Comment on the Report of the Ad Hoc Committee on Educational Uses of Tests with Disadvantaged Students." *American Psychologist* 30 (January 1975): 88–93.

Kopp, Richard Royal. "Early Recollections in Life Style Assessment and Counseling." *The School Counselor* 23 (September 1975): 22–27.

Redick, Ronald D. "A Compilation of Measurement Devices Compendia." *Measurement and Evaluation in Guidance* 8 (October 1975): 193–203.

Van Riper. B. W. "From a Clinical to a Counseling Process." *Measurement and Evaluation in Guidance* 7 (April 1974): 24–31.

Part 2

Application of Individual Analysis

IN THIS SECTION, WE SHALL DISCUSS THE TECHNICAL CONSIDERATIONS fundamental to assessment. Competency in assessment practices requires a thorough understanding of this technology. We shall assume that most students will have had some exposure to basic statistics. Therefore, material in this section highlights, elaborates on, and clarifies those technical considerations most essential for the wise use of tests.

The basic descriptive statistics presented in Chapter 3 are necessary to the counselor in understanding the meaning of various scores and in selecting appropriate normative information for use in interpreting scores. Chapter 4 includes material on correlation, reliability, and validity. The material on correlation will help the student understand how reliability and validity have been conceptualized. Recognizing the significance and understanding the concepts of reliability and validity are paramount to informed selection and use of appraisal data.

Chapter 3

Types of Assessment Data

What is a test? a test score?

Why are statistical methods of value in test development and use?

What are estimates of central tendency and variability, and how are they computed?

Why must a norm-referenced distribution be representative of and relevant to a population of persons about whom predictions are to be made?

What is the difference between intelligence quotients and deviation IQs?

TESTS AND SCORES

The principal vehicle for conducting an assessment of human behavior is a *test*. Any test worthy of the name is a representative and relevant sample of some population of behavior about which predictions may be made. To predict behavior, what is characteristic of that behavior must first be defined; then the task of measuring these characteristics must be accomplished. All tests must be planned to maximize the probability that they measure what they were intended to measure. Of course, human behavior has more specific characteristics than are possible to measure. Consequently, no test attempts to obtain measures from a population for all possible characteristics. Rather, a sample of those characteristics is assessed, which best represents the population. Furthermore, in determining this representative sample, all facets of the test plan must be relevant to the behavioral domain being examined.

A test is a plan, blueprint, or set of specifications for assessing given behavior, like plans used in constructing a building, a bridge, an automobile, or an airplane. Any number of tests could be created from a given plan; the possibilites are limited only by consumer demand, materials available, cost, and the labor of the specialists who build them. Theoretically, it would be possible to create an infinite number of forms for any test; however, in many instances, only one form of any test is ever constructed.

RAW SCORES

Most tests include many stimuli (questions to be answered, tasks to be performed) intended to elicit responses. It is possible to regard each question or task as a separate entity and to base an appraisal on each one. In most instances, however, this would be an inefficient process, if for no other reason than that of the inordinate amounts of time and effort that would be consumed by evaluating a subject's response to every question or task. Instead, responses to all test stimuli, or homogeneous subsets of these stimuli, are summarized, usually in some numerical form. These summary numbers are *raw test scores*. Typically, they represent the frequency with which an individual responded appropriately to test questions or tasks.

All raw scores are estimates rather than absolute measures of behavior. If a person were tested repeatedly on several forms of the same test, it is probable that the scores would be similar, but not identical. Fluctuations in performance, and consequently results, occur, first, because no one form of a test can be truly identical to all other forms and second, because there are natural but temporary changes in an individual over time. This fact should not be forgotten when one attaches meaning to any raw score. Furthermore, the meaning of a raw score depends on its intended use either as a criterion-referenced measure or as a norm-referenced measure. The former has been employed most successfully to evaluate the mastery of fundamental knowledge and skill. Consequently, those who have learned usually experience no difficulty in answering questions or performing tasks at the criterion level established. Those who do not attain the specified criterion score will usually fail to learn more advanced material and ought, therefore, to devote additional effort to learn the basic material assessed by the test before proceeding.

Criterion-referenced raw scores can be interpreted directly. If a criterion of 43 correct responses has been established, a raw score of 40 predicts probable failure. Criterion comparisons enable a tester to make such judgments as, "Both Carl's and Mary's basic knowledge of addition and subtraction is sufficient for them to advance to multiplication; Helen and Henry are not prepared."

COMPARATIVE SCORES

Meaning may also be attributed to raw scores by comparing them with other raw scores, provided that these latter scores have been ordered in a fashion that permits comparisons to be made. Depending on the type of appraisal desired, these comparison scores may be obtained from the same individual or from other individuals. Furthermore, these scores may represent certain levels of ability, achievement, or intensity of interest, or the presence of given personality characteristics, attitudes, or values. Comparisons of scores attained by one individual are termed *ipsative,* or self-referent; they answer questions such as, "Is this student's preparation in algebra better than her or his preparation in geometry?"

Norm-referenced data come from comparing one person's test score with the scores made on the same test by a sample of others who are representative of a group of people with whom a comparison is desired. For example, questions such as, "How does this freshman's need for academic achievement compare with that of other freshmen in the college?" call for norm-referenced data.

Most self-referenced raw scores and all norm-referenced raw scores defy intelligible comparisons unless they are ordered and transformed. Does the fact that Bill has a raw score of 27 on a sociability scale of a personality inventory and an aggression score on the same inventory of 14 necessarily mean that he is more sociable than he is aggressive? Perhaps not. Margaret has a raw score of 127 on a law school entrance examination. Will she be admitted? The outcome depends on many factors, among which are how her score compares with those of other applicants and of students known to be successful in law school. To be ordered and transformed appropriately, raw score data must be analyzed in accordance with a set of mathematical processes called *descriptive statistics.*

STATISTICAL METHODS

The construction and use of tests are associated closely with statistical concepts and techniques. The impetus for developing statistical methods came initially not from the scientific disciplines but from the needs of wealthy aristocrats who wanted principles established for setting odds in games such as roulette, dice, and cards. Sponsored by these wealthy patrons, scientists such as Bernoulli, Demoivre, Laplace, and Gauss, from the middle of the seventeenth to the middle of the eighteenth century, laid the foundation for the modern system of mathematical statistics.

NORMAL DISTRIBUTIONS

Modern statistics had their true historical beginning in the work of the Belgian mathematician Adolf Quetelet (1796–1874), who was the first person to apply Laplace and Gauss' normal law of error to the distribution of human data, both biological and social.[1] The normal law, originally developed in connection with the theory of probabilities in games of chance, had been used by Gauss to explain errors in astronomical observations. Quetelet found that certain anthropometic measurements such as the height of men or the chest measurement of soldiers in the French army were distributed in approximate accordance with this normal law, graphically depicted in the form of a symmetrical bell-shaped curve (see Figure 3.2). This type of curve has important mathematical properties and provides the basis for many kinds of statistical analyses. Essentially, the curve indicates that the largest number of cases cluster in the center of the range of scores, and that the number drops off gradually in both directions as extremely high or low scores are approached. The curve is bilaterally symmetrical, with a single peak in the center. In general, the larger the size of the sample, the more closely will the distribution resemble the theoretical normal probability curve.

Quetelet assumed that human variation might be thought to have arisen when nature, aiming at an ideal, missed by varying degrees. He hypothesized that the position in the middle of the symmetrical curve, where the distribution of errors is smallest, reflects most closely the ideal that nature sought. Thus, the average person, according to Quetelet, was nature's ideal, and deviations away from the average were nature's errors when aiming at this ideal. Quetelet is remembered not so much for his principle of nature's error as for the influence he had on thinkers who followed him. He was one of

---

[1] Kathryn W. Linden and James D. Linden, *Modern Mental Measurement: A Historical Perspective* (Boston: Houghton Mifflin, 1968), pp. 7–8.

the first people to make systematic studies of individual differences, and he interested others in the application of statistical methods in the study of human behavior. To a great extent, current use of and dependence on such statistical tools and indices as frequency distributions and measures of central tendency and variability can be traced to his work. In the next chapter, we shall deal further with the development of statistical methodologies for examining the relationship between measures.

FREQUENCY DISTRIBUTIONS

A major objective of statistical methods is to organize and summarize quantitative data in order to facilitate their understanding. A list of several hundred test scores can be an overwhelming sight. In that form, the scores convey little meaning. The first step in bringing order into such chaos of raw score data is to tabulate the scores into a *frequency distribution* (see Table 3.1). In this case, the raw scores indicate the number of correct responses given by subjects to a forty-question achievement test evaluating knowledge and understanding of basic descriptive statistics. Raw score intervals range from 7–39. Scores obtained from the eighty-one subjects included in the sample have been tallied, and the tallies have been counted to find the frequency, or number of subjects who have earned a given raw score. The sum of these frequencies equals N, the total number of cases in the sample.

This frequency distribution table permits raw scores to be organized into a framework for more efficient analysis. It is now possible to note at a glance the highest and the lowest scores and even to approximate the average score and estimate the location of the top quarter and the lowest quarter of the scores in the distribution. However, the first purpose of any frequency distribution table is simply to present and order the scores, the first step in any statistical analysis. Then, columns in frequency distribution tables can be used for actual analyses of raw test score data.

Sometimes it is desirable, when the subject sample is large and the range of scores is great, to group the scores in intervals of predetermined and uniform size. To determine the intervals to be used, first determine the range of scores (highest score minus lowest score plus 1) and divide by any odd number between 10 and 20 (yielding a midpoint of the interval that is a whole number, which makes for easier data presentation and further computations). This procedure is recommended because most experts believe that 10–

TABLE 3.1
RAW SCORE FREQUENCY DISTRIBUTION:
BASIC DESCRIPTIVE STATISTICS (N = 81)[ab]

RAW SCORE[c]	FREQUENCY	CUMULATIVE FREQUENCY
39	1	81
38	2	80
36	2	78
32	3	76
31	4	73
29	1	69
28	4	68
27	2	64
26	4	62
25	5	58
24	8	53
23	9	45
22	7	36
21	6	29
20	3	23
19	1	20
18	1	19
17	4	18
16	1	14
15	1	13
14	6	12
11	3	6
8	1	3
7	2	2

[a] mean = 22.78; standard deviation = 6.88
[b] median = 23.10; Q_1 = 20.42, Q_3 = 25.81
[c] Number of items in test (k) = 40; raw score interval size (i) = 1

20 class intervals for a given distribution are sufficient to summarize the data efficiently while not misrepresenting grossly the actual nature of the underlying distribution nor introducing excessive grouping errors in the statistics to be computed.

The information provided by a frequency distribution can also be presented graphically in the form of a distribution curve. Figure 3.1 shows the data of Table 3.1 in graph form. On the baseline, or horizontal axis, are raw score intervals. On the vertical axis are the frequencies, or number of cases falling within each raw score interval. The graph has been plotted two ways, both forms being in common use. In the *histogram* (the box-like diagram), the height of

FIGURE 3.1
HISTOGRAM AND FREQUENCY POLYGON

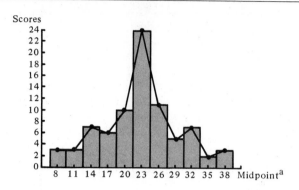

[a] Data, Table 3.1 (N = 81) grouped within class interval i = 3. Interval midpoint designated to represent raw score interval values.

the column erected over each score interval corresponds with the number of persons obtaining that score. In the *frequency polygon*, the number of persons in each interval is indicated by a point placed above the *midpoint* of the score interval and opposite the appropriate frequency. Successive points are then joined by straight lines.

MEASURES OF CENTRAL
TENDENCY AND VARIABILITY

A given distribution of test scores can be defined in terms of the average score obtained by a sample of subjects and the spread of scores (from high to low) within the distribution. Three indices of averageness can be used: the mode, the median, and the arithmetic mean. These indices are measures of the central tendency of the distribution of scores.

CENTRAL TENDENCY

MODE   The *mode* is the raw score most frequently obtained in a distribution. When frequency of scores is represented graphically, the mode is the peak of the graph. Sometimes more than one mode can be determined. This happens when two or more scores are found to occur with equal frequency in the distribution, and when this frequency of occurrence is greater than that of all remaining scores in the distribution. Such score distributions are known as bimodal (two modes) or multimodal (more than two modes). The distribution shown in Table 3.1 and Figure 3.1 is unimodal. The raw score of 23 was obtained by nine persons, a frequency greater than that found for any other raw score in the distribution. The mode is easy to determine; however, it is a crude and unstable index of central tendency. It frequently differs from sample to sample of a given population. Usually the mean or the median is a more accurate index of the average score.

MEDIAN   The *median* is the midmost score of a distribution. More exactly, it is the point on the score scale both above and below which 50 percent of the scores are to be found. Eighty-one subjects were included in the example detailed in Table 3.1; thus, the distribution comprises eighty-one raw scores. Half of 81 is 40.5; consequently, the median is a point on the score scale 40.5 raw scores from either the top or the bottom of this distribution—in this case, 23.1. Ordinarily, the median is estimated in reference to the bottom of the distribution. Since specific procedures for computing the median are presented in almost all basic statistical textbooks, we shall not detail them here.

Medians are appropriate to use because test data are ordinal scales. A raw score of 28 represents merely one more correct response than a raw score of 27, rather than one more measurement unit necessarily equal in magnitude to the other 27. The median is in fact the least biased estimate of central tendency. Modes are unstable, and arithmetic means are vulnerable to distortion caused by atypically high or low scores. Medians are used far less frequently than are means, however. Provided the sample size is large, an arithmetic mean should be sufficiently accurate to be used with test scores.

MEAN   Many important statistical indices (such as the standard deviation) require the use of an arithmetic mean for computation. The *mean*, often called the arithmetic average, is computed by adding the values of all scores in a distribution and dividing by the number of scores. When the mean for a large number of scores is to be computed, using a calculator or computational shortcuts can be quite helpful. Many textbooks in elementary statistics detail these

shortcuts, and some cover the use of formulas with calculators.[2]
The arithmetic mean estimated for the data in Table 3.1 is 22.78.
The central tendency estimates of the mean, median, and mode for
this sample round out to an approximate score of 23. This indicates
that the distribution is symmetrical. When estimates of the mean,
median, and mode are not identical, the distribution can be termed
skewed. Often the discrepancies between measures of central tendency are minor, and for all practicable purposes, the normal curve
can be used in evaluating the distribution. This is important, because traditional methods for analyzing test scores depend on the
assumption that the scores in the sample are distributed normally.
If a distribution deviates significantly from normal, serious errors
in interpreting scores can be made. Skewed distributions can be
adjusted statistically. However, it is far better for test authors to
rework their tests so that normal distributions can be elicited from
subjects than for them to use statistical wrenches to adjust skewed
data.

To discover if a distribution is normal, more information than
central tendency must be known. Attention has to be given to the
fashion in which the scores in a distribution cluster about estimates
of central tendency. To do so, measures of variability must be taken.

VARIABILITY

Indices of the dispersion of scores from high to low within a distribution, or the *variability* of scores, constitute the second major
characteristic of any set of scores. Three indices of variability are
available to interpreters of test scores: range, quartile deviation, and
standard deviation.

RANGE   The crudest index is the *range* of scores within the set.
Range can be determined easily by subtracting the lowest score
from the highest and adding 1. In our example (Table 3.1), the
highest raw score is 39 and the lowest is 7. The difference plus 1 is
33, the *exact* range of scores on the test. It is possible for a person
to earn a maximum score of 40 or a minimum score of 0 on this
test. Forty-one raw score units, therefore, constitute the *absolute*
range of scores. The closer the correspondence, or ratio, between
the exact range and the absolute range, the greater the dispersion,
or variability, of the scores in a given distribution. In our example,

---

[2] See, for instance, N. M. Downie and Allen R. Starry, *Descriptive and Inferential Statistics*
(New York: Harper and Row, 1977).

the dispersion is .80. Had the highest raw score been 35 and the lowest raw score 17, the exact range would have been less (19), and the ratio of the exact to the absolute range would have reflected this more limited variability (.46).

QUARTILE DEVIATION   The bulk of the raw scores fall in the middle of a distribution, unless the distribution is skewed markedly. With repeated testing, extremely high or low scores tend to fluctuate more than do central tendency scores. Consequently, the semi-interquartile range, or Q, is a somewhat more dependable estimate of variability than is range. Q can be found by first estimating the seventy-fifth and twenty-fifth percentiles of a distribution, then determining the difference between the two and dividing this difference by 2. For Table 3.1, the seventy-fifth percentile is 25.81, and the twenty-fifth about 20.42. The difference between the two (seventy-fifth percentile minus the twenty-fifth) is 5.39, the quartile range. Half of this difference (Q) is 2.70.

As is true of all estimates of variability, the relative size of the index is significant in relation to the absolute range of the distribution. The greater the proportion of the absolute range accounted for by Q, the greater is the variability among the raw scores that contribute to the distribution. In Table 3.1, the ratio of Q to the absolute range is .06 (rounded to two decimal places). Had the scores in the middle half of the distribution been spread over a greater range (say, Q = 3.1), the ratio of Q to the absolute range would have been .08. If Q = 2.70, as opposed to Q = 3.10, the variability of one distribution is not necessarily greater than the variability of another. (What if one test had 100 questions and another test only 30?) However, the ratio of Q to absolute range differences (.08 versus .06) does indicate that the difference among scores would be greater if Q = 3.10 than if Q = 2.70.

STANDARD DEVIATION   Since quartile deviations are appropriate for use with ordinal measures, and since most test scores are ordinal numbers, Q is theoretically the most appropriate index of variability. However, the estimate known as the standard deviation provides an efficient estimate of variability in a large distribution of scores. Computation of several other statistical indices important to test development and interpretation requires the use of the standard deviation. Consequently, it is the index most often used to determine variability.

The *standard deviation*, frequently written σ (*sigma*), is the square root of the arithmetic mean of the squared difference between scores in the distribution and the mean of that distribution.

FIGURE 3.2
RELATIONSHIP AMONG RAW SCORES, PERCENTILES,
AND SELECTED STANDARD SCORES (NORMAL DISTRIBUTION ASSUMED)

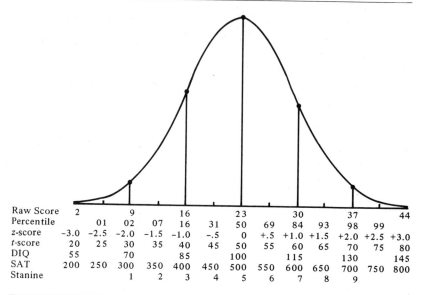

Raw Score	2		9		16		23		30		37		44
Percentile		01	02	07	16	31	50	69	84	93	98	99	
z-score	-3.0	-2.5	-2.0	-1.5	-1.0	-.5	0	+.5	+1.0	+1.5	+2.0	+2.5	+3.0
t-score	20	25	30	35	40	45	50	55	60	65	70	75	80
DIQ	55		70		85		100		115		130		145
SAT	200	250	300	350	400	450	500	550	600	650	700	750	800
Stanine			1	2	3	4	5	6	7	8	9		

(See any basic statistical textbook for procedures for computing standard deviation.) In most cases when human behaviors are measured and the number of subjects is greater than 120, the raw score distribution approximates the characteristics of the normal probability curve. Therefore, the known mathematical relationships of the standard deviation of the normal curve can be used. In a normal distribution of raw scores, the numerical value of the standard deviation divides the raw score range into approximately six equal parts, of which three are above the mean and three are below. When sample size is smaller than 120, *sigma* usually divides a range of scores into fewer than six equal parts, as there is a smaller likelihood of obtaining extremely high or low scores. For example, only 4.8 *sigma* distances encompass the range of scores presented in Table 3.1 (N = 81).

Let us assume, however, that the data in Table 3.1 were distributed normally and the N exceeded 120. The expected relationship between *sigma* ranges and the normal distribution, under these conditions, is depicted in Figure 3.2. The mean and standard deviation estimated for Table 3.1 are 22.78 and 6.88 respectively. Because the distribution is assumed to be normal, the mean approximates the median (both estimates round out to equal 23). Consequently, about half the scores are above and half below the mean. Roughly two-thirds of the scores fall between 16 and 30. Because the normal distribution is symmetrical above and below the mean, about one-third of the scores lie between the mean and a point one *sigma* above the mean; about one-third cluster between the mean and a point 1 *sigma* below the mean. Approximately 96 percent of the scores distribute themselves between minus two standard deviations and plus two standard deviations from the mean. Roughly 48 percent of the scores are distributed from the mean to a point plus two *sigma* above the mean, and another 48 percent of the scores are plotted between the mean and two *sigma* below the mean. More than 99 percent of all scores in a normal distribution occur between plus and minus three *sigma* from the mean. Less than 1 percent of all scores can be expected to exceed plus or minus 3 standard deviations from the mean.

NORMATIVE COMPARISONS

Principle 3 (see Chapter 1) stated that both idiographic and normative data are used in almost all appraisals. Here we shall give additional attention to the nature of normative data and their use. In those instances when raw test scores have no meaning unless they are compared with a body of appropriate reference data, testers refer to *normative* distribution of scores. That is, the raw scores in the distribution are assumed to be distributed normally. If the reference sample is large and representative of a population, and the behavior assessed occurs naturally, the result should approximate the normal probability distribution. The counselor must regard with caution reference distributions that may be based on small samples or that may not be representative of a population, for they may not be normal.

A norm-referenced comparison sample must be relevant to and representative of the population about which inferences are to be made. If a counselor were interested in comparing a student's performance to that of suburban high school seniors, a sample representative of rural high school sophomores would not be relevant. Furthermore, if norms were created based only on those suburban seniors who enter large midwestern universities, the sample would not represent all suburban high school seniors nationwide.

Let us assume that a student has applied for admission to graduate school in educational and psychological measurement. Researchers have found a significant and strong relationship between the knowledge of basic descriptive statistics and successful performance in such graduate programs (see Chapter 4). Consequently, the student takes an achievement test on basic descriptive statistics that is meant to help the admissions committee select applicants for admission. The student earns a raw score of 20, out of 40. Is the student's background in descriptive statistics sufficiently strong to warrant admission? If the test were a criterion-referenced measure, the score could be interpreted directly as a successful performance on only 50 percent of the items. However, let us assume that the test was designed to enable an examiner to distinguish between levels of knowledge of statistics. We can know what this raw score means only when we compare it with others.

Let us assume further that a sample of high school freshmen in California take the test. The mean score is 12, and the standard deviation is 4. Furthermore, this distribution is determined to be normal. A raw score of 20, then, is two *sigma* above the mean. Approximately 98 percent of the reference sample answered fewer than 20 questions correctly. How well has our student done? Certainly better than most high school freshmen in California. However, do these data help estimate the student's chance for admission to graduate school? No, for the student is not competing with high school freshmen for admission. The sample may be representative of California high school freshmen, but it is not representative of the population of which the student is a member. Still other reference data are required.

Other data can be obtained from a sample representative of doctoral-level mathematical statistics students nationwide. The mean and standard deviation for this reference group are 26 and 3 respectively. In comparison to this reference group, the student's raw score of 20 is two *sigma* below the mean, that is, lower than 98 percent of the other scores. Of course, the comparison is again not relevant. Additional data are needed.

Let us assume that a nationwide sample representative of applicants to graduate programs in educational and psychological measurement cannot be collected conveniently and economically. Instead, the most relevant sample available is one of master's-level graduate students nationwide who are working toward permanent certification as elementary or secondary school teachers and who took the test in question after completing a basic statistics course. Let us assume also that the data in Table 3.1 are a representative subsample of these individuals. The mean of this subsample approximates a raw score of 23 and a standard deviation of about 7. From these data, the student learns that the raw score of 20 is less than the mean, median, and mode of the reference sample. More than half of this quasi-representative sample of subjects have answered more than 20 questions correctly. Less than half have scored less well. Thus, the student's performance may be construed to be low average. Although these reference data are not absolutely relevant, their relative relevance permits the student to hazard a guess that, with effort, he or she could handle the demands of the graduate program, but that his or her chances for admission are probably low.

This situation reflects a dilemma that counselors often confront: exact data relevant to and representative of a given population about whom inferences must be made are not readily available. The counselor must use the available reference or normative data with caution.

DERIVED SCORES

A more exact estimate of the student's relative performance and chance for admission to graduate school can be provided by means of *derived* scores. At the most crude level, this could be one's rank within a subject sample. However, the size of the subject sample plays a significant role in determining the meaning assigned to a given rank (for example, a rank of 3 in a group of ten subjects has a different meaning from a rank of 3 in a group of a thousand).

PERCENTILE   A derived score that is useful in describing an individual's performance is the *percentile rank*. To calculate a percentile rank, count the number of scores at or below a given score in a frequency distribution and divide by the total number of subjects. Multiply this dividend by 100 and round to the closest whole number. The *cumulative frequency* distribution (see Table 3.1) is useful in computing percentile rank.

Although percentile rank is easy to use, standard scores are often more accurate. Percentile scores are not equal interval scores, whereas standard scores are. Recall that the standard deviation divides a normal distribution of raw scores into six equal raw score parts. The raw score difference between minus two and minus three *sigma* is equal to the raw score *sigma* difference between the mean and plus 1 standard deviation from the mean. Throughout the distribution, mean deviation scores, expressed as a ratio to the standard deviation, are equal-interval measures. This is not the case with percentile ranks. The distance between a score approximately 2 standard deviations below the mean in contrast with a score 1 standard deviation below the mean covers 14 percentile rank points (see Figure 3.2). A raw score at the mean as compared with a raw score one *sigma* above the mean covers approximately 34 percentile rank points. Yet, in each instance, these raw score differences are about 1 standard deviation apart. At the outer limits of a distribution (high and low tails), a difference of many more raw score points is required to effect a significant difference in percentile ranks than in the center of a distribution. Therefore, in regard to percentiles, a raw score distribution is fluid in the center and brittle at the tails. Whereas the percentile rank distribution depicts an ordinal relationship among scores, standard scores reflect an equal-interval relationship.

Z-SCORE   The principal standard score is the z-score. The term *standard score* means that the raw score is expressed as a ratio of the algebraic difference between a raw score and the mean to the standard deviation estimated for the distribution of scores. Raw scores that fall at the mean equal the mean. Consequently, the numerator for the computation of z in such cases is 0. Zero divided by anything is 0. Therefore, the z-value of the mean is 0. A score plus 1 standard deviation above the mean has a z-value of +1.0; a score 2 standard deviations below the mean has a z-value of −2.0

FIGURE 3.3
LINEAR TRANSFORMATION, SCALE A TO SCALE B

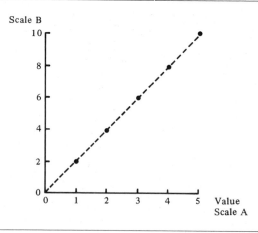

(see Figure 3.2). In effect, the derived mean and standard deviation of a z distribution are 0 and 1, respectively. In a normal distribution, almost all z-values range from -3.0 through 0.0 to $+3.0$.

The z standard score has been used for many years. Because z-scores yield decimal numbers with plus and minus algebraic signs (a raw score of 20 for the reference distribution in Table 3.1 would be equivalent to a z-score of $-.40$), they have troubled many counselors even though as equal interval numbers they can be manipulated arithmetically whereas ordinal percentile ranks cannot.

LINEAR TRANSFORMATION   Decimal and mixed-sign numbers are difficult to compute. Measurement specialists, recognizing this problem, introduced *linear transformations* of the basic z-score, which have eliminated the need to use decimal numbers and mixed signs. To transform any score scale, multiply each score in the distribution by a constant and add to another constant. A linear transformation changes only the names of the scores, not the mathematical relationships among them. In Figure 3.3, two scales are presented: 1, 2, 3, 4, 5, and 2, 4, 6, 8, 10. One is the linear equivalent of the other. Given equal intervals for distances on one scale that correspond to the same equal intervals on the other scale, the distance between 1 and 2 on scale A equals the distance between 2 and 4 on scale B. Were the points of correspondence between the two scales to be connected, they would form a straight (or *linear*) line. The constant added to a z-score to transform it is an arbitrary mean; the constant by which it is multiplied is an arbitrary value for the standard deviation of the new distribution.

T-SCORE   The first transformed standard score was the t-score. In the t-score, the arbitrary mean is 50 and the arbitrary standard deviation is 10. All t-scores are rounded to the nearest whole number. A raw score 1 standard deviation above the mean equals a z-score of $+1.0$ and a t-score of 60 ($z = 0$, the mean z plus 50, plus $+1.0 \times 10$). Because most distributions do not exceed plus or minus 3 standard deviations from the mean, the t-score distribution usually ranges from a low of about $t = 20$ to a high of $t = 80$. Decimal numbers and algebraic signs are thus eliminated.

STANINE SCORE   During the Second World War, the *stanine score* was developed, which has since had considerable impact on the use of standard score transformations. Extensive psychological research was conducted, especially on flight personnel in the Army (now the United States) Air Force, to predict job success. Many variables were studied for their predictive efficiency, and data were obtained from thousands of people. Computers at the time were cumbersome and slow, so researchers decided that the data could be processed most efficiently by reducing measures or scores to single-digit numbers ranging from 0–9. (A computer requires more than twice as much time to process two-digit numbers as single-digit numbers and more than three times as much time to deal with three-digit numbers.)

They established a standard score transformation, using 5 as an arbitrary mean and 2 as the standard deviation of the transformed standard score distribution. Scores ranging from minus 2 to plus 2 standard deviations from the mean occupied the single-digit range 1–9 (thus the standard-nine distribution, or *stanine*). (Discrimination between persons plus 2 or minus 2 standard deviations from the mean and beyond—the upper and lower 2 to 3 percent—failed to yield significant results.) Thus, the system provided a useful crude distribution for the ninety-eighth through the second percentile.

Though the stanine standard score distribution is crude, because of the imprecision of educational and psychological measurements at high and low extremes (see Chapter 4), it is a practical measurement. In recent years, the use of the stanine standard score has gained in popularity, and many tests today report normative reference data in both stanine and percentile-rank formats in order to provide data that both depict real differences between people and that counselors and others can understand and use easily. Given time and training, counselors may stop relying on percentile ranks and use standard scores such as the stanine for describing performance. Knowledge of certain basic relationships for reference points between percentile ranks and standard scores, provided a distribution of raw scores is normal, should permit the counselor to interpret standard scores as percentiles while allowing for subtleties of measurement that percentiles fail to express.

IQ SCORES

Counselors, educators, and other helping professionals often deal with the intelligence quotient (IQ). Because of its prominence and the controversy surrounding it, we shall discuss the IQ at greater length in Chapter 5. However, here are considerations regarding its properties as a test score, especially in comparison with standard scores mislabeled IQ scores.

ORIGIN

In developing the first successful standardized test to evaluate academic ability, the Frenchman Alfred Binet introduced in 1905 the concept of a mental age score. This was a measure of level of achievement. For example, a child who obtained a mental age score of 8 years, 6 months was evaluated as having achieved at a level similar to that achieved by the modal child 8 years, 6 months of age. Binet warned that the scale measured not only intelligence but also knowledge gained from school and from the environment in general.

In 1912, William Stern, an Austrian, introduced the concept of the mental quotient, the ratio of mental age score (level of accomplishment) to chronological age. A mental quotient of 1.0 implies that a child has progressed at a rate normal for his or her chronological age. A mental quotient in excess of 1.0 implies a faster than normal rate of intellectual growth, and a quotient of less than 1.0 indicates a slower than normal rate. Accordingly, rapid intellectual development has been accepted as behavioral evidence of a large capacity for mental growth and slow intellectual development as an indication of a limited capacity for such growth.

FIRST USE

Between 1910 and 1916, Lewis Terman (1877–1956) revised Binet's scale for use in America.[3] The basic measure Terman employed to report performance on his revised scale (the Stanford-Binet) was Stern's mental quotient concept, which Terman multiplied by 100 to eliminate the decimal point and renamed the *intelligence quotient* or IQ. Terman suggested a classification scheme for interpreting IQ that is still quoted without change in many textbooks. IQs from 90–110 indicate normal intelligence; an IQ below 70 indicates definite feeblemindness; an IQ above 140 indicates genius. Terman took care to point out that these limits were defined arbitrarily and that the classification scheme itself was intended only as a general guide for using the new measure. Unfortunately, these cautions were soon disregarded by many people dazzled by evidence of

---

[3] L. M. Terman, *Measurement of Intelligence: An Explanation of and a Complete Guide for the Use of the Stanford Revision and Extension of the Binet-Simon Intelligence Scale* (Boston: Houghton Mifflin, 1916).

marked contrast in school achievement and general behavior of children with high and low IQs. Even educators and psychologists came to view the IQ as an absolute, infallible index of mental capacity.

THE DEVIATION IQ
AND OTHER STANDARD SCORES

The intelligence quotient was accepted so quickly and uncritically as a standard for intelligence that ability test authors reported their raw score distributions as though they were orthodox IQs, that is, estimates of the rate of educational achievement of a child of a given age. They did this in order to sell their tests to educators enamoured of the IQ. However, with virtually no exception, these measures did not give an estimate of mental age expressed as a ratio to chronological age. Instead, the testers obtained distributions of raw scores on an ability measure, converted them to z-scores, and transformed these standard score distributions into distributions that looked like IQs. This was easy to do because, by the early 1920s, it was known that the mean of the distribution of Stanford-Binet IQ scores for children of a given age approximated 100 and that the standard deviation ranged from 14 to 16.

Many tests, including the popular series of individually administered Wechsler intelligence tests, arbitrarily used a standard score mean of 100 and a standard score *sigma* approximating 15. In fact, the rate of intellectual development cannot be inferred from these transformed distributions, in more recent years labeled *deviation IQs* (DIQs) to differentiate them from the Stanford-Binet IQ score. These standard scores reflect a level of achievement in comparison with persons of similar environment, age, and years of education. Although the relationship between Stanford-Binet IQ scores and DIQ scores is high, they are not the same. To interpret a DIQ as though it were a Stanford-Binet IQ can lead to serious misconceptions.

By the early 1950s, the Educational Testing Service, aware of this problem, decided to adopt a different system that used an arbitrary standard score transformation mean of 500 and standard deviation of 100 (the t-score multiplied by 10). This system has been employed in the *Scholastic Aptitude Test* of the College Entrance Examination Board (SAT) and the *Graduate Record Examination* (GRE). Because hardly anyone taking the test scores as low as 200 (three *sigma* below the mean), it was thought that scores on these tests, which range from 200–800, could not be confused with IQ scores.

RECAPITULATION

Let us assume, in light of what we have discussed, that a student's raw score on the test reported in Table 3.1 was 37. The corresponding percentile rank would approximate 98, the z-score $+2.0$, the t-score 70, the DIQ 130, the SAT or GRE score 700, and the stanine score 9. All these scores are different names applied to describe the student's performance in comparison with the reference sample. The scores are interchangeable in that, given a normal distribution, all signify that the raw score of 37 is 2 standard deviations above the mean in a distribution with a mean raw score of 23 and a raw-score standard deviation of approximately 7. Provided the reference distribution is representative and relevant, meaning may be derived from the score. The meaning that may be accorded to the test itself will be discussed in the next chapter.

A final point to be reinterated here relates to principle 12 (see Chapter 1), which stated that any information used in appraising an individual must be assessed accurately, fully, and economically. Test scores are not precise measures of human behavior regardless of the format used to express the measurement. Test scores should always be regarded as estimates rather than absolutes. In Chapter 4, we shall provide more detailed information on this point.

ISSUES

1. *Test data should be ordered and analyzed by only those statistical procedures appropriate for use with nominal or ordinal data.*
    Yes, because:
    1. At best, test scores depict ordinal relationships.
    2. Only statistics appropriate for the analysis of given types of data should be utilized.

    No, because:
    1. Provided N is large, statistical procedures relevant for use with interval or ratio data may be applied to ordinal data without incurring significant error.
    2. Whenever possible, practical analysis of test data requires that these data be viewed as exhibiting interval properties.

    Discussion:
    Although technically the fundamental mathematical properties of interval and ratio data are not met by test-score data, most

test-score distributions function as though they were normal in nature provided N exceeds 120 (preferably, 300) and is representative of a relevant population. All legitimate test-development work should be based on large and representative data samples. If ordinal test data function in accord with the characteristics of the normal probability distribution, the advantages of treating such data as though they were interval in nature outweigh objections to the contrary, because these data may be manipulated arithmetically.[4] Were this not the case, the characteristics of the normal probability curve could not be applied to distributions of test scores. Means and standard deviations could not be computed legitimately, and standard scores would have no basis for application. Only medians, quartile deviations, and percentiles could be employed, with considerable loss in versatility. However, it is essential that both the test developer and tester recognize that, to justify the practice of dealing with test data as though they had interval properties, test data must be ordinal in nature and must be distributed normally. If these assumptions are violated, the application of interval-dependent statistics to test data is not defensible.

2. *Specific test norms should be established for some ethnic or racial groups.*

Yes, because:

1. The experiences of different ethnic or racial groups have been found to produce differences in test scores, especially on tests of academic achievement.
2. Ethnic or racial group differences should be taken into account when interpreting any test score.

No, because:

1. Only comparisons with persons representative of the population about which inferences are to be made are appropriate.
2. For many questions that test data may help answer, normative comparisons with persons representative of specific ethnic or racial groups may provide an irrelevant and misleading basis for deriving inferences regarding an individual's test performance.

---

[4] J. C. Nunnally, "Psychometric Theory—25 Years Ago and Now," *Educational Researcher* 4 (1975); 14, 19.

Discussion:

Specialized comparisons are justified only when questions are asked or inferences are made about members of a specific population. The importance of this principle will be illustrated in the next chapter in the discussion of test validity. Suffice it to say now that, if the purpose of testing is to compare black with black, Latino with Latino, or Bulgarian with Bulgarian, special ethnic- or racial-group norms are required. However, in comparing urban high school seniors or successful employees on a particular job, the use of ethnic or racial group norms is inappropriate. Instead, comparisons should be drawn with representative samples of other urban high school seniors or successful employees. Use of inappropriate normative reference groups can only lead to error in drawing inferences about people and their future behavior.

3. *The IQ provides a useful estimate of an individual's potential for school achievement.*

Yes, because:

1. A strong and positive relationship exists between IQ scores and measures of school achievement, regardless of ethnic or racial group.
2. IQ tests measure behavior essential for success in school.

No, because:

1. IQ tests are biased in favor of the white middle class.
2. All ability measures assess academic achievement or preparation, not potential.

Discussion:

Though this question has been raised, and presumably resolved, many times over, it remains a real issue because of the failure of many to accept the fact that IQ and other ability or achievement tests do not measure intelligence directly. Rather, they enable the tester to draw inferences about the examinee's probable capacity to learn. There is no question but that a strong and positive relationship exists between performance on IQ tests and grades in school. This is true in large part because such tests measure learning that is essential to success in school. However, schools are still white middle-class, value-oriented institutions, as are most institutions in Western societies. The white middle class enjoys opportunities and experiences reinforcements that increase the chance for success in school. Perhaps, with environment, opportunity, and experience held constant, some guarded inferences may be made regarding differential capacity to learn in school. Even so, such inferences are probably not justified.

Education is not synonymous with intelligence. Furthermore, the IQ and other related tests measure considerably less than the total school experience. Moreover, there is no assurance that the environmental variables of opportunity and experience, to say nothing of the personalized variable of motivation, are constant for all members of any class. Therefore, how can one speak of assessing potential or capacity among the population for which ability measures are most relevant—to say nothing of applying this concept to those for whom these measures are much less relevant, if relevant at all?

Their shortcomings aside, ability and achievement tests have demonstrated, in assessing level of preparation relevant to success in school, and to a lesser degree success in work, an efficiency as great as, if not greater than, that of other predictor variables in our society. It has been argued that, because tests are biased in favor of the white middle class, their use penalizes certain ethnic or racial groups and that, consequently, testing is a discriminatory practice and should be discontinued. In New York and California, among other states, the use of IQ scores has been prohibited; only ability and achievement tests that yield no such score may be employed. Perhaps this is for the better, given the uninformed belief of many that IQ scores measure intellectual potential. However, IQ and other similar tests merely reflect the quality of schooling in our society.

Tests do not penalize individuals; environmental differences do. So long as schools mirror the demands of a technological society to prepare people for productive work, tests should retain their power to predict performance in school and at work, if for no other reason than that past behavior still predicts future behavior better than any other known variable.

ANNOTATED REFERENCES

Davis, F. B. *Educational Measurements and Their Interpretation.* Belmont, Calif.: Wadsworth Publishing Company, 1964, 405 pp.

Intended as a basic text and handbook focusing on the use of tests in schools and clinics, this book is organized to serve students with diverse backgrounds. The textbook demands little use of descriptive statistics;

however, a set of comprehensive appendices details these computations in simple language. For this reason, we cite this book for special consideration.

Downie, N. M. *Types of Test Scores.* Boston: Houghton Mifflin, 1968, 54 pp.

This monograph presents an easily understood coverage of different kinds of test scores as well as a comprehensive discussion of their advantages, limitations, and appropriate use. Furthermore, it includes pertinent computational guides that are easily used. The author's prose is terse and direct and affords the reader an economical guide to this topical area.

Lyman, H. B. *Test Scores and What They Mean.* 2nd ed. Englewood Cliffs, N.J.: Prentice-Hall, 1971, 186 pp.

This book was the first to deal primarily with the meaning of test scores and was intended to serve the needs of those with limited training in testing. It contains an original classification of score types and elaborates on their logical bases and interrelationships. The book includes a chapter on descriptive statistics of value to students working to master the concepts presented in this chapter.

SELECTED REFERENCES

Anastasi, Anne. *Psychological Testing.* 4th ed. New York: Macmillan, 1976, pp. 67–102.

Brown, F. G. *Principles of Educational and Psychological Testing.* Hinsdale, Ill.: The Dryden Press, 1970, pp. 15–17.

Cronbach, L. J. *Essentials of Psychological Testing.* 3rd ed. New York: Harper and Row, 1970, pp. 78–114.

Downie, N. M., and Starry, Allen. *Descriptive and Inferential Statistics.* New York: Harper and Row, 1977, pp. 40–43, 170.

Ebel, R. L. *Essentials of Educational Measurement.* 2nd ed. Englewood Cliffs, N.J.: Prentice-Hall, 1972, pp. 271–295.

Helmstadter, G. C. *Principles of Psychological Measurement.* New York: Appleton-Century-Crofts, 1964, pp. 41–57.

Horrocks, J. E. *Assessment of Behavior.* Columbus, Ohio: Charles E. Merrill Books, 1965, pp. 23–54.

Lien, A. J. *Measurement and Evaluation of Learning.* 2nd ed. Dubuque, Iowa: Wm. C. Brown, 1971, pp. 168–186, 241–243.

Mehrens, W. A., and Lehmann, I. J. *Measurement and Evaluation in Education and Psychology.* 2nd ed. New York: Holt, Rinehart and Winston, 1978, pp. 65–86, 133–156.

Noll, V. H., and Scannell, D. P. *Introduction to Educational Measurement.* 3rd ed. Boston: Houghton Mifflin, 1972, pp. 45–55, 71–80.

Nunnally, J. C., Jr. *Introduction to Psychological Measurement.* New York: McGraw-Hill, 1970, pp. 55–58, 63–67.

Payne, D. A. *The Assessment of Learning: Cognitive and Affective.* Lexington, Mass.: D. C. Heath and Company, 1974, pp. 203–206, 213.

Thorndike, R. L., and Hagen, Elizabeth. *Measurement and Evaluation in Psychology and Education.* 4th ed. New York: John Wiley and Sons, 1977, pp. 136–140, 210–233.

Chapter 4

Criteria for Test Selection and Interpretation

Why is the correlation coefficient critical to evaluating the reliability and validity of tests?

What are the major methodologies for estimating test reliability? What are the advantages and limitations of each?

What are the principal sources of reliable variance and error variance in any test score?

How reliable must a test be to warrant its use?

What are the principal methodologies for estimating test validity? What are their different functional characteristics?

What problems are associated with the definition and measurement of criteria for estimating the validity of a test?

When is a test functionally valid?

What is the difference between the standard error of measurement and the standard error of estimate? To what practical use may these statistical indices be put?

In a school, the counselor is usually the person who is most knowledgeable about tests. To be able to evaluate the utility of any test for a specific purpose and a given population, the counselor must give consideration to the relevance of the test for that purpose and those people and to the accuracy of the data. In this chapter, we shall discuss the essential criteria governing decisions about these crucial issues.

This material is essential to counselors in assessing the fundamental qualities of all tests and other appraisal methodologies regardless of type or by whom constructed and used. We cannot overemphasize the importance of developing such competence. Failure to master this body of knowledge will result in the improper selection and interpretation of appraisal data.

CORRELATION METHODOLOGY

The *correlation coefficient* is central to the experimental designs and the statistical methodology used to evaluate the utility of any test or other appraisal technique. Originated by Sir Francis Galton in the late 1800s, refined by Charles Spearman at the turn of the century, and perfected by Karl Pearson in the early 1900s (see Table 2.1), correlation methodology as a descriptive statistical procedure is the principal means of evaluating the accuracy and relevance of tests.[1]

Correlation techniques examine the relationships between sets of data obtained from a sample of subjects thought to be representative of a given population. Details of the various procedures used are beyond the scope of this book but are supplied in many statistical textbooks.[2] For our purposes, Karl Pearson's product-moment correlation (*r*) procedure is basic.[3] Most other variants of correlation methodology are related to Pearson's *r*, including that determined by Charles Spearman for rank-ordered ordinal data.[4]

VARIANCE AND COVARIANCE

The concepts of *variance* and *covariance* are essential to understanding the relationship between two or more sets of data obtained from a sample of subjects. To assess the reliability of any measure, the correspondence between responses to a set of stimuli and another equivalent set of stimuli must be determined. To the extent that correspondence is found, accuracy of measure may be inferred; if there is no correspondence, error is concluded. If appraisal data correspond to measures of behavior, one may assume that the appraisal data are valid.

The concept of variance relates directly to that of the standard deviation (see Chapter 3). As a descriptive index of a single distribution of scores, the standard deviation helps answer the question, "How much variability exists among the scores in the distribution?" Standard deviations are ranges on a scale, and as such, are

---

[1] Kathryn Linden and J. D. Linden, *Modern Mental Measurement: A Historical Perspective* (Boston: Houghton Mifflin, 1968) pp. 6–8.

[2] N. M. Downie and A. R. Starry, *Descriptive and Inferential Statistics* (New York: Harper and Row, 1977) pp. 189–202.

[3] C. J. Adcock, *Factor Analysis for Non-Mathematicians* (Melbourne, Australia: Melbourne University Press, 1954).

[4] Downie and Starry, *Descriptive Statistics*, pp. 216–218.

unidimensional measures. The variance of any distribution of scores is the square of the standard deviation. The conventional statistical symbol used to refer to the variance of a distribution of scores is σ^2 (*sigma* squared). Whereas the standard deviation answers questions of how much variability and is a unidimensional measure, variance relates to questions about why people differ and is a two-dimensional measure, or from a geometric point of view, an *area* measure. In effect, *variance* represents an estimate of the area produced by the graphic curve of a distribution of scores (see Chapter 3). This area is thought to be a reflection of the differential behaviors of subjects as explained by the reasons, both real and error-related, why people differ in terms of their test or other appraisal scores.

SOURCES OF VARIANCE
IN A TEST SCORE

Total variance equals real variance plus error variance. Typically, measures in the physical sciences are more accurate than those in the biological sciences. Even less accurate are measures in the behavioral sciences, including education. However, it is important to remember that no measure is totally free from error.

Inferential statistics (hypothesis-testing methodologies), a body of statistics other than descriptive statistics, is useful in determining which variance components are real (or error-free), and which may be allocated to error.[5] Specifically, analyses of variance procedures are useful in this regard but are beyond the scope of this book. Basic and more advanced statistical textbooks present adequate coverage of these inferential statistical procedures.[6,7]

The degree to which two or more measures relate to one another is expressed in the proportion of variance they share (covariance). In other words, a co-relationship (correlation) exists when certain reasons accounting for differences among individuals on one variable are the same reasons for their differing on another variable. The greater the number of reasons for behavior shared by two variables, the greater is the magnitude of the correlation index.

---

[5] L. J. Cronbach, *Essentials of Psychological Testing*, 3rd ed. (New York: Harper and Row, 1970), pp. 151–193.

[6] B. J. Winer, *Statistical Principles in Experimental Design*, 2nd ed. (New York: McGraw-Hill, 1971).

[7] W. L. Hayes, *Statistics for the Social Sciences*, 2nd ed. (New York: Holt, Rinehart and Winston, 1973).

RELIABILITY

THE CONCEPT

Before selecting any test or appraisal technique, a counselor must determine that the data are reliable. *Reliability* pertains to the accuracy or precision of any measure. The concepts of accuracy and precision are bound to the concept of error in measurement. To the extent that appraisal scores are free from error, a measure can be said to be reliable. The issue of reliability is further complicated by the fact that estimates of reliability are specific to a given population. Thus, scores may be reliable for one population but not for another. For example, an American history achievement test may be reliable when used with suburban high school seniors but not with minority-group seniors attending inner-city high schools. An ability test may be reliable for applicants for routine production-line assembly work but not for applicants for routine clerical work.

Unfortunately, the reliability data provided for most, if not all, tests are incomplete. No matter how conscientious test authors and publishers may be, the labor required and the cost involved prohibit the evaluation of the reliablity of any measure for all people on whom the measure may be used. Instead, only those populations are studied on whom the measure is most likely to be used. Even these efforts may at best be superficial. Counselors are usually faced with the problem of searching among reliability data provided for a test or other appraisal device to find the population that corresponds as closely as possible to the persons they intend to work with.

As is true in the case of test norms, data relevant to the persons whom the counselor serves are often not available. The counselor, therefore, must make one of two choices: to select subjectively for consideration those reliability data that are the most relevant or to obtain his or her own reliability estimates, using data specific to the people he or she serves. Because the latter requires both technical expertise and large samples of data (N in excess of 300), this solution is seldom used. Regrettably, reliability data are often inadequate. More regrettable is the fact that many counselors never question the reliability of the data they use. Either they do not realize the necessity of doing so or they accept on faith that the tests or other appraisal measures they use are reliable. Neither publication nor development by people who are highly regarded guarantees the reliability of any appraisal measure. Only appropriate data obtained from representative samples of people with whom an appraisal device is to be used demonstrate reliability.

GENERAL STRATEGY

Since the beginning of modern science, the way to evaluate accuracy has been to demonstrate that a measure can be reproduced. Physical and biological scientists repeat an experiment again and again to insure that their findings can be replicated, proving that their conclusions are accurate and that their data are relatively free from error. How often have you measured a distance two or more times when cutting a piece of wood or a piece of cloth? In checking the precision of your measurement, you use the same scientific methodology. Behavioral scientists have adopted this methodology to evaluate the reliability of appraisal data.

RELIABILITY COEFFICIENTS

The correlation coefficient is a convenient statistical index for estimating indices of relationship between distributions of test scores when a test, or some equivalent form, is administered to a single representative sample of subjects on two or more occasions.[8,9] The variance associated with one administration of the test should overlap considerably the variance of other administrations of the same test. The reasons why persons perform in a given way on one occasion should be the same reasons why they perform as they do on subsequent occasions. Consequently, if test scores are reliable, the test-retest correlation coefficient should be high, that is, high scores on one occasion should be matched by high scores on a second, and low scores should relate to low scores.

Figure 4.1 illustrates the variance overlap between the distributions of scores on testing and retesting a sample of subjects. The variance common to both occasions is labeled *reproduced variance* and is thought to be error-free, true, or reliable variance. The variance unique to each testing is attributed to error in measurement, or unreliability. Another way of viewing the reliability (correlation) coefficient is to think of it as being related to that proportion of the total variance of a distribution of scores that can be attributed to error-free variance. The greater the proportion of covariance to total variance, the closer the proportion approaches 1.0 (a perfectly reliable measure). However, no exact correspondence exists between

[8] C. Spearman, "The Proof and Measurement of Association Between Two Things," *American Journal of Psychology* 15 (1904): 72–101.
[9] H. Gulliksen, *Theory of Mental Tests* (New York: Wiley, 1950).

FIGURE 4.1
CORRELATION BETWEEN TWO ADMINISTRATIONS
OF THE SAME TEST TO A SINGLE SAMPLE OF SUBJECTS[a]

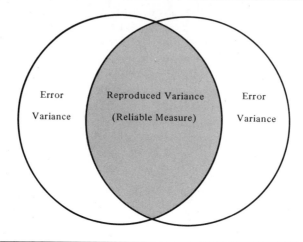

[a] Variance common to both administrations of the test provides the basis for the magnitude of the reliability coefficient. Variance specific to each administration is viewed as the consequence of measurement error.

the magnitude of a reliability coefficient and the proportion of error-free test score variance. The amount of variance overlap is estimated by squaring the correlation coefficient. Therefore, a reliability coefficient of +.90 does not imply that 90 percent of the variance is error-free; rather, it means that 81 percent ($.90^2$) of the variance is true or reliable. A reliability coefficient of +.80 indicates that 64 percent of the variance is reliable, and so on.[10]

SOURCES OF VARIANCE
IN A TEST SCORE

The total variance of any distribution of test scores is equal to the sum of error-free variance plus error variance. In short, the former is thought to be related to the real reasons why individuals differ and is thought to be systematic and orderly. The latter is viewed as related to random fluctuations in the behavior of the individual when responding to test stimuli or to random flaws in the test

[10] Cf. Cronbach, *Essentials of Testing*, pp. 173–179. Cronbach suggests that the magnitude of the reliability coefficient estimates efficiently the proportion of reliable variance.

itself. The accuracy of any test depends on the interaction of the instrument (the test form) and the subject taking the test. Reliable and error variance components are inherent in both the test form and the subject.

THE TEST   A test form should be a representative sample of the population of behaviors to be assessed. The basic blueprint, or plan, for the test may be defective in that it can fail to provide such a representative sample. However, flaws in the test are more likely to occur when efforts are made to create one or more forms of the test from the test plan. To the extent that characteristics of the test are shared or generalized in all forms, these characteristics are assumed to reflect the intended representative sampling called for by the test plan and, consequently, to contribute to reliable measure. Those characteristics of a test that are unique to a single form contribute to error in measurement in that they may introduce a bias that impairs the representativeness of the behavior sampled by the test. Thus, qualities that generalize in all test forms relate to reliable measure; those that are specific to one form are thought to introduce error.

THE SUBJECT   In most instances, individuals are tested to assess relatively permanent, lasting qualities or characteristics. However, a person's behavior is not constant. To some extent, individuals vary daily, hourly, and even from moment to moment. Both internal and external conditions influence these fluctuations. Health, mental attitude, motivation, and fatigue are but a few intraindividual variables that change frequently. A person's environment also has an effect on behavior. If the room in which a test is administered is too hot, too cold, too humid, too dry, too noisy, too quiet, too bright, too dark, or in any way less than an optimal environment, these factors can have an adverse affect on performance. Such temporary conditions inhibit the efficiency of efforts to measure a subject's lasting qualities and characteristics, thus contributing to error in measurement. In appraisal, error-free measurement exists insofar as a person's permanent characteristics influence responses.

VARIANCE ALLOCATION MODEL   This four-celled model (depicted in Figure 4.2) shows the sources of reliable and error variances associated with a test score.[11] The two factors essential to this model are the test and the subject. The test includes some components

---

[11] Cronbach, *Essentials of Testing,* pp. 173–178.

FIGURE 4.2
RELIABILITY, BASIC VARIANCE ALLOCATION MODEL

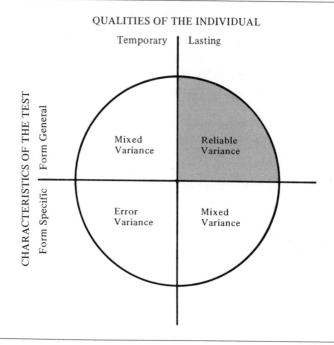

general to all possible forms and some specific to certain forms of the test. The subject exhibits both lasting and temporary qualities and characteristics. The upper-right cell, where variance associated with general qualities of the test relates to lasting characteristics of the individual, represents the portion of total test variance that is error-free. The lower-left cell indicates error: here, specific qualities of test forms interact with temporary characteristics of individuals. The goal in any appraisal is to maximize variance allocated to the upper-right cell and minimize that which must be assigned to the three remaining cells, especially the lower-left cell.

TEST-RETEST MODELS

The variance allocation model is useful in understanding test-retest methodology. Designs have been derived to estimate reliability by means of the correlation coefficient.

STABILITY COEFFICIENT   There are three basic test-retest designs.[12] The one most frequently used is the *stability* model. This design requires that only one form of a test be used. A test is administered to a representative sample of subjects on two occasions, allowing sufficient time to elapse between the two occasions to permit temporary characteristics to change. If the form of the test is identified as form *A*, the model can be defined operationally as an *A*-time-*A* design. Because only one form of the test is employed, no comparison can be made between general and specific qualities of the test. To interpret the reliability coefficient, reliable variance must be allocated to the lasting characteristics of the subjects and error assigned to temporary conditions of individuals. This variance allocation is illustrated in Figure 4.3. This design results in an overestimate of both reliable and error variance. The tester hopes that

FIGURE 4.3
STABILITY COEFFICIENT VARIANCE ALLOCATION

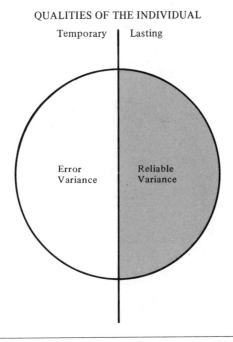

QUALITIES OF THE INDIVIDUAL

Temporary | Lasting

Error
Variance

Reliable
Variance

[12] G. C. Helmstadter, *Principles of Psychological Measurement* (New York: Appleton-Century Crofts, 1964), pp. 58–67.

the error variance and reliable variance associated with the lower-right and upper-left cells will cancel each other out so that the estimate obtained is relatively accurate.

EQUIVALENCE COEFFICIENT   A second test-retest design much less frequently used is the *equivalence* model (Figure 4.4). This design calls for administering two equivalent forms of a test to one sample of subjects with no significant time delay. If the forms of the test are designated *A* and *B*, respectively, the model can be described as *A*–no time–*B*. Reliable variance is associated with the general qualities of the test form, and error is associated with its specific characteristics. The influence of the temporary and lasting qualities of individuals cannot be isolated. As is true in the case of the stability model, the use of the equivalence model produces an overestimate of both error and reliable variance. Again, the tester must hope that these overestimates of error and reliable variance will nullify each other and render the estimated coefficient unbiased.

FIGURE 4.4
EQUIVALENCE COEFFICIENT VARIANCE ALLOCATION

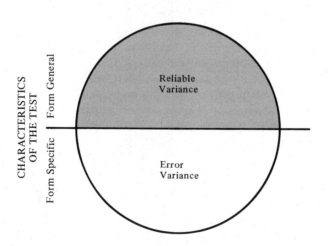

EQUIVALENT FORMS   For most tests, only one form is constructed. Published ability and achievement tests are an exception, but even here, only very few forms of a test are created. Furthermore, it is sometimes questionable that the multiple forms of these tests are truly equivalent. The criteria for equivalence are quite specific: (1) all forms must be built from the same table of specifications, or test plan; (2) central tendency estimates must be obtained from samples representative of a given population and should not differ significantly; (3) similarly, estimates of variability should not differ significantly; and (4) all forms should correlate with relevant criteria, and the magnitude of these correlations should not differ significantly.

Professional test developers usually spend considerable time, money, and conscientious effort in developing test plans and executing the development of one or more forms of a test in accordance with this plan. However, having done so, they often fail to demonstrate that their multiple forms meet these statistical criteria. One must examine carefully published information regarding a test in order to determine whether the functional equivalence of a test form has been demonstrated for those populations for whom the test is intended.

STABILITY-EQUIVALENCE COEFFICIENT   This third test-retest design (see Figure 4.5) is the logical outcome of combining the stability and equivalence models (*A*-time-*B*). Because the model requires that equivalent forms be used with an appropriate lapse of time, it is the least used of the three traditional correlational designs. The stability-equivalence model provides the most conservative estimate of test score reliability. In this case, reliable variance relates only to that cell of the variance allocation model that represents the interaction of the general qualities of test forms with lasting subject characteristics. Error variance is ascribed to all other cells.

TEST-RETEST RELIABILITY   Ability and achievement tests typically yield test-retest coefficients of the greatest magnitude. Interest, attitude, value, and personality tests tend to produce coefficients of lower order, because the behaviors they test are usually less stable than are ability and achievement. Consequently, in order to obtain accurate test-retest estimates of measures other than ability and achievement, a relatively brief time interval (a few days to a few weeks at most) should be introduced. Even when this is done,

FIGURE 4.5
STABILITY-EQUIVALENCE COEFFICIENT VARIANCE ALLOCATION

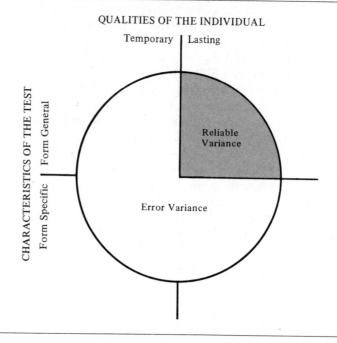

coefficients pertinent to interests, personality, or other similar *habitual performances* are usually less than those characteristic of *maximum performance* ability and achievement tests.

Furthermore, stability coefficients are usually greater in magnitude than equivalence coefficients, which in turn usually exhibit higher reliability indices than stability-equivalence coefficients. Consequently, when the question is asked, "Is this test sufficiently reliable to justify its use?," the magnitude of the correlation coefficient alone is not enough to provide an answer. In all instances, the greater the value of the coefficient, the better; however, stability coefficients for maximum performance tests suitable for use are in the low to mid .90s. In contrast, equivalence coefficients for the same tests tend to range from the low to mid .80s, and stability-equivalence coefficients are often in the low to mid .70s. Comparable test-retest reliability indices for measures of habitual behavior are frequently 20 to 30 points lower than corresponding coefficients for ability and achievement tests. Therefore, a stability-equivalence index of .50 for a personality scale can be interpreted as evidence of acceptability, whereas an ability test with the same coefficient should not be used. Other ability tests are available that provide more reliable test scores. Moreover, if one ability test yielded an equivalence index of .80 and another a stability value of .80, only the former would be appropriate to use. The latter (stability index) ought to have a significantly higher coefficient. There is no easy answer to the question of how reliable a test must be.

In order to test well and to safeguard the welfare of their clients, counselors must examine thoroughly the relevance and adequacy of the reliability data for the tests they select, administer, and interpret. Later in this chapter, we shall discuss other ways in which knowledge of estimates of error associated with test scores can be used to advantage in interpreting test data. First, however, we shall present the procedures that have been devised as substitutes for the basic test-retest designs.

INTERNAL CONSISTENCY

SPLIT-FORM PROCEDURES   It is difficult to develop truly equivalent forms of any test; nor is it easy to gather a sample of subjects together on two occasions in order to secure retest data. By the time of the First World War, efforts were being made to devise the first of a series of substitutes for the equivalence model that interpreted a single form of a test as though it were two or more equivalent forms. Because these procedures analyze data internal to a single form of the test, they are often classified as *internal consistency* methods rather than variations on the test-retest equivalence model.

THE SPLIT-HALF PROCEDURE   The first procedure is to split the content of a test into two equal halves, each an equivalent form of the total test. Scores for the first and second half of the test are then correlated.

Many tests used in the 1920s were *speeded* (allotted a time limit), because it was thought that rapidity of response as well as accuracy was a significant variable in evaluating an individual's ability. In recent years, testers have recognized that, except in the case of certain special skills, speed of response has little relationship to an individual's ability. Today, many tests are timed, but they are not speeded. Time limits are imposed for the tester's convenience rather than to introduce a factor of speed. Such tests cannot be considered

speeded because 90 percent or more of the subjects usually complete
the tasks required within the time limit stipulated. However, many
tests during the 1920s and 1930s were speeded (few if any subjects
were expected to complete the tasks in the time permitted). Consequently, near the end of the test, most subjects failed to receive
credit for correct answers simply because they did not have an
opportunity to answer the questions. Therefore, correspondence
between responses to the first half and the second half of a speeded
test is spuriously low.

Especially in earlier years (but still true of some ability and
achievement tests today), tests were also powered; that is, the second half is more difficult than the first, so regardless of time, subjects are able to answer fewer questions correctly at the end of a
test than at the beginning. The Otis series of ability tests is a classic
example of such powered tests. In this case, too, a split-half procedure yields spuriously low estimates of equivalence reliability.

THE ODD-EVEN COEFFICIENT   In an effort to remedy these problems,
another split of test content was attempted: scores from all odd-
numbered questions were compared with scores from even-num-
bered questions. On a powered test, both odds and evens include
easy and difficult questions. However, on speeded tests, the same
problem that plagued the split-half design affects estimates of odd-
even consistency, because subjects tend to perform similarly at the
end of the test: they receive no credit for questions not answered.
This results in a spurious increase of similarity in performance
between odd and even halves, produces an inflated estimate of
correspondence between halves, and yields a distorted high index
of relationship.

EQUIVALENCE CRITERIA   Perhaps more basic than any of these concerns is the fact that splitting a test into two parts in any fashion
assumes that the halves created are equivalent. The same criteria
for equivalence hold for halves of tests as for full forms of tests. For
test halves to be equivalent, they must represent the same content,
must not differ significantly in terms of estimates of central tendency or variability, and must correlate with an external criterion
to a similar extent. In most instances, it is doubtful that test halves,
no matter how determined, will satisfy all of these criteria. Therefore, the use of such a substitute procedure is suspect.

THE SPEARMAN-BROWN PROPHECY FORMULA   Even if the two halves
of a test were functionally equivalent, the coefficient estimating

the relationship between the halves might be in error, resulting in a lower-bound approximation of the relationship between two full and equivalent forms of the test. The longer a test, the greater is the probability that the test is reliable. Assume that in a 10-item test, one item is flaw-ridden, contributing to error. In this instance, .10 of the measure contributes to error. If the test were increased to 100 items, then the same error-ridden item would constitute only .01 of the total. Consequently, the impact of each error is diminished when the number of items included in the test is increased. Recognizing this principle years ago, Charles Spearman and a colleague, W. Brown, determined a formula for calculating an estimate of the maximum possible equivalence coefficient for a test. This formula, called the Spearman-Brown prophecy formula, was intended to be employed under optimal circumstances (that is, when the characteristics of half of the test are functionally equivalent to those of the other half).[13]

Test authors and publishers naturally wish to present the most impressive looking evidence of a test's utility to potential customers. Therefore, when test authors use split-form procedures, they almost always adjust their reliability estimates by means of the Spearman-Brown prophecy formula. Assume that two halves of a test form are equivalent functionally and the correlation between the halves equals +.75. Adjusted by the Spearman-Brown prophecy formula, the maximum equivalence coefficient would approximate +.82. Far too often, the reliability of the test is reported to be +.82, and the fact that this is an upper-bound optimal estimate is not made clear. It is one thing to say that the reliability of the test is +.82 and quite another to say that, if given a legitimate split-form estimate of +.75, the maximum probable equivalence reliability of a full form of the test under optimal circumstances would not exceed +.82. Of course, if counselors seriously considered the implications of the latter statement, they might conclude that the test is not worth using.

In summary, split-form methodologies and adjustments by statistical prophecy procedures frequently leave a counselor with doubts about a test's utility. For this reason, researchers have developed still other substitutes for the equivalence coefficient that do not suffer from the limitations of split-form designs. Even though these substitutes have other problems and limitations, they can produce significantly more efficient and economic estimates of reliability

---

[13] Julian C. Stanley, "Reliability," in *Educational Measurement*, 2nd ed., ed. R. L. Thorndike (Washington, D.C.: American Council on Education, 1971), pp. 394–410.

than do split-form data, provided their limitations are recognized and provided that the data analyzed are such that these limitations do not affect the procedure.

THE KUDER-RICHARDSON PROCEDURES   Beginning in the early 1930s, G. F. Kuder and M. W. Richardson began experimenting with approximating test-retest equivalence coefficients by using data from a single form of a test.[14] They elaborated on the split-form design and attempted to resolve the numerous problems associated with its use. Their strategy was to study all possible splits of test items and to determine consistency of response throughout. In effect, they considered each item to be equivalent in function to all other items on the test. (For a more thorough technical exposition of the Kuder-Richardson process, see such basic references as Downie and Starry[15] and more detailed works, such as those of Robert L. Thorndike[16] and Julian C. Stanley.[17])

In essence, the Kuder-Richardson methodologies express reliability in terms of the proportion of total test variance that is determined by the differences between total test variance and item variance, as represented by the intercorrelation among all items on a test. The extent to which subjects perform consistently on all items (the reasons why they respond to one item are the same reasons why they respond to all other items) and the extent to which the consistency of response affects total test scores yield high coefficients of internal consistency. For example, when subjects answer most questions on an ability test correctly and thus obtain high scores, their total scores and their performance on individual items are related systematically. This is also the case when they answer few questions correctly, obtaining low scores. In either case, the consistency of the subject's response to questions on a single form of a given test is high. When this is not so, the index is low. The success of this methodology is praiseworthy. However, these procedures have significant limitations.

If subjects are to perform consistently on all test items, the items should treat the same area of behavioral content and should be equally difficult. If the content of a test is mixed (heterogeneous), or if the difficulty or popularity of responses is heterogeneous, there

---

[14] G. F. Kuder and M. W. Richardson, "The Theory of the Estimation of Test Reliability," Psychometrika 2 (1937): 151–160.
[15] Downie and Starry, pp. 259–260.
[16] Robert L. Thorndike, "Reliability," in Educational Measurement, ed. E. F. Lindquist (Washington, D.C.: American Council on Education, 1951), pp. 586–599.
[17] Julian C. Stanley, "Reliability," pp. 410–415.

is a low probability that answers will be similar. Consequently, if internal consistency procedures are to be applied, both content and difficulty of a test should be homogeneous. Tests that do not fulfill these requirements are inappropriate for evaluation by internal consistency procedures.

Regrettably, since these procedures are so easy to use, many tests report such indices as evidence of their reliability. In contrast to test-retest indices, in which coefficients of variable magnitude may be interpreted as evidence of adequate reliability, depending on the type of test evaluated and the test-retest design employed, internal consistency indices should be uniformly high (.90 or greater). If they are not, either the index is inappropriate for estimating the reliability of a given test or the test is not sufficiently reliable. In either case, the test should not be used.

THE ALPHA COEFFICIENT   Cronbach[18,19] introduced still another modification of the internal consistency method that is a special case of the Kuder-Richardson formula 20. Rather than basing his methodology on correlational strategy (analysis of regression), Cronbach focused on analysis of variance procedures for comparing variance in a single subject's responses to error variance estimated for the total test. Cronbach believes that his approach is more robust than other internal consistency procedures. His *alpha* coefficient does have more universal application than do most other internal consistency methods. However, the underlying principle remains the same. To be suitable for use in estimating the reliability of any test, the content of the test and the difficulty or popularity of responses must be homogeneous.

HOMOGENEITY OF CONTENT AND RESPONSE   Early in the history of test development, little attention was paid to the homogeneity of test content or response. The use of factor analytic investigations of tests and their functions, which began in the United States with the work of J. P. Guilford[20] and L. L. Thurstone[21] in the early 1930s, has produced acceptance of the principle that accurate and relevant measures of individual behavior are fostered by the use of instruments that are unidimensional (that measure only one area of behavior) and homogeneous in terms of difficulty or popularity of

---

[18] Cronbach, *Essentials of Testing*, pp. 160–162.
[19] L. J. Cronbach, "Coefficient Alpha and the Internal Structure of Tests," *Psychometrika* 16 (1951): 297–334.
[20] J. P. Guilford, *Psychometric Methods* (New York: McGraw Hill, 1954).
[21] L. L. Thurstone, *Multiple-Factor Analysis* (Chicago: University of Chicago Press, 1947).

responses. Today, test developers favor tests that are homogeneous in content and response and therefore suitable for using internal consistency indices to estimate reliability. However, counselors must remain aware that, if a test or subtest score does not reflect homogeneity, internal consistency indices have no meaning. Only the basic and more generalizable test-retest methodologies are appropriate.

VALIDITY

The cardinal characteristic of the utility of any test is its validity. A test may be highly reliable and may have relevant and representative norms, but if it fails to demonstrate validity, it has no value whatsoever. Norms and reliability are specific to given populations; validity is even more specific. Not only is it specific to populations but it is also specific to the purpose of the test. For a given group, a test may be valid for answering some questions but not others. The high degree of specificity associated with validity complicates the matter of selecting a test for use.

Theoretically, validity is related to reliability and relevance. A test must be reliable to be valid, but reliability does not guarantee validity. Only relevance renders a reliable measure valid. *Relevance* means that the test measures what it is intended to measure, but the ultimate theoretical evidence of relevance is the power of a test to predict future behavior. Combining the two constructs, a valid measure is one that is accurate and that predicts future behavior efficiently. Though the predictive efficiency of any measure is difficult to demonstrate, the power to predict is the essence of the concept of validity.

DEFINITIONS OF VALIDITY

The literature of testing provides numerous definitions of various kinds of test validity, often employing different labels to identify the same evidence. This terminology confuses many counselors as well as the authors themselves. With the exception of some ability and achievement tests, most educational and psychological tests used to predict performance in school, or in limited instances, on certain jobs, lack evidence of predictive power. Because of the specificity of validity to purpose and population and because of the dependence of the construct on predictive evidence, fundamental validity data are difficult to obtain, a fact that frustrates test experts and counselors alike.

Although many tests give no evidence of predictive power, some test experts and counselors may nevertheless have found them to be useful. In an effort to attest to their validity (some experts argue that validity is so vague a concept as to be valueless[22]), researchers have proposed other definitions of validity that do not require proof of predictive power. Most of these definitions identify phases in the development of the test and the process of validation. They have their uses, but in failing to predict behavior, they deviate from the orthodox definition of validity itself. The extent to which evidence of these lesser validities can be shown for a test, determines the amount of confidence a counselor can have in its utility. However, with less than absolute evidence on hand, the counselor should approach the use of any test with caution and skepticism.

RATIONAL EVIDENCE OF VALIDITY

The various definitions of validity can be classified under two general rubrics: *rational* and *empirical* evidence. In the former category are face validity, content validity, and factor validity.

FACE VALIDITY   *Face validity* offers little evidence of actual validity. The term merely suggests that the content of the test appears to be relevant to the subject taking the test. If, for example, a student, told that he or she is to be evaluated for mathematical achievement, were given a reading test, the credibility of the measure should certainly be questioned.

CONTENT VALIDITY   Content relevance is basic to any test. All tests must be planned and forms of the test developed in order to take a representative sampling of a certain population of behavior as efficiently as possible. Frequently, the content of a test is determined with great care; but this is merely the first step in the development of any test and is in itself not a sufficient guarantee of validity.

FACTOR VALIDITY   With the development of factor analytic techniques in the early 1930s, test authors were able to determine if the content of a test corresponded to the test plan. If a test were in-

---

[22] R. L. Ebel, "Must All Tests Be Valid?" *American Psychologist* 16 (October 1961), 640–647.

tended to measure several dimensions of behavior, its authors were able to discover whether the questions or tasks designed to relate to each dimension actually related to one another within a given dimension. Factor analysis and related statistical procedures are most useful methodologies to employ in test development, because they enable test authors to evaluate how well a test plan has been actualized in one or more forms of a test. Notable experts in factoral analysis (for example, Thurstone[23] and Guilford[24]) have depended principally on such data to defend the validity of tests they have developed. As sophisticated and practical as these methodologies are, they are nevertheless not sufficient proof of validity. They constitute only one crucial step toward proving the validity of a test. Factor analyses are usually performed on data internal to the test; seldom do they relate test behavior to criteria external to the test.

EMPIRICAL EVIDENCE OF VALIDITY

A variety of validating techniques do relate test data to external criteria. In varying degrees, these procedures approach the predictive power design that is the most demanding of the models for establishing empirical evidence of validity.

CONGRUENT VALIDITY   Assume that a test author has determined carefully the content of the test, perhaps even demonstrating evidence of its factor integrity. The test in question is intended to assess the interest in skilled mechanical work of people considering post-secondary education in mechanics. One or more other tests or scales of other tests purported to measure similar interests are used by counselors. Also, assume that one of these tests does have evidence of at least some limited predictive power (it has been shown to contribute to predicting success by mechanics in trade school). To make a further check on the possible utility of the test, the author could administer the established test and the new test to a representative sample of subjects and correlate the two sets of scores. If the two tests correlate significantly, some variance of each is shared, indicating that some reasons for performance on one are shared by the other. The author should then be encouraged to look

---

[23] Thurstone, *Multiple-Factor Analysis.*
[24] Guilford, *Psychometric Methods.*

for additional evidence of predictive power for the new test. If no correlation exists, either the tests measure different behavioral domains or the test development work is inadequate.

In effect, this design calls for testing the validity of a test by using performance on another related test as an empirical criterion. Few tests yield predictive power coefficients greater than $+.70$ for any purpose or population. The best relationships are usually found in tests predicting academic success among middle-class individuals. In this specific instance, approximately half the variance associated with school grades and test responses is common $(+.70^2)$. Assume in the example noted that the relationship between the established mechanical interest scale and success in trade school was $+.50$ (actually a rather high relationship for an interest test). This means that one-quarter of the variance between the test and the criterion measure is shared.

Assume, further, that the congruence coefficient between the new test and the established test is $+.70$. Many test authors would be inclined to report this relationship as a validity coefficient of $+.70$, which could mislead a counselor into thinking that the test relates well to success in trade school, whereas, it actually demonstrated only some significant correspondence with another, and probably similar, interest test. Although about half the variance of each test overlaps, it is possible that the half in which the overlap occurs does not relate in any way to the variance overlap between the established test and success in trade school. In other words, it is conceivable that the new test may have no predictable relationship to success in trade school even though it correlates $+.70$ with a test that does predict such performance (see Figure 4.6). On the other hand, the new test could correlate .50 or more with the trade-school criterion. The major problem for both test author and counselor is that no one really knows for certain what data like these mean in terms of a test's predictive power. Therefore, counselors are cautioned to evaluate congruence data skeptically. Unless the relationship between one test and another is extremely high, the counselor can infer little of value about the validity of any test by comparing scores on one test with scores on another similar test. This procedure may provide useful information for the test author, but it is just another step toward developing a useful test.

CONCURRENT VALIDITY Concurrent validity indices are of two types: congruent and differentiation. The two are similar in that test and criterion data are obtained at about the same time. They differ in that the congruent method uses another test as a criterion

FIGURE 4.6
LIMITATIONS OF THE CONGRUENCE COEFFICIENT[a]

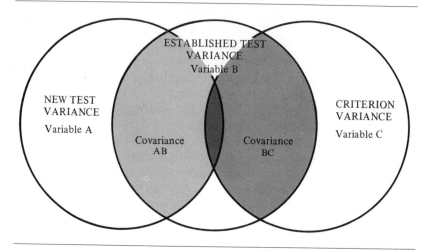

[a] Although both the AB and BC correlations may approximate .70, the AC correlation may be nonsignificant.

measure, while the differentiation method uses measures of behavior external to tests as criteria, such as grades or success in trade school. In discovering what relationship exists between a new interest test and empirical criteria, both correlation and analysis of variance can be employed. If no differentiating power is identified, the test is unlikely to have any power to predict success in trade school. Without the power to differentiate between subjects, differential prediction is impossible. On the other hand, if the test is shown to differentiate between students who do well and those who do not, then this amounts to appreciable evidence of the test's probable utility. However, the ultimate evidence of utility remains to be determined.

THE PREDICTIVE POWER COEFFICIENT   Theoretically, the essence of validity is the ability of any measure to demonstrate that a systematic relationship exists between performance on a test and future behavior. The predictive power coefficient determines this relationship. As is true in the case of the differentiation model, the criterion pertains directly to behavior. The amount of time interpolated between collecting test data and criterion task data is determined by the period of time over which predictions are to be made. If the test is meant to predict behavior two weeks hence, for example, two weeks should elapse between collecting the two sets of data for estimating the predictive power coefficient.

Many test authors and counselors hold that it is not possible to adhere to the predictive concept of validity. Subjects are frequently difficult to find and test months, let alone years, after predictor data have been obtained. Orthodox studies spanning years are rare. Notable among those that have been conducted are those of L. M. Terman,[25] who studied a sample of gifted individuals, and E. K. Strong, Jr.,[26] who conducted a longitudinal study of the interests of men.

In most instances in which predictive coefficients are estimated, the criterion employed utilizes not *ultimate* data (obtained many months or years later) but rather *intermediate* data. Even though the ultimate interest is in predicting behavior twenty years in the future, criterion data secured two years or four years after predictor testing do yield information of some value. If a test does not predict behavior after two years, it is not likely to predict behavior twenty years in the future. Fortunately, in many instances, predictions over a few months or a very few years are pertinent. In these cases, orthodox data may be obtained with less difficulty. Regardless of the difficulties involved, these validity data are sound. In recent years, especially in business and industry (although schools are not exempt), the courts have held that predictive validity data are required to justify the continued use of many tests for selecting people for training, employment, or promotion. The wishes of many test authors and counselors notwithstanding, these requirements seem to be here to stay.

THE CRITERION PROBLEM   Another consideration that has plagued test authors and counselors over the years is that of the operational definition and proper measurement of criterion behaviors. In spite of the unreliability of an individual teacher's grades or evaluations, cumulative grades or ratings over time have demonstrated acceptable reliability (errors of one teacher tend to cancel out errors of another). Therefore, cumulative academic evaluations have proven to be at least minimally satisfactory in predicting academic achievement. In routine industrial production or business detail work, suitable job performance criteria are more easily fixed, as the work

[25] L. M. Terman and Melita H. Oden, *Genetic Studies of Genius V: The Gifted Group at Mid-Life: Thirty-Five Years' Follow-Up of the Superior Child* (Palo Alto, Calif.: Stanford University Press, 1959).

[26] E. K. Strong, Jr., *Vocational Interests 18 Years After College* (Minneapolis: University of Minnesota Press, 1955).

product can be clearly defined. However, when other performance criteria are considered, the task is much more complex. For example, one could say that a person who sells the most is the most effective salesperson, but the criterion is more complex than mere sales volume. The potential for sales must be considered, and the proportion of that potential that is actualized must be determined. Someone who sells less than another may be a better salesperson because of what that person is selling and where the sales are made. More complex, relatively satisfactory methods have been developed for determining adequate criteria of this kind.

What about criteria for professional work or social adjustment? Who is the effective counselor, teacher, engineer, lawyer, or physician? What behavior characterizes a good parent or marriage partner? In instances such as these and many more, it is extremely difficult to define and to measure relative criterion behavior. Like tests, criterion measures must be relevant, representative, and reliable. The characteristics of the effective teacher have been studied for years by hundreds of investigators. The only conclusion one can come to is that there is no such person as a good teacher. Some teachers function well teaching certain students certain subject matter at one or another level, in particular ways, in specific places, and in specific administrative atmospheres or environments. These same teachers may perform most ineffectually when even one of these variables is altered.

No wonder many are looking for other ways to justify the utility of tests or to argue that something less than predictive evidence can be accepted to warrant the use of tests in order to help answer real questions regarding real people and their lives. Nevertheless, predictive utility remains the essence of validity.

CONSTRUCT VALIDITY   Cronbach and P. E. Meehl introduced the concept of construct validity.[27] The concept blends considerations of both rational and empirical validity and essentially outlines a program of worthy research and development for any test. A theoretical concept or construct regarding a given behavior is defined, a plan to sample these behaviors is determined, one or more forms of the test are created, and in time, the predictive power of the test is identified for a variety of criterion behaviors. To the extent that the test is shown to predict certain behaviors and not others, *what* the test predicts becomes evident and consequently, the construct

---

[27] L. J. Cronbach and P. E. Meehl, "Construct Validity in Psychological Tests," *Psychological Bulletin* 52 (1955): 281–303.

measured by the test can be defined operationally. The construct of intelligence can be cited as an example. In early years, it was thought that intelligence tests measured capacity or potential for learning, adaptive behavior, and so on. However, evidence collected over the years indicates that what intelligence tests measure is limited, for the most part, to an assessment of what a person learns in school.

HOW VALID MUST A TEST BE?

Overall, the content of a test should be as valid as possible; the test should correlate highly with other tests of similar type, differentiate significantly between persons in terms of pertinent criteria, and significantly predict future behavior. However, although test-task relationships must be significant statistically, a test can be useful even though the magnitude of that relationship with regard to differentiation and predictive power is low. The issues of cost and time must be considered in order to determine if the use of a particular test with certain subjects for a specific purpose is warranted.

Depending on the question at issue, it may be defensible to use a test that enables the counselor to help individuals accomplish self-selection (decisions) even if the probability of a satisfactory outcome is only a few percentage points greater than a random, or chance, selection or decision would allow. In other instances, the probability that a test will improve appreciably on chance odds must be demonstrated before the test can be considered valid enough to use.

THE SELECTION RATIO   In evaluating the validity of a test for a particular purpose, the magnitude of the relationship between test and task should be as great as possible. However, the criterion for success (easy or difficult to accomplish) and the number of persons available to evaluate for selection have a direct bearing on the percentage by which selection success based on chance procedures can be exceeded. The easier success is to obtain, and the greater the number of candidates who can be considered, the greater is the probability of making valid predictions with given test data. Under such circumstances, the *selection ratio* is favorable, and tests with low (but significant) predictive indices may be employed effectively. On the other hand, if a success criterion is difficult to achieve, and candidates must be selected from among only a few people, the probability of predicting criterion behavior well is low, unless the relationship between the predictor and the criterion task is quite high.

The judgments that a counselor must make about the validity of a test are complex and difficult. Nonetheless, the informed and responsible use of tests requires that the validity of a test in all its facets, as well as the situation(s) in which the test data are to be used, must be evaluated and interrelated with utmost care if the selection of the test is to be defensible.

EXPECTANCY TABLES   Assume that the data presented in Table 4.1 depict the relationship between performance on an interest measure and a criterion of success in a mechanical trade school. (This table has been kept simple for the purpose of illustration.) Scores on the predictor (test) and criterion (task performance) have been divided into quartile ranges. Such tables of data enable the counselor to predict the probable achievement of students depending on their performance on the predictor measure. If a trade school applicant scores within the top quartile on the predictor, according to the table, the applicant has 43 chances in 100 of performing in the top quartile on the criterion, 28 chances in 100 of scoring in the second quartile, 19 chances in 100 of placing in the third quartile, and only about 10 chances in 100 of falling in the bottom quartile.

Data of this nature may assist both counselor and client alike to estimate criterion performance realistically, provided that a known and significant relationship exists between a given predictor score and a specific criterion measure. If such data are available, relatively exact predictions can be presented to a client. Such data are sparse, and in most instances, the counselor must determine these data on his or her own. The task requires time and technical expertise, but

TABLE 4.1
ACCURACY OF PREDICTION: AN EXPECTANCY TABLE[a]
CORRELATION = +.40

QUARTER ON PREDICTOR	QUARTER ON CRITERION			
	4th	3rd	2nd	1st
1st	104	191	277	428
2nd	191	255	277	277
3rd	277	277	255	191
4th	428	277	191	104

[a] 1000 cases in each row or column

helpful information is available in determining and interpreting data of this nature.[28]

ERROR IN MEASUREMENT
AND PREDICTION

The best tests fall far short of being perfect measures, and the best predictions that can be made using test data are anything but totally accurate. We have so far discussed the use of the correlation coefficient as an index of the reliability of a test score or criterion measure and the statistical procedure whereby the validity of a test may be demonstrated. However, another statistical procedure, the standard error, is useful in selecting a test or interpreting test scores.

THE STANDARD ERROR

The *standard error* is the standard deviation of a sampling distribution. Several standard error indices are in common use, but the most basic is the standard error of the mean. We have discussed the use of score distributions obtained from single samples of subjects and the relationship, or lack of relationship, between two or more distributions in the context of correlation. Every score distribution can be described by its principal characteristics, or parameters: the arithmetic mean and the standard deviation.

The samples of persons who provide the data for constructing distributions of scores should be representative of the population from whom the samples have been selected. Usually samples do not represent a population as efficiently as they might. Errors in sampling introduce bias. Several samples drawn to represent the same population differ somewhat in terms of the parameters that define them, even if they are large in number. Assume that several hundred samples were selected to represent a given population. If the sampling procedure is done carefully, it is probable that the mean and the standard deviation of these samples would be similar, although some variability in these indices would exist. When the values for the several hundred means or standard deviations are graphed in the form of a frequency polygon (see Chapter 3), the

---

[28] H. G. Seashore, ed. "Expectancy Tables—A Way of Interpreting Test Validity," *Test Services Bulletin* 38 (New York: The Psychological Corporation, 1949): 11–15.

shape of this distribution of sample statistics should approximate that of the normal probability curve. Most would differ little, but a few would be higher or lower than the central tendency value of this special kind of data distribution. Whereas simple data distributions are made up of scores obtained from a single sample of subjects, these complex distributions are made up of estimates of statistical indices for many samples of data representative of a population. Because the distribution of data is based on sample statistics, these special distributions are called *sampling distributions.*

When the statistic in question is the mean of each sample, the distribution may be thought of as a sampling distribution of the mean of the population. The mean of this sampling distribution of means should provide a more efficient estimate of the population mean than would any mean identified by a single sample of subject data. The standard deviation of the sampling distribution is identified by a special term in order to differentiate it from a conventional single-sample standard deviation. This special type of standard deviation is identified as the *standard error* of the sampling distribution. When the statistic that constitutes the sampling distribution is the mean of each sample included, the standard deviation is known as the *standard error of the mean.* This specific standard error provides an estimate of the degree to which means that make up the sampling distribution vary in numerical value.

THE STANDARD ERROR
OF MEASUREMENT

The *standard error of measurement* is a special case of the standard error of the mean. This index has specific applicability for understanding the reliability of a test. The concept that reliability may be inferred from evidence that measures can be reproduced is fundamental to the strategy associated with the theoretical formulation of the standard error of measurement.

Theoretically, the standard error of measurement pertains to data obtained from repeated testing of the same representative sample of subjects. Assume that several hundred equivalent forms of a test were created and administered to this single sample of subjects. The mean for each form administered can be calculated and a sampling distribution of these means created. The standard deviation of this specific sampling distribution of means is called the *standard error of measurement.* This standard error provides an index of the variability in performance of a subject sample in repeated measures of the same behavior. If the measure is reliable, variability within subjects in repeated measures should be limited, and the magnitude of the standard error should be low. On the other hand, if the test is unreliable, the magnitude of the standard error index is large. Furthermore, like the conventional standard deviation, the standard error of measurement can be expressed in raw score units. This provides an explicit advantage when the standard error of measurement is applied to any given test score.

The nature of the sampling distribution associated with a standard error of measurement is assumed to be normal. Consequently, the standard error relates to the sampling distribution much as the standard deviation for a single data sample is associated with its distribution of scores (see Chapter 3). Approximately two-thirds of the repeated sample means will not deviate more than one standard error from the mean of the sampling distribution. About 95 percent of these means will fall within plus or minus two standard errors from the mean, and 99+ percent are encompassed by plus or minus three standard errors from the mean. The standard error is expressed in raw score units, thus enabling an estimate of the amount of error of any given test score to be made in raw score terms. Probability statements can therefore be made about the deviation between a given score and the score that would be obtained by a subject if that score were free of measurement error.

The theoretical process for estimating the standard error of measurement is seldom, if ever, used. Rarely are many equivalent forms of any test created, and it would be atypical to identify a representative sample for any population who would submit to repeated testing across multiple equivalent forms. A substitute procedure exists for estimating the theoretical standard error of measurement for a given test.[29] This alternative requires that only one form of a test be administered to a single representative sample of subjects and an appropriate correlational index of reliability be obtained from a data sample representative of the population in question. This substitute index is crude, and its utility is dependent on the representativeness of the sample data employed and the adequacy of the reliability coefficient used. Nonetheless, under optimal circumstances, this index does provide a practical estimate of test score error.

Assume that a standard error of measurement equal to three raw

---

[29] Downie and Starry, *Descriptive Statistics,* p. 256.

score intervals were estimated for a given attitudinal measure intended to assess motivation to study. Applying this estimate to a
subject's raw score of 40, it could be inferred that the subject's raw
score would not deviate more than three raw score intervals from
his or her true score (see Figure 4.7). In other words, the subject's
true score could be as low as 37 and as high as 43. Because only one
band width of the standard error of measurement was employed
above and below the raw score, the probability is that, in approximately two occasions out of three, the inference that the raw score
does not deviate more than three raw score intervals from the true
score would be correct.

A counselor who requires greater confidence in estimating the
discrepancy between obtained raw scores and true scores may use
two widths of the standard error of measurement. Under these
circumstances, it could be inferred that the subject's true score did
not deviate more than six raw score intervals from the obtained
score of 40, and that the true score range of 34–46 could be estimated with 95 percent confidence. A raw score range of 31–49 could

FIGURE 4.7
STANDARD ERROR OF MEASUREMENT:
A COMPARISON OF TWO RATIOS OF STANDARD ERROR TO RANGE[a]

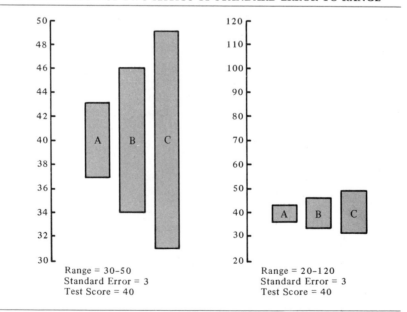

Range = 30–50
Standard Error = 3
Test Score = 40

Range = 20–120
Standard Error = 3
Test Score = 40

[a] A = .67 level of confidence; B = .95 level of confidence; C = .99 level of confidence.

be stipulated with greater than 99 percent confidence, if this degree of confidence were required.

In the latter instance, a range of eighteen raw score units must be estimated in order to obtain such a high degree of confidence. This breadth of range may be viewed as imprecise; consequently, one is left in doubt as to where the error-free score of a subject truly is. However, this is the state of testing practice as it is today. A counselor who has to view a subject's score as probably encompassing a range of raw score units on a test score scale is forced to recognize the imprecision of test scores.

Expressing the standard error as a proportion of a range of scores obtained for a given test provides a more informed basis on which to judge the reliability of any test. For example, if the range of scores were equal to 20 and the standard error of measurement were equal to two raw score intervals, the proportion of error to range would be two parts in 20, or .10. In contrast, if the range of scores were equal to 100 and the standard error of measurement were equal to two raw score units, the proportion of error to range would be two parts in 100, or .02. Two units of error on a 100-unit scale clearly is more accurate than ten units of error on a 100-unit scale. For the purpose and population intended, the test that yields the best proportion of error to range of scores is the most desirable. However, in many instances, no measure may be found to be reliable enough to justify its use.

Because of the error present in test data, the counselor must assume a conservative posture toward the interpretation of test scores.[30] Obviously, in numerous instances this would require that decisions and recommendations regarding the lives of people not be made on the basis of a single test score, or even a battery of test scores. Distressing as this posture may be to many counselors, recognition of and compliance with this position can foster an informed use of test data and should promote the personal welfare of clients.

THE STANDARD ERROR OF ESTIMATE

THE REGRESSION EQUATION   Based on data representative of a given subject population, the correlation between two variables may be

[30] S. G. Goldstein and J. D. Linden, "Paradigm to Maximize Efficiency in Clinical Prediction," *Proceedings*, 75th Annual Convention, American Psychological Association (1967), pp. 197–198.

estimated efficiently. Utilizing procedures beyond the scope of this book, it is possible to determine what is known as a *regression equation*, which permits a prediction to be made for members of a given population regarding an individual's score on one variable (criterion task) when that same person's score on a related variable (predictor test) is known.[31] Because of error associated with both the predictor measure and the criterion measure, and because of the lack of perfect correlation between predictor and criterion, criterion scores predicted by means of the use of regression equations frequently are in error. Certainly, it is possible to predict an estimate of an individual's criterion performance, to measure that criterion behavior independently, and to determine for an individual the plus or minus difference between the criterion score predicted and the criterion score obtained. For a given individual, the difference between performance predicted and performance measured represents error in prediction.

INDEX OF PREDICTIVE ERROR   The standard error of estimate may be employed to estimate the probable error in the prediction of criterion behavior. Specifically, the *standard error of estimate* is another special case of the standard error of the mean.

Assume that both predictor test scores and criterion measures were obtained for a given representative sample of subjects selected from a specific population. Based on a known correlation between predictor and criterion, criterion score predictions are made for each subject within the sample, and the difference between predicted and actual criterion behavior is determined. A distribution of the differences between predicted and actual behavior can be identified, and the mean of these differences for an entire sample can be estimated. The lower the mean difference determined, the more precise should be the predictions. Assume further that several hundred such subject samples were identified from the population in question, and that in each case, the mean difference between predicted and actual behavior was determined. A distribution of these sample mean differences could be determined. The standard deviation of this specific sampling distribution would provide an estimate of the theoretical standard error of estimate for the test when it is used to predict the criterion at issue for the population in question. In that this statistic relates to the predictive efficiency of a test, it serves as an index of the validity of that test.

As is true in the case of the standard error of measurement,

---

[31] Downie and Starry, *Descriptive Statistics,* pp. 205–214.

seldom, if ever, are orthodox data obtained to determine a standard error of estimate for a specific test and population of subjects. A substitute procedure that estimates the standard error of estimate has been devised that requires only one form of a test to be administered to a single sample of subjects, provided that an efficient validity coefficient (preferably a predictive power coefficient) has been determined.[32] Like the substitute procedures used to estimate the standard error of measurement, this procedure is crude, but under optimal conditions, it yields an index of practical value.

Again, the counselor should be cautioned to evaluate the bases for determining such substitute estimates and to judge their utility accordingly. The task is not an easy one. Test authors and publishers do not often go out of their way to detail the adequacy of their samples and the validity coefficients employed to produce the standard error of estimate data they report. Furthermore, because many test authors do not report validity coefficients at all but emphasize the content or factor validity of their tests, the counselor must determine the data necessary to produce workable approximations of the standard error of estimate. The same situation frequently applies in the case of the standard error of measurement. Granted that technical expertise on the part of the counselor is required to render these estimations possible, the actual labor is not excessive and the methodology that must be employed is not unduly complex.

Whereas the standard error of measurement yields indices expressed in terms of raw scores on a test, the standard error of estimate provides indices presented in raw score units on criterion measures. The procedures whereby the standard error of estimate is applied parallel those appropriate for the use of the standard error of measurement. For example, if a known regression equation were used to predict a criterion score of 80 for an individual, and if the standard error of estimate were calculated to be three raw score units, the subject's actual criterion score at the 95 percent confidence level should fall between 74 and 86, two band widths of the standard error applied above and below the predicted criterion score (see Figure 4.8). If the range on the criterion were only twenty units (70–90), the differential efficiency of the predictor would be nil. Having predicted a criterion score of 80, a subject could perform on the criterion from either very low to relatively high. Actual criterion performance would be most uncertain. However, if the criterion range were 100 points, it should be possible to predict criterion

[32] Downie and Starry, *Descriptive Statistics*, 210–232.

FIGURE 4.8
STANDARD ERROR OF ESTIMATE:
A COMPARISON OF TWO RATIOS OF STANDARD ERROR TO RANGE[a]

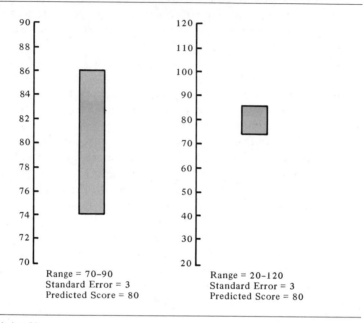

Range = 70–90
Standard Error = 3
Predicted Score = 80

Range = 20–120
Standard Error = 3
Predicted Score = 80

[a] .95 level of confidence.

behavior within a twelve-interval range (two standard errors of estimate above and below the predicted criterion score, the .95 level of confidence).

The standard error of estimate, like the standard error of measurement, must be expressed in terms of a ratio of estimate of predictive error to the range of scores on the criterion measure. If one unit in ten of predicted criterion performance were shown to be in error, the measure may be invalid for use. On the other hand, if one unit in fifty were in error, the measure may be deemed adequate for use. The utility of any measure in this regard depends on the criterion predicted and the consequences for an individual of inappropriate decisions and actions. The smaller the standard error of estimate and the smaller the ratio of prediction error to criterion score range, the better is the case. Nonetheless, depending on the criterion behavior predicted, measures that yield relatively high standard errors of estimate and relatively high ratios of predictive error to criterion range may be judged sufficiently valid.

Recognizing both the standard error of measurement and the

standard error of estimate is necessary for understanding the level of certainty with which predictor and criterion data may be used. In some instances, the imprecise nature of test and criterion scores makes the use of tests inappropriate. It is better to recognize these limitations and act accordingly than it is to continue to accept on blind faith the value of tests and to misuse test data to the detriment of clients.

ISSUES

1. Internal consistency estimates of a test's reliability may be employed in lieu of more basic test-retest procedures.

Yes, because:
1. The correspondence between the types of estimates is frequently significant, especially when more sophisticated internal consistency indices such as Cronbach's *alpha* coefficient are used.
2. Internal consistency indices are economical in that they require the administration of only one form of a test to a single representative sample of subjects and are no more difficult to compute than are test-retest estimates.

No, because:
1. To be used appropriately, internal consistency estimates may be employed only with tests that are homogeneous in content and level of difficulty or popularity of responses.
2. Frequently, the use of an internal consistency index yields an imprecise estimate of a test's reliability if the procedure requires that an adjustment be made by means of formulae such as the Spearman-Brown prophecy formula.

Discussion:
Our bias on this issue differs from that of recognized test experts (such as Cronbach and Gulliksen). In recent years, as more tests have been homogeneous in content and response, concern over appropriate internal consistency indices has diminished. However, if a test is timed or powered or includes heterogeneous content for which only a single global score is reported, the basic assumptions associated with the use of internal consistency indices have been violated and the estimates produced are suspect. The counselor must evaluate critically the adequacy and relevance of all reliability data provided for a test prior to its use.

2. *Demonstrating the content relevance of two or more forms of a test is sufficient to justify the assertion that these test forms are equivalent.*

Yes, because:
1. Content relevance for any form of a test is the primary basis on which the validity of any test rests.
2. Test plans, certainly those established for published measures, are determined painstakingly, and efforts made to actualize these plans when constructing one or more forms of a test involve great care.

No, because:
1. Content relevance is insufficient evidence to demonstrate the functional equivalence of two or more forms of a test.
2. Statistical evidence is required to demonstrate the functional equivalence of test forms.

Discussion:
Although test authors and publishers actually do devote considerable attention to developing tables of specifications for their tests in order to increase the probability that a representative sampling of behavior may be measured, the efficiency whereby equivalent forms of a test are created cannot be known with certitude unless evidence of similarity in central tendency, variability, and correlation with criteria external to the test are demonstrated. Admittedly, the latter data are obtained at cost, sometimes considerable, to the test author and publisher. However, without such empirical data, the counselor must accept the assertion of equivalence of forms on faith rather than demonstrated fact.

3. *The validity of a test may be defined in terms of its intrinsic or content relevance rather than its power to predict future behavior.*

Yes, because:
1. The concept of validity relates to the efficiency of a test in measuring the intended domain of behavior.
2. If test content is valid, it should provide an effective measure of the behavior in question.
3. Adequate definitions of criterion behaviors to be predicted are difficult to formulate and to measure.
4. Obtaining relevant evidence of the predictive power of any test is a costly, often inefficient, and impractical process.

No, because:

1. Regardless of the apparent content relevance of any test, its ultimate value is not known until the test has demonstrated utility in predicting future behavior.
2. In spite of the difficulties associated with the operational definition and measurement of behavior criteria and the labor required to obtain predictive evidence, the theoretical value of predictive power evidence cannot be discounted.

Discussion:

We have offered various definitions of validity in this chapter. Depending on which definitions counselors are willing to accept as sufficient to describe the concept, they may decide in favor in either point of view outlined above. Nonetheless, we prefer to negate the proposition. Despite the many practical problems and limitations posed, we maintain that the ultimate validity of a test is in its power to predict future behavior. We are willing to accord value to other evidence, but we feel such data to be less than satisfactory. Consequently, we think that counselors must consider with utmost diligence the nature and quality of the validity data reported for any test. Furthermore, with regard to any such information, the counselor must keep in mind that validity is specific to the purpose for which, as well as the population with whom, a test is to be employed.

ANNOTATED REFERENCES

Cronbach, L. J. "Test Validation." In *Educational Measurement.* 2nd ed. Edited by R. L. Thorndike. Washington, D.C.: American Council on Education, 1971, pp. 443–507.

This chapter updates the one written by E. E. Cureton for the first edition of this comprehensive and technically sophisticated compendium; it is viewed by many experts in the field to be the best single reference source for information on educational and psychological testing. Cronbach has built well on the foundation laid by Cureton. The concepts he presents are complex and are not intended for the casual reader. However, the serious reader can gain a thorough understanding of the construct of test validity.

Nunnally, J. C. "Psychometric Theory—25 Years Ago and Now." *Educational Researcher* 4 (1975): pp. 7–21.

Invited to address the American Education Research Association in April 1975, Nunnally presented a brief but most pertinent account of the major developments in psychometrics between 1950 and 1975, from which this piece is adapted. His remarks on test reliability and validity are easy to understand and should help counselors place these concepts appropriately in a historical perspective.

Stanley, J. C. "Reliability." In *Educational Measurement.* 2nd ed. Edited by R. L. Thorndike. Washington, D.C.: American Council on Education, 1971, pp. 356–442.

Like the chapters written by Cronbach and Cureton, Stanley's presents a complete and scholarly account of expert opinion regarding the concept of test reliability. In so doing, Stanley built effectively the foundation laid by R. L. Thorndike in the first edition. Again, the material is technically sophisticated and is intended only for the serious student. Nonetheless, the chapter provides a thorough understanding of the principles of test reliability.

SELECTED REFERENCES

Anastasi, Anne. *Psychological Testing.* 4th ed. New York: Macmillan, 1976, pp. 103–197.

Brown, F. G. *Principles of Educational and Psychological Testing.* Hinsdale, Ill.: Dryden Press, 1970, pp. 20–24, 49–157.

Ebel, R. L. *Essentials of Educational Measurement.* 2nd ed. Englewood Cliffs, N.J.: Prentice-Hall, 1972, pp. 296–302, 359–382, 407–450.

Horrocks, J. E. *Assessment of Behavior.* Columbus, Ohio: Charles E. Merrill Books, 1965, pp. 57–66.

Lien, A. J. *Measurement and Evaluation of Learning.* 2nd ed. Dubuque, Iowa: Wm. C. Brown Company, 1971, pp. 41–54, 255.

Mehrens, W. A., and Lehman, I. J. *Measurement and Evaluation in Education and Psychology.* 2nd ed. New York: Holt, Rinehart and Winston, 1978, pp. 87–132.

Noll, V. H., and Scannell, D. P. *Introduction to Educational Measurement.* 3rd ed. Boston: Houghton Mifflin, 1972, pp. 80–92.

Nunnally, J. C., Jr. *Introduction to Psychological Measurement.* New York: McGraw-Hill, 1970, pp. 77–154.

Payne, D. A. *The Assessment of Learning: Cognitive and Affective.* Lexington, Mass.: D. C. Heath, 1974, pp. 222, 251–271.

Thorndike, R. L., and Hagen, Elizabeth. *Measurement and Evaluation in Psychology and Education.* 4th ed. New York: John Wiley and Sons, 1977, pp. 163–199.

Part 3

Assessment in the Cognitive Domain

THERE ARE APPRAISAL DEVICES AND TECHNIQUES FOR ASSESSING A broad array of human behavior. This array can be ordered into two principal categories: the cognitive domain and the affective domain. The latter is the subject of Part 4. This section covers the major subcategories of appraisal in the cognitive domain. Included in this area are those behaviors associated with learning, both general and specific. The measures used to assess the cognitive domain are almost always referred to as tests of maximum performance. The premise underlying these measures is that the individual, when tested, performs at the top of his or her form.

Chapter 5 treats the assessment of intelligence or general ability and includes a brief overview of creativity measures. Chapters 6, 7, and 8 deal with appraisal devices associated with specific cognitive processes and learning products. While Chapter 6 focuses on the educational product, Chapter 7 details measures employed to diagnose learning deficits, and Chapter 8 concentrates on aptitudes or special skills basic to achievement in school and necessary for success in various kinds of work.

Chapter 5

Intelligence, or General Ability

What is the nature of intelligence?

What individual tests assess ability?

What standardized group tests are commonly employed to estimate ability and creativity?

What uses are made of ability measures?

How should scores of ability tests be interpreted, reported, and used?

THE CONCEPT OF INTELLIGENCE

Tests of mental ability were the first standardized psychological tests to be developed (see Chapter 2). Various terms (*intelligence, ability, scholastic aptitude*) have been and still are used to designate their fundamental object, which is to estimate intellectual functioning. Concerned psychologists and educators have attempted to define precisely what these tests measure since their inception in 1905. But the word *intelligence*, like *liberty, equality*, or *justice*, is hard to define and is in many ways a concept that, with some manipulation, can be made to accommodate almost any meaning a person wishes to communicate.

DEFINITIONS OF INTELLIGENCE

Definitions of intelligence fall into two categories. First is the *cognitive*, in which intelligence is viewed primarily as the ability to think in the abstract, to learn.[1,2,3] The individual who engages in

---

[1] L. M. Terman, *The Measurement of Intelligence* (Boston: Houghton Mifflin, 1916), p. 42.

[2] David Wechsler, *The Measurement of Adult Intelligence* (Baltimore: Williams Wilkins, 1944), p. 42.

[3] H. H. Goddard, "What is Intelligence?" *Journal of Social Psychology* 24 (1946): 68.

abstract thinking substitutes symbols for action and is able to manipulate ideas that represent not only what is happening on the spot but events remote in time and space. The *connative* form of definition stresses the processes of adapting to the environment and adjusting to problems and changing conditions.[4]

Intelligence has been defined as "the entire repertoire of acquired skills, knowledge, learning sets, and generalization tendencies considered intellectual in nature that are available to any one person in time."[5] T. Anne Cleary and her colleagues suggest that their definition means that (1) intelligence is not viewed as an entity; (2) learning and the constitutional basis for learning are important; and (3) a distinction can be made between the repertoire of responses (or intelligence) and eliciting those responses on a test.[6]

THE NATURE OF INTELLIGENCE

Some years ago, J. M. Hunt made a comprehensive study of the ways in which intelligence has been regarded since people first began to write on the subject.[7] He traced concepts of intelligence back to the work of Charles Darwin and his theory of the survival of the fittest. Hunt concluded, "intelligence should be conceived of as intellectual capacities based on central processes hierarchically arranged within the intrinsic portions of the cerebrum. These central processes are approximately analogous to strategies for information processing and action with which electronic computers are programmed."[8] Hunt's conception seems to be based on the belief that a person inherits a basic intellectual capacity and that both childhood learning and environment modify that basic capacity and influence its operations.

More recently, David Wechsler explored the major reasons for the continuing diversity of opinion about the nature and meaning of intelligence.[9] He identifies some unwarranted assumptions about intelligence and explains why they are untenable. These assumptions are that (1) intelligence is a quality of the mind (should be viewed as an aspect of behavior); (2) intelligence is a singular and

---

[4] G. D. Stoddard, *The Meaning of Intelligence* (New York: Macmillan, 1943), p. 4.
[5] T. Anne Cleary, Lloyd G. Humphreys, S. A. Kendrick, and Alexander Wessman, "Educational Use of Tests With Disadvantaged Students," *American Psychologist* 30 (January 1975): 19.
[6] Cleary et al., "Educational Use of Tests."
[7] J. M. Hunt, *Intelligence and Experience* (New York: Ronald Press, 1961).
[8] Hunt, *Intelligence and Experience*, p. 302.
[9] David Wechsler, "Intelligence Defined and Undefined," *American Psychologist* 30 (February 1975): 135–139.

unique trait (should be viewed as a many-faceted entity, a complex of diverse and numerous components); and (3) intelligence is concerned with how the mind functions or operates logically (intelligent behavior is not itself an aspect of cognition). Wechsler emphasizes that intelligence is a multifaceted entity, a product of many factors and subject to numerous influences. He lists certain conditions associated with intelligent behavior that might make possible a consistent definition of intelligence. These conditions, paraphrased here, include:

1. *Awareness.* To merit characterization as a manifestation of intelligence, an act must be assumed to have been performed by an individual conscious of or capable of knowing what he or she is doing and, ultimately, why.
2. *Meaning.* Intelligent behavior is not random but goal-directed.
3. *Consistency.* Intelligent behavior is capable of being deduced logically and is consistent.
4. *Worth.* To merit being called intelligent, behavior must be in accord with what group consensus deems valuable and useful.

Wechsler ends his relativistic appraisal of intelligence with a definition:

> But as to what tests measure, I am in considerable disagreement with current opinion. What we measure with tests is not what tests measure—not information, not spatial perception, not reasoning ability. These are only means to an end. What intelligence tests measure, what we hope they measure, is something much more important: the capacity of an individual to understand the world about him and his resourcefulness to cope with its challenges.[10]

Precisely what intelligence tests measure has been the subject of dispute since their origin. Scores of social scientists have checked the validity of intelligence tests. The outcome of such investigations, too many to cite here, while varied, shows that intelligence tests hold up quite well. Teachers' ratings and measured ability scores agree rather well. Children doing well in school usually have high IQ scores. Generally, the tests discriminate between normals and others. Older children give more correct answers than do younger children. Measured ability scores from several tests of verbal skill tend to agree, but agreement between scores of verbal and performance scales, although positive, is less striking.

[10] Wechsler, "Intelligence Defined and Undefined," p. 139.

No intelligence test available today measures innate ability. It is unlikely that such a test will ever be designed. Intelligence tests measure the extent to which an individual's innate potential has been modified or developed within his or her environment. Some time ago, Wechsler asserted that it was impossible to assess intelligence in action for three reasons. First, intelligent behavior represents an interaction or configuration of the abilities of which it is composed. None of these abilities, he believed, acts in isolation. Second, intelligent behavior is a function of drive and incentive as well as the more traditionally conceived components of intellectual ability. Third, varying degrees of intellectual ability result in different orders of intelligent behavior, but the possession of an excess of any one component ability does not add materially to overall intellectual effectiveness. However, despite the problem of summation, Wechsler observes that, "Although intelligence is no mere sum of intellectual abilities, the only way we can evaluate it quantitatively is by the measure of the various aspects of these abilities."[11]

PERSONALITY AND INTELLIGENCE

Personality and intelligence have been viewed by many social scientists as being interactive, if not inseparable. For example, Jean Piaget holds that intellective behaviors are stimulated by affective elements (personality). He views personality and intelligence as separate but mutually reinforcing and interacting.

> Affective life and cognitive life . . . are inseparable although distinct. They are inseparable because all interaction with the environment involves both a structuring and a valuation, but they are none the less distinct, since these two aspects of behavior cannnot be reduced to one another. . . . An act of intelligence involves. . . an internal regulation of energy (interest, effort, ease, etc.) and an external regulation (the value of the solutions sought and of the objects concerned in the search), but these two controls are of an affective nature and remain comparable with all other regulations of this type. Similarly the perceptual or intellectual elements which we find in all manifestations of emotion involve cognition in the same way as any other perceptual or intelligent reactions.[12]

[11] David Wechsler, *The Measurement and Appraisal of Adult Intelligence,* 4th ed. (Baltimore: Williams and Wilkins, 1958), p. 4.
[12] Jean Piaget, *The Psychology of Intelligence* (New York: Harcourt Brace, 1950), p. 6.

Hermann Rorschach emphasized the importance of intelligence to personality. Given his inkblot test, an intelligent person produces an orderly sequence.[13] Goldstein, while criticizing ability testing and urging abandonment of the term *intelligence*, separates behavior into concrete and abstract forms. He says, "In 'concrete' performance a reaction is determined directly by a stimulus, is awakened by all that the individual perceives. . . . In 'abstract' performances an action is not determined directly and immediately by a stimulus configuration but only by the account of the situation which the individual gives himself."[14]

THE STABILITY OF INTELLIGENCE

Measures of intelligence are essentially ranks or ratios (see Chapter 3); there is no true unit of intellectual ability. Whether individuals maintain their relative standing over time has been a question subject to much discussion and some research. It is an important issue, for if intelligence scores are unstable, predictions about an individual's educational and vocational ventures are worthless. After age 5, most individuals' scores remain stable and do not change significantly from test to test, even over a fairly long time.

This does not mean that every person's intellectual standing is fixed. Some change markedly from time to time. At least 10 percent of children's test results change at least 15 points during a period of 6–8 years. These gains or losses appear to occur because of changes in personality, emotional condition, and environment. In general, people tend to retain their relative intellectual standing when they remain in an environment that provides opportunities that nourish mental development.

Many unsubstantiated ideas about mental growth have permeated public thinking and influenced the behavior of many people. One is that attaining physical growth means that mental, emotional, and psychological growth come to an end. The myth that one doesn't keep growing after one has grown up has been accepted widely. It has wrought the greatest havoc in education, where some practitioners seem to believe that learning ends with the early years, even though this is not so.

Some time ago, Harold Jones and Herbert Conrad revealed the

---

[13] Hermann Rorschach, *Psychodiagnostics*, 5th ed. (New York: Grune and Stratton, 1951).

[14] Kurt Goldstein, *Human Nature in the Light of Psychopathology* (Cambridge: Harvard University Press, 1940).

discrepancy in the performance of different age groups on tests assessing knowledge (for example, vocabulary) versus those primarily measuring alertness (the ability to follow directions).[15] A knowledge curve usually remains almost level between ages 20 and 60, while an alertness curve declines gradually after age 17. An adult of 40, though past the peak of mental alertness, can learn new things about as well as a youngster of 13, who has not yet reached maximum mental development. In fact, an adult who is motivated strongly enough to make up some slight loss in alertness and adaptability may learn better than the thirteen-year-old.

Irving Lorge also demonstrated that the greatest difference in mental ability between younger and older persons is in speed rather than accuracy or power.[16] For example, a group of persons under 25 and a group over 40 performed equally well on a test that had no time limit. On tests with a time limit, the younger group demonstrated a clear superiority, because they worked faster.

From earliest infancy until death, mental growth is a continuing process but not an even one. There are phases when breakthroughs occur, although no one knows yet just when they come or why. It is a little like William James's metaphor of the flights and perchings of a bird. On many accounts, a child learns faster than an adult, and more effortlessly: body skills and rhythms, languages, emotional growth, leaps of intuition. Yet the creative process, which is the heart of the learning and growing experience, continues through adulthood into old age, taking subtler and more ambitious forms than in the early years. A life can hold excitement and an openness to new experience until the end. That means that one can continue growing until one grows into the unknown and unknowable.

THE NATURE-NURTURE CONTROVERSY

The question of whether intelligence is *fixed*—established at birth and unchanging—or modifiable by environmental influences was debated even prior to the origin of intelligence tests. The question of the precise proportion, but not the principle, of hereditary influences has long been a source of conflicting opinion. To determine

---

[15] Harold E. Jones and Herbert S. Conrad, *The Growth and Decline of Intelligence: A Study of a Homogeneous Group Between the Ages of Ten and Sixty* (Institute of Child Welfare, University of California, 1933).

[16] Irving Lorge, *Influence of Regularly Interpolated Time Intervals Upon Subsequent Learning* (New York: Teachers College, Columbia University, 1930).

whether environment or inheritance is the primary factor in intelligence is a complex problem, for the two forces interact. In psychological terms, one cannot exist without the other.

Of the many environmental factors influencing intelligence and performance on tests designed to measure intelligence and ability, most social scientists regard the home and education as particularly critical. Some time ago, Horatio Newman, Frank Freeman, and Karl Holzinger reported that when identical twins reared apart differed in IQ, the twin with the better education had the higher IQ.[17]

Without question, the home influences one's measured intelligence score. Newman and his colleagues reported that foster children placed in superior homes gained 5–10 IQ points after 4 years, whereas those placed in less desirable homes gained little or nothing. Hugh Gordon, in 1923, presented findings on the intelligence of canal-boat and gypsy children, who had poor socioeconomic and cultural backgrounds.[18] Mandall Sherman and Thomas R. Henry studied the intelligence of children in four mountain hollows in Virginia, comparing them with children in a typical small town nearby.[19] On every test, both verbal and performance, the children of the hollows were clearly inferior, though their inferiority showed more strikingly on verbal tests. All came from the same racial stock, but great differences were found in the economic, social, and cultural life of the various communities. In two hollows, for example, life was very primitive; little or no education, religion, or social organization existed. Few of the residents could read or write. Communications with the outer world came only by mountain path or trail. As with Gordon's canal-boat and gypsy children, IQs went down consistently as the children grew older. At ages 6–8, the hollows children had IQs between 80 and 85; after age 12, their IQs averaged about 50.

The simplest explanation is that children reared in isolated, backward sections do not receive the same experience or stimulation in their homes, schools, and communities that their more culturally normal peers obtain. With very few exceptions, tests are standardized on the performance of children reared in environments typical of the white middle class. As the test scores of average children increase with age and experience, the scores of isolated or culturally different children, who lack that experience, grow increasingly de-

[17] Horatio H. Newman, Frank N. Freeman, and Karl J. Holzinger, *Twins: A Study of Heredity and Environment* (Chicago: University of Chicago Press, 1937).

[18] Hugh Gordon, *Mental and Scholastic Tests Among Retarded Children*, Educational Pamphlet No. 44 (London: Board of Education, 1923).

[19] Mandall Sherman and Thomas R. Henry, *Hollow Folk* (New York: Thomas Y. Crowell, 1933).

pressed. Whether or not environmental influences raise or lower an individual's actual capacity for intelligent behavior, psychologists and educators generally agree that they have a considerable effect on performance on an intelligence test.

Average measured intelligence in the children of professionals tends to be high. Intelligence scores decrease as one moves down the occupational scale to unskilled labor. There is, however, much overlapping. Nancy Bayley reported that the measure of intelligence of children under 2 years is not related to the income, occupation, or socioeconomic status of their parents. From ages 2–10, Bayley reported an increasing correlation of high intelligence and high income and social and economic status.[20] These results are not surprising, since tests that assess the abilities of infants and preschool children generally evaluate a child's physical and motor development, whereas tests used with school-age children emphasize tasks related to what is taught in school. In other words, these tests do not measure the same thing. Studying a person directly does not prove whether environment or heredity is the main determinant of intelligent behavior; but measuring the mental or physical differences between two or more persons and carefully studying their backgrounds provide some data as to the importance of heredity or environment. Such a procedure involves the concept of *heritability*, which Arthur Jensen describes thus:

> A technical term in quantitative genetics, heritability refers to the proportion of the total variation of some trait, among persons within a given population, that can be attributed to genetic factors. Once the heritability of that trait can be determined, the remainder of the variance can be attributed mainly to environmental influence. Now intelligence, as measured by standard tests such as the Stanford–Binet and many others, does show very substantial heritability in the European and North American Caucasian populations in which the necessary genetic studies have been done. . . .

> No precise figure exists for the heritability of intelligence, since, like any population statistic, it varies from one study to another, depending on the particular population sampled, the IQ test used, and the method of genetic analysis. Most of the estimates for the heritability of intelligence in the populations studied indicate that genetic factors are about twice as important as environmental factors as a cause of IQ differences among individuals.[21]

---

[20] See Nancy Bayley, "Consistency and Variability in Growth from Birth to 18 Years," *Journal of Genetic Psychology* 75 (March 1949): 165–196, and Nancy Bayley, "On the Growth of Intelligence," *American Psychologist* 10 (December 1955): 805–818.
[21] Arthur Jensen, "The Differences Are Real," *Psychology Today* 7 (December 1973): 80.

Controversy over the heritability of intelligence flared anew with an earlier publication by Jensen in which he also questioned the prevailing doctrine of racial genetic equality in intelligence.[22] Jensen argued that capacity for abstract reasoning and problem solving, not learning and memory, governs intelligence test scores, and that this basic ability is unevenly distributed among populations.

Critics disputed Jensen largely on the ground that he relied excessively on what the critics regarded as questionable findings derived from comparing test scores across populations of equal socioeconomic status. For example, Theodosius Dobzhansky stated:

> After psychologist Arthur Jensen explicitly recognized that heritability of individual differences in IQ cannot be used as a measure of average heritability across populations, he tries to do just that. In fairness to Jensen he presents a detailed analysis of the environmental factors, that could account for the discrepancy, but then he concludes that none of these factors or their combinations can explain the difference in average black and white IQ scores. He appeals to studies which try to equate black and white environments by comparing populations of equal socioeconomic status. This diminishes the IQ difference between the two races, but it does not erase the difference. Jensen takes this as evidence that a strong genetic component is operating. I remain unconvinced.[23]

As Berkely Rice points out, the struggle over the relationship between heredity, environment, and intelligence has produced much turmoil, and an emotional atmosphere surrounds the issue today.[24] Without question, attempts have been made to justify hideous actions prompted by false concepts of racial differences in intelligence. To date, no definitive evidence of such differences has been produced. It is certain that both heredity and environment influence intelligent behavior, but the proportional impact of each is unknown. In contrast, the nineteenth-century theorists favored hereditary explanations of intelligence, and early twentieth-century theorists stressed the impact of environment. Most current professionals simply acknowledge that heredity probably sets limits on the extent to which environment can nurture what nature has provided.

[22] Arthur Jensen, "How Much Can We Boost IQ and Scholastic Achievement?" *Harvard Educational Review* (February 1969): 1–123.

[23] Theodosius Dobzhansky, "Differences Are Not Deficits," *Psychology Today* 7 (December 1973): 98–100.

[24] Berkely Rice, "The High Cost of Thinking the Unthinkable," *Psychology Today* 7 (December 1973): 89–93.

THEORIES OF INTELLIGENCE

Early descriptions of the organization of intelligence were based generally on a *unifactor* theory. This theory, which ascribed mental ability to a single general capacity, was adopted into psychology from biology. In 1904, after making statistical studies of test performance, an English psychologist, Charles Spearman, proposed a two-factor theory of intelligence. He concluded that each individual possesses a certain amount of general ability (g) that enters everything one does, but that there are special abilities (s) that vary for each task undertaken. Figure 5.1 depicts his theory. Intelligence was conceived as composed of a general factor, g, which was similar to the unifactor mentioned above, plus other specific factors, s. The s factor was viewed as independent of g. Spearman called them "specific mental engines." Performance on a mathematics test, for instance, depends on a person's ability as well as specific aptitude and instruction in mathematics. It also should be noted that the correlation between two or more tests depends on the amount of g factor that influences performance on each and that, consequently, they share. In Figure 5.1, the circles labeled S_1 and S_2 could be considered as independent mental tests, each with a varying amount of g and each with its specific s. Spearman believed that a special sort of energy, which he ascribed to the g factor, was particularly useful in making comparisons or drawing inferences.

Edward Thorndike, as well as other psychologists, objected to the assumption that any test can measure general intelligence. In his *Educational Psychology,* published in 1914, Thorndike questioned the existence of general ability, stressing rather the "singularity and relative independence of every mental process." Instead of general

FIGURE 5.1
SPEARMAN'S TWO-FACTOR THEORY OF INTELLIGENCE

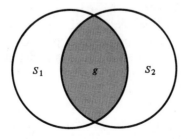

FIGURE 5.2
SPEARMAN'S GROUP FACTOR THEORY OF INTELLIGENCE

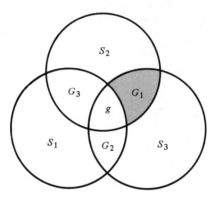

ability, he insisted that there are many special or grouped abilities, such as mathematical or mechanical ability.

Spearman continued his work and, during the 1920s, revised his theory to take into account group factors, as depicted in Figure 5.2.[25] A group factor (G_1) is shown as the darkened space in Figure 5.2. This group factor occurs because 3 (S_3) and 2 (S_2) share some common abilities and skills. This is what Spearman called a group factor. His group factors included mathematical, mechanical, musical, logical, and psychological abilities and three other factors that he labeled *perseveration, oscillation,* and *will.* British psychologists have pursued Spearman's theories or modifications of them.

The concept of ability proposed by Paul E. Vernon[26] builds on the work by Spearman. Vernon places the general intellectual factor, *g,* at the top of his schema. Below this are two major group factors, one called *verbal-educational* and the other *spatial-practical-mechanical.* Each part of the bifurcation can be subdivided further into minor group factors. The verbal-educational group usually yields numerical, scholastic, fluency, and divergent thinking factors. The other major group contains perceptual, physical, psychomotor, spatial, and mechanical factors. Vernon suggests that there are links between the two major groups such as in a test of clerical ability

[25] Charles Spearman, *The Abilities of Man* (New York: Macmillan, 1927).
[26] See Paul E. Vernon, "Ability Factors and Environmental Influences," *American Psychologist* 20 (September 1965): 723–733, and Paul E. Vernon, *The Structure of Mental Ability* (New York: Wiley, 1950).

(requiring both verbal ability and perceptual speed). Similarly, mathematics and science bring together verbal, numerical, and spatial abilities. At the bottom of Vernon's system appear specific factors related to single, simple tests.

Americans, on the other hand, have tended to follow *multiple factor* theories of ability, originated by Thorndike and advocated by the Thurstones, who found several group factors, or clusters of abilities, by carefully analyzing whole batteries of tests.[27] They administered fifty-seven tests requiring some fifteen hours of work to a large group of high school students. Treating these data statistically by factor analysis, the Thurstones were able to isolate a small group of factors they termed *primary mental abilities.* These abilities included:

N (number), the ability to carry out basic arithmetic processes rapidly and accurately
V (verbal), the ability to understand ideas expressed in word forms
WF (word fluency), the ability to write and speak with considerable ease
M (memory), recognition and recall
R (reasoning), problem solving, profiting from experience, and so on
S (spatial), the ability to visualize spatial relationships
P (perception), perceptual speed

These abilities are relatively independent, and, according to the Thurstones, a person proficient in one is not necessarily so in another.

J. P. Guilford has proposed a three-way organization of mental ability, depicted here in Figure 5.3.[28] The divisions in each of the three categories are as follows:

OPERATIONS

1. memory—retaining information
2. cognition—recognizing patterns, facts, and so on
3. convergent thinking—proceeding from information to a specific correct answer
4. divergent thinking—proceeding from information to a variety of adequate solutions as in finding titles to fit a plot
5. evaluation—making decisions concerning goodness or appropriateness of ideas

---

[27] L. and L. Thurstone, *Primary Mental Abilities* (Psychometric Monograph 1, 1948).
[28] J. P. Guilford, *The Nature of Human Intelligence* (New York: McGraw-Hill, 1967).

FIGURE 5.3
GUILFORD'S STRUCTURE-OF-INTELLECT MODEL,
WITH THREE PARAMETERS[a]

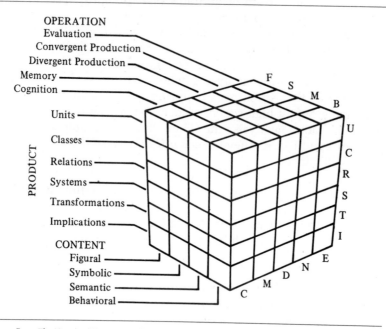

Source: From *The Nature of Human Intelligence* by J. P. Guilford. Copyright © 1967 by McGraw-Hill, Inc.
Used with permission of McGraw-Hill Book Company.
[a] Other parameters may need to be added.

CONTENT

1. figural—directly perceived objects, events, drawings
2. symbolic—letters, numbers, and so on
3. semantic—verbal meanings
4. behavioral—interpretation of human behavior

PRODUCTS

1. information—units
2. classes of units—set of objects
3. relations between units—connecting links
4. systems of information—patterns
5. transformations—changes
6. implications—something expected

The block (see Figure 5.3) made from these categories contains 120
cells (5 × 4 × 6), each of which represents an ability, a factor, or

a type of task that may appear on an intelligence test. Guilford and his colleagues have sought to demonstrate that the structure-of-the-intellect (SI) factors exist. He reports that

> at the time this was written, the number of demonstrated SI factors had grown to 82, with others under investigation. Of the total of 24 hypothesized cognition abilities, all have been demonstrated, including the 6 abilities for the cognition of behavioral products of information.[29]

Some cells, according to Guilford, contain more than one factor. While he believes that the single-score approach to intelligence has worked sufficiently well in the past, now the time has come to use a multiple-score approach. There is strong opposition to Guilford's multiple-score approach. Quentin McNemar, for example, has accused theorists like Guilford of fragmenting mental ability into more and more factors of less and less value.[30]

The similarity between the Thurstones' model and Guilford's structure of the intellect model is open to question. They do not appear highly dissimilar. When Thurstone built his factors into tests and administered them, he reported that there were positive intercorrelations among all of the factors.[31] Therefore, the presence of a g factor seems unavoidable, as this is the only way such intercorrelations can be interpreted. Actual American test practice is based on the idea of a general factor. Commonly employed individual and group tests purportedly measure general intelligence. It is true that many tests used to predict academic success provide both verbal and quantitative scores, but this seems to be the major concession made to the Thurstones' ideas, although their methods are used widely in research.

INDIVIDUAL ABILITY TESTS

Individual tests are so called because they are constructed to be administered to only one person at a time. Three general types of individual ability tests exist: highly verbal (for example, the Stanford-Binet); about half verbal and half performance (for example, the Wechsler scales); and those that primarily test performance (for example, pre-school batteries, Merrill-Palmer scales).

---

[29] Guilford, The Nature of Intelligence, p. 65.
[30] Quentin McNemar, "Lost: Our Intelligence? Why?" American Psychologist 19 (December 1964): 871–882.
[31] L. and L. Thurstone, Multiple Factor Analysis (Chicago: University of Chicago Press, 1947).

Counselors are not expected to be proficient in administering and scoring individual ability tests. Usually such work is done by psychologists. However, counselors must be familiar with the strengths and limitations of individual tests, because their work with individuals frequently requires interpretation and use of individual test data. Here, then, is an introduction to commonly used individual tests.

THE STANFORD-BINET TEST

The current edition of the Stanford-Binet, revised in 1973 (Houghton Mifflin), incorporates in a single scale, called form L-M, the best subtests from previous editions. The subtests included in the 1973 revision were selected on the basis of test records administered to 4,498 youngsters aged 2½–18 during a five-year period extending from 1950–1954. Form L-M may be administered to any person from a two-year-old to an adult. Subtests are grouped in terms of age levels. Between the ages 2–5, there is a test for each half year, and from ages 5–14, there is one test per year. These are followed by one average adult test and three superior adult tests. Each item or subtest is worth a given number of months of mental age (MA). For example, for year V, there are 6 items, and the correct response to each contributes 2 months toward an overall mental age score.

CONTENT   Most tasks set forth by the Stanford-Binet are of a verbal nature, particularly at the middle- and upper-age levels. Memory is measured by repetition of digits or sentences. Reasoning is sampled through simple and complex problems. Spatial ability is assessed through drawing geometric figures. Illustrative of these tasks are those designed for the year II-6, which consist of: (1) identifying objects by use, (2) identifying parts of the body, (3) naming objects, (4) testing picture vocabulary, (5) repeating two digits, and (6) obeying simple commands.

ADMINISTRATION   The manual identifies three conditions that must be met if valid test results are to be obtained: (1) standard procedures must be followed; (2) the subject's best efforts must be enlisted; and (3) responses must be scored correctly.[32] The time required to administer a Stanford-Binet examination involves about

---

[32] Lewis M. Terman and Maud A. Merrill, *Stanford-Binet Intelligence Scale* (Boston: Houghton Mifflin, 1973), p. 46.

30–40 minutes for the younger ages and usually not in excess of 90 minutes for older groups. The manual also advises that administration of the test be started at a level a year below the examinee's chronological age, or lower if the examinee is suspected of being below average in ability. For example, a typical seven-year-old would be given the items for year VI first, next the year VII items, followed by the year VIII, and continuing upward until an age level is reached in which the examinee misses every item. The age at which all subtests are failed is referred to as the *ceiling age*. A seven-year-old examinee who misses an item or more for year VI would be given items for year V, and this procedure would be followed downward until an age level is reached at which all items are answered correctly. This bottom age is called the *basal age*. It is assumed that the individual can answer correctly all items below the basal age and respond correctly to no item above the ceiling age. After the test is scored, the mental age values for all items passed are summed and added to the basal age. This sum is the examinee's mental age. Normally, the scattering of successes and failures spreads over several age levels.

SCORES   A major difference between the new edition and previous Stanford–Binet tests lies in the type of IQ used in reporting scores. The old ratio IQ

$$IQ = \frac{MA}{CA} \times 100$$

has been replaced with a *deviation IQ* with a mean of 100 and a standard deviation of 16 (see Chapter 3). These deviation IQs are obtained easily from an extensive table presented in the manual based on data obtained during the 1971–1972 school year. Reliability and validity evidence for the current Stanford–Binet is based on estimates of internal consistency and similarity of content and performance to the 1937 scale.[33]

CRITICISMS   The Stanford-Binet, though accepted and used widely, has been the target of criticism. First, it is a highly verbal test and thus some children are necessarily penalized, because all individuals do not possess the same amounts of all abilities. Second, many of its tasks are academic, typical of schoolroom activities. When adults are tested, these academic activities may constitute a liability in that they fail to give face validity, in that they represent behaviors

[33] Terman and Merrill, *Stanford-Binet Scale*, pp. 353–361.

which are to some degree unfamiliar, depending on how long a given individual has been out of school. Third, many psychologists affirm that a single score is a poor representation of an individual's mental ability, for they believe multiple abilities to be more characteristic of humans than one general ability. Fourth, this test and other individually administered measures like it are time-consuming to administer and to score and are, therefore, costly. Examiners who administer the Stanford-Binet must have special training in its administration, scoring, and interpretation, which usually requires a minimum of a one-semester university course. Finally, this test is held responsible by some for promoting the continued use of the IQ as a measure of mental ability.

CONTRIBUTIONS   The Stanford–Binet is well-conceptualized and well-constructed. Of course, it is the oldest such measure available. The procedures used and the time spent in developing this test could serve as criteria to be followed by all test authors and publishers. Second, the test is fairly accurate. When used correctly, it produces reliable and valid results. Third, perhaps more research has been carried on with this test than with any other ability test. Such research makes the test data invaluable.

Each new Binet revision has been an improvement over earlier ones, yet none has been free from defects. Despite its well-publicized faults, the Binet always has been considered an outstanding measure of general ability. During the last few years, its supremacy has been overtaken by the Wechsler series of intelligence scales, but there are many who still believe that the Binet has no peer.

THE WECHSLER-BELLEVUE
AND SUBSEQUENT WECHSLER SCALES

In 1939, David Wechsler published the first edition of his Wechsler-Bellevue (WB) adult intelligence scale (Psychological Corporation). The *Wechsler Intelligence Scale for Children* (WISC) was released in 1949 and revised in 1971 (WISC-R) and refined further in 1974 (Psychological Corporation). The *Wechsler Adult Intelligence Scale* (WAIS) was published in 1955 for ages 16 and older (Psychological Corporation). The WISC-R and WAIS have extended or replaced the original 1939 scale.

CONTENT   The Wechsler scales consist of eleven regular subtests and an optional maze subtest for use with children. Six of these serve to form the verbal score (the first five listed below plus vocabulary), while the remaining five (six if mazes are used) make up the performance score. The various tests are outlined briefly here:

1. Information: twenty-five questions assessing the individual's knowledge about the world and its culture
2. Comprehension: a test of practical judgment and common sense
3. Digit Span (*optional with children*): the examinee repeats from three to nine digits forward as presented orally first and then repeats another series of digits backwards in contrast to the order presented
4. Similarities: given twelve pairs of words, such as, "In what way are an egg and a seed alike?" the subject has to explain the conceptual basis for the similarity
5. Arithmetic: solution of ten timed problems of increasing difficulty
6. Picture Arrangement: six different sets of cards, much like a cut-up comic strip, are to be arranged in a logical order so as to tell a story
7. Picture Completion: shown fifteen cards containing drawings with an important part missing, the subject must tell what this part is
8. Block Design: colored designs on seven cards are to be duplicated using a set of from four to sixteen wooden cubes painted differently on each side.
9. Object Assembly: three puzzles, for example, a manikin, a profile, and a hand made of plywood or heavy cardboard, are to be put together
10. Digit Symbol: code substitution; told that the numbers 1–9 are each represented by a given symbol, the examinee then translates as many as possible of a series of numbers into these symbols within a standard amount of time
11. Vocabulary: forty-two words (thirty-two with children), ranging in difficulty from *apple* to *seclude* to *traduce*, are to be defined
12. Mazes (optional with children; not used with adults)

WAIS   The *Wechsler Adult Intelligence Scale* is highly similar to the original Wechsler-Bellevue. Some subtests were modified by raising their ceilings and clarifying their presentation and scoring procedures. New items were added to the vocabulary test. The WAIS is composed of six verbal and five performance subtests that are combined to obtain the full-scale deviation IQ score. Standard-ization of the WAIS was based on a nationwide sample of 1,700 persons divided into seven age groups ranging age 16–64. The sample matched the 1950 census in age, occupation, sex, education, urban-rural residence, geographic location, and racial group. The WAIS manual reports the full-scale reliability of WAIS as .97 with subtest reliabilities ranging from a high of .95 for vocabulary at ages 45–54 to a low of .65 for object assembly at ages 18–19.[34]

WISC-R   The revised *Wechsler Intelligence Scale for Children* (1974) yields verbal, performance, and full-scale IQs. It contains ten sub-tests and two alternative tests and takes about 50–75 minutes to administer. Verbal and performance tests are alternated to vary the testing session. One verbal test (arithmetic) and all performance tests are timed and require the use of a stopwatch. The 1974 scale is different from its 1949 counterpart in that: (1) it is used with children aged 6–16 rather than 5–15; (2) there are thirty-nine new verbal items and twenty-one new performance items, and fifteen others have been substantially revised; (3) verbal and performance tests are now given in alternating fashion; (4) different starting points for normal children are suggested, and time limits for some problems have been lengthened; and (5) items on the vocabulary test have been revised and reduced.

The standardization of the WISC-R in 1974 was based on a sample of 2,200 children; each of the eleven age levels of the test was administered to 100 boys and 100 girls. A stratified sampling plan based on the 1970 census was used. Variables included age, sex, racial group, geographic region, urban–rural residence, and so on.

The manual reports that reliability coefficients of the verbal, performance, and full-scale IQs, for the eleven age groups averaged .94, .90, and .96, respectively.[35] Reliabilities ranged from .77 to .86 among individual verbal tests and from .70 to .85 among individual performance tests. The relationship of the WISC-R to other intelli-gence tests was investigated and reported in the manual. The corre-lation between WISC-R and WAIS full-scale IQs was reported to be .95, that between the two verbal IQs to be .96, and that between the two performance IQs .83. The average coefficients of correlation of the WISC-R verbal, performance, and full-scale IQs with the Stan-ford–Binet IQ were reported as .71, .60, and .73, respectively.[36] Stan-

[34] David Wechsler, *Manual for the Wechsler Adult Intelligence Scale* (New York: Psycholog-ical Corporation, 1955), pp. 12–14.
[35] David Wechsler, *Manual for the Wechsler Intelligence Scale for Children—Revised* (New York: Psychological Corporation, 1974), pp. 27–52.
[36] Wechsler, *Manual for the WISC—R*, p. 35.

ford-Binet IQs ran about two points higher at ages 6, 9½, and 12½, while the WISC-R full scale IQ was about two points higher at age 16½.

WPPSI   The *Wechsler Preschool and Primary Scale of Intelligence,* published in 1967, was viewed as an extension of the original WISC and created to test more effectively children 4–6½.[37] A full-scale deviation IQ is derived from five verbal and five performance subtest scores. As is true of other preschool measures, WPPSI reliability and validity indices are of smaller magnitude than for Wechsler measures used with older persons. Nonetheless, the measure has been received well, because it provides scores that parallel its parent measures.

SCORING AND SCORES   Wechsler's tests are point scales, in contrast to the original Stanford-Binet, a mental age scale. Wechsler wanted a numerical score that would mean the same thing at all age levels, in the strict statistical sense of representing the same deviation from the mean. Thus, a given IQ would always be equally difficult or easy to achieve, always rating an individual in the same position relative to other persons in his or her age category. The raw scores are transformed to weighted standard scores (each has a mean of 10 and a standard deviation of 3). These are totaled and the manual consulted for the meaning of the three IQs: verbal, performance, and total or full-scale IQ. These IQs are standard scores with a mean of 100 and a standard deviation of 15 (see Chapter 3).

According to Wechsler, mental growth ceases during the early thirties. For a few years, an individual is on a plateau, and then the growth curve goes down. Because it goes down at different rates for different individuals, Wechsler argues that adults should be compared with others of the same age level. Therefore, he has established norms for thirty- , forty- , and fifty-year olds. Whether tested mental performance declines as Wechsler suggests it does is a moot question. It is possible that an individual whose adult life has been spent in an unstimulating environment and who has not performed some of the manipulations on the test since he or she left school would score lower and lower with increasing age, while an individual who deals constantly with words and numbers would show little or no decline.

Scores on the Wechsler-Bellevue correlate highly with Stanford-Binet scores. Coefficients of from .80 to .93 are usual, but this means

[37] David Wechsler, *Manual for the Wechsler Preschool and Primary Scale of Intelligence* (New York: Psychological Corporation, 1967).

not that scores on the two tests would necessarily be similar for an individual but only that an individual's rank in the two distributions would tend to be about the same. Test-bright subjects tend to score higher on the *Stanford-Binet*, while those who typically perform less well on highly verbal ability tests score higher on the Wechsler tests.

USES   During the 1950s, the Wechsler-Bellevue was more widely employed in clinics than in schools. However, a study by Kathlyn C. Silvania revealed the Wechsler adult tests to rank first as the measure of intelligence in university counseling bureaus.[38] No doubt this was so because the scale was developed for adults and based on adult data. Furthermore, the profile of verbal and performance scores available to the examiner was thought to promote differential diagnosis and greater specificity of findings.

DIAGNOSTIC CUES   The Wechsler tests have been recommended for assessing mental retardation and organic brain dysfunction.[39] The discrepancy between verbal and performance scores is particularly relevant in this regard. A difference of 15 points or more is unusual and calls for further investigation. Furthermore, discrepancies in certain subtest scores are viewed as being useful in assessing personality. In most mental disorders, impairment of function tends to be less in the verbal than in the performance area. Wechsler has suggested that this holds for psychoses of nearly every type, for organic brain dysfunction, and to a lesser degree for psychoneurosis. Differences in verbal or performance scores vary in terms of the nature of the dysfunction and the degree of the impairment. Wechsler states:

> Particularly important in diagnostic studies is the matter of sign-overlap; that is the occurrence of significantly high and/or low test scores encountered not just in a single syndrome but in several diagnostic syndromes. Thus, a low Digit Span score may be associated with organic brain disease, may be a concomitant of reading disability, or may appear as a sign of manifest anxiety. The fact that the same or a similar test sign may be encountered in different disease entities or educational disabilities has led some investigators to discount the possibility of using test patterns as a basis for differential diagnosis. The finding that a low Digit Span is charac-

---

[38] Kathlyn C. Silvania, "Test Usage in Counseling Centers," *Personnel and Guidance Journal* 34 (May 1956): 559–564.
[39] A. H. Glasser and I. L. Zimmerman, *Clinical Interpretation of the Wechsler Intelligence Scale for Children (WISC)* (New York: Grune and Stratton, 1967).

teristic of several disease entities does not make it an inconsequential diagnostic sign, any more than the fact that a high temperature may occur in respiratory infections and sunstroke, as well as in appendicitis and malaria, makes this symptom an unimportant sign. The relevance or significance of a sign or symptom depends in large measure upon *what goes with it.* Thus, a low Digit Span score plus low scores on most other tests of the Scale may simply confirm an otherwise clear manifestation of mental deficiency; a low Digit Span associated with low Block Design and very poor Coding may indicate an organic brain syndrome; a low Digit Span score along with relatively high scores on most other subtests (particularly Vocabulary and Information) may suggest an anxiety situation.[40]

Counselors should be cautious in making inferences about such discrepancies and specific clusters of Wechsler subtest scores. Regarding the former, John L. Horrocks states:

It should be remembered that in estimating the significance of verbal–performance discrepancy one must take into account ordinary variability entirely within the normal range. The standard deviation of the mean difference between verbal and non-verbal is such that a difference of more than ten points will be not found in two-thirds of all cases, a difference of fifteen points in less than 85 per cent of all cases, and a difference of twenty points in less than 98 per cent of all cases. The clinician has to decide for his own particular purposes the level of verbal performance discrepancy he is willing to regard as normal. It will probably vary from case to case in terms of its association with other variables.[41]

PERFORMANCE TESTS

A third type of individual test used to measure intelligence or general ability comes under the heading of performance tests or batteries. These require the individual to do something other than respond verbally. Some, such as the Cattell test, are especially designed for infants. Others, such as the *Minnesota Pre-School Scale* or *Merrill-Palmer Scales,* are used with the preschool child, aged 2 and up. Still others, such as the *Grace Arthur Point Scale* and

---

[40] Wechsler, *Manual for the WISC—R*, p. 7.
[41] John L. Horrocks, *Assessment of Behavior* (Columbus: Charles E. Merrill Books, 1964), pp. 216–217.

Porteous Maze, are employed with both children and adults. Usually performance tests are administered to those who have demonstrated little or very poor ability or who are deaf and mute.

These instruments consist of completing form boards or pictures, solving problems or mazes, assembling objects, composing block designs, and performing other tasks. These tests assess a kind of ability somewhat different from the verbal tests used by the Stanford-Binet; therefore, the correlation between them and the Stanford-Binet or other highly verbal tests is lower than that between the Stanford-Binet and the Wechsler tests. Most coefficients fall within a band between .50 and .80.

These performance tests are useful particularly to special education teachers and administrators. They supplement Stanford-Binet and Wechsler assessments. Most of them require special study and clinical skill to administer, score, and interpret. The *Arthur Point Scale of Performance,* designed as a means for measuring the intelligence of persons with sensory, language, and developmental abnormalities, is used widely and enjoys considerable popularity. The *Merrill-Palmer Scale,* designed for testing preschool children, is considered by many the best nonverbal battery available for assessing the intelligence of very young children, but its predictive efficiency is not great.

GROUP TESTS
OF MENTAL ABILITY

Standardized group ability tests are employed much more commonly in individual assessment than are individual ability tests, because they can be administered simultaneously to several subjects. Standardized group tests vary considerably in their reliance on verbal and nonverbal tasks, but most that are currently in use emphasize verbal skills.

Almost all standardized ability tests are timed, largely for convenience of administering them in schools. However, many tests arrange items in an increasing order of difficulty, so that by the time work on the test is stopped, most individuals have answered about as many questions as they could in any event. Today, most tests permit most subjects ample time to attempt to answer all the items. Some of the standardized tests of ability in current use, like their lineal antecedent, the *Army Alpha,* yield only a single score— a deviation IQ or other standard score or a centile score. Others provide separate verbal and quantitative scores as well as a total score expressed in standard score or centile terms.

RELIABILITY AND VALIDITY

Practically all commonly used group tests of mental ability are highly reliable. The conventional internal-consistency and stability test-retest coefficients are usually in the low .90s, although often there is too short an interval between test and retest. Parallel or equivalent form indices are in the low to mid .80s.

Authors of standardized group tests of mental ability usually attempt to demonstrate the validity of their tests in one of three ways. First, scores on a new test are correlated with those obtained from another test (congruence method). The *Stanford-Binet* has been employed as a criterion for many years. Whatever test is used, it is assumed to be valid. (For limitations associated with this assumption, see Chapter 4.) Second, ability tests are correlated with criteria such as grades, academic average, or level reached in school (amount of schooling). Third, ratings of teachers, supervisors, and others are used as criteria. As might be expected, this third approach to validation produces the lowest validity coefficients because of the unreliability of these criterion measures (see Chapter 4).

Typically, validity coefficients (estimates of predictive power) using grades as criteria fall in the .40–.60 range, with a median value of about .50. While some technical manuals report coefficients in the upper .60s and low .70s, these are exceptions. An important aspect of validity is the degree of homogeneity of the group (see Chapter 4). In elementary school, where there is great variability in student talent, correlations should be the highest, decreasing in high school and college, as the student population becomes more and more homogeneous. Concurrent or predictive power coefficients reported for the relationship between ability measures and graduate school grade-point averages (GPA) most often range from .15 to .35. Such coefficients are expected, because the range of ability among graduate students is quite circumscribed in comparison to that of the general population, and the range of grades is similarly restricted (A's and B's compose 85 to 90 percent of grades awarded).

The manuals of standardized mental ability tests usually present norms purportedly based on a representative sample of the entire country. This, of course, is a tremendous undertaking that rarely works well. Comprehensive technical manuals describe in detail the size of the samples on which norms were established, the methods used to obtain these samples, and their age and other significant demographic characteristics. One must evaluate critically the relevance and adequacy of any and all norms provided for a given test (see Chapter 3).

Here is a brief description of six group ability or intelligence tests that we believe to be among the most commonly used today in the United States. We shall not comment on the validity, reliability, or norms of these tests unless they are unusual in some way.

TESTS OF GENERAL ABILITY

CALIFORNIA TEST OF MENTAL MATURITY   The CTMM was first published in 1936 by the California Test Bureau. In 1963, a new edition (by Elizabeth T. Sullivan, Willis W. Clark, and Ernest W. Tiegs) was released for eight levels: 0 for kindergarten and grade 1, 1 for grades 1–3, 1H a transitional form for grades 3–4, 2 for grades 4–6, 2H a transitional form for grades 6–7, 3 for grades 7–9, 4 for grades 9–12, and 5 for grade 12 and up. These eight levels have been designed to provide a sequential measure of abilities from kindergarten to adult life.

Two editions are available for each of these levels, the long form, which requires two classroom periods, and the short form, which takes one period. The language section of the long form contains subtests on verbal comprehension, inferences, delayed recall, and number problems, and the nonlanguage section tests opposites, similarities, number series, numerical value, analogies, and manipulation of areas. The seven tests of the short form are similar to those of the long form. However, some are shorter, and one is entirely different (delayed recall).

The CTMM tests are organized by factor into: factor I, logical reasoning; factor II, spatial relationships; factor III, numerical reasoning; factor IV, verbal concepts; and factor V, memory. Factor II is not included in the shorter form. Scores are given for each factor plus language subtotal, nonlanguage subtotal, and total.

Both California test forms yield deviation IQs for the language and nonlanguage sections as well as for the total score. For this purpose, the relationship between scores on the short form and those of form L-M of the Stanford-Binet has been established, allowing for comparisons of IQ scores on both tests in terms of IQ distribution, means, medians, and standard deviations. The long form was equated and scaled to the short form, and all comparable derived scores were made equivalent. Answer sheets are available except for those forms used in the primary grades, on which the pupils mark their answers in the question booklet. These tests, though timed, are purported to be power tests.

COGNITIVE ABILITIES TEST   This test series (published by Houghton Mifflin, 1978) is designed to measure mental ability in kindergarten through senior high school. The *Cognitive Abilities Test* succeeds the Lorge-Thorndike series of intelligence tests originally published by Houghton Mifflin in 1954. The series consists of the Primary Battery (by Robert L. Thorndike, Elizabeth P. Hagen, and Irving Lorge) for kindergarten through grade 3 (Primary I for K-1 and Primary II for grades 2–3) and the multilevel edition series (by Robert L. Thorndike and Elizabeth P. Hagen) for grades 3–12. The term *multilevel* indicates that the *Cognitive Abilities Test* consists of three parallel batteries and eight different but overlapping levels (A–H) covering grades 3–12. The verbal battery consists of subtests on vocabulary, sentence completion, verbal classification, and verbal analogies. The quantitative battery contains subtests on number series, quantitative relations, and building equations. The nonverbal battery tests figure classification, figure analogies, and figure synthesis. Each of the batteries is administered separately. The Primary Battery contains four subtests, including oral vocabulary, relational concepts, multimental concepts (which one doesn't belong?), and qualitative concepts.

Administration time for each battery of the multilevel editions is 35 minutes, and 12–16 minutes each for four separate sessions of the regular form of the Primary Battery. A variety of MRC, IBM, and Digitek answer sheets are provided for the multilevel edition.

Scores on the multilevel *Cognitive Ability Tests* are given as standard age scores with percentile ranks and stanines, and grade percentile ranks with stanines. Scores on the Primary Battery are deviation IQs with percentile ranks and stanines, grade percentiles, and grade stanines.

These batteries are power tests with time limits. The multilevel edition provides great flexibility for a testing program and reduces both cost per pupil and the problem of storing a large number of tests.

COOPERATIVE SCHOOL AND COLLEGE ABILITY TESTS   Series I (SCAT-II) was first published in 1955 by Cooperative Test Division, Educational Testing Service (ETS), to supersede the American Council on Education (ACE) *Psychological Examination* that had been used for many years with high school seniors and entering college freshmen. The SCAT-II series, published in 1966, consists of four levels: level 4 for grades 4–6, level 3 for grades 7–9, level 2 for grades 10–12, and level 1 for grades 12–14. Two parallel forms (A and B) are available for levels 4, 3, and 2, and three forms (A, B, and C) for level 1. Administration time is 40 minutes. SCAT-II provides verbal (V), mathematical (M), and total (T) scores, which are transformed into three-digit converted scores and then into centile ranks and entered on a profile sheet, as centers of a band. Each band width acts as a safeguard against interpreting a score too precisely. The width of the band equals the standard error of measurement computed for each scale and the total score (see Chapter 4).

HENMON-NELSON TESTS OF MENTAL ABILITY   These tests were first published in 1932 by Houghton Mifflin. They were revised in 1957, and again in 1973 by Martin J. Nelson, Tom A. Lamke, and Joseph L. French. Form 1 of the 1973 edition has three levels (for grades 3–6, 6–9, and 9–12) and a primary battery for grades K–2. The Henmon-Nelson Tests of Mental Ability are spiral-omnibus tests (asking progressively difficult questions requiring verbal, numerical, and spatial reasoning) made up of 90 items for each of the first three levels and 86 items at the primary level. Items, arranged in order of difficulty, are of various types: vocabulary, sentence completion, opposites, general information, analogies, verbal classification, verbal inference, numbers series, arithmetic reasoning, figure analogies. There is an overlap in the grades covered by the forms, which allows for selecting the one that best fits the ability level of students regardless of school organization. Furthermore, it is recommended that the lowest level be used with groups believed to be below average in ability.

The Henmon-Nelson tests provide three types of scores: deviation IQs, stanines, and percentile ranks. Several norms are available. Consumable or reusable test booklets are provided, along with various types of answer sheets for the reusable booklets. The consumable forms use self-scoring carbons.

Each of the three levels of form 1 takes 30 minutes, while the primary battery has no time limit. The tests give a rapid estimate of mental ability and provide as good a prediction of success in school as do many longer tests.

KUHLMAN-ANDERSON TEST   This test, by F. Kuhlman and Rose G. Anderson, was first published in 1927; its latest revision, the seventh edition, was released by Personnel Press in 1967. The publisher now uses the title, Kuhlman-Anderson Measure of Academic Potential. Eight levels contain ten to twelve subtests, with various booklets designed for certain designated age and grade levels: booklets K, A, B, and CD for grades kindergarten, 1, 2, 3, and 4, respectively; booklet EF (grades 5–7); booklet G (grades 7–9); and booklet H (grades 9–12). Subtests include pictures, geometrical figures, mathematics, new associations, and verbal relations and information. Verbal, quantitative, and total scores are provided.

OTIS-LENNON MENTAL ABILITY TEST   The Otis-Lennon, published by Harcourt Brace Jovanovich, is a sequel to the *Otis Quick-Scoring Mental Ability Tests.* The Otis tests, revised in 1967–1969, are among the oldest ability tests, having first appeared in 1918 as the *Otis Group Intelligence Scale,* advanced examination. The Otis tests, which have been widely used in both industry and education since the 1920s, require 20 or 30 minutes.

Two forms (J and K) and six grade levels (kindergarten, 0.1–1.5, 1.6–3, 4–6, 7–9, and 10–12) of the Otis-Lennon are available. These tests (by Arthur S. Otis and Roger T. Lennon) are of the spiral-omnibus type. Both hand-scored and machine-scorable editions are available. Scores are expressed as deviation IQs or as age and grade percentile ranks and stanines. The tests give a good, rapid measure of the level of mental functioning of the general population.

COLLEGE QUALIFICATION AND
SCHOLARSHIP TESTS

Testing programs to determine qualification for college and for scholarships are administered nationally to thousands of high school juniors and seniors, and thousands of college students take either the *Graduate Record Examination* (GRE) or the *Miller Analogies Test* (MAT) to support their applications for graduate study.

ACT TEST BATTERY   The *American College Testing Program* (ACT) was initiated in 1959 as a college admission examination and is frequently revised. The ability test section is but one part of the ACT assessment administered five times a year (February, April, June or July, October, and December) at more than 2800 centers established by the publisher. The ACT assessment consists of a battery of four academic tests, a questionnaire to determine background data, high school grades, educational plans and occupational goals, and an interest inventory.

All items in the ACT ability test are multiple choice. The test yields five scores: English usage, mathematics usage, social studies reading, natural sciences reading, and a composite score. Separate MRC answer sheets are used. ACT items are direct descendants of the *Iowa Tests of Educational Development.* Percentiles and a standard score system are used for reporting results on a scale ranging from 1–36 (the maximum differs for the four subtests), with the standard deviation intentionally set at approximately 5, so that the probable error of measurement is about 1 scale-score unit, if reliability coefficients are about .91. A 1975–1976 manual reports the mean composite score for unselected first-semester high school seniors as 16 and that for college-bound seniors was 19.[42]

The ACT test takes 160 minutes. Students pay an examination fee, and test reports are sent to them, to their high school, and to three colleges (or more at extra cost).

COLLEGE BOARD SCHOLASTIC APTITUDE TEST   Two fundamental skills—verbal and mathematical—are measured by the SAT. The test, used since 1926 to choose candidates for college entrance, was revised most recently in 1973. The SAT is administered on specified dates at centers established by the College Entrance Examination Board of the Educational Testing Service. The verbal part (V) evaluates a student's knowledge of the meaning and relationship of words and his or her ability to interpret prose passages. The mathematical section (M) covers basic mathematics through elementary algebra and geometry. Scores are reported with a mean of 500 and standard deviation of 100. Actual testing time is 150 minutes.

Since 1926, there has been a tremendous amount of research on the SAT. Some results have shown that an average gain of 10 points on both sections can be expected on a second testing. Another gain, only slightly less than 10 points for each section, can be expected on the third testing. Thereafter, the effect of practice on scores is negligible. Cramming and coaching were found to cause an average increase of less than 10 points, an insignificant difference on a scale of 200–800. Studies have also shown that the three-hour battery does not bring about any noticeable fatigue or poor scores related to fatigue, and the effects of anxiety are less significant than students and parents are likely to believe.

Much attention has been given to the recent decline in SAT scores, which has continued steadily since 1964. For example, average SAT scores among 1975 high school graduates were 10 points lower on the verbal section ($\bar{x} = 434$) and 8 points lower on the mathematical ($\bar{x} = 472$) than 1964 scores. A special advisory panel, headed by Willard Wirtz, president of the National Manpower In-

---

[42] American College Testing Program, *Using ACT on the Campus,* 1975–1976 ed. (Iowa City: The Program, 1975), p. 3.

stitute, was appointed in 1975 to conduct a two-year study to investigate the decline in scores. Sidney P. Marland, Jr., president of the College Entrance Examination Board, offered four reasons: (1) the psychometric qualities of the tests, (2) the nature of the population sitting for the test, (3) factors bearing on the nature of secondary education, and (4) factors bearing on conditions of society during the past decade.[43] He denied that anything was wrong with the way SAT is constructed, administered, evaluated, or scored. He also pointed out that changes in the number of disadvantaged students taking the test is not a plausible explanation, because this number is relatively small. Moreover, the lower average is a function of both more lower scores and fewer higher ones. Finally, Marland noted that no substantial evidence exists for attributing the decline to any particular set of causes. The advisory panel, reporting in 1978, stated that the decline in scores appeared to be associated with strong educational and social influences. Among these were the proliferation of elective courses at the expense of required English and mathematics, loose standards for promotion, and the impact of television viewing.

Robert B. Zajonc and Gregory Markus speculate that the decline is a function of the birth order of those taking the test.[44] Their theory is that the intellectual environment of a family depends on the number of family members and their ages. Each family member contributes to the total intellectual atmosphere, which changes constantly as children grow, increasing each year until adulthood. They set the intellectual level of each parent at an arbitrary 30 units and that of a newborn child at 0. The first-born child enters into an intellectual environment of $(30 + 30 + 0)/3 = 20$ units. If a second child comes along when the first is a few years old and has an intellectual level of, say, 4 units, the second-born enters into an intellectual environment of $(30 + 30 + 4 + 0)/4 = 16$ units. According to the theory, the larger the family and the later a child comes in the family's birth order, the lower the child scores in intellectual performance, because that performance is diluted by his or her contact with siblings who have not reached full adult intelligence. The theory of intellectual environment proposed by Zajonc and Markus does not mean that intelligence declines automatically with birth order. What they point out is that if children are spaced so as to give the older one time to develop intellectual

[43] Sidney P. Marland, Jr., "Report to the Membership," *The College Board News* 4 (January 1976): 6.
[44] Reported in Carol Tarvis, "The End of the IQ Slump," *Psychology Today* 9 (April 1976): 69–74.

ability, the younger one will not suffer any deficit. The decline in SAT scores is attributed by Zajonc and Markus to increased family size during the late 1940s and 1950s. They predict that SAT scores will continue to drop for a few years as the last children of the 1950s take the tests. Since 1963 marked a turning point in the size of American families, by 1980 or so, SAT scores should rise as proportionately more first-born children from smaller families sit for the examination.

The SAT is used primarily to predict academic success. Thus, its scores correlate well with freshmen-year grades (.40 to .70 or higher, depending on the school). However, there are times when a freshman class is so intellectually homogeneous, especially when the cut-off score used in selection is high, that the resulting correlation coefficients are low and the battery is accused of having no functional predictive value. However, when an entering college class is so selected, one might expect practically all students to be successful; hence SAT actually does fulfill its function.

Michael A. Wallach argues that measures of academic skills (the ACT and SAT) widely used to determine admission to highly selective colleges fail in their upper ranges to predict professional achievement. Because assessments above intermediate levels demonstrate so little criterion validity, he suggests that traditional ability tests be confined to screening out those who score low. (Many schools use tests in this fashion now.) Admission to highly selective colleges, according to Wallach's proposal, would be based on demonstrating work-related competence. He recommends that the admissions committee evaluate either related work samples or public recognition provided by qualified judges (for example, research awards).[45]

PRELIMINARY SAT AND THE NATIONAL MERIT SCHOLARSHIP QUALIFYING TEST   Previously entitled the Preliminary Scholastic Aptitude Test (PSAT), the PSAT/NMQT was constructed by the Educational Testing Service to be used by the National Merit Scholarship Corporation in awarding grants. The PSAT/NMQT is administered to students in grades 10–12 each October. Three scores are derived: verbal, mathematical, and a selection index (used by the National Merit Scholarship Corporation).

---

[45] Michael A. Wallach, "Tests Tell Us Little About Talent," *American Scientist* 64 (January–February 1976): 57–63.

GRADUATE AND PROFESSIONAL TESTS

Most graduate and professional schools require applicants to submit evidence of their ability uniformly measured on a common scale for all students. Such a measure operates as a leveling agent, cutting across differences in local customs and conditions, and affording admissions committees a universal scale that, combined with other data, helps in assessing the academic potential of students.

GRADUATE RECORD EXAMINATION   The GRE, published by the Educational Testing Service, is an aptitude test from which separate measures of verbal (V) and quantitative (Q) abilities are obtained. Moreover, some twenty advanced achievement tests in undergraduate majors are available. The GRE originated in 1939 and is revised periodically. The test is administered six times a year (January, February, April, June, October, and December). Students pay an examination fee, and test reports are sent to the candidate and to three graduate schools (others at extra cost).

Working time on the GRE is 3 hours; separate answer sheets (SCRIBE) are used. Aptitude scores are reported on a scale ranging from approximately 200–800 ($\bar{x}$ = 500; SD = 100), with the third digit always 0.

MILLER ANALOGIES TESTS   The MAT (by W. S. Miller), published by the Psychological Corporation, appeared originally in 1926. Currently, four forms (J, K, S, and R) are available, with form R restricted to retesting. Forms J and R are also published under the title *Advanced Personnel Test*, for use in business and industry. A Braille edition of the MAT is available.

The MAT is administered at specified testing centers, established and controlled by the publisher. Some 600 centers are located in colleges and universities; others are in business and industries. Each center scores and reports the test data to the examinee and up to to three institutions or firms designated at the time of testing. Separate IBM answer sheets are used.

The examination fees are determined locally and vary considerably because of differences in policy, organization, and local cost. Currently, the Psychological Corporation's materials usage fee to local centers is $5.50 per examinee.

The MAT is untimed, and scores are raw scores. Tables presented in the 1970 edition of the MAT manual show means, standard deviations, and MAT raw scores at the twenty-fifth, fiftieth, and seventy-fifth percentile points of students enrolled in a variety of graduate programs leading to advanced degrees in graduate and professional schools.[46] David Hall and Frank Dyer reported that the phenomenon of gradually declining scores in the large-scale testing of undergraduate applicants did not appear in MAT scores of graduate students tested in early 1974 and early 1975.[47]

TESTS OF CREATIVITY

The early 1960s marked a period of increasing interest in the education of gifted, talented, or superior students. Until recently, a high score on an intelligence test was the criterion used most often to identify gifted individuals. New criteria have been introduced during the past few years, and new descriptive terms have evolved. As James J. Gallagher points out, whatever label is used, the individuals identified are believed to be the creators, the leaders of the next generation.[48] Failure to help gifted children reach their potential, he says, is a social tragedy.

The intelligence test remains a universally accepted means of identifying gifted children, but dissatisfaction has intensified with using the test to identify originality or creative behavior in and of itself, as well as creativity in dramatics, music, painting, or drawing. Many question whether the intelligence test identifies all the factors that contribute to superior human achievement. According to J. P. Guilford, L. M. Terman ruled creativity out of the realm of intelligence in his first Stanford-Binet test because of disappointing experiences with an ingenuity test.[49] Controversy abounds over the nature of the creative process and ways to nurture it. Creativity has become a dominant interest in the study of superior mental functioning.

Creativity has been defined in many ways, but novelty and unconventionality figure in most definitions. J. W. Getzels and J. T. Dillon point out that major conceptions of creativity may be classified according to the relative interest placed on the product, the process, or the experience of creativity.[50] They state that

---

[46] *The Miller Analogies Test Manual* (New York: Psychological Corporation, 1970).

[47] David H. Hall and Frank J. Dyer, "A Report on Miller Analogies Test Scores of Applicants to Graduate Schools in 1974 and 1975" (New York: Psychological Corporation, 1975) 4 pp. Mimeographed.

[48] James J. Gallagher, *Teaching the Gifted Child,* 2nd ed. (Boston: Allyn and Bacon, 1975), p. 9.

[49] J. P. Guilford, "Creativity: Restrospect and Prospect," *Journal of Creative Behavior* 4 (1970): 149–168.

[50] J. W. Getzels and J. T. Dillon, "The Nature of Giftedness and the Education of the Gifted," in *Second Handbook of Research on Teaching,* ed. Robert M. W. Travers (Chicago: Rand McNally College Publishing, 1973), p. 698. Copyright 1973, American Educational Research Association, Washington, D.C. Reprinted with permission.

some definitions are formulated in terms of a novel and useful *product*. . . ; other definitions are in terms of a divergent but fruitful underlying *process*. . . ; and still others are in terms of an inspired and immanent subjective *experience*. . . . One suggested omnibus definition of creative thinking is: the product has novelty and value for the thinker or the culture; the thinking is unconventional, highly motivated and persistent or of great intensity; the task involves a clear formulation of an initially vague and undefined problem.[51]

Davis, too, suggests that it is helpful to keep in mind a three-part model to unscramble the nature of creativity: attitudes conducive to creative behavior, abilities underlying creative potential, and deliberate techniques for producing new ideas.[52] *Creative attitudes* include a conscious intent to search for imaginative ideas. *Creative abilities* are those necessary for problem-solving such as abstracting, combining, perceiving novel relationships, or associating, while *techniques for producing new ideas* include brainstorming, attribute listing, and checklisting.

Despite the wide array of ideas about the nature of creativity, tests have been developed to measure it. These measures differ in that they mirror the particular sets of beliefs and preconceptions held by their authors about the nature of creativity. Donald J. Treffinger and his associates identify two sets of problems involved in measuring creativity: the theoretical description of creativity and the criterion problem.[53]

The lack of a unified, widely accepted theory of creativity makes for difficulty in establishing useful operational definitions, understanding the implications of differences among tests and test administration procedures, and understanding the relationship of creativity to other human abilities. The *criterion problem* is that of identifying acceptable external criteria for validating creativity tests. Typical criteria include judgments of teachers and peers, characteristics of adults who have made significant contributions to their professions, use of discoveries, inventions, works of art, and so on as indices of creative achievements, and statistical infrequency of response. Treffinger and his colleagues point out the difficulties involved in using such criteria as well as the need to establish differential age and sex criteria.

Getzels and Dillon categorize criteria and measures of creativity as follows:

---

[51] Getzels and Dillon, "Nature of Giftedness," pp. 698–699.
[52] Gary A. Davis, *Psychology of Problem Solving* (New York: Basic Books, 1973), pp. 8–9.
[53] Donald J. Treffinger, Joseph S. Renzulli, and John F. Feldhusen, "Problems in the Assessment of Creative Thinking," *Journal of Creative Behavior* 5 (second quarter 1971): 104–112.

1. *Achievement.* Deeds or thoughts which bespeak manifestly superior achievement may be identified, especially if they are given recognition in the form of prizes, awards or other marks of accomplishment. . . .
2. *Ratings.* Under the assumption that an observer can provide a sound judgment of another person's inventiveness or originality, evaluation by peers, supervisors and teachers has been used as a criterion of creative potential. . . .
3. *Intelligence.* As creativity is presumably a mental function; and as the best validated index of mental functioning is performance on intelligence test, a superior IQ has been used as a criterion of creative potential. . . .
4. *Personality.* Personality characteristics are evaluated in relation to an empirically derived or a priori profile of the "creative personality" and the closeness of the fit is used as a criterion. . . .
5. *Biographical correlates.* Certain items in a person's history are related to his creative performance and are then used to predict others' future performance. . . .
6. *Divergent thinking or "creativity" tests.* Among the many tests are: Remote Associates Test. . . . ; Ingenious Solutions to Problems Test. . . ; AC Test of Creative Ability. . . ; Torrance Tests of Creative Thinking; and numerous other devices such as ink-blots, block-construction, drawings and so forth.[54]

Many tests of creativity have been published and others are in experimental form. Here, two measures are summarized.

REMOTE ASSOCIATES TEST   The RAT appeared in experimental form in 1959 and was published in 1967 by Houghton Mifflin. Its authors, Sarnoff A. Mednick and Martha T. Mednick, state in the examiner's manual (1967) that the RAT "is a measure of the ability to think creatively," and that it is based ". . . on a strictly 'associative' interpretation of the creative thinking process." That is, creativity is thought to consist of seeing relationships between mutually remote ideas and forming them into new associative combinations that are considered useful or meet certain criteria.

The RAT is designed for college students and adults; it comes in two forms. It can be administered to either groups or individuals. Though it is not considered a speed test, there is a 45-minute time limit. Both forms include thirty items, each of which consists of

[54] Getzels and Dillon, "Nature of Giftedness," p. 699. Copyright 1973, American Educational Research Association, Washington, D.C. Reprinted with permission.

three stimulus words that the examinee must relate to each other by means of a single associative link. The examinee's score is the number of items answered correctly. The RAT is hand-scored with the use of a strip key. Percentile norms are based on raw scores of male and female undergraduates, male freshmen, female freshmen, freshmen liberal-arts majors, and so on. (N varies from 81 to 2,786.)

TORRANCE TESTS OF CREATIVE THINKING   The research edition of the Torrance tests is a revision of the *Minnesota Tests of Creative Thinking.* Four batteries of test activities, two verbal and two figural, were created by Paul Torrance and his colleagues and published in 1966 by Personnel Press. The two forms, designed to be used from kindergarten through graduate school, measure fluency, flexibility, originality, and elaboration. The figural forms can be administered as group tests throughout this age range, and the verbal forms can be administered to groups as low as the fourth grade.

The verbal tests, *Thinking Creatively with Words,* consist of seven parallel tests, each battery requiring about 45 minutes to administer. Each task requires the individual to think in divergent directions, in terms of possibilities. The activities include asking questions about a drawing, making guesses about the causes of an event pictured, producing ideas for improving a toy, thinking of unusual uses of tin cans. The figural tests, *Thinking Creatively with Pictures,* take 30 minutes to administer. The first task, picture construction, is designed to stimulate originality and elaboration. The other two tasks, incomplete figures and repeated figures, elicit variability in fluency, flexibility, originality, and elaboration.

The TTCT are hand-scored with guides that present clear, detailed, and comprehensive directions. Some training in scoring is recommended. In *Norms-Technical Manual,* Torrance recommends that users base their interpretations on the three verbal (fluency, flexibility, and originality) and four figural (fluency, flexibility, originality, and elaboration) scores, but he does not recommend using a composite total score.

Tables are provided for converting raw scores to *t*-scores for each of the four tests, based on the performance of fifth-grade pupils. Normative data are based on the performance of students in grades 1–12 in a California school system (N for each grade ranges from 61–113); 116 nursing students entering junior college; 52 Latin-American junior high school boys; 25 students in each grade (1–6) of the University of Minnesota Elementary School; 40 fourth-graders from a Bloomington, Minnesota, school; and others.

USES OF TEST DATA

Before we discuss the uses of ability test data, let us compare individual and group tests of ability.

Both standardized individual and group tests have long been criticized for overemphasizing the verbal aspects of mental ability. Both types of tests have also been criticized because of the cultural biases they reflect. Standardized group tests, and to a lesser extent individual tests, have been criticized for creating pressure on the examinee with established time limits.

Some practitioners have suggested that accurate measures of mental ability can be obtained only by using an individual test. If schools, colleges, universities, industry, and the military services operated on this assumption, very few people would be tested because of the time and expense involved in administering individual tests. Fortunately, the current crop of group tests yields a functionally useful estimate of most people's ability, especially academic ability. Many institutions administer individual tests to those whose group test scores place them in the bottom 10 percent of the population; group tests emphasize verbal ability and reading, and this group is thought to be deficient in these skills.

Most commonly used group tests of ability are criticized for having low ceilings; that is, they cannot measure the mental ability of superior individuals who score near the maximum. An individual test such as the Stanford-Binet or a Wechsler test is sometimes administered to those in the top 10 percent. It is believed that individual tests, particularly the WAIS, permit the superior individual to demonstrate abilities closer to maximum limits. However, individual tests have their ceiling limits too. In effect, it is not possible to differentiate reliably among the top (or bottom) 5 percent of the population.

The comparative advantages of the individual versus the group test of mental ability are:

INDIVIDUAL	GROUP
1. more valid and reliable measure	1. low instrument cost
2. enables examiner to collect more insights into an individual's behavior	2. less time to administer
	3. less costly to administer since many people can be tested simultaneously
3. greater opportunity for the individual to demonstrate limits of ability	

Despite the advantages of individual tests, we believe that in the majority of cases, all necessary information can be obtained with standardized group tests of ability. Much time is wasted giving individual tests to all clients, a not uncommon practice a decade ago in many university counseling centers. Admittedly, the individual test is a clinical instrument and many insights can be obtained by an alert, knowledgeable examiner. Observations gained in that way may be more important than scores of mental ability. But most counselors rarely have the time or the need to treat all clients in such a fashion.

APPLICATIONS
OF ABILITY TEST DATA

There are many situations in which counselors apply ability test data.

1. Ability test data are used to estimate mental ability for clients who want to verify the conceptions they hold of themselves. Usually, such people seek assistance when they are confronted with a decision or when their behaviors have not been satisfying or effective. Their counselor's interpretation of their measured ability is part of the process of verifying and understanding themselves.

2. Ability test data are used by counselors to form a working image of the client. Estimating mental functioning is part of the assessment of a client's resources that the counselor undertakes before or in the course of giving assistance.

3. Ability test data are used in predicting success in educational and vocational ventures. Measured ability scores are part of the information counselees need in order to make appropriate educational and vocational decisions. Particularly useful are estimates of the probability of success based on a client's measured ability and the ability levels of individuals in a given educational or vocational field.

4. Ability test data are used by counselors in consulting with teachers about the work of individual students. Usually, teachers confer with counselors about students who have not been functioning well in class. They seek information about the student in order to design instruction for that individual. Many teachers obtain some insight into a student's motivation by comparing his or her performance with measured estimates of capacity. Ability test scores

of students can also be useful in establishing groups within the class and in adapting instructional materials, procedures, and rates to the capacities of the students.

5. Ability test data are used by counselors in consulting with parents about their children. Parents' conceptions of what they want their children to do in school and at work are sometimes based on inaccurate information about their mental ability. Interpretation of measured ability can correct distorted expectations.

6. Ability test data are useful to the counselor in consulting with school administrators and supervisors about proposed curricular offerings or placement of students in certain courses. Measured ability data are useful in helping to decide whether certain students are to be retained or advanced. Individually administered mental ability measures have been established by most state laws or state education regulations as a major criterion for determining placement in a special-education class.

7. Ability test data are useful in writing recommendations, enabling the counselor to predict further achievement.

GENERAL PRECAUTIONS

The counselor must use group tests of mental ability and creativity with caution. It is important not to place too much confidence in scores obtained from a single measure. Though most individuals reproduce their performance from test to test, scores from a single measure may be discrepant. For every test administered and entered in a student's record, information should be inserted about the name of the test, form, level, and date of administration. The specific type of norm used in obtaining the score should also be entered, for it is important to know with what group an individual was compared. A counselor should also consider a person's motivation. Some individuals may be indifferent to a test when it is administered; an alert test administrator can frequently spot these cases. Finally, each test score should be interpreted in the light of what is known about an individual's home background, since cultural environment affects the results of mental ability and creativity tests. Group tests of ability measure what an individual has learned; they are used on the never-met principle of an equal opportunity to learn for all.

INTERPRETING AND REPORTING
TEST SCORES

A basic premise underlying assessment (see Chapter 1) is that similarities and differences exist among humans. Human idiosyncrasies, in total, form the *nomothetic* character of humankind. Individuals differ in measured ability from other people but share certain abilities with others.

There is no easy way to describe, interpret, or report individual performance on ability tests. Counselors must rely on comparisons, expressed either statistically or graphically or both, of the examinee's position in relation to his or her previous performances or that of another person on the same test. In Chapter 3, we described in some detail the advantages and disadvantages of the scores used most frequently in interpreting and reporting psychological assessments. Here, we shall provide some general suggestions and guidelines for interpreting and reporting ability test scores.

INTERPRETING
ABILITY TEST SCORES

Ability test performance is perhaps the most difficult kind of score to interpret to an individual. That is not because such data are unduly complex but because so many emotions are involved. For example, many people believe that intelligence is directly related to success. Therefore, people who have been administered an ability test want to know how well they performed and who has access to the data. They do not realize that ability test scores are variable and even fallible. Rather, they believe that their score represents a basic, permanent, and telling statement about themselves that has been assessed with a high degree of precision.

However erroneous these views of ability test performance may be, people have the right to have their performance interpreted and also have the right to be assured that only those who have a need to know will have access to these data. Secrecy about performance has made people distrust tests. It has been imposed and justified mainly on the grounds that: (1) knowledge of test performance would wound the self-esteem of those who score low; (2) test scores would be misinterpreted and misused by the individual and his or her peers, parents, and teachers; and (3) the information is too complex for the untutored to understand.

We feel that denying an individual reasonable information about his or her scores on an ability test is callous and contrary to a basic principle of counseling: facilitating self-understanding and development.

The American Psychological Association's Committee on Psychological Assessment has recommended that research be undertaken on the effects of communicating psychological information, including experimenting with different methods of feedback. But counselors cannot wait for research to be completed to start interpreting test data coherently and sensibly. They must establish a cooperative relationship with their clients so that both gain information of value from test data.

Interpretation takes time, and careful attention must be given to both the data and a client's reactions. Even though the essential information revealed by ability test scores is not particularly complex, the counselor must have a thorough understanding of the test being used. Those counselors who do so can readily communicate everything the data reveal to most individuals. Here are guidelines for interpreting ability test data.

1. *Identify and describe in nontechnical terms the test and the kind of data derived from it.* In order to use ability test data, a person must understand and accept them. A counselor's comments, therefore, ought to minimize the anxiety and threat that people commonly feel in these situations.

A good counselor neither confronts an individual abruptly with test findings nor presents data all at once or too rapidly. Rather, he or she may first ask the individual's reaction to the test with some such question as, "Well, what did you think of the ability test you took?" Some other helpful comments are:

> We need to discuss a few things before we examine your scores. You took the *Cooperative School and College Ability Test,* level two, for students in grades 10 through 12. This test provides an estimate of a person's ability to do schoolwork. Three scores are given representing certain kinds of ability. The first is a verbal score that tells how well you understand and use words, the second is a mathematical score that gives an estimate of how well you manage numbers, and the third is a total score.

> *OR*

> The ability test you took was the *School and College Ability Test.* It's designed for students in grades 10 through 12. It gives an estimate of a person's mental abilities, particularly those believed to be useful in doing schoolwork. Three scores are given. One

score estimates a person's ability to understand and use words. Another score provides a measure of a person's ability to manipulate numbers. These two scores are then combined to form a total score. The scores given here compare your ability to do schoolwork to that of other high school seniors across the nation at the same testing time.

2. *Describe clearly the type of score used in reporting results.* Many standardized group ability tests make use of deviation IQs and percentiles. To avoid the precision implied in using such scores, the counselor can turn them into score bands by adding the standard error of measurement (usually reported in the technical manual) to the raw score to establish an estimate of the upper limit and subtracting the standard error to establish a similar low estimate. (See Chapter 4 for information on this procedure.)

Many testing specialists have long urged the use of stanines to interpret test performance. They feel that stainines are broader units than other methods such as IQs or percentiles, that they give comparable test results for an individual from test to test as long as the group on which they are based is the same, and that they are relatively easy to depict and explain. Commercial scoring services provide percentile bands, stanines, and other scoring variations either as part of the total test cost or for a small additional cost.

The type of score should also be explained to a client. Try:

> Scores on this ability test are reported as an IQ. This IQ is the ratio of a person's chronological age to his or her mental age— shown by the number of test items completed correctly—multiplied by 100. The average IQ score for high school seniors on this test falls between 92 and 108.

OR

> Scores on this ability test are reported in percentiles. A centile score is a point below which falls that percentage of the cases among high school seniors. For example, an individual at centile 27 on an ability test is at a point where 73 percent scored higher. If 100 took the test, 27 scored lower than that person.

3. *Organize the test data.* A test profile form (see Figure 5.4) is one means of presenting test data coherently. Profiles have the advantage of keeping the results directly in front of the client and encouraging integration of the data during the interpretation. They also insure that all the necessary information is discussed by serving as a reminder to the counselor to deal with all the scores and their

FIGURE 5.4
PURDUE GUIDANCE CLINIC TEST RECORD PROFILE

PURDUE GUIDANCE CLINIC TEST RECORD PROFILE

CONFIDENTIAL

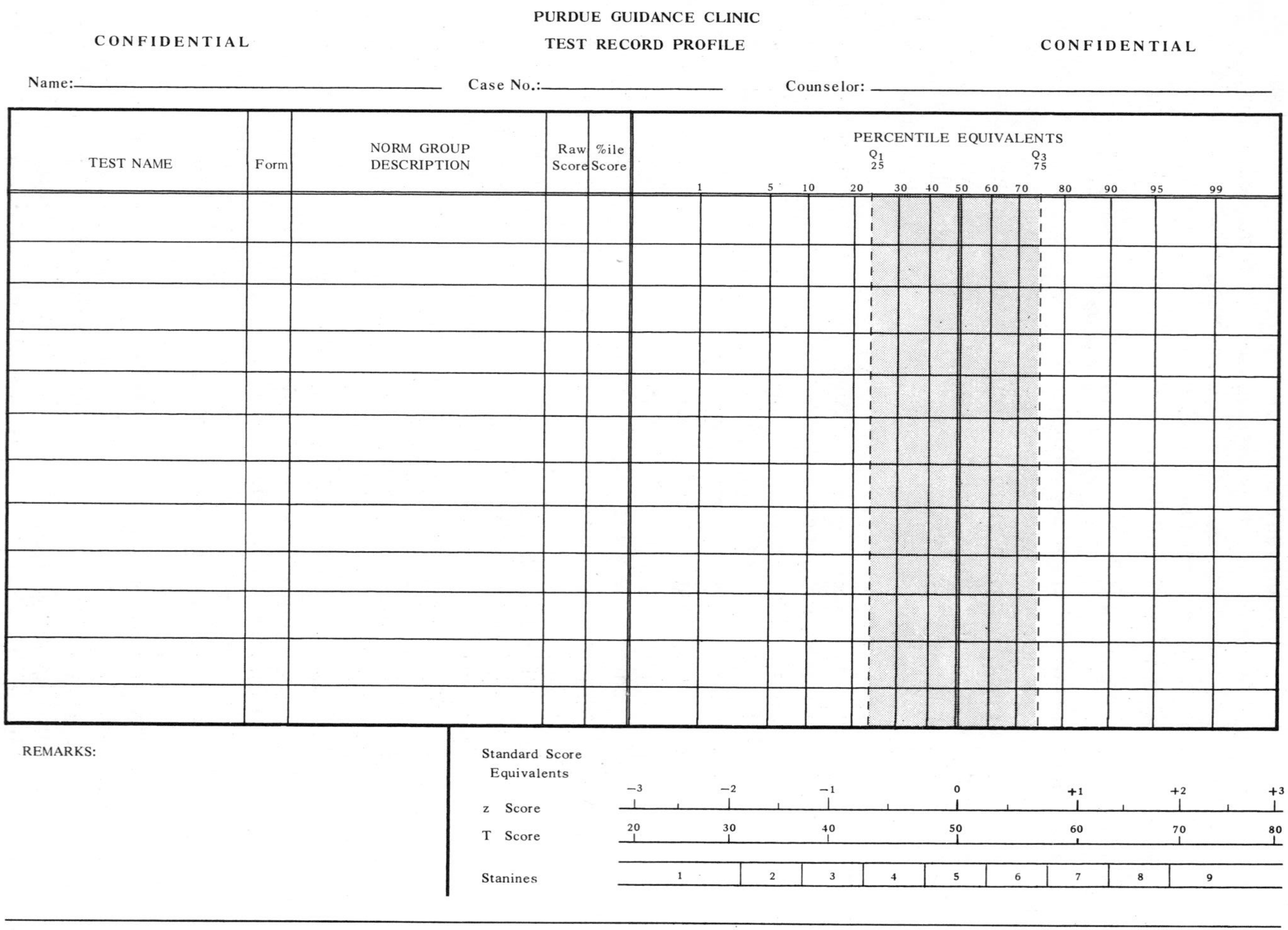

Name: _____ Case No.: _____ Counselor: _____ CONFIDENTIAL

many interrelationships as well as covering such necessary points as norm groups and types of scores. The data should not be presented all at once. Many beginning counselors err in presenting test results too rapidly, as though it were an unpleasant task that they wished to be rid of quickly. Having students complete the profiles themselves during the session can help them gain a better understanding of their scores and the meaning of the results. Remember, too, to place profile sheets so that the client can study them easily.

4. *Explain test scores simply and honestly.* Choose your words carefully. Careless remarks too often are remembered and misunderstood. Try:

> Your percentile band of 60–76 places your ability score in the sixth stanine compared with other pupils of the same age across the country. By looking at the profile, you can add the percentage of people who fall in each stanine. Because your score is in the sixth stanine, 60 percent of the group received ability scores below yours. Your score is in the high-average category.

While testing authorities do not recommend the use of terms such as *above average, average,* and *below average* to describe an individual's performance compared to the norm group, feeling that they are too imprecise, such terms have the advantage of familiarity. Without question, percentile bands and stanines are more precise than descriptive labels. However, we have found that even after percentile bands or stanines have been presented and discussed, clients still seek clarification in descriptive terms.

Express low ability test performance forthrightly but with perspective. Counselors often find it difficult to interpret or comment on low ability test scores. Evasions are noticed by the client and can cause uncertainty, confusion, and doubt.

5. *Consider relationships between verbal and quantitative mental ability scores.* Most persons, when measurement error is taken into account, usually earn similar verbal and quantitative scores. This suggests that learning in both progresses relatively evenly. However, some individuals perform significantly better in one area than in the other. When this occurs, a counselor must pay careful attention to these differences and try to understand the reasons for them. Before interpreting the results to the individual, the counselor should examine the student's record and confer with teachers about his or her work. Often, patterns of problems associated with either reading or mathematics emerge that are congruent with test results (see Chapter 7). Such research enables the counselor to provide a

context for interpreting and discussing these data with the client. Moreover, such information has diagnostic value in determining whether the individual needs remedial attention or further diagnostic testing by the counselor or psychologist (see Chapter 7).

6. *Present mental ability test scores as statements of the probability of earning certain grades or being admitted to particular college programs, or as indications of abilities characteristic of certain occupations.* Principle 16 (see Chapter 1) proposed that predictions be stated in terms of probability, supported whenever possible by actuarial evidence. To do so means that expectancy tables or regression equations must be constructed for local course offerings or programs, that the counselor must secure the test profiles of many students entering college, and must make use of the worker trait arrangement of the *Dictionary of Occupational Titles.* (See Chapter 4 on expectancy tables and regression equations.) One useful approach is to present the client with simple statistical predictions based on test data and then allow him or her to evaluate the prediction.

7. *Give the individual an opportunity to express and explore his or her reactions and feelings.* The counselor must remember that the client is emotionally involved in test results and may not always be rational or logical in thinking about, understanding, and using test data. Some people feel threatened by test results and seek to rationalize or reject data. A client may exhibit doubt about the accuracy of the score, fear, anger, embarrassment, disappointment, or satisfaction. The counselor has to be prepared to cope with these emotional reactions and attitudes in test interpretation sessions in ways that are helpful to the client. Try:

> You don't believe that these scores are good estimates of your ability? It might be helpful to review other evidence or experiences that you have had that suggest a different view.

> *OR*

> How do these ability test scores compare to other information you have about your ability to manipulate verbal and numerical concepts? . . . In what ways are they different from this other information or experience?

> *OR*

> You are disappointed with these estimates of your ability because they are not what you had hoped to see. In what ways do they suggest objectives different from those you had planned?

Using ability test scores in context with other data is helpful to the individual and is in accord with principle 6 (see Chapter 1), which states that any information about an individual that contributes to understanding his or her behavior must be given consideration. A client should regard the test data as clues to be verified by other experiences. In that way, test scores do not become goals in and of themselves, nor do they remain abstractions.

In interpreting any test—ability, aptitude, personality, interest— the beginning counselor will have to experiment for a while to find terms with which he or she feels comfortable and that are easily understood by clients. When counselors use the same words over and over to convey the meaning of scores to different clients, they sometimes feel that their interpretations are becoming boring; but the counselor is the only one who hears the description repeatedly. A useful way of describing a score to clients should be used again, within reasonable limits, for each client is unique and merits regard for that individuality. Therefore, the counselor should not fall into a habit of developing a stereotyped monologue wherein only the name of the client and the specific test scores are changed. Whether a counselor discusses scores in the third person—"People with scores like these tend to . . ."—or first person—"Your score . . ." —depends on the counselor's style and perceptions of what a client can best accept and use. Through self-evaluation of interview tapes, the counselor can discover interpretive methods most suitable for his or her use.

After interpreting the meaning of a score, it is advisable to ask if the individual understands it or wants to discuss it in greater detail. While observing the client's verbal and nonverbal behaviors provides clues to the reception of information, the counselor may still have to ask, "Is that clear?" or "Would you like me to run through that again?"

Group interpretation of ability test scores is always hazardous. However, many counselors often use small groups as a first step in interpretation. These groups may originate in a guidance class, school class, or special meeting. Interpretation of interest inventories is more commonly conducted in small groups than the more sensitive ability test data, but the same principles apply.

In group sessions given to explain ability test scores such as the SAT, the counselor normally reviews the purpose of the test and explains what the test seeks to measure. Then, the counselor checks to make sure that everyone has understood. Following this, the counselor gives each student his or her profile of test data. Scores as such are explained as precisely and as clearly as possible. In commenting on test scores, the counselor should stress that each student's scores are his or her own and that the right of privacy must be respected. Some counselors take a hypothetical score and comment on it by way of illustration. It is difficult in such group sessions to encourage discussion of test results while enabling students to retain the privacy of their test scores. Counselors have used such questions as the following to encourage student discussion:

Were the results different from what you expected?

Do you consider these estimates to be representative of your ability?

Are these data comparable to those obtained the last time you were tested?

Are these estimates comparable to other information you have about your ability?

What influence do these ability estimates have on your educational plans? Vocational plans?

Charts and profiles can be useful in explaining ability test scores to a group. The guidelines for individual interpretation of ability test data apply equally to groups. However, the meaning of such data for each person is best explored in depth in individual sessions.

REPORTING
ABILITY TEST DATA

Ability test scores must often be reported to parents, teachers, and significant others. The Family Education Rights and Privacy Act of 1974 has changed, at least in part, past practices of withholding ability test scores from parents (see Chapter 15). Counselors are obligated to make a thoughtful, considered effort to help parents understand data in order to help their children. Information given to parents about ability test scores should be as valid, dependable, and comprehensible as possible. Ordinarily, a counselor should report scores to parents as percentile bands or stanines and then discuss their meaning.

The techniques used and the amount of effort expended in reporting scores to parents depend, at least in part, on the community in which the school is located. Each community has a different socioeconomic level and attitude toward education. What may work well in reporting test data to parents in one community may not necessarily work in another, so counselors must use their initiative, skill, and knowledge in deciding which approach to use. Of course, the same general principles and practices should be followed in giving results to parents as in interpreting them to students.

Since students have some influence on their parents, the way in which students perceive testing and its value to them can influence parents' reactions. Likewise, the general attitude of the school toward conferences with parents may be conveyed to parents by students. In a school that holds parent conferences only when a child is in trouble, such meetings are looked on as something to be avoided. However, when parent conferences are seen as a process that helps students, they are welcomed by most.

A common source of friction between teachers and school counselors is the counselor's failure to discuss test results with teachers. As a professional who has a need to know, a teacher should receive results of tests administered to his or her students, especially to those whom the teacher has referred to the counselor. We are assuming, in this case, that the preservice training of the teacher has included instruction in basic measurement procedures. Thus, it is important for the counselor to know the faculty well enough to ascertain the teachers' sophistication about testing. If the teachers are deficient in this area, in-service training should be established.

Individual interpretation and reporting of ability test scores to teachers is the best method. However, this system is often not practical in terms of both the counselor's and the teacher's time. For this reason, counselors sometimes submit classified written reports summarizing students' ability test scores for their teachers' use.

Summary reports may be prepared in one of several forms. The scoring services of the test publisher can be used for this purpose at little or no cost. The information that is included and the way in which it is presented depend on a teacher's needs. The report should make clear the type of score and the norms used as a basis for comparison. Both local as well as national norms may be presented.

Here are some suggestions for presenting test data to teachers:

1. Before administering an ability test, meet with all teachers to explain the purpose of the test, the types of scores, and the purposes for which the results will be used by personnel in the school system and by others.

2. Plot and graph subtest and total scores against national and local norms for individual students and groups or classes of students.
3. At another meeting with teachers, explain the test results by using graphs, charts, and reports.
4. Prepare an alphabetical class list for each teacher's students, presenting each student's scores.
5. Hold individual conferences with those teachers who have questions about specific students' scores or profiles.

Testing reports can be misleading if the test results are not accompanied by explanatory information. See Chapter 15 for a detailed discussion of reporting test scores to teachers and parents.

ISSUES

1. Only individual intelligence tests should be used to assess mental abilities.

Yes, because:

1. The superior reliability and validity coefficients of individual intelligence tests are needed to offset the imprecise and controversial nature of ability assessments.
2. The clinical observations derived from administering a test to one person at a time add substantially to any assessment and subsequent prediction of an individual's intellectual functioning.

No, because:

1. The disadvantage of reduced reliability and validity coefficients of standardized group ability tests is not sufficient to warrant the high cost of administering individual intelligence tests.
2. Both individual and group mental ability tests can be imprecise. What is important is to know how imprecise a test is and to take that into account in using ability measures.

Discussion:

This is an old issue that has reemerged during the past few years as criticism about ability tests has mounted. Few question the superiority of individual intelligence test data, but the cost and impracticality of using only individual intelligence tests are major deterrents to using them exclusively. Besides, it is not now possible to use only individual intelligence tests, because there are not enough qualified examiners, psychometrists, and psychologists. Beyond these practical considerations lies the issue of whether individual testing would significantly improve diagnosis and prediction. It is likely that, for some time to come, only selective use will be made of individual intelligence tests.

2. *An individual's intelligence is determined primarily by heredity.*
   Yes, because:
   1. Intelligence, like other human attributes, has been subjected to the principle of natural selection. That is, the mentally superior have survived and passed on their superior qualities.
   2. Many studies have reported that an average correlation of .50 exists between the IQs of parents and their natural children while the correlation between parents and adopted children averages .25.
   3. Data from studies of identical and fraternal twins show that the correlation of IQs of fraternal twins is about .55 while that of identical twins is about .90. Even the IQs of identical twins reared in different environments correlate at a rate of about .75.

   No, because:
   1. Environmental factors such as protein deficiency during a mother's pregnancy have lasting effects on her offsprings' mental ability.
   2. Restricted experiences and little intellectual or cultural stimulation account for low ability test scores.
   3. Studies of babies removed from foundling homes where they were given only physical care and placed in homes where they were raised with love and attention report dramatic upward changes in measured ability.[55]

   Discussion:
   Most researchers are agreed that it is pointless to think in either-or terms on this issue, since both nature and nurture contribute to the development of intelligence. It is important

---

[55] H. M. Skeels, "Adult Status of Children with Contrasting Early Life Experiences," *Monographs of the Society for Research in Child Development* 31, no. 3 (1966).

to distinguish between the generally accepted notion that heredity contributes to intellectual ability and the idea that intelligence is somehow established at conception and is therefore unchangeable. Most psychologists agree that heredity sets limits but that these limits are flexible—or even permeable—and can be stretched considerably under special circumstances.

Recently, researchers have attempted to estimate the magnitude of the effect of environment and heredity on the development of intelligence. Estimates of the degree of domination of heredity range from 50 percent to 80 percent. While it is very likely true that an individual's potential intelligence may be inherited, it is equally likely that the environment determines whether or not that potential is realized, and to what degree. Conversely, it could be said that the extent to which an individual can respond to his or her environment depends on inherited capacity. Individuals respond differently to various kinds of learning environments. The question of how heredity and environment interact is more important than whether one is more influential than the other. Unfortunately, the former is even more difficult to answer than the latter.

ANNOTATED REFERENCES

Cronbach, Lee J. *Essentials of Psychological Testing.* 3rd ed. New York: Harper and Row, 1970, 752 pp.

Chapter 7 (pp. 197–226) discusses the history of ability testing and describes the Wechsler and Binet tests. Chapter 8 (pp. 227–267) covers research and theories about such factors as consistency and change in test scores and intellectual development in early childhood. Chapter 9 (pp. 268–308) discusses group tests of ability and their use and problems.

Ebel, Robert S. *Essentials of Educational Measurement.* Englewood Cliffs, N.J.: Prentice-Hall, 1972, 622 pp.

Chapter 20 (pp. 497–516) defines and describes the nature of intelligence and discusses nonverbal and culture-fair tests. IQ is discussed as a score and as a factor in the nature-nurture controversy.

Guilford, J. P. *The Nature of Human Intelligence.* New York: McGraw-Hill, 1967, 538 pp.

Chapter 1 (pp. 2–20) gives the historical background of mental ability tests including conceptions of intelligence. Chapter 2 (pp. 21–44) presents studies of intelligence. Chapter 3 (pp. 46–67) describes theories of intelligence and Guilford's structure-of-intellect model.

Sattler, Jerome M. *Assessment of Children's Intelligence.* Philadelphia: W. B. Saunders, 1971, 591 pp.

This book presents a comprehensive overview of individual intelligence testing of children, including test administration, scoring, interpretation, report writing, and recommendations. Appendices present supplementary scoring criteria, validity studies, and tables.

SELECTED REFERENCES

Albert, Robert S. "Toward a Behavioral Theory of Genius." *American Psychologist* 30 (February 1975): 140–151.

Churchill, William D., and Smith, Stuart E. "Relationships Between the 1960 Stanford-Binet Scale and Group Measures of Intelligence and Achievement." *Measurement and Evaluation in Guidance* 7 (April 1974): 40–45.

Farver, Albert S.; Sedlacek, William E.; and Brooks, Glenwood C., Jr. "Longitudinal Predictions of University Grades for Blacks and Whites." *Measurement and Evaluation in Guidance* 7 (January 1975): 243–250.

Goldman, Roy D., and Hewitt, Barbara Newlin. "The Scholastic Aptitude Test 'Explains' Why College Men Major in Science More Often Than College Women." *Journal of Counseling Psychology* 23 (January 1976): 50–54.

Hodgson, Mary L., and Cramer, Stanley H. "The Relationship Between Selected Self-Estimated and Measured Abilities in Adolescents." *Measurement and Evaluation in Guidance* 10 (July 1977): 98–105.

John, E. Roy. "How The Brain Works—A New Theory." *Psychology Today* 9 (May 1976): 48–52.

Pearson, Henry G. "Self-Identification of Talents: First Step to Finding Career Decisions." *Vocational Guidance Quarterly* 24 (September 1975): 20–27.

Prediger, Dale J., and Fought, Louise. "Local Test Validation and Use of Results." *Measurement and Evaluation in Guidance* 5 (July 1972): 366–372.

Scarr-Salapatek, Sandra, and Weinberg, Richard A. "The War Over Race and IQ: When Black Children Grow Up in White Homes." *Psychology Today* 9 (December 1975): 80–82.

Schmidt, B. June. "Prediction of Success in Clerical Occupations From Ability Test Scores." *Vocational Guidance Quarterly* 24 (September 1975): 68–72.

Slack, Charles W. "How I Tried To Tell the World How To Pass IQ Tests." *Psychology Today* 9 (January 1976): 28.

Tavris, Carol. "The End of the IQ Slump." *Psychology Today* 11 (April 1976): 69–74.

Wallach, Michael A. "Tests Tell Us Little About Talent." *American Scientist* 64 (January–February 1976): 57–63.

Wechsler, David. "Intelligence Defined and Undefined: A Relativistic Appraisal." *American Psychologist* 30 (February 1975): 135–139.

Whimbey, Arthur. "Getting Ready for the Tester: You Can Learn to Raise Your IQ Score." *Psychology Today* 9 (January 1976): 27–29, 84–85.

Chapter 6   Achievement

What types of achievement tests exist?

What standardized achievement tests are commonly employed?

What uses are made of achievement test data?

What guidelines should be followed in interpreting and reporting achievement measures?

The purpose of any education is to facilitate learning. American public education, with minor qualifications, is committed to twelve years of schooling for all children. Throughout those twelve years, potential unskilled laborers, truck drivers, and janitors sit beside embryo nuclear physicists, certified public accountants, and heart surgeons. In most schools, they read the same textbooks, participate in the same discussions, take the same courses, and are assessed according to the same criteria.

The average public high school student in 1972–1973 enrolled in more courses than did students in either the early 1960s or the late 1940s. W. Vance Grant reports that surveys by the National Center for Educational Statistics reveal that students took, on the average, 6.7 courses, compared with an average of 6.4 courses in 1960–1961 and 6.2 courses in 1948–1949.[1] Students in 1972–1973 had a wide range of courses from which to choose. English language arts enrolled the most students (24.1 million), followed by health and physical education (21.5 million.)

Data presented in Figure 6.1 disclose the percentage increase in the total number of students in public high schools and in enrollments in selected fields between 1960–1961 and 1972–1973. Enrollments in nearly all the traditional academic fields increased at

---

[1] W. Vance Grant, "Offerings and Enrollments in Public Secondary Schools," *American Education* 11 (August–September 1975): 38.

FIGURE 6.1
PERCENTAGE INCREASE IN ENROLLMENTS
IN SELECTED FIELDS OF STUDY AND IN TOTAL NUMBER OF STUDENTS
IN PUBLIC SECONDARY SCHOOLS: 1960–61 to 1972–73[a]

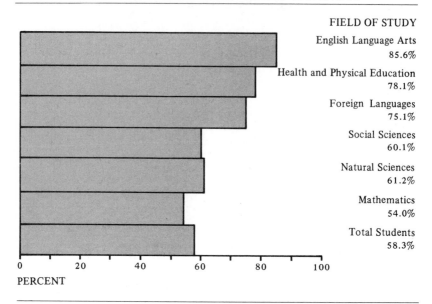

FIELD OF STUDY

English Language Arts
85.6%

Health and Physical Education
78.1%

Foreign Languages
75.1%

Social Sciences
60.1%

Natural Sciences
61.2%

Mathematics
54.0%

Total Students
58.3%

PERCENT

Source: U.S. Department of Health, Education, and Welfare, National Center for Education Statistics, *Summary of Course Offerings and Enrollments in Public Secondary Schools, 1972–73.* In W. Vance Grant, "Offerings and Enrollments in Public Secondary Schools," *American Education* 11 (August-September 1975): 38.
   [a] Includes students in grades 7–12 in public secondary schools.

a faster rate than did the total number of students. Assessment of students' attainments in these courses and collection and use of evidence of their mastery of subject matter are major areas for educational measurement. Students need and are entitled to information about their achievements and their strengths and weaknesses in mastering their courses. This information is most often collected by means of tests—either standardized tests or tests prepared by individual teachers. Any test that measures the attainments or accomplishments of a student after a period of training or learning is called an *achievement test.*

Achievement tests are designed to measure the progress students have made as a result of training. Some time ago, Lee J. Cronbach observed:

One significant contribution of standardized tests has been to break down the "time-serving" concept of education. A person's standing in school is frequently judged by the number of years he has put in, or the number of courses he has passed through. Time spent is no index of education received. In one study, where thousands of college students took standardized tests of knowledge in various fields, many college seniors knew less than the average high school senior. Since number of units accumulated tells little about proficiency, tests are being given increasing weight as evidence of educational development.[2]

In recent years, it has become clear that achievement tests have not, after all, substantially changed the "time-serving" aspect of education.

TYPES OF ACHIEVEMENT TESTS

In 1958, the Educational Testing Service classified achievement tests into three types: (1) end-of-course achievement tests that measure specifically what a student has learned in a particular subject; (2) general achievement tests that cover a student's learning in a broad field of knowledge and can be given to students who have taken quite different courses of study within a field; and (3) tests that measure the critical skills a student has learned and his or her ability to use these skills in solving new problems.[3]

The general achievement test is sometimes referred to as a *survey* test. Survey test batteries can be used from the primary grades through college, although their major application has been at the elementary and secondary school levels. Most batteries provide individual profiles of subtest scores in addition to a total score. Survey tests permit horizontal or vertical comparisons or both so that a student's relative standing in different areas can be compared to a uniform normative sample or established criteria.

Achievement tests are sometimes classified as formative and summative measures. *Formative* measures include the use of achievement tests to assess progress in the development of knowledge and skills before or during a course or unit of instruction. *Summative* measures are those given at course or unit termination to assess the outcome of instruction.

Readiness or *prognostic* tests are used to predict how well an individual may be expected to profit from subsequent training. The

[2] Lee J. Cronbach, *Essentials of Psychological Testing*, 2nd ed. (New York: Harper and Row, 1960), p. 363. Copyright, 1949 by Harper & Row, Publishers, Inc. Copyright © 1960, 1970 by Lee J. Cronbach. By permission of the publisher.
[3] *Large-Scale Programs of Testing for Guidance* (Princeton, N.J.: Educational Testing Service, 1958), p. 15.

areas most often tested are reading and number skills. Readiness tests are employed frequently for making decisions about assigning a child to kindergarten or first grade. Special emphasis in such tests is given to the abilities believed to be important in learning to read, to compute numbers, and to write. Some authors classify readiness tests as ability rather than achievement tests. We shall discuss them in the next chapter.

Diagnostic achievement tests are designed to determine a student's performance in subject matter or school skills and yield information about difficulties in reading, arithmetic, and language usage. Such tests usually have several part scores and may provide detailed checklists of specific types of errors that may be related to specific difficulties. Diagnostic achievement tests are also discussed in the next chapter.

Achievement tests can be either criterion referenced or norm referenced. *Criterion-referenced* tests are designed to assess an examinee's mastery of fundamental skills or knowledge without reference to the performance of others. The test score is translated into a statement about the behavior to be expected of a person with that score. On the other hand, *norm-referenced* tests tell where a person stands in a population who have taken the test. Most standardized achievement tests are norm referenced, but the past few years have marked the emergence and use of criterion-referenced measures. See Chapter 3 for information about both types.

COMMONLY USED STANDARDIZED ACHIEVEMENT TESTS

ELEMENTARY AND JUNIOR HIGH SCHOOL ACHIEVEMENT TESTS

Standardized achievement tests appeared first around 1910 as a result of the work of E. L. Thorndike (see Chapter 2). As time went on, and particularly during the 1920s, many achievement tests became available. These early tests concentrated on assessing how well students learned the facts presented in a course. Achievement tests currently available concentrate instead on testing learning skills.

COMPREHENSIVE TESTS OF BASIC SKILLS Intended as a replacement for the *California Achievement Tests,* the CTBS, published by the California Test Bureau/McGraw-Hill from 1968–1973, are measures of basic skills (reading, language, arithmetic and study skills). Two editions, forms Q and R, are available at four levels (grades 2.5–4, 6–8, 8–12, and an expanded edition) and form S at seven levels (grades kindergarten–1.5, .5–1.9, 1.5–2.9, 2.5–4.9, 4.5–6.9, 6.5–8.9, 8.5–12.9).

Some eleven to fifteen scores are provided, depending on level. Time required varies by level from 170–195 minutes, over four sessions. Scores are reported in stanines, grade equivalents, centiles, and expanded standard scores that have a mean of 600 and a standard deviation of 100. Regression equations have been developed for various CTBS tests and the *California Short-Form Test of Mental Maturity.* Various scoring and reporting services are provided.

IOWA TESTS OF BASIC SKILLS   The ITBS first appeared in 1937 as the *Iowa Every Pupil Tests of Basic Skills.* The latest edition was published in 1978 by Houghton Mifflin. Batteries were prepared by E. F. Lindquist, H. D. Hoover, and A. N. Hieronymus. The tests, available for grades 1–9, measure various skills applied to reading, the use of references, language, and arithmetic. The ITBS was the first battery to emphasize the fundamentals of elementary school learning rather than specific facts in history, literature, and science. Its focus on acquisition of skills rather than subject matter made the tests suitable for use in many classrooms across the country.

The ITBS covers five skill areas: vocabulary, reading comprehension, language skills (spelling, capitalization, punctuation, usage), work-study skills (reading, maps, graphs, and tables; knowledge and use of reference materials), and mathematics skills (concepts and problem solving). It comes in various levels: a primary battery, including levels 7–8 (for grades 1.7–3.5) with sixteen scores; a levels edition, including levels 9–14 (for grades 3–8) with fifteen scores; forms 1–4 (early battery, grades 3–9); six levels in a single booklet; and forms 5–6 (grades 1.7–3.5) in multilevel and separate booklet editions (original editions). The ITBS permits simultaneous administration of more than one level of the tests in the same classroom. All tests for all levels are contained in spiral-bound, reusable test booklets.

Various types of score reports are provided: grade-equivalent, stanines, age-equivalent, and percentile scores. Different types of norms are presented for each of these scores. MRC, IBM 1230 and Digitek answer sheets are available for use. Houghton Mifflin Scoring Service presents assorted scoring and reporting services.

METROPOLITAN ACHIEVEMENT TESTS   Since 1931, this achievement test battery has been used widely at the elementary school level. Though earlier forms measured knowledge of factual material, over the years, revised editions have come to test learning skills. The *Metropolitan Achievement Tests* were last revised in 1978 (authors: Walter N. Durost, Harold H. Bixler, J. Wayne Wrightstone, George A. Prescott, and Irving H. Balow) and are published by Harcourt Brace Jovanovich.

Six levels of the test battery are available from kindergarten-grade 9.5. The first three of these—primer (grades kindergarten–1.4), primary 1 (grades 1.5–2.4), and primary 2 (grades 2.5–3.4)—measure basic skills of reading, writing, and listening. Each yields from three to nine scores. The other three batteries—elementary (grades 3.5–4.9), intermediate (grades 5.0–6.9), and advanced (grades 7.0–9.5)—measure these and other skills such as work-study and problem solving. From nine to eleven scores are presented by each of these levels. Usually two forms are available at each level.

The time needed to administer these batteries ranges from about 2–5⅓ hours (six to eight sessions are recommended). Different answer sheets (IBM, MRC, NCS) are employed, and a variety of hand and commercial scoring services is available. Some subtests, such as reading and mathematics, can be given separately, while other subtests can be employed as partial batteries. Scores are reported in stanines, grade placement, and centiles.

SRA ACHIEVEMENT SERIES   These achievement tests, published by Science Research Associates in 1954 and revised periodically, were prepared by Louis P. Thorpe, D. Welty Lefever, and Robert A. Naslund. Three editions and four levels are available: level 1 (grades 1–2), level 2 (grades 2–4), level 3 (grades 3–4), and level 4 (grades 4–9). Time required varies from 210–260 minutes, to be completed in seven sessions.

Ten to twelve scores are provided: reading (verbal-pictorial association, language perception, comprehension, vocabulary, and their total), arithmetic (concepts, reasoning, computation, and their total), and a total score. Subtests from the multilevel edition (grades 4–9) that can be used separately include tests of reading, arithmetic, language arts, science, social studies, and work-study skills. Most can be either hand- or machine-scored. Four types of derived scores are available: percentiles, grade equivalents, stanines, and an SRA Growth Scale Values. This last score expresses test results in the same units for grades 1–12 for each of the subject areas also covered by the *Iowa Tests of Educational Development.*

STANFORD ACHIEVEMENT TESTS   This, another frequently used achievement test battery, has been through several modifications since its original introduction in 1923. The *Stanford Achievement Test* (authors: Truman L. Kelly, Richard Madden, Eric F. Gardner, and Herbert C. Rudman) is published by Harcourt Brace Jovanovich.

Five levels are published: primary 1 battery (grades 1.5–2.4), primary 2 battery (grades 2.5–3.9), intermediate 1 battery (grades 4.0–5.4), intermediate 2 battery (grades 5.5–6.9), and an advanced battery (grades 7.0–9.9). All test the usual language, reading, and arithmetic skills and study skills. The upper-level batteries test knowledge of facts as well as skills, especially in the social and natural sciences. Peter F. Merenda has called the format of the individual tests excellent and has said that they are attractive and appealing.[4]

Each battery yields from six to ten scores (word meaning, paragraph meaning, spelling, arithmetic computation, and so on). From two to four different forms or editions are available at each level. The tests take 120–269 minutes over five to seven sessions. Again, a variety of hand- and machine-scored answer sheets and services are provided. Scores are reported in stanines, grade placement, and centiles.

HIGH SCHOOL
AND COLLEGE ACHIEVEMENT TESTS

Some of the tests we have just described may be used in high school and beyond. In some cases, the original measures, designed for use in elementary schools, have been expanded to incorporate more of the educational program.

High school and college achievement tests can be divided into two basic types. One consists of regular achievement tests that can be used at the end of a course. Examples of these are the *Modern Algebra Test* (Gerald S. Hanna; Houghton Mifflin), the *Agribusiness Achievement Test* (Roland Peterson; Houghton Mifflin), and *Modern Geometry Test* (Gerald S. Hanna; Houghton Mifflin). The second type of test is the general survey designed to measure overall achievement at completion of certain grade levels. Some test batteries seek to measure the level of general learning expected of all students.

IOWA TESTS OF EDUCATIONAL DEVELOPMENT　This battery was originally published by Science Research Associates in 1942 and is

---

[4] Peter F. Merenda, "The Stanford Achievement Tests," *Journal of Educational Measurement* 2 (December 1965): 247.

revised periodically. The current ITED was prepared by E. F. Lindquist, Leonard S. Feldt, Robert S. Forsyth, and Esther D. Neckere.

The ITED takes nearly 8 hours to administer. Form X-4 and form
Y-4 both consist of nine subtests that may be purchased separately
or all in one booklet. Subtests include Understanding of Basic Social
Concepts, General Background in the Natural Science, Correctness
and Appropriateness of Expression, Ability to Do Quantitative
Thinking, Ability to Interpret Reading Materials (social studies,
natural sciences, literary, and total), General Vocabulary, and Uses
of Information.

Derived scores are reported in percentiles and stanines. The manual states that the major purpose of this widely used battery is to
help the classroom teacher become quickly and reliably acquainted
with the educational needs of individual pupils.[5] Thus, the battery
should be used at the beginning of the school year. The tests do not
cover any specific high school course but are broad enough to cover
several courses.

SEQUENTIAL TESTS OF EDUCATIONAL PROGRESS   The original STEP
series was published by Cooperative Tests and Services in 1956;
Educational Testing Service in 1972 published the most recent edition. The purpose of the batteries is to provide a measure of those
basic skills that all students are expected to possess by the time
they leave school. The original series consisted of seven tests including reading, writing, mathematics, science, social studies, listening, and an essay (now out of print). Series II has seven tests that
yield nine scores: English expression, reading, mechanics of writing
(spelling, capitalization, punctuation, and their total), mathematics,
computation, basic mathematical concepts, science, and social
studies.

These achievement tests are designed for grades 4–6, 7–9, 10–12,
and 13–14. Subtests are available separately. Like their ability test
counterpart, SCAT, the STEP uses standard-error band-width scores
with a mean of 500 and a standard deviation of 100. This battery is
very well constructed and is used widely in schools.

SRA HIGH SCHOOL PLACEMENT TEST   These tests, published by Science Research Associates in 1957, are revised periodically. As the
title suggests, they are designed for the placement of entering ninth-
grade students. Seven or eight scores are derived: educational abil-

---

[5] *Manual, Iowa Tests of Educational Development* (Chicago: Science Research Associates, 1972).

ity, reading achievement, language arts achievement, arithmetic, total, social studies, science methodology, and an optional score on Roman Catholic religion. Administration time is 165 minutes. Scores are reported in stanines and percentages, and both national and local norms are part of the scoring services.

TESTS OF ACADEMIC PROGRESS   The TAP were published by Houghton Mifflin in 1964 (revised 1978) to measure the progress of students in grades 9–12 toward widely accepted educational goals. Its authors are Dale P. Scannell, Oscar M. Haugh, Alvin H. Schield, Henry P. Smith, Gilbert Ulmer, and William B. Reiner. The six tests that compose the TAP include social studies, composition, science, reading, mathematics, and literature, and the administration time for each subtest is 45 minutes. MRC, IBM 1230, and Digitek answer sheets are available, as are scoring masks for hand scoring.

Scores for the six subtests and the total are reported in a variety of forms, including grade percentiles for individual students and school averages at the beginning, middle, and end of the school year. The TAP are regarded as a high school counterpart to the *Iowa Tests of Basic Skills* at the elementary school level.

TESTS OF GENERAL EDUCATIONAL DEVELOPMENT   The GED tests first appeared in 1942 and have been modified continuously since that time. A new form of the test battery is constructed each year. The test appraises the educational development of adults who want high school equivalency certificates. A satisfactory score entitles the examinee to such a certificate and enables him or her to qualify for admission to college or to any of a number of jobs that have educational requirements.

The GED was developed by the American Council on Education and is administered by the Educational Testing Service. It is composed of five tests, each with 65–100 items, covering English composition, social studies, natural sciences, literature, and mathematics. Scores are reported for each of these tests and a composite or average. Tables are provided for changing raw scores into percentiles.

The GED has civilian restricted forms that are administered for a fee throughout the year at centers established by the Educational Testing Service and military restricted forms designed for personnel on active duty and administered by the United States Armed Forces Institute. GED tests may not be used for diagnostic purposes or to determine grade levels of achievement for placement in adult education programs.

ADVANCED PLACEMENT EXAMINATION These achievement tests (College Entrance Examination Board, Educational Testing Service) are designed to assess high school students' mastery of course content for the purpose of establishing credit in college-level courses or to gain admission to advanced courses. The individual tests appeared originally in 1954 and are revised periodically. At present, fourteen tests are available: American history, biology, chemistry, English, European history, French, German, Latin, mathematics, physics, Spanish, studio art, history of art, and music. Each test has an objective section and an essay section.

The advanced placement tests are administered yearly in May at participating secondary schools and other centers established by Educational Testing Service. Most tests (there are some exceptions) are 3 hours long. The number of high school students who take one or more of these examinations continues to rise, and more are sitting for more than one examination. Also, increasing numbers of colleges and universities are accepting advanced placement scores for placement and/or credit. Sidney P. Marland, Jr., reported that in 1975, 65,000 students took 85,000 of the examinations and that 1,517 colleges participated in the program.[6]

The essay tests are evaluated by committees of readers. A five-point scale from 5—extremely well qualified or high honors—through 1—fail or no recommendation—is employed in the report to the school. The college designated as a recipient of the report receives the essay booklet, essay questions, the grade awarded by the essay committee, and interpretive information on examination scores. Colleges vary as to the score level they accept for advanced credit or placement. Alexander G. Wesman says, "Reliability estimates (Kuder-Richardson variant) as reported for the objective sections of the tests are mostly in the .80's; there is one coefficient above .90, there are several in the .70's and a startling coefficient of only .50 is reported for the English examination."[7]

COLLEGE-LEVEL EXAMINATION PROGRAM The CLEP originated in 1964, and additions and revisions are continually being made. The program is administered by the Educational Testing Service for the College Entrance Examination Board. A primary purpose of the program is that of accrediting nontraditional study or assessing an

---

[6] Sidney P. Marland, Jr., "Advanced Placement," *Today's Education* (January–February 1976): 43–44.

[7] Alexander G. Wesman, Review, in *The Seventh Mental Measurements Yearbook*, 2nd ed. O. K. Buros (Highland Park, N.J.: Gryphon Press, 1972), p. 1014.

individual's educational achievements to establish one or two years of college credit or its equivalent. CLEP consists of three types of tests. One is the General Examinations, which yield thirteen scores (English composition; natural sciences, including biological science, physical science, and a total score; mathematics, including basic skills, advanced topics, and a total; humanities, including fine arts, literature, and a total; and social sciences–history, including social sciences, history, and a total). The general examinations are six hours in length, usually taken in two sessions. Subject Examinations consist of 90-minute tests in some twenty-nine subjects such as biology, computers and data processing, educational psychology, introductory accounting, money and banking. Most tests include an optional essay. The third type, called Brief Tests, are 45-minute tests in various subjects.

CLEP is administered monthly, except for the Brief Tests, at regional centers established by Educational Testing Service. According to Alexander Astin, "Although the Score Interpretation Guide reports satisfactory K-R 20 reliabilities (above .90 for the General Examinations, above .85 for most Subject Examinations, and between .77 and .85 for the Brief Tests), no information on retest reliability is presented."[8] General examination scores are based on a representative national sample of 2,582 sophomores from 180 colleges. The score employed is the scale familiar to users of the *College Board Scholastic Aptitude Test* (see Chapter 5) with the reference group mean set at 500 and a standard deviation of 100. Norms for college sophomores, freshmen, and seniors are presented, as are separate norms for men and women. Norms for the Subject Examinations are reported in two formats: the percentile equivalents of scaled scores at five-point intervals from 20–80 are presented in tabular format; and each set of norms is depicted in a graph showing the distribution of scaled test scores that correspond to each letter grade for the course assigned by teachers.

Use of CLEP shows steady growth as more and more colleges and universities give credit for individual study programs, television courses, special lectures, adult education courses, correspondence, and other nontraditional educational experiences. CLEP serves, in many ways, as a means of certifying achievement at any stage of life. Certainly, the current emphasis on life-long learning encourages increasing use of CLEP to demonstrate competence.

---

[8] Alexander W. Astin, Review, in *The Seventh Mental Measurements Yearbook,* 2nd ed. O. K. Buros (Highland Park, N. J.: Gryphon Press, 1972), p. 1014.

SPECIAL
ACHIEVEMENT TEST BATTERIES

Certain achievement tests have been assembled into special batteries for specific purposes. For example, criterion-referenced tests have moved increasingly to the forefront in assessing achievement during the past five years. Many companies have sought to redesign and repackage for criterion-referenced tests items used in norm-referenced tests. One example is the *Individual Pupil Monitoring System* designed by Houghton Mifflin. This system is composed of criterion-referenced achievement tests in mathematics (eight levels, each one corresponding to a grade) and reading (six levels). Comprehensive reporting materials are provided to help maintain records of pupils' performances in meeting behavioral objectives.

Other special test batteries have been constructed for use in assessing achievement among applicants to law school and medical school and for certain jobs. These tests assess the applicants' knowledge of relevant subjects. Many include a general ability test. These are some special achievement test batteries.

NATIONAL TEACHER EXAMINATIONS   This battery, now administered by the Educational Testing Service, was first issued in 1940; the most current edition is dated 1970. It serves to assess those qualities thought to be essential to effective classroom teaching. No one claims that this battery is a measure of the ability to teach. The various tests assess knowledge of subject matter, cultural background, mental ability, cognitive knowledge, and the understanding of principles associated with success in teaching. The battery covers general education, professional education, and subject-matter specialization. The tests are administered four times a year (January, April, July, and November) at centers established by the publisher.

The battery is composed of two parts. The Common Examinations yield seven scores: professional education, weighted subtotal, general education (English, mathematics, weighted subtotal) and weighted total. The second part, the Teaching Area Examinations, consists at present of twenty-seven separate tests, including art, biology, French, German, guidance counseling, home economics, and speech pathology. Each examination is designed to measure an individual's attainments in an area of concentration. Generally, each test has about 150 multiple-choice items. College seniors and teachers take the test battery, usually in two sessions.

The seven-part scores are reported at three levels. The first is a single-digit scaled score. (Part scores have low reliability—K-R 20 estimates range from .59 to .82—presumably because of the small number of test items.) These scores range from 3–9 with a mean of 6 and a standard deviation of 1. The second level of scaled scores consists of four two-digit standardized scores, one for each of the major tests, ranging from 30–90 with an expected mean of 60 and a standard deviation of 10. The four tests have reliability estimates (K-R 20) ranging from .84 to .87. The third score is a three-digit scaled score, known as the weighted Common Examinations total score. This score, summarizing the candidate's performance on all four of the Common Examinations, ranges from 300–900 and has a mean of 600 and a standard deviation of 100.

The *National Teacher Examinations* are used in some states for certification and related purposes. Some local school districts require job applicants to submit NTE results.

LAW SCHOOL ADMISSIONS TEST   The LSAT, developed by the Educational Testing Service, first appeared in 1948 and is revised periodically. The test gives two scores: aptitude and writing ability. The aptitude score is derived from six subtests that include reading comprehension, data interpretation, reading recall, principles and cases, and figure classification. The writing ability score is drawn from three subtests including error recognition, organization of ideas, and editing. The LSAT is administered five times a year (February, April, July, October, and December) at centers established by the Educational Testing Service. The fee covers reporting scores to three law schools. Most schools require applicants to submit scores from this six-hour battery.

MEDICAL COLLEGE ADMISSIONS TEST   The MCAT originated in 1946 and is updated periodically. The latest edition, published in April 1977, is believed to be a good gauge of a student's ability to solve problems. The new MCAT takes a full working day to complete, twice as long as older versions. The test is administered twice a year (spring and fall) at centers established by the American College Testing Program. There are four parts to the battery: verbal, science, quantitative, and general information. Scores are reported with a mean of 500 and a standard deviation of 100.

Applicants seeking admission to member colleges of the Association of American Medical Colleges must submit MCAT scores. Over the years, the MCAT has been found to be effective in selecting students who do well in medical school.

When either the LSAT or the MCAT is used alone, it is often no better a predictor of success in academic work than are college grades. Over the years, an individual tends to repeat his or her performance in similar learning situations. Prediction is generally improved, however, when it is based on a combination of grade averages and scores on selection tests or batteries. Scores on these achievement test batteries, like those obtained from special aptitude batteries (see Chapter 8), all depend to a great extent on general ability and previous learning experience.

USES OF
STANDARDIZED TEST DATA

Standardized achievement test data are used toward such purposes in schools and other educational institutions as promotion or retention, classification and placement, or evaluation and diagnosis (see Chapters 2 and 15).

Since achievement test batteries are expensive, both from the point of view of cost and the amount of school time devoted to them, they should be used so as to offer as much information as possible. Here are some uses of achievement test data.

1. *Promoting client self-understanding.* Standardized achievement test data are used by counselors to help a client find out about himself or herself. That is not to say that a student who comes to a counselor and says, "I'm worried because it takes me so long to complete an assignment," should immediately be administered a battery of achievement tests. But, if in the course of discussing his or her difficulties, the client remarks, "I'm often worried about whether I'm really as prepared in math [or English or science] as other students. Do you have some test results that would tell about that?" the counselor ought to supply the client with appropriate test data.

Achievement test data enable a client to find out about himself or herself. A seeming advantage of achievement tests over ability tests is that clients usually find it easier to accept unfavorable evidence about their achievement than evidence of what they take to be low intelligence. More important, the strong and weak points in a person's schoolwork can be revealed by achievement tests. The results make it possible for the clients to reflect on his or her performance in light of his or her personal characteristics.

2. *Helping in decision-making.* Students who come to the counselor with such questions as "Should I go to college?" or "Should I study mathematics when I go to college?" or "How about medicine?" or "Should I try to be a lawyer?" may find their questions answered, at least in part, by their achievement test scores. Data

about an individual's performance can be used to support or reject alternatives.

3. *Encouraging further self-study.* The most helpful single principle of testing (see Chapter 1) is that test scores are data on which to base self-study. Achievement test data, coordinated with background facts and verified by repeated comparison with other data, encourage clients to learn about themselves. Test scores and test performance suggest topics to be treated in the counseling relationship.

4. *Assisting in diagnosis.* Counselors use achievement test scores in diagnosing school problems of individual clients and planning constructive remedial or corrective programs. Students may show gross irregularities in achievement in particular courses and even in the same course from time to time. In such cases, the counselor can make use of achievement test data to document and explore the reasons for irregular performance. Where there is no evidence of neurotic symptoms and no marked deviation from normal behavior, the procedure may be largely psychometric in nature. For example, a high school student, Bill, who was failing in algebra, had made high scores on a mathematics achievement test. His failures in algebra stemmed from the fact that he could do simple equations without resorting to the laborious, step-by-step, written procedure demanded by his teacher. Conferences with the teacher and with Bill resulted in compromises in methods and special arrangements for advanced work in mathematics. As a result, he passed the course. Another student, Ellen, was having trouble learning new vocabulary as it was introduced in a physics course, and her classmate Tom's failure in English was the result of his missing an important unit of work. The reasons for both students' difficulties were revealed by item analysis of an achievement test. It should be noted that test data do not, in themselves, automatically disentangle the complex interaction of factors that produce irregular performance. When a counselor finds disparities between test performance and behavior, he or she must look for explanations in a client's responses to environment and experience.

ASSESSING, INTERPRETING, AND REPORTING TEST DATA

As students move beyond early elementary school, counselors may depend more on data from standardized achievement tests than on tests of general ability (described in Chapter 5), because differential effects of experiences, rates of learning, and opportunities to learn produce significant differences in achievement. Achievement test scores make it possible to think in terms of verbal factors, numerical factors, spatial orientation, and mechanical performances. These should not, of course, be overlooked when they appear on ability tests. But, as increasing specialization is demanded by occupations and by higher education, such factors assume great importance. Achievement test data, particularly those designed to measure learning skills, may be substituted for (some school districts now use them in place of) general mental ability tests. Many research studies demonstrate that the communality of functions between the general ability test and a general achievement test is approximately 75 percent to 90 percent. General achievement tests are not used frequently in lieu of general ability tests, however, because group-administered general ability tests are adequate in normal situations and are much more economical in time and cost to administer, score, and interpret. Beyond elementary school, there is little reason to continue administering general ability tests gradewide. Such tests are more usefully employed on an individual, need-to-know basis.

The guidelines we proposed in Chapter 5 for interpreting and reporting ability test data apply equally well to achievement test data. Here are some additional recommendations specifically for interpreting achievement test data.

1. *Use achievement test data cautiously.* Test publishers have obtained the highest validity and reliability coefficients in measuring school achievement, but even achievement measures are not foolproof, and they do not always give dependable results even in the hands of experts. However, the reliability, validity, and objectivity of achievement tests, in light of the norms provided for comparative purposes, can, when used with caution, be invaluable to individuals making educational and vocational decisions or learning more about their areas of competence.

2. *Supplement achievement test data with grades.* Though the reliability and validity of grades given by teachers are variable, grades remain important indicators of performance. Counselors assessing individuals or interpreting achievement test scores cannot ignore teachers' marks, even though they are aware of their limitations.

3. *Search for patterns in achievement test performance.* This guideline follows principle 8 (see Chapter 1), which states that appraisal must be based on a pattern of information rather than

drawn from a single datum. Putting achievement test data into usable form is not an easy task. It requires painstaking and meticulous study of each subtest score, of data obtained from other sources such as grades, of the relationships among data; and it calls for sorting out and assembling all data that form a pattern. For example, a pattern of high subtest scores and high grades in mathematics may suggest conceptual learning strengths. The burden of collating and organizing data is great. In the future, it may be possible to put numerical values on achievement data and to apply statistical techniques so that the relationship of results from many sources may be computed. Contingency coefficents or some new method may then reveal the degree of relationship among data. It may also be possible at some time in the future to develop a forecasting technique that serves the same purpose for the individual as the regression equation does for groups. At present, however, such techniques have yet to be perfected for individuals.

For the time being, practicing counselors should examine achievement test data and other performance indices for relationships and trends in order to improve their assessments and interpretations. By noting subscores, counselors arrive at a conception of a pattern; having grasped a pattern, they can understand and reinterpret the meaning of the parts as well as the whole.

4. *Remember that the test data represent an individual.* This guideline amplifies principle 1 (see Chapter 1), which states that appraisal is the process of arriving at an understanding of an individual. Norms for achievement test scores are usually given in terms of age, grade, and percentile position in a group or in terms of deviation from the average of certain actual or theoretical populations. These norms provide the counselor with many reference points and measures of deviation from these points. However, these points must not be interpreted as standards that all individuals are expected to attain. When interpreting a test to a person, a counselor must be concerned not only with a score on an achievement test but, more specifically, with the reasons why the score is high, average, or low.

Tests do not come equipped with weights to be attached to the quality of instruction, the kind of school or home, the quality of textbooks, and many other factors that may influence a person's achievement test performance. If such factors as these have had adverse influence, counselors may expect the client's achievement test scores to be below (or even, sometimes, above) average, but the test gives no guide as to how much variation from the average is to be expected.

It is possible that a low achievement test score is a high score for the individual in view of the opportunities he or she has had. Counselors must be aware of the differences between low scores in general and low scores of an individual. For a particular client, it may mean the difference between recommending remedial treatment or discouraging further study in a particular field. If two students achieve the same low score on a mathematics test, one may be given special tutoring or assistance in that field as a preparation for an education in engineering while the other may be discouraged from entering that field because it requires so much mathematics. Counselors must interpret and reinterpret achievement test scores in the light of all they know about a particular client.

5. *Remember that achievement test scores are no guarantee that the measured performance is a typical performance.* The only way to get evidence about performance is to measure achievement on selected tasks. However, counselors must keep in mind that inferences about a score may be seriously in error. A student who has put forth less than maximum effort or who habitually attacks a problem emotionally may produce a below-average performance. It is unwise, however, to infer that his or her performance will always be at that low level. In order to avoid error, it is useful to interpret achievement test scores (tests of maximum performance) in terms of an individual's habitual modes of response. In Chapter 1, principle 11 stated that longitudinal data should be considered in appraisal, and principle 13 stated that an individual's behavior is to be considered consistent and understandable in terms of his or her motives and values. Here it should be noted that statistical tables for such interpretations are not provided in test manuals. The counselor must make a subjective analysis of an objective measurement. Records of the achievement test performance, school marks, and other indices of attainments over a period of years provide indispensable data for counseling purposes.

ISSUES

1. *Achievement tests are best administered at the beginning of the year.*

   Yes, because:
   1. Administering achievement tests in the fall of the year reveals the overall achievement picture of a class and enables the teacher to know where to start instruction.

2. Tests at the beginning of school take into account loss of achievement over the summer vacation.
3. Reading and other instructional groupings can be established at the outset, based on students' current status.
4. Individual diagnosis and treatment procedures can be best derived from administering achievement tests in the fall.
5. Administering tests at the beginning of the school year discourages use of such data for evaluating teachers.

No, because:
1. Students aren't ready in early fall to put forth the maximum effort required in achievement testing; they are more ready at the end of the school year.
2. Too much time elapses even with an early fall administration between administering, scoring, and reporting and using the data. The teacher can't wait that long to obtain information from counselors in order to form instructional groups.
3. Giving tests at the end of the school year makes achievement test data available for decisions about grades, promotion, and retention.
4. Testing at the end of the school year gives teachers time to study the performance of each student entering his or her class, enabling the teacher to anticipate their needs in the fall (the loss during summer months is but temporary).

Discussion:
Again, this is an old but perennial issue. Both positions present some worthwhile and useful reasons. Ideally, fall achievement testing is more logical and, therefore, preferable. However, more schools engage in year-end testing than fall testing. This, of course, is not the first case in which practice does not conform to the ideal.

Most likely, the practice of end-of-year achievement testing evolved because of the need for objective data to support decisions about grading, promotion, and retention. Once instituted, spring testing remained, even though the need may no longer be as urgent as it once was. Of course, some elementary school principals, directors of curriculum and/or personnel, and school superintendents prefer end-of-year achievement tests, because they use these data to make assessments about teacher's performance and to decide whether teachers should be offered contracts for the next year. We do not recommend this use of test data (see Chapter 15). Surely, far better ways exist to evaluate a teacher's performance and the effectiveness of his or her instruction.

2. *Achievement test batteries are best administered by teachers.*
   Yes, because:
   1. Teachers have established rapport with their students that encourages them to do their best. Counselors or psychometrists who enter classrooms to administer tests, particularly in elementary schools, create anxiety, because children don't know them.
   2. Placing the responsibility for administering achievement tests on teachers gives them the incentive to make use of data derived from the test battery.
   3. It is not practical to employ the numbers of counselors or psychometrists needed to administer grade-wide or system-wide achievement test batteries. The administration of such tests is neither difficult nor rigorous and does not require or demand the use of specialists.

   No, because:
   1. It is important to follow precisely the directions given in the manual. Having each teacher administer achievement tests to his or her class increases variability and hence influences results.
   2. Teachers find it difficult to remain objective or to refrain from giving help to a student who asks about a test item or needs more time.
   3. The use of specialists who are familiar with test directions and administrative procedures, rather than teachers, assures uniformity of administration and leads to more confidence in the test results.

   Discussion:
   Standardized achievement tests can be given by any teacher or competent adult. Because it is expensive to employ psychometrists or counselors to administer achievement tests, and because teachers have the confidence of their students, it seems appropriate that teachers administer achievement tests. To most individuals, any testing situation is threatening. Some elementary school students become so anxious when tests are given that they have been unable to function. The tension is not as great when a teacher administers the test. Teachers encourage students to produce scores that are representative of their true level of performance.

The person in charge of testing for the school district should bring teachers together before any testing period to go over the test, especially the instructions. Suggestions can be made to prepare them for possible problems. A good administrator of a standardized group test of achievement is alert and interested in what is going on, is a good oral reader familiar with test directions, and is able to keep time accurately. A good way to become familiar with a test is to administer it to oneself.

The best practice is to administer achievement tests in the morning. Because achievement test batteries are long, they should be broken into two, four, or more sections and administered on consecutive mornings.

ANNOTATED REFERENCES

Ebel, Robert S. *Essentials of Educational Measurement.* Englewood Cliffs, N.J.: Prentice-Hall, 1972, 622 pp.

Chapter 18 (pp. 465–480) treats the differences between standardized and classroom achievement tests. The types of items used in achievement tests are described and explained. Test score profiles and subtest scores are examined.

Hoepfner, Ralph, et al., eds. *CSE Elementary School Test Evaluations.* Los Angeles: University of California, Center for the Study of Evaluation, 1970.

Some 204 instruments designed for measuring elementary school objectives are grouped by both testing areas and grade levels. Measures for grades 1, 3, 5, and 6 are classified into twelve areas (affective, arts-crafts, cognitive, mathematics, music, science, and others).

Hoepfner, Ralph, et al., eds. *CSE Secondary School Test Evaluations: Grades 7 and 8.* Los Angeles: University of California, Center for the Study of Evaluation, 1974.

Approximately 3,300 tests for measuring secondary school educational goals at specified grade levels are grouped (1,100 per volume) by test areas. These instruments were evaluated by certain criteria and a grade assigned to each. Two other volumes, one for grades 9 and 10 and one for grades 11 and 12, are also available.

Horrocks, John E. *Assessment of Behavior.* Columbus, Ohio: Charles E. Merrill Books, 1974, 736 pp.

Chapter 15 describes the characteristics of good achievement test items. Methods of conducting item analysis are identified and explained. Attention is given to the use of achievement test data.

Scannell, Dale P., and Tracy, D. B. *Testing and Measurement in the Classroom.* Boston: Houghton Mifflin, 1975, 288 pp.

Chapter 3 (pp. 49-70) describes the planning process for classroom measurements. Chapter 9 (pp. 241-266) illustrates good practices in reporting progress to students and deriving grades for schoolwork.

SELECTED REFERENCES

Biggs, Donald L.; Mayer, G. Roy; and Lewis, Ernest L. "The Effects of Various Techniques of Interpreting Test Results on Teacher Perception and Pupil Achievement." *Measurement and Evaluation in Guidance* 5 (April 1972): 290-297.

Bauer, David H. "Error Sources in Aptitude and Achievement Test Scores." *Measurement and Evaluation in Guidance* 6 (April 1973): 28-34.

Johnson, Richard W., and Thomas, W. F. "Prediction of Performance on CLESP General Examinations." *Measurement and Evaluation in Guidance* 6 (October 1973): 168-170.

Khan, S. B. "Sex Differences in Predictability of Academic Achievement." *Measurement and Evaluation in Guidance* 6 (July 1973): pp. 88-92.

Lynch, Daniel O., and Smith, Billie Clifton. "Item Response Changes: Effects on Test Scores." *Measurement and Evaluation in Guidance* 7 (January 1975): 220-224.

Pascale, Pietro J. "Changing Initial Answers on Multiple-Choice Achievement Tests." *Measurement and Evaluation in Guidance* 6 (January 1974): 236-238.

Pazandak, Carol H. "Self-Estimate of Level of Effort as a Predictor of College Grades." *Measurement and Evaluation in Guidance* 8 (April 1975): pp. 43-50.

Prendergast, Mary A., and Binder, Dorothy M. "Relationships of Selected Self-Concept and Academic Achievement Measures." *Measurement and Evaluation in Guidance* 8 (July 1975): 92-95.

Reilly, Richard R. "Student Placement by a Maximum Likelihood Procedure." *Measurement and Evaluation in Guidance* 7 (April 1974): 8-15.

Chapter 7

Academic Deficits and Status

What is the nature and function of diagnosis?

What types of academic deficits exist?

What diagnostic tests are used widely to measure academic deficits?

What guidelines may be set forth for using diagnostic measures?

THE NATURE
AND FUNCTION OF DIAGNOSIS

Diagnosis as a concept and as a function has had a checkered history in counseling. A term commonly associated with medicine, its definition and function have been clear: the identification of disease from symptoms so that treatment can be undertaken. The diagnostic process employed by a physican follows certain logical and systematic procedures, in that the physician (1) recognizes the problem presented by the patient, (2) collects data that clarify the problem, (3) thinks over the facts and possible solutions, (4) reasons out the implications of the suggested solutions, and (5) compares the facts with the suggested solutions to determine if there is an identity between the known facts and the suggested solutions. The use of the term *diagnosis* in counseling has been based primarily on this definition, with certain qualifications and drawbacks.

DIAGNOSIS AND COUNSELING

In the early days of counseling, diagnosis was accepted as an inevitable and desirable function—inevitable because counseling (at least in its published accounts) followed the medical model. *Diagnosis,* as employed then, referred to the counselor's statement of the client's problems, to causal factors, to suggested counseling procedures, and to a prediction of future adjustment. The process of diagnosis consisted of reducing case data by eliminating irrelevant material and arriving at a best judgment of the individual's problems by formulating and testing hypotheses. The hypotheses about the person and/or situation were based on generalizations from research and experience, intuition and insight. The term *best judgment,* unlike the phrase *definite conclusion,* implied that an interpretation was based on the data at hand and was revised as counseling progressed.

The advent of client-centered counseling cast doubt on the desirability of diagnosis as part of counseling. The original objections to the practice, stated by Carl Rogers, were that diagnosis: placed the locus of evaluation on the counselor and thereby encouraged dependency by causing the client to believe that responsibility for improvement rested with the counselor; and that it resulted in certain long-range adverse social and philosophical implications (such as social control of the many by the few).[1]

Even prior to the introduction of client-centered counseling, the question was being raised as to whether diagnosis could be applied to psychological problems. Medical diagnosis *distinguishes* an illness or disease and *differentiates* it from other diseases. Both C. H. Patterson[2] and Leona Tyler[3] have discussed the hazards and difficulties of applying diagnosis as such to emotional disorders. They feel, first, that the classification of diseases into discrete, mutually exclusive categories (each of which has a common origin, a common course, and a common prognosis) does not apply to psychosocial disturbances. While patients who have the same physical disease follow the same course rather closely, those who have been diagnosed as having the same emotional disorder do not necessarily follow similar courses. Second, the etiology of physical disease is always a specifiable, and ultimately a verifiable, physical or external agent (chemical, bacteriological, or viral), whereas emotional disturbances may be related to multiple factors. Third, specific remedies exist, either known or unknown, for physical disease, but none have yet been devised for personality problems.

---

[1] Carl Rogers, *Client-Centered Therapy* (Boston: Houghton Mifflin, 1951), pp. 223–224.
[2] C. H. Patterson, *Counseling and Psychotherapy: Theory and Practice* (New York: Harper and Brothers, 1959), pp. 219–230.
[3] Leona Tyler, *The Work of the Counselor,* 3rd ed. (New York: Appleton-Century-Crofts, 1969), pp. 65–72.

Still another reason why medical diagnosis does not apply to counseling is that the degree of participation by the medical patient differs greatly from that of the counselee. More reliance is placed on the counselee's active participation in the process, and more weight is given his or her self-reports. Doctors do not ignore such reports, but they can use physical tests to verify them. This difference extends to treatment as well. Physicians are able to do things *to* patients, while counselors must depend to a greater extent on working *with* clients.

Tyler believes that diagnosis can be thought of as a means of obtaining a comprehensive picture of the individual.[4] Used in this fashion, *diagnosis* means understanding an individual in order to take intelligent action. From the first moment of contact, the counselor begins to form a working image of the counselee. Hypotheses or impressions—of the individual's development to date, of the nature of his or her interpersonal relationships, of his or her habits and work—go into this picture and make the counselor aware of alternative courses of action. Background data and the outcome of tests, interviews, and observations modify the image and fill in the details. Therefore, as Tyler suggests, diagnosis may be viewed as the counselor's asking himself or herself such questions as, "Shall I continue working with this client?" or, "What does this individual need most?" She points out that the diagnostic act in and of itself does not help or hinder the counseling relationship or the person. For example, the counselor's knowledge of a person's fears does not remove the fears. Any diagnosis must assume that somewhere, sometime the client is going to be able to benefit from the diagnosis.

Patterson, however, cautions against extending the concept of diagnosis as understanding of the client because it represents a failure to distinguish understanding of from knowledge about a client.[5] Diagnostic knowledge or understanding, according to Patterson, is understanding from an external view and represents knowledge about a client rather than knowing that individual. Furthermore, it contains an evaluative element that is detrimental to counseling.

The concept of diagnosis can be considered from many levels and viewpoints. In its broadest sense, however, a certain amount of diagnosis takes place in all counseling relationships. Diagnosis does

---

[4] Tyler, *The Work of the Counselor*, pp. 65–72.
[5] Patterson, *Counseling and Psychotherapy*, pp. 219–230.

not necessarily ascertain the basic cause of an individual's problem or bestow a permanent label on the individual. It may be simply the counselor's hypothesis as to what has taken place, the current status of the individual, or the nature of the help the client needs most.

DIAGNOSTIC TESTS

In many ways, all tests are diagnostic instruments in that they permit classification, a major element of diagnosis. Even more important, they provide information that, if given to the individual, enables him or her to correct mistakes or misconceptions. Certain tests have been labeled diagnostic because they are designed to measure an individual's proficiency in performing learning components within an area in which the individual has been least successful. For example, diagnostic reading tests measure various skills associated with reading and provide scores for each component. Presumably, these scores identify sources of reading difficulty so that corrective methods can then be applied.

Useful diagnostic tests are difficult to construct. First, they must be highly reliable if they are to have diagnostic value. Because each part of a test has to be sufficiently brief to be administered with ease, adequate reliability is often difficult to achieve. A second reason is that, before a test can be used for diagnostic purposes, it is necessary to demonstrate not only that each part measures what it purports to measure but that the elements measured are fundamental to the overall skill. This too has been difficult to accomplish.

In a strict interpretation of the term, diagnostic tests do not diagnose the causes of learning difficulty. They identify only those aspects of learning with which the individual has had difficulty, not necessarily the root of this difficulty. Say, for example, that John's word-meaning score on the *Iowa Silent Reading Test* is at the fifteenth percentile. This datum does not necessarily reveal the reason for John's poor vocabulary, but it does pinpoint an area in which correction can be applied.

In Chapter 6, we pointed out that achievement tests designed to measure performance in a particular area use only small samples of the subject matter or skill being tested. Each small sample in and of itself is insufficient for drawing precise diagnostic conclusions about an individual's overall proficiency in that area. In contrast, a diagnostic test includes rather large samples from limited aspects of the area of achievement. Diagnostic tests are more properly viewed as screening devices to identify the *what* and *how* involved in inadequate learning performances.

TYPES OF ACADEMIC DEFICIENCIES

It is a paradox that counseling as practiced in educational settings has made little progress over the years in treating students with academic disabilities. Every educational institution has sizable numbers of students whose academic performance is deficient in one way or another. All too often, meetings between such students and their counselors result in prescriptive conclusions, suggesting that students unfortunate enough to do poorly in school ought to try harder or that such students are emotionally disturbed and, therefore, need help beyond the competencies of the counselor. Here is an overview of common types of academic deficits.

READINESS DEFICIENCIES

A child entering school is assumed to have certain abilities and certain degrees of skill in various types of activities. The people responsible for arranging the school curriculum must assume a commonly agreed-upon level of ability that can be used as a base. Schools are designed for the so-called normal child. Therefore, this base represents the abilities displayed by average children when they begin school.

Many schools test the extent to which each child conforms to this profile through readiness tests, judgments by teachers, and other informal assessments. The skills and abilities assessed by readiness tests, however, do not represent the starting point of learning for the child as they do for the school. These skills and abilities are the culmination of a very extensive and rapid period of learning—the preschool years.

One of the tasks generally demanded of a child starting school is that he or she draw a reasonably good representation of a square. This is a task on many standardized readiness tests and some intelligence tests. It involves control of gross motor activities, eye-hand coordination, including laterality and directionality, temporal–spatial translation, and form perception. Demonstration of this skill is one reflection of the child's readiness to cope with the complex activities demanded in school that depend on basic sensory-motor skills.

UNDERACHIEVEMENT

Though readiness deficiencies can lead to underachievement in school, many counselors, teachers, and parents are confronted by children who appear ready but who do not do well in school. All educational personnel are familiar with the able but unmotivated student whose report card always carries the notation, "Should be doing better." They are equally aware of discrepancies between certain students' ability and their performance. The term *underachievement* has been employed to describe this condition. A tongue-in-cheek definition given some years ago was that the underachiever is anyone "who sits on his potential, resisting various [devices] to get him off his potential, and possibly needing an adroitly directed kick in that same potential."[6]

Underachievement has been defined rather consistently as the discrepancy between measured potential, as demonstrated by ability test scores, and achievement, as shown by grades or achievement test scores. Variations exist in what is set forth as the amount of the discrepancy, but 1 or 2 standard deviations in test scores or 1 or 2 grade levels is the usual magnitude of difference. Underachievement is a broad classification label incorporating many classes of learning problems.

Underachievement has been a popular persistent research area in education, and abundant literature exists reporting investigations in which comparisons have been made between underachievers and normal achievers as well as the highly gifted. Some variables that have been investigated are historical antecedents, socioeconomic factors, personality and interest differences, study habits, and personal and social adjustment problems.

Here is an overview of the underachiever, generalized from the research literature. At school, most underachievers are unhappy and bored. They are frequently absent from school and dislike teachers and course work. Underachievers tend to be poor readers and do not read for pleasure. The male underachiever is likely to be a source of disturbance in a social group, although he is strongly swayed by

---

[6] Donald W. Russell, "A Plea to Beam in the Underachiever," *High School Journal* 42 (December 1958): 66.

what the crowd does. The classroom behavior of school underachievers is usually disruptive. No clear pattern emerges from the research on the personality characteristics of the underachiever. Some claim that the underachiever is hostile and suspicious, whereas others disagree. Moreover, the underachiever has been described as both an introvert and an extrovert. Serious maladjustment has been noted by some researchers but not by others. A rather consistent finding is that the underachiever tends to be unrealistic in self-appraisal and to lack self-confidence and self-acceptance. He or she has a narrow range of strong interests and stated vocational goals or aspirations lower and less well-defined than those of achievers.

Three rather consistent findings emerge from the research literature on underachievers. First, underachievers are predominantly males. Although nearly every study shows this sex factor, few researchers have followed it up experimentally. Presumably, males have a wider range of activities and more freedom in choosing them than females have had in American culture. This means that there is more competition for a boy's time. Because there are many avenues open to him that are neither academic nor scholarly, a boy may turn away from education at an early age.

The second finding is that underachievers are unable to delay rewards, to postpone gratification. External, frequent, and immediate rewards are needed to counter the lack of reinforcement experienced frequently in their academic efforts. Productivity and success in school seem to underachievers a very lonesome road. They need to be sustained, to feel that they belong. They can be influenced by identifying with teachers and counselors or other adults, for underachievers lack a built-in system of reinforcement and need reinforcement from others.

The third prominent finding is that underachievement is not an *emergent trait*. This means that underachievement does not usually appear suddenly. Most underachieving college students were underachievers in high school. Some years ago, John C. Gowan demonstrated that the high school achievement pattern is established in grade school.[7] The discrepancy between ability and achievement shows up as early as the third grade.

Although the psychological implications of underachievement have been explored in many research studies, almost all share a common limitation. These studies are *correlative*, that is, they

[7] John C. Gowan, "Starting a Program for Giftd Children," *Education* 70 (February 1960): 337–340.

explore and reveal variables that are concomitant with underachievers. Although this does not minimize their value, it does make it necessary to avoid separating cause from effect. Some of the factors mentioned above, like home environment, can be inferred as causes rather than consequences because of their historical priority. The studies, however, do not demonstrate this. Other factors, such as personality characteristics or maladjustment, could just as easily be effects as causes. Counselors must guard against using imprecise words when they deal with human dynamics. For example, it cannot be said as an explanation that a person underachieves because of lack of motivation. Rather, the counselor should think of underachievement as the evidence of lack of motivation. The problem of underachievement, reduced to its simplest terms, is that certain students withdraw from rather than approach certain activities that teachers think important, while they approach certain activities that teachers deem to be less important.

SLOW LEARNING

This term, like *underachievement,* is a broad one that designates a group of children who never seem quite able to learn what others are learning readily and eagerly. Even in the first grade, they experience difficulty in the readiness work that precedes reading, writing, and arithmetic. As the school year progresses, these children fall behind until they are no longer able to work with the rest of the group. The longer they remain in school, the more confused they become, and the more constantly they are faced, both formally and informally, with their failure to achieve.

Many children designated as slow learners come to school lacking in basic perceptual-motor skills. As a consequence, they are unable to participate satisfactorily in formal education, and they are unable to learn as quickly or as much as others do. For many, artificial means have to be designed to provide additional practice in perceptual-motor skills in order to build up to the more complex skills involved in reading, writing, and arithmetic.

Newell C. Kephart suggests that the inability to generalize is the prime cause of difficulty for slow learners.[8] They learn facts and acquire specific skills but are unable to integrate and organize data so as to make generalizations. Slow learners, confronted by a prob-

---

[8] Newell C. Kephart, *The Slow Learner in the Classroom,* 2nd ed. (Columbus, Ohio: Charles E. Merrill, 1971), p. 52.

lem whose solution depends upon data, must inventory their knowledge item by item, selecting and rejecting each in turn. As a result, in any assigned task, slow learners are likely to overlook a fact or piece of information that they have been taught and know well. They put together things that do not belong together, while composite wholes such as forms or words tend to fall apart on them.

Kephart places two groups in the slow-learner category: the *learning disabled* and the *culturally deprived.* Children with learning disabilities are unable to generalize because of disturbances in the functioning of the central nervous system. One or more units of the system fail to work (masses of nervous tissue fail to function in concert, making integration of information impossible). The culturally deprived have intact nervous systems but suffer from limited or chaotic learning experiences. Kephart suggests that their generalizations are inflexible and limited in extent, and while qualitatively adequate, are based on too few data.[9] They frequently fail because insufficient information has gone into their solution of problems.

LEARNING DISABILITIES

This term is currently fashionable, and its use incorporates a range of disorders including educational handicaps, brain injury, brain dysfunction, psycholinguistic disabilities, reading problems, perceptual difficulties. Patricia Myers and Donald Hammill apply the term to those students displaying marked underachievement in school-related activities.[10] They note that no rigid formula exists for determining the discrepancy, but that elementary school children who read 1½ years below level and secondary school students who are 2 years below level are considered candidates for special instruction. Learning disabilities, according to Myers and Hammill, are usually related to one or more prelinguistic and/or linguistic functions: loss of established basic perceptual process (visual decoding, auditory decoding, kinesthetic decoding, visual encoding, graphic encoding, connecting associations); inhibition of the development of such a process; interference with the function of such a process. They exclude from the category all those whose primary problems stem

---

[9] Kephart, *The Slow Learner,* p. 54.
[10] Patricia I. Myers and Donald D. Hammill, *Methods for Learning Disorders* (New York: John Wiley and Sons, 1969), p. 3.

from mental subnormality, educational or cultural deprivation, severe emotional disturbance, and/or sensory defect. Learning disability, as a term, is used to describe those whose discrepant performance stems from faulty motor activity, emotionality, perception, symbolization, attention, memory, or a combination of these characteristics.

EMOTIONAL DISTURBANCES

Emotional disturbances often cause or are linked to poor school performance. Many authorities suggest that emotionality precipitates or augments motor disorders, perceptual problems, and memory disorders. Frequently, the terms *maladjustment* and *behavior disorder* are used interchangeably with the term *emotional disturbance*. A useful example of a description of the emotionally disturbed student is found in the administrative manual of the Bureau of the Educationally Handicapped and used with Title VI of the Elementary and Secondary Education Act. In this source, the disturbed student is described as one who suffers from: (1) an inability to learn that cannot be explained by intellectual, sensory, or health factors; (2) an inability to establish or maintain satisfactory interpersonal relationships with peers and teachers; (3) inappropriate types of behavior or feelings under normal circumstances; (4) a generally pervasive mood of unhappiness or depression; and (5) a tendency to develop physical symptoms such as pains or fears associated with personal or school problems.

Of all school personnel, counselors and school psychologists are most concerned with the emotional state of a child. Both groups possess some expertise in recognizing and managing pupils thought to be disturbed. In some schools, negative attitudes toward the emotionally disturbed create a climate in which assistance is viewed so narrowly that few ways of helping them are available short of exclusion from school. Some educators believe that the school has no business serving the disturbed. The emotionally disturbed individual is often viewed as a classroom problem, disruptive of the education of the many and best removed from school.

Estimates of the number of students found each year to exhibit some emotional, behavioral, or psychosomatic problem vary widely. This variation is related to the lack of a uniform definition and to differences in the cutoff points used in categorizing a student as disturbed. The criteria employed in making judgments stem from definitions and that affects the precision of decisions. In general, estimates vary from 4 percent to 20 percent. Whichever extreme of this range applies, in the total American school and college population, there exists a tremendous number of individuals who need help.

HYPERKINESIS

Some children are *hyperkinetic.* They appear to be put together with springs. They are always under tension. Any movement is accompanied by excess tension throughout the entire musculature. They cannot confine increased muscle tone to those muscles essential to the task.

Teachers are concerned by the behavior of hyperkinetic children. Their movements are quick, explosive, and uncontrolled. As a consequence, they frequently destroy materials and supplies, break furniture or equipment, and appear clumsy and careless. Reprimands for such behavior have no effect. The child appears cowed by the teacher's anger but immediately makes the same mistake again because he or she has not learned to attend to and control specific movements. A progression often takes place among hyperactive children: hyperactivity → lack of attention → poor memory → academic failure → increased hyperactivity. Often relaxation techniques (Jacobson procedures[11]) or even more commonly, drugs such as Ridilin, are used with such individuals, but with questionable effects on the child's learning and health.

HEARING DEFICITS

Sensorimotor difficulties occur in varying degrees. Hearing defects, for example, range from slight hearing problems to partial deafness to deaf-muteness. Behaviors symptomatic of those with poor hearing include:

peculiar listening posture; habitual turning of head to position one
  ear toward speaker
inattention and slow response; lack of interest in general
  conversation

---

[11] E. Jacobson, *Progressive Relaxation* (Chicago: University of Chicago Press, 1938).

mistakes in carrying out spoken instructions; frequent requests to
  have instructions repeated
irrelevant answers
vocal peculiarities such as monotone, high pitch, excessive softness
  or loudness
repeated colds, earaches; ear discharge
tendency to look at another person's lips rather than eyes in face-
  to-face encounters

  Many schools administer hearing tests early in a child's school
career, because some severe hearing disabilities can be prevented
with early diagnosis and treatment. Those who have even mild
hearing defects usually experience difficulty in auditory discrimination. To compensate, some teachers emphasize visual approaches
to identifying and recognizing words. Hard-of-hearing students may
develop feelings of inadequacy and emotional stress unless teachers
encourage special efforts to make them feel that they belong in
class and play activities.

SPEECH DEFICIENCIES

Speech defects can also interfere with school performance. Some
students with speech deficiencies become painfully embarrassed
when asked to read aloud or to take part in class discussions. Astute
teachers, to avoid aggravating the embarrassment, use tact in their
requests and suggestions to such students. However, these teachers
realize that it is not appropriate or helpful to exempt such students
altogether from oral work. Modern schools provide speech training
and remedial work by speech teachers. The relationship between
speech and mental health is circular. Good speech can contribute
to good adjustment; poor speech can contribute to poor adjustment.
Words are used to express feelings, tensions are released, and people,
by doing so, gain some understanding of themselves. Some speech
therapists maintain that every speech problem is a manifestation
of emotional conflict. Even if this is not always the case, emotional
problems are a very common consequence of impaired speech.

VISUAL DEFICITS

Some students' academic work is impaired by visual defects. Behaviors symptomatic of visual problems include:

holding a book abnormally near or far from the eyes

walking overcautiously; faltering, stumbling, or running into objects not directly in the line of vision

rubbing the eyes frequently as if to brush away the blur

frowning or distorting the face when using the eyes; tilting the head at odd angles when looking at objects

showing undue sensitivity to normal light levels by squinting or other signs of irritation

inconsistency in reading print at different distances, such as on the blackboard and in a book

Many visual defects such as ordinary myopia, hyperopia (extreme farsightedness), astigmatism, and muscular imbalance can be remedied by properly fitted glasses. A small number of children have visual deficiencies that cannot be fully corrected by glasses. In some schools, sight conservation programs have been established to keep watch over all children who are diagnosed to be in need of it by a competent eye specialist. When a person has visual acuity no better than 20/50 in the better eye after correction, he or she is probably in need of the special care provided in sight-saving classes.

READING DEFICIENCIES

The so-called tool subjects, particularly reading, are frequently the source of academic deficiencies. Most children are introduced to reading through the home or head-start programs in which reading is used to obtain information. Most quickly absorb the rudiments of the reading process, but some children's initial experiences with reading are overwhelming. When they enter school, where reading is taught as a skill, they lack motivation, because they cannot recognize its value.

Deficiency in reading among both children and adults has long been a concern of educators. Proficiency in reading is essential throughout an individual's scholastic career. Reading is estimated to be a requirement for 80 percent to 90 percent of learning activities in secondary school and college. At least moderate reading ability is necessary for most jobs, and job advancement is frequently dependent on reading skills.

Many surveys have sought to document the extent of reading disability. While variations exist in the magnitude established as a deficit, the findings are remarkably consistent: some 10 percent to 20 percent of the school population have varying degrees of reading disability. The proportion of seriously retarded readers (one year behind in lower grades and two years or more behind at the higher levels) ranges from about 10 percent to 15 percent. Most authorities estimate that about four-fifths of these individuals would probably respond well to special instruction while the other one-fifth would require special clinical diagnosis and intensive, perhaps prolonged, remedial training.

Survey after survey has revealed that more boys than girls are retarded readers. It is not unusual for twice as many boys as girls in a group to have reading disabilities. In reading clinics, it is not uncommon to find a ratio of ten boys to every girl.

The causes of reading deficiencies are legion and varied. Undoubtedly, the more profound the disability, the more numerous are the factors that operate, each contributing to the disability singly and in association, to impede reading proficiency. Reading difficulties range from minor to very severe. The minor problems often go unrecognized and therefore uncorrected, with deleterious effects that become cumulative and result in severe difficulty. Reading difficulties probably result from both environmental and hereditary or predisposing conditions, but for the most part, they are brought about by factors in the child's environment at home, at play, and in the school.

There seems to be no single cause of reading disability. Physical conditions such as visual, hearing, and speech deficiencies, motor adjustments, brain damage, and lateral dominance are often involved. Various emotional, intellectual, educational, and environmental factors play their part, often linked to and interacting with one or more physical causes. Each reading disability problem is unique, requiring careful study for diagnosis and specific remediation.

Some years ago, Emmett Betts outlined reading levels as follows:[12]

1. *Independent reading level.* This is ascertained from the level of a book that an individual can read with no more than one error in word recognition (pronunciation) in each 100 words and with a comprehension score of at least 90 percent. At this level, the individual reads aloud in a natural conversational tone; the reading is rhythmical, well-phrased, and free from tension. Silent reading is faster than oral reading and free from vocalizations.

---

[12] Emmett A. Betts, *Foundations of Reading Instruction* (New York: American Book, 1957).

2. *Instructional reading level.* This is determined from the level of a book that the individual can read with no more than one error in word recognition in each twenty words with a comprehension score of at least 75 percent. At this level, the individual reads aloud, after silent study, without tension, in a conversational tone, and with rhythm and proper phrasing. This is the level at which a student is able to make successful progress in reading under a teacher's direction.

3. *Frustration reading level.* At this level, an individual bogs down in the book, reading without rhythm and in an unnatural voice. Errors and hesitations are numerous, tensions are present, and comprehension is no more than 50 percent.

4. *Probable capacity reading level.* This level is demonstrated by the highest book in any reading program series in which a student can comprehend 75 percent of the material when it is read aloud by the examiner. The examinee answers questions about and discusses the material and is able to pronounce and use properly many words in the selection.

Teachers have been preached at for years about employing either sight or oral methods of reading instruction. People outside the school have sought to persuade teachers to adopt an extensive array of new reading programs and techniques. Often, teachers feel that the advocates of new reading practices are cavalier in their comments and attitudes about existing reading programs and that they seem insufficiently aware, much less appreciative, of what teachers have accomplished in reading instruction.

A variety of approaches to reading instruction is employed in current classroom practice. No single approach is suitable for every student or in all reading situations. For that reason, classroom teachers do not confine themselves to a single approach but rather employ many oral and visual strategies.

DYSLEXIA

A wide range of meanings is associated with the term *dyslexia.* It is often used as a synonym for *word blindness, strephosmbolia, specific language disability,* and the like. The term has been applied to individuals without mental deficiency, brain damage, or emotional disturbance who fail or fall behind in school despite instruction that enables others to succeed. Such individuals experience difficulties specific to language that range from mild to severe. The

World Federation of Neurology defines *dyslexia* as "a disorder in children, who, despite conventional classroom experience, fail to attain the language skills of reading, writing and spelling commensurate with their intellectual abilities."[13]

Dyslexia is a perceptual defect, possibly genetic in origin or possibly the result of a childbirth trauma such as lack of oxygen. Some authorities rule out birth trauma. Opinion varies widely as to its prevalence. Some estimate that one in every ten children has dyslexia. Others hold that it may have an emotional etiology. However, most authorities prefer to use the term to designate those with cognitive difficulties of constitutional origin, composing no more than 2 or 3 percent of the population.

Dyslexia as a specific neurological difficulty occurs in children at all socioeconomic levels. The left hemisphere of the brain supposedly controls language abilities. Dyslexics are believed to use both hemispheres when they read. They confuse symbols in space and sounds in time. For instance *b* becomes *d*, or 24 comes out 42. Letters and words get switched upside down or backward (*was* for *saw*), and dyslexics have trouble in following a sequence of words or lines. They may not hear sounds correctly, confusing *b* with *v* or *th* with *f*, or they may mispronounce words.

Hand–eye coordination is a problem for many dyslexics. They may not shine at skipping rope or riding a bike. Visual–motor exercises such as walking on a balance beam, bouncing balls, and tracking a moving object with the eye are often prescribed, but because of controversy in the field over the efficacy of such techniques, most authorities recommend that they be used only as a supplement to a child's remedial training program.

Parents, teachers, and counselors ought not to be alarmed if a five-year-old nursery school student reads and writes some letters backward or makes *biscetti* out of *spaghetti*. That's about par. But if the student has such habits at 7, concern is warranted. Children with dyslexia appear normal enough in other than school behavior, so the problem often goes undetected. They are frequently branded underachievers and put in remedial reading groups, where their problems may only get worse.

LANGUAGE DEFICIENCIES

Students from homes where a foreign language is spoken may have little or no command of English and may be unable to understand

---

[13] Announcement by the Research Group on Developmental Dyslexia, World Federation of Neurology, April 1968.

or speak English well enough to participate in ordinary classroom activities. Any language deficiency makes accurate measurement of intelligence or achievement difficult, if not impossible.

The procedures used in teaching the academic fundamentals are based on the assumption that each child has already learned to understand and speak the dominant language of the society. Those who fail to meet this assumption need a program to improve their understanding of English. Two instructional activities are of prime importance: building a basic vocabulary and improving facility in oral communication. Too often, children who have a meager knowledge of English receive no special training to eliminate their handicap. They often become disabled readers, and their underachievement worsens.

MATHEMATICAL DEFICIENCIES

Considerable numbers of students have difficulty with arithmetic. For some time, such difficulties have been ascribed to visual–spatial disorders. Mathematics deals with groups of objects, the characteristics of groups, and grouping phenomena. Students who have not developed an adequate concept of space and its manipulation have trouble with math. Abstractions of space (Euclidean geometry) grow from perception of space. Observation of relationships (concept formation) is vital to arithmetic, indeed to most advanced thinking.

Manipulating the relationship between or among numbers is what makes arithmetic intelligible; otherwise, it is only a series of memorized facts. The concept of *threeness* as a grouping in space and in symbols, pictures, and diagrams must be comprehended and interpreted. Reading mathematical problems is a difficult task demanding intensive concentration. Some time ago, L. C. Fay adapted the SQ3R procedure (Survey, Question, Read, Recite, Review) for arithmetic study (SQRQCQ), as follows:

> S—The problem is read rapidly to determine its nature.
> Q—What is the problem?
> R—Reread for details and interrelationships.
> Q—What processes should be used?
> C—Carry out the computation.
> Q—Is the answer correct? Check the computation against the problem facts and the basic arithmetic facts.[14]

---

[14] L. C. Fay, "Reading Study Skills: Math and Science," in *Reading and Inquiry* (Newark, Del.: International Reading Association, 1965), p. 93.

DEFICIENT STUDY SKILLS

A number of skills are subsumed under this heading. Developing efficiency in locating information by means of such aids as tables of contents, indexes, and card catalogues constitutes one of these skills. Acquiring proficiency in the use of general reference material is a second. This category includes activities from simple alphabetizing to use of dictionaries, encyclopedias, and the like. A third skill is interpreting pictures, maps, graphs, and charts. The fourth skill, or group of skills, includes organizing materials, outlining, classifying materials under main headings and subheadings, ordering selected materials in proper sequence, and constructing time lines and two-way charts. The ability to organize materials and data is essential to developing efficient study skills.

Students who have deficient study skills often demonstrate poor reading comprehension. Students have to develop a wide variety of reading skills to study effectively: reading for specific information, reading to organize, reading to evaluate, and reading to interpret, for example. The importance of reading to proficient study skills is amply demonstrated in the SQ3R method described by Frances R. Robinson.[15]

REPRESENTATIVE
DIAGNOSTIC TESTS

Here is a list of some representative diagnostic tests. Few counselors administer these tests themselves. Such testing is usually done by school psychologists, special educators, reading specialists, speech therapists, and others. Nonetheless, the counselor must be familiar with these tests if he or she is to work effectively with these specialists for the benefit of the student.

READINESS TESTS

BOEHM TEST OF BASIC CONCEPTS The BTBC assesses mastery of basic concepts and is designed for grades K-2. The test (by Ann E. Boehm) was published in 1971 by the Psychological Corporation in two forms. It is administered aloud in 30–40 minutes (in one or two

---

[15] Frances R. Robinson, *Effective Reading* (New York: Harper and Row, 1962).

sessions) to small groups or individual students. Percentile norms are provided. The BTBC tests knowledge of fifty general concepts.

ANALYSIS OF READINESS SKILLS This test (authors: Mary C. Rodrigues, William H. Vogler, and James F. Wilson) was published in 1972 by Houghton Mifflin. It is designed to assess the extent to which children in grades K–1 are ready for reading and arithmetic. The test consists of three subtests of 10 items each: visual perception of letters (recognizing lower-case and upper-case letter forms), letter recognition (pupil marks letter named by teacher), mathematics (child identifies numerals 1–11 and counts from 1–11).

The six raw scores (visual perception, letter identification, mathematics, number identification, counting, and a total score) are converted into percentile ranks. No time limit is established, but the test usually takes 30–40 minutes. The test can be used with either individual pupils or small groups. It is hand-scored, and separate norms are provided for English-speaking and Spanish-speaking pupils.

GATES-MACGINITIE READING TESTS: READINESS SKILLS This test, by Arthur I. Gates and Walter H. MacGinitie, is designed for kindergarten and grade 1. The 1978 edition (Houghton Mifflin) has but one form and takes about 120 minutes (in four sessions). Nine scores are provided: listening comprehension, auditory discrimination, visual discrimination, following directions, letter recognition, visual–motor coordination, auditory blending, word recognition, and a total score.

Separate norms have been provided for students finishing kindergarten and those beginning first grade. Performance (total test score) correlates about .60 with late first-grade reading test scores. The manual states that 4,500 children in thirty-five communities served as the norming sample. Subtest reliabilities are given.

LEE-CLARK READING READINESS TEST Among the older and better-known readiness tests, the Lee-Clark was originally published in 1931, and its latest edition (authors: J. Murray Lee and Willis Clark) came out in 1962. The test is designed for pupils in grades K–1 and is published by the California Test Bureau (McGraw-Hill). Four scores are given: letter symbols, concepts, word symbols, and total. Administration time is 15–20 minutes. The manual reports split-half reliability coefficients ranging from .87 to .96. Predictive validity coefficients range from .13 to .72 (median .54) when compared with teacher ratings and .14 to .79 (median .45) when compared with scores from a reading test.

METROPOLITAN READINESS TESTS   This test (1933) is one of the older readiness measures. Its 1976 edition (authors: Joanne R. Nurss and Mary E. McGauvran) is published by the Psychological Corporation. Two levels are available. Level I, for use in kindergarten or entry into grade 1, consists of six subtests: auditory memory, rhyming, letter recognition, visual matching, school language and listening, quantitative listening, and an optional test, copying. Administration time is about 80–90 minutes, and the test can be either hand- or machine-scored. Percentile ranks and stanines are provided for most subtests, and norms are available for November and midyear of kindergarten. Level II is a replacement for the 1964 edition of the test. It yields six scores: auditory, visual, language, quantitative, pre-reading skills composite, and battery composite. Administration time for the battery is about 100 minutes. Norms are provided for the end of kindergarten and for the beginning of grade 1 for each skill area. Stanine and percentile ranks are provided for most subtests. The *Technical Handbook* was published in 1977.

PERCEPTUAL
AND PSYCHOMOTOR TESTS

BENDER VISUAL-MOTOR GESTALT TEST   The Bender test, developed in 1938 (revised in 1946) by Lauretta Bender and published by the American Orthopsychiatric Association, purports to estimate the visual-motor development of the child aged 4 and over. The test consists of nine designs, each on a separate card, that are exposed one at a time. The examinee copies each one on a sheet of paper. No time limit is imposed. Reproduced designs are judged in terms of distortion, rotation, perseveration, method of reproduction, and other factors. Data have not been presented on reliability. E. M. Koppitz has designed and standardized a scoring technique for the Bender that may be used with children as young as 5 years of age; it yields derived scores related to developmental age and school grade equivalents.[16]

MARIANNE FROSTIG DEVELOPMENTAL TEST OF VISUAL PERCEPTION Frostig, in collaboration with D. Welty LeFever, John R. B. Whittlesey, and Phyllis Maslow, devised and published (Consulting Psychologists Press, 1963) the third edition of a battery of five discrete

[16] E. M. Koppitz, *The Bender Gestalt Test for Young Children* (New York: Grune and Stratton, 1963).

tests of visual perception. The tests may be administered to children aged 3–8, individually or in small groups. The test assesses eye-motor coordination, figure-ground discrimination, form constancy, position in space, and spatial relationships. A total score and a perceptual quotient are derived. The standardization group included 2,116 subjects from southern California schools. Test-retest reliability of the perceptual quotient was .80 for a small group of 72 first- and second-graders tested two weeks apart, with subtest reliabilities ranging from .42–.80. Little information has been provided about validity.

PURDUE PERCEPTUAL-MOTOR SURVEY This scale, developed in 1966 by E. G. Roach and N. C. Kephart and published by the Charles E. Merrill Publishing Company, is designed to rate perceptual-motor development. Five areas—balance and postural flexibility, body image and differentiation, perceptual-motor match, ocular control, and form perception—are assessed in eleven subtests for children aged 6–9 years. A test-retest reliability of .95 was obtained by different examiners who tested thirty subjects one week apart. Part-score reliabilities have not been reported.

READING TESTS

Several tests have been constructed for assessing reading proficiency. These tests are generally classified as either reading survey tests or diagnostic reading tests. Reading survey tests are designed to be used as initial screening instruments to identify reading disability. These survey tests yield a measure of the grade level at which a pupil can read. Comparing this measure with a measure of mental ability identifies the degree to which the student is behind in reading. Survey reading tests usually begin with relatively easy items and progress to more difficult ones. Norms for interpreting scores usually extend over a range of several grades. The typical survey test measures vocabulary, comprehension of sentences or paragraphs or both, and sometimes speed and accuracy. The achievement batteries described in Chapter 6 include reading survey tests. Consequently, we shall mention only three reading survey tests here. The rest are diagnostic reading tests.

DAVIS READING TEST This test (authors: Frederick B. Davis and Charlotte C. Davis) was published by the Psychological Corporation in 1958 and was revised in 1962. Two series are available, each with four equivalent forms. Series 1 is used for grades 11, 12, and 13, and series 2 for grades 8, 9, 10, and 11. Each test has 80 items arranged in two sets of 40 items each. Administration time is 40 minutes.

Each Davis test form provides two scores: level of comprehension and speed of comprehension. Raw scores are converted to scaled scores and percentile ranks. Norms for series 1 forms were derived from 5,857 eleventh-grade students, 5,596 twelfth-grade students, and 6,922 college freshmen. Norms for series 2 were based on 4,936 eighth-grade students, 5,292 ninth-grade students, 6,649 tenth-grade students, and 5,017 eleventh-grade students from 52 high schools located in 25 states.

Intertest (three-week intervals) reliabilities reported in the manual for series 1 range from .70 to .83 for level of comprehension and from .82 to .89 for speed of comprehension. Averages of the correlations between level and speed scores from two different forms of series 1 were .74 for grade 11, .77 for grade 12, and .80 for college freshmen. Average correlation between two different forms of series 2 were .84 for grade 8, .84 for grade 9, .78 for grade 10, and .77 for grade 11. The 1962 manual reports validity correlations between Davis scores taken at beginning of year and English grades at mid-year that average .50.

The directions and scoring of the test are simple. The manual reports that the major skills tapped include remembering word meanings, finding answers to questions, grasping the central thought of ideas, making inferences, recognizing tone and mood, and following the structure of a page.

GATES-MACGINITIE READING TESTS   These tests, by Arthur I. Gates and Walter H. MacGinitie, for grades 1, 2, 3, 2.5–3, 4–6, and 7–9, are revisions (1978) of previous tests by Gates published in 1926 by the Bureau of Publications, Teachers College, Columbia University. The tests are now published by Houghton Mifflin Company. Two editions are available for the 4–6 and 7–9 levels. Administration time is 40–50 minutes over two sessions. Most levels yield vocabulary and comprehension scores and some test speed and accuracy. Both hand-scored and machine-scored editions are available. The level manuals and the technical manual report the standardization process and reliability coefficients (alternate-form reliabilities range from .78 to .89 except on speed and accuracy subtests).

GATES-MACGINITIE READING TESTS: SURVEY F   These tests are for grades 10–12 and were published in 1969–1970 by the Psychological

Corporation. Two editions are available, and each test yields three scores: speed and accuracy, vocabulary, and comprehension. Administration time is 49 minutes. Alternate-form reliability ranges from .64 to .81 for the speed and accuracy subtest, .90 for the vocabulary, and .88 for comprehension. Normalized standard scores and percentile ranks for three points during the school year are provided. Both machine- and hand-scored forms are available.

This and the previous two reading survey tests are designed primarily for determining a pupil's average reading level, but they are also diagnostic. Scores on word recognition, vocabulary, sentence completion, or paragraph comprehension yield information about the individual needs of a student experiencing difficulty in reading. There are, however, analytical tests that are more diagnostic in nature. Such tests are believed to be superior to general survey reading tests for diagnostic purposes because they provide a profile of reading abilities that indicates strong and weak areas in an individual's skills. Some diagnostic reading tests have but a small number of subtests, others a large number. Here are a few typical examples of analytical tests.

CLASSROOM READING INVENTORY   The second edition of this inventory by Nicholas J. Silvaroli was published in 1973 by the William C. Brown Company. It is designed for elementary school classroom teachers (grades 2–10) who have not had prior experience with individual diagnostic reading measures. Three forms are available, and each form contains three parts. Parts I (word lists) and II (oral paragraphs) are designed for use with individual children, and part III (spelling survey) can be administered individually or to a class. Part I takes 5 minutes to administer and part II about 7 minutes.

The inventory provides information about the individual's independent, instructional, frustration, and hearing-capacity reading levels. Most important, this popular inventory assesses the individual's word-recognition and comprehension abilities.

Here is a brief description of the three parts of form A (form B and form C are optional but similar).

1.   Graded Word Lists. Eight lists of twenty words are presented, starting at pre-primary level. The child pronounces each word, and the test is continued until the child mispronounces or does not know five of the words. Each correct response is worth 5 points. The purpose of the Graded Word Lists is to identify errors in word recognition and to estimate approximate starting level for oral paragraphs (part II).

2. Graded Paragraphs. Ten paragraphs, graded in difficulty, are used to assess the child's independent and instructional reading levels. Word recognition and comprehension are tested.

3. Spelling Survey. Six levels of ten words each are presented. When the child makes five spelling errors in any one level, the test is discontinued.

The inventory contains a record or profile for recording the percentage of correct words and estimated reading levels (independent, instructional, frustration, and hearing capacity) by grades. The directions for administering and scoring are clear and easy to follow.

DURRELL ANALYSES OF READING DIFFICULTY   These tests, now published by the Psychological Corporation, consist of a manual of directions, a booklet of reading paragraphs, a tachistoscope for quick exposure of words, and various series of words on cards to use in the tachistoscope. An individual record blank for each person to be tested asks for such information as identifying data, a profile chart, difficulties observed and recorded, home history, and an outline of remedial plans. The test series is designed for grades 1–6 and takes from 30–90 minutes to administer to each student. It measures such crucial reading skills as oral reading, silent reading, listening comprehension, word recognition, visual memory, and hearing of sounds. The Durrell series also includes a learning rate test for severely retarded readers that determines the degree of difficulty a child has in remembering new words.

Administering the *Durrell Analysis of Reading Difficulty* is uncomplicated. The checklist of errors, which are detailed and quite complete, are more important than the norms. The series is thought to be highly useful in diagnosing reading disability, particularly among students with less than severe deficits.

MONROE DIAGNOSTIC READING EXAMINATION   This diagnostic reading procedure was developed, standardized, and used on children referred for poor reading and other problems at the Institute for Juvenile Research in Chicago.[17] A control group of 101 normal readers was used for comparative purposes. Reading achievement, chronological age, arithmetical achievement, and mental age are considered in identifying reading deficiency. An average reading score is derived from: (1) Gray's *Oral Reading Paragraphs*; (2) either

---

[17] M. Monroe, *Children Who Cannot Read* (Chicago: University of Chicago Press, 1932).

the *Haggerty Reading Examination, Sigma* 1, test 2 (for primary grades) or the *Monroe Silent Reading Test* (for intermediate grades); and (3) the *Monroe Iota Word Test* for reading isolated words. Monroe derived the grade score for arithmetic from the *Stanford Test in Arithmetic Computation*. Mental ages were obtained from the *Stanford Revision of the Binet-Simon Tests*. Tables are provided to transform mental age and chronological age into grade scores.

A single measure of reading proficiency is given by the reading index, which compares a child's reading grade with the average of his chronological and mental ages and arithmetic grades. The index identifies reading disability cases quite well. Those individuals who have a reading index of .80 or below almost always require remedial instruction, while indexes between .80 and .90 are borderline.

In addition to this basic series of diagnostic tests, Monroe lists several supplementary tests to be used as needed. These include tests of mirror-reading, mirror-writing, auditory word discrimination, visual-auditory word learning, sound blending, and handedness and eyedness tests. The tests place considerable emphasis on phonetics. The Monroe series is believed to be especially useful for identifying profoundly retarded readers. Though it is time-consuming, exacting, and somewhat laborious, the series is a carefully worked-out system of diagnosing reading difficulty and has proved its value in many reading clinics.

GATES-MCKILLOP READING DIAGNOSTIC TESTS   This test series was published 1926–1962 by the Bureau of Publications, Teachers College, Columbia University and is described fully in a textbook.[18] Diagnosis of reading disability, according to Gates and McKillop, requires a measure of mental age, a measure of silent-reading ability, and the individual's actual grade placement. Mental age scores are best derived from either the Stanford-Binet or estimated from the WISC. One or more standardized silent reading tests are given. Mental age and silent-reading scores are converted to grade scores. Average silent-reading grade is compared to actual grade placement. An important comparison is between average silent-reading grade and mental grade to reveal the degree of reading retardation in relation to the individual's intelligence level. Comparisons of reading grade either with actual grade placement or with mental grade is made by referring to a table that indicates ratings that are average (at grade), low, or very low. The degree of retardation that is given

---

[18] *Gates-McKillop Reading Diagnostic Tests*, 3rd ed. (New York: Bureau of Publications, Teachers College, Columbia University, 1962).

a rating of low or very low varies with grade level. The skilled examiner rarely needs to give all the tests in the program to discover a student's specific difficulty but rather selects those necessary to secure the information.

The Gates-McKillop series consists of three types of materials: (1) the manual of directions, which contains detailed instructions for administering, recording, and scoring the tests; (2) two booklets of four cards each containing test materials that are presented visually for oral responses; and (3) the pupil record booklet, which provides space for identifying data, raw scores, grade scores, and ratings for intelligence, silent-reading tests, and all diagnostic reading tests.

The Gates-McKillop program is comprehensive and capable of screening a variety of reading disabilities. The program presents helpful suggestions for treating reading difficulties, even profound ones. The tests are designed primarily for skilled clinical use in reading centers. Their scoring is long and laborious.

LANGUAGE TESTS

Considerable numbers of tests are available for assessing language disabilities. They measure language ability that is not influenced by speech inadequacies. These are two such tests.

ILLINOIS TEST OF PSYCHOLINGUISTIC ABILITIES   The test was developed originally in 1961 by Samual A. Kirk and its latest revised edition was published in 1968 (by Kirk, James J. McCarthy, and Winifred Kirk). It is published by the University of Illinois Press. The ITPA consists of ten discrete subtests and two supplementary subtests standardized on some 1,000 children between the ages of 2–10. It is a test of language, perception, and short-term memory abilities. Six of the subtests measure reception, association, and expression. Others measure sequential memory and closure (the ability to complete or recognize an incomplete stimulus event). Normative data enable the examiner to derive age equivalents and scaled scores, giving an objective point of reference in judging individual performance in any of the twelve abilities tested. The twelve subtests and a composite at each of eight levels result in 104 internal consistency coefficients. Of the 104 uncorrected reliabilities, 51 fall below .80, 23 below .70, and 15 above .90. The tests appear to be reasonably reliable at each level. The test-retest (six-month interval) reliabilities for the subtests range from .12 to .86. The ITPA is a comprehensive test of language but is a fairly complicated battery to administer.

STANFORD LANGUAGE TESTS These subtests of the Stanford Achievement Test, by Truman L. Kelley, Richard Madden, Eric F. Gardner, and Herbert C. Rudman, measure mastery of spelling and the mechanics of language and language study skills. The Stanford Language Tests (1964–1965) are published by the Psychological Corporation. Three forms are available: intermediate I for grades 4.0–5.4; intermediate II for grades 5.5–6.9, and advanced for grades 7.0–9.9. Administration time is approximately 60 minutes for each of the three levels. Grade equivalents, percentiles, and stanines are given for each test, which can be either hand-scored or machine-scored.

MATHEMATICS TESTS

Most arithmetic tests have no set of separate norms for oral administration. Those students who have difficulty with mathematics should be tested for both arithmetic computation and arithmetic reasoning. They should be permitted to demonstrate their status in arithmetic reasoning by having problems read aloud to them. Any test of mathematics from the achievement batteries (see Chapter 6) can be used to assess arithmetic competence for those students who read well. Younger students who manifest arithmetic deficits can be assessed with readiness test batteries.

STANFORD DIAGNOSTIC MATHEMATICS TEST This test, published in 1976 by the Psychological Corporation, was developed by Leslie S. Beatty, Richard Madden, Eric F. Gardner, and Bjorn Karlsen. The test is for grades 1.5–13 and is designed to identify specific arithmetic strengths and weaknesses. It assesses the students' understanding of the number system and its properties, their facility in computation, and their ability to manipulate numbers in problem-solving and measurement.

Two forms are available at each of four levels: grades 1.5–4.5; grades 3.5–6.5; grades 5.5–8.5, and grades 7.5–13. Each level is color coded, and administration time is 1½–2 hours. Percentile ranks, stanines, grade equivalent scores, and scaled scores are given.

MODERN ALGEBRA TEST   This test, written by Gerald S. Hanna and published in 1972 by Houghton Mifflin, is for grades 9–10. It assesses a student's mastery of first-year algebra, including the number system and terminology; fundamental processes and evaluation; factoring; exponents, roots and radicals; equations and inequalities; and systems of equations. Administration time is 40 minutes. Both hand- and machine-scoring services are available.

ORLEANS-HANNA ALGEBRA PROGNOSIS TEST   This test originated in 1928 and was revised in 1968 by Joseph B. Orleans and Gerald S. Hanna and published by the Psychological Corporation. It is designed to estimate a student's probability of success in learning first-year algebra. Administration time is 40 minutes. The test consists of fifty-eight work-sample items in multiple-choice form that correspond to an instructional lesson. Norms have been established for 5,109 students completing eighth-grade mathematics and for a subgroup of 2,860 enrolled in first-year algebra. Predictive validities range from .39 to .82 (median .71) for both midyear and full-year algebra performance. Test-retest coefficients (two-week interval) range from .91 to .96 for total scores.

ORLEANS-HANNA GEOMETRY PROGNOSIS TEST   This test was authored by Joseph B. Orleans and Gerald S. Hanna and published in 1968 by Harcourt Brace Jovanovich. It is designed to estimate eight- to eleventh-grade students' success in learning geometry. Administration time is 40 minutes. The test consists of a set of test questions and a questionnaire, each with a maximum score of 40 points. The questionnaire asks for past course marks in four subjects and the grade the student expects to receive in geometry. The test uses a work-sample approach. The five lessons are followed by questions. Percentile ranks, stanines, and expectancy tables are provided. Normative data are based on 3,525 students completing first-year algebra and 2,218 completing algebra and enrolled in geometry. Validity data for midyear and final geometry grades (745 students) are .42 and .47 for the work sample and .67 and .68 for the questionnaire.

STUDY SKILLS TESTS

COLLEGE ADJUSTMENT AND STUDY SKILLS INVENTORY   The CASSI (author: Frank A. Christensen) was published in 1968 by the Personal Growth Press. It contains fifty-seven questions, to which the examinee responds on a four-point scale from *very often* to *very seldom*. The author suggests that the primary purpose of the CASSI is to serve as a counseling tool to evaluate characteristics believed to contribute to success in college.

Six scores are derived from the CASSI: time distribution, attitude and personal adjustment, reading and class participation, taking notes, taking examinations, and total. The table that sets forth means and standard deviations is based on an *N* of 146 students from midwestern universities. Reliability data were not reported. Subtests correlate from .25 to .53 with each other and from .51 to .83 with the total test score. Validity evidence is scant, but the manual reports a rank order correlation coefficient of .19 between the test and grade-point averages for 98 students.

SURVEY OF STUDY HABITS AND ATTITUDES One of the better known inventories, the SSHA appeared originally in 1953; its latest edition was published in 1967 by the Psychological Corporation. Its authors (W. F. Brown and W. H. Holtzman) designed the inventory to assist counselors in helping students succeed in high school and college.

The attitudes and work habits assessed by the 100 items are thought to relate significantly to academic success (grades) but only moderately with ability test scores. Form H is designed for students in grades 7–12 and form C for college students. Both forms yield a seven-score diagnostic profile drawn from basic scales (delay avoidance, work methods, study habits) and three combined scores (teacher approval, education acceptance, study attitudes). The SSHA consists of numbered statements, arranged in two columns per page, to which the examinee responds in one of five ways: *rarely, sometimes, frequently, generally,* or *almost always.* The inventory is untimed; most students complete it in 20–25 minutes. Both hand- and machine-scoring services are available.

Percentile norms for college freshmen, based on 3,054 cases from nine colleges, are given for form C. Form H norms were derived from 5,425 students in grades 7–9 and 5,793 from grades 10–12.

The lowest reported form C subscale reliability coefficient (K-R20) was .87; the lowest four-week test-retest coefficient was .88, and the lowest 14-week test-retest was .83. The lowest reliability coefficient reported for form H was .93, with a four-week interval. Validity evidence presented includes low correlation coefficients (mean .21 for form C and .27 for form H) between SSHA and aptitude tests and higher correlations (mean .36 for form C and .49 for form H) between SSHA and grades. Intercorrelation coefficients of SSHA subscale scores range from .51 to .75.

The SSHA is easy to administer and score. Its directions are clear and complete. Each answer sheet includes a diagnostic profile that can be completed by the examinee. Areas in which a student's performance is most different from the performance of those who do well are identified.

INTERPRETING AND REPORTING
TEST DATA

Counselors today are more aware of students who need help than were counselors in the past. Until recently, it was not unusual to label individuals with learning difficulties dull or mentally incompetent. The current means for diagnosing learning deficits are better than they were twenty-five years ago. Test program results yield accurate information on which diagnosis and remedial work can be based.

Academic deficits are generally accompanied by problems with personal and social adjustments. The degree to which any academic deficiency is a cause or an effect of emotional maladjustment is never very clear. For example, the emotional stress produced by the failure to learn to read may become a handicap to further learning. All too often, there is a vicious cycle, a reciprocal relationship between the emotional condition and the academic deficiency. In many such cases, both counseling and remedial instruction should be extended to break up the cycle.

Professional counselors constantly study the strengths and weaknesses of their clients, alert for any sign of physiological or psychological limitations. The tests available for assessing academic status and deficits enable them and other professionals to detect and institute procedures to correct many learning difficulties before they become serious.

Some years ago, L. J. Brueckner and G. L. Bond defined three levels of educational diagnosis: general diagnosis, analytical diagnosis, and case-study diagnosis.[19] Some individuals' problems require only a general study of their educational achievement and intellectual abilities. Other individuals' difficulties may require more differential or analytical study in order to locate the specific area of limitation. Some of these situations may be so subtle and complex that a detailed case study is required before a remedial

---

[19] L. J. Brueckner and G. L. Bond, *Diagnosis and Treatment of Learning Difficulties* (New York: Appleton, Century Crofts, 1955).

program can be designed. Information for a general diagnosis is usually obtained from standardized group tests of ability and achievement as well as from consultations with teachers and parents. An analytical diagnosis systematically explores specific strengths and weaknesses, locating the difficulty and indicating the skills wherein lies the weakness. Information for an analytical diagnosis often comes from diagnostic tests and clinical experience. Case-study diagnosis is usually made from diagnostic tests and procedures; study of the individual, including intellectual appraisals, evaluation of vision, hearing, and physical condition; and information about relevant environmental factors.

Here are some guidelines for using tests of academic status and deficits.

1. *Diagnostic test data should be used to formulate methods directed at assisting an individual.* While etiological diagnostic data—finding out what initially caused a person's difficulty—are often unavailable, diagnostic tests can yield information about current conditions that can give direction to a corrective or remedial program. The tests can also identify specific problems and strengths that may be helpful to the student and his or her teachers and parents.

2. *Diagnosis involves more than appraisal of school achievement and ability.* This guideline is in accord with principle 9 (see Chapter 1). The complex nature of educational disability and the large number of potential contributing factors make it necessary for the counselor to explore many traits, personality characteristics, and habits in order to arrive at an adequate diagnosis. The physical, sensory, and environmental factors that impede or facilitate learning need to be taken into account.

3. *Diagnosis should be efficient.* Diagnosing the problems of some students who are having difficulty with their schoolwork requires time and is highly complex, while the difficulties of others can be identified with relative ease. A diagnosis, therefore, should proceed as far, and only as far, as is necessary to formulate a treatment program. The diagnosis should be arrived at by collecting and analyzing data assessing relatively common types of problems (reading, for example) and proceeding toward the more complex, unusual ones. As we have suggested, diagnostic procedures employed by counselors are like successive screenings, in which only the more complex and subtle cases are retained for further measurement and study. Diagnostic appraisals, therefore, can occur at several levels:

appraisals made routinely for all students or for all those referred for special study; appraisals that are more detailed in character and are made when more than exploratory study is warranted; and appraisals that are highly individual in nature and are made when the counselor is confronted by subtle, serious, or long-standing academic deficits.

4. *Informal methods of obtaining information about academic status and deficits may be useful.* Counselors often find it useful to explore further, by informal means, leads about the nature of academic deficits that come to light from the use of standardized diagnostic tests. Consultations with teachers and parents often supply additional useful insights. Most counselors combine formal testing with informal inventories of study skills, observations of a student's classroom work, and discussions with teachers and other professionals in order to arrive at the best understanding of the student's difficulty. Needless to say, the information acquired by these various practices should be obtained as systematically as possible and interpreted and used with caution. Many misjudgments are made because of personal bias or pet theories.

5. *Diagnostic decisions must be based on score patterns.* Principle 8 from Chapter 1 is reflected in this guideline. Information obtained from standardized diagnostic tests must be arranged so that various numerical scores can be compared with one another. High as well as low scores must be taken into account in estimating the status of students with academic deficits. Deficits may occur as a result of an unfortunate stress of the instructional program. For example, a student's sight vocabulary may be low because he or she has been successful in employing word-recognition techniques and therefore has had little need to remember words at sight.

Failure to compare a student's performance of separate skills with general reading ability may result in making mistakes and ignoring strengths. For example, the difficulties experienced by an eighth-grade student who has only sixth-grade achievement in syllabication may seem to the counselor a result of the student's inability to break words into syllables. However, if the student's reading ability is only that of the typical fourth-grader, the student's ability to syllabify becomes a strength rather than a weakness.

Most standardized diagnostic tests are so arranged that such comparisons are made easily. Even the range of tolerance (standard error) is indicated frequently so that the counselor will not be disposed to place too much emphasis on any one high or low score that is not significantly out of range.

6. *Indiscriminate diagnostic testing should be avoided.* The individual should be given every consideration when administering tests for diagnostic purposes. All too often, counselors, psychologists, and others give test after test in their routine diagnostic procedures. The time, energy, and cost involved in testing are so great that counselors should evaluate the diagnostic tests being used to make sure that they are efficient and useful. While it is true that anything worth measuring at all should be measured well, it is equally true that wasteful and nonessential tests should be avoided. We do not recommend cutting down on the information needed to diagnose correctly, but we do feel that counselors should be alert to and avoid indiscriminate and inefficient measurement.

7. *Care must be exercised in interpreting normative data from standardized survey and diagnostic tests.* The norms supplied for many of these tests indicate the performance of typical pupils on a sample of typical subject matter in the field that is being measured. That is the source of the strength as well as the greatest weakness of standardized diagnostic tests. By definition, students who exhibit severe academic deficits are far from typical learners. Caution and insight are in order in interpreting the results of the measurements obtained. For example, if a child in the sixth grade with a reading expectancy of 6.0 measures 4.0 in reading, an inexperienced counselor might assume that the child needs reading materials and methods suitable for the typical fourth-grade child. This may not be the case, for the sixth-grade child is not a typical fourth-grade reader. The child may have sixth-grade interests, drives, motivations, and friends. Standardized diagnostic test data can yield information on which to make judgments as to what will help the atypical learner.

ISSUES

1. *Poor attitudes toward education on the part of parents are responsible for the academic deficiencies of students.*
   Yes, because:
   1. The parents of many students who do poorly in school are contemptuous of books, learning, educational toys, and musical records, instruments, and lessons; their attitudes are communicated to their children and adversely influence achievement.
   2. Families in the lower socioeconomic classes are often marked by child neglect, irregular meals, inadequate cloth-

ing, sickness, accidents, and beatings. Children from such homes may be less ready for school than their more fortunate counterparts because they may be read to less often, receive less affection, may be punished more, and share less mealtime conversation.

3. Children from families that exist on the knife-edge of disaster use all their energies to survive. Parents of such children tend to train their children to conform, to be subservient, to be passive; such attitudes do not facilitate learning.

No, because:

1. Poor academic performance occurs among children at all socioeconomic levels.
2. Student achievement or underachievement is more likely associated with good or poor teaching practices than with family background.
3. The child comes to school, not the parents, and it is the individual, not his or her family, who succeeds or fails.

Discussion:

There is little doubt that disadvantaged children are sometimes hungry, physically ill, and fatigued from lack of sleep in noisy and overcrowded living quarters. Many such children do not approach school with a desire to know and understand equal to that of their more fortunate peers, let alone with the readiness skills necessary to implement the desire. Not surprisingly, they often fall behind in their schoolwork. The wonder is that so many of them manage to succeed in school.

Underachievement has been ascribed to numerous causes. Not uncommonly, college professors place the responsibility on high school teachers, who in turn, blame elementary school teachers, who say that the fault lies with the parents and the home. They may all be right. Neither family attitudes nor inadequate teaching has been demonstrated clearly or consistently in the research literature to be the major cause of poor achievement. To date, remedial or compensatory educational measures have not been uniformly successful in providing enriched learning experiences that are sustained over the years. Besides, many families who do all the right things produce some children who are average or high achievers and others who are underachievers or poor achievers.

It seems unlikely that a single cause will ever be established for underachievement. Whatever the cause, counselors and teachers are committed to providing assistance to those students who need special instruction and counseling to achieve at a level commensurate with their abilities. The effectiveness of the services they render to such students depends on their professional competence and their ability to diagnose factors that contribute to the student's difficulty and to plan and conduct informed practices that correct deficiencies.

2. *Diagnostic tests used in assessing academic status and deficits are of little value.*
   Yes, because:
   1. Diagnostic tests fail to uncover or identify the causes of academic deficits or deficiencies.
   2. The psychometric properties (reliability, validity, norms) of many published diagnostic measures are inadequate and fail to meet the minimum standards set forth for such measures by professional associations.

   No, because:
   1. Assessment based on diagnostic tests provides feedback to students, which, properly given, often functions as reinforcement in mastering basic skills.
   2. Diagnostic tests provide a detailed analysis of a student's strengths and weaknesses. This information can be used by teachers, counselors, and the students themselves to plan and implement efforts to improve their performance. Without such information, it is practically impossible for a counselor or teacher to make systematic efforts to change things for the better.
   3. Diagnostic test data, despite their known limitations, serve as a catalyst or as an incentive to undertake corrective actions.

   Discussion:
   The use of diagnostic tests is beset with many difficulties, particularly if diagnosis is viewed in the traditional sense of deciding on the nature of a thing. Viewed in another way, diagnosis may be seen as the most important single activity engaged in by a counselor. Whether overt or covert, intentional or unintentional, diagnosis, in terms of understanding a student's academic status and functioning, underlies every decision made by the counselor. Without diagnostic test information, the counselor knows little more than the student does about his or her

behavior or academic difficulty. The value of diagnostic test data lies in providing information that permits hypotheses to be made about students' problems. Diagnostic test data are used, then, to formulate rudimentary propositions about corrective procedures to be applied in given situations.

School, like life itself, is a series of continually changing situations. No reputable diagnostic test author or publisher claims to have captured all the significant aspects involved in poor school achievement. Their aspirations are less ambitious, and so they simply scan academic performance in given areas and classify its relationship among groups of people.

ANNOTATED REFERENCES

Deutsch, Martin; Katz, Irwin; and Jensen, Arthur R. *Social Class, Race and Psychological Development.* New York: Holt, Rinehart and Winston, 1968, 423 pp.
This is a collection of eleven papers that address issues concerning research and theory in the education of children. The volume is sponsored by the Society for the Psychological Study of Social Issues. Basic assumptions about class, race, and environmental and biological differences on children's educational development are examined.

Horrocks, John E. *Assessment of Behavior.* Columbus, Ohio: Charles E. Merrill Books, 1964.
Chapter 13 (pp. 392–417) presents tests used to assess maturation and readiness, and Chapter 14 (pp. 418–458) describes tests of subject-matter readiness. These discussions are comprehensive.

Minuchin, Patricia; Biber, Barbara; Shapiro, Edna; and Zimiles, Herbert. *The Psychological Impact of School Experience.* New York: Basic Books, 1969, 521 pp.
This book reports the results of an investigation to determine how different kinds of education affect children's learning and development. Fourth-grade students in four different urban schools were studied. School philosophies and practices ranged from traditional to modern.

Schopler, Eric, and Reichler, Robert J., eds. *Psychopathology and Child Development.* New York: Plenum Press, 1976, 395 pp.
This book is a compendium of papers delivered at the First International Leo Kanner Colloquium on Child Development, Deviations, and Treatment. Leo Kanner (who identified autism) presents a historical perspective on developmental deviations. Six papers deal with biological research, six with developmental research, and six with intervention practices. The relationships between experimental research and interventions for deviant behavior are explored.

SELECTED REFERENCES

Beery, Richard G. "Fear of Failure in the School Experience." *Personal and Guidance Journal* 54 (December 1975): 190–205.

Bijou, Sidney W. "Development in the Pre-School Years: A Functional Analysis." *American Psychologist* 30 (August 1975): 829–837.

Crissey, Marie Skodak. "Mental Retardation: Past, Present and Future." *American Psychologist* 30 (August 1975): 800–808.

Dowd, E. Thomas, and Moerings, Bette J. "The Underachiever and Teacher Consultation: A Case Study." *The School Counselor* 22 (March 1975): 263–266.

Eder, Sid. "Learning On the Rocks." *American Education* 12 (April 1976): 16–21.

Gardner, Howard. "Developmental Dyslexia: The Forgotten Lesson of Monseiur C." *Psychology Today* 7 (August 1973): 62–67.

Gerler, Edwin, R., Jr. "The School Counselor and Multimodal Education." *The School Counselor* 25 (January 1978): 166–171.

Lebsock, Marjean S., and DeBlassie, Richard R. "The School Counselor's Role in Special Education." *Counselor Education and Supervision* 15 (December 1975): 128–134.

Lewin, Roger. "Starved Brains." *Psychology Today* 9 (September 1975): 29–34.

Morse, Dee. "Counseling the Young Adolescent with Learning Disabilities." *The School Counselor* 25 (September 1977): 8–16.

Newton, Fred B. "How May I Understand You? Let Me Count the Ways." *Personnel and Guidance Journal* 54 (January 1976): 256–261.

Reilly, Robert. "Student Placement By a Maximum Likelihood Procedure." *Measurement and Evaluation in Guidance* 7 (April 1974): 8–15.

Sherman, Stanley R.; Zuckerman, David; and Sostek, Alan B. "The Antiachiever: Rebel Without A Future." *The School Counselor* 22 (May 1975): 311–324.

Sugar, Marilyn Susman, and McKelvey, William. "Case Analysis: Consultation and Counseling." *Elementary Guidance and Counseling* 10 (March 1976): 218–221.

Thomas, Jerry R., and Chissom, Brad S. "Relationship Between Teacher Ratings and Objective Tests of Aptitude for Early Elementary School Children." *Measurement and Evaluation in Guidance* 6 (April 1973): 54–56.

Thweatt, William H. "The Vicious Circle in Study Problems." *Personnel and Guidance Journal* 54 (May 1976): 468–472.

Chapter 8   *Aptitudes*

What is the nature of aptitude tests?

What standardized aptitude tests are commonly used?

How are aptitude measures used?

What guidelines govern interpreting and reporting aptitude test data?

THE NATURE
OF APTITUDE TESTS

Chapter 5 outlined the development of general ability or intelligence tests. Recall that as a result of factor analysis, ability is separated into factors, or special abilities (for example, numerical or spatial). Since the Second World War, there has been considerable development and application of tests that permit analysis of performance in order to discover different attributes of intelligence. Special aptitude tests have been constructed that assess skills other than verbal or numerical abilities. Factor analyses of these special abilities or aptitudes demonstrate that they are composed of the same factors as is intelligence, in addition to some other very specific abilities.

The term *aptitude* has been used in connection with tests that predict future performance or status on the basis of an individual performance, whereas a test of *ability* measures an individual's current status. The word *aptitude* does not necessarily have to be applied to the tests discussed in this chapter, as any test used to predict future performance may be so classified. Both achievement and intelligence tests as well as interest inventories may all be thought of as aptitude tests when they are used to predict future behavior. However, we prefer to apply the term only to tests that assess specific skills and behavior rather than academic achievement or general mental ability.

FIGURE 8.1
SCHEMATIC REPRESENTATION OF CLUSTERS OF SPECIAL ABILITIES
SERVING FOUR RELATED APTITUDES[a]

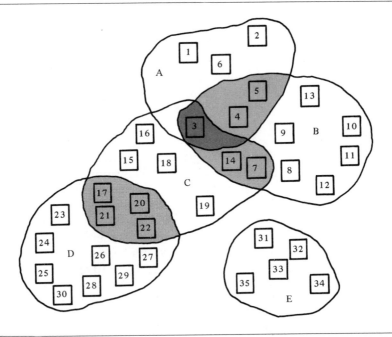

[a] Small numbered squares represent single special abilities; large lettered circles represent aptitudes.
Source:John E. Horrocks, *Assessment of Behavior* (Columbus, Ohio: Charles E. Merrill, 1964), p. 299. Reprinted with permission.

THE CONCEPT OF APTITUDE

Factor analysis of ability (see pages 131–135) produces clusters of special abilities deemed central to performing some task or function. These clusters of special abilities have been called *aptitudes*. Used in this way, an aptitude is to a cluster of abilities as general ability is to the cluster of components subsumed under the terms *intelligence* or *general ability*.

Horrocks has provided a schematic representation of a small number of related aptitudes, and his representation is depicted in Figure 8.1.[1] Aptitude *A* in Figure 8.1 consists of a cluster of six special abilities, and aptitude *B* is a cluster of eleven special abilities. Three

[1] John E. Horrocks, *Assessment of Behavior* (Columbus, Ohio: Charles E. Merrill, 1963), p. 299.
p. 299.

of these eleven special abilities are shared by aptitudes *A* and *B*. Aptitude *C* shares one special ability with *A* and two with *B*, but only one is held in common by *A*, *B*, and *C*. Aptitude *E* shares nothing with *A*, *B*, *C*, or *D*. (The five aptitudes depicted in Figure 8.1 are not meant to present a complete picture of all special abilities or aptitudes. They are far too numerous.) According to Horrocks, an aptitude is interpreted by means of what an individual has learned to do. He uses musical pitch discrimination as an example. Some people are able to discriminate precisely and accurately among various pitches. Through learning, an individual can recognize and identify the pitch, saying, for example, "That is middle *C*." Tests assess the extent to which an individual is capable of such discrimination. The assumption is that the individual has a background of hearing music that makes identifying the pitch possible. No one is born knowing that a given sound is middle *C*. Musical aptitude, according to Horrocks, includes not only pitch discrimination but also a cluster of associated special abilities such as perception of rhythmic patterns or melodic memory.

Job aptitude, according to Horrocks, is a second-order aptitude (first-order aptitudes include numerical, verbal, and reasoning skills) because it is much more comprehensive than the ordinary cluster of special abilities that make up a relatively homogeneous first-order aptitude. He defines a *job aptitude* as a group of related aptitudes necessary for performing an occupation such as that of mechanic, clerk, teacher, musician, or engineer. Job aptitude viewed in this way consists of several "different but more molecular aptitudes operating under specified conditions of general ability, interest, attitude and past learning."[2]

DIFFERENCES BETWEEN
APTITUDE TESTS AND OTHER TESTS

Differentiating among aptitude, intelligence, and achievement tests is not easy. People assume, often naïvely, that aptitude tests measure innate capacity while achievement tests assess the outcome of instruction. Counselors should recognize that all tests measure a person's current behavior, which inevitably reflects prior learning. Anne Anastasi makes two distinctions between aptitude and achievement tests.[3] One distinction involves the uniformity of rel-

---

[2] Horrocks, *Assessment of Behavior*, p. 300.
[3] Anne Anastasi, *Psychological Testing*, 4th ed. (New York: Macmillan, 1976), pp. 398–403.

evant antecedent experiences. Generally, achievement tests measure the outcomes of standardized school experiences, such as courses in mathematics or social studies, while aptitude tests measure the cumulative influence of a multiplicity of daily experiences. The other distinction between aptitude and achievement or intelligence tests lies in their uses. Aptitude test data predict subsequent performance; they are employed to estimate the extent to which individuals will profit from training or to forecast the level or quality of their achievement in a new situation. Achievement test data, on the other hand, frequently are used to evaluate an individual's status at the end of a period of training.

TYPES OF APTITUDE TESTS

Horrocks classifies aptitude tests into these four types.[4]

1. *Differential test.* Also widely known as *multifactor* or *analytic* tests, the differential test assesses a number of special abilities that compose one or more aptitudes. An examinee's performance is measured by a battery of separate tests and analyzed by scores drawn either from each component test or from a single total score. Since each measurable aptitude is useful in a number of occupations, these standard test batteries are constructed and normed in such a way as to yield scores for a number of specific occupations. Most differential tests include a verbal component and have been used in predicting success in training programs and in the labor market.

2. *Component ability test.* This kind of test assesses a single special ability, such as space perception. Such aptitude tests are published as either single measures or component parts of a differential test.

3. *Analogous test.* Such tests present the basic activities of a job either by duplicating the pattern of the job in miniature or by simulating the job. Analogous tests are based on the theory that a job is performed as a whole and that the interrelationship among the components of the job task is as important as the components themselves. An advantage of analogous tests is that the abilities that underlie a particular task need not be identified.

---

[4] Horrocks, *Assessment of Behavior*, pp. 332–334.

4. *Work-sample aptitude tests.* A work-sample test requires the examinee to perform all or part of a given job under the conditions that exist on the job. An example of a work-sample test for an automobile mechanic would be repairing a faulty carburetor. Scoring of work-sample tests is usually based on the rate of performance and the amount of improvement after a certain period of practice. Such tests are often used in hiring and classifying of job applicants.

COMMONLY USED APTITUDE TESTS

MULTIPLE APTITUDE TESTS

DIFFERENTIAL APTITUDE TESTS   The DAT is one of the oldest multiple aptitude batteries. It appeared first in 1946 and was revised in 1959, 1966, 1972, and 1974. Devised by George K. Bennett, Harold G. Seashore, and Alexander G. Wesman and published by the Psychological Corporation, the DAT is designed for use with students in grades 8–12 and in college, and with adults. The battery consists of eight tests: (1) verbal reasoning (VR); (2) numerical reasoning (NR); (3) abstract reasoning (AR); (4) space relations (SR); (5) clerical speed and accuracy (CSA); (6) mechanical reasoning (MR); (7) spelling (SP, language usage I); and (8) grammar (GR, language usage II). Scores are derived from these eight tests in addition to a special score, the index of scholastic ability, that combines verbal reasoning and numerical ability. The tests are packaged in a variety of ways: all eight tests in a single booklet; each test in a separate booklet (form T); two booklets, one containing VR, NA, AR, and CSA and the second containing MR, SR, SP, and GR. The DAT tests are all presented in objective form and are all power tests, except those tests on speed and accuracy. Administration time for the complete battery is 181 minutes, over two or more sessions. A variety of scoring services is available. The DAT manual has long been praised for its comprehensiveness. It is well written and informative without being patronizing.

One group of 1,463 students who had taken the DAT was followed up seven years after graduating from high school.[5] In general, those students who had graduated from college had been graded above average on all the tests. This result was most pronounced on

---

[5] George K. Bennett, Harold G. Seashore, and A. G. Wesman, "The Differential Aptitude Tests: An Overview," *Personnel and Guidance Journal* 35 (October 1956): 81–91.

the verbal reasoning, numerical ability, spelling, and grammar tests. Those students who had attended college but did not graduate were higher than the average of their high school group but not so superior as those who finished college; those who had attended training schools tended to fall around the average or slightly below; and those who had had no further education after high school tended to be slightly below their class average. When the occupations of the examinees were analyzed, among men, engineers were shown to have been far above average on all tests. Draftsmen, technicians, and business and sales personnel had scored around the average on all tests. Supervisors, foremen, factory workers, construction workers, and other skilled laborers had fallen slightly below to far below average on all tests. Among the women, teachers had generally scored highest on all tests, followed by nurses, stenographers, and clerks. These results demonstrate that groups of persons in various occupations can be effectively differentiated from each other on the basis of their level of DAT performance. But, as M. Y. Quereshi pointed out, this does not present evidence of differential validity, for similar discrimination can be made on the

> basis of VR & NA scores alone or on the basis of global scores on group mental ability tests. The proper evidence of the differential value of DAT should present (a) the appropriate combination of scores which sets one occupational group apart from another and (b) the contribution that a particular test makes to the discriminant function identifying people in a particular occupation.[6]

A DAT Career Planning Report may be purchased (see Chapter 9). It is a computer-printed profile that interprets students' DAT scores with their responses to a DAT Career Planning Questionnaire. The report, devised by Donald Super, presents in simple terms the student's occupational choices in relation to measured ability, preference, and plans.

GENERAL APTITUDE TEST BATTERY   The GATB was developed in 1947 by the U.S. Employment Service for use by state employment offices in providing career counseling and placement for individuals aged 16 years and older. The manual for the GATB is published in four separate sections: section 1, Administration and Scoring; section 2,

---

[6] M. Y. Quereshi, "DAT Review," *The Seventh Mental Measurement Yearbook*, vol. 2 (Highland Park, N.J.: Gryphon Press, 1972), p. 673.

Norms, Occupational Aptitude Pattern Structure; section 3, Development; and section IV, Norms, Specific Occupations.

The GATB comes in an expendable booklet edition or an edition with a separate answer sheet. Book 1 (B-1002A) contains four tests: 150 name comparisons, 50 computation problems, 40 three-dimensional space problems, and a 60-word vocabulary. Book 2 is composed of three tests: 49 tool-matching items, 25 mathematical reasoning items, and 60 form-matching items. Three other tests, pegboard (place-and-turn or manual dexterity), finger dexterity board (assembly and disassembly), and part K (marking for motor coordination) complete the GATB. Nine aptitudes are assessed by the GATB, including general ability; verbal, numerical, and spatial abilities; clerical ability; form perception; motor coordination; and manual and finger dexterity.

The GATB norms were derived initially from 519 employed workers; more recently, 4,000 cases were selected by means of a stratified quota method to be proportionally representative of the working population. Only workers 18–54 years of age were included. GATB test scores are expressed in standard scores ($\bar{x} = 100$ and standard deviation $= 20$). Multiple cut-off scores are used to determine whether an individual passes or fails the minimum qualifications for a job or group of jobs (occupational aptitude pattern). Each OAP consists of the cut-off scores of the three most important aptitudes required by a family of similar occupations. Thus, a family of occupations might require G (intelligence), N (numerical), and V (verbal) aptitudes and the minimum scores required on each are stated. An individual's profile is compared with these profiles in order to discover which fields of work are most suited to his or her measured abilities.

The manual (section 3: development) reports that the GATB has been widely used in the vocational counseling of high school seniors during the past twenty years (most recent norms were established in 1967–1968 based on 200,000 seniors). Release agreements between the U.S. Employment Service, schools, and state education agencies have made it possible for the GATB to be used on eighth- and ninth-grade students. The Employment Service has developed a test battery for disadvantaged individuals who lack sufficient literacy to take the GATB.

ARMED SERVICES VOCATIONAL APTITUDE BATTERY The ASVAB was designed in 1966 by test experts from each military service to serve all services. Since 1970, the ASVAB has been made available at no cost to participating schools. The test being used currently is AS-

VAB form 5 (1976). The twelve tests that comprise the battery are identified in Table 8.1. Six aptitudes or composite factors are drawn from the twelve tests:

Electronic/electrical (EL). Aptitude for electrical and electronic occupations is assessed by the arithmetic reasoning and electronic
information tests.
Communications (CO). Aptitude for operating communications and
other such equipment is measured by a combination of scores
drawn from the arithmetic reasoning, mechanical comprehension,
and space perception tests.
General Technical (GT). Aptitude for occupations requiring superior learning ability is assessed by a combination of scores on the
word knowledge and arithmetic reasoning tests.
Motor/mechanical (MM). Aptitude for engine repair, maintenance,
and operation is assessed by the mechanical comprehension, au-
tomotive information, and mathematical knowledge tests.
General mechanical (GM). Aptitude for mechanical and trade occupations is measured by the space perception, shop information,
and arithmetic reasoning tests.

TABLE 8.1
CONTENTS OF THE ASVAB FORM 5

NAME OF TEST	NUMBER OF ITEMS	TESTING TIME IN MINUTES
(GI) General information	15	07
(NO) Numerical operations	50	03
(AD) Attention to detail	30	05
(WK) Word knowledge	30	10
(AR) Arithmetic reasoning	20	20
(SP) Space perception	20	12
(MK) Mathematical knowledge	20	20
(EI) Electronic information	30	15
(MC) Mechanical comprehension	20	15
(GS) General science	20	10
(SI) Shop information	20	08
(AI) Automotive information	20	10
Total number of items	295	
Total testing time		135
Administrative time		30
Total test session		165

Source: Department of Defense, *ASVAB Counselors Manual* (Washington, D.C.: GPO, 1976), p. 4.

Clerical administrative (CL). Aptitude for clerical and administrative occupations is measured by combining scores from the word knowledge, attention to detail, and numerical operations tests.

A student's raw scores on the six composites are converted to percentiles and graphically displayed on a color-coded profile (see Figure 8.2).

The norm, validity, and reliability data of previous ASVAB editions were subject to much criticism. Reliability estimates, while adequate, were based on small sample sizes, and the internal consistency reliability indices were surprisingly high (suggesting that the items on the test were of a relatively similar level of difficulty, though the test is supposed to be a power test). The validity data were extremely limited, being restricted to a few Air Force studies using training success as the only criterion. Reference or norm data were based on large subject samples, but the subjects were incidentally available. Criticism was also directed at the practice of correcting correlation coefficients for both restricted range of talent on the part of the subjects and for the unreliability of the measures. (See Technical Research Report 1161, U.S. Army Behavior and Systems Research Laboratory, February 1970.) This practice has been discontinued. The volume of validity data is now somewhat more substantive and informative than previously.[7] Providing expectancy tables is a helpful service beneficial to counselors in interpreting test results to students. Improvements have been made in reporting norm data with the publication of regional data for grade and sex. Moreover, further plans have been made to obtain additional validity and reliability data.

Normative data for the ASVAB, form 5 are based on 1.25 million students in 16,000 schools. The manual (1976) reports that the reliability of form 5 was determined from a stratified sample of 610 males and females drawn from 1,500 young people applying for enlistment at selected recruiting stations "representing each geographic area of the country." Internal consistency coefficients (K-R 20) for ten tests (the numerical operations and attention to detail tests were excluded) ranged from .67 to .91 (7 in the .80s, 1 in the .70s). Validity data reported in the manual still leave much room for improvement. The data given include coefficients of .43 between vocational course grades and ASVAB scores for high school students

---

[7] See, for example, "A Concurrent Validity Study Relating the Armed Forces Vocational Aptitude Battery To Success in High School Vocational-Technical Courses" (University City, Tex.: Research Division, Armed Forces Vocational Testing Group, May 1976), 43 pp.

FIGURE 8.2
ASVAB STUDENT SCORE SHEET

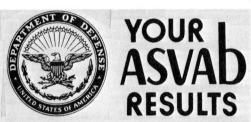

STUDENT ALICE T   GRADE 11
SSAN 162672630 SEX F CC 02
ASVAB 5D   76 SEP 15
MAIN HIGH SCHOOL
GRAND RAPIDS   MI

YOUR ASVAB RESULTS

ASVAB PERCENTILES

Composites	Raw Score	
EL	17	XXXXXX-12
CO	21	XXXXXXXXXXX-21
GT	22	XXXXXXXXXXXX-24
MM	23	XXXXXXXXXXXXXXX-30
GM	29	XXXXXXXXXXXXXXXXXX-37
CL	77	XXXXXXXXXXXXXXXXXXXXXXXXXXXXXXXXX-63

To acquire your ASVAB profile for your grade and sex, use the raw scores to the left of the graph, and the conversion tables which are available through your counselor. With this information, you can create your own histogram in the space provided below.

	10	20	30	40	50	60	70	80	90
EL									
CO									
GT									
MM									
GM									
CL									
	10	20	30	40	50	60	70	80	90

YOUR ASVAB SCORE SHEET

Your Armed Services Vocational Aptitude Battery (ASVAB) results are displayed in the histogram above. The scores can tell you a lot about yourself and can be useful when considering your future plans.

The score sheet is divided into several sections. The portion on the left contains general information such as your name, school, and the date you took the ASVAB. The colored section contains bargraphs (rows of Xs) representing your ASVAB composite scores. Each bargraph shows how well you did compared to a national sample of high school students who took the same tests. The lower half of this section has space where you can graph a more personal ASVAB profile. Your school counselor has been given the information and tables needed to help you complete this portion.

Source: Department of Defense, *ASVAB Counselors Manual* (Washington, D.C.: GPO, 1976), p. 11.

and .61 for post–secondary-school students. In addition, according to the manual, "Based on the results of a study of the intercorrelation of student performance on Form 2 and Form 5, the validity of the composite scores from Form 5 are expected to approximate those reported for Form 2."

The ASVAB has been subjected to other criticism, for example, that administering the test in schools is a means of recruiting for the Armed Forces and that, though the ASVAB is promoted in schools as having great value in career counseling, there have been no studies demonstrating the relationship between civilian jobs and ASVAB scores.[8] We believe that the psychometric properties of the revised ASVAB have been improved and that the manual has been greatly improved but still needs to report more validity, reliability, and norm data. Approximately 1 million high school students take the ASVAB each year. The Department of Defense has issued directives to its military personnel that the data are to be handled in accordance with provisions of the Privacy of Information Act of 1974 (information will be revealed only as authorized in a student's release statement) and that recruiting personnel must encourage high school students to stay in school and graduate before applying for enlistment (if enrolled students try to enlist, the recruiter must notify the school and, in some cases, obtain parental consent before processing the enlistment).

FLANAGAN APTITUDE CLASSICATION TESTS   The FACT was developed by John C. Flanagan in 1951–1960 and published by Science Research Associates. It is available as separate test booklets or as a booklet including nineteen tests and is designed for use with students in grades 9–12 and adults. Both machine- and hand-scored answer sheets are available.

The FACT represents an attempt to develop a comprehensive battery of tests based on the job elements approach basic to performance in a wide range of job classifications. Flanagan describes the approach:

> The first step in this procedure is to obtain a comprehensive list of critical behaviors involved in the job or jobs being studied. These critical behaviors are obtained by systematically determining which behaviors really make a difference with respect to on-the-job success and failure. These critical behaviors are then classified into job elements in terms of initial hypotheses regarding the

---

[8] See, for example, "Aptitude Test Probes Continue," APGA *Guidepost*, June 20, 1976.

precise nature of the aptitudes involved. The hypotheses that specific types of variation in job performance are all due to the same aptitude are then tested. Comprehensive and precise definitions of the job elements are prepared so that other workers may readily identify these job elements in jobs which they study.[9]

Administration time for the various FACT tests ranges from 5–40 minutes. Approximately 8 hours are required to administer the complete battery. Percentile and stanine norms are provided.

CLERICAL APTITUDE TESTS

Clerical positions require a wide variety of abilities. Most tasks performed by clerical workers call for aptitude in both arithmetic and language. Most good clerical workers process numbers and symbols rapidly and accurately, so rapid observation is an important factor in clerical ability. Tests that measure this skill are called *perceptual tests.* Certain clerical personnel also need skill in spelling, rapid calculation, taking dictation, running business machines, and so on. Though no test measures all these abilities, here is a selection of tests that measure some clerical skills.

APPRAISAL OF OCCUPATIONAL APTITUDES   The AOA was developed by Aurelius Abbatiello and published by Houghton Mifflin in 1971. The AOA was designed to assess aptitudes and skills believed to be important in office jobs in business and industry. The eight tests can be administered separately or as a battery. Percentile norms for high school students and adults are provided.

MINNESOTA CLERICAL TEST   The MCT is probably the most widely used test of clerical ability. Originally it was entitled the *Minnesota Vocational Test for Clerical Workers.* The MCT was developed by Dorothy M. Andrew, Donald G. Patterson, and Howard P. Longstaff and was published in 1933 by the Psychological Corporation. It consists of two parts: number-checking and name-checking. The examinee goes through 200 pairs of numbers and 200 pairs of names as rapidly as possible and puts a check on a line between the pairs that are identical. This is a true speed test with time limits of 8 minutes for part 1 and 7 minutes for part 2.

---

[9] John C. Flanagan, *Flanagan Aptitude Classification Tests: Technical Supplement* (Chicago: Science Research Associates, 1954).

This clerical test is designed for individuals aged 13 to adult. Percentile norms are provided for both sexes, for grades 8–12, and for groups of employed clerical workers and applicants. The test is hand-scored and has been shown to be useful in such diversified activities as predicting grades in accounting (r = .47, .49), differentiating between rapid and slow typists, separating people currently employed as clerical workers from workers in general, and predicting different types of clerical success. Age, except for a slight slowing-down after age 40, seems to have no effect on scores. Individuals with many years of clerical experience do not seem to have any advantage on the test over younger clerks. Sex differences are significant: the manual reports that only about 16 percent of male workers in the general population reach or exceed the median of women on both parts of the test. Among employed clerical workers, only 21 percent of the males reach or exceed the median of female workers.

GENERAL CLERICAL TEST   The GCT appeared originally in 1944 as the *Psychological Corporation General Clerical Test* and has been revised and updated several times, most recently in 1972. The GCT is designed to be used in selecting and upgrading all types of clerical personnel.

The test identifies three kinds of abilities believed important in office work: clerical speed and accuracy, numerical ability, and verbal fluency. The test is published in two booklets and is designed to be used with individuals from age 15 to adult. It takes 47 minutes to administer and is hand-scored. Percentile norms are provided based on males and females in specifically defined positions in various business and industrial organizations, as well as for groups of high school and business school students. Separate norms are available for the three subscores as well as for the total score. This test produces typical validity coefficients (.40 to .50) when used to predict success in different clerical occupations.

SRA CLERICAL APTITUDES   This test was prepared by Richardson, Bellows, Henry and Company and published by Science Research Associates in 1947, with a revision in 1950. It was constructed for use with students in grades 9–12 and adults.

Three subtests compose the battery: office vocabulary, office arithmetic, and office checking. The test yields scores for each part and a total score. Administration time is about 25 minutes, and the test is scored with the SRA self-scoring grid. The total score is the unweighted sum of the three subscores. Percentile norms were established based on 2,226 applicants for clerical jobs, 2,866 female students in grades 9–12, and 1,602 male students in grades 9–12.

MECHANICAL APTITUDE TESTS

Attempts to define mechanical aptitude have not been successful. So many definitions describe job activities or performances that George K. Bennett and R. M. Cruikshank commented, "A mechanical job as the term is ordinarily used covers a wide variety of occupations ranging in level from day laborer to graduate engineer and in another direction from locomotive repairman to watchmaker."[10] They set forth three major components of mechanical ability: (1) the capacity to understand mechanical relationships, including the complex abilities of spatial perception and imagination, (2) manual and finger dexterity and manipulative ability and the muscular coordination required by most mechanical jobs, and (3) motor abilities of strength, speed of movement, and endurance.

T. W. Harrell conducted a factor analysis of thirty-one tests and such other information as ratings by supervisors; his report was based on data collected on ninety cottonmill machine repairmen.[11] He isolated five group factors: (1) perception, (2) verbal skill, (3) youth or inexperience, (4) agility (manual dexterity), and (5) spatial aptitudes. Two additional factors, general mental alertness and motor speed, overlapped the first five factors, linking them together. In a similar vein, the War Manpower Commission administered fifty-nine tests to 2,156 male subjects and obtained markedly similar results.[12]

Mechanical aptitude, instead of being a single trait, is made up of a cluster of abilities. Because many occupations require the same basic abilities, occupations so related have been grouped together in fields. Given even a relatively small number of test scores, one can predict performance in a number of mechanical occupations. The tests discussed here are tests of mechanical information and experience, tests of spatial ability, and tests of manual and finger dexterity.

---

[10] George K. Bennett and R. M. Cruikshank, *A Summary of Manual and Mechanical Tests* (New York: The Psychological Corporation, 1942).

[11] T. W. Harrell, "A Factor Analysis of Mechanical Tests," *Psychometrika* 5 (March 1940): 17–33.

[12] War Manpower Commission, Division of Occupational Analysis, "Factor Analysis of Occupational Aptitude Tests," *Educational and Psychological Measurement* 5 (Summer 1945): 147–155.

BENNETT MECHANICAL COMPREHENSION TEST   The BMCT was published by the Psychological Corporation in 1940 and has gone through several revisions, the latest dated 1970. Its authors (G. K. Bennett, William A. Owens, and Dinah E. Fry) designed the test to assess the knowledge of mechanical relationships, general principles of mechanics, and elementary physical laws in practical situations. The BMCT is used in selecting personnel and apprentices for mechanical work and students for technical and engineering training.

Forms *S* and *T* represent revisions of previous forms AA, BB, and WI. Tape recordings of the questions are available for testing applicants with limited reading skills. The tests are also available in Spanish. The test takes 30 minutes, is hand-scored, and yields a single score. The BMCT is meant for older adolescents and adults. Percentile norms are available based on the performance of industrial applicants, industrial employees, and eleventh- and twelfth-grade students in both academic and technical high schools.

SRA TEST OF MECHANICAL CONCEPTS   This test was developed by Steven J. Stanard and Kathleen A. Bode and published by Science Research Associates in 1975 to assess the understanding of mechanics and mechanical relationships. There are three subtests: identifying mechanical interrelationships, identifying mechanical tools and devices, and understanding spatial relationships.

The SRA test is untimed but generally takes 35–40 minutes. It is designed for high school students and adults. Percentile norms for students in vocational and industrial high schools are provided. Information about reliability and validity was not available at the time this book was written.

REVISED MINNESOTA PAPER FORM BOARD TEST   This paper-and-pencil test is probably one of the most widely-used measures of spatial ability. The original test was constructed by Donald D. Patterson, Richard M. Elliott, L. Dewey Anderson, Herbert A. Toops, and Edna Heidbreder in 1930. The 1948–1970 revisions are by Rensis Likert and William H. Quashe. The test is published by the Psychological Corporation.

It consists of 64 items, each showing a cut-up geometrical figure. The items are multiple-choice, with 5 responses each. The examinee must assemble the pieces mentally and mark the response that is the correct assembly. The test is used with students 14 or older and adults. Administration time is 20 minutes, and percentile norms are provided based on such groups as apprentices, job applicants, and engineers. Both hand-scored and machine-scored answer sheets are available.

The validity studies conducted on this test are too numerous to cite here. Test performance has been found to be related to academic work in engineering, art, and dentistry. Scores on it correlate significantly with ratings of success for such workers as toolmakers, aircraft engine inspectors, certain machine operators, and various assembly workers. The manual accompanying the test recommends many uses.

PURDUE PEGBOARD   This test of manual and finger dexterity appeared originally in 1941 and was revised in 1968. It was originated by Joseph Tiffin, published by the Purdue Research Foundation, and is distributed by Science Research Associates. The pegboard has a double row of holes. At the top of the board are four bins holding plugs, collars, washers, and pegs. Tasks include (1) putting pegs from the right-hand cup into the right-hand row of holes using the right hand, (2) a similar task for the left hand, (3) using both hands to put pegs in simultaneously, and (4) an assembly task, consisting of inserting a peg with the right hand, a washer with the left, a collar with the right, and another washer with the left. Five time scores are derived: right hand, left hand, both hands, right plus left plus both hands, and assembly.

The pegboard test was designed to be used with students in grades 9 through college and adults, with the examiner giving directions of varying levels of complexity. The pegboard has been used to assess applicants for small-parts assembly-line work.

DAILEY VOCATIONAL TESTS   The DVT were designed by John T. Dailey and published in 1964–1965 by Houghton Mifflin. The battery, for students in grades 8–12 and adults, comprises three tests: (1) a *Technical and Scholastic Test* (TST) that yields three scores for males and females in grades 8–10 (technical, scholastic, and total) and eleven scores for others (technical, with subscores in electricity, electronics, mechanics, and science; scholastic, with subscores in arithmetic, algebra, and vocabulary; mechanical, with subscores in mechanics and arithmetic; and total); (2) *Spatial Visualization Test* (SVT); and (3) *Business English Test* (BET). Administration time for the TST is about 65 minutes, for the SVT 20 minutes, and for the BET 30 minutes.

Only hand-scoring answer sheets are available. Age and grade percentile norms for the TST are extensive and are based on 24,000 students of both sexes in grades 8–12 in a stratified sample of public schools, and some 5,500 technical and business school students. However, norms for the SVT do not include females, and those for the BET do not include males. There is little evidence of predictive validity for screening students in various specialties for training programs or for selecting personnel for jobs in business and industry.

SENSORY AND PSYCHOMOTOR SKILLS   Usually, tests that evaluate mechanical ability seek information on vision, color blindness, hand strength, auditory acuity, and so on. These abilities are classified as either sensory or psychomotor skills. Vision is often tested by means of a wall chart, usually the Snellen Chart, and hearing by means of an audiometer. Color blindness is tested by such devices as the Ishihara plates. Each plate consists of a background of dots of one color. A number is traced over this in dots of another color. Both colors are light in value, similar to pastels. An individual who is color blind is unable to see the numbers. Because color blindness varies from total to just color blindness for red or green, responses to the plates differ depending on the examinee's degree of color blindness. Two newer tests for color blindness have been published by the Psychological Corporation. One of these is the *Farnsworth Dichotomous Test for Color Blindness*. In this test, the examinee arranges fifteen caps in order according to color. The other is the *Farnsworth-Munsell 100-Hue Test for Color Blindness* in which the examinee sorts eighty-five caps of varying hues into four different series.

Measuring the various psychomotor skills frequently requires special and sometimes rather expensive equipment. Many modern physical education departments have dynamometers, which are used to measure strength of grip. In addition, numerous tests measure reaction time, steadiness, coordination, and body sway.

MUSICAL APTITUDE TESTS

SEASHORE MEASURES OF MUSICAL TALENTS   This is one of the oldest musical aptitude tests, published by the Psychological Corporation in 1919; it was last revised in 1957, and the manual was revised in 1960. The tests were designed for use with students in grades 4–college and adults. Norms have been presented only for various educational levels.

This battery, presented on recordings, tests six variables: pitch, loudness, rhythm, time, timbre, and tonal memory. Administration time is 30 minutes; two sessions are recommended for younger subjects. The tests can be scored either by hand or by an IBM test-scoring machine. Norms are provided for students in grades 4–5, 6–8, and 9–16. Norm groups for each scale and for each level vary considerably in size. Percentiles are used. Despite the test's longevity, definite evidence of its predictive validity has not been presented.

MUSICAL APTITUDE PROFILE   The MAP was developed by Edwin Gordon and published by Houghton Mifflin in 1965. It is designed to evaluate the musical ability of students in grades 4–12 as an aid in making educational plans. It also helps teachers adapt music instruction to individual needs and abilities.

Three music factors are assessed by the battery: musical expression, aural expression, and kinesthetic musical feeling. These factors are classified into three main divisions, each consisting of two or more subtests: test I—*Tonal Imagery,* including melody and harmony; test R—*Rhythm Imagery,* including tempo and meter; and test S—*Musical Sensitivity,* on phrasing, balance, and style. The tests consist of 250 original short selections composed by the author for violin and cello and played by professional artists. The complete battery is recorded on high-fidelity magnetic tape, and students record their answers on either hand- or machine-scored answer sheets. Students are asked to compare a selection with a musical answer and decide if the selection and the answer are alike or different, exactly the same or different, or to decide which is indicative of a more musical performance. The test takes 110 minutes over three sessions.

Eleven scores are produced by the MAP, one for each of the subtests, a total score for each of the three main divisions, and a composite score for the entire battery. Percentile norms are provided for grades 4–12 and additional norms for students participating in school musical organizations in elementary school, junior high, and senior high. Norm data appear to be adequate.

ART APTITUDE TESTS

Most art aptitude tests are directed toward assessing the abilities used in drawing and painting. Some time ago, Ray Faulkner grouped the evaluation methods into five types: (1) drawing scales, (2) art-judgment tests, (3) art ability tests, (4) achievement tests, and (5) evaluation of artistic products.[13] The first of these, drawing scales, consists of a series of scales that assess the drawing ability of young children. It employs standards based on realism rather than expression. The second technique, art-judgment tests, is widely used. These are some examples.

MEIER ART TESTS   In 1930, Norman Charles Meier and Harold Seashore issued the *Meier-Seashore Art Judgment Test.* It consisted of 125 pictures of art works, in black and white, including Old Masters, Greek vases, and Japanese prints. The revised edition (1963) by Norman Charles Meier was published by the Bureau of Educational Research and Service, University of Iowa, and consists of sections on Art Judgment and Aesthetic Perception. The Art Judgment test contains 100 items, each one consisting of two parts: an original work of art and a copy that has been altered in some way to change the symmetry, unity, or rhythm of the original. The individual's attention is directed to that part of the work that has been changed. The examinee marks in each pair the picture or drawing he or she prefers. Scores depend on the number of original pictures selected, with double credit assigned to a few. This test assesses six factors: manual skill, volitional perseveration, aesthetic intelligence, perceptual facility, creative imagination, and aesthetic judgment. The test can be used with students in grades 7–college and adults. Percentile norms were established for some 3,500 students taking art classes in 2,500 schools. Reliability coefficients for the revised edition run between .70 and .84. Correlations of test scores with intelligence test scores are very low or equal to 0. Correlations of art grades and test scores tend to fall in the .40s. Correlations between rated creative ability and Meier test scores are between .40 and .69.

In 1963, the second part of the *Meier Art Tests*—Aesthetic Perception—was published. It is composed of 50 items based on art works ranging from ancient to modern, including paintings, abstract designs, and sculptures. The examinee studies four versions of each piece of art, one of which is the original, the other three differing in design, form, pattern of lights and darks, or in a combination of these characteristics. The examinee ranks them from aesthetically best to poorest. Tentative norms exist for high school students

---

[13] Ray Faulkner, "Evaluation in Art," *Journal of Educational Research* 35 (March 1942): 544–552.

taking art courses and for groups of college students. Reliability and validity data have yet to be published.

GRAVES DESIGN JUDGMENT TEST   This test was designed by Maitland Graves and published originally in 1946 (copyright renewed 1974) by the Psychological Corporation. Ninety sets of two- and three-dimensional designs, all but eight in pairs, are presented to examinees, who then select the ones they prefer. Items are scored on the bases of agreement of art teachers, more frequent selection of one design over another by art students, and item analysis.

The test is untimed and takes about 20–30 minutes. Scoring is by hand or by machine. Percentile norms are provided based on 152 high school and 1,035 college art and other students. To date, very little research on this test has been published.

Art ability tests, the third evaluation method, generally assign tasks that help determine whether individuals can actually draw or paint. These tests are frequently long, are preferably used on an individual basis, and are administered only to those who profess a real interest in artistic training. They may be considered work-sample tests. Two such tests are the *Knauber Art Ability Test* and the *Horn Art Aptitude Inventory*.

Some time ago, Charles A. Horn and Lea F. Smith reported a correlation of .53 between scores on their inventory and instructors' mean ratings for a group of 52 art school graduates.[14] They also presented data showing a correlation coefficient of .66 between freshmen's grades in art and their inventory scores. Again, scoring such a test involves subjective judgments.

A fourth approach to appraising aptitude for art is the achievement test. Some of these tests are parts of achievement batteries, such as the art education test of the *National Teacher Examination* or the fine arts subtest of the *Cooperative General Culture Test*, described in Chapter 6. Such tests measure an individual's knowledge of art history and contemporary art.

Finally, artistic ability can be assessed by having competent judges appraise the merits of a person's artistic production. Most authorities believe that this method is as good as, if not better than, other assessment techniques. Art aptitude tests do not predict success but do screen out those most likely to fail.

---

[14] Charles A. Horn and Lea F. Smith, "The Horn Art Aptitude Inventory," *Journal of Applied Psychology* 29 (October 1945): 350–359.

USES OF TEST DATA

At present, no clear-cut, incontrovertible evidence exists concerning the structure of the mind, and no definite and dependable proof
of the presence or absence of general and special abilities has as yet
been demonstrated. Consequently, counselors must proceed as best
they can without this proof and use those methods and instruments
that, in the absence of other information, seem best for their purpose of assisting individuals in educational and vocational planning.

The transition from school to work has never been easy, and
there is evidence that increasing numbers of youth are experiencing
difficulty in making the transition. For example, in 1974, the National Assessment of Educational Progress questioned a national
sample of seventeen-year-olds about their achieving certain objectives toward a career. These objectives included (1) preparing to
make career decisions, (2) improving occupational capabilities, (3)
possessing skills useful in the labor market, (4) practicing effective
work habits, and (5) having positive attitudes toward work. Among
other findings, Ralph W. Tyler reported that

> With regard to knowing their own characteristics relevant to career
> decisions, only 40 percent of the 17-year-olds have ever taken an
> aptitude test. . . . Their knowledge of the educational requirements
> for these occupations was on the average about 75 percent correct.
> With regard to career planning, 62 percent had discussed it with
> their parents, only 38 percent with their peers, 35 percent with a
> school counselor and only 14 percent with a teacher. In preparing
> a job-wanted ad, 62 percent correctly stated the job sought, but
> only 47 percent listed their own qualifications relevant to the
> job.[15]

These findings suggest that the process and procedures employed
for assisting young people in planning a career are complex, multifaceted, and far from perfect. Certainly, the psychological information about individuals that describes their aptitudes, skills, interests, and personality traits, and the social information that
describes their environment, the forces that influence them, and
the resources at their disposal underlie the process of planning a
career. In such a process, it is important for the counselor and the
client to explore certain special aptitudes. Data concerning

---

[15] Ralph W. Tyler, "The Competencies of Youth," in National Commission for Manpower
Policy, *From School To Work: Improving the Transition* (Washington, D.C.: U.S. Government
Printing Office, 1976), pp. 100–101.

strengths or weakness in verbal comprehension, arithmetic reasoning, spatial ability, and especially in the aptitudes that play a part in clerical, technical, musical, artistic, and manual activities must be collected and made known to the person planning a career.

A primary objective of career counseling is to help the client develop an understanding of his or her personal characteristics in relation to the requirements of various occupations. This, by definition, is a broad and complex task that relies on both test and nontest data and other information obtained subjectively. Effective career counselors know when and how to use testing, when and how to rely primarily on nontest data, when and how to help counselees obtain the insights and information they need.

Some progress has been made in aptitude testing since the Second World War. The advent of the multiaptitude test battery was hailed as a major achievement that would make possible differential predictions, and, therefore, improved placements in educational and vocational ventures. For example, a series of articles appeared in each issue of Volume 35 (1956–1957) of the *Personnel and Guidance Journal* devoted to a multiple-aptitude test battery. Each article was written by at least one of the authors of the battery and each was followed by a comments written by Donald E. Super. In the lead article for the series, Super listed the characteristics required of tests used in counseling.[16] First, tests should describe a person's intelligence, interests, attitudes, special abilities, and overall adjustment. Second, a test should predict. It should reveal what an individual's status, behavior, and attainments will be like in the future. It must tell not only what an individual will be like but what he or she will do. Third, a test should be timeless. The *Meir Art Judgment Test* is of this nature, and many of the individual tests do not lose their value with age. Finally, Super states that a test should measure more than one kind of potential, because people, by nature, possess many potentials. A test should also be constructed so that it can be applied to a large number of individuals in a large variety of jobs.

Super went on to demonstrate that multiple-aptitude test batteries are descriptive and timeless and that they test a variety of potentials but that they are less useful as predictors than are other types of tests. Multifactor batteries usually attempt to achieve factorial purity for each test. Thus, their items tend to be abstract and

---

[16] Donald E. Super, "The Use of Multifactor Test Batteries in Guidance," *Personnel and Guidance Journal* 35 (September 1956): 9–15.

general in content, quite unlike work-sample tests. Custom-designed work-sample tests, then, are better than multifactor tests for selecting employees for specific jobs, but they are not as good as multifactor tests for counseling.

Quentin McNemar[17] and P. E. Vernon[18] individually investigated earlier versions of the DAT and came to similar conclusions about its differential predictive powers. They agreed that the verbal reasoning scale was the best single predictor of school achievement, with the language usage test a close second. Furthermore, the numerical ability test was the best predictor of achievement in mathematics. Finally, they felt that the remaining scales in the battery failed to demonstrate differential power in prediction but that they did provide clues that might possibly be useful in counseling. The DAT has been revised since these studies were concluded; however, it is improbable that similar studies conducted today would produce marked deviations from their findings.

In summary, it appears that multiple-aptitude test batteries do predict but not in the differential manner intended. Those parts of the batteries that contain the factors or measure the abilities present in commonly used intelligence tests do predict grades in the basic academic subjects but usually do no better than many intelligence tests. Many have observed that the verbal and numerical tests in the batteries have carried most of the load in predicting.

A prominent study was conducted by Robert L. Thorndike and Elizabeth Hagen, who sought to determine the relationship between aptitude test scores and vocational success.[19] They sent a questionnaire on educational and vocational activities to 17,000 former Air Corps personnel approximately twelve years after they had been separated from service. Each man had taken the battery given to Air Corps Cadets in World War II and had completed a biographical data blank. This battery, forerunner of the ASVAB, measured general intellectual, numerical, perceptual-spatial, mechanical, and psychomotor abilities. The follow-up questionnaire requested such information as monthly salary, number of persons supervised, self-ratings of job satisfaction and success, and length of time in the occupation. Thorndike and Hagen reported that, while there were real differences among various occupational groups, success in an occupation could not be predicted by these tests or by items on the

[17] Quentin McNemar, "Lost: Our Intelligence? Why?" American Psychologist 19 (December 1964): 871–872.

[18] P. E. Vernon, "Ability Factors and Environmental Influences," American Psychologist 20 (September 1965): 723–733.

[19] Robert L. Thorndike and Elizabeth Hagen, 10,000 Careers (New York: John Wiley, 1959).

biographical questionnaire. That conclusion led to considerable controversy. Various authorities questioned its wisdom and pointed out: (1) that Thorndike and Hagen were dealing with a very homogeneous group, because Air Cadets were a select group both mentally and physically (correlations between traits and criterion measures of such groups tend to be low); (2) that only the most successful individuals tended to return their questionnaires (this is often the case in such research); (3) that the battery was established originally to predict success in the military, but the survey covered a civilian labor force; (4) that although the occupational groups used by Thorndike and Hagen bore specific titles, they all included many different types of jobs; and (5) that many other factors believed to be associated with ability in occupational success, such as interests and attitudes, were disregarded.

There has yet to be realized a comprehensive test battery, with test weights established for all major occupational fields, that would enable differential predictions to be made with confidence. It may be that both people and occupations are too complex and too dynamic for such a test to become a reality. Though aptitude test data cannot be used for the purposes of differential prediction, they do have several important uses. While aptitude test data have been used for selection, classification, placement, and promotion in industrial, business, military, and government organizations, our concern is to show how these data may be employed beneficially by counselors.

Aptitude test data are useful in helping individuals explore occupations. Used in this way, they can identify the vocational, academic, and avocational activities from which a person will be most apt to profit. Such data may suggest general occupational areas that an individual may wish to investigate. The limits of reasonable occupational choices may be estimated from such data, particularly the amount of training that the person can undertake with profit. Estimating an individual's constellation of aptitudes yields information that permits the areas in which that person may operate most effectively to be identified. For example, a student who intends to go to engineering school ought to demonstrate high general ability, for such schools are academically demanding. In addition, an individual's clusters of specific aptitudes—such as numerical ability or spatial aptitude—ought to be identified. It is less expensive, less discouraging and less difficult for a high school or college student or an unemployed man or woman or an adult in midcareer who is considering a change of work to take a series of aptitude tests to discover his or her abilities than it is for that person to take on a job in the hope of finding out whether he or she is suited to it.

All aptitude test data, particularly music and art aptitude tests, can be used effectively to screen out those individuals who seem unlikely to profit from further education in certain areas. Those who score low on the tests usually have little chance of succeeding in those occupations.

Finally, aptitude test data are often useful in uncovering undiscovered abilities. This function is of fundamental importance to counselors in helping their clients who are engaged in career planning or who are involved in the transition from school to work.

INTERPRETING AND REPORTING
TEST DATA

The guidelines set forth in Chapter 5 on assessing ability apply equally well to interpreting and reporting aptitude test data. Here are some additional guidelines.

1. *Before interpreting test data, restate the purpose for which the tests were taken.* Tell the client that the major purposes for administering the aptitude test were (1) to survey his or her abilities in order to plan further education and/or vocations or (2) to analyze one or two areas intensively in order to better understand and evaluate assets already known to exist or (3) to help make decisions about immediate entry into the labor market. Restating the primary objective of administering the test helps both the client and the counselor gain a perspective on the values illustrated by the test data. In schools and colleges, many students take tests as a matter of routine because they are asked to do so rather than because they want to do so. Other individuals take them because they are confronting educational and vocational decisions. Members of both groups can be helped by a brief explanation of the reason for testing. A client's attitude toward test results is important in the interpreting sessions. Restating the objective prevents or removes any confusion about the results.

2. *Relate aptitude test data to the individual's educational, leisure-time, and work experiences in order to reveal occupational possibilities.* Aptitude test data are best used in conjunction with a review of the client's previous achievements and interests to formulate hypotheses concerning vocational promise. The counselee, assisted by the counselor's mature judgment and facilitating

skills, can determine which hypothesis seems most suitable. The hypothesis can be tested by embarking on certain activities. Career plans can be reviewed and revised as more information becomes available. Lee J. Cronbach has written:

> The safest way to interpret scores is in terms of items that constitute the test; i.e., "This score shows that you do well on problems like this." Any more elaborate interpretation leads quickly to misunderstanding. Mechanical reasoning is misinterpreted as "mechanical aptitude" though the test does not cover dexterity. The clerical test is misinterpreted as a predictor of success in stenography and typing whereas it actually covers rapid checking of details, important chiefly in routine office jobs. The student may connect spatial ability to art, geometry and shop courses even though the validity coefficients discourage such an interpretation. Some degree of vagueness is absolutely essential. The student should be made to feel that he can improve many of his aptitudes. He should regard the test findings as hints to be checked in other experiences. Nothing in our experience with testing justifies making firm decisions on the basis of differential abilities.[20]

3. *Remember that refinements in making occupational applications of aptitude test scores depend on the counselor's acquisition and use of occupational information.* A counselor judgment of occupational promise revealed by test scores is of critical importance and is a potential source of grave error. As we have noted, relatively few of the aptitude tests have been validated for many occupations. Therefore, counselors must not only acquire an intimate knowledge of the test but must also possess a great fund of information concerning occupational activities and requirements. A good counselor ought to be familiar with the worker trait requirements and the functions, duties, and tasks of workers presented in the *Dictionary of Occupational Titles* and other published occupational guides. In some cases, these materials may be too general to provide the insights a counselor needs to apply aptitude test data. The counselor may have to augment his or her knowledge by observing workers in action and discussing with them the knowledge, tools, and processes that are involved in performing their operations. Such information is not gained quickly but is acquired over

---

[20] Lee J. Cronbach, *Essentials of Psychological Testing*, 3rd ed. (New York: Harper and Row, 1970), p. 374. Copyright, 1949 by Harper & Row, Publishers, Inc. Copyright © 1960, 1970 by Lee J. Cronbach. By permission of the publisher.

time by professional counselors committed to improving the quality of vocational counseling.

4. *Be alert to the feelings of a client who expresses levels of aspiration higher or lower than his or her measured ability.* This guideline was stated in Chapter 6 but warrants repetition here. Such discrepancies are warning signals that emotions are likely to be aroused. The counselor's ability to accept and reflect a client's feelings makes it possible for the client to discharge such feelings, accept the facts, and discuss the situation and its implications for planning. Recognizing and accepting the client's attitudes encourage the client to examine and discuss his or her aspirations, disappointments, strengths, and weaknesses.

5. *Communicate scores honestly and forthrightly.* Communicating scores inconsistent with the individual's previous impressions of himself or herself forces that person to reexamine his or her plans. Some students overestimate and others underestimate their ability and interest in the vocational fields they have chosen. Test data that challenge these false impressions can be beneficial. Challenging distortions generates emotional conflict that counselors can respond to. By doing so, counselors encourage clients to plan constructively.

Some years ago, Donald E. Super and John O. Crites stated six principles that should be observed in reporting aptitude test data.[21]

1. Each test score should first be interpreted in terms of the appropriate norm groups.
2. Any behavior that might have influenced the client's performance, such as resistance to the test, undue tension, or systematic attention, should be identified and discussed with the individual so as to temper any hypotheses generated.
3. The relationship of each test score to others that might have a bearing on its interpretation should be reviewed and the implications noted. Examples are discrepant scores on two tests of the same aptitude or the congruence or lack of agreement between two tests of different types of traits such as aptitude and interests important in the same occupation.
4. Interpretations based on norm group references should be modified in the light of personal data such as age, sex, and educa-

---

[21] Donald E. Super and John O. Crites, *Appraising Vocational Fitness,* rev. ed. (New York: Harper and Brothers, 1962), pp. 629–632.

tion. For example, the case of a twenty-three-year-old whose DAT score reference group is based on high school seniors aged 17–19 calls for a modified interpretation.

5. Test scores should be expressed first in psychological and then in educational or vocational terms. This improves the chances that the data will be understood as intended. Counselors must explain scores in common terms that help a person understand to which educational and occupational possibilities his or her aptitudes are most relevant.

6. A summary should give a picture of the person tested, including his or her educational and vocational potential and liabilities. This summary should bring together the information that has been brought out by the tests and should integrate these findings into a picture of characteristics from which occupational hypotheses may be drawn.

ISSUES

1. The inefficiency of multifactor test batteries in differential prediction renders them useless for educational and vocational counseling.

Yes, because:

1. Such batteries cost too much and take too long to administer.

2. Counselees are served equally well by predictions of educational and vocational success based on the verbal and numerical scores of general ability or intelligence tests.

No, because:

1. Multifactor test batteries yield data that are useful in identifying types and levels of occupations that a client may do well to explore in courses, extracurricular activities, or summer jobs.

2. Multifactor test data supply information about the skills and aptitudes of individuals beyond that provided by general ability tests.

Discussion:

Predicting success in any occupation is very difficult. The disappointing differential prediction outcomes associated with multifactor tests may be related to several reasons, not the least being that certain occupational characteristics may be acquired in training or even on the job itself. It has yet to be proved, though it is often assumed, that a person holding a job is unchanged since the time when he or she began training for that job. Nor is a counselee certain to retain current characteristics while he or she trains for and begins a job.

Aptitude test data have proved useful in helping individuals clarify their strengths and weaknesses and narrow their range of choices among vocations. They have also proved beneficial in encouraging adult clients to explore both their personal characteristics and their occupations.

2. *Multifactor test batteries should be included as a regular part of the school's testing program.*

Yes, because:

1. They yield differential information that is not provided by any other test but is needed by every school.
2. The information yielded by differential test batteries is needed by every student in the upper grades for educational and vocational planning, including selection of curriculum and courses.

No, because:

1. Testing programs and, therefore, the tests that make up the programs should be tailored to the needs of individual schools.
2. Students who go on to college need not be given multifactor tests, because general ability tests can be used as effectively to assess their potential for college study.

Discussion:

Counselors and their colleagues in education have to decide whether multifactor test batteries would be beneficial in their school. There does appear to be a current swing away from the general ability test, but counselors who plan to follow the trend may be disappointed with the instruments that have been designed to replace them. Counselors must remember that general ability tests are not meant to provide reliable evidence of the presence or absence of special abilities, that they are not valid measures of fitness for particular occupations, and that they must not be used independently of other measures or evidence. Furthermore, we believe that most schools test too much and use the results too little.

A long-established but too often ignored principle of testing is that multifactor tests, like other tests, should be used in order to provide information needed by counselors and their clients. No doubt the need for differential measures increases as students move on in high school and as special opportunities, achievements, training, and interests begin to exert their influence. We feel that the cost and long administration time forbid *carte-blanche* inclusion of multifactor tests in most school testing programs. Such test batteries are best used on a selective basis with those individuals who need the information provided by the tests. Furthermore, it is not always necessary to administer the complete test battery. Selective use can be made of differential battery subtests. Counselors, guided by their knowledge of an individual's prior academic performance, expressed and surveyed interests, work habits, and vocational goals, can suggest mechanical, clerical, spatial, musical, and/or other aptitude tests that will help that individual make choices and act on them. We recommend that counselors depend on tests carefully selected to meet a client's needs. In making hypotheses based on such tests, counselors should remember that these hypotheses must be substantiated by other sources. Test scores in and of themselves answer few questions completely and solve few problems. Nevertheless, the hints, leads, suggestions, and cues obtained from differential test data are likely to help in vocational planning even though such tests do not automatically match individuals to suitable courses of study and occupations.

ANNOTATED REFERENCES

Bennett, George K.; Seashore, H. G.; and Wesman, A. G., eds. *Counseling from Profiles.* New York: The Psychological Corporation, 1951.
Cases are reported of thirty students in grades 8–12 who exhibit a variety of realistic problems that aptitude profiles are useful in solving. The editors comment on the ways in which the test interpretation was handled by the counselor. Although the data discussed pertain to earlier DAT editions, the monograph remains most useful to the beginning counselor, as the principles it establishes for interpreting profiles apply to all test data.

Buros, Oscar K., ed. *Vocational Tests and Reviews.* Highland Park, N.J.: Gryphon Press, 1975, 1114 pp.
This monograph presents 649 vocational tests, 675 test reviews, 65 excerpted reviews, and 6,652 specific test references. It treats tests in the

business education, multi-aptitude and vocations sections of the seven *Mental Measurement* yearbooks.

Harkness, Charles A. *Career Counseling.* Springfield, Ill.: Charles C. Thomas, 1976, 311 pp.
Chapter 9 (pp. 126–139) discusses the use of tests in career counseling. Aptitude test data are covered briefly and generally.

Mehrens, William A., and Lehmann, Irvin J. *Standardized Tests in Education.* 2nd ed. New York: Holt, Rinehart and Winston, 1975, 369 pp.
Aptitude measures are covered in a chapter that is well-written, concise, and understandable.

SELECTED REFERENCES

Bauer, David H. "Error Source in Aptitude and Achievement Test Scores: A Review and Recommendations." *Measure and Evaluation in Guidance* 6 (April 1973): 28–34.

Carbuhn, Wayne M., and Wells, Ivan C. "Use of Nonreading Aptitude Tests (NATB) for Selecting Mental Retardates for Competitive Employment." *Measurement and Evaluation in Guidance* 5 (January 1973): 460–467.

Cochran, Donald J.; Vinitsky, Michael H.; and Warren, Penelope. "Career Counseling: Beyond 'Test and Tell.'" *Personnel and Guidance Journal* 52 (June 1974): 659–664.

Cohen, Charles, and Drugo, John. "Test-Retest Reliability of the Singer Vocational Evaluation System." *Vocational Guidance Quarterly* 24 (March 1976): 267–270.

Droege, Robert C. "GATB Longitudinal and Maturation Study." *Personnel and Guidance Journal* 44 (May 1966): 919–930.

Goldman, Roy D., and Hewitt, Barbara Newlin. "The Scholastic Aptitude Test 'Explains' Why College Men Major In Science More Often Than College Women." *Journal of Counseling Psychology* 23 (January 1976): 50–54.

Heath, Douglas H. "Adolescent and Adult Predictors of Vocational Adaptation." *Journal of Vocational Behavior* 9 (August 1976): 1–20.

Heikkinen, Charles A. "Counseling Rejected Applicants: Feedback for Career Development." *Personnel and Guidance Journal* 53 (February 1975): 446–452.

Ingersoll, Ralph W., and Peters, Herman J. "Predictive Indices of the GATB." *Personnel and Guidance Journal* 44 (May 1966): 931–937.

Ivancevich, John M. "Predicting Job Performance by Use of Ability Tests and Studying Job Satisfaction as a Moderating Variable." *Journal of Vocational Behavior* 9 (August 1976): 87–98.

Lewis, Michael D., and Warren, Phyllis. "The Counselor and Armed Forces Recruitment." *Personnel and Guidance Journal* 53 (January 1975): 357–362.

Lister, James L., and McKenzie, D. H. "A Conceptual Framework for the Improvement of Test Interpretations In Counseling." *Personnel and Guidance Journal* 45 (September 1966): 61–65.

Mastie, Marjorie M. "Test Review: Differential Aptitude Tests, Form S and T, with Career Planning Program." *Measurement and Evaluation in Guidance* 9 (July 1976): 87–95.

Nevo, Barukh. "The Effects of General Practice, Specific Practice and Item Familiarization on Change in Aptitude Test Scores." *Measurement and Evaluation in Guidance* 9 (April 1976): 16–21.

Noeth, Richard J. "Converting Student Data to Counseling Information." *Measurement and Evaluation in Guidance* 9 (July 1976): 60–69.

Pearson, Henry G. "Self-Identification of Talents: First Step in Finding Career Directions." *Vocational Guidance Quarterly* 24 (September 1975): 20–27.

Schmidt, B. June. "Prediction of Success in Clerical Occupations from Ability Test Scores." *Vocational Guidance Quarterly* 24 (September 1975): 68–72.

Scott, Owen, and Castles, Janice. "Aptitude, Motivation, and Life History as Predictors of the Non-Academic Accomplishments of High School Seniors." *Measurement and Evaluation in Guidance* 8 (April 1975): 37–42.

Sharf, Richard S. "Evaluation of a Computer-Based Narrative." *Measurement and Evaluation in Guidance* 11 (April 1978): 50–53.

Thompson, Albert P. "Client Misconceptions in Vocational Counseling." *Personnel and Guidance Journal* 55 (September 1976): 30–33.

Thorndike, Robert L. "The Prediction of Vocational Success." *Vocational Guidance Quarterly* 11 (Summer 1963): 179–187.

Wolfson, Karen P. "Career Development Patterns of College Women." *Journal of Counseling Psychology* 23 (March 1976): 119–125.

Part 4

Assessment in the Affective Domain

In this section, we shall consider the measures designed to assess individual interests, attitudes, values, and personality characteristics. These tests reveal people's day-to-day habitual or typical performances and preferences and therefore differ from tests that require an individual to demonstrate his or her peak performance. In typical behavior testing, an examinee is instructed to respond in a way that reflects how he or she usually thinks, feels, or acts. Considerable evidence supports the relative stability of people's behavioral patterns beyond midadolescence.

In Chapter 9, we shall discuss interests, and the relatively recent emphasis in testing on the conceptualization of and measurement of vocational maturity and career development. The concepts of attitude, values, personality, and motivation are detailed in Chapter 10. Measurements of such phenomena often describe only the whats of behavior. If one is to attach meaning to these behaviors, one must discover why people behave as they do.

Chapter 9   *Interests and Vocational Maturity*

Why do people behave as they do?

What is the nature of interests, career development, and vocational maturity?

What principal features characterize widely used interest inventories?

How do measures of career development and vocational maturity differ from conventional interest inventories?

What special considerations are pertinent to interpreting data about interests, career development, and vocational maturity?

MOTIVATION
AND VOCATIONAL INTERESTS

A basic premise of the behavioral sciences is that behavior is purposive. If behavior were totally random, there could be no science of behavior, for science requires system, order, and purpose in order to permit prediction. Random behavior provides no basis for prediction. Human behavior can be predicted, albeit imperfectly. In that it suggests order, system, and purpose, human behavior is *motivated.*

Abraham Maslow speculated that human behavior may be explained in light of the efforts of individuals to satisfy certain needs.[1] He described a hierarchy of such needs in ascending order from physiological and survival needs through social needs to philosophical needs. The awareness of social needs does not emerge until an individual has satisfied the basic physiological needs. We feel that Maslow's highest category of needs—the philosophical needs—are

---

[1] Abraham H. Maslow, *Motivation and Personality* (New York: Harper and Brothers, 1954).

an academic's dream. Very few people are free to pursue knowledge, truth, and beauty for the sake of becoming all that their potential permits. The motivations of most people are linked to the more fundamental survival and social needs. Efforts to satisfy these needs consume their daily lives. Other people, whose survival needs have for the most part been met, are motivated to assume and advance in positions of social significance and responsibility. A person who holds a position of value to the community is to some extent guaranteed that his or her survival needs will be met. Those lacking in such social value often are subject to the whims of their environment. Social attitudes in favor of providing for the continued existence of economically nonproductive individuals come and go. Thus, the fate of nonbeing exists for those who are unable to or who do not contribute to the economic foundation of their social order.

Maslow's scheme of human behavior has implications for determining the interests of individuals. John C. Darley and Theda Hagenah have stated:

> Below some cut-off point in the occupational hierarchy, work primarily is the means to an end of survival and minimal subsistence. The tasks of jobs are not in themselves intrinsically interesting, challenging or satisfying. Above the cut-off point survival and subsistence needs are met and the task of the job may appeal to intrinsic satisfactions, interests and needs. Job satisfaction studies are implicitly founded on some continuum of extrinsic-intrinsic satisfaction elements. . . .[2]

The modal interest inventory usually asks questions about people's intrinsic needs ("What do you want to do?") rather than questions with an extrinsic orientation ("Under what circumstances do you wish to work?" or "What do you wish to receive as a consequence of your labor?"). Recently, interest and career maturity inventories have shown an improved approach to extrinsic issues. Nonetheless, the bulk of such inventories still reflect a bias in favor of the individual who, by virtue of social condition, is free to take the intrinsic view of his or her needs and desires. The suitability of these measures for use with all people is suspect, for a variety of reasons.

---

[2] John C. Darley and Theda Hagenah, *Vocational Interest Measurement, Theory and Practice* (Minneapolis: The University of Minnesota Press, 1955), p. 169.

THE CONCEPT OF INTERESTS

Economists have generally assumed that people are motivated to work in order to gain profit. Sociologists see one's choice of work as a result of one's sex, family traditions of occupation, and social class, and the social forces that surround an individual. Anthropologists attribute a person's place in the world of work as a function of interaction with cultural forces. Psychologists feel that work supplies a person with experiences and relationships that, in turn, fulfill unique personal needs.

People have long believed that certain temperaments and certain occupations are closely related. However, attempts to document scientifically certain anecdotally observed relationships between personality and occupation have failed to support such popular conceptions.

In 1931, D. Freyer published a comprehensive review of the literature of interests. Freyer distinguished between *subjective* interests (those pursued because they bring pleasure or avoided because they are unpleasant) and *objective interests* (behavior that can be observed by others). He thought of both subjective and objective interests as "acceptance-rejection activity . . . observed in the behavior of the individual and in his(her) estimates of pleasure and displeasure when stimulated by an interest situation."[3]

At about the same time, Edward K. Strong, Jr., was working at the Carnegie Institute of Technology developing an interest inventory. Like Freyer, Strong postulated a learning theory explanation of interest.[4] In contrast to Freyer, he placed interest clearly within the domain of motivation, and he expressed confidence that clusters of related interests, attitudes, and personality factors would eventually be defined and be shown to be associated with the choice of and satisfaction with an occupation.

THE DYNAMIC
CHARACTER OF INTERESTS

In 1940, H. D. Carter introduced the concept of the dynamic character of interests and took into account the social forces that affect adolescents in the process of developing interests, choosing a career,

---

[3] D. Freyer, *The Measurement of Interests* (New York: Henry Holt, 1931), p. 16.
[4] Edward K. Strong, Jr., *Vocational Interests of Men and Women* (Stanford, Calif.: Stanford University Press, 1943), pp. 4, 6.

and achieving both an acceptable self-concept and satisfaction with one's status in life.[5] He also noted the role played by one's value system in narrowing one's range of possible occupations.

In 1941, John Darley suggested that differential interests reflect the process of personality development.[6] He felt that measured vocational interests are dynamic factors and should be considered a phase of personality measurement. Congruent with this dynamic theme, Edwin S. Bordin asserted that, in responding to an interest inventory item, an individual expresses an acceptance or rejection of the self performing a given stereotyped occupational role.[7] Therefore, in responding to the broad range of items included in a typical interest inventory, a person reveals the self in a dynamic way through a pattern of perceived role performance, likes, and dislikes.

Donald E. Super defined interest with even greater precision.[8] According to his definition, *expressed interest* is the verbal statement of liking for any stimulus such as an object, an activity, a task, or an occupation. *Manifest interest* refers to evidence of participation in an activity, task, or occupation and can be observed by others (recall Freyer). *Tested interest* refers to interests measured by such objective devices as free-association measures or information measures (recall Freyer). *Inventoried interest* he defined essentially in terms that refer to instruments such as the *Strong Vocational Interest Blanks*; that is, the assignment of an empirically determined weight to every possible response to extended lists of activities or occupations based on the study of the responses of various social groups. Super also pointed out that the term *interest* has been used to mean both degree of interest or strength of motivation and drive or need. In this latter usage, Super's position is similar to that of Bordin.

Psychologists trained in clinical skills during the Second World War brought a variety of projective, objective, and other clinical methods (such as the *Rorschach Diagnostik*, the *Thematic Apperception Test*, the *Minnesota Multiphasic Inventory*, and unstructured interviews) to bear on measuring the relationship between personality and career. One of the most imposing series of studies of the relationship between personality and occupation began with

[5] H. D. Carter, "Resources for the Consultant: The Development of Vocational Attitudes," *Journal of Consulting Psychology* 4 (1940): 185.

[6] John G. Darley, "The Theoretical Basis of Interest," in *The Strong Vocational Interest Blank: Research and Uses*, ed. Wilbur Layton (Minneapolis: University of Minnesota Press, 1960), p. 123.

[7] Edwin S. Bordin, "A Theory of Vocational Interests as Dynamic Phenomena," *Educational and Psychological Measurement* 3 (1943): 49–65.

[8] Donald E. Super, *Appraising Vocational Fitness*, 1st ed. (New York: Harper, 1949).

Anne Roe's initial Rorschach studies of scientists and technicians,[9] was extended and summarized in her book, *The Psychology of Occupations*,[10] and culminated in a major test of her hypotheses, the results of which were published in 1964.[11] Anne Roe and M. Siegelman concluded that accurate predictions were possible only at low levels of probability.

A number of other efforts such as those by R. H. Schaffer, who conceived an interest measurement as a general type of need measurement, were also published.[12] Schaffer reported moderate correlations, which revealed that a job can fulfill personal needs, and when it does, there is subjective experience of satisfaction. When one's most important needs are not satisfied, job satisfaction is low even if less important needs are met. Bordin, Barbara Nachmann, and S. J. Segal published a paradigm for analyzing specific occupations for the types of personality needs each was able to satisfy.[13]

THE STRUCTURAL
APPROACH TO INTERESTS

In 1954, J. P. Guilford reported the results of a factor analytic study intended to examine the basic dimensions of interests.[14] In general, Guilford's data verified other factor studies of the *Strong Vocational Interest Blanks*. The mechanical, scientific, aesthetic, social-welfare, business-detail, and business-contact factors reported in Guilford's study are similar to those that have been found to be characteristic of score clusters in the *Strong Vocational Interest Blank*. To this list, Guilford added a factor involving interest in outdoor work.

For many years, John Holland studied the career patterns of National Merit scholars. In 1959, these studies culminated in the postulation of a theory of career development that describes in detail the personality types thought to be stereotypic for certain careers. Holland theorized that career choices are an extension of

---

[9] Anne Roe, "A Rorschach Study of a Group of Scientists and Technicians," *Journal of Consulting Psychology* 10 (1946): 317–327.

[10] Anne Roe, *The Psychology of Occupations* (New York: Wiley, 1956).

[11] Anne Roe and M. Siegleman, "The Origin of Interests," *APGA Inquiry Studies*, no. 1 (Washington, D.C.: American Personnel and Guidance Association, 1964).

[12] R. H. Schaffer, "Job Satisfaction as Related to Need Satisfaction in Work," *Psychological Monographs* 364 (1953).

[13] Edwin S. Bordin, Barbara Nachmann, and S. J. Segal, "An Articulated Framework for Vocational Development," *Journal of Counseling Psychology* 10 (1963): 107–118.

[14] J. P. Guilford et al., "A Factor Analytic Study of Human Interests," *Psychological Monographs* 68, no. 375 (1954).

personality and represent an attempt to implement broad personal behavioral styles in the context of one's work.[15]

A person choosing a vocation responds to the environment in certain ways that Holland terms *modal personal orientations.* These orientations correspond to six occupational environments, designated *realistic, investigative* (previously labeled *intellectual*), *social, conventional, enterprising,* and *artistic.* Each orientation represents a somewhat distinctive lifestyle, characterized by preferred methods for dealing with daily problems and including such variables as values and interests, preferences for playing various roles and avoiding others, interpersonal skills, and other factors. Each person's orientations may be ranked according to their relative strength. The lifestyle heading the hierarchy determines one's major direction of choice (see Table 9.1). The clarity, persistence, and stability of a person's choice depend on the order of the other five orientations. (This presumes a stereotypic order of the orientations within each occupation.) To the extent that his or her pattern matches the stereotype, a person may be said to be in the proper occupation.

Holland introduced the notion that people project their views of themselves and the world of work onto occupational titles. He states that interests are reflections of personality. Studies by D. H. Nafziger and S. T. Helms,[16] Carol M. Toenjes and Fred H. Borgen,[17] and Robert Schussel[18] provide evidence of the validity of Holland's occupational classification.

**THE CONCEPTS
OF CAREER DEVELOPMENT
AND VOCATIONAL MATURITY**

In 1951, a multidisciplinary team, Ginzberg, Ginzberg, Axelrod, and Herma, published a book that became a focus of debate.[19] They charged that vocational guidance professionals never produce theoretical statements that can be tested by research. They also stated that they had found the personal-need theory of occupational choice

[15] John L. Holland, "A Theory of Vocational Choice," *Journal of Counseling Psychology* 6 (1959): 32.

[16] D. H. Nafziger and S. T. Helms, "Cluster Analysis of Interest Inventory Scales as Tests of Holland's Occupational Classification," *Journal of Applied Psychology* 59 (1974): 344–353.

[17] Carol M. Toenjes and Fred H. Borgen, "Validity Generalization of Holland's Hexagonal Model," *Measurement and Evaluation in Guidance* 7 (July 1974): 79–85.

[18] Robert Schussel, "Circularity of Vocational Interests: Spherical Analysis of VIP Items," *Measurement and Evaluation in Guidance* 7 (July 1974): 86–91.

[19] E. Ginzberg *et al., Occupational Choice* (New York: Columbia University Press, 1951).

TABLE 9.1
HOLLAND'S TYPOLOGY OF PERSONAL ORIENTATION

TYPE	VOCATIONAL INTERESTS	BEHAVIORAL DESCRIPTION	PERSONALITY CHARACTERISTICS
REALISTIC	Agricultural Technical Skilled	Exhibits aggressive behavior; emphasizes activities involving motor coordination; prefers concrete "down to earth" activities; avoids interpersonal contact	Unsociable, mature, masculine, extroverted, persistent
INVESTIGATIVE	Scientific	Thinking rather than acting; organizing and understanding rather than dominating or persuading; avoids close interpersonal contact	Unsociable, masculine, radical, self-sufficient, dedicated to scholarly work, introverted, persistent
ARTISTIC	Musical Artistic Literary Dramatic	Strong desire for self-expression; dislikes structure; feminine; little self-control; expressive of emotion; tasks emphasize physical skills or interpersonal interactions	Immature, effeminate, guarded, introverted
SOCIAL	Educational Therapeutic Religious Social Service	Needs attention; seeks interpersonal relations; avoids problem solving, use of physical skills, or highly ordered activities	Sociable, cheerful, adventurous, verbal, conservative, feminine, dominant, dependent, responsible, humanistic
ENTERPRISING	Social-Persuasive Roles	Use of verbal skills for manipulating and dominating; aspires to power and status	Sociable, dominant, cheerful, adventurous, conservative, dependent, impulsive, nonintellectual, playful, extroverted
CONVENTIONAL	Clerical Computational	Concern for rules and regulations, self-control; seeks structure and order; subordination of personal needs; strong identification with power and status	Conforming, masculine, conservative, dependent, playful, extroverted, responsible

to be so lacking in confirmation that they had stopped collecting data on the issue early in their investigation. They presented an alternative position based on the theory that occupational choice is a developmental phenomenon that involves a series of choices. In the first stage, during ages 6–11, one's choice is based on fantasy. During adolescence, one's tentative choice is based on subjective criteria. In the third and last stage, early adulthood, one's realistic choice reflects the use of objective criteria in evaluating the suitability of an occupation.

Donald Super answered Ginzberg's criticisms with a ten-point theory of occupational choice.[20] He defined vocational choice in terms of implementing one's self-concept. Later, Super reformulated his theory into a developmental theory of vocational behavior, which postulated certain vocational tasks that must be accomplished in specific stages and sequences. Donald Super and Phoebe L. Overstreet instituted a longitudinal career pattern study that terminated data collection in 1978.[21] A major purpose of this study was to gather developmental data for a sample of males first evaluated as ninth-grade students and systematically evaluated thereafter for a period of fifteen years as they moved through the process of occupational exploration, preparation, entry, and establishment, in order to compare each subject with peer norms at each developmental stage.

Career development has been defined as "the total constellation of psychological, sociological, educational, physical, economic and chance factors that combine to shape the career of any given individual."[22] The concept of stages of development is central to many theories. Jean Piaget's[23] emphasis on the importance of resolving cognitive development problems at one stage in order to permit coping with those of the next stage is similar to that of Harry S. Sullivan[24] on the developmental handling of interpersonal problems. From such theories have come the emphasis of the Career Pattern Study on the definition, assessment, and development of

---

[20] Donald E. Super, "A Theory of Vocational Development," *American Psychologist* 8 (1953): 188–198.

[21] Donald E. Super and Phoebe L. Overstreet, *The Vocational Maturity of Ninth Grade Boys* (New York: Teachers College Bureau of Publications, 1960).

[22] National Vocational Guidance Association and American Vocational Association, *Career Development and Career Guidance, Joint Position Paper* (Washington, D.C.: National Vocational Guidance Association, 1973), p. 6.

[23] J. H. Flavell, *The Developmental Psychology of Jean Piaget* (New York: Van Nostrand, 1963).

[24] Harry S. Sullivan, *The Interpersonal Theory of Psychiatry*, ed. H. S. Perry and Mary L. Garvel (New York: Norton, 1953).

vocational maturity.[25] The idea of vocational maturity began with
the work of the Career Planning Study.[26] It was continued in a
career development study during the 1950s and 1960s.[27] A major
step ahead was taken by John O. Crites,[28] who built on work that
he and other Career Pattern Study staff members had accomplished.
Since then, B. W. Westbrook[29] and Super and D. J. Forrest[30] have
launched projects that have advanced the boundaries of knowledge
and have improved the instruments needed for its application.

The concepts of maturity and adjustment are often confused.
Adjustment is the outcome of behavior. *Maturity* is best defined as
a repertoire of coping behavior that leads to outcomes and is thus
developmental in nature. However, the two concepts are related.
Adjustment is a determining factor in maturity, for past adjustments can facilitate or impede the development of modes of behavior appropriate to new stages in life. As a case in point, the Career
Pattern Study has found ability to be a major factor in vocational
maturity. In a more recent work, A. S. Thompson and his colleagues[31] and Super and Forrest[32] have found planning or future-
orientation to be the first factor in establishing vocational maturity, followed by exploration and decision-making.

Adolescents vary greatly in their vocational maturity and related
behaviors. For most, adolescence is a period of exploration rather
than actual preparation, in the sense of acquiring specific vocational
skills. The exploration continues, in many cases, for several years
after the end of formal schooling. That the vocational development
of the majority of people in their early 20s has not reached a degree
of maturity that permits vocational commitment underlies the importance of both maturing experiences and methods of estimating
degree of vocational maturity so as to plan further exploration and
to make decisions.

[25] Donald E. Super, "The Dimensions and Measurement of Vocational Maturity," *Teachers College Record* 57 (1955): 151–163.

[26] Donald E. Super et al., *Vocational Development: A Framework for Research* (New York: Bureau of Publications, Teachers College, Columbia University, 1957).

[27] W. D. Gribbons and P. R. Lohnes, *Emerging Careers: A Study of 111 Adolescents* (New York: Teachers College Press, 1968).

[28] John O. Crites, "Measurement of Vocational Maturity in Adolescence: I. Attitude Test of the Vocational Development Inventory," *Psychological Monographs* 72, no. 595 (1965).

[29] B. W. Westbrook, *The Cognitive Vocational Maturity Test* (Raleigh, N.C.: North Carolina State University, 1971).

[30] Donald E. Super and D. J. Forrest, *Career Development Inventory, Form 1: Preliminary Manual for Research and Field Trial* (New York: Teachers College, Columbia University, 1972).

[31] A. S. Thompson et al., *The Educational and Career Exploration System: Field Trial and Evaluation in Montclair High School* (New York: Teachers College, Columbia University, 1970).

[32] Super and Forrest, *Career Development Inventory*.

Super has summarized well the importance of the development stages associated with career choice and advancement and of one's readiness to cope with each of these developmental stages.

> The career model which is used in career guidance or developmental vocational counseling is one in which the individual moves along one of a number of possible pathways through or ladders up the educational system and into and through the world of work. Readiness to make decisions at each branch of the career tree as he (she) climbs it is crucial to the success of his (her) efforts. The speed with which he (she) moves is determined largely by psychological and social characteristics, but speed is no asset if the goal is unclear. He (she) enters the world of work at a point which is determined in part by the rung on the educational ladder which he (she) has reached at the time of leaving education for work, but leaving the educational for the occupational ladder may take place prematurely. He (she) progresses through an entry job into one or more other jobs which may or may not be related to each other in the sense of constituting a career field, one of progressive attainment and advancement. He (she) comes frequently to decision points or branches on the career tree but he (she) may face decisions before he (she) is ready to make them. Career guidance is thus the essence of vocational counseling when more is involved than the decision about a specific job. . . . Of great importance to career guidance and career education is an assessment of the readiness of the individual to make the decisions that are called for at a given point.[33]

To recapitulate, the starting point in any conceptual formulation of interest, career development, or vocational maturity is to distinguish between interest and ability. It is useful to consider ability as representing what E. K. Strong, Jr., called *efficiency variables*— means to reach certain goals. Such goals should be included in a definition of interest. What people want out of life is related in part to their choice of occupation.

Methods have been devised for classifying occupations functionally and efficiently. However, from a conceptual prospective such as those set forth by John Holland, Anne Roe, and Donald Super,

---

[33] Donald E. Super, "Vocational Maturity Theory," in *Measuring Vocational Maturity for Counseling and Evaluation*, ed. Donald E. Super (Washington, D.C.: National Vocational Guidance Association, 1974), p. 10. Copyright 1974 American Personnel and Guidance Association. Reprinted with permission.

developments of the past decade and a half clarify but generally reiterate long-established themes.

An occupational continuum has been postulated in which, at the upper end, intrinsic satisfactions can be found in work itself while at the lower end, satisfactions are, for the most part, extrinsic to the tasks that make up the job. There is support for some of the personality stereotypes thought to be characteristic of certain occupational groups. Clearly, there is evidence that a person's degree of concern with people in general and with social activities tends to influence his or her choice of a profession or higher-level business occupation.

Patterns of individual personality development may provide an understanding of the many ways in which interest and career patterns can emerge. For many, occupation reflects personality; for all, occupation provides an opportunity to fulfill certain personal needs and drives. Choices made are, in effect, products of individual development. They form bridges and determine the path whereby each individual discovers and pursues his or her role in life.

MEASURES OF INTEREST

The various techniques developed for measuring interest include self-estimates, interviews, questionnaires, checklists, and tests known as inventories.

Interest inventories began as measures to aid in personnel selection, but since their initial development, they have been used principally in vocational and educational guidance. They are more satisfactory in some ways than are interviews because they ask a large number of specific questions representative of a broad range of careers. A typical interest inventory consists of a list of activities to each of which an individual responds by indicating whether he or she likes, dislikes, or is indifferent to the activity or by indicating his or her relative preferences within a group of stimuli. These responses yield a score or scores of general interest from which, directly or by comparison, interest in particular occupations or fields of activity can be estimated. This approach assumes that each group of people under investigation has a pattern of interest in common that is different from that of some other group, for example, E. K. Strong's men-in-general group (MIG). Identifying response patterns that differentiate between criterion groups is one major strategy for constructing an interest inventory.

STRONG
VOCATIONAL INTEREST BLANKS

E. K. Strong, Jr. (1884–1963) was a pioneer in the field of identifying and measuring interest. He constructed the first form of the *Strong Vocational Interest Blanks* (SVIB) in 1927.

In designing the SVIB, Strong used several different formats, as he was interested in comparing different ways of presenting items. Most of the items were arranged in a way that permitted the choice of one of three responses: *like, indifferent to,* or *dislike.* However, he tried other formats, such as the choice-between-two-items response and a forced-choice format that required a subject to select three items he or she liked most (or thought most important) and three items he or she liked least (or thought least important) from a set of ten.

After constructing the original forms of his inventory, Strong developed additional scales, continuing his MIG strategy to maintain a common point of reference. In each instance, he differentiated between given criterion groups and MIG. By 1931, he had created scales for thirty-one occupations.

1966 EDITION Strong revised the inventory in 1938. It was again revised in 1966 (form T399), by David Campbell, following Strong's death in 1963.[34] The SVIB (form T399, male) consists of 399 vocational and avocational items grouped into eight sections: occupations, school subjects, amusements, activities, types of people, order of preference of activities, preferences between two items, and abilities and characteristics. Three hundred of these items were transferred unchanged from the 1938 edition, except for the rewording of approximately 40 items in order to lower the required reading level. The remaining items replaced obsolete items and items that failed to reflect certain areas such as philosophy, art, and modern technology. Fifty-four occupational scales and five nonoccupational scales, all empirically derived in accordance with Strong's scale construction strategy, were determined for this revision of the SVIB. In addition, twenty-two rationally derived basic occupational area scales were also included.

The original normative data for various occupational groups were reanalyzed to provide norms for the scales of the 1966 revision. The

---

[34] David P. Campbell, *Handbook for the Strong Vocational Interest Inventory* (Stanford, Calif.: Stanford University Press, 1971), p. 33.

MIG norm group was assembled from data obtained between 1927 and 1964 from men who comprised the criterion groups other than the specific group involved in a given normative enterprise. Normative data were presented in standard score format (mean, 50; standard deviation, 10) for which the mean standard scores of given criterion groups are all 50 and corresponding mean scores for MIG are well below 50. Despite Campbell's protestations to the contrary, the procedures employed to norm the 1966 form of the SVIB are questionable because of the fact that form M criterion group data, much of which were 30 or more years old, were rescored on the revised scales to provide current norms.

STRONG-CAMPBELL INTEREST INVENTORY   The 1966 (T399) and 1969 (TW398) revisions of the SVIB came out at the time of the emergence of the women's liberation movement. At the point when women were demanding equal treatment at work, this interest inventory with separate forms for men and women seemed discriminatory. Pressure for change from a variety of sources led to a reexamination and rejection of the rationale behind the separate tests. Accordingly, in the fall of 1971, David Campbell decided to combine two forms into a single inventory, form T325. For two years, researchers worked to determine how the revision should be done, and a third year was spent in putting the new procedures into practice. Thus, major modifications brought the SVIB "in line with changing requirements of our society; collectively they represent the most substantial revision of the instrument in its more than 45-year history."[35]

Campbell and his associates integrated John Holland's theory of career development with the empirical approach traditionally used in scoring and interpreting the SVIB. The best items from the two forms of the SVIB for men and women, T399 and TW398R, were retained to develop the SCII. Of the 325 items on the SCII, 180 were common to both SVIB forms T399 and TW398R; 74 were abstracted from the SVIB for men; 69 were derived from the SVIB for women; two are completely new. All items have been expunged of sexual references, with the exception of the term *draftsmen*. Although Campbell's primary concern was to purge the inventory of sexist items, the test was also modified in several other ways. The forced-choice items presented in sets of 10 were eliminated; culture-bound items were deleted so that the inventory could be translated more

---

[35] David P. Campbell et al., "A New Edition of the SVIB: The Strong-Campbell Interest Inventory," *Measurement and Evaluation in Guidance* 7 (July 1974): 95.

easily for use in other countries. A few dated items were deleted. Items for which certain responses were either very popular or very unpopular were dropped because they did not differentiate well. Some items retained were reworded to render them more up to date, make them easier to read, or to remove ambiguities.

The inventory is easy to administer, but scoring procedures are complex. As with the SVIB, it is necessary to use a computer for scoring. More scores are presented on the SCII profile than on the two profiles provided for the SVIB for men and women combined. A total of 179 scales is reported on the new SCII profile (see Figure 9.1). For the first time, subjects receive scores on scales based on the Holland typology, occupational scales based on opposite-sex norms, and response pattern indices for all content areas of the inventory.

Most SCII occupational scales are abridged versions of occupational scales developed for the SVIB T399 and TW398R. Scales, which formerly averaged approximately 75 items each, now average approximately 45 items because of the elimination of some items and a change in the criteria for selecting items. Campbell increased the minimum percentage difference between occupational criterion group members and the MIG/WIG reference sample from 12 percent to 16 percent in an effort to strengthen the validity of the scale. Despite a drop in the number of items, the occupational scales lost little in the magnitude of reliability estimates. Median test-retest reliability coefficients dropped from .91 to .88 (thirty-day interval). Concurrent validity, as measured by percentage overlap between occupational members and MIG/WIG, changed little; the median overlap percentage increased for both men and women by 1 percent.

The arrangement of the profile for the occupational scales has been changed so that average scores between standard score 25 and standard score 45 are presented in a narrow strip in the middle of the profile. As a result, the SCII profiles for many individuals appear to be relatively flat. Because of the uncertain validity of occupational scores based on the opposite sex, only the scores for the same-sex scales are plotted on the profile. Such occupational scores could be misleading if they were to tap an interest area that reflects large sex differences. Where such differences are shown to exist, separate norms should be used in reporting the occupational scores for men and for women. The interpretation of the profile of scores for the occupational scales is facilitated by the use of Holland's letter codes to classify the scales. These letter codes, arranged in descending order of importance, are based on the mean scores of the occupational criterion groups on the Holland theme scales,

FIGURE 9.1
SVIB-SCII PROFILE

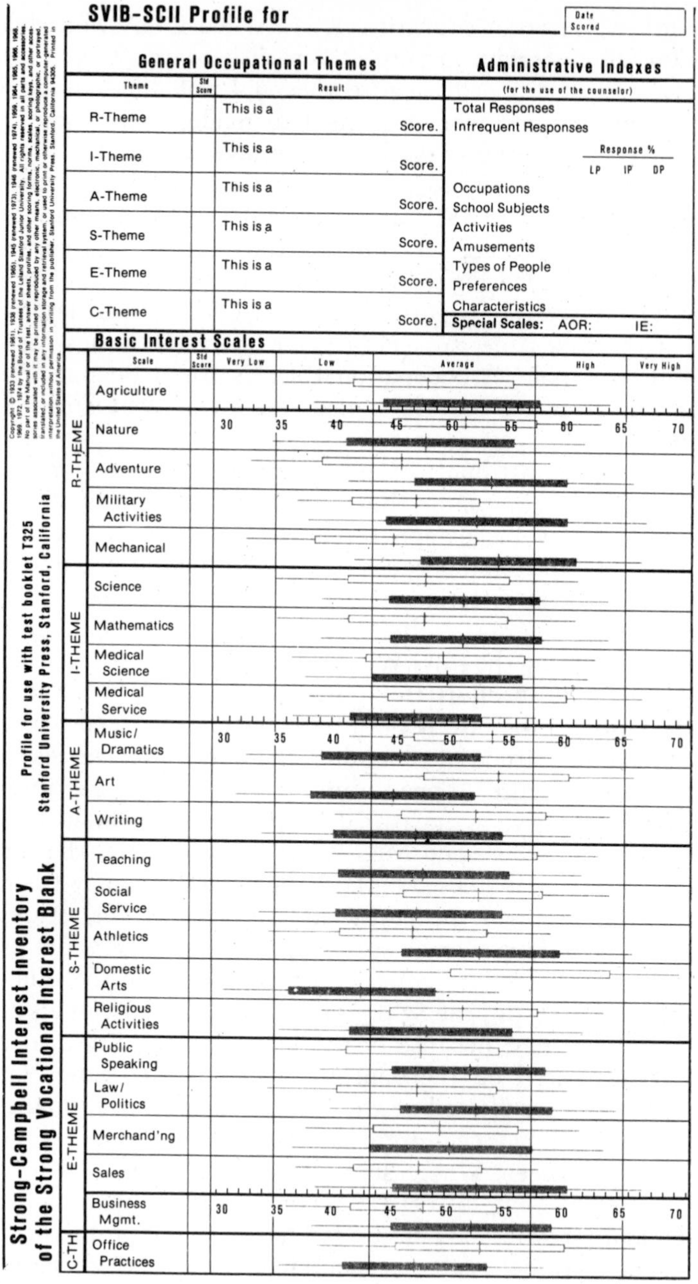

Reprinted from *Strong-Campbell Interest Inventory,* Form T325 of the *Strong Vocational Interest Blank* by Edward K. Strong, Jr., and David P. Campbell with the permission of the publishers, Stanford University Press. Copyright © 1974 by the Board of Trustees of the Leland Stanford Junior University.

Occupational Scales

Code	Scale	Sex Norm	Std Score	Very Dissimilar	Dissimilar	Avg	Similar	Very Similar
RC	Farmer	m						
RC	Instrum. Assembl.	f						
RCE	Voc. Agric. Tchr.	m						
REC	Dietitian	m						
RES	Police Officer	m						
RSE	Hwy. Patrol Off.	m						
RE	Army Officer	f						
RS	Phys. Ed. Teacher	f						
R	Skilled Crafts	m						
RI	Forester	m						
RI	Rad. Tech. (X-Ray)	f						
RI	Merch. Mar. Off.	m						
RI	Navy Officer	m						
RI	Nurse, Registered	m						
RI	Veterinarian	m		15	25	45	55	
RIC	Cartographer	m						
RIC	Army Officer	m						
RIE	Air Force Officer	m						
RIA	Occup. Therapist	f						
IR	Engineer	f						
IR	Engineer	m						
IR	Chemist	f						
IR	Physical Scientist	m						
IR	Medical Tech.	f						
IR	Pharmacist	f						
IR	Dentist	f						
IR	Dentist	m		15	25	45	55	
IR	Dental Hygienist	f						
IRS	Phys. Therapist	f						
IRS	Physician	m						
IRS	Math-Sci. Teacher	m						
ICR	Math-Sci. Teacher	f						
IC	Dietitian	f						
IRC	Medical Tech.	m						
IRC	Optometrist	m						
IRC	Computer Progr.	f						
IRC	Computer Progr.	m						
I	Mathematician	f						
I	Mathematician	m		15	25	45	55	
I	Physicist	f						
I	Biologist	m						
I	Veterinarian	f						
I	Optometrist	f						
I	Physician	f						
I	Social Scientist	m						
IA	College Professor	f						
IA	College Professor	m						
IS	Speech Pathol.	f						
IS	Speech Pathol.	m						
IAS	Psychologist	f						
IAS	Psychologist	m		15	25	45	55	
IA	Language Interpr.	f						
ARI	Architect	m						
A	Advertising Exec.	f						
A	Artist	f						
A	Artist	m						
A	Art Teacher	f						
A	Photographer	m						
A	Musician	f						
A	Musician	m						
A	Entertainer	f						
AE	Int. Decorator	f						

Code	Scale	Sex Norm	Std Score	Very Dissimilar	Dissimilar	Avg	Similar	Very Similar
AE	Int. Decorator	m						
AE	Advertising Exec.	m						
A	Language Teacher	f						
A	Librarian	f						
A	Librarian	m						
A	Reporter	f						
A	Reporter	m						
AS	English Teacher	f						
AS	English Teacher	m						
SI	Nurse, Registered	f						
SIR	Phys. Therapist	m						
SRC	Nurse, Lic. Pract.	m						
S	Social Worker	f						
S	Social Worker	m						
S	Priest	m		15	25	45	55	
S	Dir., Christian Ed.	f						
SE	YWCA Staff	f						
SIE	Minister	m						
SEA	Elem. Teacher	m						
SC	Elem. Teacher	f						
SCE	Sch. Superintend.	m						
SCE	Public Administr.	m						
SCE	Guidance Couns.	m						
SER	Recreation Leader	f						
SEC	Recreation Leader	m						
SEC	Guidance Couns.	f						
SEC	Soc. Sci. Teacher	f		15	25	45	55	
SEC	Soc. Sci. Teacher	m						
SEC	Personnel Dir.	m						
ESC	Dept. Store Mgr.	m						
ESC	Home Econ. Tchr.	f						
ESA	Flight Attendant	f						
ES	Ch. of Comm. Exec.	m						
ES	Sales Manager	m						
ES	Life Ins. Agent	m						
E	Life Ins. Agent	f						
E	Lawyer	f						
E	Lawyer	m		15	25	45	55	
EI	Computer Sales	m						
EI	Investm. Fund Mgr.	m						
EIC	Pharmacist	m						
EC	Buyer	f						
ECS	Buyer	m						
ECS	Credit Manager	m						
ECS	Funeral Director	m						
ECR	Realtor	m						
ERC	Agribusiness Mgr.	m						
ERC	Purchasing Agent	m						
ESR	Chiropractor	m						
CE	Accountant	m						
CE	Banker	f		15	25	45	55	
CE	Banker	m						
CE	Credit Manager	f						
CE	Dept. Store Sales	f						
CE	Business Ed. Tchr.	f						
CES	Business Ed. Tchr.	m						
CSE	Exec. Housekeeper	f						
C	Accountant	f						
C	Secretary	f						
CR	Dental Assistant	f						
CRI	Nurse, Lic. Pract.	f						
CRE	Beautician	f						

noted below. However, the sex of the occupational criterion group was not taken into account in assigning Holland codes. Because separate-sex norms are used in interpreting Holland codes for individuals, separate norms must also be used in assigning Holland codes to occupational scales.

The twenty-two basic occupational area scales of the SVIB T399 and the nineteen basic scales in the SVIB T398R have been integrated to form twenty-three basic occupational scales in the SCII. The item content of the new scales differs somewhat from that of the earlier scales with similar titles. The scales range in length from 5–24 items, with a median length of 11 items. The scales are reported to be reliable over short interpolated time intervals. These basic interest scales have been standardized on the same combined sample of men and women used to standardize the other scales reported for the SCII. Sex differences are indicated by mean scores and significant percentile point bench marks that are presented graphically for each sex on the profile sheet in order to communicate the same information for all scales to both men and women. Males and females have been reported to differ 5 standard score points or more in mean scores on thirteen of the twenty-three scales. Such differences between men and women conform to sex role stereotypes. Again, separate sex norms should be used in interpreting these scores.

New general occupational theme scales are intended to measure the six types of personality and occupational environments identified by John Holland. The six types—realistic, investigative, artistic, social, enterprising, and conventional—are represented by 20 items, each selected to fit Holland's description. The scores on the six theme scales have been standardized with a mean of 50 and a standard deviation of 10 on the combined standardization sample of men and women. Interpretation of the standard scores is facilitated by means of printed statements based on separate norms for males and females. Seven descriptive statements ranging from *very high* to *very low* are employed for this purpose. Scores for men and women have been found to diverge most on the realistic and artistic scales. Such differences support the need for separate interpretive statements for men and women on these scales. The basic occupational area scales have been ordered according to the Holland categories, based on the intercorrelations between the two sets of scales. Each of the six theme scales is highly correlated with at least one of the basic area interest scales. In effect, because of their brevity, the basic area scales may be viewed as subscales of the Holland theme scales. Therefore, the Holland theme scale data do not provide unique information; however, they do contribute a conceptual framework within which to organize and interpret the data reported on the total SCII profile for both men and women.

The SVIB Masculinity-Femininity scale has been eliminated; only two SVIB nonoccupational scales have been retained as special scales. The Academic Achievement (AACH) scale has been renamed academic orientation (AOR) to reflect the fact that this scale is a better predictor of academic persistence than of academic achievement. The AOR was normed on a combined sample of male and female Ph.D.s with a mean of 60 and a standard deviation of 10. High scores reflect interest in investigative and artistic activities. The Occupational Introversion-Extroversion scale (OIE), now simply called Introversion-Extroversion (IE), has been reconstructed for the new profile. The IE score has been normed on a combined sample of male and female occupational groups who obtained average scores on the old OIE scale. High scores (60 or above), obtained if an individual dislikes social and enterprising activities, indicate introversion; low scores (40 or below) indicate extroversion.

The number of administrative indices on the profile has been increased. The percentage of responses labeled *liked, indifferent to,* or *disliked* in each of the seven sections of the SCII booklet are printed on the profile sheet. Base-rate percentages for the different content areas are reported in the manual.[36] The total response index has been retained. The T399 and T398R form check scale has been eliminated. The unpopular responses category has been revised and renamed *infrequent responses.* Separate infrequent response indices have been constructed for men and for women because of the sex differences in certain preferences.

Interpretations of SCII should be made only by persons with special training and supervised experience in assessing objective interest. Results can be faked by a sophisticated subject. Furthermore, the SCII remains applicable for use only with those persons who are oriented toward professional, semiprofessional, or managerial occupations that attract college graduates. For others, the relevance of the instrument is questionable.

KUDER PREFERENCE RECORDS

Despite the long history of use of and research with the *Strong Vocational Interest Blanks,* the measures created by G. Frederick Kuder, another pioneer in the field of interest measurement, are

[36] David P. Campbell, *Manual for the Strong-Campbell Interest Inventory (Form T325)* (Stanford, Calif.: Stanford University Press, 1974).

more extensively used. Form C, the *Kuder Preference Record—Vocational*, which dates back to 1932, retains its popularity and continues to be the most commonly employed of the Kuder inventories, because of its relevance for use with the total age range of high school students, its relatively low cost, and its ease of administration and scoring. Our discussion pertains principally to form C, although much of it applies equally to the other Kuder measures.

FORM C, THE KUDER PREFERENCE RECORD—VOCATIONAL[37]   Whereas Strong's initial motivation for creating the SVIB was to devise an efficient instrument for industry, and whereas Strong employed an empirical methodology in constructing scales, Kuder's initial motive was to develop a measure for the guidance of students in school. For many years, his test-development strategy was dominated by a rational bias. Only with the development of the more recent forms D and DD did Kuder adopt Strong's empirical orientation. Authors who take the rational approach to test construction have some theory they want to examine or a construct they wish to measure. Their method assumes a universe of possible items for use with a given measure. The test author logically samples this universe, selecting those items that appear to measure the construct. On the other hand, the empirical approach requires that each item discriminate between two or among several criterion groups. In this instance the author usually begins with the rational selection of items but then checks them empirically to be certain that each item does in fact differentiate. Kuder's form C was constructed using the rational approach without any empirical check. Instead, homogeneity was the basis of the scales developed for the preference record, that is, the scales were assembled from items that are analogous in content, that are significantly intercorrelated, and that reflect some specific area of interest. In other words, the items are functionally related to each other.

With respect to form C, Kuder has demonstrated reasonable homogeneity for each of the ten scales included in the inventory. A frequent criticism of completely homogeneous interest inventories has been their transparency, that is, that results can be intentionally influenced by the examinee. In contrast, the empirically scaled interest inventory is less susceptible to attempts to distort responses. This is true in part because the subject cannot know all the interests that might be distinctive to different occupations,

---

[37] G. Frederick Kuder, *Manual, Kuder Preference Record—Vocational* (Chicago: Science Research Associates, 1946).

especially because he or she is likely to overlook negative preferences or dislikes. However, for a person who wants to explore his or her pattern of interests honestly, the homogeneous inventory is a useful instrument. People taking the test at counseling centers are unlikely to answer insincerely, but the probability of faking increases sharply when the test results may determine whether or not a person obtains a job. In forms C, D, DD, and E, Kuder introduced a verification scale intended to estimate the sincerity of an examinee's responses. Foster conducted an investigation of the verification scale for form D, in which he attempted to fake sincere scores.[38] Highly significant results were obtained. He found that if an examinee answers according to some plan, errors are likely to occur. Furthermore, he determined that these errors are not distributed randomly.

Differential response modes determine two common types of report inventories—the ipsitive scale and the normative scale. *Ipsitive* scales allow for intraindividual comparisons (comparisons within the individual). Such scales are derived from inventories on which the individual must select one activity over another in a forced-choice format. The acceptance of one activity and concomitant rejection of another forces some scale scores to be high while others are low. In contrast, *normative* scales allow subjects to accept or reject each item and thus permit interindividual comparisons, using appropriate reference group data. With a normative scale, for example, a counselor may report the degree to which a person has interests similar to those of other persons in a given occupational criterion group or some other criterion group. Difficulties arise when normative interpretations are used with ipsitive data.

Kuder forms employ a forced-choice, three-item response format. That is, an examinee selects the item he or she prefers or would like most, given sufficient training, and the one that he or she least prefers. Kuder's form C scales do not all contain the same number of items. Also, there are triads in which two (sometimes only one) content areas are represented. There is thus a greater probability of selection associated with the area that is uniquely sampled by a triad. No matter what the response is, the area is weighted. Because of the interdependence of raw scores, a difference between two individuals' percentile ranks on the same scale may not represent a true difference in interest in the activities represented by the

---

[38] R. Foster, "Kuder-D Verification Key Sensitivity to Various Faking Techniques, *Psychology* 2 (1973): 4–6.

scale. This has created problems in the interpretation of form C profile data. "A given individual's results are far more complicated than the apparently simple and straightforward scales and percentile values suggest."[39]

Raw scores for each scale defy interpretation. Raw score comparisons are obscured by unequal representation of the various scales and by the considerable range in the frequency with which various scales are pitted against each other in the form C triads. In form C, an ipsitive response mode and normative interpretive procedures tend to nullify each other, making any comparison or interpretation dubious. Kuder himself urges users of form C and form E (for junior high school students) to interpret the direct, or surface, meaning of the scales rather than to attempt to match profiles directly with occupations or to hazard making any other more demanding interpretation.[40]

Still other problems pertain to form C. Although the items deal with common activities with which most people are familiar, the forced-choice triads are objectionable to many people because they like or dislike all the items equally. Furthermore, subjects' responses to certain triads may reflect the differential social desirability of the items rather than an individual's real preferences.

Finally, form C occupational data were gathered more or less as opportunity permitted and did not sample various professions representatively.[41] Form C (as is true of all other Kuder forms) has not been investigated sufficiently with respect to reliability and validity in order to provide any guarantee of maximum predictability or usefulness in counseling.

FORMS D, DD, AND E   The forced-choice triad format has also been employed for these Kuder interest inventories. Form E (general interest survey for grades 6–12) is a downward extension and revision of earlier vocational forms (form B and form C) and includes the same scales: outdoor, mechanical, computational, scientific, persuasive, artistic, literary, musical, social service, and clerical occupational areas and a verification scale. The reading level of form E is designed for the sixth grade.

[39] Barbara Kirk, "The Kuder Preference Record—Vocational, Form C" (review), in The Seventh Mental Measurements Yearbook, ed. Oscar Buros (New Brunswick, N.J.: Gryphon Press, 1972), p. 1422.

[40] See Lee J. Cronbach, Essentials of Psychological Testing, 2nd ed. (New York: Harper and Row, 1970).

[41] G. Frederick Kuder, Manual, Kuder Preference Record, Form E (Chicago: Science Research Associates, 1964).

The items in both form D (preference record—occupational) and form DD (occupational interest survey) represent all of the ten occupational areas listed above and also the five areas of the personal form (form A): group activity, stable situations, working with ideas, avoiding conflict, and directing others. Two more personal areas were added: working independently and acting spontaneously. Form D is a one hundred-item inventory that provides a verification scale and approximately fifty-two empirically derived scales, each based on a study of responses found to be representative of men in a given occupation. The items of form D and form DD are the same.

Form DD introduced a new Kuder concept in scoring that results in improved discrimination between occupational groups.[42] Moreover, scores showing congruence with interest patterns characteristic of thirty-three college major groups have been developed. In all, 157 scales have been determined empirically for form DD. For men, 79 occupational scores and 20 college major scores are reported; for women, 56 occupational scores and 25 college major scores are available. Of the scores reported for women, 23 are based on scales developed for men. A verification scale and 8 experimental scales are also reported.

All forms are administered easily; the directions are explicit and may be understood readily. Although no time limit is specified for any Kuder form, most individuals are able to complete forms D and DD in approximately 30 minutes and form E in about 45 minutes. Form D may be scored either by IBM machine or by hand. Because of the numerous occupational keys required for form D, hand-scoring is extremely time-consuming when there are several tests to score. Form DD is scored only by the publisher. The pen-punched, self-scoring answer pattern for form E is a convenient scoring device.

Form D high school percentile norms are based on the responses of 3418 boys and girls in grades 9–12 from schools across the country. Adult percentile norms for form D were developed concurrently with form C (revised vocational) and form A (personal) from the responses of a stratified sample of 3000 male telephone subscribers (1000 per form) living in 138 cities and towns across the country and ranging in age from 25–65. Form DD percentile norms were developed from data collected from 100–500 adults in each of seventy-nine occupational groups and from 11,000 seniors in twenty

[42] G. Frederick Kuder, Manual, Kuder Occupational Interest Survey (Chicago: Science Research Associates, 1966).

colleges and universities primarily during the period 1960–1965. Only the responses of those individuals who reported satisfaction with their choice of occupation and college major were used.

Each occupational sample is identified in the manual in terms of source, size, age, and education. Forty-two of these samples were used to develop form D criterion groups. Form E percentile norms for grades 6–12 were developed in the spring of 1963 for data obtained from a stratified sample of boys and girls in public elementary and secondary schools throughout the United States. The sample is not identified further. Adult norms for form E appear to be based on revised form C norms.

The form D manual reports test-retest reliability estimates based on a sample of 117 students at Northwestern University and a sample of 96 Evanstown (Illinois) High School students. The samples involved both males and females and used a one-month interval between testings. The estimates derived for the college sample ranged from .77 to .91 with a median scale estimate of .85. A high school sample provided estimates that varied from .61 to .90 with a median reliability estimate of .78. Two separate stability studies are cited in the form DD manual. For one study involving four samples of equal size ($N = 25$) of high school seniors and college students, separated by sex, stability estimates were obtained for each sample with a two-week interval between testings. The median estimate for the four samples was .90. For both high school senior boys and girls, the median estimate was .91, while for each of the college groups, the median was .90. In a second study cited in the form DD manual involving ninety-two high school senior boys and fifty college senior women (both samples unidentified), test-retest coefficients computed for 142 occupational scales yielded median r's of .93 (senior boys) and .96 (college women). Form E stability data were derived from data obtained from 328 girls and 311 boys who were tested in the sixth or seventh grade with a prepublication form of form E and then retested four years later, in 1963. The average stability estimate for raw scores was .50 for the male sample and .43 for the female sample.

The form D and form E manuals report no data on predictive validity. The form D manual does present studies indicating that various occupational groups scored high on appropriate scales of the inventory. Studies reported for form DD were concerned with errors of classification and the rank of scores of criterion group members on the selected occupational scales ($N = 100$ for each thirty criterion groups). In the form E manual, attention is devoted to studies based on forms B and C of the *Kuder Preference Record,* in which measured interests were compared to a measure of job satisfaction obtained seven to ten years later.

The manuals for all Kuder forms include directions for gross interpretation. Specific interpretive aids are provided as part of the publisher's scoring service for form DD. Although Kuder profiles and profile brochures given to examinees are intended to aid self-interpretation, it is doubtful that adequate interpretation can be made by an examinee. An interpreter of any Kuder form should be trained in the use of these instruments in order to safeguard against inaccurate interpretation of results.

We feel that all Kuder forms should provide more complete reliability and validity data. Since the development of the first form of the *Kuder Preference Record* in 1932, with the exception of form E, little change has been made in the content of the items in the forced-choice triads. For all forms, the impact of social desirability on responses has not been investigated. Furthermore, the use of forced-choice derived scores in a normative interpretive framework is a questionable psychometric practice. Nonetheless, today the Kuder series of inventories, especially the familiar form C, remain the most widely employed measures of interest in the United States.

In 1972, Donald Zytowski concluded that neither the *Strong Vocational Interest Blanks* nor the *Kuder Occupational Interest Survey* (form D) proved to be better than the other in identifying subjects' occupations and, thus, neither can be judged as more valid than the other. Zytowski expressed an oft-mentioned caution in interpreting results of interest inventories:

> Rather than suggesting that person's future occupation is identified by his highest scores on either inventory . . . it seems more appropriate to employ scores as possibilities to be investigated and considered, or as indicators of a general area, just as the authors of each implore the user.[43]

CAREER ASSESSMENT INVENTORY

Developed by C. B. Johansson, this 305-item inventory is suitable for individuals interested in beginning work immediately or in careers requiring some post-secondary education in technical school, business school, or college. The *Career Assessment Inventory* (CAI)

---

[43] Donald Zytowski, "A Concurrent Test of Accuracy-of-Classification for the Strong Vocational Blank and the Kuder Occupational Interest Survey," *Journal of Vocational Behavior* 2 (July 1972): 250.

requires 30 minutes to complete and is computer-scored in three categories: theme scales, basic interest area scales, and occupational scales similar to the categories employed by the SCII.[44] Presented in the CAI report are data pertinent to Holland's general occupational themes. Each person is ranked on each theme, and scores are discussed in terms of their relevance to the occupational scales.

The basic interest scales are ranked from high to low for each subject, and the highest and lowest scores are explained further with occupational examples and cross-referenced to the *Occupational Outlook Handbook*. Occupational scales are ranked and grouped from very similar through average to very dissimilar. In addition, the four highest and lowest scales are listed with *Dictionary of Occupational Titles* and *Occupational Outlook Handbook* references. Applicable government reprint pamphlets are noted, and books written about fields of interest are cited by author, title, and publisher.

MINNESOTA
VOCATIONAL INTEREST INVENTORY

The MVII, in contrast to the SVIB and SCII, was designed to measure the interests of males in occupations for which a college education is not required.[45] The instrument presents 158 triads within which the examinee is required to choose the statement he likes best and the statement he likes least. Item content is oriented heavily toward occupational activities familiar to young men, specifically, the types of activities performed by skilled workers and Navy personnel. Nine occupational area scales (mechanical, health service, office work, electronics, food service, carpentry, sales–office, clean hands, and outdoors) and twenty-one specific occupational scales are provided. Both consumable-booklet and reuseable-booklet formats are available.

Directions for completing the MVII are printed on each booklet and are easy to understand. No time limit is specified, but most individuals complete the inventory in less than 45 minutes. The MVII may be scored either by hand or by one of two machine-scoring services. Hand-scoring directions are clear and explicit; however, the number of keys required may render hand-scoring

---

[44] Charles B. Johansson, *Manual, The Career Assessment Inventory* (Minneapolis: National Computer Systems Interpretive Scoring Systems, 1976).

[45] Kenneth E. Clark and David P. Campbell, *Manual, Minnesota Vocational Interest Inventory* (New York: The Psychological Corporation, 1965).

uneconomical. The consumable booklet is scored by National Computer Systems. Separate answer sheets are scored by the Measurement Research Center. In each instance, the cost is nominal and competitive with that charged by the other scoring service.

Test-retest estimates (thirty-day interval) for both occupational area and specific occupational scales vary from a low of .70 to a high of .80. Corresponding means and standard deviations are presented in the manual. These data were obtained from ninety-eight students who attended the Dunwoody Industrial Institute in Minneapolis. All specific occupational scales were developed empirically. Each specific occupational scale has been shown to differentiate men in a given occupation from a reference group of tradesmen in general (TIG). The reported index used to estimate the validity of these MVII scales was the percentage of overlap between each criterion group (N varied from 72–349) and TIG ($N = 240$). The median overlap was 40 percent. The criterion and reference groups were drawn from tradesmen in the Minneapolis area, from Navy enlisted personnel, and from experienced industrial-education teachers attending summer sessions in 1959 at four midwestern colleges and universities. No validity index is provided for the occupational area scales. By inspection of the item content, central themes were identified subjectively for each area scale. The manual also lists the occupational groups found to score high on each respective scale.

Standard score norms (mean, 50; standard deviation, 10) are provided for each of the twenty-one occupational scales and the nine occupational area scales. In the case of each specific scale, the standard scores were based on the means and standard deviations of an appropriate criterion group. Standard scores for the area scales were determined by using the mean and standard deviation of TIG.

An individual's MVII standard scores are reported on a profile sheet. The specific occupational scales are grouped according to the intercorrelations demonstrated among the scales. For each scale on the profile, a shaded area representing the range of scores provided by the middle one-third of the TIG sample distribution is indicated in order to assist in making decisions about the significance of an examinee's scores. Interpretation should be made only by counselors with training and supervised experience in the use of objective interest inventories.

The scores appear relevant for a limited sample of nonprofessional occupational orientations. These measures are not related, to any substantial extent, to measured intelligence or to special skills. The representativeness reflected by the sampling accomplished by the occupational scales needs to be improved. Lack of use of this measure may lead to its demise. As with all tests of this type, the possibility of response distortion must be taken into consideration; caution must be applied to any interpretation of results.

OHIO
VOCATIONAL INTEREST SURVEY

The OVIS was designed to be used by students in grades 8–12 in their educational and career planning and by counselors and planners in developing better educational and vocational programs.[46] The OVIS is a further development of the *Vocational Planning Questionnaire* created by the Division of Guidance and Testing, Ohio Department of Education, in 1953. The OVIS consists of a survey, a scoring service, a career exploration guide describing the twenty-four OVIS job clusters, and various interpretive materials, including a special report series that has been developed during the past several years.

The unique value of OVIS, according to the authors, lies in its compatibility with major occupational and guidance tools such as the *General Aptitude Test Battery*, the *Dictionary of Occupational Titles*, and the *Occupational Outlook Handbook*. The survey was derived rationally from the cubistic model of vocational interest reported by D'Costa and his colleagues, which is based on the data-people-things structure used in the 1965 edition of the *Dictionary of Occupational Titles*.

The OVIS consists of two parts: the Student Information Questionnaire lists twenty-seven kinds of work activities and also asks for information about the school subject the student likes best, the high school program he or she is taking or plans to take, and the kinds of education he or she plans to have after leaving high school; the Interest Inventory presents 280 job activities defining twenty-four scales or clusters of statements, each scale consisting of from 11–15 items. Subjects respond to the items in terms of a five-point Likert-type scale ranging from *like very much* to *dislike very much*. The items for nineteen of the scales are common for males and females; certain items in five of the scales are differentiated by sex.

[46] Ayres G. D'Costa *et al.*, *Manual, Ohio Vocational Interest Survey* (New York: Harcourt Brace Jovanovich, 1969).

The scoring system provides percentile ranks and stanines for comparing a student's interest with those of other students. Local norms or national norms or both may be employed.

SELF-DIRECTED SEARCH
FOR EDUCATIONAL
AND VOCATIONAL PLANNING

The Self-Directed Search (SDS) is the product of more than twenty years of research by John L. Holland.[47] The SDS makes it possible for an individual to engage in a self-directed effort to facilitate planning for education and for work. The subject administers the SDS to himself or herself and then tabulates the results. A companion booklet, the *Job Finder*, provides assistance in interpreting the results. Holland maintains, and rightfully so, that people can and should do a good deal of the work required for vocational and educational planning themselves.

Form E is an abridged form of the SDS that was published in 1970; it was designed for students as young as the fourth grade as well as for adults with limited reading skills. Requiring approximately 40 minutes to complete, the SDS booklet guides an individual through a series of questions related to occupational daydreams, preferences for activities, competencies, preferences for occupations, and an estimate of the subject's abilities in a number of occupational areas. Each subsection of the SDS presents items related to the six vocational and personality types that form the basis for Holland's theory of vocational choice. An attempt has been made in each section to provide items that range across broad educational and socioeconomic levels.

The directions are clear and straightforward. When a subject completes the SDS, he or she is provided with a summary code comprising the types that rank first and second across all subtests. With this code in hand, the respondent is referred to the *Job Finder*, which contains information about 456 jobs listed in terms of two-letter SDS codes. Each entry in the *Job Finder* includes the job title, the *Dictionary of Occupational Titles* reference number, and the level of general educational development required for that occupation. Having made a list of jobs that correspond to a summary code,

[47] John L. Holland, *Professional Manual, The Self-Directed Search* (Palo Alto, Calif.: Consulting Psychologists Press, 1972).

the individual is provided with a list of suggested next steps to be undertaken in order to continue orderly planning for education and for vocation. The manual contains extensive technical data. It presents a thorough discussion of the appropriate uses of the instrument and also includes a complete discussion of the origins of the SDS. Validity and reliability data are discussed in the manual.

Last, but not least, Holland has given thought to the basic knowledge that counselors and others ought to possess in order to use the SDS properly. To accomplish this end, Holland has included a mastery test in the manual.

MEASURES
OF CAREER DEVELOPMENT
AND VOCATIONAL MATURITY

The first model of vocational maturity was developed in the Career Pattern Study, Teachers College, Columbia University.[48] Three concepts from developmental psychology and two characteristics of mature behavior served as guides in developing this model:

1. Development proceeds from random, undifferentiated activity to goal-directed specific activity.
2. Development is in the direction of increasing awareness in orientation to reality.
3. Development is from dependence to increasing independence.
4. The mature individual selects a goal.
5. The mature individual's behavior is goal-directed.

Twenty possible measures or indices of vocational maturity were identified in a study of the relevant literature. Preliminary empirical work led to the regrouping of these indices and to a theoretical model of vocational maturity consisting of six dimensions. This model was tested empirically with ninth-grade boys and was revised.

Crites built on the work of the Career Pattern Study, first at the University of Iowa and later at the University of Maryland.[49] He sought to refine the model and to develop a battery of instruments for measuring the least well-measured variables specified by the

---

[48] Super and Overstreet, *Vocational Maturity.*
[49] John O. Crites, *Theory and Research Handbook for the Career Maturity Inventory* (Monterey, Calif.: California Test Bureau/McGraw-Hill, 1973).

model. Instead of comparing the vocational coping behaviors of an individual with those of age peers, as did the Career Pattern Study, Crites felt that comparison ought to be made with the oldest individuals in the same vocational stage. Thus, ninth-graders were compared not with other ninth-graders but with twelfth-graders. Crites postulated eighteen variables, patterns of behaviors, or characteristics that he deemed to constitute vocational maturity. The important contribution of his model is the distinction it makes between cognitive and attitudinal variables.

Both the Career Pattern Study and Crites's models focused on the structure of vocational maturity. Since vocational maturity is a developing set of traits, it may be expected to differ somewhat from one stage to another.[50] A model for vocational maturity must be both structural, as were the Career Pattern Study and Crites's models, and developmental, as none is at present. A developmental model, supplementing structural models, clarifies age changes. Evidence suggests increasing correlations between various vocational maturity variables and appropriate criteria as people mature and as the predictor measures relate closer in time to criterion measures. Here are some examples of measures intended to assess patterns of career development and an individual's vocational maturity.

ASSESSMENT OF CAREER DEVELOPMENT

The *Assessment of Career Development* affords a summary of the career development status of student groups.[51] This program is designed to inform counselors and school administrators how much students know about occupations and career planning, what they have done about career explorations, what kinds of help they need, and what effect the school's career development program has had upon them. The program elicits information to aid counselors in designing effective guidance programs, and it may also be used in assessing the outcomes of such programs.

The *Assessment of Career Development* is divided into three basic categories: occupational awareness, self-awareness, and knowledge of and involvement in career planning. Occupational awareness includes knowing about the characteristics of and preparation required by various occupations and, in addition, explora-

[50] Super, "Vocational Maturity Theory," 1974.
[51] American College Testing Program, *Handbook for the Assessment of Career Development* (Boston: Houghton Mifflin, 1974).

tory occupational experiences. Three types of information that are included in the self-awareness category are preferred job characteristics, career plans, and perceived needs for help with career planning.

This program can be administered in three separate 45-minute periods or in one 125-minute continuous session. Students record their responses on a single answer sheet that can be scored only by the Houghton Mifflin Scoring Service. Two types of reports are provided: group summary reports, including score distributions, means, and standard deviations for three knowledge scales and eight experience scales; summaries of student responses to forty-two critical questions; the percentage of students attaining locally designated expected performance levels on each of three program-knowledge scales; and, summaries of student responses to nineteen locally developed questions. Counselors can establish the expected performance levels for their students based on the objectives of given career development programs and the content of the instrument. These data can be reported to the scoring service, which in turn can compute the number and percentages of students reaching or surpassing an expected performance level. The handbook provides a full description of the program, what it measures, for whom it is intended, and how it can be used. Annotated references to diverse career guidance activities and materials are keyed to the program content outline.

CAREER DEVELOPMENT INVENTORY

The CDI is an objective, multifactor, self-administered, paper-and-pencil inventory that measures the vocational maturity of adolescent boys and girls.[52] It yields three scale scores, two of them attitudinal and one of them cognitive, plus a total score. Scale A, Planning and Orientation, contains 33 items; scale B, Resources for Exploration, 28 items; and scale C, Information and Decision-Making, 30 items. The questions are appropriate for both boys and girls, and there is no sex difference. The reading difficulty of the CDI makes its use appropriate at and above the sixth-grade level, and its vocabulary and content make it acceptable for junior and senior high school students (a college form uses suitable vocabu-

---

[52] Donald E. Super and D. J. Forrest, *Career Development Inventory, Form 1, Preliminary Manual for Research and Field Trial* (New York: Teachers College, Columbia University, 1972). Mimeographed.

lary). Administration is relatively easy and is self-explanatory. The inventory requires about 30–40 minutes to complete. Scoring by hand is difficult, but a computer-based format is available. Completion of all items is essential.

Data are reported suggesting that, for short time intervals, scale reliabilities equal or exceed .70 and that, over a six-month interpolated interval, the lowest scale test-retest coefficient obtained was .63. Content validity for the CDI was established by design, judgment, and psychometric evaluation. Criterion-related validity remains to be determined but has tentatively been demonstrated by relating scale scores to grade level and to educational treatments. Construct validity has been inferred from relationships with two status characteristics, two behavioral characteristics, and three other measures of vocational maturity. Each of these relationships has demonstrated that the CDI is related in expected ways to variables considered relevant in describing vocational maturity. The CDI seems to be useful in assessing the degree to which established educational objectives have been obtained by career, educational, and vocational guidance programs.

CAREER MATURITY INVENTORY

The CMI was developed in the context of theory and research associated with the Career Pattern Study.[53] This project introduced the concept of vocational maturity. Crites constructed a model including four factors involved in choosing a career (consistency, realism, competencies, and attitudes) and built on three interrelated levels: (1) career behaviors that supposedly mature with time, (2) clusters of interrelated factors, and (3) degree of career development, that is, the sum of the four group factors (see Figure 9.2). In this model, a hierarchy of variables combines to determine a person's degree of career maturity. Crites felt that the Career Pattern Study measured his first two group factors—consistency and realism of career choices—adequately, so he concentrated on career choice attitudes and career choice competencies in developing the CMI. He devised items designed to tap all five attitude factors, but he treated them as one for purposes of scoring and validation. His competency tests go farther in that they do attempt to measure the five types of competency.

[53] Crites, *Theory and Research Handbook.*

FIGURE 9.2
A MODEL OF CAREER MATURITY IN ADOLESCENCE

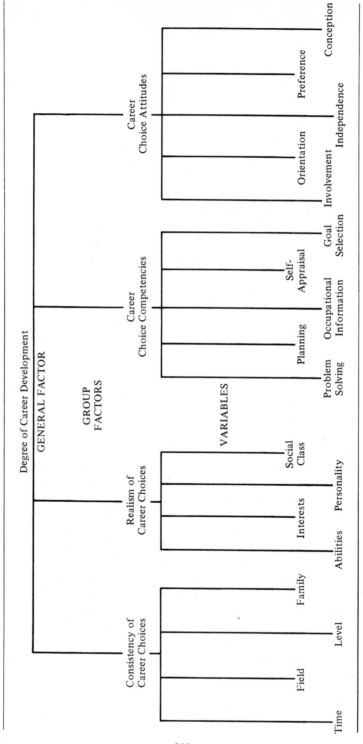

Source: John O. Crites, "The Career Maturity Inventory," in Donald E. Super, ed., *Measuring Vocational/Maturity for Counseling and Evaluation* (Washington, D.C.: National Vocational Guidance Association, 1974), p. 26. Copyright 1974 American Personnel and Guidance Association. Reprinted with permission.

The CMI is a machine-scored, paper-and-pencil inventory that has been standardized on large samples of students primarily in grades 5–12, though it includes some in college. The rationale behind the CMI is that any measure of a developmental variable must be related systematically to time. Crites assumed that, because development is usually interpreted as a unidirectional and irreversible process, the form of the relationship to time should be a generalized upward or downward curve. Accordingly, he selected for the CMI only those items with responses that systematically increase or decrease with time. In addition, he retained only those items that reflect accepted psychological theory. Consequently, all items of the CMI are thought to measure theoretically relevant behaviors that differentiate among the various developmental levels in late childhood and adolescence.

Only cross-sectional standardization data have been analyzed for both CMI scales. Two types of reliabilities have been determined for the attitude scale: internal consistency coefficients and test-retest reliability estimates. Data reported are comparable to those of other nonintellectual measures. Only internal consistency estimates of reliability are reported for the competence tests. How stable the competence tests part scores are over time remains to be established. It is speculated that they will change significantly over the course of developing a career, but not as much as will the maturity of career attitudes, which probably are more susceptible to day-by-day learning experience.

The validation process for the CMI has only begun; however, preliminary findings are promising. Additional data will be forthcoming as Crites continues his work and as the CMI is used more widely.

To date, interpretation of research data suggests that the attitude measures may prove more cognitive than attitudinal in function. Such a test may not apply to some persons who do not subscribe to the work ethic, despite their maturity in other respects. Individuals from certain cultural backgrounds may appear immature in light of dominant culture norms even though they may be very mature vocationally, given their environment. Furthermore, sex role development is another variable that must be taken into account in assessing the vocational maturity of women. Finally, it is important to consider not just the broad spectrum of development from childhood to old age but also specific cycles and subcycles of development as new situations are encountered, new choices are made, and role reestablishment takes place again and again throughout life.

DIFFERENTIAL APTITUDE TEST
CAREER PLANNING QUESTIONNAIRE

The DAT Career Planning Questionnaire (CPQ) was developed by Donald E. Super, in collaboration with the authors of the DAT, as part of the work that resulted in the 1973 revision and restandardization of the *Differential Aptitude Test* battery (forms S and T). Combined used of the DAT and the CPQ permits access to what is known as the DAT Career Planning Program.[54]

Combined questionnaire DAT answer sheets must be sent to the Psychological Corporation Scoring Service, where students' occupational preferences are compared by computer with the level and pattern of their DAT scores, the school subjects and activities they like best, and their reported educational plans. The CPQ requires students to provide data on: sex; grade; age; interest preferences among ninety-two school subjects, activities, and sports; expected educational goals; class standing by quarters; and preferences among one hundred specified occupations.

These occupations were selected for their representativeness and familiarity. A glossary of school subjects and occupations is provided. The CPQ can be completed in less than one classroom period. A Career Planning Report provided by the Psychological Corporation Scoring Service includes a profile of students' DAT scores and preprinted descriptions of the aptitudes measured by the DAT, and the school subjects, activities, and occupations listed in the CPQ. This report may confirm the appropriateness of a respondent's occupational choice, or it may suggest alternative occupational areas to explore if the choices seem inappropriate. A manual written by Super provides background information with suggestions for using and interpreting the Career Planning Report in both individual and group counseling and in interviews with clients or with clients and their parents.

INTERPRETING
AND REPORTING SCORES
AND IMPLEMENTING ACTION

Although the reliability of interest, career development, and vocational maturity scales usually approaches that typical of mental

---

[54] Donald E. Super, *Counselor's Manual for the DAT Career Planning Program* (New York: The Psychological Corporation, 1973).

ability measures, evidence of validity and the adequacy and relevance of most related normative data do not measure up to the standards set by mental ability tests. Most objective tests of interest, career development, vocational maturity, and personality can be administered and scored easily by counselors who have had only limited training in standardized testing. Furthermore, the guidelines and cautions stipulated for interpreting general ability measures (see Chapter 5) hold in total when it comes to interpreting, reporting, and using data about interests, career development, and vocational maturity. Counselors who are responsible for interpreting such data must be far more sophisticated and better trained than persons who work only with data from most objective ability and aptitude tests. Counselors who work with interest and career inventories require specialized training and supervised experience, if for no other reason than that these inventories yield a profile of many scores rather than one score or a few scores.

Creative interpretation requires skill in integrating such profile data with what is known about the abilities, education, motivation, and opportunities of individuals and with what is known about the nature of various occupations. To become truly proficient, the counselor must invest the time and effort required to permit postulating hypotheses about future behavior and eventually obtaining the behavioral information that either verifies or refutes these hypotheses. Thus, over time, a counselor can develop the subjective conceptual framework and reference data base that are essential to the efficient interpretation of behavior profiles.

Interest, career development, and vocational maturity inventories can be administered to large groups, and an initial interpretation of profile data can be carried out in group discussions rather than in individual counseling sessions. However, in private discussion of vocations, persons may reveal certain problems that only a trained counselor can help solve.

Important distinctions differentiate among vocational preferences, selection, and attainment. Vocational *preference* refers to the career an individual would like to follow. Vocational *selection* refers to individual action and the acceptance of its outcome. Vocational *attainment* is reflected in the actual position an individual comes to hold.

> Preference carries with it the concept of what would be done assuming all things are possible; selection includes the results of the compromise the individual makes in the face of his (her) per-

ceived limitations; and attainment reflects the ability of the individual to implement his (her) selection.[55]

While one person's vocational preference, selection, and attainment may all be identical, this is not always the case.

PERSONAL DEVELOPMENT
AND TEST SCORES

Habitual behavior profiles, regardless of the inventory from which they have been obtained, tend to reflect a developmental characteristic clearly related to the concept of vocational maturity. Owing to perceived stereotypes and limited exposure to work experience, many early and mid-adolescents are unable to make systematic and informed choices among work activities. Consequently, responses to such inventories may be random, with scale scores tending to be unexceptional or falling in the average normative range. Such profiles are bland and reveal little about personal choice. People with profiles of this type may be viewed as being vocationally immature. Interest inventories with similar results may be thought to reflect individuals for whom extrinsic considerations are dominant.

Interest measures are pertinent for persons entering professions or skilled jobs, but many jobs require little skill, are routine, and offer little possibility for self-fulfillment. In these jobs, a worker's satisfaction must come not from the work itself but from extrinsic considerations such as companionship, good working conditions, and/or freedom from responsibility. An unskilled, routine job probably cannot command active interest.

Persons with strong intrinsic values are able to identify what they dislike at an earlier stage of development than what they like. Consequently, low profile scores or negative profile configurations emerge before any orderly pattern of positive profile clusters can be identified. The full profile configuration, not isolated parts of it, must be evaluated. Although a mature profile with distinct positive and negative characteristics can be interpreted with greater confidence, emerging profiles, reflecting for the most part negative or below-average scale scores, are of practical value. For example, on the SVIB (T399), negative score clusters frequently appear in the science and nonscience profile areas before positive configurations

---

[55] S. H. Osipow, *Theories of Career Development*, 2nd ed. (New York: Appleton-Century-Crofts, 1973), p. 12.

are reported. These data have value for counselors, because it is probable that when positive clusters do emerge later, they will be found in the bland, unexceptional areas rather than in areas reflecting low or negative scores. Therefore, it is appropriate to advise students to explore those occupational areas devoid of clusters of negative scores.

The vocational maturity, or the readiness of an individual to respond in a sensible way to an interest inventory, and the known abilities of that individual and the circumstances of his or her life are important in evaluating the ability of certain measures to serve the needs of certain persons and in interpreting the meaning of the scores derived. In the hands of counselors knowledgeable of interpretive schema such as those postulated by Roe or Holland, both negative as well as positive results may be used to advantage.

SYSTEMS OF INTERPRETATION

FIELDS AND LEVELS   Interests are a special case of motivation and are related to the developing personality of the individual. Anne Roe has detailed the development of what she calls a *field and level* description of occupations, and she relates these fields and levels to personality and motivational variables. Roe has postulated eight fields of occupations (discussed later in this section), each one of which can be divided into a hierarchy of six levels, extending from high status and responsible positions of a professional and managerial nature to basically unskilled work. Associated with this hierarchy are several parameters, most of which are continuous in nature, for example, the relationship between intrinsic motivation and extrinsic motivation. Individuals who occupy positions at the highest levels—level 1 or level 2—are for the most part thought to be motivated toward the choice of occupation largely by intrinsic considerations (for example, what one does is more significant than what one receives for one's labor). At the lower end of the level continuum—levels 5 and 6—it is probable that extrinsic motivations dominate. The relatively recent career development and interest maturity inventories show a greater emphasis on extrinsic variables, and so they are seen as a significant move toward providing the majority of the labor force and potential labor force with relevant guides for choosing an occupation.

Education is another of Roe's parameters. Generally speaking, the more formal education an individual has, the higher is the level at which he or she enters the labor market and the higher is the level he or she ultimately attains. Relatively uneducated individuals, with diligence, may attain an intermediate position—level 3, which represents a high level of skills learned through experience on the job. In contrast, the college graduate may enter the labor market at level 3 and eventually move to positions in level 1.

Responsibility is yet another parameter associated with this continuum. Individuals with positions in levels 1 and 2 have considerable responsibility for the direction of their own work and the work of others. Frequently, such persons have little direct contact with the majority of individuals for whose work they are responsible. Persons who occupy intermediate positions—levels 3 and 4—have more limited responsibilities for the conduct of their own work and the work of others, but are frequently in more direct contact with the majority of other workers. Persons at the lowest levels—levels 5 and 6—usually have little responsibility in the conduct of their own work and that of others. Especially at level 6, workers are generally told what to do, when to do it, and how to do it.

Anne Roe's occupational fields bear systematic intrinsic relationships to one another. Her research suggests that persons in field I, social service, are humanistically oriented and sincerely interested in other people. Field II, business contact, is like field I in that persons in such occupations are interested in dealing with people; however, they tend to be assertive and independent in their daily behavior and, in contrast to those in field I, are probably motivated more by materialistic than by humanistic goals. (The materialistic motive characterizes individuals in field II and most other fields in the Roe schema.) Persons in field III, business detail, also deal with people, but they view them as data to be organized, directed, and dealt with relatively impersonally. The verbal skills of individuals in field III tend to be relatively strong, but in contrast to persons in fields I and II, their applied quantitative skills are also strong.

At its highest levels, Field IV, technology, perhaps better labeled physical sciences and technology, is characterized by individuals who have both verbal and quantitative skills. This quantitative orientation tends to be theoretical at higher levels, unlike the similar orientation of field III individuals. However, at intermediate levels within this field, verbal skills tend to be mediocre while quantitative skills remain strong, though similar to those of persons in field III. People in field IV are the most non–person-oriented in Roe's scheme. They exhibit far more interest in ideas, numbers, and machines than they do in relations with people. They often have few close personal relationships and are content to spend long hours in isolation. Such an orientation is thought by many to be essential for success in scientific research.

Field V, outdoors, is perhaps better labeled biological sciences. Like persons in field IV, those in field V tend to exhibit relatively little interest in dealing with other people; however, in contrast, they do deal with living organisms. At the upper levels, individuals manifest strong verbal skills and high-level quantitative skills.

In field VI, science, perhaps better termed medical science, people at the higher levels exhibit relatively strong verbal skills and stronger-than-average quantitative skills. They are interested in working with people, but like their counterparts in field III, they deal with people as objects, in this instance, objects to be treated. Roe postulates that people in field VI who do not acquire an impersonal orientation would be unable to tolerate the emotional stress of their work.

Field VII, cultural heritage, might better have been labeled person persuaders. Again, at the higher levels, verbal skills are well developed and strong; however, as in fields I and II, quantitative skills are mediocre. Persons in field VII are oriented toward dealing with people, but like their counterparts in field VI and field III, they deal with them as objects, in this instance, objects whose thoughts and behaviors are to be influenced. Journalists, lawyers, politicians, many teachers and clergy, and advertising and public relations specialists characterize the field. In many ways, they share the characteristics of persons in the business contact field, but they differ from such people in that some vehicle intervenes between the individual and the public to be persuaded or influenced. This contributes to the impersonal character of the field.

At its upper levels, field VIII, arts and entertainment, is represented by individuals who, like persons in fields I, II, and VII, are adept verbally but often only average with regard to quantitative skills. They are oriented toward dealing with people, but as in field VII, a vehicle intervenes between the artist and his or her audience. Furthermore, unlike individuals in field I, whose humanistic and service motives appear dominant, many artists need an audience more than the audience needs the artist.

THEMES The application of Roe's schema has merit in that it provides a conceptual basis for interpreting such occupational scales as the *Strong Vocational Interest Blanks* and the *Kuder Occupational Interest Survey*. Although by no means totally congruent, the points of view of Anne Roe and John Holland do overlap considerably. This is seen most readily on the profile established for the SCII, which represents the major use of the Holland orientation to date. The relationship between the occupational scale profiles for the SCII and the SVIB (T399) still obtain.

Holland's realistic theme corresponds most directly to SVIB groups 3 and 4, which are similar to Roe's fields III, IV, and V. Holland's investigative theme is represented strongly within SVIB groups 1 and 2, and it also relates to Roe's fields IV, V, and VI at the highest levels. Holland's artistic theme relates primarily to the SVIB group 6 and, to some degree, group 10 and overlaps Roe's field VIII and, to some degree, field VII. Holland's social theme is reflected almost exclusively in SVIB group 5 and Roe's field I and, to some extent, field III. Holland's enterprising theme bears a direct relationship to SVIB groups 9, 10, and 11 and can be associated with Roe's fields II, III (at the highest level), and VII. On the other hand, Holland's conventional theme is reflected little in the SVIB (and the SCII) and pertains primarily to intermediate-level occupational groups representative of SVIB group 8 and perhaps groups 5 and 3. This theme is associated with intermediate-level occupations in several of Roe's fields, especially field III, and is testimony to the fact that the Strong series of interest measures are oriented primarily toward upper- rather than intermediate- or lower-level positions in any occupational field.

COMMITMENT TO WORK   With specific reference to measures of career development and vocational maturity, a person's commitment to or involvement in work, a job, or a career plays an important part in several conceptual models, especially those of Crites and Super. Work has varying degrees of importance to different people. For some people, especially those subscribing to the Protestant work ethic, jobs, independent of their content, have an important motivational and organizational function. There are those to whom their work is important as a challenging, engrossing, and rewarding activity in its own right. For others who greatly value work, an occupation itself is of relatively little importance; rather it is the industry that matters, whether it is coal mining, textile manufacturing, finance, education, or government. The nature of the work may change, the occupation itself may change, but this individual is committed to an area of enterprise and becomes a specialist in it.

For still other people, work itself is not important. They consider work only as a means to leisure. Work has no place in their system of values and in their lives. Instead, they choose work that frees them from both external and internal compulsions to structure time, to organize energy, and to see the product of an activity. A new work ethic may develop to accommodate this kind of person. However, it seems unlikely that society will ever accept those who are inactive, who are drifters.

ISSUES

1. *Interests and abilities are directly related.*
   Yes, because:
   1. Individual interests may emerge because ability is reinforced by our culture, and individuals learn preferences in response to such reinforcement.
   2. Knowledge of the abilities required for success in certain occupations is essential if one is to choose an appropriate role. Realistic persons pursue education and job training that capitalize on their assets and avoid their liabilities.

   No, because:
   1. Interests are a product of motivational and personal variables that have little, if any, relationship to ability.
   2. For many, interests are determined by the opportunities for employment available to them when they enter the labor market. For these people, it is important to have access to a job that gives them the extrinsic satisfaction of meeting survival needs.

   Discussion:
   Interests tell nothing about abilities. A high interest score indicates that if a person is trained and enters the occupation, he or she is likely to enjoy the work. A person with suitable abilities but unsuitable interests for an occupation can do well but may not. A person with low aptitude will do poorly regardless of interest. For persons who, by privilege of ability, education, and socioeconomic status, can choose selectively among many opportunities, ability may bear a strong relationship to the occupation they choose. In their case, intrinsic motives, those concerning the nature of the work and its relationship to the satisfaction of social needs, dominate their choice. For the majority of workers, minimal levels of ability are required for successful performance of a job, and extrinsic considerations, such as the availability of a job, work conditions, and benefits, determine their choice. Consequently, for them, ability bears minimal relationship to career entry and advancement.

2. *Interests, motivation, attitudes, and personality are inter-*
related.

Yes, because:

Interests are an aspect of habitual behavior. They bear a strong relationship to other facets of such behavior and are influenced by these other behavioral variables.

No, because:

Interests can be independent of other aspects of habitual behavior, as Freyer postulated, and can be thought to be related as much to cognitive variables as to connative and affectual considerations.

Discussion:

We feel that interests are a special case of motivation, and that, although they are influenced by cognitive experience and opportunity, their evolution and consistency are associated significantly with the development of a self-concept and the emergence of personality, especially as personality is a product of the awareness of need and those modes of behavior that satisfy these needs.

3. *Most interest inventories, as currently constituted, are biased*
in favor of males and against females.

Yes, because:

1. In instruments that provide specific scale scores for females (such as the SVIB), data for females reflect cultural stereotypes.
2. Inventory norms compare females' scores only with those of males in the case of male-dominated occupations.
3. The language employed in interest inventories uses sex-related personal pronouns to describe job activities, encouraging females to respond in stereotypic fashion.

No, because:

1. Recent modifications in interest inventories (for example, the development of the SCII) have reduced bias in item content and availability of normative data.
2. It now is possible for females to compare their interests with those of other females in heretofore male-dominated occupations. Also, it is now possible for males to compare their responses with those of other males working in occupations that have employed many more females than males.

Discussion:

Today, most if not all people in the field honor the principle that measures of development and vocational maturity must be as free as possible of any bias, in both content and norms. Such instruments are needed if all individuals are to be given maximal opportunity to evaluate their opportunities and abilities in the context of the entire spectrum of the labor market, and to be assisted in all possible ways to attain maximal realization of their potential.

For many years, inventories such as the Kuder series have provided both male and female norms for all scales. In July 1974, the SCII, suitable for use with both sexes, was published, leading the way to reform of those inventories, such as the SVIB, that had published separate forms for males and females or did not provide normative data for both sexes for all scales. However, recent definitions of sex bias in interest inventories focus on factors that limit the career opportunities considered by persons taking the inventories. The restrictive effects of interest inventories do not constitute the only element of sex bias. The predictive validity of inventory scores for all persons oriented toward certain occupations and levels must be demonstrated as well.[56] Such data have not been provided; until they are, some persons, especially women, may still be misled in exploring, preparing for, and entering suitable occupations. Unless a distinction is made between the sex restrictiveness and sex bias in reporting inventory scores, the current definition of sex bias as restrictiveness only delays the elimination of bias.

4. *Measures of career development and vocational maturity are distinct from measures of interest.*

Yes, because:

1. Such measures, unlike the typical interest inventory, focus on both cognitive and affective dimensions.

2. A person's level of awareness of occupation and occupational demands is subsumed in interest inventories. Such assumptions are absent from the typical career development and vocational maturity inventory, wherein specific knowledge of occupations, entry requirements, and opportunities are assessed rather than taken for granted.

---

[56] Dale J. Prediger and Gary R. Hanson, "The Distinction between Sex Restrictiveness and Sex Bias in Interest Inventories," *Measurement and Evaluation in Guidance* 7 (July 1974): 96–103.

No, because:
1. Interest inventories assume no knowledge of occupational requirements and opportunities, merely a liking of or a dislike for certain activities.
2. For the able, well-motivated, and well-educated, opportunities for employment are available, given persistence and patience.

Discussion:
Career development and vocational maturity inventories differ from interest measures in that they assess additional practical concerns regarding the labor market and its requirements. However, to a considerable degree, both types of measures ask subjects what they would like to do rather than what rewards they wish to receive and under what conditions. The counselor is urged to emphasize those aspects of the career development and vocational maturity inventories that deal with an individual's recognition of ability and opportunity.

ANNOTATED REFERENCES

Campbell, D. P. *Handbook for the Strong Vocational Interest Inventory.* Stanford, Calif.: Stanford University Press, 1971.

The *Handbook* is intended as a definitive professional reference for the *Strong Vocational Interest Blanks.* Included are all aspects of a test manual, technical information and test development data, brief commentaries on use in various settings, and a few case studies. Test results are summarized for more than 100,000 adults in more than 400 occupations, some tested as many as four times in forty years. Several thousand statistics are reported. Unfortunately, the development of the SCII postdated the publication of this weighty reference; however, the *Handbook* provides a comprehensive record of the history of the SVIB between its introduction approximately fifty years ago and 1970. It may be viewed as the complete SVIB. When the SCII has had opportunity to mature, it may merit a handbook of its own.

Clark, K. E. *Vocational Interests of Non-Professional Men.* Minneapolis: University of Minnesota Press, 1961.

Clark combines a sound knowledge of psychometric and statistical theory with a real concern for the empirical problems of interest measurement. Outstanding in technical detail, this work reports the results of ten years of research that led to the development of the *Minnesota Vocational Interest Inventory.* Clark also provides an excellent summary of future steps in interest measurement that need to be considered, detailed in the context of past accomplishments.

Holland, J. L. *The Psychology of Vocational Choice: A Theory of Personality Types and Modal Environments.* Waltham, Mass.: Blaisdell, 1966.

In this volume, Holland presents the bases in theory and research for the development of his classification of broad occupational areas and for the foundation of his hexagonal model of occupations. Although technical in detail, this reference is essential to learning to apply Holland's conceptualizations effectively to the interpretation of data about interest, career development, and vocational maturity.

SELECTED REFERENCES

Campbell, David P. "The Strong Vocational Interest Blank: 1927–1967." In *Advances in Psychological Assessment.* Vol. 1, edited by Paul McReynolds. Palo Alto, Calif.: Science and Behavior Books, 1968.

Campbell, David P., and Holland, John L. "A Merger in Vocational Interest Research: Applying Holland's Theory to Strong's Data." *Journal of Vocational Behavior* 2 (October 1972): 353–376.

Cole, Nancy S. "On Measuring the Vocational Interests of Women." *Journal of Counseling Psychology* 20 (March 1973): 105–112.

Crites, John O. *The Development of Vocational Attitudes in Adolescence.* Washington, D.C.: American Personnel and Guidance Association, 1972.

Diamond, Esther E. "Minimizing Sex Bias in Testing." *Measurement and Evaluation in Guidance* 9 (April 1976): 28–33.

Gottfredson, Gary D., and Holland, John L. "Vocational Choices of Men and Women: A Comparison of Predictors from the Self-Directed Search." *Journal of Counseling Psychology* 22 (January 1975): 28–34.

Hansen, Jo-Ida C., and Johansson, C. B. "The Application of Holland's Vocational Model to the Strong Vocational Interest Blank for Women." *Journal of Vocational Behavior* 2 (October 1972): 479–493.

Harmon, Lenore W. "Sexual Bias in Interest Measurement." *Measurement and Evaluation in Guidance* 5 (January 1973): 496–501.

Holland, John L. *Making Vocational Choices: A Theory of Careers.* Englewood Cliffs, N.J.: Prentice-Hall, 1973.

Holland, John L.; Gottfredson, Gary D.; and Nafziger, Dean H. "Testing the Validity of Some Theoretical Signs of Vocational Decision-Making Ability." *Journal of Counseling Psychology* 22 (September 1975): 411–422.

Zytowski, Donald G., ed. *Vocational Behavior.* New York: Holt, Rinehart and Winston, 1968.

Zytowski, Donald G., ed. *Contemporary Approaches to Interest Measurement.* Minneapolis: University of Minnesota Press, 1973.

Chapter 10

Personality
and Self-Concept

How do descriptive and dynamic theories of personality differ?

What are the major types of personality measures?

Which personality and self-concept inventories are the most appropriate for use by counselors?

What two factors or areas of content matter typify most, if not all, personality inventories?

What special considerations and cautions must be taken into account by counselors when reporting and using personality and self-concept data?

THEORIES OF PERSONALITY

The term *personality* is derived from the Latin word *persona*, the mask used by actors performing on the stage in ancient Greece and Rome. To enable the audience to differentiate among the characters being portrayed, the actor would hold up the mask identifying a character with whom the audience was familiar. In this sense, for hundreds of years, the word *personality* has connoted the superficial impression created by an individual's behavior. This is the term's most widely accepted meaning, and it is basic to the descriptive emphasis of the majority of personality and self-concept inventories.

In contrast, when many professionals use the term today, a dynamic rather than a descriptive meaning is intended. That is, they view personality as the ever-changing product of physiological status and/or environmental experience. This causal orientation can be traced back to the early contributions of Sigmund Freud, who was among the first to ask questions about why people behave as they do. Freud believed that the standard practice of his colleagues during the late 1800s, who sought only to describe and classify what

314

behavior was, was inadequate to an understanding of human behavior, both normal and deviant. A dynamic orientation provides the theoretical basis for the majority of performance and projective tests of personality and self-concept and permits causal inferences to be made by informed and experienced professionals.

Theories of personality arose in the context of medical practice in response to the need of physicians for a rationale and procedures for dealing with their patients' psychological problems. These clinically derived theories differed from experimentally based psychological theories of behavior. Both personality theory and behavior theory in psychology underwent rapid development in the first two decades of the twentieth century. During the next three decades, there were indications of convergence between the two types of theoretical formulations.[1] Academic psychologists, such as J. Dollard and N. E. Miller, attempted to integrate experimental findings into the framework of personality theories.[2] In recent years, however, there has been a movement away from grand-scale theorizing in favor of an emphasis on experimentation in limited behavioral domains with both personality theory and behavior theory.[3]

Theories about the determinants of behavior and the conditions that change behavior dictate the choice of data studied and the specific procedures and criteria used to evaluate them.[4] Descriptive, or trait theories, and dynamic, or state theories, represent two main approaches to the study of personality. Most theoretical controversies concern the utility of certain techniques for making inferences about the substantive content, structure, and organization of the personality. The majority of current personality theories assume an internal structural dynamic hierarchy. The implication in all hierarchical personality models is that some internal factors underlie others, and that their dynamic interrelations determine or produce behavior.[5]

The term *trait* is confusing. At the simplest level, a trait is merely an observable, stable, individual difference in behavior. "A trait is any distinguishable, relatively enduring way in which one individual varies from others."[6] However, traits have been viewed both as psychological realities that exist in some tangible form in the person

[1] Jerry S. Wiggins, *Personality and Prediction: Principles of Personality Assessment* (Reading, Mass.: Addison-Wesley Publishing Company, 1973), p. 512.

[2] J. Dollard and N. E. Miller, *Personality and Psychotherapy* (New York: McGraw-Hill, 1950).

[3] Wiggins, *Personality and Prediction*.

[4] Walter Mischel, *Personality and Assessment* (New York: John Wiley and Sons, 1968).

[5] N. Sanford, "Personality: Its Place in Psychology," in *Psychology: A Study of Science*, vol. 5, ed. S. Koch (New York: McGraw-Hill, 1963), pp. 488–592.

[6] J. P. Guilford, *Personality* (New York: McGraw-Hill, 1959), p. 6.

and also as the causes of behavior.[7] A chief aim of the *trait approach* to the study of personality is to infer the underlying personality structure of individuals and to compare people's trait dimensions. Professionals who accept the basic assumptions of trait theory believe that personality is made up of certain definite attributes. They also assume that particular traits are common to many people, that they vary in amount, and that they can be inferred by measuring behavioral indicators. Most important, they assume that traits are relatively stable and enduring predispositions that exert fairly generalized effects on behavior.

Dynamic theory, like trait theory, assumes that the underlying personality is more or less stable, or that during childhood, an individual develops a basic personality core that does not change much in its essentials. Dynamic theory contends that all a person's responses ultimately reveal enduring basic concerns and personality organization that permit the underlying meaning of behavior to be interpreted. In clinical situations, the assessor who holds to this theory may pay as much attention to seemingly irrelevant and casual behavior as to evidence that the subject says is important (See principle 6, Chapter 1). This practice is based on the psychoanalytic principle that an individual is largely unaware of his or her most important motives.[8] The dynamic perspective holds that people develop elaborate defenses in order to avoid anxiety and to come to terms with instinctive impulses that conflict with reality.[9] These complex disguises help individuals hide from themselves as well as from others and may produce pathological behavior. The meaning of behavior and of signs of underlying dynamic motives and states are interpreted symbolically.

Dynamic theorists often object that trait theorists, because of their concern for discrete, quantifiable traits, miss the dynamic, interactive aspects of internal functioning and the configuration of relationships among different aspects of personality. Both dynamic and trait theorists study responses as signs (direct or indirect) of pervasive underlying mental structures. Both assume that these underlying inferred dispositions (whether called traits, states, processes, dynamics, or motives) exert generalized and enduring causal effects on behavior. Both search for signs that serve as reliable indicators of these hypothesized underlying dispositions.

Few doubt that previous experience and genetic and constitu-

---

[7] Gordon Allport, "Traits Revisited," *American Psychologist* 21 (1966): 1.

[8] Sigmund Freud, "Analysis of a Phobia in a Five-Year-Old Boy," in Sigmund Freud, *Collected Papers,* vol. 3 (London: Hogarth Press, 1953).

[9] R. W. White, *The Abnormal Personality* (New York: Ronald Press, 1964).

tional characteristics affect behavior, resulting in vast individual differences among people. Perhaps the most striking finding in personality psychology is the fact that different persons respond differently to the same objective stimulus. The existence of enormous differences among persons is recognized by all psychologists, regardless of theoretical orientation.

Most personality theories fail to measure up to the formal criteria that are employed to evaluate scientific theories. In general, they are lacking in clarity and explicitness and are not sufficiently formalized to allow for the generation of hypotheses by formal deduction. In order for a personality theory to facilitate prediction, it must be relevant to a particular criterion, must be explicit enough to suggest a selection of specific testing instruments, must have definite implications for criterion performance, and must be capable of being evaluated. Despite the predilections of psychologists for one type of theorizing over another, the personality models that are likely to be of the greatest value are those the principal constructs of which can be translated most directly into concrete testing procedures. Although some models appear more promising than others as theoretical frameworks for guiding assessment, too few personality models have been implemented in practical assessment fully enough to permit any general conclusion about the role of theory in behavioral prediction.[10]

TYPES
OF PERSONALITY MEASURES

Personality assessment is a threefold process involving: (1) an understanding of the environment in which the individual to be assessed is to act; (2) an understanding of the individual subject; and (3) the study of the congruence between the data obtained from an analysis of the individual and the characteristics of some theoretical model of human behavior.[11] Behavior is a function of the relationship between the person and the environment (see principle 9, Chapter 1). It is difficult to determine the most effective methodology for evaluating this relationship.

Analytic assessment methods are time-consuming, requiring a functional analysis of the environment, the administration of tests,

---

[10] Wiggins, *Personality and Prediction.*
[11] George G. Stern, Morris I. Stein, and Benjamin S. Bloom, *Methods in Personality Assessment* (Glencoe, Ill.: Free Press, 1963), pp. 244–245.

analyses of data, case conferences, and the like. The cost of any such project is high. Furthermore, the relative scarcity of professional personnel and the high costs of hiring them add to the price. Finally, only a relatively small number of persons can be assessed in a certain period of time. The cost of the *empirical* assessment method depends in large measure on the number of techniques that are used and the number of persons to be assessed. Cost for staff need not necessarily be as high as those of the analytic assessment method. Clerical personnel can administer and score tests; professional personnel are required only for integrating and interpreting the data. The majority of analytic procedures use performance and projective measures, whereas most empirical strategies require the use of standardized, self-descriptive questionnaires and inventories.

PERFORMANCE TESTS

Under optimal conditions, performance tests of personality are quantitative measuring instruments. Such tests are also used for impressionistic assessment, being integrated with other data in an evaluation of the whole person.[12] The performance test may be contrasted with the time sampling method of observation (see Chapter 11). A performance test is an observation of the way in which a person performs a standardized task designed to elicit a particular type of response. Since the purpose of such testing is concealed, ethics require the counselor to provide afterwards a frank disclosure to each subject that explains any deception and to allow the subject to ask questions and discuss his or her feelings. Performance tests vary greatly in design. The tests may measure only one narrowly defined behavior or they may be employed as a basis for evaluating a person's total lifestyle. Tasks range from highly structured to almost totally unstructured.

FREE-ASSOCIATION TESTS   The development of scientific association tests can be traced to the work of the eminent English scholar, Sir Francis Galton.[13] In Galton's work, associations were evoked experimentally and studied quantitatively. This method has been most popular in the study of abnormal personalities. Carl Jung, an early associate of Sigmund Freud, saw in the association technique

---

[12] Lee J. Cronbach, *Essentials of Psychological Testing*, 3rd ed. (New York: Harper and Row, 1970), pp. 659–665.
[13] Francis Galton, "Psychometric Facts," *Nineteenth Century* 5 (1879): 425–433.

a method of diagnosing mental disturbance. Jung developed a free-association test that consisted of one hundred words, to each of which the subject was to respond as quickly as possible with the first word that came to mind. The list, constructed after many years of experimentation, was intended to reveal emotional states of various types by prolonged reaction time and by the responses themselves. While the free-association test using words as stimuli had less than moderate success as a diagnostic device, it was the forerunner of the projective instruments that have been widely used in the description of personality.[14]

RORSCHACH PSYCHODIAGNOSTIK A Swiss psychiatrist, Hermann Rorschach, who had studied at Zurich and was familiar with Jung's verbal free-association test, was the first to use inkblots as stimuli for the systematic study of personality. After many trials, Rorschach selected ten inkblots as ambiguous stimuli to be interpreted, one at a time, by a subject.[15] He regarded the interpretation of random forms having no intrinsic meaning as a matter of perception rather than a matter of imagination. In his formulation of the projective hypothesis, Rorschach assumed that a subject's responses are a reflection of wishes, attitudes, and conceptions of the world, a hypothesis clearly in accord with an analytic perspective.

From the very first, responses to the Rorschach inkblots have been evaluated not primarily in terms of the content of the associations evoked but rather in terms of the classes or types of associations—whether and to what degree they correspond to the actual forms, whether there is a perception of movement, and whether there is a reaction to color in certain of the inkblots. Rorschach's diagnostic method has been elaborated by subsequent investigators seeking a description of psychodynamics. In the United States, the technique was extended in the 1930s and 1940s by the scoring systems and theories of Samuel Beck[16] and Bruno Klopfer.[17]

THEMATIC APPERCEPTION TEST The Rorschach Psychodiagnostik illustrates a projective technique for studying a subject's style of handling a problem. Stylistic tests may be contrasted with thematic tests in which the interpreter is concerned especially with the content of thoughts and fantasies. This distinction is like that between

---

[14] Philip H. DuBois, A History of Psychological Testing (Boston: Allyn and Bacon, 1970).
[15] Hermann Rorschach, Psychodiagnostics (New York: Grune and Stratton, 1951).
[16] Samuel J. Beck, Rorschach's Test: I. Basic Processes (New York: Grune and Stratton, 1961).
[17] Bruno Klopfer et al., Developments in the Rorschach Technique, vol. 1 (Yonkers, New York: World Book Company, 1954).

trait questionnaires that focus on response tendencies and techniques for studying stimulus meanings such as the semantic differential (see Chapter 12). The stylistic and thematic categories are not mutually exclusive. However, the thematic test comes nearer to examining the whole person at once than does any other projective testing technique.[18]

H. A. Murray's *Thematic Apperception Test* (TAT), consisting of a series of rather ambiguous pictures, has had, after the Rorschach, the widest acceptance by clinicians and investigators of personality of any projective test.[19] In the TAT, a series of pictures, generally with human figures of recognizable age and sex, is shown one at a time to a subject, who is instructed to make up a story to explain the situation—what is happening, what led up to the scene, and what will be the outcome. Responses are thought to be dictated by the experiences, conflicts, and wishes of the subject. Essentially, a subject must project himself or herself into the scene, identifying with a character. The TAT consists of twenty pictures (different pictures are used to some degree for men and women). Because the test takes two one-hour sessions, counselors ordinarily use selected cards. The subject is led to believe that his or her imagination is being tested.

The interpreter gives particular attention to the themes that underlie the plots of the stories reported. The interpreter considers, in addition to these aspects of the responses, their style, that is, the description of the whole picture rather than parts; fluency; concern with accuracy; and fitting the story to the picture. The interpreter looks at each story in turn, deriving hypotheses from the plot, the symbolism, and the style.

OTHER PROJECTIVE AND SEMIPROJECTIVE MEASURES   A. F. Payne was the first to use sentence completion in assessing personality.[20] A subject is instructed to complete a sentence stem, working as quickly as possible. How the sentences are completed is thought to provide clues to the examinee's motives and internal status. Many people have worked on developing this procedure, especially during the Second World War. Notable among them are Benjamin Willerman and Julian B. Rotter, who developed a forty-item test.[21]

---

[18] Cronbach, *Essentials of Psychological Testing.*
[19] C. D. Morgan and H. A. Murray, "A Method for Investigating Fantasies: The Thematic Apperception Test," *Archives of Neurology and Psychiatry* 34 (1935): 289–306.
[20] A. F. Payne, *Sentence Completion* (New York: New York Guidance Clinic, 1928).
[21] Julian B. Rotter, "The Incomplete Sentences as a Method in Studying Personality," *American Psychologist* 1 (1946): 286. Abstract.

Florence Goodenough, in her original work with children's drawings, noted that children with psychopathic tendencies sometimes make drawings that differ from those of normal children. She believed that children's drawings, properly understood, contribute to knowledge of their interests and personality traits.[22] In 1948, J. N. Buck developed the *House-Tree-Person Test,* which requires a subject to draw a house, a tree, and a person. In 1949, Karen Machover published a monograph presenting the drawing of the human figure as a method of investigating personality. Her method involved the impressionistic interpretation of various signs by which drawings were placed in diagnostic categories.[23] Over the years, a wide variety of ambiguous stimulus materials have been explored, including cloud pictures, unstructured sounds, puppets, dolls and other toys, figure paintings, and comic strip characters.

An experienced professional who has employed a projective device conscientiously and thoughtfully for many years, formulating hypotheses about behavior from test data and verifying or refuting these hypotheses, thereby developing a subjective interpretive framework within which to evaluate projective data, can employ such projective measures to advantage. Nonetheless, because they are relatively inexpensive and because they promise good results with less professional time than that required for projective data gathering, structured, paper-and-pencil, objectively scored personality questionnaires and inventories have dominated the personality assessment field since the early 1950s.

QUESTIONNAIRES AND INVENTORIES

During the First World War, Robert S. Woodworth applied a questionnaire technique to the study of emotional stability.[24] He invented what was at first called a *personality data questionary,* the ancestor of all subsequent personality inventories, schedules, and questionnaires. The Woodworth scale was followed by several adjustment inventories that list problems and symptoms or grievances to be checked. These instruments are not descriptive, and they often yield only a single score representing level of adjustment. Adjustment inventories single out persons who check symptoms

---

[22] DuBois, *History of Psychological Testing.*
[23] DuBois, *History of Psychological Testing.*
[24] Robert S. Woodworth, in *History of Psychology in Autobiography,* vol. 2, ed. Charles Murchison (New York: Russell and Russell, 1951), pp. 359–381.

PERSONALITY AND SELF-CONCEPT

and self-criticisms. While the information they provide is superficial, their transparency may make them easier to justify for use in schools. Individuals who cause trouble in social settings are easily recognized. However, children and adults who are withdrawn and insecure may not attract the attention of observers. Consequently, an adjustment inventory may be useful in that it draws attention to many of these cases.

During the period 1920–1945, most psychologists in the United States were behaviorists. They considered the adjustment inventory to be a primary substitute for observation. Its questions placed more emphasis on what an individual did than on what he or she felt or thought. Dozens of instruments were produced, each taking items from its predecessors, adding a few new ones, and scoring them in new combinations.

The second generation of personality questionnaires, which appeared after 1940, were vastly more sophisticated than the questionnaires of the first generation. Developments in inventories since the 1940s have amounted to changes in detail rather than radical alterations.

The construction of inventories for practical use has tapered off in recent years, in part because competitors in the clinical field were crowded out by the popularity of the *Minnesota Multiphasic Personality Inventory* and in part because, since the Second World War, the rise of psychotherapy as a prestigious activity reduced the interest of clinical and counseling psychologists in diagnostic problems.

New tests have been developed for use with those who function adequately in daily life, but their authors have made little attempt to justify using them. Psychologists sophisticated in personality measurement have concentrated increasingly on theoretical research. Construct-oriented personality tests of both the self-report and performance varieties have made possible inquiries into social relationships, character, learning, the effects of drugs, economic behavior, and the like.

Personality and self-concept measurements have been classified among attempts to assess typical behavior. This phrase is common in *behavioristic psychology,* which directs attention to overt, observable responses to stimuli. The behavioristic outlook is somewhat limiting, however, and personality assessment can be better understood if it is also conceptualized in the context of phenomenological psychology. *Phenomenological psychology* is concerned with the ways in which the world appears to an individual. Such ideas as self-concept, feelings of hostility, and attitude toward authority are perceptions and reactions that occur within the individual.

In the next section, we shall examine some personality and self-concept inventories in common use today. Each is representative of a rational, empirical, or factorial strategy for inventory test construction. Some are suitable for employment in clinical settings only; most have more universal utility in the hands of a trained and experienced examiner. The vast majority reflect the behavioristic outlook and permit relatively precise comparisons between persons in a classical normative framework. However, to the extent to which the counselor is able to integrate a phenomenological posture with a behavioristic orientation, richer inferences about personality may be derived.

PERSONALITY INVENTORIES

This discussion does not provide a complete description of each of the inventories listed. To do so would involve repeating material that can be found in the manuals published for the various inventories. We recommend that the reader study the manual for each inventory and consult a copy of the inventory itself, in order to understand the nature of the items of each scale scored in the inventory. Trait names assigned to scales are often abstract and are occasionally misleading.[25] This is true particularly with respect to rationally derived scales. Critical reviews and evaluations of personality inventories can be found in *Personality Tests and Reviews.*[26] The inventories reported below are ordered alphabetically within each of three principal construction strategies: rational, empirical, and factorial.

RATIONALLY CONSTRUCTED INVENTORIES

STUDY OF VALUES: A SCALE FOR MEASURING THE DOMINANT INTERESTS IN PERSONALITY The ASV, developed originally in 1931, was based on Eduard Spranger's sixfold classification (1928) of evaluative attitudes: the theoretical, the economic, the aesthetic, the social, the

---

[25] Allen L. Edwards, *The Measurement of Personality Traits by Scales and Inventories* (New York: Holt, Rinehart and Winston, 1970).

[26] Oscar K. Buros, ed., *Personality Tests and Reviews* (Highland Park, N.J.: Gryphon Press, 1970).

political, and the religious.[27] Subjects are required to make choices designed to reflect evaluative attitudes toward specific situations. The six scores reveal the relative importance to the individual of the six basic values. The instrument may be used in vocational guidance and personnel work and in various areas of personality research. In counseling college students or college graduates, this test frequently serves as a useful supplement when it is employed in combination with other tests of personality or interest.

EDWARDS PERSONAL PREFERENCE SCHEDULE   The EPPS was designed to assess the relative importance to the individual of fifteen key needs or motives selected from H. A. Murray's need system.[28] It consists of fifteen scales: achievement, deference, order, exhibition, autonomy, affiliation, intraception, succorance, dominance, abasement, nurturance, change, endurance, heterosexuality, and aggression. A forced-choice format purported to inhibit falsification of responses pairs one of nine statements from each need area with statements from each of the remaining fourteen need areas, so that each pairing is made twice. Subjects are required to choose the statement in each pair that best represents themselves. To indicate consistency, fifteen pairs are presented twice, providing the basis for an auxiliary consistency score. In total, the inventory includes 225 forced-choice item dyads.

The EPPS is easy to administer either to individuals or to groups. The inventory is untimed, but total administration time usually varies from 40–55 minutes. The EPPS may be hand-scored, scored by IBM machine, or scored by National Computer Systems. One raw score is obtained for each of the fifteen personality variables and for the consistency scale. Both percentile and standard score norms (mean, 50; standard deviation, 10) are presented for college students, based on 760 males and 749 females drawn from a number of colleges throughout the country. Percentile norms for adults are based on 4,031 males and 4,932 females who participated in a nation-wide survey of heads of households. High school norms developed from the responses of 700 male and 760 female students exist but are not presented in the manual.[29]

---

[27] Gordon W. Allport, Philip E. Vernon, and Gardner Lindzey, *Manual, Study of Values: A Scale for Measuring the Dominant Interests in Personality*, 3rd ed. (Boston: Houghton Mifflin, 1960).

[28] Allen L. Edwards, *Manual, Edwards Personal Preference Schedule* (New York: Psychological Corporation, 1959).

[29] C. J. Klett, "Performance of High School Students on the Edwards Personal Preference Schedule," *Journal of Consulting Psychology* 21 (1957): 68–72.

A profile depicting normative comparisons can be plotted graphically on the reverse side of the answer sheet. Each of the fifteen personality variables is described briefly in the manual. However, interpretation should be limited to persons with professional training in objective personality assessment.

The instrument can be recommended for experimental use; its value for counseling has yet to be demonstrated. An additional caution should be noted: the use of normative data with results obtained from forced-choice responses is a questionable psychometric practice. Interpretations that compare a person's frequency of endorsement of statements from one scale with that person's frequency of endorsement of statements from the other scales provide the best basis for evaluating self-reports (see our comments regarding the interpretation of forced-choice inventories later in this chapter).

EDWARDS PERSONALITY INVENTORY   The EPI was designed to measure a large number of personality traits that vary in normal individuals.[30] The EPI consists of five lengthy booklets, each containing 300 items, although a few items in some of the booklets are not scored. All items are true-false. Booklets 1a and 1b were intended as comparable forms and provide scores on the same fourteen scales. Booklets 2, 3, and 4 provide scores on eleven, fifteen, and thirteen scales, respectively. The complete EPI thus provides scores on fifty-three personality traits.

The EPI differs from other personality inventories in a number of ways. For example, almost all items that might be regarded as offensive have been eliminated. There is no item in the EPI inquiring into an individual's religious and political beliefs, and there is no item that asks about the individual's health or bodily functions. Another way in which the EPI differs from a number of other personality inventories is that instead of asking an individual whether he or she believes the items to be true or false, it asks the subject to indicate how he or she believes that the people who know him or her best would answer. In other words, individuals are asked to take an objective look at themselves.

In some inventories, a considerable number of items is scored on more than one scale, and the resulting correlation is spurious because of the overlap. In the EPI, no item is scored in more than one scale.

[30] Allen L. Edwards, *Manual, Edwards Personality Inventory* (Chicago: Science Research Associates, 1966).

The items in the EPI were developed from three major sources: (1) interviews in which individuals were asked informally to speak about the personality of someone known well to them, (2) published biographies and autobiographies, and (3) statements written specifically to represent a certain personality trait. The original item pool consisted of 2,824 statements. Items from this pool have been used in a number of Edwards' research studies on social desirability and response sets. No validity information and no statement regarding the intended uses of the instrument are reported in the manual. Consequently, we recommend this measure only for research use.

MYERS-BRIGGS TYPE INDICATOR   The MBTI, an objective self-report personality test, consists of 166 forced-choice items based on Jungian theory.[31] The forced-choice format is supposed to provide choices equated in terms of social desirability. According to Jung, four basic preference extremes structure an individual's personality: introversion-extroversion, sensing-intuition, thinking-feeling, and judgment-perception. For example, the sensing-intuition dimension is designed to reflect a person's preference between two opposite ways of perceiving, in this case, relying on the direct evidence of one's senses as opposed to perceiving indirectly by way of the unconscious, which attaches ideas or associations onto what it perceives. The judgment-perception dimension contrasts a judging attitude (which shuts off all perception, makes a decision, and gets things settled) with a perceptive attitude (which shuts off judgment, assumes that all evidence is not in, and delays a decision).

The test is designed for use with individuals in grades 9–16 and adults. Internal consistency reliabilities range from .75 to .85. A large body of validity data is offered in the manual. These data consist mostly of concurrent studies, for example, the test's relationship to other tests, ratings, and differences between groups. The inventory is easy to administer and score. Scores on the eight scales are reduced to four bipolar scores that can range to approximately 50 at either pole. Only limited norms are provided.

Items are nonthreatening and are standardized on college students. The manual is good; however, the instrument has several technical limitations. There are no directions for part 2. Item stems and second or third response choices do not complete a thought because some necessary information is contained in the first response choice. Descriptions presented for the various types tend to

---

[31] Katherine C. Briggs and Isabel Briggs Myers, *Manual, Myers-Briggs Type Indicator* (Princeton, N.J.: Educational Testing Service, 1962).

be positive and optimistic, resembling horoscopes. The MBTI does not put Jungian concepts into operation successfully. Nevertheless, it does appear to have uses for research and counseling, so long as scores are interpreted in the light of their empirical relationships rather than their assumed theoretical significance.

PERSONALITY RESEARCH FORM   Developed by Douglas N. Jackson,[32] the PRF is unquestionably the best example of a large-scale personality inventory developed to conform to the construct point of view.[33] Although various specialized instruments have been devised for construct-oriented procedures, and the construct validity of numerous scales has been appraised after their development, the PRF is the only published multitrait personality inventory the development of which was guided explicitly by the substantive, structural, and external considerations of the construct viewpoint. As applied to the development of the PRF, these considerations took the form of a set of four interrelated principles: (1) the overriding importance of psychological theory; (2) the necessity of depressing variations in response style; (3) the importance of scale homogeneity as well as scale generalizability; and (4) the importance of fostering convergent and discriminate validity at the very beginning of a program of test construction.[34]

Jackson maintained that the sytem of variables emphasized in H. A. Murray's theory of personality (1938) possessed the advantage of "covering broadly, if not exhaustively the spectrum of personality needs, states and dispositions, of possessing carefully worked out published definitions and of having a good deal of theoretical and empirical underpinning."[35] After reviewing the available research and theoretical literature on twenty personality variables, Jackson developed a set of mutually exclusive substantive definitions for these variables. The final scales of the PRF were derived from a pool of approximately 3,000 items. An attempt was made to generate a roughly equal number of items reflecting the positive (having a trait) and negative (not having a trait) pole of each of the traits.

Forms A and B are intended to be comparable or equivalent forms. Each form contains 300 items and provides scores on the same

[32] Douglas N. Jackson, *Personality Research Form Manual* (Goshen, N.Y.: Research Psychologists Press, 1967).

[33] Wiggins, *Personality and Prediction.*

[34] Douglas N. Jackson, "A Sequential System for Personality Scale Development," in *Current Topics in Clinical and Community Psychology*, vol. 2, ed. C. D. Spielberger (New York: Academic Press, 1970), p. 63.

[35] Jackson, *Sequential System*, p. 67.

fifteen traits: achievement, affiliation, aggression, autonomy, dominance, endurance, exhibition, harm/avoidance, impulsivity, nurturance, order, play, social recognition, understanding, and infrequency. The last scale is intended as a reliability check on random or nonpurposive responses. Forms AA and BB each consist of 440 items. They include the same scales that are in forms *A* and *B* as well as seven other scales.

Elaborate item analysis procedures were employed to derive the PRF scales. These procedures were designed to insure optimal levels of homogeneity within each scale. In addition, a variety of procedures was used to achieve homogeneity on the basis of content saturation rather than on the basis of irrelevant responses. Considerable evidence indicates that the final PRF scales are relatively uncontaminated by sources of stylistic variance. Of greater methodological interest is a series of studies that demonstrate that the suppression of variance in response style increases the content homogeneity of personality scales. Finally, there is a considerable range of validity coefficients across different PRF variables. All are statistically significant, and most are quite respectable in comparison with those typically reported for personality inventories.

The PRF was constructed more than twenty years after the *Minnesota Multiphasic Personality Inventory* and more than half a century after the *Woodworth Personal Data Sheet*. There is not as yet sufficient evidence to substantiate the assumption of the construct viewpoint that careful attention to considerations of substantive and structural validity, typical of the PRF, guarantees significant empirical validity. This issue is among the most important in personality assessment today.[36]

PIERS-HARRIS CHILDREN'S SELF-CONCEPT SCALE   The PHCSCS was developed from Jersild's extensive list of things children say they like and dislike about themselves.[37] The scale was constructed from a pool of 164 statements to which examinees responded either yes or no, indicating which statements were congruent with their perception of themselves. The current form of the scale includes only 80 items, the rest having been deleted by the authors.

The PHCSCS was developed for use with children over a wide age range and was designed to control to some extent acquiescent responses by alternating keyed responses (40 percent yes, 60 percent

---

[36] Wiggins, *Personality and Prediction.*
[37] E. V. Piers and D. B. Harris, "Age and Other Correlates of Self-Concept in Children," *Journal of Educational Psychology* 55 (1964): 91–95.

no). Internal consistency indices for grades 3, 6, and 10 were reported by the authors as ranging from .88 to .93, except for tenth-grade girls (.78). Four-month test-retest reliabilities for grades 3, 6, and 10 were reported as .72, .71, and .72, respectively. Validity was determined by testing a group of 88 institutionalized retarded females. As predicted, the mean score for this group was found to be significantly lower than that obtained from public school children.

Factor analysis of scores derived from the PHCSCS by the authors results in the identification of ten factors. However, Piers and Harris indicated that only the scores obtained by the sixth-grade children were included in the analysis ($N = 457$).[38] Six of the ten factors identified were reported as interpretable and were labeled: behavior, intellectual school status, physical appearance and attributes, anxieties, popularity, and happiness and satisfaction.

Douglas J. Stanwyck and Donald W. Felker, using correlational techniques, compared the factor structure of the PHCSCS responses for three groups of children and derived clusters that they considered to be similar to Piers and Harris's results.[39] However, only five of Piers and Harris's six factors were discerned. These five aspects of the global self-concept were labeled: feeling self-concept, school self-concept, behavior self-concept, social self-concept, and body self-concept. Additional evidence for validity of the PSCSCS was reported by C. L. Mayer,[40] as well as by A. S. Bolea, D. Felker, and M. D. Barnes.[41] Elsewhere, this measure has been used for inferring self-concept change, and scores derived from the scale have been found to be predictive of self-evaluative behavior.[42]

TENNESSEE SELF-CONCEPT SCALE Developed for persons aged 12 and above who have at least a sixth-grade reading level, the TSCS may be used with both healthy and maladjusted people. It is designed to be easy for the subject, widely applicable, well standardized, and multidimensional in its description of self-concept. The original purpose of the TSCS was to develop a research instrument that might contribute to the solution of a difficult criterion problem in

[38] Piers and Harris, *Correlates of Self-Concept.*

[39] Douglas J. Stanwyck and Donald W. Felker, *Measuring the Self-Concept: A Factor Analytic Study* (Paper presented to the National Council on Measurement in Education, New York, 1971).

[40] C. L. Mayer, "A Study of the Relationship of Early Special Class Placement and the Self-Concepts of Mentally Handicapped Children," in E. V. Piers, *Manual for the Piers-Harris Children's Self-Concept Scale* (Nashville, Tenn.: Counselor Recordings and Tests, 1969).

[41] A. S. Bolea, Donald W. Felker, and M. D. Barnes, "A Pictorial Self-Concept Scale for Children in K-4," *Journal of Educational Measurement* 8 (1971): 223–224.

[42] Donald W. Felker, "The Prediction of Specific Self-Evaluations from Performance and Personality Measures," *Psychological Reports* 31 (1972): 823–826.

mental health research.[43] The scale consists of 90 items, equally divided for positive and negative responses. The counseling form yields fifteen profiled scores; the clinical and research form, thirty.

Test-retest reliability estimates of all major scores on both forms range from .60 to .92. Other evidence of reliability comes from the remarkable similarity of profile patterns found in repeated measures of the same individuals over long periods of time. Reliability coefficients for the various profile segments used in computing the number of deviant responses fell, for the most part, in the .80 to .90 range. Intercorrelations of the scores on the scale are reported in the manual. Some of the correlations are part-whole correlations and consequently are spuriously high. Other correlations are independent with regard to item overlap but are predictable from theory. The intercorrelation network is an important aspect of this scale. Deviations from typical patterns contribute significantly to the meaning of individual profiles.

Three kinds of validation procedures are reported in the manual: content validation, discrimination between groups, and correlation with other personality measures. Items on the scale were judged by seven psychologists to be classified correctly. Thus, the test's author assumes that the categories used in the scale are logical and publicly communicable. Factor analysis of twelve subscale scores yielded two factors—one interpreted as self-esteem and the other as a conflict-integration dimension of the self. Factor analysis of the 90 × 90 matrix of item correlations extracted twenty-two factors. Twenty of these factors were such external dimensions of self as family, physical, moral–ethical, personal, and social self. Some 369 psychiatric patients were compared with the 626 nonpatients of the norm group. The analysis demonstrated highly significant differences between patients and nonpatients for almost every score on the scale. At least four more studies by different researchers arrived at the same conclusion. It was also found that the scales differentiate types of disorders as well as degrees.

The scale is self-administering and requires no instruction beyond those on the inside cover of the test booklet. The answer sheet is arranged so that the subjects respond to every other item on the answer sheet and then repeat this procedure to complete the answer sheet. Some subjects may be momentarily confused by this instruction. Counselors must be aware of this possibility. The scales of TSCS are scored either by hand or by a computer service. The scoring procedures are explained on the score sheets and on the templates for the empirical scales for form CR (clinical and research form). The group from which the norms were developed was a broad sample of 626 people, including people from various parts of the country whose ages ranged from 12–68. There were approximately equal numbers of males and females. Black and white subjects were representative of all social, economic, and intellectual levels and educational levels from the sixth grade through the Ph.D. level. Subjects were obtained from high schools and colleges, institutions, and various other sources. Norms are provided for males and females combined in the form of percentile and standard T-scores.

The TSCS counseling form (form C) is easy to interpret. The score sheet may be presented directly to the client for interpretation and discussion. However, with form CR, feedback to a client is difficult and requires professional training.

EMPIRICALLY CONSTRUCTED INVENTORIES

CALIFORNIA PSYCHOLOGICAL INVENTORY   The CPI is constructed for persons 13 years of age or older. Harrison Gough developed the test to provide a comprehensive, multidimensional personality description of normal persons in a variety of nonclinical settings.[44] The CPI is made up to 480 true-false items (12 of which are duplicates) and yields scores on eighteen scales. Approximately half the items used were selected from the relatively nonpathological items included in the *Minnesota Multiphasic Personality Inventory* item pool. The items range over a wide variety of manifest behavior content that are classified into the following categories: (1) poise, ascendancy, and self-assurance; (2) socialization, maturity, and responsibility; (3) achievement potential and intellectual efficiency; and (4) intellectual and interest modes. The strength of the CPI is that it represents personality characteristics important for social living relevant to such variables as social class membership, grades in introductory psychology courses, prominence as a leader, and the like.

Stability estimates reported for 200 male prisoners, retested from one to three weeks later, ranged from .49 to .87, with a median estimate of .80. High school subjects retested one year later provided

---

[44] Harrison Gough, *Manual, California Psychological Inventory* (Palo Alto, Calif.: Consulting Psychologists Press, 1966).

median test-retest correlations of .65 (males) and .68 (females).[45] The validity of most of the CPI scales was estimated by comparing groups between which a given scale ought to discriminate. All but four of the scales were developed by item analysis procedures using criteria external to the inventory. The socialization scale, for example, was shown to discriminate between delinquents and non-delinquents and to relate to descriptions of normal persons. The four rationally derived scales were formulated by means of content integrity criteria and were refined by item analysis for internal consistency. Intercorrelations of CPI scores with several other widely used tests of personality are presented in the manual.

The CPI is mainly self-administering. There is no time limit, and most examinees complete this inventory in less than an hour. The CPI may be scored locally by hand or by IBM machine. An economical scoring service is provided by National Computer Systems. Standard score norms (mean, 50; standard deviation, 10) were developed separately for males and females, based on samples of over 6,000 males and over 7,000 females. Although these normative groups are not represented as a random sample of the general population, they are purported to include a wide range of ages, socioeconomic groups, and geographical areas. In addition, the manual presents separate mean profiles for college and high school subjects of both sexes and includes tables showing the raw score means and standard deviations of thirty special educational, professional, and other groups for each of the eighteen CPI scales. Interpretation of the CPI should be limited to persons with professional training in objective personality assessment.

There would seem to be no limit to the number of criteria for which one might undertake to establish scoring keys for the CPI. The evidence, however, is not clear as to how many of these criteria are of unique and practical value. The scales may provide an inefficient and superfluous method of conceptualizing individuals. For the most part, they are found to be highly intercorrelated, in some cases approaching the reliability values of the individual scales. The fact that the scales appear to overlap considerably raises the problem of parsimony in the inventory; that is, could the inventory be modified and still give reliable and valid personality assessment? James Mitchell and J. Pierce-Jones concluded from a factor analysis of the CPI that the scales represent a much smaller number of personality dimensions than the eighteen suggested.[46] In an unpub-

[45] Gough, *Manual, CPI.*

[46] James V. Mitchell, Jr., and J. Pierce-Jones, "A Factor Analysis of Gough's California Psychological Inventory," *Journal of Consulting Psychology* 24 (1960): 453–456.

lished study, Richard Schnell verified these findings and extracted two principal factors representative of the feeling and action content typical of self-report personality inventories.[47] Furthermore, Gough's suggestion that considerable weight should be given in interpretation to interactions among scales, to patterns of profiles, and to the internal variability of the profile is not substantiated by the evidence published to date. Nevertheless, the CPI has been accepted for wide use, especially in academic counseling.

MINNESOTA MULTIPHASIC PERSONALITY INVENTORY In the mid-1930s, psychologists working in mental health settings, psychiatrists, and other mental health professionals had little other than interview procedures to aid them in diagnosing persons afflicted with mental or emotional disorders. The few who had followed Woodworth's lead in the development of personality inventories were for the most part academics. Their instruments were little known and seldom employed in clinics. Although the *Rorschach Psychodiagnostik* had been introduced in the United States in the early 1930s by Samuel Beck, widespread acceptance and use of this measure did not occur until the Second World War. When they did use tests, psychologists relied principally on the Stanford-Binet as the measure of choice. For the most part, efforts to employ a test intended to assess the mental ability of children to evaluate the emotional status of both children and adults were unsuccessful.

Influenced by the success of the work of E. K. Strong, Jr., and his colleagues in using an empirical methodology to develop the *Strong Vocational Interest Blank* for men, Stark Hathaway, a psychologist, and J. C. McKinley, a psychiatrist, both affiliated with the University of Minnesota, undertook work in 1936 to develop empirically a personality test that would facilitate the diagnosis of clinic patients and fill the void of unavailable or inadequate instrumentation required to accomplish this task.

Construction of personality questionnaires according to empirical methodology was slow to develop, chiefly because the criteria for measuring personality are debatable at best. However, Hathaway and McKinley were encouraged to believe that one obvious point of departure was psychiatric classification. The MMPI was finally published in 1942, was accepted rapidly, and remains today the most widely used and the most widely investigated of all personality questionnaires.[48] Although strictly empirical in its original concep-

---

[47] Richard Schnell, *Factor Scales for the California Psychological Inventory* (masters thesis, Purdue University, 1961).

[48] Stark R. Hathaway, *Manual, Minnesota Multiphasic Personality Inventory,* rev. (New York: Psychological Corporation, 1951).

tion, it proved to be ineffective in allocating patients to diagnostic groups. Nonetheless, the inventory has grown in prominence because accumulated research and clinical experience have provided a basis for other practical types of interpretation.[49]

In the development of the MMPI, use was made of Woodworth's procedure of writing items that seem to have clinical significance and establishing their validity by contrasting the responses of normal and abnormal subjects. Furthermore, using the model of the *Strong Vocational Interest Blanks*, a large item pool was created with the idea that only a relatively small subset would be included in any one key or scale. The entire pool of 550 items, selected from more than 1,000 items and covering health conditions, habits, personal and social attitudes, and psychiatric symptoms, was administered both to normal people and to individuals exhibiting a defined pathological condition. Items that showed the greatest differentiation were selected for the scale and then were cross-validated on new groups of cases. The items, written as declarative sentences, were printed on small cards to be sorted by the subject into three groups: *true, false,* and *cannot say.*

Constructed for use with persons 16 years of age or older, the MMPI consists of 566 items (including 16 duplicated items), representing different areas of experience. More than 400 special scales have been developed utilizing this item pool.[50] Some are rational scales. In addition, some of the MMPI scales simply consist of shorter forms of versions of other MMPI scales. One innovation was the development of several validity (reliability) scales, designed to indicate such factors as the degree to which the subject consistently selects socially acceptable responses rather than tell the truth.[51]

The original MMPI scales were designed primarily to be of interest to clinical psychologists and psychiatrists concerned with diagnosis and treatment of psychopathology. Because of the pathological content of many of the MMPI items, many individuals may consider it offensive to be asked to answer true or false to some of them.

As published, the MMPI includes four auxiliary (verification) scales and ten clinical scales. The auxiliary scales are labeled question score (?), lie score (L), validity score (F), and K score (K). The

[49] Edwards, *Measurement of Personality Traits.*
[50] W. G. Dahlstrom, G. S. Welsh, and L. E. Dahlstrom, *An MMPI Handbook: A Guide to Use in Clinical Practice and Research,* 2nd ed., vol. 2 (Minneapolis: University of Minnesota Press, 1975).
[51] DuBois, *History of Psychological Testing.*

clinical scales include hypochondriasis (Hs), depression (D), hysteria (Hy), psychopathic deviate (Pd), masculinity–femininity (Mf), paranoia (Pa), psychothenia (Pt), schizophrenia (Sc), hypomania (Ma), and social introversion (Si). Most of the scales were developed by comparing the responses of persons judged to be normal with persons classified in given diagnostic groups. Because of the common item content included in these scales, rather high interscale correlations are obtained. A group form R presents the MMPI items in a new order that allows all fourteen regular scores to be determined from only the first 399 items. The remaining items, used for research only, are grouped as numbers 400–566. The form R hardcover booklet facilitates completion of the MMPI where a desk or other writing space is not available.

Reliability estimates from only three separate studies are reported in the manual. However, a relatively large number of MMPI reliability studies reported elsewhere provide considerable evidence of the test's reliability for various groups.[52]

According to the manual, a high score on a given scale has been found to predict positively a corresponding final clinical diagnosis for more than 60 percent of new psychiatric admissions. A summary of research studies concerned with the question of the diagnostic validity of the MMPI supports the conclusion that this instrument can differentiate normal individuals from abnormal but that it is not sensitive enough to discriminate within the abnormal population itself.[53] Few psychological measures have been subjected to greater scrutiny than has been the MMPI, with research reports numbering in the hundreds. Factorial studies indicate that very few factors do account for the major proportion of the variance in the MMPI.[54] G. S. Welsh, in seeking to obtain pure factor scales, found only two.[55]

The validity of the MMPI still is in doubt. The diagnostic groups used to build the instrument were based on questionable, and perhaps inaccurate, psychiatric classifications. The total number of items and the number of items that involve markedly pathological content are both excessive. In contrast, items relevant to variables considered important in current personality theories are excluded or deemphasized.

Untimed, the MMPI is administered easily to most persons in

[52] Buros, *Personality Tests and Reviews.*
[53] Buros, *Personality Tests and Reviews.*
[54] Paul Horst, *Personality: Measurement of Dimensions,* (San Francisco: Josey-Bass, 1968).
[55] G. S. Welsh and W. G. Dahlstrom, eds., *Basic Readings on the MMPI in Psychology and Medicine* (Minneapolis: University of Minnesota Press, 1956).

40–90 minutes. Directions for administering both individual and group forms are explicit and clear. Hand-scoring is feasible for all forms. Computer-scoring and computer-interpreting services are available; however, the validity of computer-based actuarial interpretation has yet to be demonstrated. No system has been developed to date that does not require monitoring by an experienced counselor.

Interpretation should be attempted only by persons who have had special training and supervised experience in the use of the MMPI. This inventory was developed for use in a clinic population by experienced clinicians. The MMPI has demonstrated utility in the hands of persons who work with such clientele. Untrained persons and inappropriate individuals or groups should not use this instrument. The tendency to overinterpret results should be avoided. However, appropriately used as a clinical instrument, together with other tests and inferential media, the MMPI can make a definite contribution to the process of personality evaluation.

FACTORIALLY CONSTRUCTED
INVENTORIES

EYSENCK PERSONALITY INVENTORY   Constructed for use with college students and adults, the EPI[56] is a further development in assessing the relatively independent personality dimensions measured by the *Maudsley Medical Questionnaire* and the *Maudsley Personality Inventory* (MPI): extroversion-introversion (E) and neuroticism-stability (N).[57] Extroversion refers to the outgoing, uninhibited, impulsive, and sociable inclinations. Neuroticism is the tendency toward a generalized emotional overresponsiveness under stress. Over 30,000 subjects were employed in the series of investigations that culminated with the development of the EPI. They included university students and various English middle-class and working-class groups who varied in age and sex composition, as well as samples purported to be representative of the whole population of England.

The content of the EPI is very similar to that of the MPI. Some changes have been made, such as the introduction of two equivalent forms, the elimination of the significant low-order correlation between the two MPI factor scales, the rewording of the items to

[56] Hans J. Eysenck and Sybil B. G. Eysenck, *Manual, Eysenck Personality Inventory* (San Deigo, Calif.: Educational and Industrial Testing Service, 1963).
[57] Robert R. Knapp, *Manual, Maudsley Personality Inventory* (San Diego, Calif.: Educational and Industrial Testing Service, 1962).

make them less difficult for subjects of low ability or educational level, and the addition of a lie scale (L, abstracted from the MMPI) that identifies examinees who falsify their responses. Forms A and B are provided for use with college students and adults. Each form includes 57 items: scale E, 24 items; scale N, 24 items; and scale L, 9 items. A specially printed form is available for use in industry.

Correlations reported in the manual between the extroversion and neuroticism scales range from −.04 (neurotics) to +.05 (psychotics) for form A and from −.09 (normals) to −.22 (neurotics) for form B. The relationship between extroversion and neuroticism was also investigated in seven separate English samples that involved a total N of 1,478. No significant correlation was obtained. In an American college sample, correlations between the scales were +.01 for form A ($N = 1,003$) and −.11 for form B ($N = 239$). These findings were viewed by the authors as support for the hypothesis that two statistically independent factors had been determined for the EPI. When Hans Eysenck suggested, in 1947, that two important personality dimensions (neuroticism and extroversion) exist, there was much argument about the scheme. However, the major alternative factor-analytic schemes, namely those of Cattell and Guilford, result in second-order factors that resemble closely those postulated by Eysenck. The Eysencks contend that their factors E and N contribute more to a description of personality than do any other set of factors in the noncognitive field. Acceptable reliability indices of sufficient magnitude are reported in the manual; however, associated N is small.

Few validity data are reported for the EPI. However, the test authors and others have conducted several experimental studies using the EPI's predecessor, the MPI, in which the MPI scales were shown to predict circumscribed real-life behavioral criteria. EPI-MPI correlations are sufficiently high to support assertions that the experimental findings reported for the MPI may also apply to the EPI.

Factor N (neuroticism) may be related closely to the inherited degree of liability of the autonomic nervous system, while factor E (extroversion) is thought to be associated with the degree of excitation and inhibition prevalent in the central nervous system. Introverts have demonstrated better performance on vigilance tests than have extroverts, have longer afterimages, preserve visual fixation better, have greater tolerance for sensory deprivation but less tolerance for physical pain, and yield better performance when a measure is made of their critical flicker fusion thresholds. The use of the EPI has been associated with general inquiries into various forms of mental or physical illness. Hysterics and psychopaths have been found to be significantly more extroverted than anxiety neurotics, and neurotic groups studied have scored higher on the neuroticism scale than have normal groups. Better adjustment appears to be associated with low-average neuroticism scores and with middle to above-average extroversion scores. Further research in educational settings has demonstrated the importance of dimensions of extroversion and neuroticism to academic attainment and learning theory. The scales have been shown to be independent of intelligence and, in general, within given academic groups, individuals having slightly elevated scores on the neuroticism scale and scores toward the introverted pole on the extroversion scale can be expected to achieve greater academic success.

The EPI is administered easily and requires no time limit. Ten to 20 minutes are usually required to complete each form. Instructions printed on each booklet may be read aloud to groups of subjects or may be read silently by the subjects themselves. The tendency for subjects to answer questions in a socially favorable manner has not been found to play an important part under ordinary administration conditions. An exception noted in the manual is the use of the EPI for selection in industry. Both forms of the EPI may be hand-scored by the same set of stencils. A FORTRAN computer program, developed and distributed by the publisher, is also available to score data suitably prepared for computer processing.

Correlations by sex are not large, because items suggesting large sex-related response differences were eliminated from the inventory. However, women do tend to score higher than men on scale N and to score lower on scale E. In addition, there is a general tendency for working-class groups to have higher scale N scores than middle-class groups; no difference has been observed with respect to scale E. Urban samples have been shown to score higher on both scales N and E when compared with rural samples. These findings suggest that particular care should be taken when selecting normative reference data to aid in the interpretation of results.

For both EPI forms, British percentile norms based on a total of 1,931 normal adults (1,055 males and 876 females) are available. The manual presents tables of means and standard deviations for the normative sample ordered by occupation and for a sample of 483 abnormal British subjects (203 males and 280 females) separated into neurotic groups, psychotic groups, female prisoners, and hospitalized alcoholics. Percentile norms for college students are provided separately for form A and form B. Norms for form A are based on 1,003 cases and for form B on 239 cases tested at various colleges and universities throughout the United States. Tentative norms for

236 college cases for forms A and B combined are presented in the manual. All norms provided for the EPI should be used with caution. Although the authors wisely suggest that it may be desirable for counselors to develop their own local norms, it is their responsibility to provide more relevant and representative reference data than they have to date. Certainly, interpretations of the EPI should mirror these considerations and be limited to persons with professional training and supervised experience in objective personality assessment.

GUILFORD-ZIMMERMAN TEMPERAMENT SURVEY J. P. Guilford's research program, in relation to the factors eventually included in the *Guilford-Zimmerman Temperament Survey* (GZTS), began as far back as 1930 with a discussion of the concepts of extroversion and introversion.[58] In 1933, Guilford published what was perhaps the first attempt to apply the new factor analytic methods to a personality questionnaire in order to determine what common personality variables might be represented therein.[59] Guilford continued his research and published the GZTS.[60] Of the ten factor trait names employed in the GZTS, seven have the same letter symbols that they had in the earlier inventories: S, T, and R from the *Inventory of Factors STDCR;* G, A, and M from the *Inventory of Factors GAMIN;* and O from the *Guilford-Martin Personnel Inventory.*

Constructed for use with high school seniors, college students, and adults, the GZTS was intended to provide a profile of traits thought to be useful for assessing normal individuals. The GZTS consists of 300 items, with each of ten factors or traits measured by 30 items. The ten GZTS scales have been labeled general activity (G), restraint (R), ascendance (A), sociability (S), emotional stability (E), objectivity (O), friendliness (F), thoughtfulness (T), personal relations (P), and masculinity (M).

Internal consistency estimates based on the consensus of results obtained from a sample of 912 college students (523 males and 389 females) and a random sample of 100 males varied from .75 (objectivity and friendliness) to .87 (sociability).[61] The college sample data were analyzed by use of Kuder-Richardson formulas applied separately by sex and for the combined sample, while both split-half

[58] J. P. Guilford and K. W. Braly, "Extraversion and Introversion," *Psychological Bulletin* 27 (1930): 96–107.
[59] J. P. Guilford and R. B. Guilford, "An Analysis of the Factors Present in a Typical Test of Introversion-Extroversion," *Journal of Abnormal and Social Psychology* 28 (1934): 377–399.
[60] J. P. Guilford et al., *Manual for the Guilford-Zimmerman Temperament Survey* (Beverly Hills, Calif.: Sheridan Supply Company, 1948).
[61] Guilford et al., *Manual, GZTS.*

and odd-even corrected estimates were derived from random male sample data.

The manual asserts that factorial validity is assured by factor analytic studies together with successive item analyses directed toward internal consistency and uniqueness. Although no specific evidence of predictive validity is presented, the manual states that evidence of validity has accumulated, based on correlational studies of the GZTS with criteria of adjustment.

Findings derived from other research on the GZTS report that the GZTS may be used effectively at the high school level if appropriate norms are constructed. Furthermore, the manual includes a table containing recommendations as to the most favorable and least favorable score ranges in relation to performance of industrial supervisory and administrative personnel.

Adequate directions for self-administration are printed on the test-booklet cover. Although the time required varies with the individual, usually 45 minutes is sufficient. The scales of the GZTS are scored easily by hand with stencils or by scoring machine. GZTS norms are provided for males and females separately in the forms of percentile ranks and of two normalized standard score scales: T-scores (mean, 50; standard deviation, 10), and C-scores (mean, 5; standard deviation, 2). These norms were established for all GZTS scales, except thoughtfulness, on data obtained from 523 college men and 389 college women sampled from one university and two junior colleges in southern California. The male sample, with a mean age of approximately 23, included many veterans of the Second World War. In addition, data for the norms were obtained from an unspecified number of high school seniors and their parents in southern California, who were administered the final form of the GZTS with thoughtfulness items included. Because no significant difference was found between the mean scores of parents (age range, 37–62) and their children, the data were combined for norming purposes.

The GZTS is difficult to interpret properly, unless the interpreter is familiar with the instrument and has received professional training in objective personality assessment. In most cases, optimal scores do not extend to the top of the scale but are at some moderate position between the mean and the highest score for each scale. Two test-taking attitude scales have been derived for use with the GZTS.[62]

---

[62] A. Jacobs and A. Schlaff, *Falsification Scales for the Guilford-Zimmerman Temperament Survey* (Beverly Hills, Calif.: Sheridan Supply Company, 1955).

SIXTEEN PERSONALITY-FACTOR QUESTIONNAIRE Constructed for persons 16 years of age or older, the 16 PFQ was devised to measure sixteen factor-analytically determined personality variables for use in occupational guidance and individual counseling and as a tool in clinical evaluation.[63] Forms A and B consist of 187 items and include 10 to 13 items for each of sixteen personality factors: reserved-outgoing, less intelligent–more intelligent, affected by feelings–emotionally stable, humble-assertive, sober–happy-go-lucky, expedient-conscientious, shy-venturesome, tough-minded–tender-minded, trusting-suspicious, practical-imaginative, forthright-shrewd, placid-apprehensive, conservative-experimenting, group-dependent–self-sufficient, casual-controlled and relaxed-tense. A shortened and simplified form C contains only 105 items and adds a seventeenth scale, motivation. The majority of statements for all forms concern interests and preferences. The remaining statements represent the customary self-reports of behavior. The sixteen PFQ scales were developed by factor analytic techniques that resulted in correlated factors rather than uncorrelated factors. Consequently, the scores of the sixteen PFQ scales are correlated.

Split-half internal consistency estimates ($N = 450$) for the sixteen scales, adjusted by the Spearman-Brown Prophecy Formula, ranged from .71 to .93 for the previous editions of forms A and B combined and from .54 to .87 for single forms.[64] The sample studied was not identified. No reliability datum is reported for forms C and X. Factor loadings ranging from .73 to .96 are presented as estimates of the validity of the 16 PFQ. Tables in a handbook provide data for predictive use of the 16 PFQ in the form of profile matching and criterion estimation for twenty-eight occupational profiles. Profiles for nine clinical syndrome groupings are also presented. However, no statistical datum is given regarding the power of 16 PFQ scores to discriminate among the occupational or the clinical groups.

Easily administered, forms A and B require approximately 50–60 minutes to complete, while form C may be completed in 30–40 minutes. Form X is presented either in booklet form with tape-recorded directions for use with semiliterates or entirely on tape for use with illiterates. This form requires 50–70 minutes for administration. The 16 PFQ may be scored by hand or by machine. Hand-scoring is simple and is viewed by the authors of the test to be

[63] Raymond B. Cattell and H. W. Eber, Manual, Sixteen Personality Factor Questionnaire (Champaign, Ill.: Institute for Personality and Ability Testing, 1963).
[64] Buros, Personality Tests and Reviews.

superior to machine-scoring when fewer than 1,000 examinees are to be tested. National Computer Systems offers an economical scoring service for this questionnaire.

The 16 PFQ yields sixteen or seventeen scores, depending on which form is used. Normalized standard score norms (Sten: mean, 5.5; standard deviation, 1.5) are presented for the 1961–1962 editions of forms A and B in a handbook and as a separate supplement of norms. Separate norms tables for each form, and for forms A and B combined, are provided for American college students, ordered by sex. A handbook supplement (form C) presents normalized standard score norms for both male and female general population and college students. Several thousand subjects made up the normative samples for these forms of the 16 PFQ. However, specific characteristics of these samples, such as source, occupation, social class, and specific sample size, are not identified. Data relevant to form X are available in mimeographed form from the publisher.

The 16 PFQ should be interpreted only by those persons who have had professional training and supervised experience in objective personality assessment. A prodigious amount of careful statistical work has gone into the development of the 16 PFQ. However, it should be regarded primarily as a research instrument. The number of items that make up each of the factor scales, especially in the case of form C, is perhaps too low to obtain reliable measures. Some doubt remains concerning the independence and reliability of each of the factor scales. Furthermore, critical examination is needed of both the scale structure and the number of factors measured by this instrument.

INTERPRETING PERSONALITY
AND SELF-CONCEPT INVENTORIES

A CONCEPTUAL FRAMEWORK

Many researchers have attempted to reduce a seeming chaos of personality traits and human behaviors into orderly two-dimensional models. These attempts have resulted from factor analytic work on studies with parent-child interaction and small-group interaction and with personality ratings and questionnaires. Timothy Leary presented his classification of interpersonal behaviors in a circular structure incorporating the dimensions of dominance-submission and love-hate.[65] Emanual Shapiro concluded that Leary's

---

[65] Timothy Leary, *Interpersonal Diagnosis of Personality* (New York: Ronald Press, 1957).

two-dimensional conceptualization was quite similar to that of Hans Eysenck.[66]

These dimensions are not new. Eysenck has drawn a comparison with the four temperaments discussed by Wundt, Kant, and Galen. Wundt's slow-quick dimension would appear to correspond to the introversion-extroversion dimension, while Wundt's strong-weak dimension seems to correspond to the neurotic-stable dimension of Eysenck.[67] The relationship between Eysenck's dimensions and the four classical temperaments is illustrated in Figure 10.1. The terms on the periphery of this figure represent the results of Eysenck's factor analytic work with personality ratings and questionnaires.

Eysenck suggests that such a dimensional system would allow individuals to be perceived as occupying a position located along two continua. He concludes that this system might prove to be more reliable than the diagnostic system now widely used.

SPECIAL
CONSIDERATIONS AND CAUTIONS

Questionnaires may be valid on certain levels of interpretation and completely invalid on others, or they may have varying degrees of validity at different levels. Various distortions prevent the acceptance of personality questionnaires as frank and valid self-descriptions.

ITEM AMBIGUITY   The first difficulty is that items are often ambiguous. "Do you make friends easily?" seems to be a straightforward question, but it is hard to say just what behavior the question refers to and what the examiner means by *easily* or by *friend*. Similar difficulty arises because most questionnaires ask about a hypothetical typical situation, instead of asking about well-defined situations. Many self-report inventories ask for responses such as *always, frequently,* or *never*. Simpson (reported in Cronbach[68]) examined what such ratings might mean quantitatively. He asked students what they meant by saying they usually did something. Twenty-five percent of them replied that it meant at least 90 percent of the time; another 25 percent said that *usually* includes frequencies below 70 percent.

[66] Emanual Shapiro, *An Investigation of the Utility of Two Dimensional Models for the Assessment of Personality* (doctoral diss., Purdue University, 1966).

[67] Theodore M. Sharpe, *An Investigation of the Adequacy of the Eysenck Personality Inventory in the Prediction of Client Behavior and Optimal Therapeutic Objectives* (doctoral diss., Purdue University, 1972).

[68] Cronbach, *Essentials of Psychological Testing.*

FIGURE 10.1
RELATIONSHIP BETWEEN EYSENCK'S PERSONALITY DIMENSIONS
AND THE CLASSICAL FOUR TEMPERAMENTS

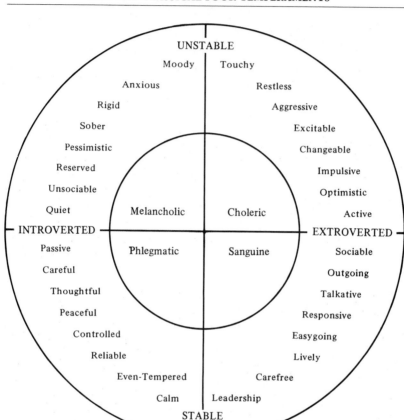

Source: Hans J. Eysenck, "Principles and Methods of Personality Description, Classification and Diagnosis,"
British Journal of Psychology 55 (August 1964): 285. Reprinted with permission of Cambridge University Press.

FAKING   Though an examiner may view an inquiry as a scientific project to which a subject is willing to contribute valid information, the subject may see it differently. In the clinical setting, the subject may wish to avoid a threatening diagnosis. In business, the subject's first concern is to obtain a job. In vocational guidance, the subject may set out to convince the counselor that he or she should enter a certain occupation rather than learn the truth about his or her suitability for it. Most subjects pick a socially desirable response to any item. Some tests have social desirability keys that count how often a person gives socially accepted responses. A high social desirability score may mean that the person truly has an admirable interpersonal orientation, but it also may mean that he or she has been less than frank in filling out the questionnaire. Nor can one dismiss the possibility that subjects may be deceiving themselves and have never realized some of the faults in their behavior. On the other hand, some subjects deliberately paint an unfavorable self-portrait.

A number of methods, such as the L scale of the MMPI, has been devised to identify certain contaminating influences on personality test performance. A few, for example, the K scale of the MMPI, may be used to correct scores.[69] For the California Test of Personality, H. C. Lindgren devised an idealization scale that consists of the 30 items most easily faked.[70] A correlation of .85 between the scores on this scale and total scores led him to conclude that the inventory measured the tendency to idealize oneself. In another study, Harrison Gough selected MMPI items that drew different responses when students were asked to respond normally and as if they were attempting to make a good impression.[71] A high score indicates an attempt to make a good impression. Still another method attempts to reduce the possible effects of differences in the social acceptability of items on test scores by the use of the forced-choice technique.

THE FORCED-CHOICE TECHNIQUE The forced-choice technique is radically different in many respects from older devices that have proved to be inadequate.[72] This method is a procedure for constructing items designed to control certain biasing variables that may influence an individual's score on a test. Desirable and undesirable personality traits are learned, culturally determined phenomena. The social desirability values of given statements, therefore, may vary from culture to culture or from group to group.[73] In any event, the bias toward social desirability may be controlled by requiring

---

[69] Paul E. Meehl and Stark R. Hathaway, "The K Factor as a Suppressor Variable in the Minnesota Multiphasic Personality Inventory," *Journal of Applied Psychology* 30 (1946): 525–564.

[70] H. C. Lindgren, "The Development of a Scale of Cultural Idealization Based on the California Test of Personality," *Journal of Educational Psychology* 43 (1952): 81–91.

[71] Harrison G. Gough, "On Making a Good Impression," *Journal of Educational Research* 46 (1952): 33–42.

[72] E. L. Runyon and E. L. Stromberg, "Forced-Choice Evaluation Form for Clinical Psychology Practicum Students," *Educational and Psychological Measurement* 13 (1953): 170–178.

[73] Edwards, *Measurement of Personality Traits.*

subjects to choose among items that are equal in that respect but as different as possible with respect to some index of validity.[74]

The term *forced-choice* had its origins in the fact that the original method asked individuals to pick one of two items most descriptive of themselves. When only two stimuli are presented, the forced-choice method is a special case of paired comparisons. However, it differs from this method in that ordinarily in the forced-choice method not all possible combinations of stimuli are presented to the subject; and the items are grouped together in a set on the basis of certain characteristics that are obtained from the study of each item in a yes-no format.

A given item may consist of two alternatives of equal social desirability. The individual is instructed to check the one that he or she believes best describes him or her. If more than two alternatives are presented, subjects check the one that they believe least describes them as well as the one that best describes them.

Promoters of the forced-choice technique do not hold that the forced-choice method prevents an individual from falsifying results. Rather, "it reduces the . . . ability to produce any desired outcome of obviously good or obviously bad traits. It, thus, diminishes the effect of favoritism and personal bias."[75]

Critics of the forced-choice technique suggest that forcing the choice of one item over another as descriptive of an individual creates a situation in which the individual may have no logical basis for making a choice. However, a more serious criticism pertains to the fact that, by virtue of their mathematical properties, forced-choice scales yield scores that cannot be manipulated by conventional arithmetic procedures.[76] Thus norms should not be provided for such scales, although Cattell, Edwards, Kuder and others have done so. Certain measures, such as the EPPS, can be interpreted from an ipsative, or a self-referent, conceptual framework, wherein an individual's responses are compared with one another rather than with those of other persons. The EPPS provides an equal opportunity to endorse each of the fifteen scales of the inventory. The fact that the raw frequency of endorsement of one scale is greater or less than that of other scales has interpretive significance in and of itself.

---

[74] Staff, Personnel Research Section, AGO, "The Forced-Choice Technique and Rating Scales," *American Psychologist* 1 (1946): 267 (Abstract).

[75] E. D. Sisson, "Forced-Choice, The New Army Rating," *Personnel Psychology* 1 (1948): 365–381.

[76] R. H. Bauerfiend, "The Matter of Ipsative Scores," *Personnel and Guidance Journal* 40 (1962): 210–217.

Figure 10.2 shows an example of an EPPS profile created from both normative and ipsative data. A subject has twenty-eight opportunities to respond to the content of each scale. If responses are random, a scale score of 14 should be expected. The extent to which scores exceed or are less than 14 can take on interpretive meaning with no reference to a normative comparison. A study of Figure 10.2 reveals probable discrepancies between interpretations based on these two evaluative postures.

The counselor is cautioned to attend to ipsative modes of profile interpretation when using forced-choice inventories. Unfortunately, most such measures do not permit equal choice among scale content as does the EPPS. Consequently, it well may be that scores constituting the profiles of forced-choice measures that fail to provide this opportunity are not interpretable.

ITEM CHARACTERISTICS AND INVENTORY LABELS   Another masking device is the use of subtle items that have little seeming relevance to the decision being made. While a score derived wholly from subtle items may be nearly fake-proof, the majority of empirical scales are loaded with transparent items. A noteworthy proposal is to score separately the subtle and the transparent items.[77] When the two scores agree, some confidence can be placed in the results. If they disagree, separate validity data are needed. D. N. Wiener developed separate keys for five MMPI scales. No direct validity study was carried out on them, but there is evidence that subtle and transparent (obvious) keys differ in their susceptibility to response biases.

Some questionnaires are openly called measures of adjustment. More commonly, the title is unrevealing, for example, the *California Psychological Inventory*. Often, a subject does not know what scores will be recorded and what interpretation will be made. Perhaps the use of subtle scale content is the most legitimate to employ, provided that a counselor has encouraged the client to provide the best information he or she can. This sort of rapport is a complex interpersonal relationship, depending on many factors other than a counselor's technique. Counselors can never safely assume that they have created an ideal relationship and that a client will tell the whole truth and nothing but the truth. A subject may shift back

[77] D. N. Wiener, "Subtle and Obvious Keys for the MMPI," *Journal of Consulting Psychology* 12 (1948): 164–170.

FIGURE 10.2
NORMATIVE VERSUS IPSATIVE PROFILE MODE

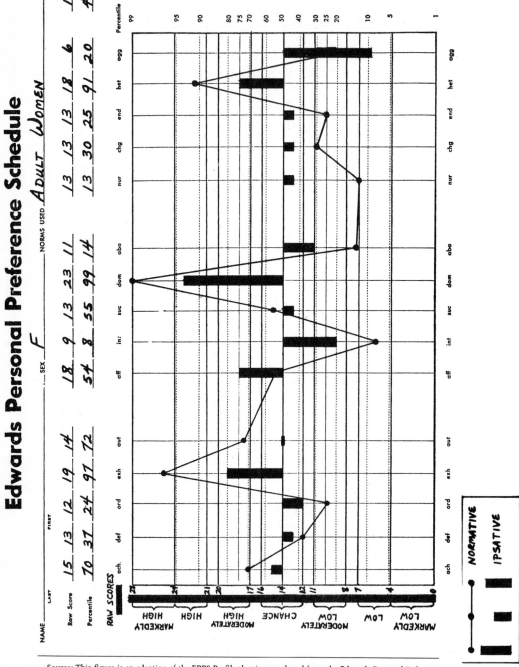

and forth between concealing and revealing, but there is little chance that "he (she) will come to rest at 'objectivity'."[78]

RESPONSE SETS AND STYLES Acquiescence has been described as a generalized tendency of persons to be agreeable (a set), but it has also been defined operationally in terms of a disproportionate tendency to select a certain response category (a style). Acquiescence response style is a nuisance in true-false tests of ability and achievement. The estimated ability of the highly acquiescent individual rises or falls depending on whether the test-maker presents more true statements than false statements or vice versa. The subject tends to agree or to offer a positive response regardless of what questions are asked. A test developer who views this behavior as a response bias will try to eliminate or reduce its influence. For instance, authors write items in such fashion that there are as many items keyed like as there are items keyed dislike. Others believe that response tendencies such as acquiescence reflect significant personality characteristics.[79] Some writers suggest that the patterns of response tell more about an individual's true characteristics than does the content of the responses themselves. The acquiescent person is thought to be submissive and conforming; the one who evades questions with cannot say may also withdraw from challenges in daily life. There is evidence that persons who experience difficulty in adapting to their environment respond disagree more often than agree on attitude or self-descriptive items. Hence, a tendency to disagree may be a diagnostic indicator of sorts.

An extensive body of research exists relating to response styles, sets, and biases as they affect personality test scores. A deviation hypothesis assumes that statistically deviant response patterns are general and that deviant behavior patterns in real life are associated with deviant behavior patterns in responses to structured tests. A corollary of this hypothesis is that the content of personality test items is relatively unimportant in the sense that discrimination between behavior criterion groups can be achieved on the basis of deviant response patterns to almost an infinite variety of test stimuli.[80]

In his article entitled "The Great Response-Style Myth," Leonard G. Rorer disclaims the assertion that response styles are an important source of variance in personality and self-concept inventories.[81]

---

[78] Cronbach, Essentials of Psychological Testing, p. 502.
[79] Cronbach, Essentials of Psychological Testing.
[80] Wiggins, Personality and Prediction.
[81] Leonard G. Rorer, "The Great Response-Style Myth," Psychological Bulletin 63 (March 1965): 129–156.

Rorer clearly distinguishes between the terms *response style* and *response set*. He defines *set* as what happens when a respondent employs some systematic posture while evaluating item content to formulate a response; an example of a set is defensiveness. Such behavior may account for a significant portion of the response variance on personality inventories. Their measurement and control are essential if the predictive validity of personality inventories is to be increased. On the other hand, the term *style* is used to refer to a way or manner of responding, such as the tendency to select some particular response independent of item content. Whereas sets affect responses in relation to item content, styles affect responses in the absence of consideration of item content.

In assessing the extent to which styles affect answers to items, it is necessary to distinguish between achievement measures and personality, attitude, and interest inventories.[82] On examinations, the examiner knows the right answers, and the respondent must sometimes guess. On such tests, inferences concerning an individual's response style may be made on the basis of his or her behavior on a number of examinations and by comparing the proportion of answers selected from any given response category. No such inference is possible on inventories, because the correctness of answers is unknown and because there is no basis for assuming that the individual guessed at any of the answers. When people do guess, they are exhibiting a response style, if by this it is meant that the distribution of their answers is not random. Available data indicate that not more than 20 percent of the response variance on ability and achievement tests may be attributed to the tendency to guess in a consistent manner on questions to which the subject does not know the answer. Guessing tendencies are easily changed and, therefore, are more likely related to hypotheses concerning item keying than to personality traits.[83] There is no reason to believe that subjects are guessing when they respond to objective personality, attitude, or interest inventory items. Therefore, it should not be assumed that results obtained from guessing can be generalized to apply to inventory responses.

Jerry Wiggins is not as certain as Rorer that response style has no value in explaining differences in inventory scores. Although he may not assign much weight to the impact of response style, Wiggins asserts that a complete understanding of the relations between test responses and criterion behaviors can come about only through

---

[82] Rorer, "Response-Style Myth."
[83] Rorer, "Response-Style Myth."

recognizing each of the many components that determine response and through an understanding of their relations to each other.[84]

METHODS OF INTERPRETATION

INTERPRETATION AS A PUBLISHED SELF-CONCEPT No matter what special procedures are used to reduce distortion, inventory responses depend on how much of the truth the subject is willing and able to report. It is reasonable to interpret a self-report more as a public self-concept (a statement of the reputation that the individual would like to have) than as a statement of typical behavior or private self-concept. To be sure, one's public self-concept should correspond in some measure to one's behavior, but the ambiguity of test items and the inevitable distortion in self-description reduce this correspondence. The fact that an individual is unable to admit certain kinds of socially undesirable impulses may be highly informative. People who present too perfect a picture of themselves may be expressing their fears that others are critical and that they can maintain the respect of others only by keeping their social image bright. The counselor should suspect that the person who presents a perfect picture on an inventory maintains a similar façade in the majority of his or her social relations. A posture of perfect control can be maintained only at considerable emotional cost.

The person who admits to certain emotional problems may also be building up a public image. These may not be the most important problems of which he or she is aware. People often do not bring out major problems in counseling until after several interviews have passed. When a person admits to problems that call for counseling, the report often is an invitation to open up counseling with an examination of the areas mentioned. Serious personal concerns may be concealed completely by questionnaire responses, and an individual who is unwilling to admit these concerns on an inventory is probably also unwilling to deal with them in counseling.

CLINICAL INTERPRETATIONS The clinical counselor is concerned not with the number of times a client becomes emotionally upset but with the conditions under which this happens. Drawing conclusions about personality dynamics even from an extended series of counseling interviews is difficult. Although inventories can offer only hypotheses of questionable validity, they are frequently used

[84] Wiggins, *Personality and Prediction.*

as a basis for dynamic interpretation. Every act is seen as having a purpose, even when a given act is inconsistent with other observations of an individual's behavior. The task of the clinical counselor is to seek some underlying unity that resolves as many of these contradictions as possible. To do this, the counselor needs extensive data about an individual's environment and problems as well as test data and knowledge of personality theory and behavior disorders.[85]

Dynamic interpretations may be contrasted with another clinical approach, *behavioral counseling,* in which a counselor attempts to identify stimulus situations that produce an ineffective or undesirable response and then to recondition the individual so that the problem response is replaced by a desirable one. This procedure requires a careful individual analysis, ordinarily by interview and by observation in controlled situations. Analyses used in behavioral counseling are conservative rather than speculative and make few claims to understand individuals and their behavior.

AUTOMATED PREDICTION   Automated prediction methods yield interpretive statements that are standardized and may serve as the basis for a computer program that generates interpretive reports. Such predictions are formulated on the basis of known empirical regularities between predictor data and criterion data. At present, the most widely employed automated clinical interpretation procedures are those developed for use with MMPI data. These programs differ from one another primarily in the complexity and readability of the final computer-written psychological evaluation. Benjamin Kleinmuntz suggests that predictions generated by a program that simulates clinicians' or counselors' judgments tend to be more accurate than the professionals themselves.[86] Nonetheless, the authors contend that computer interpretation has not been extended to a level of sophistication to permit its use without professional review and modification.

ACTUARIAL INTERPRETATION   Personality inventory responses may be interpreted as self-descriptive or as "an act of verbal behavior that is correlated with inner nature." These two approaches have been characterized as the sample and sign approaches.[87] If responses

[85] Cronbach, *Essentials of Psychological Testing.*
[86] Benjamin Kleinmuntz, "Personality Test Interpretation by Computer and Clinician," in *MMPI: Research Developments and Clinical Applications,* ed. James N. Butcher (New York: McGraw-Hill, 1969), pp. 97–104.
[87] Cronbach, *Essentials of Psychological Testing,* p. 506.

are signs, item content is irrelevant. Even distorted responses may have significance. In a strict actuarial interpretation, there is no assumption of honest self-report. Scales with empirical keys are not seen as self-ratings. Instead, empirical keying capitalizes on the assumption that a given criterion group exhibits distinctive psychological qualities that cause it to differ from other groups. The validity of an empirical key depends entirely on the adequacy of the data utilized to establish empirical weights. Large samples of persons representative of the subjects on whom the test will be used are crucial. Otherwise, such scales are extremely sample-specific. Moreover, criterion validity must be high. Because of sample, inventory, and criterion flaws, the validity of empirical scales in use today is only moderate at best.

CLINICAL VERSUS STATISTICAL (ACTUARIAL) PREDICTION   To compare the products of clinical and statistical prediction, the same subject data are given to a clerical worker (or to a computer) and to a clinician. Each is asked to make specific predictions concerning socially relevant criteria. In reviewing fifty studies then available, Paul E. Meehl concluded that thirty-three demonstrated the superiority of statistical procedures over clinical prediction, and the remaining seventeen studies indicated that the two methods were approximately equal in predictive accuracy.[88] Other authors have challenged this conclusion on methodological grounds. Many of the studies reviewed by Meehl: (1) involved prediction tasks that are inappropriate for counselors; (2) deprived the counselor of information that is usually available; (3) unfairly compared the counselor's work with cross-validated statistical procedures; and (4) failed to recognize the contribution of judgmental measurement. "Of the foregoing methodological criticisms, the failure to recognize the contribution of judgmental measurements is the most telling."[89] Sawyer examined forty-five of the studies reviewed by Meehl and concluded that the best method of prediction appeared to be that in which both judgmental (clinical) and mechanical (statistical) data were available for statistical combination.[90]

Table 10.1 summarizes the principal types of interpretations cited above. Any inventory may be used in all three ways and, when it is appropriate to do so, an interpreter may shift from one point of view to another.

---

[88] Paul E. Meehl, *Clinical Versus Statistical Prediction: A Theoretical Analysis and a Review of the Evidence* (Minneapolis: University of Minnesota Press, 1954).
[89] Wiggins, *Personality and Prediction*, p. 221.
[90] J. Sawyer, "Measurement and Prediction, Clinical and Statistical," *Psychological Bulletin* 66 (1966): 178–200.

TABLE 10.1
COMPARISON OF THREE STYLES OF INTERPRETATION

	TEST TAKEN AS SELF-DESCRIPTION
KINDS OF ITEMS EMPHASIZED	Transparent statements on actions and feelings.
GROUPING OF ITEMS INTO KEYS	Correlated items or items logically fitting a category are treated together.
ASSUMPTION AS TO SUBJECT'S ATTITUDE IN TAKING TEST	Answers are assumed to be as honest as an interview would elicit.
USE MADE OF FACE CONTENT OF ITEMS	Statements taken at face value as descriptions.
USE MADE OF PERSONALITY THEORY	Only a superficial sampling concept is required.

Source: Lee Cronbach, *Essentials of Psychological Testing,* 3rd ed. (Englewood Cliffs, N.J.: Prentice Hall, 1970), p. 508. Copyright, 1949 by Harper & Row, Publishers, Inc. Copyright © 1960, 1970 by Lee J. Cronbach. By permission of the publisher.

USING AND REPORTING DATA

The general guidelines for the use and reporting of test data presented earlier in this book hold for personality and self-concept inventories as well. In addition, because of the sensitive nature of such information, the ethical considerations detailed later in this chapter must be applied as well. Finally, it must be remembered that under no circumstance should personality descriptions be shared with others unless the communication is ethically defensible and the person with whom such data are shared is trained to check the interpretation critically in the light of other evidence. The following brief commentary is ordered according to the three principal situations in which personality and self-concept data are employed.

VOCATIONAL SELECTION AND COUNSELING Personality inventories should not be used directly for hiring employees. As part of a battery

DYNAMIC INTERPRETATION	ACTUARIAL INTERPRETATION
Any type. Items that allow rationalizations and denial of symptoms important. May ask what stimuli elicit a response rather than how often the response occurs.	Any type. Subtle items are favored in theory, but rarely predominate.
Any type of key may be used.	Items are grouped according to correlation with a criterion. Internal homogeneity is not sought.
Distortions, conscious and unconscious, are expected.	Subject is assumed to take the attitudes of person in the keying or weighting sample.
Content of statement is often seen as an expression of defense mechanisms.	Content ignored.
Interpretation relies on complex theory, usually derived from psychoanalytic concepts.	Theory plays no part.

of measures, they may provide some data of limited value. We cannot dismiss entirely the hope that information about one's personality will contribute to an understanding of job performance and satisfaction. Counselors should be able to make good use of personality theory as that understanding develops. Unfortunately, to date, personality inventories have been shown to be poor predictors of employee behavior, especially for semiskilled and unskilled workers.

EDUCATIONAL SELECTION AND COUNSELING   Attempts to predict academic performance from personality and self-concept data have been disappointing. In 1963, the College Entrance Examination Board warned member colleges that "a very serious risk . . . would certainly attend to the actual use of [personality] tests in making admissions decisions."[91] Such problems could arise as possible misunderstanding by the public, faking, coaching, the absence of parallel forms, an overemphasis of scales that correlate only slightly

[91] College Entrance Examination Board, "A Statement on Personality Testing," *College Board Review* 51 (Fall 1963): 11–13.

with grades, and the inability to allow for the fact that adolescent personalities reflect a period of dynamic change. However, it is possible that the relationships of personality variables to academic performance may have theoretical interest even though they may lack practical uses.

PERSONAL COUNSELING   In counseling, the personality inventory may be used to help an individual to examine himself or herself. The inventory permits comparisons of oneself with others and may provide an appropriate initial topic for counseling. Single-score instruments are of little use in counseling, because they pose few questions for discussion. The descriptive inventory that reports several scores is of potential value in that it may open the discussion of significant traits. Descriptions in terms of preferred activities and values are somewhat better suited to vocational counseling than are scales that describe emotional reactions. A problem checklist may be of special value in personal counseling, because it draws attention to a client's concerns. In many ways, a personality inventory may be viewed more as a preliminary interview than as a measuring device. A second major use of inventories in personal counseling is to provide others with insight into an individual. The validity of these descriptions is difficult to assess. Descriptive interpretations for normal subjects are generally suspect; however, results tend to be better for hospitalized individuals, because salient characteristics tend to be reported more emphatically, thus yielding more dramatic and more readily interpretable personality pictures. Inventories do measure individual differences reliably, and those differences do have some relation to personality.

ETHICAL CONSIDERATIONS   Valuable as information about the personality can be, any test is nevertheless an invasion of privacy if a subject does not wish to reveal information about himself or herself. While some people object to tests of knowledge and mental ability, the personality test is more often regarded as a violation of rights. Every individual has two personalities: public and personal. The personality measure probes into feelings and attitudes that people normally conceal and regard as private. While questions had been raised by psychologists, counselors, and others regarding the use of personality tests, during the 1960s, professionals were shocked to find themselves accused of wholesale violations of human dignity. These attacks involved political, personal, and moral considerations.[92]

---

[92] Paul Horst, *Personality: Measurement of Dimensions* (San Francisco: Jossey-Bass, 1968).

POLITICAL CONSIDERATIONS   It is not unusual for a person who has failed the civil service test to complain to his or her Congressional representative or state legislator, who then insists on seeing a copy of the test and challenges the validity of the individual items.

PERSONAL CONSIDERATIONS   Some critics say that personality measures violate the American tradition of individual liberty and freedom. Members of extremely conservative groups as well as more temperate and progressive citizens have made such feelings known. They attack this invasion of personal privacy without detailing the disadvantages that might result from taking the test. Their criticism seems to be more theoretical and ideological than practical or empirical.

MORAL CONSIDERATIONS   Perhaps a more sincere objection to personality inventories is the moral implication of some of the items. Counselors know well that social taboos concerning eliminative and reproductive functions are recurring themes in many behavior disorders, in neurotic symptoms, and directly or indirectly, in manifestations of many personality problems. Consequently, the stimuli of many personality scales relate to various aspects of these taboo topics. Enterprises that are associated directly or indirectly with these taboos invite criticism on moral grounds.[93]

Little or no evidence supports those who oppose personality tests on moral grounds. Nevertheless, pressure from critics has at times forced reputable investigators to cease their work. The public has to be convinced that questions asked in personality measures are fully in the public interest. A balance must be struck between the intrusiveness of a question and the benefits that can come from asking it. Has an employer the right to question an applicant about any aspect of life not directly related to his or her work? Has a teacher any right to ask children about their fears, hatreds, and home life? Counselors can eliminate many objections simply by checking the acceptability of inventories and discarding those their public finds objectionable.

PUBLIC VERSUS PRIVATE CONSIDERATIONS   No one knows just how much validity would be lost if objectionable questions were no longer asked. Use of the MMPI in selecting government employees was criticized because of some items that dealt with religion. The Constitution does not allow screening for public office on the grounds of religious belief. In rebuttal, Stark Hathaway stated:

---

[93] Horst, *Measurement of Dimensions.*

If the psychologist cannot use those personal items to aid in the assessment of people, he suffers as did the Victorian physician who had to examine his female patients by feeling the pulse in the delicate hand thrust from behind a screen . . . it is obvious that if we were making a new MMPI, we would again be faced either with being offensive to some groupings of people by personal items they object to or, if we did not include personal items and were inoffensive, we would have lost the aim of the instrument.[94]

Although public outcry over privacy has centered on personality questionnaires, similar objections can be raised to observation and performance tests when a person is unaware of the observation or believes that he or she is revealing less than he or she is. The same defenses of relevance to the public interest must be prepared if any procedure invades personal privacy. Many tests outwit a subject so that the subject cannot guess what information is being revealed. Trying to extract the truth from an unwilling subject can place an investigator in an indefensible position. Using a diagnostic procedure that the subject does not understand is acceptable provided that the information obtained is what the person would allow others to know. Also, when the public interest overrides the individual interest, a strictly objective look at the person can be justified.

The counselor should ordinarily introduce evaluative procedures with as frank an account as possible. In testing, Cronbach recommends the following approach:

It should help to solve your problem if we collect as much information as we can. Some of our tests use straightforward questions whose purpose you will readily understand. Others dig more deeply into the personality. Sometimes they bring to light emotional conflicts that the person is not even conscious of. Few of us admit to the whole truth about our feelings and ideas, even to ourselves. I think I can help you better with the aid of these tests.[95]

Perhaps a basic fault in personality testing is that tests are occasionally used for no constructive purpose. There is no point in evaluating a person unless something constructive can be accomplished. Without this purpose, personality testing is unwarranted.

It is in the public interest to understand what sort of persons break under stress, what sort become delinquent, and so on. While in recent years there has been some decline in the use of personality

---

[94] Stark Hathaway, "MMPI: Professional Use by Professional People," *American Psychologist* 19 (1964): 204–210.

[95] Cronbach, *Essentials of Psychological Testing,* p. 513. Copyright, 1949 by Harper & Row, Publishers, Inc. Copyright © 1960, 1970 by Lee J. Cronbach. By permission of the publisher.

questionnaires for decision-making, their use in theoretical research has been increasing steadily. While studies are not entirely consistent, there is a large body of significant findings. Personality theory generates understanding, permitting parents, schools, clinics, and informal groups to act wisely.

Techniques of personality measurement are in flux. The privacy issue is just one of the several factors influencing change. Most personality theories have some utility, but professionals are sensitive to limitations of current personality appraisal and personality theory. The interaction of a person with situations must be assessed more effectively. Traits and type descriptions that portray what a person is like cannot account for his or her actions as the situation changes. More than descriptions must be known and, given time and effort on the part of many, professionals and subjects alike, will be known.

ISSUES

1. *The use of personality measures constitutes an unwarranted invasion of personal privacy.*

   Yes, because:
   1. The highly personal nature of the content of personality measures renders inappropriate their use for educational and vocational counseling and for employee selection.
   2. Personality measures ask questions about the private thoughts, feelings, and actions of individuals, the answers to which persons do not wish to reveal but do so either inadvertently or in the belief that they must respond.
   3. The Constitution and the law, as well as professional ethics, protect individuals from the disclosure of private personal information against their will.

   No, because:
   1. With informed consent, the use of personality measures is permissible in professional settings.
   2. Provided that it can be demonstrated that personality test data predict criteria relevant to educational and vocational counseling and employee selection, use of personality measures is both legally and ethically appropriate.

   Discussion:
   Research has demonstrated that personality data do add to the power of test data to predict significant behavior. Provided that

proper personal safeguards are employed, their use should not be construed as an unwarranted invasion of privacy. Furthermore, criticisms and concerns about the use of personality assessment could be reduced if such measures eliminated or reduced highly sensitive content. It is probable that much of this content could be eliminated without affecting the predictive power of personality measures in educational and vocational counseling and in employee selection. More sensitive material may have to be included in measures designed for clinical use, but then it is probable that such content is required if these measures are to predict significant clinical criteria.

2. *Projective measures of personality evaluate the whys of behavior, whereas structured measures (personality inventories) merely describe the whats and hows of behavior.*
   Yes, because:
   1. Projective measures have been established according to dynamic theory and are designed to answer questions regarding the whys of behavior.
   2. Structured measures are based on behavioristic theory, which requires only behavior description.

   No, because:
   1. Experienced examiners have learned that dynamic explanations can be given for specific patterns of behavior.
   2. Dynamic data can be used to predict behavior.

   Discussion:
   Inferences derived from data obtained from projective and structured stimuli are interchangeable. Descriptive inferences may be concluded from projective data, and dynamic interpretations may be proposed from the careful scrutiny of structured-measure data. This can be done if a counselor formulates hypotheses about future behavior and a rationale for current behavior, and then verifies or refutes these hypotheses. These procedures should develop a personalized subjective reference base for data interpretation.

3. *Although most self-report personality measures are trait measures, they actually measure the state of the individual's personality.*
   Yes, because:
   1. Personality test data tend to be unstable over time.

2. What is depicted is a picture of the person at the moment, not a description of lasting characteristics.

No, because:
1. Many specific scales do demonstrate stability over time.
2. Although individuals do vary somewhat with retesting, for many scales, individuals tend to score within a relatively restricted range.

Discussion:
Some personality scales do exhibit relative consistency over time and may estimate trait characteristics. Others appear to be much more variable, even though evidence attests to their internal consistency reliability at the point when data were collected. Counselors must study the internal consistency and retest reliabilities of personality scales before using them. Regardless of the labels attached, scales should be regarded as state or trait measures as both reliability and validity data dictate. The use of content-homogeneous subscales increases the probability of content validity and internal consistency reliability and enables the counselor to employ data with greater confidence. However, when a scale is demonstrated to be stable, data may be interpreted in the context of a lifestyle or trait perspective. At all times, counselors must remember that personality data may reflect only the thoughts, feelings, and actions that an individual is willing to endorse at the moment.

ANNOTATED REFERENCES

Mischel, Walter. *Personality and Assessment.* New York: John Wiley and Sons, 1968.
This work is recommended to the student who is curious about the evaluation of the basic assumptions of personality assessment in the context of empirical research, especially the prediction of behavior and personality change. Mischel synthesizes various concepts of social learning and cognitive processes as they pertain to the measurement and modification of personality. This book fosters the development of a conceptual framework within which the understanding, interpretation, and application of personality data are enhanced. The book is well-referenced and is useful to the student who wishes to learn more. For the casual student, the excellent chapter summaries are an economical overview of the content of the book.

Wiggins, Jerry S. *Personality and Prediction: Principles of Personality Assessment.* Reading, Mass.: Addison-Wesley, 1973.

Intended for the serious student, this book provides a relatively up-to-date technical presentation of the art and science of personality assessment, with special emphasis on methodology and research findings pertinent to the prediction of socially relevant criteria. Personality assessment models and strategies are included, as well as detailed coverage of observation and structured measures as vehicles for the collection of personality data. An extensive and comprehensive bibliography references the text well. In addition, this bibliography provides an excellent guide to primary source material dating back to significant pioneer publications of the mid and late 1800s. At times, the text is difficult, especially for the reader with limited background in statistics and measurement theory and methodology. Nonetheless, mastery of the content of this book is essential to developing a solid, informed conceptual framework for the professional selection, use, and interpretation of personality measures and the application of such findings.

Wylie, Ruth C. *A Review of Methodological Considerations and Measuring Instruments, The Self Concept.* Vol. 1. Lincoln, Neb.: University of Nebraska Press, 1974.

The Self Concept is far more than a compendium of measures. It is a review of the history of interest and self-relevant constructs and of phenomenological theories and the problems they present for measurement and research design. It is an exhaustive and critical review of pertinent empirical studies. Wylie lists and discusses a substantial number of self-concept research instruments. The general tone is scholarly. The reader is led to think, conceptualize, reconceptualize, and face underlying issues concerning various instruments.

SELECTED REFERENCES

American Psychological Association. "Testing and Public Policy." *American Psychologist* 20 (1965): 857–1002.

Bentler, P. M.; Jackson, D. N.; and Messick, S. "A Rose by Any Other Name." *Psychological Bulletin* 77 (1972): 109–113.

Block, J. "On Further Conjectures Regarding Acquiescence." *Psychological Bulletin* 76 (1971): 205–210.

Edwards, Allen L. *The Measurement of Personality Traits by Scales and Inventories.* New York: Holt, Rinehart and Winston, 1970.

Fowler, Raymond D., Jr. "Automated Interpretation of Personality Test Data." In *MMPI: Research Developments and Clinical Applications.* Edited by James N. Butcher. New York: McGraw-Hill, 1969, pp. 105–126.

Goldberg, L. R. "Man Versus Model of Man: A Rationale Plus Evidence for a Method of Improving on Clinical Inferences." *Psychological Bulletin* 73 (1970): 422–432.

Jackson, D. N. "A Sequential System for Personality Scale Development." In *Current Topics in Clinical and Community Psychology.* Vol. 2. Edited by C. D. Spielberger. New York: Academic Press, 1970, pp. 61–96.

———. "The Dynamics of Structured Personality Tests: 1971." *Psychological Review* 78 (1971): 229–248.

Kleinmuntz, B. "Personality Test Interpretation by Computer and Clinician." In *MMPI: Research Developments and Clinical Applications.* Edited by James N. Butcher. New York: McGraw-Hill, 1969, pp. 97–104.

Loevinger, Jane. "Some Principles of Personality Measurement." *Educational and Vocational Measurement* 15 (1958): 3–17.

Peabody, D. "Evaluative and Descriptive Aspects in Personality Perception: A Reappraisal." *Journal of Personality and Social Psychology* 16 (1970): 639–646.

Rosenberg, S., and Olshan, K. "Evaluative and Descriptive Aspects in Personality Perception." *Journal of Personality and Social Psychology* 16 (1970): 619–626.

Sundberg, Norman. *Assessment of Persons.* Englewood Cliffs, N.J.: Prentice-Hall, 1976.

Part 5

Nonstandardized Tools and Techniques

A RELATIVELY LARGE VARIETY OF NONSTANDARDIZED TOOLS AND techniques is available for gathering information about individuals, which, when employed appropriately and cautiously, can enhance a counselor's understanding of a client. In this section, we shall discuss nonstandardized methods for assessing a variety of behaviors, except for those measured by classroom tests.

In Chapter 11, we shall examine the functions of direct observation, including methods of systematic, controlled, and informal observation. Chapter 12 presents various types of rating methods and their interpretation and use. Chapter 13 offers a variety of methods for assessing social and environmental behavior. In Chapter 14, we shall discuss content analysis and the case study as methods of interpretation, integration, and use of assessment data.

All of these tools and techniques are tests, even though many described in this part appear to be different from the measures of maximum and habitual performance described in Parts 3 and 4. A major difference between standardized and nonstandardized measures is that the latter group of assessment tools and techniques is usually not developed or normed by means of data obtained from well-defined populations.

Even when information about an individual is obtained from both types of measures, the resulting pool of information, complete as it may appear to be, can represent only a small portion of the whole individual, albeit a larger portion than is possible to achieve without the use of both types of measures. Therefore, counselors must be aware constantly that much of what makes a person an individual remains hidden from observation.

Chapter 11   *Observation*

What functions do methods of observation serve?

How can observations be classified?

What observational methods are employed frequently in making individual and/or group appraisals?

What are the advantages and limitations of the various observational methods?

GENERAL
DESCRIPTION OF OBSERVATION

Observation can be described as humankind's first educational tool and first method of appraisal. A number of more or less specific purposes and functions have been identified for various observational methods that are relevant for appraising behavior in schools and in similar settings. Observation is bound intimately to obtaining criterion data for the development and validation of assessment tools and techniques. Moreover, observation provides the basic and most practical means of testing the validity of the hypotheses proposed in both experimental and descriptive research studies of behavior.

Behavioral observations can be viewed as samples drawn from a "stream of behavior."[1] This metaphor was meant to call attention to the fact that behavior is a lifelong continuum that can never be seen in its entirety.[2] Many different information-gathering methods, techniques, and procedures can be devised to fit the nature of the

---

[1] R. G. Barker, ed., *The Stream of Behavior* (New York: Appleton-Century-Crofts, 1963).

[2] Herbert F. Wright, "Observational Child Study," in *Handbook of Research Methods in Child Development*, ed. Paul H. Mussen (New York: John Wiley & Sons, 1960), p. 73.

THIS CHAPTER WAS WRITTEN BY KATHRYN W. LINDEN.

phenomena being studied and the conditions under which the information must be obtained.

Regardless of the form of the data collected, how they are recorded, or the purpose for which they are employed, three forms of activity are involved in the collection of data: empathy, participation, and observation.[3] *Empathy* refers to feeling with the individual being observed, or understanding how the individual feels about something. *Participation* involves the degree of intrusiveness that is introduced by the presence or absence of an observer. The participant observer does something with people in order to observe their behavior. The nonparticipant observer is separated from the setting in which the behaviors occur. *Observation* involves any sensory perception of external cues (not merely visual perception) that aid the understanding of human behavior.

A wide range of methods and procedures is available for making observations in natural settings such as classrooms, clinics, counseling centers, personnel offices, or in any other context that requires individual evaluation.[4,5] Procedures for deriving direct observations range from brief, narrowly circumscribed and highly controlled systematic procedures, as illustrated by the time-sampling or event-sampling methods, to long-term, comprehensive, and less controlled techniques, such as the analysis of personal documents or the longitudinal case study. All observational procedures are concerned with what a given individual does in natural settings over relatively long periods of time. The length of a single observation may vary from less than one minute to several hours, days, or years, depending on the nature and the purpose of the observation. Observations may be concentrated into one day or several days, or they may be spaced over several months or years. Observations may be concerned with the total behavior of an individual or a group that occurs during the specified observation period. However, observations are often limited to a specific kind of behavior, such as language, interpersonal interactions, or aggressive actions.

To assist observers in making and/or recording observations, such tools as observation schedules, coding systems, record forms, and various mechanical recording devices have been employed. Recordings made on film, tape, or videotape are excellent tools, and the

[3] Raymond L. Gordon, *Interviewing: Strategy, Techniques and Tactics*, rev. ed. (Homewood, Ill.: Dorsey Press, 1975), p. 33.

[4] Richard R. Jones, John B. Reid, and Gerald R. Patterson, "Naturalistic Observation in Clinical Assessment," in *Advances in Psychological Assessment*, vol. 3, ed. Paul McReynolds (San Francisco: Jossey-Bass, 1975), chapter 2.

[5] Jerry S. Wiggins, *Personality and Prediction: Principles of Personality Assessment* (Reading, Mass.: Addison-Wesley, 1973), pp. 295–327.

use of radio telemetry has also been explored as a recording medium.[6,7] Three major purposes of instrumentation in observational methodology were identified by Charles D. Hopkins:

1. It provides a purely objective record of what happened as the events occurred; however, each record is limited to the scope of the recording device.
2. It provides a means of gathering sensations not available through human senses. This contribution is limited to the extent of the sophistication of the device; some are very refined, but some are relatively crude.
3. It provides a way to quantify many behavioral variables.[8]

Two basic approaches to recording observations were differentiated by Clifford Froehlich and Kenneth Hoyt: observer description and observer evaluation.[9] Observer-description techniques require the observer to function as nearly as possible as an objective but flexible human camera or recording machine.[10] This function is discussed in connection with each of the specific observational methods presented in this chapter. The observer-evaluation method of recording requires the observer to function not only as a recorder of observations but also as a judge who must weigh and interpret observations.

METHODS OF OBSERVATION

Methods of observation may be classified in a variety of ways. For example, Robert L. Thorndike and Elizabeth Hagen used the terms *behavioral tests, systematic observation,* and *informal observation* to denote the means of gathering samples of an individual's behavior as the basis for personality appraisal.[11] Anne Anastasi differentiated between situational tests, in which the stimulus situation is con-

---

[6] O. Ivan Lovaas, Gilbert Freitag, Vivian J. Gold, and Irene C. Kassorla, "Recording Apparatus for Observation of Behaviors of Children in Free Play Settings," *Journal of Experimental Child Psychology* 2 (1965): 108–120.

[7] Donald R. Miklich, "Radio Telemetry in Clinical Psychology and Related Areas," *American Psychologist* 30 (1975): 419–425.

[8] Charles D. Hopkins, *Educational Research: A Structure for Inquiry* (Columbus, Ohio: Charles E. Merrill, 1976), p. 88.

[9] Clifford Froehlich and Kenneth Hoyt, *Guidance Testing,* 3rd ed. (Chicago: Science Research Associates, 1959), pp. 225–227.

[10] Robert L. Thorndike and Elizabeth Hagen, *Measurement and Evaluation in Psychology and Education,* 4th ed. (New York: John Wiley & Sons, 1977), p. 507.

[11] Thorndike and Hagen, *Measurement and Evaluation,* pp. 491–532.

TABLE 11.1
CLASSIFICATION OF OBSERVATIONAL PROCEDURES

TYPE	SETTING	METHOD[a]
Systematic	Natural	Director observation by time or event sampling of behaviors
Controlled	Controlled	The interview
	Contrived	Situational "test" In-Basket method
Informal	Natural	Anecdotal observation Developmental records Unobtrusive measures Sociometric methods

[a] Rating methods are not classified, as they are employed in all of the settings subsumed under the three major types of observational procedures. Moreover, the case study also is not classified because it represents an integrated product of all types of observations. Both rating methods and the case study are discussed in separate chapters.

trolled, and naturalistic observation, ranging from comprehensive, long-term methods to narrowly circumscribed and highly controlled observations.[12] On the other hand, Jerry Wiggins offered a classification of observational procedures that is based on the degree of control exercised over observational settings and the degree of intrusion introduced by the presence or absence of an observer.[13] Wiggins' classification model may have relatively little value for counselors because of its complexity. Consequently, a more simple classification model is presented in Table 11.1.

In this model, methods of observation are classified as systematic, controlled, and informal. *Systematic* observation techniques employ procedures for quantifying the behavior observed in naturalistic settings. Time-sampling procedures and event-sampling procedures are the two principal strategies employed. *Controlled* observation techniques are designed to evoke particular behaviors or specific responses. The three major controlled techniques are the interview, the biographical data inventory, and the situational test. *Informal* observation is neither controlled in terms of what behaviors are to be observed nor systematic in the sense of observations' being timed or directed to specific significant events. Informal techniques include a variety of self-observation methods, as well as the spontaneous, informal observations derived from significant others.

[12] Anne Anastasi, *Psychological Testing*, 4th ed. (New York: MacMillan, 1976), pp. 588–620.
[13] Wiggins, *Personality and Prediction*, pp. 295–304.

For some methods of observation, the distinction between the systematic, controlled, and informal nature of the observation is somewhat blurred, and such distinctions are noted later, where applicable. Certain observational tools may transcend a given category and setting. For example, an interview can be conducted in either a natural, a controlled, or a contrived setting, depending on the purpose of the interview. Direct observation of a counseling or classroom situation could be classified as any one of the three types of observation, depending on its focus and the nature of the setting. Informal observation depends primarily on the degree of planning exercised in obtaining the observational data.

SYSTEMATIC OBSERVATION

The primary purpose of systematic observation is to obtain an accurate and representative picture of an individual's learning, development, and adjustment. In systematic observation, as in all types of observation, the ability of the observer to identify the factors that initiate behavior and to describe accurately the manner in which the subject reacts to a given situation is of crucial importance. Thus, an observational procedure should be as objective and reliable as possible, with a minimum of dependence on the idiosyncrasies and whims of individual observers.

Systematic observation methods were developed in order to meet the needs of measurement, as distinct from the qualitative description that is typical of less formal methods of direct observation. Because quantitative measurement requires the use of procedures that permit statements of quantity or amount to be made, it is necessary to use either direct systematic methods that involve time-sampling and/or event-sampling techniques or unobtrusive measures, depending on the purpose to be served by the observation.

TIME SAMPLING Time sampling is a method of observing the behavior of individuals or groups under the ordinary conditions of everyday life. Observations are made in a series of short periods distributed in such a way as to yield a representative sampling of the behavior under observation. The validity of time sampling is primarily a function of the amount and distribution of the time spent in observation or of the number, length, and distribution of the separate observations, or *time samples*. The essential function of time sampling is to measure accurately the incidence of certain behaviors or patterns of behavior under specified conditions.

Time sampling is applicable to a wide variety of behaviors that can be observed in several situations or several stages of development. Interrelationships among the different aspects of a person's behavior are appropriate for study by time-sampling methods. Moreover, the time-sampling methodology is also useful in delineating the successive stages of social development, determining the sequence in which common social patterns are acquired, and measuring stability and change in individual patterns of social behavior over a period of time.

A situation that lends itself to the systematic study of habitual behavior must afford a relatively constant opportunity for free expression of the behaviors being studied; must be one with which the individuals being observed are familiar; must consist of observation periods of approximately uniform duration from day to day; and must involve a group of people that remains relatively constant during the period of observation.[14] The range of situations meeting these requirements and the types of situations appropriate for a time-sampling study of behavioral characteristics are limited only by the creative expertise of the observer.

In determining the optimal length of the observation, or time sample, several factors in addition to frequency of the occurrence of the behavior must be considered. The amount of time available for observation, the number of individuals to be observed, the number of behavioral characteristics to be recorded at one time, and the probable frequency of interruptions all influence the length of a time sample.

The time sample should be long enough to permit accurate recording of the focal behavior and to avoid unnecessary waste of time between successive observations. It should be short enough to afford uninterrupted observation of the individual or group for the specified length of time and to permit the accumulation of enough samples to encompass the typical variations in the behavior being observed.

The number of samples required to provide stable measures varies with the frequency of the behavior, the length of the time sample, the day-to-day variation in the conditions of observation, the variability of the individuals being observed, and the method of measuring frequency within the time sample. In general, the number of time samples required to provide reliable and valid observations increases as (1) the conditions in which samples are derived increase

[14] Ruth E. Arrington, "Interrelations in the Behavior of Young Children," *Child Development Monographs* 8 (1932): 99.

in variability, (2) individuals behave inconsistently, and (3) behaviors occur less frequently.

The utility of time sampling as a method of measuring direct observations of behavior depends on its ability to provide either more reliable information than can other methods or information that cannot be obtained as easily by other means. Time sampling requires no prior acquaintance with the individuals being observed. Moreover, time sampling is a more reliable method than are ratings, because time sampling yields measures that are not based on judgments or impressions and are not dependent on memory. Time-sampling methodology is based on a carefully selected and recorded sample of observed behavioral incidents. Time sampling is applied more easily than is a controlled experimental method, because it requires no special apparatus and can be employed on a much more extensive scale.

A limitation of the time-sampling method is that it requires a great expenditure of time in order to obtain accurate and representative samples. Also, important, highly relevant behaviors that occur infrequently may not be observed when timed samples are drawn. Moreover, such segmented behavioral snapshots have been criticized as lacking continuity and adequate context. For these reasons, the method of event sampling was developed as a means of obtaining observations of a complete behavioral unit.

EVENT SAMPLING   The *event-sampling* technique involves selecting for observation integral behavior occurrences of a particular class, as opposed to the time-sampling method of observing behavioral units at different times.[15] Examples of integral behavior occurrences are fights and quarrels, verbal interchanges on specific topics, silence in counseling sessions, classroom interactions between teacher and students, and interactions between counselor and counselee. Because event sampling involves natural events, it has an inherent validity not usually demonstrated by time samples. Moreover, an integral event has a continuity of behavior factor that the piecemeal behaviors reflected in time samples usually do not have. For example, a problem-solving situation observed from beginning to end offers the observer a natural and complete unit of individual or group behavior rather than the segmented snapshots characteristic of time samples. Event sampling was developed as a means of counteracting the lack of continuity, lack of adequate context, and to a certain extent, lack of naturalness typical of time sampling.

[15] Wright, "Observational Child Study," ch. 3.

TIME AND EVENT SAMPLING COMBINED Sometimes it may be desirable to use a combination of time-sampling and event-sampling procedures to study certain kinds of behavior. For example, in studying a counselor's questioning strategies, a random sample of the counselor's interviews could be drawn, allowing each session to be observed in its entirety and all questions posed by the counselor during the sampled periods to be recorded and analyzed. Used either singly or in combination, these methods provide a means of learning something about the dynamics of the teaching and counseling processes and their relationship to learning, development, and adjustment, especially when an attempt is made to gain insight into the nature of effective teaching or effective counseling. Moreover, these methods are also appropriate for measuring the effectiveness of guidance programs and procedures.

INSTRUMENTATION FOR SYSTEMATIC OBSERVATION More than one hundred category systems, or category instruments, designed to quantify the behaviors observed during classroom instruction had been developed by the early 1970s. The anthology *Mirrors for Behavior* contains sixty-two instruments designed for categorizing affective behaviors and forty-eight instruments for categorizing cognitive behaviors.[16] These instruments are organized into four categories: (1) instruments having an explicit theoretical or empirical base; (2) instruments having an implied theoretical or empirical base; (3) modification or synthesis of existing category systems; and (4) author-original category systems.

Three elements appear to differentiate among the various observational systems: the recording procedure, the scope and specificity of the items, and the format used to code the individual events.[17] When an event is recorded each time it occurs, the instrument is labeled as a *category system*. When an event is recorded only once if it occurs within a specified time period, regardless of how often that event ordinarily occurs, the recording instrument is called a *sign system.*

Items appearing in these instruments can be classified as (1) low-inference, behaviorally specific items, such as "Teacher gives directions" and "Teacher asks questions"; (2) moderate-inference

---

[16] A. Simon and E. G. Boyer, eds., *Mirrors for Behavior: An Anthology of Classroom Observation Instruments* (Philadelphia: Research for Better Schools, vols. 1–6 [1967], vols. 7–14 and summary [1970]; supplementary vols. A and B [1970].

[17] Barak Rosenshine and Norma Furst, "The Use of Direct Observation to Study Teaching," in *Second Handbook of Research on Teaching,* ed. Robert M. W. Travers (Chicago: Rand McNally College Publishing Company, 1973), ch. 5.

items, such as "Teacher uses student ideas" and, "Teacher criticizes"; and (3) high-inference items such as "Teacher is responsive," "Teacher is harsh," and "Teacher is pleasant." Category and sign systems were originally developed to measure behaviors that were specific and required less inference by the observer than did the high-inference behaviors included in many rating scales. However, as more observation systems are developed, this distinction has become blurred.

An example of a rather well-known category instrument that utilizes a multiple-coding format employed for time-sampling studies of teacher-student interaction is *Flanders' Interaction Analysis Categories* (FIAC).[18] Interested in the impact of verbal interactions in the classroom, Ned Flanders first studied the effect of indirect influence in a teacher's approach as compared to direct influence. The FIAC can be adapted for studying the verbal interactions of counselors and students as well as teachers and students. However, a number of the instruments presented in *Mirrors for Behavior* might also serve this purpose effectively.

RELIABILITY AND VALIDITY Experience has demonstrated that the most important factors affecting the accuracy of observation in uncontrolled situations include the amount of behavior observed, the degree of precision with which the observed behavior is defined, and the simplicity, or complexity, of the method of recording observations. The fewer the behavior categories included in the record, the more precise the definitions of the behavior categories should be. The more simple the recording process, the more reliable the observations will be. In general, measures of reliability should be based on a comparison of the simultaneous records taken by several different pairs of observers, with the series of observations for each pair planned to include similar proportions of easy and difficult recording situations. Moreover, checks on the reliability of measures should be repeated, if possible, at intervals during the course of the observation.

The validity of measures derived from time sampling, event sampling, and related techniques is generally a function of three factors: the naturalness of the behavior being observed, the adequacy with which behavior is sampled, and the accuracy with which behavior is recorded. When the indices obtained are interpreted solely as measures of the frequency of the behavior under the conditions of observation, the validity of measurement is synonymous with the

---

[18] Ned A. Flanders, *Analyzing Teaching Behavior* (Reading, Mass.: Addison-Wesley, 1970).

reliability of measurement. However, when such indices are interpreted as being representative of the habitual behavior of the individuals observed in a particular situation or in similar situations, the validity of observation depends not only on the accuracy of the records but also on the representativeness of the observational samples. However, one must be cautious in interpreting systematic behavioral observations as being representative of habitual behavior. Because time sampling, event sampling, and combinations of the two cannot be guaranteed to produce data that are necessarily representative of habitual behavior, other assessment techniques are required.

CONTROLLED OBSERVATION

Controlled observation is structured in order to evoke certain behaviors or responses that are thought to be significant for understanding a given individual. Three major observational methods are classified as controlled observation: the interview, the self-report biographical inventory, and the situational test. The *interview* is an undisguised, controlled observation of an individual's behavior obtained, usually, in one-to-one conversation. The *self-report biographical inventory*, developed as an alternative to the interview, requests information in a standard format that can be scored objectively. A *situational test* disguises the purpose of the evaluation by forcing the individual to respond in a contrived, but realistic, problem situation.

INTERVIEW   The interview has been described by Raymond L. Gordon as "one specific form of empathizing, participating and observing that takes place between two people."[19] The interviewer participates by determining the setting or social context in which the interview takes place and asking questions or presenting other stimuli in order to elicit information from the person being interviewed. Empathy is reflected in his or her anticipating probable reactions to questions. Observation consists of making notes not only of the content of the messages being transmitted by the respondent but also the tone of voice, facial expressions, and bodily movements.

Although the interview as an information-seeking tool can be classified in various ways, two approaches seem to be represented

[19] Gordon, *Interviewing*, p. 33.

in the literature more frequently than others: classification according to interview structure or form and classification by interview function. The structure, form, or style of interviews can be categorized as either standardized or nonstandardized. The *standardized* interview is designed to collect exactly the same kinds of information from any number of respondents. Moreover, the answers of all respondents must be comparable and classifiable. Thus, any difference in answers should be caused by differences among the respondents.

Standardized interviews can be either scheduled or nonscheduled. The term *schedule* refers to a list of questions used by the interviewer. Interview schedules vary widely in the degree to which they specify details of context, wording of questions, sequence of topics, and form of answers. The completely scheduled standardized interview defines the objectives to be accomplished in terms of specific questions that must be asked in a fixed sequence and in the same wording. This type of interview restricts both the techniques employed by the interviewer and the form of the information given by the individual being interviewed. In the completely nonscheduled interview, the interviewer is guided only by a central purpose. Consequently, the interviewer is free to decide the means by which the objective may be accomplished.

Between the two extremes of completely scheduled and unscheduled standardized interviews, there are varying degrees to which communication between interviewer and respondent is specified and controlled by a prepared schedule. Moreover, the interviewer allows the respondent various degrees of freedom in selecting topics and sequences of topics.

In order to keep within the requirements of the standardized interview, an interviewer who employs a nonscheduled format or other than a completely scheduled format must record the responses of the individual on a standard form either during the course of the interview or later. The recording of responses on a standard form is much easier to accomplish if the interviewer uses a moderately scheduled format. If the interview information is not transferred to a standard form, individuals cannot be compared clearly, and the aggregate response of a group cannot be summarized statistically.

The *nonstandardized* interview does not require the presentation of the same questions or same topics to all persons interviewed. Consequently, the resultant information cannot be summarized statistically in order to reflect the aggregate response of a group or to compare one individual's responses with those of another. Therefore, whenever the purpose of an interview does not include making a comparison or summarizing the responses of a group, there may be no need to adhere to any prearranged interview schedule no matter how unstructured and loosely controlled it may be. The nonstandardized interview is essentially formless, and its variations are identified according to purpose or function rather than by form.

Because of the variety of purposes that the nonstandardized interview can serve, there are many ways of classifying such interviews by their functions. In the *fact-finding* interview, both the content and the structure of the interview are determined largely by the interviewer. Although the ultimate goal of the fact-finding interview is to help the person being interviewed, the immediate goal is to provide the interviewer with information. The fact-finding interview supplements information gathered by other means, verifies information that has been collected previously, and permits observation of physical characteristics, mannerisms, and other nonverbal clues. Success of the fact-finding interview is determined largely by the relevance of the questions asked and the degree of honesty with which the person being interviewed answers the questions. Decisions regarding the subsequent steps to be taken are made primarily by the interviewer, rather than by the person being interviewed. The fact-finding interviewer also makes relatively greater use than does the counseling interviewer of direct questions requiring specific answers and of specific leading remarks, such as probing, interpretative, and informative statements.

The structure of a *counseling* interview is determined by the counselor, but the content is influenced by the client to a much larger extent than is true in a fact-finding interview. Neither the topics to be discussed nor the order in which they are discussed can be, or should be, predetermined by the counselor in a counseling interview. Froehlich and Hoyt suggested that four major goals are served by the counselor in a counseling interview: (1) helping clients understand themselves and their environment; (2) helping clients make decisions in light of these understandings; (3) helping clients accept responsibility for the decisions they have reached; and (4) helping clients initiate a plan of action for effecting these decisions.[20]

The success of a counseling interview depends on a counselor's ability to perceive shades and degrees of feeling underlying a client's remarks and to respond appropriately to the expressions of feeling. In such instances, the counselor's skill in responding, rather than the counselor's skill in leading the client, is crucial. Decisions

[20] Froehlich and Hoyt, *Guidance Testing.* pp. 261–262.

regarding subsequent actions are made primarily by the client, because although some decisions may be made by the counselor, the primary objective of the counseling interview is to enable the client to make his or her own decisions.

As compared with other methods of observation, interview methodology provides an immediate opportunity for the observer (the interviewer) to motivate the respondent to supply accurate and complete information about past and current events. Moreover, most interview formats permit an observer to guide a respondent in interpreting the questions being asked, to be flexible in questioning, and to have greater control over the observational situation than is possible in most other methods. For example, the exploratory value of the interview is impossible to attain by other observational methods, such as standardized tests, questionnaires, personal documents, and even direct observation, which allow no opportunity to formulate new questions or to probe in depth those lines of inquiry that seem most relevant and productive.

The interview requires great skill in gathering and interpreting data. Wrong decisions are made frequently, either because important data were not elicited or because data were interpreted inadequately or incorrectly. Thus, probably the most important limitation of the interview as an appraisal technique is the skill of the interviewer. The successful interviewer is sensitive in identifying clues in the respondent's behavior and in the facts reported that require further probing for other facts to support or contradict the original hypothesis.

A second limitation of interview methodology is all those factors that inhibit communication by making the respondent unwilling and/or unable to provide relevant information to the interviewer. Such factors as threatened self-concept, traumatic experiences, competing demands of time, and interview etiquette may influence the respondent's willingness to give information. Forgetfulness, confusion about the sequence of events or the inferential meaning of the observer's questions and/or respondent's feelings, and unconscious behavior all may make the respondent unable to give relevant information.

As a psychometric technique, the typical interview is neither precise nor efficient. Interview methodology is basically subjective; variable in format, content, and style; and heavily dependent on the skills of the interviewer. Evidence of the reliability and validity of the conclusions derived from interviews is contradictory, although it has been demonstrated repeatedly that the impressions different interviewers gain of the same individual are quite varied. This variability results from two major sources: variation in the questions asked and in the lines of inquiry pursued in depth, and differences in interpretation and evaluation of the responses elicited. However, for a skilled interviewer, the advantages of interview methodology may be of considerable value.

BIOGRAPHICAL INVENTORY   The self-report questionnaire method, developed as an alternative to the interview, has the dual advantages of economy of time and uniformity in both presentation format and evaluation procedure. The biographical inventory includes a standard set of questions concerning an individual's life history, feelings, preferences, or actions that are presented in a standard format and scored with a standard scoring key. Most of the interest, attitude, and personality measures that we have discussed are essentially self-report questionnaires. Such measures are economical and efficient in terms of the time required to gather information. They permit comparison of results from person to person. They can be scored objectively, and estimates of their reliability can be obtained quite readily. However, the self-report questionnaire method is not flexible, nor is it adaptable to the individual case.

This questionnaire technique does provide a type of anonymity that is not possible under interview conditions: responding to a printed form is quite different from responding directly to another person. Often, it is much easier for an individual to reply to questions presented in written form than it is to answer the questions presented directly by some stranger (or even an acquaintance or friend). The questionnaire technique designed to elicit specific factual information concerning an individual's personal history is called by various names, such as personal history questionnaire, personal data record, biographical data inventory, and personal or biographical data blank. Because this type of self-report questionnaire focuses primarily on biographical or developmental facts, we shall use the term *biographical inventory*. Other types of developmental records will be identified and discussed in the section dealing with informal observation techniques.

Biographical inventories attempt to obtain a host of relatively objective and verifiable facts concerning an individual's developmental history. Such items as date and place of birth, family background, the amount and nature of educational experience, special skills, hobbies and other recreational activities, and job experiences are typical questions on biographical inventories. Some include items that seek reactions, asking which school courses the individual likes best or least or what the individual has liked best and least about his or her jobs. Moreover, biographical questionnaires sometimes include items that are similar to those found in interest inventories. However, the basic purpose of carefully designed biographical inventories is to obtain factual information under uniform conditions and in situations in which it is not possible to conduct individual interviews. The particular appeal of this method is its economy and its efficiency.

A second purpose of the biographical inventory is to facilitate and to expedite an individual interview: "One appropriate use of self-report inventories of all types is to provide a jumping-off place for an interview, the questionnaire providing leads that may be followed up in the interview."[21] The inventory is filled out in advance by the client and is used by the interviewer in preparing for the interview.

Most biographical data blanks employed for school, counseling, and personnel selection combine specific-answer and open-ended formats. However, these data blanks do vary widely in both purpose and presentation. An example of a data blank that combines specific-answer and open-ended items is presented in Figure 11.1. The items in this biographical inventory, designed for use in a university guidance clinic, are organized into sections denoting several relevant areas of student characteristics.

Arranging items by topical areas has several advantages: (1) interpretation is facilitated; (2) the inventory appears to have organization and purpose so that it is viewed by the student less as an intensive grilling exercise than as a systematic way for the counselor to become better acquainted with the student; and (3) the collection of such information helps the student to organize his or her thoughts and possibly gain additional insight into the kind of person he or she is becoming. It should also be noted that this biographical inventory is loaded with specific items that have normative characteristics. In other words, such items enable the counselor to obtain information regarding the degree to which a student can be considered different from typical students and to form conclusions regarding the characteristics of typical students. A simple frequency count of the number of school activities a student engages in, the number and/or types of offices he or she has held, and the number of years of participation are examples of the normative content of some of these items. Thus, this type of instrument can permit, to a limited extent at least, comparisons among students.

The value of the biographical data blank as an observational

---

[21] Thorndike and Hagen, *Measurement and Evaluation*, p. 401.

FIGURE 11.1
PURDUE COUNSELING AND GUIDANCE CLINIC
PERSONAL DATA INVENTORY

Case no. _____

Date _____

Counselor _____

Please complete this inventory as carefully as you can. The purpose of collecting this information is to be of assistance to you in making choices and decisions. All information which you provide about yourself will be treated confidentially.

Name _____
Last   First   Middle

Address _____

School _____ Grade _____

Age _____ Birthdate _____ Phone _____ Sex _____

School information:

	Name of school	Grades attended	Years attended	Course of study
Elementary				
Jr. high				
Sr. high				
College-				
Other				

Best-liked subjects _____ Easiest subjects _____

Least-liked subjects _____ Hardest subjects _____

Out-of-school leisure time activities and hobbies _____

What magazines do you read regularly? _____

What types of books do you enjoy? _____

Activities and hobbies:

School activity	Number of years of participation	Offices held	Kind of activity

Class offices held _____

Work experience: Job held   When   What did you like best about it?

1. _____   _____   _____
2. _____   _____   _____
3. _____   _____   _____
4. _____   _____   _____

Figure 11.1 (continued)

Family and home:

	Name Last	First	Live at home	Age	Occupation	Years of schoolir completed
Father						
Mother						
Bro/Sis						

Health:

Do you have normal eyesight? _____ Normal hearing? _____ Briefly summarize important factors in your health history:

_____

_____

Underline any of the following words which seem to describe you fairly well:

Active, ambitious, self-confident, persistent, hard working, nervous, impatient, impulsive, quick-tempered, excitable, imaginative, original, witty, calm, easily discouraged, serious, easy-going, good-natured, unemotional, shy, submissive, absent-minded, methodical, timid, lazy, frequently gloomy, hard-boiled, dependable, reliable, cheerful, sarcastic, jittery, likeable, leader, sociable, quiet, retiring, self-conscious, often feel lonely.

Plans:

What are your plans for the future? _____

What occupations have you seriously considered as possible goals? Why? _____

_____

What topics would you like to discuss with the counselor? _____

_____

_____

_____

Comments:

instrument depends on four factors: (1) the comprehensiveness with which the instrument asks for data regarding individual characteristics; (2) the accuracy with which the individual describes himself or herself; (3) the perspective that the instrument provides counselors, teachers, and other personnel on areas of individual characteristics and behavior that should be explored in interviews or counseling sessions; and (4) the opportunities that this technique affords individuals for obtaining an increased degree of self-understanding.

Two important conclusions have been derived from research on biographical data inventories. First, as with other types of self-report documents, reasonably satisfactory levels of reliability and validity can be achieved, particularly if the data obtained are analyzed carefully. Second, it has been found that individuals will report facts concerning themselves consistently and accurately if the conditions under which the data are obtained are favorable. When the data are intended for a counselor's use, for example, it is extremely important that students know how confidential their responses will be. Moreover, the person who administers the instrument must be viewed by students as one who is sincerely interested in helping them, who can be trusted, and who is able to help them.

The biographical inventory does not usually provide details regarding the exact nature of an individual's problem, nor does it yield direct evidence regarding the causes of behavior. However, this observational tool is valuable in identifying students who are likely to have problems and in providing clues that may be useful in studying such students intensively. Although the biographical data inventory is an appraisal procedure that frequently raises as many questions as it answers in terms of understanding students, it is valuable both for what it tells counselors and for what it leads them to ask clients.

SITUATIONAL TEST   The fundamental difference between the *situational test* and other testing instruments is that many situational tests direct the observation of individuals in a highly controlled simulation of a natural situation. Consequently, it is appropriate to categorize this technique as a method of controlled observation. Although some situational methods simply set the stage for an individual to react to a contrived naturalistic situation, others rely on deliberate deception. In such situations, individuals are lied to or tricked deliberately. Moreover, stress factors may be introduced into the contrived situation in order to induce anxiety and other emotional states. This method is called a *situational stress test.* In recent years, this concept has been applied to certain interviewing situations, resulting in the term *stress interview.*

A simplified version of the situational test, without the stress component, employs a leaderless group as a device for assessing such characteristics as initiative, resourcefulness, cooperation, teamwork, and leadership. A variation of this type of situational test is the *Leaderless Group Discussion* (LGD). Because LGD requires a minimum of both time and equipment, it has been used widely for the selection of such groups as teachers, social workers, sales trainees, industrial executives, management trainees, civil service supervisors and administrators, military officers, and clinical psychology trainees.[22] Moreover, the LGD technique has also been employed in research on the effects of counseling.[23] In an LGD situation, a small group of individuals (six is optimal) is assigned a topic to discuss or a problem to solve within a specified period of time. During the discussion period, the group is observed by a team. A record is made of the nature and extent of each individual's contribution to the group, and/or summary ratings are made of each participant with respect to certain important behaviors.

The LGD technique can be employed effectively in classroom, counseling, and many other small-group settings. Direct observation of individuals working in small groups on simulated real-life problems has been an integral part of the multidivision introductory educational psychology course at Purdue University since the fall of 1975.[24] LGD serves both as a teaching strategy and as a means of gathering information regarding the behavioral characteristics of students. It also serves as a means of gathering information concerning the adequacy of the solutions produced for the simulated problems. In this context, the LGD becomes a situational proficiency test.

Even though LGD has been employed frequently under informal and nonstandardized conditions, there is a considerable body of evidence to support the conclusion that the reliability of observers' reports for LGD and other situational tests is reasonably strong.[25] Such tests have demonstrated validity for predicting performance in positions that require verbal communication, verbal problem-

---

[22] Anastasi, *Psychological Testing,* p. 597.

[23] H. B. Pepinsky, L. Siegel, and A. Vanatha, "The Criterion in Counseling: A Group Participation Scale," *Journal of Abnormal and Social Psychology* 47 (1952): 415–419.

[24] John F. Feldhusen, Kathryn W. Linden, and Russell E. Ames, "Using Instructional Theory and Educational Technology in Designing College Courses: A Three-Stage Model," in *Improving College and University Teaching, Yearbook 1975,* ed. Delmar M. Goode (Corvallis, Ore.: Oregon State University Press, 1975), pp. 64–69.

[25] J. M. Greenwood and W. J. McNamara, "Interrater Reliability in Situational Tests," *Journal of Applied Psychology* 51 (1967): 101–106.

solving, and acceptance by colleagues and peers. Thus, the use of LGD techniques should have strong appeal for both counselors and teachers in evaluating the dynamics underlying small-group counseling sessions or the interpersonal behaviors occurring in small problem-solving task groups in the classroom.

All situational tests appear to be most effective when they approximate actual work samples of the criterion behavior to be predicted and when the performance of the observed group is interpreted in relation to the work sample. A serious limitation of situational tests is that, because these tests are so task specific, behavior elicited under preplanned and controlled conditions may not be duplicated under natural conditions or even under other simulated conditions.

The major research conclusion regarding situational tests is that they are an interesting and potentially useful tool for appraising a variety of behaviors. However, the use of certain situational stress tests involves serious ethical considerations.[26] Such issues led the American Psychological Association to issue a policy regarding the use of measures involving deception. The use of situational tests for research purposes might be justifiable if it can be demonstrated that participants will not suffer either physical or emotional stress, that the research problem has scientific significance, and that there is no other practical method to use for the investigation.[27] Because of the time and expense required, and the ethical considerations raised by the use of some situational tests, counselors should confine this procedure to the appraisal of the interpersonal dynamics of small groups.

INFORMAL OBSERVATION

A number of informal methods of observation may be used to accumulate objective factual information about individuals that do not require as much preplanning and careful control as do the other methods. The principal tools of informal observation include records of anecdotal observations and various developmental records.

ANECDOTAL RECORDS As a medium for recording informal observations of significant incidents, anecdotal records provide primarily

---

[26] Zack Rubin, "Jokers Wild in the Lab," *Psychology Today* 4, no. 4 (December 1970): 18, 20, 22–24.
[27] American Psychological Association, "Ethical Standards for Psychologists," *American Psychologist* 23, no. 5 (May 1968): 357–361.

qualitative descriptions of selected aspects of an individual's behavior. Careful recording of anecdotal observations can yield dependable data to be used when needed.

Anecdotal records can provide information that is useful in helping an individual understand himself or herself and in interpreting the individual to his or her teachers, parents, employers, and significant others. Objective recording of behavioral incidents can help school or other personnel gain practice in obtaining factual observational data, acquire skill in identifying causes of behavior in its total context, and recognize the importance of the peer culture code and the cultural standards of a person's family in determining the individual's behavior at school or at work.

School personnel, students, and others can benefit from a program of anecdotal observation with its resultant anecdotal records. Both counselors and teachers can gain information about a student's cumulative pattern of development and can increase their skills of objective observation and interpretation of student behavior.

A good anecdotal record reports behavior; it does not interpret behavior. Moreover, a good anecdotal record describes behavior in specific terms; it does not describe behavior in terms of general impressions. Nevertheless, it is appropriate for a good anecdotal record to include mood cues such as gestures, postures, facial expressions, and vocal qualities that can yield inferences about an individual's feelings at the time.

A good anecdotal record is selective in that the event it describes either represents an individual's habitual behavior or differs significantly from the individual's typical behavior. When the behavior being observed differs from the individual's usual behavior, that fact is noted. The setting in which a behavorial incident occurred is described in order to provide meaning for the event. For example, such factors as time, place, and persons involved should be described clearly.[28]

The most desirable type of anecdotal record is the *specific descriptive* type that presents an accurate record of what was said and done by the persons involved in the observed incident. Anecdotal records of student behavior increase in diagnostic value as they become clear word pictures, free from language suggesting any specific trait, or combination of traits, to be associated with the action described.

A special case of anecdotal observation, known as the *critical incident technique,* was proposed by John C. Flanagan as a means

---

[28] Jane Warters, *Techniques of Counseling,* 2nd ed. (New York: McGraw Hill, 1964), p. 24.

of studying individuals.[29] Only incidents that point to a critical strength or weakness in an individual's personal and/or social development are singled out and recorded. This method permits the development of a graphic record of the changes in an individual's behavior pattern. Critical incident records have become a popular vehicle for studying and analyzing the dynamics involved in a variety of natural settings.

Just as a response to a single test item provides a single bit of information about an individual, a single anecdotal record provides one item of information. A series of records provides a set of items, just as a series of test items make up a test. In each case, a series of items must be organized, summarized, and interpreted in order to be meaningful. No single item, either as a test item or as a behavioral incident, can yield a comprehensive picture of an individual. Even though the significant elements in a set of anecdotal observations cannot be summarized as simply as those in a set of test items, it is usually desirable to make an attempt to organize the significant items of information in a set of anecdotes into a coherent picture of the individual in question.

Anecdotal records on students should be reviewed carefully at regular intervals, usually once a semester or possibly more often if a particular student is being studied intensively. Recurring patterns of behavior should be noted, and any progressive change should be identified. An attempt should be made to relate the anecdotal material to other known facts about the individual, such as academic achievement or ability, physical characteristics, general state of health, home surroundings, and family pattern. When this has been accomplished, a tentative interpretation of the behavior patterns may be made (of course, any interpretation is regarded as a set of very tentative hypotheses).

Anecdotal records can suffer from problems associated with the method itself, with the selection of behavior to be assessed, and with the individuals making the appraisals. Four problems are involved: the selection and sampling of behaviors to be observed and recorded, the wording of the anecdote itself, the use of anecdotal information, and the amount of work involved in collecting and keeping anecdotal records. An additional very serious problem has been raised by the Family Educational Rights and Privacy Act of 1974. This act, designed to protect the privacy of students, permits both parents and students access to student records.

---

[29] John C. Flanagan, "The Critical Incident Technique," *Psychological Bulletin* 51 (July 1954): 327–358.

The recording of anecdotal observations may create serious problems for school personnel. Consequently, it is necessary for a school faculty or other agency to decide whether or not records of informal anecdotal observations are worth the risk of being charged with invasion of privacy and/or the investment of staff time and effort. As is true for all methods of appraisal, if records of informal anecdotal observations can assist individuals in their self-understanding and also provide information that will aid counselors, the work involved is well worthwhile. However, if the anecdotal method is to be of any use in a school guidance program, for example, counselors, teachers, and administrators must be convinced of its value and must also receive detailed instructions and practice in its operation.

AUTOBIOGRAPHY   As a tool for understanding individuals, the autobiography not only reveals behavior but also frequently indicates the personal attitudes and emotions that underly the behavior of an individual. In educational settings, the autobiography provides a means by which an individual can think about himself or herself in a systematic way. Moreover, counselors are able to gain additional insights into a student's self-concept. A third purpose for using an autobiography is to collect facts concerning students and their environments.

Because the autobiography is an intimate tool involving direct expression, it is essential to establish a climate of trust and confidentiality. The amount of revealing information to be expected in an autobiography varies widely, depending not only on the conditions under which the autobiography is written but also on the personality of the individual and the degree to which he or she is experiencing difficulty. In addition, the form of the autobiography appears to influence its effectiveness as an observational tool.

As is true of interview formats, the most widely accepted terminology for the two basic forms of the autobiography are structured and unstructured, or controlled and uncontrolled. Both sets of terms refer to the same basic types: *structured* or *controlled* autobiographies employ an outline to be followed or present specific questions or topics; *unstructured* or *uncontrolled* autobiographies permit a freely written account of an individual's life without regard to any organizational format, specific question, or topical content. Sometimes these two basic formats are combined within a single autobiographical form; as in some interview formats, it is possible to vary the degree of structure of a given form.

The fact that an autobiography enables individuals to learn more

about themselves can be considered a primary purpose of the autobiography. Although this criterion has not been subjected to experiment, it seems reasonable to expect that a structured form
might have greater potential than an unstructured form in helping
individuals organize their thoughts. Moreover, a structured form
permits easy scanning by counselors, teachers, and others interested
in obtaining information in specific areas. There is no evidence to
support the notion that individuals are less likely to reveal information regarding their self-concepts when a structured form of the
autobiography is used rather than an unstructured form.

For these reasons, the structured or semistructured forms may be
preferred for use in school guidance programs, although the unstructured form may have greater value in other circumstances. For
example, an unstructured topical autobiographical form was used
by Everett L. Davis, who asked 408 students to tell, in their own
words, what kind of person they were.[30] Approximately 38,000
words submitted by the students were classified into various categories and topics. The most popular topics were such socially approved ones as school, family, athletics, self, and friends. Socially
disapproved topics, such as drugs and sex, were listed infrequently.
In view of the danger of negative reaction to structured autobiographical items, it is probably unwise to include items that are
socially disapproved, especially in light of the Family Educational
Rights and Privacy Act of 1974.

When interpreting and using autobiographical information, three
crucial questions should be considered: (1) To what extent has
writing an autobiography led the student to think more clearly
about himself or herself? (2) What has the counselor or teacher been
able to learn regarding the student's self-concept? and (3) What new
information was obtained from the autobiography? Although the
first question is of major importance, it is almost impossible to
answer by examining the autobiography, so it must be explored
during further contacts with the student in counseling or teaching
situations. The second and third questions can be answered by
careful study of the autobiography; but interpretation requires time,
careful attention to detail, and at least some background knowledge
of the individual.

As we have pointed out, the amount of self-revealing information
depends on the conditions under which the autobiography is written, the personality of the student, and the degree to which he or

---

[30] Everett L. Davis, "An Analysis of Autobiographical Statements of Adolescents," *Measurement and Evaluation in Guidance* 6 (October 1973): 152–156.

she is experiencing difficulty in working out problems. The auto-biography, therefore, is an extremely personal document having the same weaknesses that are inherent in any subjective technique. Many people are prone to overlook their weaknesses and limitations and to build up either real or imagined strengths when judging themselves. On the other hand, some people tend to understate their strengths and dwell primarily on their weaknesses and limitations. The method of content analysis, discussed in Chapter 14, provides a means for interpreting self-report documents, including the autobiography, as well as other observational data.

Although the autobiography is one of the counselor's most potentially useful tools, a surprising number of authorities in the field give scant attention to this essential aid to counseling. The major problems encountered in using the autobiography to elicit facts and feelings are those of communication. Even when questions are formulated carefully and responses are written, misunderstanding may occur either in the respondent's interpretation of the questions or in the counselor's interpretation of the responses. Unless there is some personal interaction, such misunderstandings cannot be resolved. Consequently, it is extremely important that counseling sessions be held with individuals subsequent to the collection of autobiographical data.

RELATED PERSONAL DOCUMENTS   In addition to the autobiography, there are several related personal documents that can be useful tools for counselors and teachers: the daily record or time log; the diary or journal; and other writing, such as letters, themes, and poems. All of these tools are potential sources of supplementary information, and no tool that permits individuals to tell their own stories as they want to tell them should be overlooked. Such documents as these may have value for showing the general pattern of an individual's life, the activities in which the person customarily engages, and perhaps some special interests.

As with autobiographies, fantasy and self-interest rather than truth may sometimes supply the basis for the report. Moreover, the validity of the data obtained from these documents depends a great deal on the student-teacher or student-counselor relationship. When such relationships are positive, students may report accurately about what they think while they are engaged in some activity and how they spend their days. These sources may suggest new meaning for old data by bringing into focus details that may have been overlooked or little noticed. All data derived from students' writings must be interpreted with caution, and the counselor must be extremely careful not to read personal feelings, hopes, fears, aspirations, and sensitivities into the students' documents.

CUMULATIVE PERSONNEL RECORD The summarized cumulative personnel record is an instrument for recording the past and, as such, is capable of yielding a maximum of information in a minimum of space.

The primary purpose of cumulative personnel records is to provide a comprehensive picture of individuals and their backgrounds obtained over a period of time. In the best of worlds, cumulative personnel records present an up-to-date, organized, and progressive record of information about individuals that distinguishes each of them from every other person. Objective information is sought that will portray significant and representative characteristics of given individuals. The cumulative record can be used by counselors, teachers, and other personnel workers to help students make effective adjustments and to assist them in understanding themselves and their physical, academic, social, and emotional development. Moreover, when used effectively, the cumulative record can help counselors identify the degree to which the school is meeting an individual student's needs.

In order to fulfill its objectives and purposes, a cumulative personnel record should be maintained carefully and kept up to date. It is important for all entries to be dated, because this helps to provide a clear picture of the scheme and development of the information. Moreover, entries should be initialed so that the counselor can seek clarification or locate additional resources. The cumulative record should not be a depository for odds and ends; rather, it should be a valuable source for the kind of information that helps to create an understanding of students and to promote realistic planning with them. Finally, the cumulative record folder or record card should make it easy to forward information to other schools or organizations.

In recent years, many school districts, colleges, and universities have shifted from manually maintained cumulative records to automated records. The advantages of computerized record systems include easy access to information, convenient collation of information, compactness and efficiency of record keeping, and speed of retrieval and reproduction. In the future, the use of automated data processing and retrieval systems is likely to be increased.

There has likewise been growing concern about computerized information that can be retrieved and communicated rapidly and widely. The fear that such information will be misused has increased dramatically, and this fear has led directly to the development of policies, guidelines, and federal laws regulating the collection and disclosure of such data. As we have said, any data that have been obtained from students or others under conditions of confidentiality should not be entered into the cumulative record. Confidential information can be kept in a counselor's private file and a notation entered on the cumulative record that additional information is available from the counselor on a need-to-know basis. However, when and to whom such information ought to be made available is a complex issue involving professional ethics. The issues of an individual's right to privacy and of professional ethics are discussed in Chapter 15.

PROBLEMS IN OBSERVATION

One major deterrent to the widespread use of observational methods is that individuals usually know when they are being observed and are likely to adapt their behavior, consciously or not. For this reason, it is important to secure rapport with the individuals to be observed or to conceal from them either the fact that observations are being made or the exact nature of the observations. Consciousness of being observed appears to be a function not only of the age and degree of sophistication of the individual being observed but of a variety of other factors as well.

Familiarity with a particular observer and with observers in general, previous experience in being observed, the type of situation in which observations are made, the number of individuals observed in a given situation, and the frequency with which observations are rotated among the various members of an observed group all influence the consciousness of the target individuals. The presence of observers is least disturbing in regular informal situations in which freedom of movement is unrestricted and in situations wherein visitors are common and the observer's attention shifts frequently from one individual to another. Nevertheless, the possibility of bias resulting from the awareness of being observed should always be considered.

A second major problem concerns the relatively limited range of situations in which individuals can be observed over a sufficiently extended period of time to insure an adequate sampling of behavior. In the context of the representative sampling of characteristic individual behavior patterns or traits in all situations of a given type, the accepted criterion of validity has been agreement of the measures obtained with corresponding indices derived by other methods.

Ratings obtained from teachers, parents, counselors, supervisors, and others have been used to validate observational data, and observational data derived from uncontrolled situations have been compared with measures of the incidence of the same behavior derived from experimental situations. However, none of these approaches affords conclusive proof of validity for either of the measures compared.

When observational measures indicate substantial agreement with measures obtained from experimental situations, it is assumed that both of the indices constitute valid measures of the behavior under observation. However, when two indices purporting to measure the same behavior in the same individuals are markedly inconsistent, it is assumed that one was, or both were, unrepresentative or invalid. Behavior is variable, and observation is selective. Therefore, evaluations based on observation are subject to sampling error and observer bias. Nevertheless, methods of observation can be valuable assessment tools, supplying information that cannot be gathered by other techniques.

ISSUES

1.   *Observational tools and techniques have questionable value because they lack both reliability and validity.*
     Yes, because:
     1.   Observation methods are subject to both sampling error and observer bias; hence, reliability and validity of observational data are suspect.
     2.   Both records of observations and interpretations of the resulting data are influenced by the special sensitivities, premature hypotheses, and selective memory of observers.
     3.   Viewing observations methods with skepticism is justified by the misuse of these techniques in many situations.

     No, because:
     1.   Observation provides information that cannot be obtained by any other technique.
     2.   These methods provide the facts that may confirm or refute tentative hypotheses derived from other sources.

     Discussion:
     Observation is a basic investigative tool of all who study behavior. Observation provides criterion data for the development and validation of all kinds of appraisal instruments. The method

is subject to sampling error and observer bias, but so is every other kind of assessment tool. Admittedly, the measurement error associated with standardized test data is usually known and can be incorporated into interpretations. Moreover, the precision with which measurements are obtained represents only one part of the total picture to be considered in judging any method of appraisal. Other issues involve the need to consider the perspective that the assessment tool affords, the significance of the behavioral area that it measures, and the possibility of obtaining more precise measurements by some other means. In this context, observational tools are worthy of serious consideration.

Although the evidence regarding reliability and validity of observational data varies according to the method employed, there is ample evidence to support the contention that these tools have value. The extensive sampling of real-life behavior made possible by observational techniques employed in natural settings provides data that cannot be obtained from standardized tests, although each source supplements the other. The more extensive the behavior samples are, the greater is the probability that the samples are representative of an individual's true behavior.

Information derived from observational instruments and methods has been misinterpreted and misused in countless situations. However, the fact that such cases are common is the fault of the way in which the observation techniques were used and not necessarily the fault of the techniques themselves. As with all methods of appraisal, observational tools should be employed with care and precision. The more skilled observers are in applying interpretive techniques, the more valid, reliable, and useful will be their interpretations. All data provide only estimates of the behavior patterns of individuals and, therefore, demand cautious interpretation.

2.   *Only skilled and experienced personnel should be permitted to employ observation methods and to interpret observational data.*
     Yes, because:
     1.   The determination of what to observe and how to evaluate observational data requires both skill and experience in using a given method.
     2.   Untrained observers tend to bias observations by their failure to record the observed events objectively, to avoid praise and blame, and to keep their own emotions, attitudes, and prejudices under control.

3. Effective observation involves grasping clearly, concisely, and as completely as possible the essential behavior of individuals in given situations.

No, because:
1. All people utilize observation as a basic educational tool and assessment technique.
2. Some observation methods do not require as much formal training as others.

Discussion:
The observational tools discussed in this chapter and in the next three chapters require a great deal of expertise in interpretation. However, the collection of observational data involves the relatively more simple process of recording observed behavior. For some of the methods, such as biographical data inventories and personal documents, the individual being studied makes the observations. In such instances, the validity and reliability of the facts reported are not crucial, although the facts reported in a biographical data inventory are readily verifiable.

Often it is true that many self-report documents and much interview data contain distortions and inaccuracies, but these errors may reveal as much concerning the individual as the information reported accurately. Whether or not the information is accurate, the counselor must make valid interpretations of the data. Consequently, the more skilled the counselor is in the application of interpretative techniques, the more valid, reliable, and useful the interpretations will be. This is equally true of interpretations made of all observational data. (Suggestions for integrating and interpreting data are presented in Chapter 14.)

No matter how simple an observational technique may appear to be, it should be employed with care and caution. The more skilled and experienced an observer is, the greater the probability is that he or she can obtain a representative and unbiased sample of relevant behavior. All interpretations must be viewed as tentative hypotheses to be verified or refuted by further evidence. Moreover, the conscientious professional also recognizes that any pool of data on an individual represents only a small portion of the complete person (see principle 8, Chapter 1). The more crucial the decision to be made, the greater must be the degree of expertise required of the observer.

ANNOTATED REFERENCES

Kerlinger, Fred N. *Foundations of Behavioral Research.* 2nd ed. New York: Holt, Rinehart and Winston, 1973.
For individuals interested in research design and applications of behavioral research, this book is an excellent resource. Chapter 28 is concerned with interviews and interview schedules, and systematic observation is discussed in Chapter 31.

Rosenshine, Barak, and Furst, Norma. "The Use of Direct Observation to Study Teaching." In *Second Handbook of Research on Teaching.* Edited by Robert M. W. Travers. Chicago: Rand McNally College Publishing Company, 1973, ch. 5.
This resource presents a rather detailed discussion of various instruments used in systematic observation. Characteristics of the instruments are detailed. This is a valuable resource for the consumer of data obtained from systematic observation methods.

Simon, A., and Boyer, E. G. *Mirrors for Behavior: An Anthology of Classroom Observation Instruments.* Philadelphia: Research for Better Schools, vols. 1–6 (1967); vols. 7–14, summary, supplementary vols. A and B (1970).
The documents that make up this anthology present more than one hundred instruments that have been designed to assess behavior in real-life settings. Consequently, this anthology should be a valuable resource for persons interested in systematic observation in classrooms, counseling offices, or other natural settings.

SELECTED REFERENCES

Allport, Gordon W. *The Use of Personal Documents in Psychological Sciences.* Bulletin 49. New York: Social Science Research Council, 1942.

Flanders, Ned A. *Analyzing Teaching Behavior.* Reading, Mass.: Addison-Wesley, 1970.

Gordon, Raymond L. *Interviewing: Strategy, Techniques and Tactics.* Rev. ed. Homewood, Ill.: Dorsey Press, 1975.

Gronlund, Norman E. *Measurement and Evaluation Teaching.* 3rd ed. New York: Macmillan, 1976.

Jones, R. R.; Reid, J. B.; and Patterson, G. R. "Naturalistic Observation in Clinical Assessment." In *Advances in Psychological Assessment.* Vol. 3. Edited by Paul McReynolds. San Francisco: Jossey-Bass, 1975, ch. 2.

Miklich, D. R. "Radio Telemetry in Clinical Psychology and Related Areas." *American Psychologist* 30 (1975): 419–425.

Payne, David A. *The Assessment of Learning: Cognitive and Affective.* Lexington, Mass.: D. C. Heath, 1974.

Chapter 12   Rating

What major events mark the development and use of rating techniques for assessing behavior?

What functions do rating methods serve?

What types of rating scales and other rating methods are available?

What are the major problems associated with rating methods?

How can the results of rating be interpreted and used appropriately?

A BRIEF HISTORY

Formal rating scales have been employed for at least two centuries in various scientific fields. As early as 1805, meteorologists in the British navy used a rating to judge wind velocities. The scale ranged from 0, indicating complete absence of wind, to 12, which indicated a hurricane. Another ten-point rating scale was used to estimate the mugginess of the weather, with 0 indicating bright, brisk, or stimulating weather and 1, the highest rank, describing the muggiest conditions.

Many psychologists credit Sir Francis Galton with the first use of rating methods in psychology for the scientific assessment of the personal, psychophysiological, and social characteristics of people. Galton, who was interested in the investigation of individual differences, particularly with regard to the influence of heredity, suggested that various kinds of rating scales could be used in "rude experiments" that would yield results capable of being submitted to statistical analysis.

The use of a scientifically developed rating scale for measuring

THIS CHAPTER WAS WRITTEN BY KATHRYN W. LINDEN.

an educational product was introduced in 1909 by Edward L. Thorn-dike, when he presented his Handwriting Scale (see Chapter 2). This scale made possible the quantitative description of an essentially qualitative product. Based on the premise that differences in quality are equal when they are noted with equal frequency by competent observers, Thorndike secured a set of handwriting specimens that were rated consistently by experts as being qualitatively different. These specimens were arranged in order of increasing merit to form the scale. A student's handwriting sample was measured by match-ing it with the division of the scale that the example resembled most closely in general merit.

By the time that the man-to-man rating method was introduced during the First World War, the use of ratings had become a rela-tively routine feature of the application of psychology to human affairs. Developed by Walter Dill Scott and his colleagues, the man-to-man scale was employed as a device for rating officers. Although this rating method has been employed primarily in military and industrial situations, its use has declined in the last several decades. However, with ingenious improvements, it might still be a very useful tool in certain situations.

The graphic rating scale appears to have originated in the Scott Company Laboratory in 1920.[1] Described by Freyd as the "latest development" in rating methodology, with promise of becoming the most popular, the graphic model's only original feature was its combination of the methods of rating on a line and checking de-scriptive terms, both of which were in prior existence. By 1923, several graphic rating scales were being used by the Scott Company and the Bureau of Personnel Research at the Carnegie Institute of Technology.

The first of several methods of scaling psychological measures was reported by L. L. Thurstone and E. J. Chave in 1929.[2] This method, known as the method of equal-appearing intervals, was first used to develop a scale to assess attitudes toward religion. In this scale, the lower the value, the more positive is the attitude. Subsequent work by Thurstone and his colleagues demonstrated how scales of attitudes could be constructed for any topic and how items could be developed to reveal various strengths of feeling toward an object or a situation. In 1927, Thurstone introduced the method of paired comparisons (or pair comparisons), which requires

[1] M. Freyd, "The Graphic Rating Scale," *The Journal of Educational Psychology* 14 (1923): 83–102.

[2] L. L. Thurstone and E. J. Chave, *The Measurement of Attitude* (Chicago: University of Chicago Press, 1929), pp. 61–63, 78.

a rater to compare each member or object in a given group to every other member in the group. Employed primarily for purposes of determining scale values, this method also has been used widely as a method of measurement. During the early 1930s, Rensis Likert reported his development of the method of summated ratings for measuring attitudes toward internationalism, imperialism, and the Negro.[3] Likert employed items of the multiple-choice type consisting of three-response options or five-response options: yes, ?, no, or strongly approve through undecided to strongly disapprove. His final approach was to scale the responses using the category-scale method and to use the resulting scale values as weights for the responses. However, he found that using the integral values of 1–5 for the five-option items and 2–4 for the three-option items yielded scores as reliable as those resulting from the category-scale values, and the two scores correlated almost perfectly. Consequently, the more simple weighting method was used, and a rater's score became the sum of the weights assigned to his or her responses for all items.

A Likert scale is easier to construct than one employing the Thurstone procedure; therefore, the former has become the most widely used technique for developing rating scales. A significant contribution to rating scale methodology was the forced-choice rating technique introduced during the Second World War by a number of psychologists working in the military services and in industry. During this time, there evolved a considerable folklore of more or less subjective rules governing the construction of rating scales. Rating methods for use in judging behavioral characteristics have now come of age. Their widespread use in industrial, military, and educational settings seems to have exceeded the application of all other methods of assessment except the interview and tests.

GENERAL DESCRIPTION OF RATING

Observers using the observational methods discussed in the previous chapter function primarily as accurate recorders of the behavior being observed. Synthesis and interpretation of the observations are separate processes. Rating methods, however, involve an evaluative summary of present or past experiences "in which the 'internal computer' of the rater processes the input data in complex

---

[3] Rensis Likert, "A Technique for the Measurement of Attitudes," *Archives of Psychology* 132 (1932): 101–107.

and unspecified ways to arrive at the final judgment."[4] Several limitations of direct observational methods—including the extreme subjectivity of unstructured statements, the lack of a common core of content or standard of reference from observer to observer, and the difficulty of quantifying materials—contributed to the emergence and rapid rise in popularity of rating techniques. Rating techniques attempt to overcome these deficiencies.

In rating methodology, each observer is presented with an observation system consisting of some kind of rating form comprising a set of characteristics or attributes to be evaluated and a scale that indicates the degree to which each attribute or characteristic is present in the observed object, person, or event. The rating form itself is merely a tool for reporting the rater's assessment. The rater must make his or her assessment on the basis of past observations or on the basis of his or her perceptions of what the observed person, object, or event is like and/or what future behavior is likely.[5]

The value of rating methods depends primarily on the care with which the rating form is developed and the appropriateness with which it is employed. As with other assessment methods, rating scales should be constructed in accordance with the behaviors to be evaluated, and their use should be confined to those areas of concern for which there is sufficient opportunity to make the observations needed for reliable, relevant, and valid information. When these two principles are applied appropriately, rating scales serve several important functions. They provide:

1. direct observation of specific, clearly defined aspects of behavior
2. a common frame of reference for comparing individuals, objects, or events on the same set of characteristics
3. a convenient method for recording the judgments of the observers

Thus, rating scales are employed in order to obtain appraisals for a common set of characteristics that are expressed on a common quantitative scale for all raters and for those persons, objects, or events being rated.

---

[4] Robert L. Thorndike and Elizabeth Hagen, *Measurement and Evaluation in Psychology and Education,* 4th ed. (New York: John Wiley and Sons, 1977), p. 449.

[5] Fred N. Kerlinger, *Foundations of Behavioral Research,* 2nd ed. (New York: Holt, Rinehart and Winston, 1973), p. 547.

RATING METHODS

Any rating method should accomplish two major objectives: it should classify individuals, objects, or events according to some trait or variable, and it should identify the reasons for placing an individual, object, or event in one category rather than another. In accordance with these objectives, Leonard W. Ferguson classified rating methods into two broad categories: *analytical,* if the rating method provides both classifications and supporting reasons, and *nonanalytical,* if the method provides classifications without supporting reasons.[6] J. P. Guilford identified five major types of rating methods: numerical, graphic, standard, cumulated points, and forced choice.[7] Kerlinger labeled ratings in terms of numerical, graphic, forced-choice, checklist, and category methods.[8]

Even though these authors and others appear to disagree about the labels assigned to the major types of rating methods, the disagreement is more apparent than it is real. The basis for most rating methods is essentially the same. A behavioral continuum is defined as precisely as possible, and a rater is asked to evaluate and to allocate samples of the specified behavior either along an unbroken continuum or in ordered categories along the continuum. Attaching numbers to the allocated behaviors is a common end product of all types of ratings. However, rating scales differ in the operations regarding categorizing the behaviors, the kind and number of aids or cues provided, the fineness of the discrimination required of the rater, and certain other minor details.

Rating scales that employ either a word, a short phrase, or a sentence to describe the points along a behavioral continuum are usually labeled *graphic* scales. However, these same scales can become *numerical* scales simply by adding numbers to the scale points. On the other hand, many numerical scales do not contain verbal descriptions of the scale points. *Ranking* scales, regardless of the specific label that may be attached to this type of rating, represent an approach different from those of both numerical and graphic scales. Moreover, techniques that sample actual behavior or give a description of a behavioral sample or a hypothesized behavioral sample are still another method.

We shall classify rating methods into five broad categories: numerical, graphic, criterion-related, ranking, and checklist methods.

[6] Leonard W. Ferguson, *Personality Measurement* (New York: McGraw-Hill, 1952), pp. 288–334.

[7] J. P. Guilford, *Psychometric Methods,* 2nd ed. (New York: McGraw-Hill, 1954), pp. 263–278.

[8] Kerlinger, *Foundations of Research,* pp. 547–548.

Forced-choice, pair comparisons, Q-sort, and semantic differential techniques are special cases of these rating categories. Sociometric techniques, which are also special rating tools, are discussed in Chapter 13.

NUMERICAL SCALES

Numerical rating scales usually take the form of a sequence of defined numbers. The numerical values of this sequence may or may not be defined in verbal terms. Verbal definitions of the numbers might be made in terms of degree of pleasantness, favorableness, frequency, or agreement with a statement. The task of the rater is to assign to each stimulus a number appropriate to a given definition or description. Guilford illustrated a numerical scale with scale points defined by statements:
  How serious-minded is he or she?

  7 takes everything as if it were a matter of life and death
  6 ordinarily serious and conscientious about things
  5 slightly on the serious, conscientious side
  4 neither serious nor unconcerned
  3 slightly on the relaxed and unconcerned side
  2 ordinarily unconcerned and carefree
  1 seems not to have a care in the world[9]

These seven defined points could be reduced to five defined points quite easily. In fact, many numerical scales contain only five defined numbers.
  Research on rating scales appears to indicate that as many as twenty categories may be used, depending on the nature of the traits being assessed and the sophistication of the rater. However, the more defined points a scale has, the greater is the probability that semantic confusion will cloud the rater's judgments, thus lowering both the reliability and validity of ratings. One approach for overcoming this problem is to specify the frequency of occurrence that applies to each term. David A. Payne recommended this scheme based on the results of a study conducted by R. Simpson in 1944, who asked samples of high school and college students to indicate what certain terms connoted for them:

[9] J. P. Guilford, *Personality* (New York: McGraw-Hill, 1959), p. 142.

5   almost always (86 to 100 percent of the time)
4   generally (66 to 85 percent of the time)
3   frequently (36 to 65 percent of the time)
2   sometimes (16 to 35 percent of the time)
1   rarely (0 to 15 percent of the time)[10]

Even though there is still some latitude in interpreting what the various terms mean, indicating the frequency of occurrence should provide a clearer and more consistent frame of reference. Nevertheless, numerical scales often are rejected in favor of other types of ratings because of their vulnerability to biases and errors.

LIKERT SCALE   This scale is the most widely-used technique for measuring attitudes. Developed by Rensis Likert in the early 1930s, the technique has gained wide popularity in recent years for measuring many affective behaviors other than attitudes. Probably the most frequently employed such format consists of five response choices that range from strongly agree through undecided to strongly disagree and yield numerical values of 1–5. Each rater responds to every item, and the total score is the sum of the numerical values assigned to the rater's responses.

Interest in educational accountability has led to the use of the numerical type of rating scale for assessing both affective and cognitive behaviors of teachers, particularly at the college and university level. Students' ratings of instructors and courses are being employed not only to assist instructors in identifying areas of strength and weakness but also to help make administrative decisions about raises, promotion, and tenure.

The issue of whether or not it is appropriate to employ student ratings in assessing the effectiveness of a teacher for such purposes as giving a promotion or granting tenure remains to be resolved. Regardless of the empirical evidence concerning the reliability and validity of such ratings, some educators believe that student ratings should not be included in the credentials submitted for administrative decision-making. Others argue that because student ratings have proven to be both reliable and valid, such evidence should be submitted in support of a teacher's effectiveness. At any rate, the number of new instruments designed to assess various aspects of teaching has increased substantially in recent years.

Other types of personal service are assessed as well, including

[10] David A. Payne, The Assessment of Learning: Cognitive and Affective (Lexington, Mass.: D. C. Heath, 1974), p. 381.

counselor's effectiveness. The twenty-one-item Counseling Evaluation Inventory intended for client use has demonstrated reliability and validity.[11] Similarly constructed scales have been employed in many businesses and industries.

SEMANTIC DIFFERENTIAL TECHNIQUE   A special case of numerical rating, the semantic differential technique, was developed by C. E. Osgood and his associates as a means of indexing the manifold implications of persons, objects, and ideas for the human observer.[12] The construct of meaning is inextricably interwoven with psychological and philosophical theory, for it is axiomatic that human behavior is governed by the meaning of events rather than by the intrinsic properties of events.

Semantic differential is based on the hypothesis that certain important components of meaning can be measured by rating objects or ideas with respect to bipolar adjectives, such as good-bad, emotional-rational, humorous-serious, pleasant-unpleasant, sincere-insincere, or valuable-worthless. Each set of bipolar adjectives comprises a scale in the semantic differential. A great number of empirical studies have used this rating technique, ranging from studies of dream symbolism to cross-cultural studies of language.

A concept is measured and portrayed in three dimensions of meaning, or semantic space: evaluation (good-bad), potency (strong-weak), and activity (fast-slow). The number of scales included in a given semantic differential varies widely; studies have employed as few as half a dozen scales to more than thirty. Each scale contains a 7-point continuum for each set of bipolar objectives, and the concept to be rated is written at the head of a page above the bipolar scales. Moreover, the same set of scales is used to rate all of the concepts being studied, each on a separate page. Many current educational applications of the semantic differential have deviated from Osgood's orthodox approach in several ways. More than one concept may be presented on a single page of the instrument, and the scales used to measure each concept are not always the same. Moreover, the major concern is with the value that a concept has for a given student rather than whether the scales are pure measures of a given dimension. Thus, the notion of semantic meaning is

[11] James D. Linden, Shelley C. Stone, and Bruce Shertzer, "Development and Evaluation of an Inventory for Rating Counseling," *Personnel and Guidance Journal* 44 (November 1965): 267–276.

[12] C. E. Osgood, G. J. Suci, and P. Tannenbaum, *The Measurement of Meaning* (Urbana, Ill.: University of Illinois Press, 1957).

ignored, and each scale is interpreted directly. In spite of its rather brief history, the semantic differential measurement technique has been useful in a wide variety of applications in many fields and has become a standard assessment technique.

GRAPHIC SCALES

Even though numerical rating scales have been increasing in popularity during the past few years, the most popular rating method is still the graphic rating scale. This type of scale can have numerous variations in format, for there are many ways in which a straight line can be presented and combined with cues to aid the rater in making assessments. The straight line can be either continuous or broken into units, and the number of scale points can be varied. Although the line can be presented either horizontally or vertically, most graphic scales are horizontal.

One of the difficulties of the horizontal-line format is that there is room for only very short verbal cues. Moreover, a cue cannot be located at a single point on the continuum but must be spread out along the line, leaving its exact scale position in doubt. Both of these difficulties were adjusted by the vertical line format of the *Fels Behavior Rating Scale,* designed and introduced by H. Champney for assessing various aspects of a child's home environment.[13]

Raters seem to prefer the graphic rating scale to any of the other types of rating methods. Moreover, it has been stated that "the virtues of graphic rating scales are many, their faults are relatively few."[14] Graphic scales are relatively easy to construct and to administer. The simplicity of format also makes it easy for the rater to grasp what is involved in a rating dimension. Because such scales are interesting to most raters, little additional motivation is required. Moreover, depending on where the rater places check marks, the ratings can be as discriminating as the rater chooses, and the sensitivity of scoring can be great. Finally, no outside criterion is required in order to develop and/or use graphic scales. Thus, graphic scales appear to have no disadvantage that does not apply to other types of scales.

---

[13] H. Champney, "The Measurement of Parent Behavior," *Child Development* 12 (1941): 131–166.
[14] Guilford, *Psychometric Methods,* p. 268.

CRITERION-RELATED SCALES

Criterion-related scales, sometimes called standard or sample scales, are distinguished from other scales in that they present either an actual sample of behavior or a description of a sample, or they ask the rater to hypothesize a sample. The rater then uses this sample as a criterion and compares it to that which is being rated. Thorndike's Handwriting Scale, cited earlier in this chapter, is an example of a criterion-related scale. Probably the best known of this type of scale is the man-to-man scale developed by W. D. Scott and his associates during the First World War. Unfortunately, the man-to-man technique is cumbersome and time consuming. Consequently, it is little used outside the military.

RANKING METHODS

The ranking of persons, objects, or events can be either a simple or a complex process. The best known of the ranking methods is the simple *rank-order method* for assessing intragroup differences with respect to some characteristic or set of characteristics. The names of the members of a given group (set of objects, ideas, or events) are arranged in serial order from high to low in keeping with their status in terms of the characteristics being judged. The rank of 1 is assigned to the highest placed member, 2 to the next highest, and so on, until the last member is ranked. This procedure is easy to employ when the characteristic being ranked is represented in numerical terms, such as grade-point averages, scores on a test, the time required to perform a certain task, or the number of yards gained in a football game. However, the ranking task becomes very cumbersome and difficult when the characteristic being judged is, for example, the overall quality of an oral presentation or of class participation. In such instances, the rater may rank the group members from the ends toward the middle, ranking the highest first, then the lowest, then the next highest and the next lowest, and so on. This strategy simplifies the ranking procedure and may increase the probability that the students are ranked appropriately. Nevertheless, this approach is both cumbersome and difficult, especially when the group to be ranked is large.

One variation of this approach requires raters to place specified proportions of their samples into defined groups. For example, grading on the curve is, in effect, this type of ranking. An instructor may decide to assign 10 percent of the students the letter grade of

A, 20 percent *B*, 40 percent *C*, 20 percent *D*, and the lowest 10 percent a failing grade. In effect, the rater is forced to distinguish differences that may or may not exist in order to yield a normal distribution of ranks. Thus, even though a valid rationale may exist for assigning a stipulated percentage of cases to each category, rarely is such a practice justified. However, assigning persons or things to different groups for the purpose of assigning letter grades could be a useful approach if no percentage is stipulated. Dividing persons, or objects, into defined groups is used frequently as the first step in a complete ranking procedure and in many selection procedures employed by a wide variety of businesses, industries, government agencies, and schools.

PAIR-COMPARISON RATING   More precise although more time consuming than either of the rank-order methods described above, the method of pair-comparison requires the rater to compare two stimuli at a time until each stimulus has been compared with every other stimulus. This method can be used to provide the same kind of information as can be obtained by other ranking methods, but the results tend to be more reliable because the rater must make many judgments. The number of comparisons required severely curtails the use of the pair-comparison method in many applied settings. However, when the number of persons or objects to be rated is small, this method is excellent.

Q-SORT TECHNIQUE   Developed by William Stephenson and his colleagues as a means of recording and measuring multiple judgments, impressions, or preferences, the *Q*-sort technique is another variation of a complete ranking method.[15] A rater is presented with a set of cards containing statements, phrases, pictures, or other kinds of stimuli, and is asked to sort them into piles of cards according to their relative standing in terms of a single criterion. However, instead of being required to rate each item according to its applicability to the concept, as is the case with the traditional ranking procedure, the rater is asked to sort the item cards into a specific number of piles, each containing a given number of item statements. The trait continuum can be described in many ways: most important to me to least important to me, or extremely characteristic to extremely uncharacteristic. The number of cards assigned

[15] William Stephenson, *The Study of Behavior: Q-Technique and Its Methodology* (Chicago: University of Chicago Press, 1953).

to each pile usually is determined in advance in order to approximate a normal frequency distribution. Hence, the basis of this procedure is not unlike that described for the defined-group ranking method. In other words, the rater is required to distribute the Q-sort items in such a way as to produce a forced normal distribution.

The Q-sort technique may be employed in a variety of ways: to describe the rater or his or her interests or attitudes, or to rate others on the same traits. This technique has been employed widely in research on counseling effectiveness. An individual may describe himself or herself with one Q-sort, re-sort the statements to reflect his or her ideal self, and perhaps sort a third time in order to describe how the rater thinks the counselor perceives him or her. The sorted piles can then be correlated to determine the amount of agreement between the various sets of results.

In comparison to most other rating methods, the Q-sort technique can be employed for a wide variety of material, thus providing a means for investigating many kinds of problems that would otherwise be unmanageable. Moreover, the Q-sort method emphasizes the representativeness of the sample of items in the item set. The Q-sort rating technique has been used to investigate a wide variety of problems, particularly in studies on counseling and psychotherapy. In general, however, the time and effort required to administer and score Q-sorts, together with their focus on a single trait, tend to inhibit their widespread applicability, especially in comparison to such scales as the Likert-form numerical scale and the semantic differential method.

BEHAVIORAL CHECKLISTS

Perhaps the most simple method of recording observations is the behavioral checklist, which rarely requires complex judgments. Consequently, relatively naïve raters can use this procedure easily. The basic difference between checklists and other rating procedures is in the type of judgment required. A checklist calls for a simple yes or no judgment regarding the presence of a characteristic or an action. Other rating procedures require the rater to indicate the degree to which a characteristic is present or the frequency with which a behavior occurs. Moreover, checklists usually can be employed both to describe and to evaluate behavior, while other rating methods are used primarily for evaluation.

Checklists can serve many of the purposes served by other types of rating scales. However, they have special utility for evaluating performance skills that can be divided into a series of specific, clearly defined actions. The score for an individual or object is either the sum or the average of the number of points. When the evaluation is based on direct observation rather than on memory or general impression, the checklist becomes a testing procedure instead of a rating procedure.

A well-known commercially available instrument is *The Adjective Check List* (ACL).[16] The ACL was constructed originally for use in measuring self-concept in the research program of the Institute for Personality Assessment and Research. It provides an alphabetical list of 300 adjectives ranging from *absent-minded* to *zany*. Individuals mark all the adjectives that they feel describe themselves. Individuals who mark many adjectives generally are active and enthusiastic; individuals who mark few adjectives usually are quiet, reserved, and cautious. A total of twenty-four basic scales can be scored, including one labeled counseling readiness. This scale was developed by comparing the answers of counseling clients indicating positive counseling responses to those of clients indicating less positive responses. All scales are experimental, according to the authors. The ACL has been employed in a tremendous variety of research problems drawn from such areas as occupational choice, psychopathology, political and economic behavior, and patient reactions to orthodontia and contact lenses.

The checklist is a convenient method for recording evidence of growth toward specific learning outcomes in the area of personal and social development. However, merely noting the presence or absence of such characteristics as general activity, initiative, aggressiveness, sociability, and emotional maturity has little value in assessment. It is more meaningful to assess the degree or frequency of the characteristic. Consequently, other types of rating scales are more appropriate for such assessment needs.

PROBLEMS IN RATING

The use of ratings is based on the assumption "that the human observer is a good instrument of quantitative observation, that he (she) is capable of some degree of precision and some degree of objectivity."[17] In rating methodology, two psychological processes

---

[16] Harrison G. Gough and Alfred B. Heilbrun, Jr., *The Adjective Check List Manual* (Palo Alto, Calif.: Consulting Psychologists Press, 1972).
[17] Guilford, *Psychometric Methods*, p. 278.

must be combined into one judgment: observing and recording performance and evaluating performance. Consequently, several factors are involved in determining the effectiveness of rating methods. Ratings are highly susceptible to inaccurate observation, inaccurate recording, and inaccurate evaluation. The rater's task is to report his or her general estimate, based on direct observation, of the strengths and limitations of an individual, object, or event with regard to the characteristics named in the scale. Of course, no rating is an unbiased, objective assessment. In contrast to carefully designed tests of cognitive achievement or ability, rating methods are highly subjective.

SOURCES OF SYSTEMATIC ERROR

Any evaluation of rating methods should consider first the errors involved in ratings.

GENERAL RATER BIAS   Sometimes referred to as the leniency error, personal bias, or personal equation, *general rater bias* is the general, constant tendency for a rater to rate too high or too low on a scale, no matter what characteristic or trait is being assessed. When the rating is too high, the error is one of *positive leniency;* when the rating is too low, the error is one of *negative leniency,* or severity. Because positive leniency error is found more often than negative leniency error, control for the social desirability of responses is built into many scales. In other words, scale points are defined primarily by words, phrases, or statements having favorable connotations.

Another type of general rater bias is reflected by the tendency of some raters to avoid the extremes of a scale, resulting in displacement in the direction of the mean or median of the group. When a single individual is being assessed on a number of traits, this *error of central tendency* is manifested by a rater's endorsement of the scale points located at or near the midpoint of the scale. As a means of counteracting the influence of central tendency error, Guilford recommended that the intermediate descriptive phrases in graphic scales be spaced distinctly apart from each other.[18] Similarly, the strength of the descriptive adjectives employed in numerical scales can be adjusted in order to counteract the error of central tendency. "Greater differences may be introduced between steps near the ends of the scale than between steps near the center."[19]

---

[18] Guilford, *Psychometric Methods,* p. 278.
[19] Guilford, *Psychometric Methods,* p. 279.

RATER-RATEE INTERACTION   Perhaps the most widely known systematic error concerns the nature of the relationship between the rater and the person being rated. Nearly every rater falls victim to this source of error at one time or another. Identified more than seventy years ago by F. L. Wells,[20] this error was named the *halo effect* by E. L. Thorndike in 1920. An overall impression, either positive or negative, of an individual, object, or event can influence the rater's judgment concerning the specific traits being assessed, thus making the ratings of at least some of the traits less valid than they ought to be.

Because a rater tends to rate each individual similarly in all traits, overrating some individuals while underrating others, a spurious amount of positive correlation is introduced between the traits being assessed. The influence of rater-ratee interaction error appears to be more pervasive in rating traits that are not easily observable, that are not singled out or discussed frequently, that are not defined clearly, that involve interactions with other people, and that have strong moral importance. Consequently, a number of strategies has been employed to reduce the influence of this type of error, including a practice of rating one trait at a time for all persons being rated, listing one trait per page of the scale rather than one ratee per page, and using the forced-choice technique. Moreover, averaging the ratings from several raters, canceling out rater-ratee interaction errors, increases reliability.

RATER-TRAIT INTERACTION   Similar in basic concept to the rater-ratee interaction error, the rater-trait interaction error involves the rater's attitudes toward specific traits. First identified by Guilford, this source of error is caused by a rater's tendency to judge others to be like himself or herself (similarity error) or to be the opposite (contrast error).[21] For example, a person who sees himself or herself as being extremely orderly, neat, and meticulous may tend to rate others in the opposite direction. Similarly, raters who are themselves low on these traits may tend to see others as being more orderly, neat, and meticulous than they actually are. Conversely, people who expect others to be like themselves may tend to rate others in the same direction that they would use to rate themselves.

LOGICAL ERROR   Inaccuracies in rating may also occur because the traits in the scale are not defined clearly. Many rating forms require ratings of relatively broad, abstract traits, leaving the examinee to

---

[20] F. L. Wells, "A Statistical Study of Literacy Merit," *Archives of Psychology* 1, no. 7 (1907).
[21] Guilford, *Psychometric Methods*, p. 280.

wonder what exactly is meant by serious-minded, energetic, initiative, emotional stability, and integrity. People are likely to attach slightly different meanings to such abstract concepts. To the degree that a term is abstract, its meaning varies from person to person. A major problem associated with obtaining consistent, accurate ratings is acquiring consistent interpretations of the traits being rated.

A second source of logical error is derived from the lack of a uniform standard of reference for the scale categories or scale points. The more abstract the scale categories or scale points are, the more variable are raters' interpretations of those categories. How good is good? Does good in the four-option scale mean the same as good in the six-option scale? Does superior mean the top 10 percent of the reference group? The top 25 percent? Does poor or unsatisfactory mean that an individual has little of the trait in question or none? Is the standard for interpretation absolute (criterion referenced) or relative (norm-referenced)?

Other logical errors arise from the failure to discriminate the meanings of trait concepts. For example, a rater who believes two or more traits to be similar in meaning tends to assign a similar scale value to each trait when in fact the two traits should be rated independently. In this case, the rater regards the traits as being more or less synonymous and decides that the person being rated must possess the two traits to the same, or similar, degree. A rater may also interpret two or more traits as being quite independent of one another and may rate them quite differently for an individual when, in fact, the traits are closely related. In each case, the resulting ratings are inaccurate.

OTHER SOURCES OF ERROR

The major source of what is regarded as *unsystematic errors* are factors that affect a rater's willingness to rate honestly and conscientiously in accordance with the instructions for rating. Usually, it is assumed that each rater is trying to follow the instructions for the rating instrument to the best of his or her ability. In addition, it is assumed that any shortcomings in his or her ratings are the result of systematic errors either in the instrument itself or in human fallibility.

UNWILLINGNESS TO RATE   When rating forms are complex, raters sometimes are unwilling to spend the time required to make careful, accurate ratings. The man-to-man-scale was discarded primarily because of the unwillingness of military officers to spend the time it required. Graphic scales, on the other hand, became popular principally because they are both easy to use and easy to construct.

Perfunctoriness in carrying out the operations of rating may lower the effectiveness of many rating programs. The task of preparing periodic ratings of students, clients, or employees is decidedly onerous when the number of persons to be rated is large. In such situations, a counselor may make judgments that are superficial and hurried. In order to make accurate analytical judgments, raters must accept the importance of the ratings.

IDENTIFICATION WITH RATEES   In some situations, a rater is more concerned with providing a break for the people he or she is rating than in providing objective, accurate information. This may be true especially when rating information is requested by an outside agency such as the military, a large company or business, a university or some other school. Often the rater is closer to the person being rated than to the agency requesting the ratings. The morale in any organization depends on the principle that the leader cares for the members of the group. Whenever ratings are required, caring for becomes making certain that the members of one's group fare at least as well as, if not better than, members of competing groups. Hence, in these situations, counselors and teachers tend to rate their counselees and students higher than would be the case if the information were to be used for a different purpose.

VARIABLE RELIABILITY

It is difficult to make universally applicable statements regarding the reliability of ratings because of the many types of scales in use, the widespread variability both within and among raters, the large variety of traits assessed by ratings, and many other conditions that affect ratings. Moreover, the manner in which the reliability of ratings is estimated also influences the size of the reliability estimates obtained. Within-rater reliability estimates (stability estimates) are obtained from ratings made by the same raters of the same ratees over a period of time. Between-rater reliability estimates (congruence estimates) are derived from comparing the ratings of different judges for the same ratee or group of ratees.

A number of factors influences the stability of ratings made by the same raters for the same group of individuals. Functional fluctuations of the trait or traits involved and of the trait indicators lower stability reliability estimates. For example, a rater remembers and forgets information, and new information is added. Changes in the rater's conception of the meaning of the trait or traits, changes in the group with which the rater is being compared, and the memory of ratings given previously influence the consistency of ratings over time. Some of these influences give an increased appearance of stability; others lead to an impression of instability. In general, stability reliability coefficients in the range of .70 to .80 are reported frequently in the rating literature, although many others are considerably below this range. Nevertheless, it should be noted that test-retest stability estimates for ratings ranging between .70 and .80 compare favorably with stability estimates derived from many well-known measures of maximum performance.

Certain conditions also affect the size of interrater correlations. Differences in the amount of information available to the various raters lower the degree of agreement among raters. Differences in definitions of the traits being rated, in the indicators selected and used, and in the weighting of the indicators all lower interrater correlations. The common systematic errors discussed earlier contribute to unreliability because the biases are not identical for the various raters. Evidence of interrater agreement varying from correlations of 0 to above .90 has been reported in the literature. Correlation estimates between two raters of .50 to .60 are not uncommon. Several studies concerning the reliability of ratings were examined by Percival M. Symonds,[22] who concluded that the relationship between the ratings made by two independent raters for the conventional type of rating scale is approximately .55. Thorndike and Hagen stated that "there seems to be no good reason to change this conclusion after the lapse of years."[23] However, when the ratings of two or more raters are summed or averaged, correlations between either total rating scores or average rating scores for the persons being rated are usually higher than those obtained from correlating trait by trait ratings, because bias is cancelled somewhat by averaging or summing rating scores.

Pooling the ratings of several independent raters who know the persons being rated equally well can increase reliability substantially. Pooling ratings is similar in concept to lengthening a test. Unfortunately, it is often impossible to obtain additional equally qualified raters. For example, in most elementary schools, usually only one teacher knows a particular child well during a school year.

[22] Percival M. Symonds, *Diagnosing Personality and Conduct* (New York: Century Books, 1931).
[23] Thorndike and Hagen, *Measurement and Evaluation*, p. 460.

In many high schools, the large number of students prevents teachers from knowing all students equally well, even though several teachers could rate a student.

The same restriction applies to many other settings. Employing additional raters who may have limited acquaintance with the person being rated may weaken rather than strengthen the reliability of the ratings. Moreover, the use of more than three to five raters in combination usually adds little to the dependability of ratings.

Research in both industrial and military settings has demonstrated the effectiveness of training raters for increasing the reliability and consequent validity of ratings by reducing systematic errors. Certain rating methods tend to be more reliable than others, and the informed counselor selects or constructs the rating tool that is the most relevant to the intended purpose and the most reliable one available. In addition, the rater must be willing to rate carefully and accurately. Once these conditions are met, the ultimate measure of the value of any assessment tool is its validity.

VALIDITY OF RATINGS

Neither the validity of rating methods nor the resulting ratings of behavior traits should ever be taken for granted. Nevertheless, recent studies of the validity of ratings definitely support their use. Ratings made by teachers, instructors in specialized courses, job supervisors, military officers, school counselors, co-workers, classmates, club-members, and other groups of associates have been employed in validating a host of appraisal instruments and methods designed to assess academic achievement, performance in specialized training, or job success. Ratings are especially useful in providing criteria for validating personality tests, because objective criteria are difficult to obtain. Moreover, ratings of distinctly social traits, based on personal contact, may constitute the most logically defensible criterion. Although ratings are subject to error, they represent a valuable source of data when obtained under carefully controlled conditions.

These principles or guidelines for constructing effective rating forms are a means of controlling at least some of the errors that are related to rating effectiveness.

1. Decide what data are needed to provide for increased understanding of individual students. Sort out the various ways in which these data may be obtained.

TABLE 12.1
SELECTED BEHAVIOR RATING SCALES AND SCHEDULES

NAME OF INSTRUMENT	LEVEL	DATE(S)
ADJECTIVE CHECK LIST (ACL)	Grades 7–16 and Adults	1952–1972
CALIFORNIA Q-SET: A Q-SORT FOR PERSONALITY ASSESSMENT & PSYCHIATRIC RESEARCH (CQS)	Adults	1961
CHILD BEHAVIOR RATING SCALE (CBRS)	Kgtn–3	1960–1962
COLLEGE AND UNIVERSITY ENVIRONMENT SCALES, SECOND EDITION (CUES)	College	1962–1969
DEVEREAUX ADOLESCENT BEHAVIOR RATING SCALE (DAB)	Ages 13–18	1967
DEVEREAUX ELEMENTARY SCHOOL BEHAVIOR RATING SCALE (DESB)	Kgtn–6	1966–1967
FELS PARENT BEHAVIOR RATING SCALES (FPBRS)	Adult use	1937–1949
HOW WELL DO YOU KNOW YOURSELF? (HWDYKY)	High School, College, Office and Factory	1959–1961
INTERPERSONAL CHECKLIST (ICL)	Adults	1955–1956

AUTHOR(S)	PUBLISHER	DESCRIPTION
Harrison B. Gough and Alfred B. Heilbrun, Jr.	Consulting Psychologists Press, Inc.	300 items organized into 24 basic scales, including "counseling readiness."
Jack Block	Counseling Psychologists Press, Inc.	Observer ratings of 100 statements and sorted into 9 categories, from most to least salient, with a fixed number of statements being assigned to each category.
Russell N. Cassel	Western Psychological Services	Ratings by teachers or parents yielding 6 adjustment scores: self, home, social, school, physical and total. Reliability of sub-scales is questionable.
C. Robert Pace	Educational Testing Service	Students' conceptions of campus climate yielding 7 scores: practicality, community awareness, propriety, scholarship, campus morale, quality of teaching and faculty-student relationships.
George Spivack, Jules Spatts and Peter Haines	The Devereaux Foundation Press	Suitable for normal and emotionally disturbed youth, the DAB yields 12 factor scores, 3 cluster scores and 11 item scores for problem behaviors.
George Spivack and Marshall Swift	The Devereaux Foundation Press	Ratings of problem behaviors in school yield 11 factor scores and 3 item scores.
A. L. Baldwin, et al.	Fels Research Institute	Appraisal of parent-child relationships by trained home visitor yields 30 scores.
Thomas N. Jenkins, John H. Coleman and Harold T. Fagin	Executive Analysis Corporation	Scale yields reliable scores on 19 traits, but no evidence of practical validity is presented.
Timothy Leary, Rolfe LaForge and Robert Suczek	Psychological Consultation Service	Eight interpersonal traits are reflected by the 128 items. Intended as a self-rating checklist, ICL has practicable utility.

TABLE 12.1
SELECTED BEHAVIOR RATING SCALES AND SCHEDULES (cont.)

NAME OF INSTRUMENT	LEVEL	DATE(S)
KD PRONENESS SCALE (KDPS)	Grades 7–12	1950–1956
MOONEY PROBLEM CHECKLIST (MCPL)	Grades 7–16 and Adults	1950 revision
MULTIPLE AFFECT ADJECTIVE CHECKLIST (MAACL)	Grades 8–16 and Adults	1965–1966
PERSONALITY RATING SCALE (PRS)	Grades 4–12	1944–1962
PERSONALITY RECORD (REVISED) (PR)	Grades 7–12	1941–1958
RATING SCALE FOR PUPIL ADJUSTMENT	Grades 3–9	1950–1953
VINELAND SOCIAL MATURITY SCALE (VSMS)	Birth to Maturity	1935–1965

2. Include only observable traits or characteristics in the rating scale. (More reliable ratings can be obtained for overt characteristics than for inner qualities.)
3. Avoid general terms for the behaviors to be studied. The traits selected and the terms used in defining them should be explained clearly and specifically. If ratings are to be valid and reliable, the variation in judgments must be small.

AUTHOR(S)	PUBLISHER	DESCRIPTION
William Kvaraceus	Western Psychological Service	Ratings by teachers of delinquency proneness; 25 scales.
Ross L. Mooney and Leonard V. Gordon	Psychological Corporation of Harcourt, Brace Jovanovich, Inc.	Yields 7–11 scores, depending upon level used, for several problem areas, including physical development, social relations and concerns about self.
Marvin Zuckerman and Bernard Lubin	Educational and Industrial Testing Service	Yields 3 scores: anxiety, depression, hostility.
S. Mary Amatora	Educators'-Employees' Tests and Services	Contains 22 separate 10-point scales to be employed as ratings by classmates, teachers or self-ratings.
Committee of the National Association of Secondary-School Principals	National Association of Secondary-School Principals	Teacher ratings of 8 personal traits—no reliability or validity datum is provided.
Gwen Andrew, et al.	Science Research Associates	Teacher ratings of 11 areas of adjustment and one on physical handicaps useful in improving accuracy of referrals.
Edgar A. Doll	American Guidance Service, Inc.	Contains 117 items on performances of self-help, self-direction, locomotion, occupation, communication, and social relations; yields social age and social quotient scores.

4. Provide specific instructions on the rating scale form. Include such cautions as:
   a. Make judgments independently without consulting others.
   b. Rate all students for one trait before rating any student for the next trait on the scale.
   c. Rate only on the basis of actual experience with the student.
   d. Do not guess or infer anything that you cannot determine

through observation. Be reasonably sure of your judgment;
if you are uncertain, do not give a rating. (The scale should
provide a "no opportunity to observe" category.)

  e. Make your ratings as honest as possible. Try to avoid the
     influence of gossip, prestige, personal likes and dislikes.
     Complete integrity is essential.
5. Give a period of training and practice in the use of the scale.
6. Combine the ratings of several observers whenever possible.
   (From three to five is optimal.)
7. Apply in actual practice the data obtained through the use of
   rating scales. Practice should include providing individuals
   with experiences rich in preventive and developmental value,
   as well as experiences of therapeutic value.

   In view of the amount of technical knowledge and experimentation required to produce an effective rating instrument any individual, group, or agency should investigate the various published rating
scales that are available before attempting to develop a brand-new
product. Descriptions and reviews of published rating instruments
can be found in *Personality Tests and Reviews,* edited by O. K.
Buros.[24] A selected list of published instruments that may be of
interest to counselors is presented in Table 12.1.

INTERPRETING
AND REPORTING DATA

The use of rating methods for assessing the personal and social
characteristics of students in schools is not as widespread today as
it has been in the past. Colleges and universities still employ them
as part of the conventional procedures used to evaluate applicants
for admission. Moreover, rating methods continue to be a popular
tool for many personnel executives in business in evaluating prospective employees and providing recommendations about assignments, reclassification, and promotion. In schools, rating methods
still are used as an adjunct to other observational data, especially
in assessing personality. Recent federal legislation and administrative regulations having to do with the right to privacy and access
to records concerning oneself and one's children have rendered the
use of ratings and similar evaluative data a sensitive issue.

[24] Oscar K. Buros, *Personality Tests and Reviews* (Highland Park, N.J.: Gryphon Press, 1970).

The legal consequences of evaluating a person unfavorably may constrict the responses of raters, impairing or perhaps even destroying the validity of ratings. The somewhat diminished popularity of ratings may become even more limited. In the case of ratings of students by other students, students are less likely to be influenced by the legal consequences of recording subjective impressions of others; however, young people are generally reluctant to assign any rating to a fellow student that may be construed as negative. Certainly the vulnerability of such data must be recognized by the counselor.

As is true of any other appraisal technique, the use of rating data alone to make decisions regarding others should be avoided. Rating data, when available, must be integrated, as their quality merits, with what else is known about an individual. Ratings can supply information that cannot be obtained readily by other appraisal procedures. However, more reliance can be placed in the central tendency estimates of several informed raters than on one rater, however informed, or on a few informed raters, especially when the variance among rater response is small.

Students' ratings of counselors' or teachers' effectiveness serve as appropriate examples of the proper use of rating methods to derive information that is difficult to obtain by other means. Moreover, self-ratings, compared with the ratings of such significant others as peers, teachers, and counselors can provide useful data for counseling. Businesses, industry, and government agencies and organizations can find value in using employees' ratings of supervisory and management personnel as a method of assessing accountability for the actions of those in authority. At their best, rating procedures are a means of quantifying observations of an individual made by several informed persons who are accurate and reliable. At their worst, rating methods have no validity at all.

ISSUES

1. *The utility of rating scale data should be viewed with extreme caution because of their questionable reliability and validity.*
    Yes, because:
    1. The typical rating scale employed in schools is constructed by persons untrained in the development of rating instruments.
    2. Usually only one or two raters provide data for a given individual or group.

3. Within-group comparisons based on rating data are frequently inappropriate, because no common set of raters is employed to rate each individual in a given group.

No, because:
1. Carefully constructed rating instruments employed by informed raters *do* provide reliable and relevant data.
2. When reliable, relevant data are available, ratings contribute information that is not obtained readily by other means.

Discussion:
The basis of effective rating data lies in the nature of the instrument used to obtain the data. Specific and careful delineation of the scale units to be employed by raters in responding to the elements of the rating instrument is essential. Moreover, it is also essential that raters agree on the meanings of the various rating scale categories. In order to obtain such consensus, the steps must be defined clearly and concisely, leaving no room for variation in interpretation. Such precision requires expert training in scale development; most people who need the data that can be obtained by rating methods do not have the expertise necessary for developing a precise instrument. Consequently, data obtained from most rating tools should be viewed as suspect.

Not only must a rating instrument be constructed carefully and precisely, it must also be used with care and precision. Ratings obtained from only one rater are suspect; too many personal response biases may be involved. However, often only one rater is available and willing to supply accurate, relevant ratings. Even when more than one person is willing and able to rate an individual or group of individuals known equally well to each rater, the subjective biases of the various raters (of which the rater may be unaware) may interfere with the accuracy of the data. Moreover, it is difficult in most situations to find several able raters who know equally well each individual in the group.

In spite of these problems, carefully constructed rating tools are capable of providing reliable and relevant data that can help students better understand themselves. Research indicates that some rating methods are nearly as reliable as most measures of maximum performance and as reliable as most standardized measures of habitual performance.

2. *In spite of the concern expressed by many people regarding the utility of rating data, their continued use is essential because important kinds of data cannot be obtained readily by other means.*

Yes, because:

1. For assessing both the process and the outcome of teacher and counselor education and the effectiveness of in-service teaching and counseling, rating scales are the only accessible means of obtaining the needed data.
2. Rating data continue to be employed as criteria for validating measures that assess habitual behavior.
3. Rating methods permit significant others to rate an individual objectively and in a systematic and consistent manner.
4. Rating methods permit comparisons between self-ratings and ratings of significant others.

No, because:

Realistically, most rating instruments are constructed poorly; the raters usually are uninformed about the proper use of such instruments; and even if they are informed, they frequently have inadequate opportunity to observe the object or person rated. As a result, the data have little if any practical value and should be discarded.

Discussion:

Although use of rating scales has declined in popularity over the past few years, rating methods continue to be employed in assessing variables associated with observable performance including both cognitive and affective behaviors of counselors, teachers, supervisors, and others who have direct contact with individuals. Strong evidence suggests that rating instruments, when employed wisely and precisely, yield reliable and valid information for judging the effectiveness of such professionals.

No other means of assessing many kinds of observable behaviors are as readily accessible and precise. Moreover, in spite of their limitations, rating data continue to provide the primary criteria for validating other measures intended to assess habitual behaviors. No other system is as capable of reflecting performance-based criteria.

Whether used in research investigations or in other less controlled situations, rating tools do provide a systematic format for people to rate others. Moreover, when raters are trained so that they reach agreement as to what kinds of behaviors reflect what kinds of characteristics, the resulting data may be employed with great confidence.

Because the carefully derived ratings of significant others can be compared to the self-ratings of individuals and groups, the resulting data provide a good basis for discussion of individual or group strengths and limitations, leading to increased understanding of oneself as well as of others.

Realistically, however, most rating instruments are constructed so poorly and employed so imprecisely that the data they yield have little real value. The declining popularity of rating scales may reflect recognition of the myriad problems associated with the proper development and use of rating methods. The time and effort required to construct reliable and valid instruments and to train raters are significant deterrents. However, when no other measure is available for obtaining the data needed for comprehensive appraisal of an individual or group, it is worth the effort required to obtain reliable, valid data. Counselors are encouraged to use rating methods.

ANNOTATED REFERENCES

Guilford, J. P. *Psychometric Methods.* 2nd ed. New York: McGraw-Hill, 1954.
This work continues to be a primary source for in-depth study of the basic theory and methods of scale development. Chapter 11 deals with the specific treatment of rating scales. The method of pair-comparisons is discussed thoroughly in Chapter 7, and a detailed discussion of the rank-order method is included in Chapter 8.

Horrocks, John E. *Assessment of Behavior.* Columbus, Ohio: Charles E. Merrill, 1964.
Chapter 18, "Measurement of Personality: Ratings," presents a thorough discussion that is easy to understand. The author provides historical background for the rating method as an assessment tool, giving the reader a perspective for the use of ratings. This work is recommended highly, even though it is somewhat dated.

Kerlinger, Fred N. *Foundations of Behavioral Research.* 2nd ed. New York: Holt, Rinehart and Winston, 1973.
Excellent discussions of semantic differential and Q-methodology are presented in Chapter 33 and Chapter 34, respectively. Theory, procedures, methods of analysis, and research uses of these methods are discussed in detail. Some discussion of general rating methods is presented in Chapter 28, but the primary value of this resource lies in the thorough treatment given semantic differential and Q-method.

SELECTED REFERENCES

Gronlund, Norman E. *Measurement and Evaluation in Teaching.* 3rd ed. New York: Macmillan, 1976, pp. 435–451.

Lien, Arnold J. *Measurement and Evaluation of Learning.* 3rd ed. Dubuque, Iowa: Wm. C. Brown, 1976, pp. 254–265.

Payne, David A. *The Assessment of Learning: Cognitive and Affective.* Lexington, Mass.: D. C. Heath, 1974, pp. 374–412.

Stanley, Julian C., and Hopkins, Kenneth D. *Educational and Psychological Measurement and Evaluation.* Englewood Cliffs, N.J.: Prentice-Hall, 1972, pp. 282–301.

Chapter 13

Sociometric and Environmental Assessment

What are the functions and uses of sociometric measures?

What types of sociometric and environmental measures are available?

What value do sociometric and environmental data have?

GENERAL DESCRIPTION
OF SOCIOMETRIC MEASURES

Many of the problems brought by clients to counselors lie in the clients' relationships with other people. An individual's self-perception is influenced strongly both by the reactions of others (especially significant others) and by his or her perceptions of these interactions. That basic premise is found in most theories relevant to human relations and related fields of inquiry.

Marvin E. Shaw estimated that the average person in our society today belongs to at least five or six different social groups at any given time, and that the total number of existing small groups may be as high as 4–5 billion.[1] This network of interpersonal relationships is of particular concern to counselors, psychologists, and others interested in studying the effects of social influences on individual behavior.

An interpersonal network consists of all the attractions, repulsions, and indifferences that affect individuals in their daily interactions and that reflect the dynamics of the organization, formal or informal, of various groups. Moreover, interpersonal relationships influence the social status of individuals, as well as such other

---

[1] Marvin E. Shaw, *Group Dynamics: The Psychology of Small Group Behavior* (New York: McGraw-Hill, 1971), p. 4.

THIS CHAPTER WAS WRITTEN BY KATHRYN W. LINDEN.

variables as economic, class, race, ethnic group, and caste distinctions. Various aspects of interpersonal networks can be measured effectively by means of sociometric techniques that have been "designed specifically to provide a sensitive and objective picture of the interpersonal relations existing within a group and between pairs of individuals."[2]

Measures of social relationships have been used by many investigators, but an important first step in the development of sociometry occurred in 1934 with the publication of *Who Shall Survive?*[3] In this volume, Jacob L. Moreno reported a series of group studies that had been carried out in public school and institutional settings using a variety of data-gathering techniques, including sociometric measures. He also presented both theory and applications of methods and their results to problems of broad social significance. *Sociometric* measures are designed to yield data capable of being analyzed mathematically, similar to biometric and psychometric measures. Sociometric measures refer to all measuring devices that focus on social behavior, whereas *biometric* measures deal with biological behavior, and *psychometric* measures focus on individual behavior.

By using various types of observation reports and rating scales, counselors can learn about the opinions that people in authority hold about certain individuals. In addition, counselors can learn something about an individual's opinion of himself or herself by means of interviews and data derived from various inventories, self-ratings, creative writings, and other personal documents. However, counselors also need to know the extent to which individuals are accepted by their peers. Knowledge of an individual's reputation among those of his or her own age, position, and status in classes, teams, clubs, and other such groups increases understanding of the individual. Every group constitutes a learning laboratory, and the quantity and quality of an individual's relationships with his or her peers determine, to a considerable extent, the quantity and quality of what the individual learns. Some of this information can be obtained by means of the various techniques described in preceding chapters, but more accurate and comprehensive information can be derived from *peer-appraisal* methods, which disclose the patterns of belonging within the groups of which the individual is a member.

---

[2] Gardner Lindzey and Donn Byrne, "Measurement of Social Choice and Interpersonal Attractiveness," *The Handbook of Social Psychology: Research Methods*, vol. 2, 2nd ed., ed. Gardner Lindzey and Elliot Aronson (Reading, Mass.: Addison-Wesley, 1968), p. 452.

[3] Jacob L. Moreno, *Who Shall Survive?* (Washington, D.C.: Nervous and Mental Disease Publishing Company, 1934).

Interest in the use of sociometric techniques in public schools was stimulated by the three-year experimental study on intergroup education conducted by the American Council on Education.[4] In this study the value of sociometry for promoting the emotional development and social adjustment of individual students was demonstrated clearly. Data obtained from sociometric measures can be employed as a basis for either organizing or reorganizing groups to the psychological advantage of all members. Certain arbitrary or artificial barriers between students can be reduced gradually. Divisions between group members can be eliminated: between boys and girls; between fast and slow learners; and between students of different cultural origins, national backgrounds, and socioeconomic levels.

While sociometric techniques are employed to study the social structure of various kinds of groups and the influence of counseling and classroom and school practices and innovations on students, their real value lies in the use of the information obtained from these studies to promote optimal organizational patterns for effective counseling and for classroom groups in order to improve personal adjustment and individual achievement. Sociometric methods also have been employed in a wide variety of investigations designed to study the relationship between social adjustment and personal adjustment. The positive relationship between the two has been well-established by a large variety of studies employing different age groups. One implication of this relationship is the use of sociometric data as an index of change in adjustment. For example, if counseling is an effective agent of behavioral change, sociometric status should improve with successful counseling.

Numerous studies have been reported in which sociometric status has been correlated with such demographic variables as age, sex, family size, socioeconomic status, and educational level. Most of the studies that have related sociometric variables to intelligence and performance skills have found a positive association. Thus, there appears to be evidence for substantial relationships between aspects of behavior measured by sociometric techniques and a great many other variables. Gardner Lindzey and Donn Byrne suggest that, on the basis of the data now available, it would be possible to construct a relatively complex description that contrasts individuals at the high and low extremes of sociometric status.[5] However,

---

[4] Helen H. Jennings, *Sociometry in Group Relations*, 2nd ed. (Washington, D.C.: American Council on Education, 1959).

[5] Lindzey and Byrne, "Measurement of Social Choice," p. 495.

for the school counselor, the greatest value in using sociometric measures is in describing group structure and assessing behavioral change.

METHODS
OF SOCIOMETRIC APPRAISAL

A number of techniques have been devised to study complex inter-personal relationships in various social settings. Methods for col-lecting sociometric data include sociometric tests, various other nominating techniques, social distance scales, social acceptance scales, and sociogames. Methods for summarizing and analyzing sociometric data include the summary-data matrix, the sociogram, and the sociomatrix.

THE SOCIOMETRIC TEST

A sociometric test is an instrument designed to measure the struc-ture and organization of social groups. This technique asks individ-uals to reveal their personal feelings about others by choosing those group members they wish to be associated with in given situations. These situations can range from selecting luncheon partners to choosing seatmates, fellow committee members, laboratory part-ners, partners for a project, members for a counseling group, or partners for recreational activities.

For most purposes, it usually is desirable to restrict the number of choices to five. Results derived from sociometric research indi-cate that reliability of the data increases up to five choices, with no increase beyond that number.[6] Moreover, because it is sometimes difficult to satisfy everyone's first several choices, using five choices makes it easier to arrange sociometric groups. At the lower ele-mentary grades, however, it usually is necessary to limit the num-ber of choices to two or three, because very young children tend to find it difficult to discriminate beyond this number. Moreover, if the resulting data are to be represented in a sociogram, limiting the number of choices to no more than three facilitates interpretation of the data.

It is crucial to keep the students' preferences confidential. To the

---

[6] Norman E. Gronlund, *Sociometry in the Classroom* (New York: Harper and Row, 1959).

degree that students trust the person who administers the sociometric method and know that their choices will be used for the
stated purpose, their responses can be expected to be spontaneous,
truthful, and valid. It might be helpful to have the students assist
in formulating sociometric questions, especially those to be used
in forming counseling groups. This strategy helps insure that the
students understand the exact nature of the choices presented by
the questions.

The degree to which the students understand what they are to do
in the sociometric situations also affects the accuracy and truth-
fulness of their choices. The names of absent students should be
listed on the blackboard so that they will not be overlooked as
possible choices, although it is best to provide each student with a
list of all the students. Having a list of names alleviates the need
to look around while responding. Moreover, students should sit
where they will not be able to see one another's papers.

Sociometrc test questions can be formulated to elicit rejections
as well as acceptances. However, there is some disagreement among
sociometric experts concerning the desirability of using questions
that call for negative choices. Negative choices identify rejected
students who can be helped; and they help avoid interpersonal
friction in the arrangement of new groups. On the other hand,
negative questions make students more conscious of their feelings
of rejection, so both group morale and the emotional development
of students may be disturbed. In most school situations, it probably
is best to avoid the use of negative choices, unless they are essential
to the purpose for which the technique is being used. For some
counseling purposes, it may be desirable and helpful to obtain both
acceptance and rejection choices. However, rather than ask "Whom
would you like most—or least—to have in your counseling
group? " have the students identify the individuals they would select
first and last. The use of these terms is less threatening than is the
use of *most* and *least*. In any case, all student responses should be
optional rather than required. Again, the students' trust in the
administrator is crucial.

THE SOCIOGRAM

The sociogram is a figure or map that depicts the underlying structure of a social group and the position each member has within the
group at the moment when group members responded to a particular sociometric measure. A sociogram maps out the choices of

each individual in the group to a single question. In order to obtain a broad picture of the social interactions of a given group, it is necessary to administer several sociometric tests involving various situations, each resulting in a specific sociogram. Individuals do not always choose the same people for different activities, nor do they necessarily choose the same individuals for the same activity at different times.

SOCIOMETRIC TERMINOLOGY   Before we discuss how to construct and interpret a sample sociogram, we must identify common sociometric terms. See Figure 13.1 for these definitions and the symbolic representations of the terms.

SUMMARIZING SOCIOMETRIC DATA   In order to interpret and use sociometric data appropriately, students' choices must be organized in some fashion. A simple tally of the number of choices each student receives indicates the degree of social acceptance but does not provide information about who made the choices or whether two students chose each other (a mutual choice); nor does a simple tally illustrate the social structure of the group.

A complete record of the sociometric results can be obtained by tabulating the choices in a matrix table, such as the one illustrated in Table 13.1. In this matrix, the names of students are listed in the left-hand column and are numbered 1–27. The numbers corresponding to the students' names are listed across the top of the matrix table so that each student's choices can be recorded. For example, Alice chose Jack, Mark, and Joe as her three choices of students with whom she wanted to work on a class project. These choices were recorded in the table to the right of Alice's name by placing number 1 in column 17 to indicate Jack as her first choice, number 2 in column 21 to indicate Mark as her second choice, and number 3 in column 22 to indicate Joe as her third choice. The circled numbers in the table represent mutual choices. For example, Alice (number 1) and Jack (number 17) chose each other as their mutual first choice, and Carl (number 15) and Jim (number 18) chose each other as their mutual second choice. In the matrix table, mutual choices always appear in an equal number of cells from the diagonal line in each corresponding row and column. For this sociometric question, students were not asked to make rejection choices. However, when the sociometric question does call for rejection choices, the symbol x is used, and a circled x can be employed to represent mutual rejection choices.

FIGURE 13.1
SOCIOMETRIC TERMS

TERM	DEFINITION	REPRESENTATION
Star	A student who receives a large number of choices, or a number larger than chance	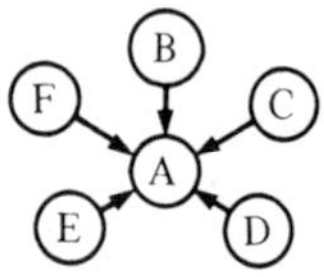
Mutual Choice	Students who choose each other	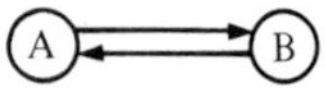
Isolate	A student who receives no positive choices (e.g., student C)	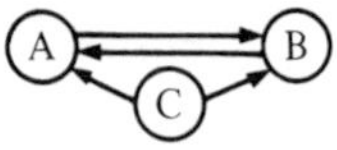
Rejectee	A student who is actively rejected by group members (if rejection data are gathered)	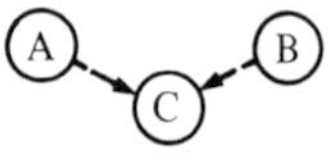
Neglectee	A student who receives very few positive choices (e.g., student C)	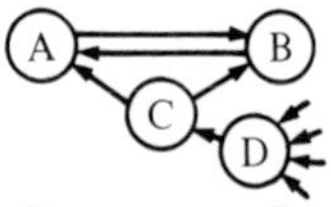
Sociometric Clique	A number of individuals who choose each other but make very few choices outside the group	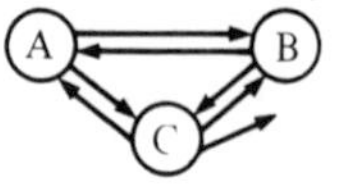
Sociometric Cleavage	A lack of sociometric choices between two or more subgroups, e.g., boys and girls	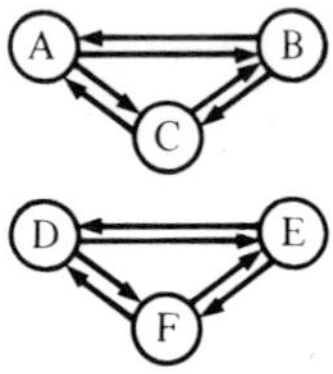

Source: Adapted from David A. Payne: *The Assessment of Learning* (Lexington, Mass.: D. C. Heath and Company, 1974), p. 392. By permission.

For the matrix illustrated in Table 13.1, girls and boys are grouped separately, dividing the main part of the table into four quarters. Thus, girls' choices of girls are found in the upper left-hand quarter of the table, and boys' choices of boys are in the lower right-hand quarter. The diagonal line through the empty cells, unused because students were asked not to choose themselves, cuts through these two quarters. Thus, the upper right-hand quarter and lower left-hand quarter contain only cross-sex choices. Organizing the matrix table in this manner makes the number of choices given to the same sex and to the opposite sex readily apparent and easy to summarize.

When the number of choices received were totaled, each choice was assigned a value of 1, regardless of the level of choice. Although some counselors and teachers prefer to weight the choices so that a first choice has more value than a second choice and so on, there is no empirical basis for assigning such weights. Various arbitrary weighting systems have been employed, but none has demonstrated superiority to the simple method of counting 1 for each choice made. However, the level of choice still should be recorded in the matrix table, because such information is useful for organizing groups based on sociometric data and for determining the social acceptance of individual students.

CONSTRUCTING A SOCIOGRAM   The data recorded in a matrix table are used to construct a sociogram depicting the social relationships among group members. Usually, males are distinguished from females by the use of figure symbols, such as triangles and circles that contain the students' names, initials, or matrix table numbers for ready identification. Moreover, different types of lines, or lines differentiated by number, are employed to designate which choice (first, second, third) the line represents.

In building the sociogram, start with the most frequently chosen students and place them at the center of a sociometric grouping, surrounded by the students who chose them. Represent mutual choices by closely adjacent figures, and place students who are rejected or chosen least often on the periphery of the sociogram. The lines depicting choices should be as short as possible, and the intercrossing of lines should be held to a minimum. The plotting of a sociogram such as that illustrated in Figure 13.2 (based on the data in Table 13.1) probably would have to be undertaken several times in order to reduce the crossing of lines and to present a clear, uncluttered result.

The figures must be arranged and rearranged until the interrelationships are depicted as clearly as possible. The conventional graphic sociogram in Figure 13.2 is relatively uncluttered because the sociometric question required only three positive choices rather than five, and called for no rejection choice. A sociometric question calling for additional positive choices as well as negative choices could result in such a maze of lines that the sociogram would be very difficult to interpret. Consequently, the conventional graphic

TABLE 13.1
MATRIX OF SOCIOMETRIC CHOICES FOR A SEVENTH-GRADE CLASS

STUDENTS CHOSEN

		1	2	3	4	5	6	7	8	9	10	11	12	13
ALICE	1													
BARBARA	2						①	②				3		
BERTHA	3													
BETTY	4						②	1					3	
BEVERLY	5								①					
JANE	6		①		②			3						
JENNY	7		②				1							
JOYCE	8					①								
JUDY	9		1				3	2						
KATHY	10								3					
MARIA	11	2												
SALLY	12		2				1							
SHARON	13													
BENNY	14	1												
CARL	15													
DICK	16													
JACK	17	①												
JIM	18													
JOE	19													
JOSÉ	20											①		
MARK	21	②				1								
MARTIN	22	2												
MIKE	23													
PAUL	24					1			③					
PETE	25													③
RICARDO	26													
ROB	27					1								
CHOICES RECEIVED		5	4	0	1	4	5	4	3	0	0	1	2	1

					STUDENTS CHOSEN									MUTUAL CHOICES (all levels)
14	15	16	17	18	19	20	21	22	23	24	25	26	27	
			①		3		②							2
														3
		2										1		0
														1
			2				3							2
														3
										3				2
									③				2	2
														0
										1			2	0
						①								1
					3									1
			2					1			③			1
														0
		③		②					1					3
	③				②				①					3
								3			2			3
	②				③				1					2
		②		③					1					3
					2		3							1
			3											2
			1						3					1
	2	①			3									3
							2							1
			1										②	3
	2				1				3					0
											②			1
0	3	5	6	2	7	1	4	2	6	3	3	1	3	

FIGURE 13.2
SOCIOGRAM OF A SEVENTH-GRADE CLASS

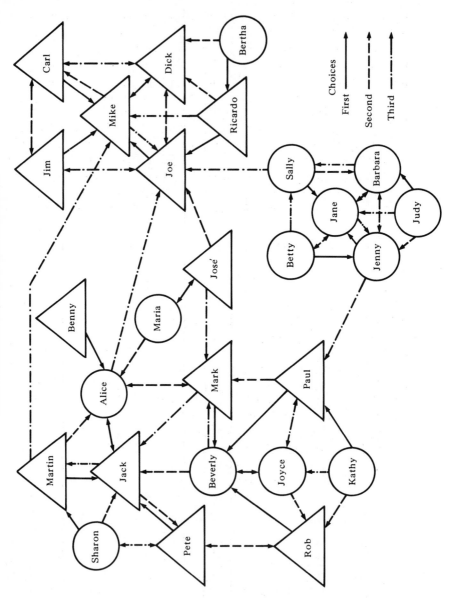

sociogram has two limitations: for groups of thirty or more, the diagram becomes too complex to be interpreted easily, unless only first choices are included; and considerable trial and error are required before an effective placement of the individuals can be achieved.[7] Because of these limitations, some experts advocate the use of a target diagram,[8] or target sociogram.[9] Moreover, for many situations, the ease of construction and interpretation of a target sociogram permits sociometric analysis that would not be possible with the conventional graphic sociogram.

The *target sociogram* consists of concentric circles that represent the number of times each person has been chosen. The "stars" are placed in the center ring of the target, the bull's eye, and the neglectees, isolates, or rejectees (if the sociometric question asks for negative choices) are placed in the outermost concentric ring. The remainder of the group is placed in the two (of perhaps three) concentric rings between the inner core and the outside ring. These intermediate rings may be defined according to the number of choices received greater than the overall mean but less than enough to indicate star status, or to the number of choices received less than the overall mean but greater than those received by the neglectees, isolates, and rejectees.

Such definitions would produce a target sociogram with four concentric rings. Usually, males are placed in half of the target diagram and females in the other half in order to identify easily any sex-based division in the group. Arrows and/or lines representing direction of choice can be drawn on a target diagram, although indicating the degree of selection can produce a target sociogram as complex and difficult to interpret as a conventional sociogram.

The target sociogram represented in Figure 13.3 portrays the data presented in Table 13.1 and depicted in Figure 13.2. In this target sociogram, students are identified by their corresponding matrix numbers rather than by name as in the conventional sociogram (Figure 13.2) in order to conserve space. However, it is appropriate to use either name or identification number in both forms. Although information regarding the number of choices each group member receives may be indicated more clearly by the target sociogram than by the conventional sociogram, the matrix table also presents the information very clearly. Both types of sociograms

[7] M. E. Bonney, "Sociometric Methods," in *Encyclopedia of Educational Research*, 3rd ed., ed. C. H. Harris (New York: Macmillan, 1960), pp. 1319–1324.

[8] Julian C. Stanley and Kenneth D. Hopkins, *Educational and Psychological Measurement and Evaluation*, 5th ed. (Englewood Cliffs, New Jersey: Prentice-Hall, 1972), p. 407.

[9] Gronlund, *Sociometry in the Classroom*; Payne, *Assessment of Learning*, p. 393.

FIGURE 13.3
TARGET SOCIOGRAM FOR A SEVENTH-GRADE CLASS

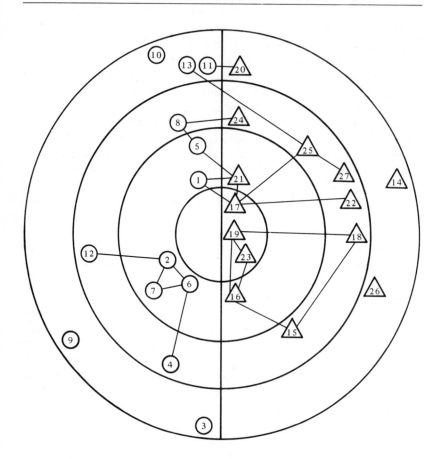

depict a group's social structure quite clearly with respect to the sociometric question that was presented. Consequently, either format is appropriate for use, and the selection of one form over the other is basically a matter of personal preference.

THE SOCIOMATRIX

An alternative to the conventional sociogram and target sociogram, called the *sociomatrix,* was proposed by Forsyth and Katz as a

FIGURE 13.4
SOCIOMATRIX OF CHOICES IN A SEVENTH-GRADE CLASS[a]

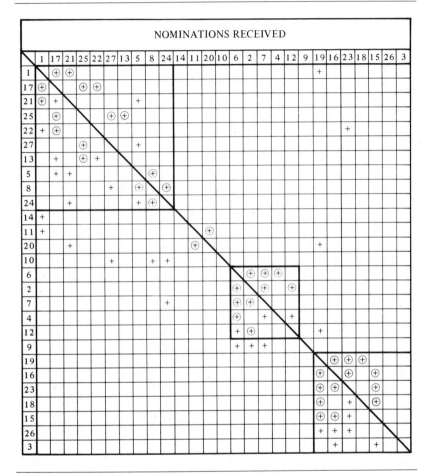

[a] Based on data in Table 13.1 and Figures 13.2, 13.3.

means of analyzing sociometric data.[10] In the development of a sociomatrix, the rows and columns of the original summary-data matrix (see, for example, Table 13.1) are rearranged to show the social structure of the group. The sociomatrix based on the summary-data matrix presented in Table 13.1 is illustrated in Figure 13.4.

[10] E. Forsyth and I. Katz, "A Matrix Approach to the Analysis of Sociometric Data: Preliminary Report," *Sociometry* 9 (1946): 340–347.

In constructing a sociomatrix, the rows and columns of any two students having a mutual choice are moved to the top left-hand corner of the matrix. The next step is to shift individuals having mutual choices with the original two to the upper left-hand corner. When all mutual choices have been positioned, a search is made for those who chose, or were chosen by, one of the mutual-choice students. This process of rearrangement is continued, adding anyone chosen by at least half the members of the subgroup. A subgroup is complete when no other individual can be found who satisfies the criterion. Additional subgroups are constructed in the same manner, beginning with two persons who make a positive mutual choice but are not included in the first subgroup. Consequently, a sociomatrix represents (1) a series of subgroups based on mutual choices, (2) the extent to which individuals within subgroups make choices outside their subgroup, and (3) individuals who do not belong to any subgroup.

The matrix approach to the analysis of sociometric data has attracted considerable interest during the past thirty years because of its several advantages. These methods are explicit and repeatable, and they are amenable to statistical analysis.

Some matrix methods deal with large amounts of data relatively efficiently, and they have certain graphic features. Moreover, the matrix method is the only approach that is relatively unrestricted as to the size of the group that may be examined; this advantage alone may be a sufficient reason for using the method. Nevertheless, a number of difficulties and limitations are evident: (1) the matrix operations are laborious unless a computer is employed; (2) identification of social patterns of a given definition leaves many other patterns unidentified, requiring either retreatment or neglect of the data; (3) the limitation to unweighted choices or rejections may be restrictive; and (4) the holistic view of group structure presented by sociogram approaches is not possible with matrix methods, except for the Forsyth and Katz method.

OTHER TECHNIQUES
FOR ANALYZING SOCIOMETRIC DATA

In addition to graphic, tabular, and matrix methods, there are a number of quantitative techniques for analyzing and summarizing sociometric data. Sociometric scores or indices can represent the individual, the group as a whole, and the individual in interaction with other members of the group. For example, in *Who Shall Sur-*

vive! Moreno summarized what appeared to be important characteristics of the choices and rejections within a group in terms of simple scores or ratios that provided the basis for a large number of individual and group indices developed later by other investigators. The simplest index is a numerical count of the number of times an individual was nominated for a specific function. This index can be treated as his or her peer rating of social status. Many variants of this simple index are presented in the literature.

Various statistical models and techniques have been employed to test the significance of observed findings and to provide derived scores or indices. For example, the use of matrix multiplication appears to have strong potential for the development of standardized techniques for identifying group structures and channels of communication. The application of factor analysis to sociometric data has been suggested many times, although only a few studies have been reported. According to B. Wright and Mary S. Evitts, who presented factor analytic data derived from a *Q*-sort of interpersonal relations in the form of sociograms: "Not only do the sociograms make accessible objective yet comprehensive maps of social structure, but the analysis of congruence provides an orderly basis for the inferences of fundamental sociometric laws."[11] Thus, there has been a steady transition during the past thirty years from using descriptive, nonstatistical analytic procedures to using quantification and statistical analysis of sociometric data in virtually all social-science investigation.

INTERPRETATION AND USE
OF SOCIOMETRIC DATA

Although the "increase in quantitative sophistication of social-science investigators is nowhere better reflected than in the use of sociometric measures and their derivatives,"[12] the counselor is concerned primarily with the use of descriptive, nonstatistical analysis of sociometric data. The two fundamental concerns in interpreting sociometric data are individual social status and group social structure. For each concern, the sociogram, target sociogram, and sociomatrix illustrate the nominations of group members but do not indicate why these choices were made. The counselor, teacher, or

---

[11] B. Wright and Mary S. Evitts, "Direct Factor Analysis in Sociometry," *Sociometry* 24 (1961): 97.

[12] Lindzey and Byrne, "Measurement of Social Choice," p. 460.

other personnel worker who employs sociometric techniques
should try to discover why choices were made as well as what
choices were made.

When interpreting sociometric data with respect to group structure, perhaps the basic question to ask is, "How cohesive is the
group as a whole?" It is quite clear that in the group represented in
Figures 13.2 and 13.3, there are three fairly well-organized
subgroups. The largest subgroup, consisting of boys and girls, appears to be organized somewhat loosely. The two other subgroups
represent a sex-based division: one subgroup is composed entirely
of girls and the other of boys. The number of individuals making
choices outside their subgroup suggests that the social structure of
this class may be in the process of transition. For example, Martin
(number 22) chose Mike (number 23) as his third choice for working
on a project; both Alice (number 1) and Sally (number 12) chose Joe
(number 19) as their third choice; and Jenny (number 7) chose Paul
(number 24) as her third choice. These choices suggest that the two
sex-based subgroups may be in the process of breaking up. The
teacher can use these crossover choices to form new groups that
will facilitate integration in the class.

A number of other questions can be asked in order to achieve an
in-depth understanding of the group's social structure. For example,
what is the leadership structure within the group? In Figures 13.2 and 13.3, Jack (number 17) is the leader of the large
subgroup, Jane (number 6) is the leader of the girls' group, and Mike
(number 23) is the leader of the boys' group. If there are two or more
well-organized groups, what are the attitudes of their leaders toward
each other? Are the reasons for division into subgroups similar to
those in adult society, such as segregation by ethnic group, nationality, or social class? Is any group isolated from, or rejected by, the
rest of the class? Is there any evidence of maladjustment or delinquency in these isolated groups? Is there any self-contained clique
of students; if so, what are its characteristics? Maria (number 11)
and José (number 20) appear to be an isolated clique, although each
makes one other choice. (These choices should be used to draw
these students into the social life of the class.) These two students
probably do not view themselves as an isolated clique. They may
simply reflect characteristics of their national group and/or social
class. To what extent have mutual choices been made? Here, nine
mutual choices were made in the large mixed-sex group, eight were
made in the boys' group, and five were made in the girls' group. If
the sociometric question permitted out-of-group choices, what percentage of the total choices were made within the group?

Still another question concerns the number of isolates, neglectees, and fringers in the social structure of the group. The socio-metric data illustrated in Figures 13.2 and 13.3 show that seven students (including Maria and José) appear to be on the periphery of the three subgroups: Kathy (number 10), Maria (number 11), and Benny (number 14) on the periphery of the integrated group; José (number 20), Ricardo (number 26), and Bertha (number 3) outside the boys' group; and Judy (number 9) on the edge of the girls' group. Each of these students made choices within a subgroup but was not chosen by anyone clearly established as a member of that subgroup. Consequently, for the sociometric question presented, the data suggest that seven of the twenty-seven students in the class, approximately 26 percent, are outsiders looking in. This finding might be viewed to be undesirable for a happy, comfortable, and positive social climate. However, this interpretation should be viewed with caution, because these seven students might have been chosen by established subgroup members if the sociometric question had permitted more than three choices. If the conclusion that slightly more than one-fourth of this class is neglected and/or rejected by the others is verified by evidence derived from other assessment techniques, then the social climate of the class is undesirable, and steps should be taken to draw the outsiders into the group as well as to integrate subgroups into a cohesive whole.

After directing attention to the social structure of the group as a whole, the counselor or teacher should ask himself or herself a number of questions regarding the status characteristics of individuals within the group. For example, is the Maria-José clique really based on their minority association? Is Benny a fringer for ethnic reasons? Is Bertha hovering on the fringe of the boys' group because she is an early adolescent? Is Mike the leader of the boys' subgroup because he has strong athletic abilities? Is Jane the star of the girls' group because her father is influential in the community? Is Jack the leader of the large, integrated group because he is handsome, bright, and kind to others? Questions can be, and should be, asked about every individual in the group. In general, these questions can serve as a guide:

1. What do the students most often chosen (stars and leaders) have in common (high social status, personality characteristics, religious denomination, length of residence in the community, participation in afterschool activities)?
2. What do the neglectees, fringers, and rejectees have in common (nationality; low socioeconomic status; newness to community and/or classroom; or residence in trailer camp, housing project, or orphanage)?

3. Are the students on the periphery of, or isolated from, the group also peripheral to, or isolated from, home and neighborhood groups, or are their positions in one social group counterbalanced, at least in part, by their positions in another group? (This phenomenon frequently occurs when ethnic group or social class is the basis for isolation or fringe status.)

4. Is a given student realistic about his or her social position in the group? ("Some isolates are quite realistic about their social status in the class, indicating their desire to associate with one or two students with whom there is some basis for establishing friendships. Other isolates are quite unrealistic, listing the most popular members of the group as friends."[13])

It is extremely important to remember that sociometric measures provide information concerning only what nominations were made; they do not and cannot provide information regarding why choices were made. Moreover, because the why of social choice is viewed to be an important, pervasive influence on self-concept, it is an important question to answer if the counselor is concerned about the self-actualization of individuals.

The sociometric interview is one tool that can be employed to gain insight into the dynamics underlying social choice. In the interview, individuals are asked, in confidence, to explain their choices. Care must be taken to avoid placing an individual on the defensive. It is better to ask, "How did you decide to choose (or to reject) Mike?" than to ask, "Why did you choose (or reject) Mike?"

An alternative to the sociometric interview would be to obtain written responses from all individuals in the group regarding the reasons for their nominations. However, written statements of this kind seldom are very effective unless the counselor or teacher has excellent rapport with and is trusted by the group. Although interviews and written statements can provide some insights into the reasons why nominations were made, getting in-depth answers requires the use of the other investigative techniques discussed in this book.

When the group structure and social status of individuals in the group have been identified, the original purpose for asking the sociometric question must be fulfilled. Thus, for the group illustrated in Table 13.1 and Figures 13.2, 13.3, and 13.4, project committees

---

[13] Georgia Sachs Adams, *Measurement and Evaluation in Education, Psychology, and Guidance* (New York: Holt, Rinehart and Winston, 1964), pp. 285–286.

must be formed that are patterned as closely as possible to the students' nominations. The most effective way to rearrange groups is by starting with the outsiders and working toward the students receiving the largest number of choices. By beginning with the students on the periphery of or isolated from the group, it is possible to satisfy at least two of their highest choices, placing them in contact with the students with whom they have the best chance for developing social relationships.

RELATED SOCIOMETRIC METHODS

A number of sociometric methods have been devised that do not require the formation of new groups. However, all sociometric data, regardless of how it was obtained, should be used to achieve healthy interpersonal relationships. Variants of the sociometric test question include other nominating techniques, sociometric scales, ratings of interpersonal attractiveness, group preference records, sociometric self-ratings, and various combinations of related procedures. Data derived from most of these methods may be summarized, represented, and analyzed by the various descriptive, quantitative, and statistical techniques used for any sociometric question.

THE GUESS-WHO TECHNIQUE

One of the simplest methods devised for obtaining peer judgments is the guess-who technique, developed for use with young children. Presented originally as a guessing game, this technique uses a casting-characters format. When it is employed with older students or adults, the guess-who or casting-characters format is dropped, and the directions merely require respondents to supply the names of those who best match each behavior description.

A set of guess-who items lists many kinds of acceptable and unacceptable behaviors, or descriptions of such behaviors, including friendly versus unfriendly, dominating versus submissive, quiet versus noisy, neat versus sloppy characteristics. Although this technique is particularly valuable for appraising personality characteristics, character traits, and social skills, it can be employed to evaluate many kinds of behaviors. Paul Torrence suggested using this approach to assess various aspects of creative thinking:

1. Who in your class comes up with the most ideas? (fluency)
2. Who has the most original or unusual ideas? (originality)
3. If a situation changed, or if a solution to a problem wouldn't work, who in your class would be the first to find a new way of meeting the problem? (flexibility)
4. Who in your class does the most inventing and developing of new ideas, gadgets, and such? (inventiveness)
5. Who in your class is best at thinking of all the details involved in working out a new idea and at thinking of all the consequences? (elaboration)[14]

The major advantage of the guess-who technique is its simplicity. It is relatively painless to administer and to score, and it can be used with persons of all age levels. Scoring is accomplished by simply counting the number of nominations received for each description. When both positive and negative descriptions are used, the number of negative nominations is subtracted from the number of positive nominations received for each characteristic. Compared to the conventional sociometric test that deals with only one behavioral characteristic at a time and is limited to a few choices, the guess-who approach can yield data on a variety of characteristics at the same time for all students in the group, thus providing a more representative and complete picture of the personal and social characteristics of the group. The major limitation of this method is that it does not provide very much information about patterns of interaction or communication in the group. The method is limited primarily to data on individual status and reputation.

SOCIAL DISTANCE/ACCEPTANCE
SCALES

The concepts of social distance and psychological distance were defined by Jacob Moreno in his conceptualization of sociometry. *Social distance* is the "undifferentiated attitude of an individual (or group) toward a class of people," and *psychological distance* refers to the "degree of distance or nearness an individual (or group) has toward another individual (or group) on the basis of the accumulation effect of the individual affinities and disaffinities between them."[15] Evidence for both concepts is secured by sociometric test-

---

[14] E. Paul Torrence, *Guiding Creative Talent* (Englewood Cliffs, N.J.: Prentice-Hall, 1962).
[15] Moreno, *Who Shall Survive?*, p. 10.

ing. The Bogardus *Social Distance Scale* was one of the first scoring scales developed in social psychology, and a number of modified sociometric instruments have been adapted from the Bogardus design.[16] Labeled frequently either social-distance or social-acceptance scales, such instruments as the Bogardus scale have been designed to indicate the degree to which an individual accepts, and is accepted by, every other member of a group. A good example of this class of sociometric instruments is the *Classroom Social Distance Scale* employed in a study by Ruth Cunningham and her associates of the behavior of elementary and junior high school students.[17] Described as a "short-cut in finding the place of the individual in a group," this scale employs five intervals:

1. would like to have him (her) as one of my best friends
2. would like to have him (her) in my group but not as a close friend
3. would like to be with him (her) once in a while but not too often or for a long time
4. do not mind him (her) being in our room, but do not want to have anything to do with him (her)
5. wish he (she) were not in our room

Students rate every member of the class, including themselves if they wish. The person who administers these scales should give a copy of the class or group roster to each student so that no one is left out inadvertently.

A similar sociometric scale is the *Ohio Social Acceptance Scale*, in which each student rates other students under these categories: (1) very best friends; (2) other friends; (3) not friends, but okay; (4) don't know them; (5) don't care for them; (6) dislike them.[18] The last two categories can be pooled under the category of "others in the group," so that students do not have to reject others overtly. From the prevalence of 1, 2, and 3 ratings, the degree of acceptance by one student of another can be ascertained. The prevalence of 4 ratings suggests an isolate, while ratings of 5 and 6 (or 5, if these categories are pooled) identify the rejected and/or neglected.

A variety of other scales have been developed to measure such

[16] Emory S. Borgardus, "Measuring Social Distance," *Journal of Applied Psychology* 9 (1925): 299–308.

[17] Ruth Cunningham and associates, *Understanding Group Behavior of Boys and Girls* (New York: Bureau of Publications, Teachers College, Columbia University, 1951).

[18] L. L. Young, "Sociometric and Related Techniques for Appraising Social Status in an Elementary School," *Sociometry* 10 (1947): 168–177.

concepts as social relations, group participation, and interpersonal attractiveness. In an attempt to incorporate traditional psychometric considerations into the framework of sociometric measurement, E. F. Gardner and G. G. Thompson developed the *Syracuse Scales of Social Relations*, an instrument designed to elicit an individual's ratings of members of the group in terms of their capacity for satisfying these needs: affiliation; play and mirth; succorance; and achievement and recognition.[19] These scales involve a series of forced-choice comparisons that result in a rating by each and for each group member on each variable. Even though this method is somewhat complex and cumbersome, the Syracuse scales possess "clear measurement superiorities over most or all similar instruments."[20] Because the Syracuse scales use a frame of reference that extends beyond the classroom group, it is possible to compare the social-relations status of a student to status in a number of subgroups to which he or she belongs, such as teams and clubs. Norms are provided in which the class average is the unit. Consequently, the counselor or teacher can compare the average social-relations status of a class with the average of a large number of classes included in the normative group. The authors report evidence of the positive relationship between this information and group morale.

An approximation of the Thurstone Method of Equal Intervals (see Chapter 12) was employed by H. B. Pepinsky, L. Siegel, and E. L. Vanatta in an attempt to develop a sociometric measure that would reflect "effectiveness of participation in group activity."[21] Their twenty-four item *Group Participation Scale*, representing each of eight scale positions, has been employed primarily in research on counseling.

SOCIOMETRIC SELF-RATING

Most, if not all, sociometric methods can be adapted easily to the use of *sociometric self-rating*, or predicting one's choice by others. For example, changing the emphasis from, "Whom do you choose. . . ?" to, "Who do you think will choose you for. . . ?" produces a self-rating format. This method was mentioned first by Moreno in connection with the training of individuals' perceptions of others

---

[19] E. F. Gardner and G. G. Thompson, *Syracuse Scales of Social Relations* (New York: Harcourt, Brace and World, 1958).

[20] Lindzey and Byrne, "Measurement of Social Choice," p. 457.

[21] Harold B. Pepinsky, L. Siegel, and E. L. Vanatta, "The Criterion in Counseling: A Group Participation Scale," *Journal of Abnormal Psychology* 47 (1952): 415–419.

by means of repeated sociometric trials. This technique has been employed with widely divergent groups, including children at a summer camp, high school groups, French army officers, U.S. Air Force enlisted personnel, and female college students.

MEASURES
OF ENVIRONMENTAL STATUS

SOCIOECONOMIC STATUS

The concept of socioeconomic status (SES) is utilized widely in education, psychology, and sociology. SES is related closely to many characteristics of students, including motivation to achieve, reason for dropping out of school, level of academic achievement, level of intelligence, and occupational choice. Because the concept of SES is so pervasive, a counselor should know how to measure it, even though he or she does not expect to make frequent formal SES assessments. Several different SES measures have been devised, all of which employ some combination of the following variables: educational level, occupational level, type of residence, amount of income, source of income, and residential area.

The most widely used measure is the *Index of Status Characteristics* (ISC).[22] The ISC contains seven levels for each of four factors: occupation, source of income, housing, and dwelling area.[23] A score is obtained by using the category ratings from the four factors in the following equation:

$$\text{ISC} = (4 \times \text{occupation}) + (3 \times \text{source of income}) + (3 \times \text{house type}) + (2 \times \text{dwelling area})$$

A social class rating is assigned to the score according to the following system:[24]

ISC SCORE	SOCIAL CLASS RATING
12–22	upper class
23–37	upper-middle class
38–51	lower-middle class
52–66	upper-lower class
67–84	lower-lower class

[22] W. L. Warner, M. Meeker, and K. Eells, *Social Class in America* (Chicago: Science Research Associates, 1949).

[23] For a detailed explanation of each category, see C. M. Bonjean, R. J. Hill, and S. D. McLemore, *Sociological Measurement: An Inventory of Scales and Indices* (San Francisco: Chandler, 1967), pp. 442–448.

[24] Warner, Meeker, and Eells, *Social Class in America,* 1949.

Because of the difficulty and expense involved in obtaining information about residential area, other SES scales were developed that do not require such information. Perhaps the most widely used of these scales is the *Two-Factor Index of Social Position*, which yields an index based only on occupational and educational scales, each of which is divided into seven levels.[25] A total Index of Social Position (ISP) is obtained by employing the following equation:

ISP = (7 × occupational rating) + (4 × educational rating)

ISP scores are classified as one of five social classes, ranging from high to low social position:

ISP SCORE	SOCIAL CLASS
11–17	I
18–27	II
28–43	III
44–60	IV
61–77	V

Other scales provide a differentiated picture of home environment, including not only the characteristics of the parents but also such data as the size and nature of the home; the availability of such material possessions as telephones and television sets; the presence of books, magazines, and newspapers; and the degree of aesthetic and sociocivic involvement of the family. Data for these scales may be gathered by means of questionnaires, interviews, home visits, or some combination of these procedures.

SOCIAL CLIMATE

The social climate of an institution—whether family, school, business organization, correctional institution, hospital, or therapeutic program—provides a social environment that tends to support some kinds of behavior and to weaken others. Thus, social climates of various institutions have been described in such terms as supportive, controlling, structured, flexible, intellectual, artistic, and practical.[26]

The most direct measure of the social climate of an environment

[25] August B. Hollingshead and F. C. Redlich, *Two Factor Index of Social Position* (New Haven, Conn.: published by the authors, 1957).

[26] Anne Anastasi, *Psychological Testing,* 4th ed. (New York: Macmillan, 1976), p. 619.

is the consensus of individual perceptions of that environment. Several scales have been designed to measure this consensus, including the *College Characteristics Index* (CCI).[27] Other versions of this instrument have been developed for use in high schools and evening colleges, and a generalized form of the CCI was designed to be applicable to any organization, regardless of setting.[28] A similar instrument, called the *Stern Activities Index* (SAI), is applicable to individuals. Both types of measures are based on Murray's theoretical model of individual needs and environmental press, and 10 items are employed to measure each of thirty needs that are similar to those sampled by the EPPS (see Chapter 10). Results of factor analyses have identified certain broad descriptive variables representative of both first-order and second-order factors for both the CCI and the SAI. When these two instruments are employed together, they can provide "a basic taxonomy for characterizing both persons and situations in comparable terms."[29]

The *College and University Environment Scales* (CUES) originated in the same research project as the CCI and was designed for the same purpose. However, rather than reflect Murray's need-press categories, the CUES employs dimensions derived from factor analysis of data obtained from a representative sample of fifty colleges and universities.[30] CUES yields scores for five factors: practicality, community, awareness, propriety, and scholarship. More recently, a series of nine *Social Climate Scales* was developed for use in such environmental settings as hospital-based and community-based treatment programs, correctional facilities, military companies, community groups, university student residences, high school classrooms, families, and work settings.[31] Each scale contains 80–100 true-false items that are organized into seven to ten subscale scores, based on the ability to discriminate among the various environmental settings. The scales have demonstrated the ability to discriminate among environmental units, a high degree of temporal stability, and only a minimal relationship to the personality characteristics of respondents. Moreover, because these *Social Climate Scales* were designed for relatively small environmental units

[27] G. G. Stern, *People in Context: Measuring Person-Environment Congruence in Education and Industry* (New York: John Wiley and Sons, 1970).

[28] G. G. Stern, *Stern Environmental Indexes* (Minneapolis: National Computer Systems, 1972).

[29] Anastasi, *Psychological Testing*, p. 619.

[30] G. G. Stern, *College and University Environment Scales*, 2nd ed. (Princeton, N.J.: Educational Testing Service, 1974).

[31] R. H. Moos, *The Social Climate Scales: An Overview* (Palo Alto, Calif.: Consulting Psychologists Press, 1974); "Assessment and Impact of Social Climate," in *Advances in Psychological Assessment*, vol. 3, ed. Paul McReynolds (San Francisco: Jossey-Bass, 1975), ch. 1; *Evaluating Correctional Environments: With Implications for Community Settings* (New York: John Wiley and Sons, 1975).

within complex, heterogeneous institutions (for example, a class-room rather than an entire school, a university residence rather than an entire university, or a treatment program rather than an entire hospital), they have to be capable of yielding data that are more readily interpretable and less ambiguous than data obtained from a composite assessment of an entire organization.[32]

Although these various measures of social status and environmental climate have been employed primarily for research purposes, they also have utility for educational and vocational counseling. They can provide reliable supplemental information of value in curriculum and vocational planning, particularly at the high school and post-high school levels.

SOCIAL AND AFFECTIVE NEEDS

An interesting use of socometric data combined with teacher ratings was proposed by James R. Barclay, who recommended gathering sociometric data on a variable such as cooperativeness and having teachers rate their students on the variable.[33]

This notion of multiple-input measurement of social and affective needs is reflected in three recent assessment instruments: the *Barclay Early Childhood Assessment* (BECA) for children 3–6 years of age; the *Barclay Classroom Climate Inventory* (BCCI) for students in grades 3–6; and the *Barclay Learning Needs Inventory* (BLNI) for students in junior high school through junior college.[34] The BECA, designed to measure skills related to learning readiness in nine critical developmental areas, is based on direct observation of children by teachers, aides, and parents. The BCCI integrates self-report, peer nominations, and teacher judgments, yielding thirty-six scale scores and six factor scores for each student. The BLNI provides both self- and group comparisons and is criterion-referenced to the local group. Results obtained for each of these instruments are reported in the form of computer-written reports on each individual, in language that can be understood easily by parents and students as well as by counselors and teachers.

---

[32] Anastasi, *Psychological Testing*, p. 620.
[33] James R. Barclay, *Controversial Issues in Testing* (Boston: Houghton Mifflin, 1968).
[34] James R. Barclay, *Barclay Early Childhood Assessment; Barclay Classroom Climate Inventory; Barclay Learning Needs Inventory* (Lexington, Ky.: Educational Skills Development, 1976).

MARITAL AND FAMILY
RELATIONSHIPS

Among the most important of social relationships are those that pertain to marriage and the family. Marriage and family counseling practices are changing rapidly and profoundly, thanks to both conceptual developments and new methods of data collection. Relationships of, communications between, and roles enacted by marriage partners and family members have become the subject of study. The family is seen in family counseling practice and in theory building as a system of interacting personalities.

Good measures of marital adjustment have been difficult to develop and to standardize, for marriage is a complex phenomenon. Here, briefly, are three measures:

CARING RELATIONSHIP INVENTORY The CRI was published first in 1966 (research edition) by the Educational and Industrial Testing Service (author: Everett L. Shostram). Forms for males and for females are available; administration time is about 40 minutes.

The CRI yields seven scores: nurturing love, peer love, romantic love, altruistic love, self-love, being love, and deficiency love. The manual defines these terms. Albert Ellis, who reviewed the CRI for the *Seventh Mental Measurement Yearbook*, said, "The scales of this test have split half reliabilities ranging from .66 to .87. A validity group of successfully married couples showed significant mean differences on almost all the scales between a group of troubled couples and a group of divorced couples."[35] Ellis said that the clinical usefulness of the CRI in assessing and treating married couples had yet to be established.

DYADIC ADJUSTMENT SCALE The DAS is a 32 item scale, devised by Graham B. Spanier and reported in 1976, designed to measure the quality of marriage and other similar dyads. The DAS can be used with either married or unmarried cohabiting couples. It contains four subscores: dyadic consensus, dyadic satisfaction, dyadic cohesion, affectional expression, and a total score.

Graham B. Spanier[36] has described the construction and development of the DAS. He reported reliability coefficients (Cronbach's

---

[35] Albert Ellis, "Caring Relationship Inventory," in Oscar Buros, *The Seventh Mental Measurements Yearbook*, vol. 2 (Highland Park, N.J.: Gryphon Press, 1972), p. 950.

[36] Graham B. Spanier, "Measuring Dyadic Adjustment: New Scales for Assessing the Quality of Marriage and Similar Dyads," *Journal of Marriage and the Family* 38 (February 1976): 15–28.

coefficient *alpha*) ranging from .73 to .96 between and among component total scales. Construct validity estimates of .86 and .88 (married and divorced respondents) were obtained between the Locke-Wallace marital adjustment scale and the DAS.

LOCKE-WALLACE MARITAL ADJUSTMENT QUESTIONNAIRE The MAQ was devised originally by H. J. Locke in 1951 to discriminate between successful and unsuccessful marriages. The questionnaire contains 23 items. Twelve of the items have multiple-choice responses, and nine question the extent of agreement or disagreement on marital issues. The other two consist of a checklist and a seven-point scale to indicate the degree of happiness with one's marriage. Douglas Kimmel and Ferdinand Van Der Veen factor analyzed the MAQ and reported that sexual congeniality and compatibility were the two components that compose the total score.[37] Factor scores were found to be stable after a two-year test-retest interval.

USES OF SOCIOMETRIC
AND ENVIRONMENTAL DATA

It is easy to view sociometric and environmental assessments as a kind of rating scale (see Chapter 12), because members of a given group (even $N = 2$) are asked to nominate, or rate, members of the group or features of the environment in terms of their attractiveness or desirability. Sociometric and related measures are more limited than are rating scales in the variables that can be assessed and in the settings wherein they can be employed. A main advantage of rating methods is their versatility for use in a wide variety of situations; however, they require the difficult and time-consuming task of producing common frames of reference for raters and homogeneous criteria against which to assign ratings.

The reliability and validity of most social and environmental measures differ somewhat from the conventional applications of these concepts. Most of these measurements involve relatively simple questions about friendship, living arrangements, or physical environment. Four types of reliability have been investigated: interjudge consistency, consistency over time, consistency in equivalent forms of measurement, and internal consistency. Several generalizations have been drawn by Lindzey and Byrne.[38] Among the

---

[37] Douglas Kimmel and Ferdinand Van Der Veen, "Factors of Marital Adjustment in Locke's Marital Adjustment Test," *Journal of Marriage and the Family* 36 (February 1974): 57–63.

[38] Lindzey and Byrne, "Measurement of Social Choice," pp. 475–479.

more important ones were: (1) that most investigators report a relatively high degree of consistency over time, especially if the time period is relatively short; (2) test-retest reliability tends to increase as the age of subjects increases from preschool through adulthood; and (3) stability of choices appears to increase with the passage of time.

The validity of sociometric and environmental assessments depends primarily on the reality value of the criterion, that is, the situation for which the choices are made and the extent to which persons are acquainted with each other and aware of the environment. For any criterion to have reality value, the basis for making choices must be real, not hypothetical. In order for the results to indicate valid patterns of social relations, individuals must have confidence that their choices will be used for the purpose expressed, and the purpose must be one that is important to them.

Sociometry and other environmental assessments contribute to individual growth and adjustment when used to improve group and organizational climates. Organizing or reorganizing a group on the basis of such data improves personal communication and understanding.

ISSUES

1. *Sociometric techniques are valuable tools for counselors, because these measures provide accurate and comprehensive information about individual social needs and interpersonal relationships within social groups.*

Yes, because:
1. Sociometric techniques are designed for the purpose of disclosing the patterns of acceptance or belonging within peer groups in order to improve interpersonal relationships and social climates.
2. The quantity and quality of the relationships of individuals with their peers determine, to a large degree, the quantity and quality of their personal intellectual, social, and emotional development.

No, because:
1. The situations for which peer nominations of social choices are to be made usually are limited to a specific purpose at a given time; hence, data derived from one social situation

may not represent an individual's general pattern of social behavior.
2. More information than that generated by sociometric techniques is needed in order to provide a complete picture of an individual's social needs and interpersonal relationships.

Discussion:
Although considerable information concerning social relationships may be obtained by means of direct observation and other assessment methods, only sociometric techniques reveal with whom individuals would like to associate and how their wishes compare with the attitudes of others toward them. How people feel toward each other strongly influences their personal development. Every group serves as a learning laboratory, and group members learn best when they are comfortable in the group, when they feel that they belong and are accepted, wanted, and appreciated. Learning is frustrated when individuals are in groups in which they feel more tolerated than enjoyed, not well-accepted, unwanted, or rejected. Therefore, in order to help individuals to find a comfortable place in social groups, counselors and teachers need to identify the patterns of acceptance and belonging within peer groups. Sociometric techniques can sensitize counselors and teachers to the interpersonal and intergroup difficulties among students.

Data obtained from every type of assessment technique must be interpreted carefully and cautiously, and sociometry is no exception to this principle. Moreover, sociometric measures must also be developed and administered carefully for the results to be of maximum value. Sociometric data reveal what social choices were made, but not why. Further study is necessary in order to understand the dynamics underlying social choice. Nevertheless, sociometric techniques do aid the counselor and teacher in appraising the social structure of peer groups and in identifying individuals who need help in achieving satisfying relationships.

2. *Conventional interpretations of reliability and validity concepts are inappropriate for sociometric techniques.*
  Yes, because:
  1. Traditional interpretations of the reliability of measurement seem to be contradictory to the primary purpose of sociometry, which seeks to measure peer acceptance and social status. Stability of peer nominations is usually an undesirable outcome of sociometry.

2. The assessment of sociometric attraction is not analogous to other types of appraisal designed to measure some general disposition or underlying characteristics.

No, because:
1. There is considerable evidence to support the stability and reliability of sociometric choices, especially when the time between successive measurements is relatively short; consequently, sociometric measures are technically as dependable as most other assessment techniques.
2. Even though sociometric measures are inherently valid when limited to interpersonal choices, rankings, or ratings, evidence of their relationship to relevant independent variables should be obtained.

Discussion:
Studies concerned with the reliability of sociometric measures have concentrated primarily on the question of temporal consistency. The meaning of test-retest stability coefficients as estimates of the reliability of sociometric measures is clouded by the fact that changes in interpersonal attraction should occur with concomitant changes in interpersonal relationships. Thus, sociometry requires a different conception of test-retest reliability than does psychometry. Given relevant changes in the situation, in the individual being rated, or in the person making the rating, changes in the sociometric measure are not only expected but required as evidence of its adequacy. However, if no change occurs or if only a short period of time is involved, an appropriately reliable sociometric measure should be as stable as a reliable ability or achievement measure.

When the situations for which sociometric choices are to be made have reality value for peer group members, no other evidence of validity is necessary. External criteria are not needed to demonstrate that a sociometric measure is made up of interpersonal choices or attraction ratings. However, the relationship between sociometric responses and other criterion variables, such as overt behavior, may have value and interest. If sociometric measures are employed to estimate or predict overt behavior, for example, the magnitude of the relationship is crucial and may be conceptualized as a validity coefficient. Nevertheless, the most important point about data obtained from sociometric techniques is that they ought to be used to enhance personal adjustment and interpersonal relations and improve the social climate of peer groups.

ANNOTATED REFERENCES

Fox, R.; Luszki, Margaret B.; and Schmuck, R. *Diagnosing Classroom Learning Environments.* Chicago: Science Research Associates, 1966.
A series of twenty-three diagnostic tools for gathering reliable classroom data that can help the teacher or counselor to change the learning environment are described in easily understandable terms.

Gronlund, Norman E. *Sociometry in the Classroom.* New York: Harper and Row, 1959.
Directed toward the practical application of sociometry, this book presents a comprehensive integration and interpretation of the sociometric literature.

Lindzey, Gardner, and Byrne, Donn. "Measurement of Social Choice and Interpersonal Attractiveness." In *The Handbook of Social Psychology,* 2nd ed., Vol. 2. Edited by Gardner Lindzey and Elliot Aronson. Reading, Mass.: Addison-Wesley, 1969, pp. 452–525.
The authors present an overview of sociometric techniques, discuss the application of traditional measurement concepts to sociometric measures, and present a comprehensive review of the related research.

SELECTED REFERENCES

Conyne, Robert K. "Environmental Assessment: Mapping for Counselor Action." *Personnel and Guidance Journal* 54 (November 1975): 150-155.

Getzels, Jacob W. "A Social Psychology of Education." In *The Handbook of Social Psychology,* 2nd ed., Vol. 1. Edited by Gardner Lindzey and Elliot Aronson. Reading, Mass.: Addison-Wesley, 1969, pp. 459–537.

Gronlund, Norman E. *Measurement and Evaluation in Teaching.* 2nd ed. New York: Macmillan, 1976, pp. 452-479.

Haskell, Martin R. *An Introduction to Socioanalysis.* Long Beach, Calif.: California Institute of Socioanalysis, 1972.

Reiss, A. J. "Systematic Observation of Social Phenomena." In *Sociological Methodology.* Edited by Herbert L. Costner. San Francisco: Jossey-Bass, 1971, pp. 3–33.

Schuessler, Karl. *Analyzing Social Data.* Boston: Houghton Mifflin, 1971.

Chapter 14

Integration of Standardized and Nonstandardized Data

What methods are used by counselors to integrate assessment data?

What are the characteristics and functions of case studies?

What are the characteristics and functions of case conferences?

Counselors can gather a wealth of information about an individual by means of standardized and nonstandardized assessment techniques. Having data on hand is not enough; it is necessary to integrate information in order to be able to derive coherent hypotheses about an individual. In this chapter, we shall present the two principal methods for summarizing and integrating appraisal information: the case study and the case conference.

As counselors work with clients, they accumulate an enormous array of information that they must process. They must think about the information, order it, estimate their validity, draw inferences about the individuals, determine its meaning, and communicate this meaning to their clients and sometimes to others. This process of integrating data is a basic function of counseling. It occurs naturally and simultaneously with providing assistance to clients. The intervention that occurs is a product of this process.

Above and beyond the usual process of integrating data, there are occasions when counselors need more structured and formal methods of integrating information about individuals. For example, students who are more seriously disturbed emotionally or mentally deficient or those students for whom conventional counseling does not seem appropriate may require careful study. Moreover, students

THIS CHAPTER WAS WRITTEN BY KATHRYN W. LINDEN.

who are absent frequently, students from adverse home situations, students involved in crises, students whose vocational plans are unusually complex, students who are exceptionally gifted, or others may all require more formal and deliberate study.

In the best of all possible worlds, these formal and deliberate methods would be used with most clients. However, this cannot happen. Case conferences consume the time of several professionals, and case studies are a tremendous undertaking on the part of the counselor. These activities are time-consuming and costly. Consequently, they are reserved for special cases. While the time and effort that these methods require limit their use, nevertheless, when they are employed alone or in combination, they provide a powerful means of understanding individuals and designing strategies for helping them.

THE CASE STUDY

A *case study* can be defined as a report of an intensive analytical and diagnostic investigation of an individual or other social unit, in which attention is focused on factors contributing to the development of particular personality patterns and/or problems. Two other terms, *case history* and *life history,* also have been employed to describe this analytical and diagnostic tool. Although these terms have been defined somewhat differently by various writers, they all describe the same general technique—the comprehensive study of an individual. Consequently, these terms frequently are used interchangeably.

The major function of a case study as an assessment tool for counselors is to provide a means of integrating and summarizing all available information about an individual in order to determine what further steps should be taken to enhance his or her development. The case study is the most comprehensive of all analytical techniques; it can make use of all other assessment methods. The collection of case study data should not be regarded as a simple stockpiling of information. Rather, the purpose of a case study is to present an individual as a fully functioning totality within his or her environment. It must be recognized, however, that many aspects of an individual's private life never can be known to others. Consequently, counselors always must be aware that much of what makes a person an individual remains hidden from view even in the best, most intensive, and thorough of case studies.

CHARACTERISTICS
OF A GOOD CASE STUDY

Case studies of children were devised originally for use in child-guidance clinics, where clinicians were concerned with investigating maladjustment and providing therapeutic treatment. From this source, the term *clinical approach* became attached to the case study method. Although the desire to understand maladjusted and other problem students may be the primary motivation underlying most case studies, counselors also ought to develop case studies that focus on students who exhibit socially desirable behavior and high levels of performance.[1]

A good case study is concerned not only with a person's past and present but also with the future. By analyzing, synthesizing, and presenting in organized form the data collected from different sources at different times, the counselor can develop a full-length portrait of an individual that portrays the continuum of his or her development and the interrelationships among the various factors influencing growth and development, current status, and outlook for the future. Information can be obtained from the individual, the individual's peers, and significant others such as family, neighbors, counselors, teachers, or employers. Both standardized and nonstandardized instruments and techniques can provide data for a full-length case study.

A good case study is dynamic and longitudinal rather than static and cross-sectional. It is designed to enable counselors and others to understand a student well enough to accomplish effective planning for the next steps in his or her development. Therefore, a good case study contains all available reliable data about an individual that are relevant to the problem presented, together with interpretations, recommendations for future action, and provisions for reviewing the effects of the prescribed problem. It is important to include a provision for review, for it provides a vehicle by means of which the validity of the recommended course of action can be assessed.

A study may encompass an entire life or investigate merely a selected segment; it may concentrate on specific factors or consider the totality of an individual's life and behavior. The formality of a case study varies widely and depends on several factors: (1) the age

[1] John W. M. Rothney, *Methods of Studying the Individual Child: The Psychological Case Study* (Waltham, Mass.: Xerox College Publishing, 1968), p. 3.

of the client; (2) the purpose of the evaluation; (3) the working situation; and (4) the experience of the counselor.

ORGANIZATION

The organization of a case study can be theory based, test oriented, problem oriented, or some admixture of various schemes.[2] Organization involves not only providing a sequence format or outline but also developing and executing a logical plan for presenting information as significant elements in an integrated, functional entity. The organization of a case study depends on two major issues: the purpose for which the case study is being prepared, and the competencies or skills of the counselor in collecting, organizing, and using information. The purpose of the case study is determined by the needs of the client, the counselor, the client's parents, the counselor's colleagues, and any referral agency to which the case study may be presented later.[3] Some needs require an extensive case study; others require only a relatively brief psychological report.

No set of criteria exists for identifying which data may or may not be important to a case study. Moreover, there is no pattern that dictates the order, emphasis, or form of the case study. Two general categories can be used to classify the various types of information: (1) identifying data, such as name, age, sex, height, weight, place of residence, date and place of birth, referral source; and (2) personal data, such as developmental history, family background, school and work experiences, school activities, interests and hobbies, test and other observational data, personal and social adjustment, and goals. Both types of data serve to identify and to aid understanding of an individual, but the relative emphasis afforded the two may differ significantly, depending on the case.

In general, most case studies include: (1) identifying data; (2) a statement of the specific problem, including observable symptoms; (3) family background, including home environment, family relationships, and socioeconomic status; (4) physical history; (5) information on personality and social adjustment; (6) school history, including scholastic achievement, activities, peer and teacher relationships; (7) test and other observational data; (8) work experience;

---

[2] Michael P. Maloney and Michael P. Ward, *Psychological Assessment: A Conceptual Approach* (New York: Oxford University Press, 1976), pp. 106–116.

[3] William C. Cottle and Norville M. Downie, *Preparation for Counseling,* 2nd ed. (Englewood Cliffs, N.J.: Prentice-Hall, 1970), pp. 105–115.

(9) goals, including educational and/or vocational plans; (10) general appraisal and hypotheses, including the analysis, synthesis, and evaluation of the case; (11) recommendations for action; and (12) follow-up reports regarding the effects of the plan.[4]

Some criteria must be established in order to guide the counselor's choice of the areas to be investigated, the tools to be used, and the methods to be employed. Without such criteria, the counselor may collect useless information and/or overlook important data. None of the many available case study forms may be adequate for a given individual study; the counselor must adapt such forms to fit particular circumstances.

ANALYSIS
AND CONCEPTUALIZATION

Because it is much wider in scope than other observational techniques, the case study requires multiple methods of analysis and interpretation. Individual components, such as various types of test data and other observational results, may require different analytical techniques; each component must be analyzed and interpreted independently. When this has been accomplished, the counselor must integrate and synthesize the various component interpretations into a coherent whole in order to conceptualize the individual accurately and to develop a plan of action for the future that can be shared with the individual and appropriate others. The basic concepts underlying the method of content analysis are useful in synthesizing case study information.

Content analysis may be defined as "any technique for making inferences by systematically and objectively identifying specified characteristics of messages."[5] More than three-fifths of all empirical content analysis research investigations have dealt with five areas of inquiry, each of which accounts for at least 10 percent of the total: psychological-psychoanalytical research, media inventories, propaganda analyses, journalistic studies, and the study of social values.

Three major purposes for content analysis have emerged from the research literature: (1) to describe the characteristics of content; (2) to make inferences about content; and (3) to make inferences about

---

[4] Bruce Shertzer and Shelley C. Stone, *Fundamentals of Guidance*, 3rd ed. (Boston: Houghton Mifflin, 1976), p. 270.

[5] Ole R. Holsti, "Content Analysis," in *The Handbook of Social Psychology*, vol. 2, 2nd ed., ed. Gardner Lindzey and Elliot Aronson (Reading, Mass.: Addison-Wesley, 1968), p. 607.

the effects of content. Counselors depend on various types of communication in their efforts to understand the dynamics underlying the behavior of students. Therefore, any method that helps a counselor derive meaning and draw inferences from student communications is a valuable tool in the repertoire of assessment techniques. Personal documents and other written materials can be content-analyzed to infer the personality traits of their authors. Videotapes and tape-recordings of counseling interviews, individual and group therapy sessions, classroom groups, and other school activities can be content-analyzed. Moreover, content analysis can be used to derive meaning and to draw inferences from the results of projective devices, open-ended questionnaires, and related techniques.

Among the characteristics of content analysis about which there is wide agreement are objectivity, system, and generality. *Objectivity* requires that the analysis be conducted on the basis of explicitly defined rules in order to enable different persons to obtain the same results from the same documents. For a content analysis to be *systematic,* the decision to include and exclude content or categories is carried out according to consistently applied criteria of selection. The characteristic of *generality* requires that the findings have theoretical relevance, that is, the results must be related to other attributes of content or to the characteristics of the sender or recipient of the message. Purely descriptive information about the content has little value by itself. Thus, content analysis has the same requirements as any other method of inquiry and can be regarded as the application of scientific principles to the analysis of the content of communication.

In developing a system of content analysis, the first step is to select and define the categories into which content units are to be classified. There are as many potential categorization systems for classifying content data as there are questions that may be asked about data.

A content analysis design that has potential value for counselors was developed by Bucklew for the purpose of case history analysis.[6] A case history may be developed from interviews, self-reports, or a combination of the two. In Bucklew's content analysis paradigm, several categories are defined, and constructs (units of analysis or recording units) are listed and briefly characterized. Graphic symbols, or diagram elements, corresponding to each construct are depicted in Figure 14.1. Bucklew's content analysis paradigm permits a visual reconstruction of a case history that is somewhat similar

---

[6] J. Bucklew, *Paradigms for Psychopathology: A Contribution to Case History Analysis* (Philadelphia: J. B. Lippincott, 1960).

FIGURE 14.1
MAJOR CONSTRUCTS AND DIAGRAM ELEMENTS
IN BUCKLEW'S PARADIGMS FOR CASE HISTORY ANALYSIS

CATEGORY OF CONSTRUCTS	DIAGRAM ELEMENT
A. Behavioral Unit Constructs	Rectangles with rounded edges
1. Ego 2. Role	
3. The complex (Inside the rectangles, phrases summarize the leading characteristics of the unit. Right-hand rectangles stand for ego or roles; left-hand rectangles, for ego alien motives.)	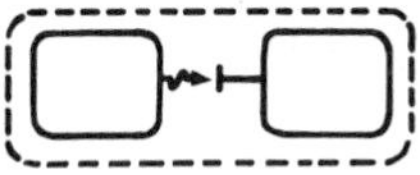
4. Symptom formation	
5. Anxiety	
B. Process Constructs	Lines suggesting either motivation or conditions of the units (such as being regressed)
1. Conflict (two arrows pointing at one another)	
2. Repression (wavy-lined arrow blocked by an opposing line indicating counter motivation)	
3. Regression (lines pointing upward)	
4. Fixation (blocked lines pointing down)	
5. External conflict	
C. Life Event Constructs	Rectangles with square corners
1. Precipitating events 2. Traumatic events 3. Conditioning events	
D. External Constructs	
1. Social and legal restrictions	
E. Developmental Sequences	

Source: J. Bucklew, *Paradigms for Psychopathology: A Contribution to Case History Analysis* (Philadelphia: J. B. Lippincott, 1960) p. 51. Reprinted with permission.

to the sociogramming techniques described in Chapter 13. In both analytical approaches, the recording unit and unit of quantification are combined. However, a sociogram is based on quantitative data, while Bucklew's paradigm is an example of qualitative content analysis.

According to Bucklew, diagraming a case history analysis proceeds as follows:

> In diagramming cases, it is usually easier to start with symptoms first and then go back to the complex, or else, skipping this stage temporarily, to reconstruct earlier life events first, and then the complex as the final step.[7]

The resulting content-analysis diagram represents a chronological sequence of the case history, from early life to personality status at the time the history was recorded. In order to illustrate Bucklew's method, a content analysis diagram derived from the case history report of a depressed scientist is presented in Figure 14.2.

Interpreting case histories is complex and difficult, regardless of whether the case history suggests psychopathology or relatively more normal modes of adjustment. Although considerable effort and ingenuity are required in order to develop content analysis paradigms, such as those suggested by Bucklew, they can be utilized to bring order out of the morass of interview, case history, and other personal record data. Content analysis applied to counseling and therapeutic materials, particularly when it is used in conjunction with other assessment data, appears to offer a fertile area for the study of the dynamics within individuals as well as that underlying various communications.

Content analysis provides a firm base for conceptualizing clients and their behaviors, strengths, limitations, and needs. A useful system appropriate for counselors has been developed by Clifford H. Swensen for the purpose of conceptualizing information about a client.[8] This model focuses the counselor's attention on a broad range of categories to be considered before any diagnosis and intervention strategy can be formulated. In this context, Swensen's model acts as a guide for observation. Among the content categories in this system, some of which may overlap, are environmental

---

[7] Bucklew, *Paradigms for Psychopathology*, p. 52. Reprinted with permission.
[8] Clifford H. Swensen, *An Approach to Case Conceptualization*, Guidance Monograph Series (Boston: Houghton Mifflin, 1968).

FIGURE 14.2
PARADIGM FOR DEPRESSION IN A SCIENTIST

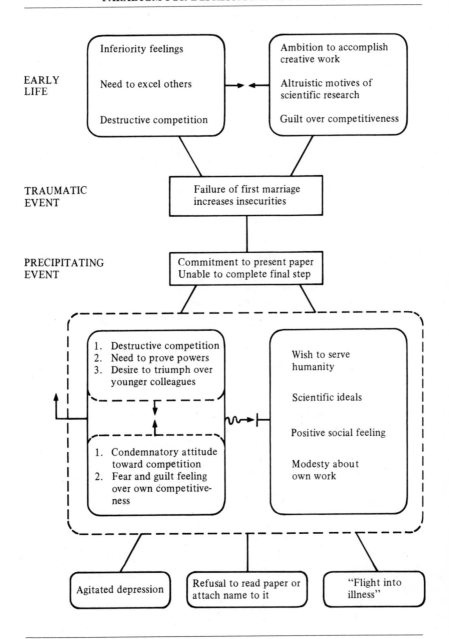

Source: J. Bucklew, *Paradigms for Psychopathology: A Contribution to Case History Analysis* (Philadelphia: J. B. Lippincott, 1960), p. 103. Reprinted with permission

supports, environmental stresses, adaptive habits, maladaptive habits, ego strength, defense-reaction patterns, and deviant behaviors reported by the client and by others. A major strength of Swensen's model is that it provides counselors with a positive-negative balance in conceptualizing the individuals being studied that "makes it difficult to view the client with a jaundiced eye or through rose-colored glasses."[9]

ADVANTAGES AND LIMITATIONS

For counselors, the case study can provide a more complete basis for understanding an individual than can the various data components taken independently; thus, it inhibits superficial and premature judgments. Because case studies are intensive, they may bring to light important variables, processes, and interactions that suggest viable hypotheses for further investigation or action. In interpreting case data, multiple causation and constellations of contributing factors can be identified, and key factors can be isolated where conflicting accounts may tend to confuse interpretation. The case study also may indicate what the counselor can expect of the individual in similar situations if the proposed intervention strategies are not successful.

Probably the greatest limitation of the case study method is the amount of time it requires. Another limitation concerns the reconstruction of the client's life history. The case study is not always a reliable document, and cross-validation of the case study is necessary if it is to contribute to understanding the client's behavior as completely as possible. This criticism, however, is directed at the ways in which case studies are collected, presented, and used, not at the method itself. The case study method is individualized and limited in scope to its relevancy to the problem at hand.

THE CASE CONFERENCE

The case conference and case study methods share objectives, use the same types and sources of data in studying individuals, and are employed in counseling for the same basic purposes. The primary difference between the two methods concerns the number of persons actively involved in studying an individual rather than any

---

[9] Shertzer and Stone, *Fundamentals of Guidance,* p. 271.

difference in purpose and function. A case study of an individual is developed by a counselor primarily for use in counseling that person. A case conference involves two or more professionals who meet in order to evaluate, make recommendations about, and plan a strategy of assistance for a client. Consequently, the decisions that emanate from a case conference tend to be more reliable than those derived by a single counselor.

The case study and case conference are not interchangeable methods of appraisal. In some situations, the case study may be the preferred method, while the case conference may be the most appropriate method for use in other situations. Moreover, the simultaneous use of both methods may be necessary for effective casework. Thus, the variety and sources of data introduced in a case conference, the kinds of cases presented, and the function of the conference depend on the purpose of the conference and the levels of training and experience of the participants. Nona F. Tollefson[10] identified three types of case conferences: the individual case consultation, the staff conference, and the case conference. These conferences have different participants and different purposes.

The *individual case consultation* conference typically involves one counselor and a supervisor or colleague. It is used primarily as a learning tool for counselors in training and in service. This type of conference is particularly helpful in demonstrating how to use the case study method. It is the most informal type of conference and offers the greatest flexibility in procedure. In consultation with a counselor skilled in case analysis, the inexperienced counselor can focus on the particular aspects of casework or case analysis for which he or she needs to develop increased skills. Moreover, the use of the case study method is more effectively taught when real clients, rather than hypothetical cases, are the subjects. The individual case consultation also can be employed effectively when experienced counselors need to consult one another concerning some aspect of a case that may be difficult to interpret.

The *staff conference* is a procedure employed by professional workers in order to share ideas regarding planning, reviewing, and evaluating their work with clients. When counselors participate in a staff conference, they are, in effect, performing a case analysis, even though a counselor may not be the one who presents, or staffs, the case. As a counselor's skill in case analysis increases, the staff conference becomes a particularly useful form of in-service training. Moreover, the staff conference is especially useful in helping the

---

[10] Nona F. Tollefson, *Counseling Case Management* (Boston: Houghton Mifflin, 1968), p. 32.

counselor to decide on appropriate referrals either in the school or in the social services of the community. When a counselor refers a client to an outside agency, a staff conference with professionals in the agency can be helpful in deciding the client's qualifications for the agency's services.

Both the individual consultation conference and the staff conference may be viewed as special cases of the general *case conference* conducted in a school. They differ primarily with regard to the participants and possibly the degree of formality. All counselors use conferences as a means of checking their hypotheses and inferences about clients with other professionals in order to evaluate and improve their effectiveness. The importance of the case conference as a method of individual appraisal has been accepted widely by counselors, clinicians, and other professional workers. However, there has been a tendency, especially among counselors, to replace the formal case conference with informal discussions with teachers and/or other personnel, perhaps because of the time required for a formal case conference.

Although counselor-teacher and other consultations are indispensable to a guidance program, such conferences are not substitutes for the formal case conference, the purpose of which is "to provide an official forum to generate, discuss, and evaluate program alternatives and the interface of those alternative programs with a given child."[11] Thus, a formal case conference provides a means for educational professionals with several perspectives to share their ideas and, through discussion, to specify behavioral outcomes and alternatives for the student being studied. Finally, the case conference, as well as the case study, must provide due process and equal protection safeguards.

A CASE CONFERENCE MODEL

If executed appropriately, the case conference not only safeguards the rights of clients but also may facilitate quality control in the delivery of services to individuals. The case conference model developed by Fred Kladder and Michael Tracy,[12] using systems-approach principles, begins with the initial referral of a client and continues until the client leaves the educational service system. In

---

[11] Michael I. Tracy, Spencer Gibbons, and Fred W. Kladder, *Case Conference: A Simulation and Source Book* (Indianapolis: Indiana Department of Public Instruction and the Indiana University Developmental Training Center, 1976), p. 44.

[12] Tracy, Gibbons, and Kladder, *Case Conference*, pp. 39–62.

this model, the case conference committee meeting, or *convocation*, is but one element in a continuous process. The flow chart presented in Figure 14.3 illustrates the continuous nature of this model.[13] By means of the feedback loop, the intervention program can be monitored periodically as progress is compared with the projected goals.

FIGURE 14.3
A CASE CONFERENCE MODEL

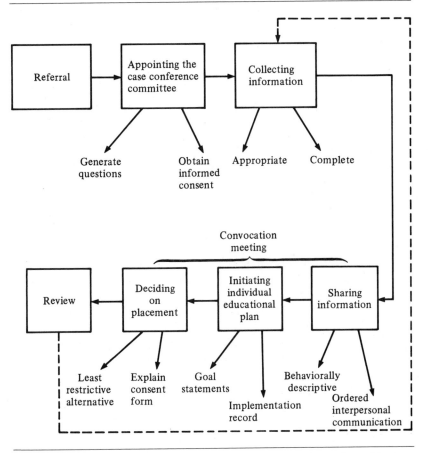

Source: Fred W. Kladder and Michael L. Tracy, "A Case Conference Model and the Delivery of Services to Individuals," in Michael L. Tracy, Spencer Gibbons, and Fred W. Kladder, *Case Conference: A Simulation and Source Book* (Indianapolis: Indiana Department of Public Instruction and the Indiana University Developmental Training Center, 1976), p. 41.

[13] Tracy, Gibbons, and Kladder, *Case Conference*, p. 40.

Three interrelated and interdependent processes are involved in the case conference process: decision-making, information collection, and implementation. The critical issues in the decision-making process are informed parental participation, due process procedures, development of an individual educational plan, least restrictive placement, and periodic review. Decision-making is dependent on the basic building blocks of information about the individual and his or her situation and potential placement. Consequently, the quality and quantity of the information collected greatly influences the decisions to be made.

The flow chart presented in Figure 14.4 illustrates the sequence of the case conference process, based on the model depicted in Figure 14.3, and shows when the case conference committee might meet and the possible outcomes of each meeting. Tracy, Gibbons, and Kladder view the case conference committee as being composed of two sets of individuals—the technical experts and the decision-makers. The technical experts are the professionals (school psychologist, counselor, speech therapist, school nurse, teacher, social worker) who may have relevant data to provide for a case. Their tasks are to collect and specify information (assessment), develop individualized educational plans, determine eligibility for placement, and consult on the implementation and elaboration of the agreed-upon alternatives of the individual education plan and placement for the student concerned. Because these experts do not participate directly in the decision-making process, they are free to facilitate, record, chair, and perhaps arbitrate in the staffing if appointed to do so by the school superintendent or his or her agent.

The decision-makers in the case conference process are a student's parents or their representative and the administrator or other representative of the local education agency. They must agree on a specific alternative program comprised of an individual educational plan and a suitable placement. Whenever the two factions do not agree, they must appeal to a higher authority for arbitration, such as a state board of education or one of its special divisions. Equal protection and due process procedures and safeguards must be provided in each phase of the case conference process.[14] (See Chapter 15 for further discussion of these issues as they relate to individual appraisal.)

---

[14] For a thorough discussion of how these legal issues are involved in each phase of the case conference process, together with criteria and guidelines for each phase, see Tracy, Gibbons, and Kladder, *Case Conference.*

FIGURE 14.4
FLOW CHART FOR A CASE CONFERENCE COMMITTEE

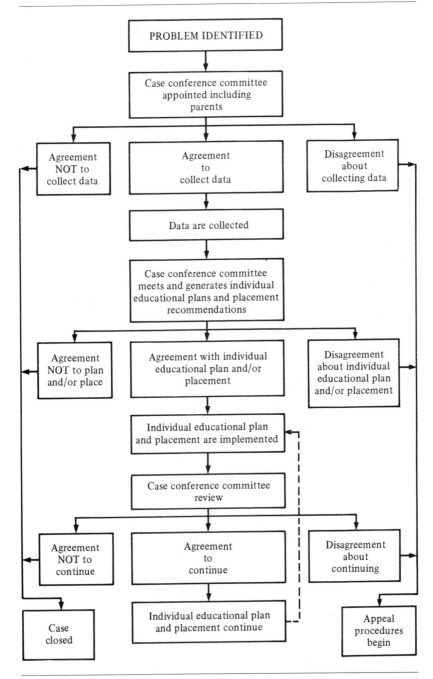

Source: Fred W. Kladder and Michael L. Tracy, "A Case Conference Model and the Delivery of Services to Individuals," in Michael L. Tracy, Spencer Gibbons, and Fred W. Kladder, *Case Conference: A Simulation and Source Book* (Indianapolis: Indiana Department of Public Instruction and the Indiana University Developmental Training Center, 1976), p. 47.

LIMITATIONS AND CAUTIONS

Effective as the case conference undoubtedly is, the method does have certain limitations. Perhaps the major drawback involves legal issues. Confidential data cannot be presented in a case conference unless the individual (or the parents, if the case involves a minor) gives written consent. Moreover, data that are not pertinent to the specific purpose of a case conference should not be introduced by any participant.

The question of the confidentiality of data is complex, involving more than just consent. Participants must be capable of understanding the data presented.[15] Confidential data, though essential for diagnosis, planning, treatment, or evaluation, cannot be discussed in a case conference. Nevertheless, cases in which the major issue is that of special education services require a formal case conference. The school administrator must appoint to the committee professionals who are qualified to interpret the data accurately, to plan an appropriate educational or remedial program, and to evaluate the effectiveness of the program for the student.

Another limitation is time. The length of time required for a case conference depends on the complexity of the problem and the participants' familiarity with the techniques of gathering data. The more complex the student's problem is, the more time is required to develop an understanding of the case. Moreover, as the number of participants involved in a case conference increases, so do the problems of scheduling the conference and providing sufficient time for it. Some counselors have had to abandon the case conference method for in-service training, because they found it almost impossible to schedule meetings that were convenient for everyone.

The issues of reliability and validity apply to the case conference method, as they do for all other methods of individual appraisal. There is little hard research evidence on the reliability and validity of the case conference method, so the reliability and validity of each individual case conference must be judged according to the outcome of the treatment.

PROBLEMS IN THE USE OF
CASE STUDIES AND CONFERENCES

In summary, the techniques that we have described in this chapter require a great deal of time, effort, and expertise. Case study and

---

[15] Tollefson, *Counseling Case Management*, pp. 43–44.

case conference methods can be very valuable in both the pre-service and in-service training of counselors and teachers, and we encourage the use of these methods for training purposes. However, the identity and rights of the person being studied must be protected, regardless of whether the material is being employed for training or for actual diagnosis and placement.

The pooling of information from a variety of sources can lead to a reliable and valid analysis of an individual's strengths and limitations and to an informed decision on placement. It is, however, essential to obtain true informed consent from those affected by the procedures in order to insure their rights and to obtain information that is both complete and appropriate. The ethically and legally mandated criteria of completeness and appropriateness of information mean that the data must be valid for the individual and must provide as many choices as possible concerning the source of the problem and its possible alleviation, without violating personal privacy. Professionals involved in the assessment of children for special services are frequently asked to justify the use of test instruments and other data-gathering methodologies in terms of their relevance to the problem at hand.

The use of the case study and case conference methods will increase as the legal issues associated with individual rights become increasingly well-defined. It is imperative for counselors to know about and gain experience with the techniques presented in this chapter and the other chapters in Part 5, as well as those dealing with more conventional procedures and techniques.

ISSUES

1. *The time required for careful analysis, integration, and summary interpretation of observational data is more than a counselor should be expected to employ for a single student.*

Yes, because:
Counselor-student ratios are so large that there is not enough time in a school day for studying individual students.

No, because:
The major reason for having counselors in schools is to help individual students with their concerns and problems.

Discussion:
It is true that the counselor-student ratio is extremely large in most schools. Moreover, no school day is ever long enough for

any counselor to fulfill all of his or her obligations. On the other hand, it also is true that many counselors are required to perform tasks that have little to do with counseling, such as scheduling students into courses and supervising extracurricular activities. Relieving counselors of these duties would give them more time for aiding students. They would then be free to engage in the content analysis of individual products (interviews, autobiographical data, other case data) and the time-consuming activities of case studies and case conferences.

2. *Many, if not most, school counselors are not skilled in the use of content analysis techniques, the development of case studies, and participation in case conferences. Therefore, they should not use these techniques.*

Yes, because:

In many states, certification for a school counselor requires only a minimum of training; consequently, many counselors are not skilled in using complex assessment techniques.

No, because:

Counselors can be trained on the job to employ and/or to participate in content analysis, case study, and case conference methods for studying individual students.

Discussion:

As we have noted, these methods are useful in both pre-service and in-service counselor training. Even though many counselors may not be skilled in the use of individual appraisal techniques, they nevertheless can acquire the required skills and experience. Supervision of the novice by an experienced counselor can only enhance the utility of these summary methods. Moreover, the legal mandates for the use of special educational services require that data must be valid for the individual. Consequently, it is imperative that counselors become skilled in interpreting and using individuual appraisal methods.

These methods enable a counselor to synthesize relevant information from all potential sources into a valid, dynamic portrait of an individual, permitting the counselor, school psychologist, and other professionals to develop and implement an effective plan of action. Any method requiring information from more than one source and using experts from a variety of disciplines is more reliable and valid than is one that depends on only one professional and limited data. The case conference and case study methods permit valid diagnosis and evaluation of a program of action.

ANNOTATED REFERENCES

Bucklew, J. *Paradigms for Psychopathology: A Contribution to Case History Analysis.* New York: J. P. Lippincott, 1960.
The author elaborates on his method of content analysis and applies it to numerous case histories. This is an excellent resource for counselors who wish to study the topic in depth.

Holsti, Ole R. "Content Analysis." In *The Handbook of Social Psychology.* 2nd ed. Vol. 2. Edited by Gardner Lindzey and Elliot Aronson. Reading, Mass.: Addison-Wesley, 1969.
Chapter 16 offers an in-depth discussion of the conceptulization, method, and issues of content analysis as a research tool. It should be required reading for counselors and other practioners, including researchers, who wish to draw inferences and derive hypotheses from various types of communication.

Swensen, Clifford J. *An Approach to Case Conceptualization.* Boston: Houghton Mifflin, 1968.
This book presents a method of determining the strengths and weaknesses of an individual who seeks counseling. The author devotes considerable attention to the processes of arranging, conceptualizing, and using various types of data about the client. This book is a practical introduction to the topic.

Tollefson, Nona F. *Counseling Case Management.* Boston: Houghton Mifflin, 1968.
The author presents a well-written, concise discussion of the case study and case conference methods of appraisal. In addition, the uses and maintenance of counseling records are discussed, and an illustrative case study is presented.

Tracy, Michael I.; Gibbons, Spencer; and Kladder, Fred W., eds. *Case Conference: A Simulation and Source Book.* Indianapolis: Indiana Department of Public Instruction and the Indiana University Developmental Training Center (pursuant to grant DEG no. 0-74-2773, U.S. Office of Education), 1976.
The authors present a model for the case conference process that emphasizes the legal principles of equal protection and due process in the professional activities of data collection, development of individual educational plans, implementation, and review. Numerous illustrations are provided as well as various sample forms that are required as a result of due process and equal protection issues. This book is timely and is an excellent source for various educational agencies as well as individual counselors and other professional workers.

SELECTED REFERENCES

Brown, Joe, and Koltveit, Thomas. "Individual Assessment: A Systematic Approach." *Personnel and Guidance Journal* 55 (January 1977): 271–276.

Cottle, William C., and Downie, Norville M. *Preparation for Counseling.* 2nd ed. Englewood Cliffs, N.J.: Prentice-Hall, 1970, pp. 105–143.

Davis, Everett C. "An Analysis of the Autobiographical Statements of Adolescents." *Measurement and Evaluation in Guidance* 6 (July 1973): 117–121.

Freijo, Tom D., and Ward, Annie M. "A Case Study of the Development of a Career Education Achievement Test." *Measurement and Evaluation in Guidance* 9 (January 1976): 51–59.

Gagné, Robert M. "Task Analysis—Its Relation to Content Analysis." *Educational Psychologist* 11 (1974): 11–18.

Kerlinger, Fred N. *Foundations of Behavioral Research.* 2nd ed. New York: Holt, Rinehart and Winston, 1973, pp. 525–535.

Maloney, Michael P., and Ward, Michael P. *Psychological Assessment: A Conceptual Approach.* New York: Oxford University Press, 1976, ch. 4.

McReynolds, Paul, ed. *Advances in Psychological Assessment.* Vol. 3. San Francisco: Jossey-Bass, 1975.

Wang, Margaret C., and Stiles, Billie. "An Investigation of Children's Self-Concept of Self Responsibility for Their School Learning." *American Educational Research Journal* 13 (Spring 1976): 159–179.

Westbrook, Bert W. "Content Analysis of Six Career Development Tests." *Measurement and Evaluation in Guidance* 7 (October 1974): 172–180.

Part 6

Perspective and Prospectus

THIS FINAL SECTION HIGHLIGHTS ESSENTIAL PRINCIPLES APPROPRIATE in the use of assessment techniques and appraisal devices. Projections are made about probable future developments in individual analysis. Chapter 15 discusses school testing programs and establishes guidelines for interpreting and communicating test data to students, parents, educators, and the public. We point out prominent ethical and legal considerations that govern the responsible use of tests. Chapter 16 forecasts changes in the field of assessment, particularly those bearing on the practice of counseling.

Chapter 15

Responsible
Use of Data

What is an adequate K-12 school testing program?

What can counselors and other personnel do to prepare to use and interpret assessment data?

What assessment principles are among the most fundamental to observe when counselors interpret data to students and parents or make recommendations?

What use is made of appraisal data in guidance accountability programs?

What ethical and legal considerations govern the proper use of tests?

SCHOOL TESTING PROGRAMS

Teachers, counselors, and school administrators need information about students—their measured abilities, interests, problems, and their academic strengths and limitations—if they are to assist them. Certain aspects of a modern appraisal program apply to the entire school and the entire school system. Decisions concerning the types of measurement data that should be obtained and recorded for all students must hold for at least the entire school.

The phrase *testing program* is intended to depict an organized school-wide or system-wide program for the administration of standardized tests. Many tests serve needs that are common from one school to another. However, any testing program must always be appropriate for a specific setting.

Test data are used by several groups in a school. Although the distinctions among the functions are by no means clear-cut, the data provided by a testing program can be used to implement certain administrative and supervisory functions, instructional functions, and guidance functions.

From an administrative and supervisory point of view, measurement data for classes and grades can help determine the need for supervisory assistance or for a revision of curricular activities and instructional materials. Measurement data are indispensible in evaluating the progress of students toward educational goals, and they can aid in making administrative decisions concerning the appropriate classification of students. Assessment data serve four major instructional functions: (1) they determine the extent to which students are making progress toward instructional goals; (2) they provide evidence to students and their parents about their progress; (3) they ascertain group and individual attainments as a basis for forming groups in a class or offering individualized corrective instruction; and (4) they aid in developing hypotheses concerning basic causal factors behind any deficiency. Counselors use assessment data to assist students in making educational and vocational decisions; to help teachers better understand students' needs in areas of personal and social adjustment; to help students toward improved self-appraisal and self-direction; to increase parents' understanding of their children; and to assist in the identification of students whose special abilities or disabilities require modifications of the educational program or referral to specialists.

David A. Goslin concluded that at least three-quarters of the public school systems in the United States, and a large proportion of independent schools, have regular testing programs, and that all school systems make use of tests to some extent.[1] He found that there are more than a dozen national school, scholarship, and college testing programs, in addition to other testing programs sponsored by numerous state and local agencies. School-wide testing takes place somewhat more frequently at the elementary levels, while external testing programs are more common from junior high school through college.

Goslin was not able to discern clearly just how test results were being used, but he found little disagreement that tests frequently play an important part in a wide range of decisions that critically affect the lives of young people. He also thought it likely that test results have an effect on the aspirations and expectations of children and their parents. He concluded that testing has become an important factor in American education, and that no one can afford to overlook testing or to be indifferent to test results. Indeed, the value of standardized testing is directly related to the diligence and prudence with which the results are interpreted and used.

[1] David A. Goslin, *The Search for Ability* (New York: Russell Sage Foundation, 1963).

GENERAL CHARACTERISTICS
OF TESTING PROGRAMS

Many school counselors are responsible for managing school testing programs. Those not involved in the direct management of the program nevertheless participate in its planning or use its results.

A good testing program demonstrates relationship to use, integration, and continuity. *Relationship to use* means that tests should be offered at a time that insures that the information they provide will be available and current when it is needed. *Integration* means that the testing program should be viewed as a whole: the information that is needed on sixth-graders is not unrelated to information that is obtained from fifth-graders or to the information about seventh-graders. In an integrated program, tests that are administered in the junior high school are selected in relation to those given in the elementary school and those administered in senior high school. The third characteristic, *continuity,* suggests that the same tests be used year after year, unless some mitigating circumstance intervenes. Advantages of continuity are twofold. On the one hand, comparable data may be accumulated in all students' records. Continuity also enables the school system's personnel to become more knowledgeable about specific tests. Getting to know tests means getting to know what they measure, as well as establishing local standards of expectation.

Many years ago, Ralph A. Spence suggested that a "good testing program should be supplementary not duplicative, usable not confusing, economical not burdensome, comprehensive not sporadic, suggestive not dogmatic, progressive not static."[2] These prescriptions are still applicable, though fulfilling them is just as difficult today as it was then.

William C. Daley presented four principles that should characterize school testing programs:

1. The program should be continuous. Occasional testing may serve immediate needs, but fully effective use of tests is possible only when they are part of a continuing program that permits measurement of growth and progress and systematic evaluation of changes.
2. The testing program should be comprehensive. Spot testing in one subject or another or periodic use of intelligence tests is

---

[2] Ralph A. Spence, "A Comprehensive Testing Program for Elementary Schools, *Teachers College Record* 34 (1933): 279–284.

of value; but results of all tests are enhanced when they are part of a comprehensive evaluation program and when they may be studied in relation to each other.

3. Because test data are of concern to the teacher, the counselor, the administrator, and others, decisions relevant to the selection of a test, the scheduling of the test, reporting the test results, and other aspects of the program should be made jointly. Only in this way can there be common understanding of the purposes of testing and an awareness of the benefits to be derived.

4. The testing program should be integrated with the total educational program of the school. Standardized testing should be thought of not as extrinsic to or independent of the school's total program but as an essential part of it, intimately related to instructional goals and counseling activities.[3]

PLANNING A TESTING PROGRAM

As there is no one best appraisal device, so there is no one best testing program for use in each school system. A remarkable characteristic of American public education is the tremendous diversity of its school systems. The approximately 16,000 school districts in the country range in size from a few square miles to almost 100,000 square miles, and in enrollments from fewer than ten to more than a million. Nevertheless, some principles can be suggested to serve as guides to school personnel in planning a testing program.

A major weakness of many school testing programs is their lack of purpose. Many just "growed," like Topsy, and continue their existence without examination to determine whether any useful function is being served. The professionals planning a school testing program must know toward which educational objectives changes in student behavior are directed. The major purpose of a testing program is to provide information about students' attainment of these objectives. Therefore, the purposes served by a testing program should be formulated clearly and presented in written form to school staff members. Also, forming a testing committee to plan a testing program or to review an existing program is a good way to focus on the measurement needs of the many professionals in the school system.

---

[3] William C. Daley, "Test Scores: Fragment of a Picture," *Test Service Notebook No. 24* (New York: Harcourt, Brace and World, 1959).

In summary, here are some of the steps involved in planning a school testing program:

1. Specify the information needed by the system, when and where it is needed, and who will use it.
2. Identify those tests to be given system-wide. Most schools assign testing at each educational level, usually starting with elementary school grades, then senior high, followed by junior high grades. Sequence-developed ability tests are usually initiated first, followed by achievement tests, then prognostic and diagnostic instruments, followed by interest inventories, aptitude measures, and then personality inventories.
3. Coordinate the use of test data by counselors, teachers, and administrators.
4. Implement ways of reporting test data to those who need the results and of interpreting tests to students and their parents.
5. Evaluate the testing program in terms of its objectives.

In planning any school testing program, decisions must be made early about the frequency of the testing and the grade levels at which particular tests are to be given. These matters are determined by the purposes for which the testing is intended and are further affected by such considerations as the kinds of measuring instruments used and the amount of money and time available. It is far better to undertake a modest program and put the results to effective use than to attempt a more extensive and ambitious program that produces no practical outcome.

Table 15.1 represents a basic testing program for a system organized on a 6–3–3 basis. Of course, the organization of the school district and the purposes of the tests and the intended use of test results, rather than any arbitrary scheme, should dictate the testing system.

In the elementary school, the purpose of education is to help students master the tools of learning and communication while they are learning to live and work in a group. For this reason, the first tests given in elementary school usually are tests of school readiness or reading readiness. Reading is the principal means of acquiring organized knowledge. Thus, a valuable testing program should provide early identification of poor progress in reading and should keep track of progress in reading through the school years. Understanding various aspects of students' achievement, particularly the achievements of those who do not progress at normal rates, brings into use measures of general ability and achievement.

TABLE 15.1
A BASIC TESTING PROGRAM

GRADE	ACHIEVEMENT	ABILITY	APTITUDE	PERSONALITY	INTEREST
			TYPE OF TEST		
K–1	x[a]		As needs	As needs	As needs
2			dictate	dictate	dictate
3		x			
4					
5					
6	x				
7					
8					
9	x				
10					
11					
12					

[a] School readiness.

Given the practical realities of time and cost, most schools settle for group-administered ability tests as a minimal testing program. However, the data derived from group tests given as early as the beginning of the third grade do not have satisfactory reliability or stability over time (see Chapter 4). If a school can afford only one group intelligence test, it should probably not be administered until the end of the third grade or the beginning of the fourth grade. Individually administered intelligence tests have definite advantages over group tests, particularly in the early grades. If a community has adequate resources and trained personnel available, it would be worthwhile to give an individual test to each child toward the end of kindergarten or early in the first grade.

Most school testing programs include an achievement battery that covers basic skills and subject content. This can replace a separate reading test. If the battery is to be given only once, it is probably best to administer the test in grade 3 or grade 4 and use the results in planning individual programs of instruction or in placing students in remedial programs. However, it is preferable to test children on more than one occasion with such a battery.

The time at which tests are administered is an important factor to be considered in planning a program. The need for evidence on which to base sound judgments is particularly acute when students enter a new stage in their education. Tests, then, are generally given at such points as: entering the first grade; completing the third or beginning the fourth grade; leaving elementary school for junior high school; beginning senior high school; and entering a college or university or other post–high school education or work. There is also need for test data to help a student make plans for later life, whether or not these plans are based on graduating from high school.

At each of these points (except the first, when making estimates of reading readiness is crucial), it is helpful to have evidence gained from tests of scholastic ability and/or achievement, supplemented by interest inventories for high school students. The use of other tests such as diagnostic, personality, and special aptitude tests, and tests that assess achievement in specific school subjects should be undertaken only as needed. Little is to be gained by forcing teachers to use tests when neither they nor their students see any real need for them.

Personality inventories and other specialized tests are best used on an individual basis for curriculum selection or vocational and personal counseling. Often these tests are given early in the fall. The results then can be used by students, teachers, counselors, and others throughout the school year.

Many tests administered late in the spring are filed and forgotten, a waste of considerable time and money. No more tests should be administered than are needed. The overwhelming majority of tests are given in schools as part of a grade-wide test program. Everyone in a given grade receives the same test on the same day regardless of any one person's readiness or needs. It is, therefore, not surprising to find that the results of many tests are never used and that for only a small minority of students do tests make any difference. Leo Goldman suggested that answers to the question "In what way is this test necessary?" respond equally to the question "What information does this test add to what we already know?"[4]

Rather than administer a test to an entire group, professionals should plan testing for different people, taking into account such factors as: previous test data; the presence of various signs of congruence among tests, grades and other data; any behavior that suggests unusual changes since previous testing; and the person's readiness to think about himself or herself, to examine information about himself or herself, and to begin planning for the future. This is the ultimate objective of any worthy school testing program.

All counselors should become acquainted with referral testing

---

[4] Leo Goldman, "Tests Should Make a Difference," *Measurement and Evaluation in Guidance* 2 (Spring 1969): 53–59.

resources available in the school and the community. These may include specialized personnel capable of administering and interpreting individual ability tests; other psychological tests, projective and otherwise, used to study problem cases; and tests of reading, speech, hearing, neurological impairment, and so on. These may be oral, performance, or written tests or a combination of all three. Usually they are administered individually. Teachers can identify students in need of special attention. Large school systems often have specialized personnel on staff to assist in this process. Small school systems usually have referral arrangements with city, county, or college and university agencies. Such testing represents an important supplement to the general testing program of the school.

LARGE-SCALE TESTING PROGRAMS

A matter of concern to educators in recent years has been the proliferation of large-scale testing programs external to the school but imposed on schools and serving some purposes other than those of the school itself. College admissions testing is one such example. In addition, there are national scholarship testing programs, armed forces entry programs, large-scale research testing programs, and quality control testing programs administered by large city units, states, and even federal agencies. Each of these is designed to serve a valid educational purpose; but the question has arisen in recent years as to whether these purposes conflict with other purposes of the schools.

Concern about the impact of these testing programs on students, especially during the last year or two in secondary school, arises on two counts: Do students spend too much time taking tests? Does the time spent in taking such tests interfere with their regular school work? Although the scheduling of these tests may be a nuisance for school counselors, the burden on the time of the students is not to be taken lightly. Furthermore, there is concern that external testing programs may subvert the educational objectives of the school because unwisely employed tests can adversely influence the curriculum and motivate teachers to prepare for these tests. This problem is most likely to arise when external tests focus on specific segments of the curriculum. Teachers may fear that, if their students perform poorly on these tests, they and the school may all be judged negatively and unjustly. Even when a test is not tied closely to the curriculum, it may affect the curriculum. Thus, it is important that external testing programs present desirable models, emphasize the important goals of education, and do not distort the objectives of a given school.

COLLEGE ADMISSIONS AND SCHOLARSHIP PROGRAMS   Testing programs used in connection with college admissions and scholarships (see Chapters 5 and 6) have arisen because substantial scholarship funds come from sources outside the universities. Consequently, some general appraisal of applicants that is not related to the programs or policies of any single institution is needed. The most ambitious scholarship testing program is the one administered by the National Merit Scholarship Corporation. Other extensively used scholarship testing services have been developed by the Educational Testing Service and the Psychological Corporation.

CITY-WIDE AND STATE-WIDE PROGRAMS   A number of cities and some states have centrally administered programs of ability and/or achievement tests. Response to these programs has been relatively favorable. The advantage of any centralized and uniform testing program is that records from one school can be compared to those of another. However, if a rigid uniform testing program is applied throughout a large educational unit, there is a danger that the tests may not relate well to the specific circumstances of given schools. They may not reflect the goals and methods of teachers, and they may not fit the characteristics of a particular school's population.

Some city school districts and state educational agencies provide advisory testing services to local educational units. A number of different possible testing programs are offered to local schools as guides. State educational agencies may keep files of specimen tests suitable for different purposes to help local school committees select tests that meet their needs. Consultant and advisory help may also be offered. Such a service may be more useful than a program specified and directed from a central administrative office.

NATIONAL ASSESSMENT   A national educational assessment scheme was formulated by Francis Keppel, John Gardner, and others concerned with the needs of education in the United States and the criticisms that were leveled against education in the early 1960s. Defenders of education have been hard pressed to present direct evidence that American schools meet the needs of society as those needs have been expressed in the objectives that schools set for themselves. National assessment is an educational project designed to provide information about many of the direct outcomes of education: knowledge, skills, understanding, and attitudes in a variety of subject areas.

The purpose of national assessment is to improve the educational decision-making of legislators, board of education members, professional educators, or anyone vitally concerned with improving American education.[5] National educational assessment has the potential for focusing attention on current status, past performance, and the direction in which the nation is moving in education. However, after more than a decade of effort toward implementing this idea, a truly functional program for national assessment remains a dream. The locus of school testing programs is still the local school district or corporation or even the individual school, the place where many sincerely concerned individuals believe it should be. However, large-scale testing for college admissions and scholarships, and tests given by state and national programs, must be taken into account in planning any school testing program.

ALLOCATION OF RESPONSIBILITY

Almost every member of a school staff who is charged in any way with responsibility for the instructional program of the school is vitally concerned with test data. Rare is the administrator, supervisor, counselor, psychologist, or director of research who has no need of such data in his or her work. Each has a stake in the planning of testing and the application and interpretation of test results. Test selection is accomplished best if it takes account of their respective needs. Their interests are sometimes common, sometimes diverse.

An appraisal program of any consequence is undertaken with the cooperation and responsibility of several people. The program may involve only classroom teachers, counselors, and their supervisors or principals, or the work may be planned and carried out with the cooperation of the entire staff of the school system. In the latter case, it is customary to entrust most of the active direction to one qualified person or to a representative committee. When a testing program is carried out to meet needs that teachers or counselors

[5] Frank B. Womer, "National Assessment of Educational Progress," in *Perspectives in Educational and Psychological Measurement*, ed., Glenn H. Bracht, Kenneth D. Hopkins, and Julian C. Stanley (Englewood Cliffs, N.J.: Prentice-Hall, 1972), pp. 26–40.

regard as important, and when those teachers or counselors participate actively in the planning of and the execution of the program,
it has a good chance of success. Parents ought to understand the
reasons for testing so that they too will support the program. If
parents can see that the results of tests help to bring about better
learning and adjustment, their confidence in the usefulness of tests
will increase.

THE TESTING COMMITTEE

A vehicle that many school systems have found effective in giving
voice to all interests in the school is the testing committee, which
is charged with the responsibility for planning a school system's
total appraisal program and keeping it under continued review. The
chairperson of this committee may be a director of testing or research, a director of instruction, a director of guidance, a psychologist, a counselor, the superintendent, or some other staff member,
according to local organizational practice. The first duty of any
testing committee is to formulate an explicit policy statement for
the appraisal of all students in the school system. A committee
discharges its responsibilities best if its members have been trained
for this task and informed about the criteria that should prevail in
selecting tests and about the various uses for which test data can
be employed.

The scope of an appraisal and evaluation program in a school is
as broad as the range of the instructional goals of the school itself.
Many of these goals do not lend themselves to assessment through
standardized tests, so the evaluative contributions of teachers constitute an integral component of any comprehensive program of
appraisal.

The testing committee must consider the frequency with which
tests should be administered, establish priorities among testing
needs, choose appropriate grades in which to administer tests, decide the time of the year at which tests should be administered,
arrange for scoring, determine the types of reporting systems, and
formulate ways in which test data will be disseminated. Of course,
the committee also has the crucial task of selecting, or at least
recommending the selection of, the test or tests to be used. Responsibility for testing, therefore, is shared by many persons in a
school system. Each contributes his or her special knowledge and
interest.

TEST SELECTION

The first requirement for test selection is that the testing committee or others responsible know what tests are available. This information may be obtained from the catalogs provided by the various test publishers. Sample tests and manuals also can be obtained for modest prices. Test manuals should be examined carefully, for they can answer many questions. In making specific selections, the committee should evaluate the technical attributes of each test, giving consideration to the mechanics of the instrument, its ease of administration, its scoring, and so on. Consideration should also be given to the availability of certain services: Can arrangements be made for external scoring, analysis, preparation of student reports? Furthermore, the school budget should provide for the purchase of standardized test materials. Finally, the committee should plan far enough in advance to allow for ordering and distributing the test in ample time for testing. Appendix E presents a form for collecting the data essential for selecting a test.

SPECIFIC CONSIDERATIONS Counselors should investigate carefully the time needed for test administration to make certain that the daily routine of the school will be disrupted as little as possible. Many tests are constructed to be administered in 30–45-minute periods, though frequently, more time is needed to administer the test than the time limit specified by the publisher. Time is needed to settle the group, to pass out the test materials, to read directions, to complete practice items, and to collect the materials.

The ease with which a test is administered also should be considered. A test that requires special skills and training for administration has limited use in a school testing program. Directions should be evaluated for comprehensibility, simplicity, and clarity. Furthermore, some programs require classroom teachers or counselors to score the materials, though most teachers and counselors believe that they have enough to do without having to score tests. This problem can be solved in a variety of ways. First, clerks can be engaged to score tests and record the results. Second, materials can be sent to a scoring center to be scored by machine or computer. Large urban school systems often have their own scoring services. In some counties, a group of schools jointly purchases a scoring machine or contracts for computer services. Third, some tests provide self-scoring examination booklets or answer sheets. These tend to cost a bit more than regular answer sheets, but the time saved may be well worth the extra cost. However, the economical and efficient scoring services now being offered by the major test publishers render this issue relatively inconsequential.

Tests are expensive. The chief way to keep testing costs down is to purchase tests with reusable booklets. Each time the test is given, all the school needs to order are additional answer sheets and possibly some sort of scoring service. In addition, a testing program should be staggered so that several groups can take the test at different times. The maximum number of individuals who will take the test at any one time can be determined, and test booklets and other materials ordered accordingly.

Frequently, it is desirable to have two or more parallel forms of a test on hand. Sometimes a test is given at the beginning of a year and another at the end of the year to measure progress. It is best to use a parallel form of the test for the second administration. Also, tests that are available for different levels—that is, tests with forms for primary, elementary, intermediate, and higher levels—are especially useful. First, some individuals who do very well on a test should not have been given that level in the first place; it was too easy. Second, slow readers may score badly. A higher test level would be appropriate for the former and a lower level for the latter.

Using different levels of the same test throughout a school system has the additional advantage of consistency and, perhaps, comparability. If tests are similar in content and structure at different levels, then there may be some justification in comparing the scores that a student makes at different levels. However, scores obtained on different tests, even if they have the same label, should not be thought of as being equivalent. In addition, the best type of test to employ is one that provides norms based on individuals representative of the school or school system. This is particularly true of achievement tests and, to some extent, of general ability measures. In evaluating norms that are associated with interest measures, it is wise to consider the number of different occupational groups for which norms are available and also the size of the sample on which these reference data have been based.

A useful test does not require specialized graduate work on the part of examiners. If tests are to be used in an elementary or secondary school, teachers and counselors, at least after limited training, should be able to understand what the test measures, what the scores mean, and how they can make use of these scores. In addition, when tests are used for counseling, results should be able to be easily understood by students, parents, teachers, and administrators.

PACKAGE TESTING PROGRAMS Another service that has grown in recent years is the package testing program offered by many test publishers to schools at all levels. The various kinds of programs differ considerably both in the variety of tests and the services offered. For elementary schools, the package usually consists of a general scholastic ability test and achievement tests in basic skills. For secondary schools, the package typically consists of a general scholastic ability test or a multifactor ability test and achievement tests in reading, mathematics, language, science, and social studies. A school pays so much per student tested, a cost that usually includes the rental or purchase of test materials, test scoring, and the preparation of test score distribution and report forms by grades or by classes.

Any school that considers the purchase of a package program should examine each test in the package carefully to determine whether or not it meets its needs. If the tests are of good quality, and if they provide the school with the information it needs, then buying the package may be both economical and efficient. However, a package program is not necessarily an efficient testing program for a specific school. School officials must weigh the components of the package in terms of needs and objectives of their school.

TEST ADMINISTRATION

For the effective administration of a testing program in a school or school system, responsibility must be centralized in a group of people who are trained for such responsibility. The persons administering a test must be prepared adequately and must adhere to standardized instructions. The tests should be administered under optimal physical conditions and optimal conditions of communication and rapport. Examinees must be well-motivated, and the scoring and reporting of tests must be accurate.

Probably the most important aspect of test administration is following exactly the directions in the manual. If directions are to be read aloud, that is exactly what the examiner must do. When a test is timed, great care should be taken to adhere to the limit. If a test is being administered to large groups, proctors are needed. One individual can handle twenty-five or thirty students adequately, but for each additional twenty-five or thirty examinees, an additional proctor should be available to aid in handing out and collecting materials, to answer questions, to help students complete practice items, and to observe once the test is under way.

Students, particularly those in elementary schools, do their best when they are tested in familiar surroundings. Therefore, whenever possible, they should be examined in small groups in their own classrooms by their own teachers. Older students are frequently tested in large groups, and many individual problems go unattended because of the size of the operation. In addition, such factors as temperature, lighting, humidity, and distracting noises should always be considered in selecting a location for administering a test.

Most standardized group tests can be given by any competent teacher. All test administrators should confer before beginning testing in order to review the test and the directions and to make suggestions about solving anticipated problems. Tests that are administered as part of the school routine or on an individual basis by a counselor present no problem as to time of administering. In elementary school, it is best to administer tests in the morning. At any level, a long test should be broken into two or three segments and administered on consecutive days, preferably in the morning.

An important problem in administering a test is how to motivate students to do their best. Most children from middle-class homes are strongly motivated and tend to turn in relatively credible performances on tests. In contrast, lower-class parents frequently see little value in school and seldom offer their children encouragement. Such a child may treat a test as if it were just another one of those things to be endured because he or she has to go to school.

On the other hand, some individuals are so strongly motivated at times that they perform miserably. When examinations mean a great deal, such as passing or failing a course or winning a scholarship, many students become so distraught that they can't work.

RECORD KEEPING

The ultimate value of any testing program lies in the variety and extent of its uses. The scores from tests given school-wide should be recorded carefully and filed in a permanent cumulative record. No counseling program can operate effectively without such records. Continuing application of test results calls for a system in which to record all essential test and life history data in a readily understandable fashion.

The summarizing and recording of data can be a time-consuming, mechanical process. On the other hand, record-keeping can be carried out so as to provide new understandings of students by putting together current data on various aspects of behavior and perceiving their interrelationships and by building up a longitudinal picture of a student's development. The process of reporting results to students and to their parents can also be routine drudgery, or it can be a valuable and stimulating process of sharing insights and planning. In order to make all three processes (summarizing, recording, and reporting) as functional as possible, it is necessary to keep in mind that they are means to an end, not ends in themselves.

EVALUATION

Most counselors are aware that the ultimate use of any effective school testing program is to place the results into the hands of counselors, teachers, administrators, students, and parents and to interpret and apply them. Counselors should insist on periodic evaluations of a school's testing program by all personnel involved in testing and test usage.

PREPARATION FOR TEST USE

George E. Hill has suggested that two standards for test use are paramount: (1) the most important user of tests in schools is the individual who takes them; and (2) taking a test, or responding to an inventory, is a self-relevatory process; therefore, the person being tested must be helped to capitalize on the information produced by the test.[6]

THE SCHOOL COUNSELOR

Secondary schools now accept the responsibility for providing each student with counseling concerning educational and career plans. Furthermore, schools also have assumed a measure of responsibility for helping students at all levels to cope with emotional problems or other areas of adjustment. The increasing use of counselors in the elementary school for this purpose is one of the most promising educational developments of recent years.

The requirement that tests be used only by appropriately qualified counselors is one step toward protecting students and others against

---

[6] George E. Hill, "Standards for Test Users," *Measurement and Evaluation in Guidance* 2 (Fall 1969): 141.

the improper use of tests. The necessary qualifications vary with the type of test. A relatively long period of intensive training and supervised experience is required for the proper use of individualized intelligence tests and most personality tests (seldom used by counselors), whereas a minimum of specialized psychological training is needed for giving group-administered general ability tests or tests of educational achievement or vocational proficiency. The preparation required for the proper use of interest inventories falls somewhere between these extremes and, for most counselors, constitutes the area of test usage wherein they need to develop the greatest degree of expertise and sophistication.

Well-trained counselors use tests that are appropriate for both the purpose for which they are testing and the person to be evaluated (see principle 4, Chapter 1). Counselors also must be familiar with the research literature on tests and be able to evaluate their technical merits with regard to such characteristics as norms, reliability, and validity. In administering the test, the counselor must be alert to the many conditions that may affect a person's performance. Furthermore, a counselor should make recommendations about a student only after considering the test scores in light of all other pertinent information (see principle 3, Chapter 1). Above all, the counselor should be sufficiently knowledgeable to guard against unwarranted inference.

No counselor is qualified equally in all areas of test use. Ethical standards require counselors to recognize the limits of their competence and to act accordingly. Virtually all states require the certification of counselors who practice in the public schools. Certification requires at least basic preparation in testing. A violation of ethical practice is usually sufficient cause to revoke any certification or license. Therefore, counselors are well advised to know their limitations and to practice only as they are qualified.

If the counseling profession is to meet public expectations, its members must understand what it is that counselors ought to do and then prepare themselves so that they can function accordingly. No longer can educators move into counseling positions without full and adequate preparation to insure their competence. The 1973 ACES standards represent the best thinking of the profession to date regarding the preparation of counselors.[7] Eugene T. Buckner

---

[7] Association for Counselor Education and Supervision, "Standards for the Preparation of Counselors and Other Personnel Services Specialists," *Personnel and Guidance Journal* 55 (June 1977): 599–601.

has suggested ways in which counselors can place their profession on a more sound basis:

1. Counselors should survey their own ranks to see that those occupying counseling positions have the training and expertise necessary to perform those duties proposed by professional counseling organizations.
2. Counselors prepared to function as qualified professionals should actively acquaint administrators, teachers, students, and parents with the accepted professional code.
3. Counselors should attend workshops and training programs and participate in professional organizations that will help them develop and maintain their skills.
4. Counselors in individual schools should sponsor programs designed to demonstrate to teachers, administrators, students, and parents the services that they can offer.[8]

Counselors must contribute substantially to the total mission of the school if they are to maintain their hard-earned and necessary reputation as an asset to and an essential component of education.

THE TEACHER

Teachers play an important role in guidance in every school. Many schools do not provide the services of trained counselors at the lower grade levels, and at the secondary level, particularly in small schools, counseling may be so inadequate that a major guidance and testing burden falls on the classroom teacher. Teachers who employ tests should be able to make observations and decisions about students that have a great degree of accuracy and significance. A teacher needs to know how to use tests to solve practical problems and to plan instruction. A teacher also needs to know how to formulate classroom examinations that evaluate and build on what students have learned.

The teacher must be familiar with the procedures for combining test scores for rating classroom and laboratory performance, and other means of obtaining valid, fair, and reasonably accurate estimates of performance. A teacher also must know how to select

---

[8] Eugene T. Buckner, "Accountable to Whom? The Counselor's Dilemma," *Measurement and Evaluation in Guidance* 8 (October 1975): 191.

standardized tests. Furthermore, teachers must be able to talk intelligently with parents, school administrators, counselors, and school psychologists about the achievements and accomplishments of students and to understand and use the products of research reported in professional educational journals.

Since the early 1960s, there has been evidence of movement toward a closer association between testing and teaching practices. Nowhere has this been more apparent than in the individualization of instruction through the use of carefully programmed instructional materials that make repeated checks of attainment. Teachers usually have minimal preparation in the use of tests and measurements before they start to teach. Teacher education programs are still weak in testing and measurement, in spite of the fact that teachers remain the largest single group of consumers of test data, both the standardized and homemade varieties. Training has improved. Nevertheless, teachers must become better prepared to develop and use tests and test data within the next decade, the indifference of teacher education programs not withstanding. Failure to make the classroom teacher an efficient partner in the total appraisal enterprise of the school can result in its untimely and regrettable demise.

THE STUDENT

The development of sound student-teacher-counselor relationships rests on the recognition by each that they are working toward a common goal: the student's immediate and ultimate welfare. However, few persons, children or adults, are so secure that they can contemplate taking any test without some feelings of personal threat. Because poor performance on a test may incur the displeasure of parents, teachers, and others, lower prestige among peers, and cause a loss of self-esteem, it is not hard to understand the anxiety that testing may produce. Text anxiety is a fact in the lives of children. Persistent efforts must be made to reduce this effect and to lessen undue competitiveness in testing. The improper use of tests that can produce and stimulate excessive tension stems largely from the students' failure to understand the proper role of tests and teachers' and counselors' failure to understand the emotional problems posed for some children by any ego-threatening evaluation.

Most testing can be conducted in such a fashion as to elicit willing and interested cooperation: if tests are used for legitimate instructional, counseling, or administrative purposes; if students are told why the tests are being used and how they contribute to self-understanding; and if counselors and teachers interpret and use the results to benefit the students. What a counselor or teacher says to students before or during testing is much less important in creating attitudes on the part of students toward testing than what that professional does after testing. It is in the actual use of the test results that the counselor and teacher reveal the real purposes of testing, and it is here that students must be convinced that testing is done for their benefit.

Leo Goldman suggested that if test results are to influence behavior, students must understand and be willing to accept the interpretations and the implications of the scores.[9] Yet, how often do students respond with resistance, rationalization, and defensiveness? When they do, the test data are probably wasted. It makes sense to establish acceptance of the test before it is administered. Students should be helped to identify pertinent questions to bring to a test interpretation—some doubt or a tentative plan needing confirmation. Unless the process in which test results are reported and discussed touches something of recognized importance to them—values, goals, feelings, or self-concept—it is not likely to make much difference to them.

Finally, if tests are to have a place in counseling and the education process, they should contribute to behavior change. Such change cannot be expected in all cases, but change should be a more frequent outcome than is often the case today. If tests were used more selectively, and if persons tested were actively involved in determining the need for testing, had some understanding of its purpose, and had demonstrated some willingness to receive the results, more change would be realized. The entire testing process requires the active collaboration of the student.

THE PARENT

Modern educational practice emphasizes the importance of bringing parents as partners into the business of education. The school and the home should have a common understanding of the ability, achievement, and interests of a student. Many parents are curious

---

[9] Leo Goldman, "Tests Should Make a Difference," pp. 53–59.

about testing programs, and most parents are interested in learning about information that concerns their child. Many parents can be helped to become more effective in cooperating with the school and its objectives.

Those who work with children and adolescents should be well aware of the fact that often the parents rather than the children are most in need of information provided by tests and other appraisal methods. Certainly, the school is responsible for keeping parents informed of the progress of their children. Therefore, test data should be shared with parents. However, the effective reporting of test results to parents requires careful education about tests and their use. Test publishers and others have tried hard to help parents understand what testing in schools is all about, but published resource materials mean little unless schools make an effort to enlighten parents in this regard.

In communicating test information to parents, counselors often make the mistake of assuming that a parent, unlike a child, is reasonable and objective about the matter. Frequently this is not the case. Counselors and teachers must spend enough time with parents to deal with their feelings about their children's test data (see the guidelines at the end of Chapter 5). Parents should be provided with as much information as they need and can understand to be effective in helping their child develop.

A group meeting with parents to discuss broad topics concerning an appraisal program should help parents acquire a general understanding of the program and should offer background information for individual conferences on test interpretation. Furthermore, some schools have found that parents appreciate the opportunity to take samples of the ability, achievement, and interest measures used with their children. However, the parent conference is the crucial vehicle for helping parents understand and accept test results.

Parents can and do make significant contributions to their child's developing self-concept. If these contributions are to be supportive and are to help the student develop a realistic picture of his or her abilities and achievements, parents must be consulted and informed from the primary grades onward as they, with counselors, teachers, and others, seek to achieve a growing understanding of a particular child's development. Ability and achievement testing, and later interest assessment, can contribute to this process. Parents and school personnel may help one another place appraisal data in their proper perspective together with many other facts about a child's growth and development. The parent-school partnership should be a continuous venture, one that lasts from the preschool through the secondary school years.

INTERPRETATION
AND USE OF TEST DATA

Chapters 3 and 4 dealt with the technology of test evaluation and test score interpretation. This material is crucial to this discussion. We have made suggestions in each chapter for interpreting and using various tests and other assessment techniques. We shall now present some general considerations for interpreting and using appraisal data. Some of them repeat points made earlier in order to provide a summary of principles that we believe to be essential to the appropriate use of appraisal data by counselors. These remarks are intended for all who make use of tests, but the needs and responsibilities of the school counselor are particularly emphasized.

The interpretation and use of standardized test results are crucial topics facing educators in today's schools. They are among the most difficult topics to discuss, primarily because of the many variables to be considered. If such discussions are to have any effect, it is necessary to specify the kind of test under discussion and whether or not the test yields a single-score or a multiscore profile of scores derived from a battery of related tests. The purpose of the analysis of test data is to produce individual and group results for clear interpretation and practical application. Although each interpretation is unique, counselors must plan to interpret the results to themselves, to one another, to their students, and to the parents of their students.

These principles should be observed in using and interpreting test data: (1) use the best available test for the purpose; (2) make certain that you are competent to interpret the data; (3) consider test data in the context of all other available information; (4) interpret test results and other evaluation data in terms of probabilities rather than certainties; (5) make certain that evaluation data help meet a need and are presented objectively and impersonally and that you encourage students to make their own interpretations and express their reactions; (6) interpret with special caution data from all tests on which students can vary their responses at will; (7) temper your approach with the realization that a student may react emotionally to the test data; (8) use both group and individual approaches to help students engage in self-appraisal and planning.

TEST SCORES

The meaning of a test score is determined by numerous factors. The pattern into which the score is fitted must be constructed from all the quantitative and qualitative data known about a student. This process requires subjective interpretation by the counselor. Inappropriate use of test scores most often results not from faulty tests or test scores but from the lack of preparation or experience or both on the part of the counselor, teacher, or administrator responsible for interpreting the data. In interpreting test scores, all evidence at hand and all possible avenues of investigation should be used. Such procedures are essential if evaluations and predictions are to be reliable. Furthermore, interpretations should be directed toward positive and constructive action. They should be factual rather than judgmental. Test results and other evidence should be reported truthfully and accurately, and the objective should always be to work with the student to realize common goals. Testing will be more significant to students and others if they can realize something in terms of the outcome and uses of the testing. Any report, of course, must be adapted to the maturity of the individual.

Arnold J. Lien listed seven principles to follow in interpreting data to students, parents, and others:

1. Make sure that both the examiner and the person to whom test results are interpreted have a clear, immediate goal in mind that serves as a reason for the interpretation.
2. Avoid the use of specific scores whenever possible.
3. Never discuss the implication of scores in terms of absolute answers.
4. Concentrate on increasing understanding rather than posing as an expert.
5. Remember that understanding and acceptance are not synonymous.
6. Never directly compare one student with another.
7. After the tests have been interpreted, continue the discussion with the student and/or the student's parents if necessary.[10]

USE WITH STUDENTS AND PARENTS

An effective interpreter understands a student and his or her parents. Accepting a student's perceptions, feelings, and ideas as well as those of the parents can improve the effectiveness of test reporting. To accept a student's or a parent's right to argue with the test's

[10] Arnold J. Lien, *Measurement and Evaluation of Learning*, 2nd ed. (Dubuque, Iowa: W. C. Brown, 1971), p. 259.

implications or to aspire too high or too low or to choose a school program or occupation that is inappropriate is not the same as approving of or agreeing with these choices. Rather, such acceptance illustrates: first, an expression of the humanistic regard for other people; second, an appreciation of some facts about human behavior; and third, a belief that, in the long run, counselors and teachers should work with rather than against students and their families.

USE WITH TEACHERS
AND OTHER PROFESSIONALS

Counselors have a splendid opportunity to enlarge the effectiveness of tests by communicating findings to teachers, administrators, and other professionals. Some large-scale testing programs have encouraged reports to teachers and administrators by providing forms for that purpose and, in some instances, statistical summaries of test results for entire classes and grades in a school. On occasion, counselors make formal reports of test results for other counselors, psychiatrists, or social workers. A number of problems can arise in connection with this practice. Each school or school corporation must establish a general policy regarding what kinds of information to release, to whom, and with what provisions. Judgments must be made for each case. Unfortunately, all too frequently, confidential information is released indiscriminately or to unqualified individuals.

USE WITH THE COMMUNITY AT LARGE

Recently, the concern, interest, and participation of the public in school matters have increased tremendously. These developments have affected the work of all school personnel, but their effects have been felt most strongly by administrators and others in supervisory positions whose job it is to explain and to justify what schools are attempting to accomplish and to present evidence that these objectives are, in fact, being achieved. When people ask about their children's education, the results of testing programs are among the first kinds of evidence to be presented. Evaluation and measurement provide an excellent means of interpreting schools to the community.

However, this use of test data creates additional problems. One is the tendency of the community or individuals to react negatively to test results that do not support what they want to believe. Also, the public may not understand the terms and concepts used in measurement and the meaning of different types of test scores. Public reports of data related to the appraisal of a school's students may mislead more than inform. Nonetheless, it seems reasonable to believe that appraisal data, when properly presented and understood, can be useful in interpreting schools to the community.

Data must be tallied for each class and school, and separately for significant subtests and for the test as a whole. Interest scores ordinarily should be converted to relevant scores for a particular grade. In each instance, measures of central tendency and variability should be obtained for each student group. Emphasis should be placed on interpretive reporting of group results to show what the scores signify in terms of progress toward realizing school objectives or vocational plans.

Individual test results must never be made public. A school has many confidences to keep. Through testing and daily exposure to students, school administrators, teachers, and especially counselors inevitably come to know a great deal of private information. Seldom should an individual's accomplishments be made public, except for announcing a prize or a scholarship.

USE IN CONTEXT

Tests are designed to show what an individual can do at a given time. Tests cannot tell why a student performs as he or she does. To answer that question, it is necessary to investigate the individual's background, motivation, and other pertinent details. Nor can tests tell how able a student from a minority cultural or educational background might have been if he or she had been reared in a more conventional environment. Moreover, tests cannot compensate for cultural differences. On the contrary, tests should reveal such differences so that appropriate remedial steps can be taken. To conceal the effects of cultural differences by rejecting tests or trying to devise tests that are insensitive to such effects can only retard progress toward a genuine solution of social problems. While social stereotypes may distort interpersonal evaluations, tests can provide a safeguard against favoritism and arbitrary or capricious decisions. With regard to personnel selection, tests can serve an important function in preventing irrelevant and unfair discrimination. They also provide a quantitative index of the extent of any cultural handicap as a necessary first step in remedial programs.

EXPECTANCY TABLES

An expectancy table is a useful device for communicating test results and giving meaning to test interpretation. It also helps teachers, counselors, and others identify which students are performing below, at, or above expectations. Technically, an expectancy table shows the relationship between performance level intervals and criterion categories. Counselors with no special training in testing or statistics can make expectancy tables. Especially helpful in doing so is Bulletin 38 of the Psychological Corporation Test Service (see Chapter 4).

An expectancy table should include a large number of students and should be kept up to date with as much correct data as possible. A counselor must compare current students with previous students of similar age or grade in performance on the variables under consideration. School counselors can build expectancy tables for teachers to use for a grade or in certain subjects.

Howard B. Lyman recommends that, in interpreting the results of an expectancy table, counselors should:

1. Use the same test (including the same form, level, edition).
2. Understand that the table is based on past results and may not be relevant to an individual at present.
3. Be aware that an expectancy table based on the performance of people from another office, company, school, or college may not apply.
4. Realize that more confidence can be placed in expectancy levels that are based on large numbers of scores (percentages are sometimes used to disguise small numbers).
5. Use expectancy tables to spot individuals (or subgroups) that do not perform as expected, and noting instances in which predictions miss, check back to discover possible reasons for the failure.
6. Think of an expectancy table as a set of norms in which one's test score is compared with a criterion performance of others who have made the same score.[11]

MISUSE OF DATA

There may be more misinformation in circulation concerning the use and misuse of tests than on any other subject in the counseling

[11] Howard B. Lyman, *Test Scores and What They Mean*, 2nd ed. (Englewood Cliffs, N.J.: Prentice-Hall, 1976), p. 70.

field. Different opinions are that tests are good, bad, immoral, unfair, un-American, useless, infallible. Tests, of course, are none of these things. A test is merely a sample of behavior taken under standardized conditions from which other behavior is inferred.

Tests are only devices for making observations. It is only when the users of test information make inferences from these observations that the possibility arises of being unjust, biased, or just plain mistaken. To allow test scores to outweigh other judgmental data, or to ignore test scores in favor of other judgmental data, is to misuse these scores. Counselors must apply stringent requirements to the use of information gained from tests. George Hill suggested that counselors ask these questions about appraisal data: Is this information true? Is this information fresh? Is this information developmental? Is this information complete?[12] Test information never constitutes an end in itself but is merely a tool to be used to attain important counseling goals. Counselors should always involve the student and significant others in an active interpretation of the test information.

There are many ways to improve the use of testing. Henry S. Dyer recommended looking beyond the numbers and viewing tests as an integral part of the educational process.[13] Mastering statistical thinking and drawing careful inferences are fundamental to the proper use of test results; the failure to do so demonstrates a lack of professional responsibility (see principles 5 and 14 in Chapter 1). However, a test score indicates more than probabilities. It points inward to the mental processes and attitudes that generated the score. Educators too often neglect such meanings.

Neither published research nor informal observation offers assurance that tests necessarily result in changes in behavior. Tests may have little impact on students' thinking, self-concepts, or planning. Goldman said that any significant improvement will have to come from the ways in which counselors, teachers, and others use tests rather than from changes in tests themselves.[14] Tests have been greatly refined, especially during the past twenty-five years. Test publishers now provide a good deal of information about the reliability and validity of their tests, as well as more adequate normative information. A main problem that remains today is that tests continue to be misused.

[12] Hill "Standards for Test Users," 1969.
[13] Henry S. Dyer, "Needed Changes to Sweeten the Impact of Testing," in *Perspectives in Educational and Psychological Measurement,* ed. Glenn H. Bracht, Kenneth D. Hopkins, and Julian C. Stanley (Englewood Cliffs, N.J.: Prentice-Hall, 1972), pp. 321–327.
[14] Goldman, "Tests Should Make a Difference," 1969.

The potential of tests will be realized only when they are used to do more than just assess the status quo. Tests have a large role to play in helping counselors assess students' minds and attitudes in order to help them understand their behavior and to make better choices and predictions regarding this behavior.

ASSESSMENT IN
GUIDANCE ACCOUNTABILITY PROGRAMS

In the last few years, the people responsible for educational programs, including guidance, have begun to demonstrate more formally the outcome of their efforts. This effort is summed up by the term accountability. *Accountability* refers to a set of procedures that collate information about outcomes and costs of facilitating decision-making. Applied to guidance programs, it involves (1) defining the objectives of guidance, (2) establishing and conducting practices that enable the objectives to be met, (3) assessing how well the objectives were met, (4) determining program costs, (5) judging whether the outcomes were worth the costs, and (6) planning and devising methods based on evaluative data.

A commonly used approach to accountability has been the planning-programming-budgeting system (PPBS), which is similar to management-by-objectives long used in business and industry. PPBS allocates resources so as to maximize benefits at reasonable cost. It provides a structured mechanism for identifying needs, planning programs, choosing among various courses of action, allocating and controlling resources, and evaluating outcomes.

John D. Krumboltz has proposed a system of accountability that enables counselors to (1) obtain feedback on the results of their work, (2) select counseling methods on the basis of demonstrated success, (3) identify students with needs that have not been met, (4) devise short cuts for routine operations, (5) support increased staffing to reach attainable goals, and (6) request training for problems requiring new competencies.[15] The accountability system suggested by Krumboltz is a method of summarizing accomplishments and failures, specifying how much each costs and recommending changes to correct deficiencies. The system requires counselors to record their activities each day, collect information about the outcome of their work, acquire information from others about what

[15] John D. Krumboltz, "An Accountability Model for Counselors," *Personnel and Guidance Journal* 52 (June 1974): 639–646.

their counselees are doing, and disseminate all this information to the public. None of this is easy. It takes time, particularly if the research is done systematically, as it should be. Continuous experimentation is necessary if the benefits of becoming accountable are to outweigh the costs.

There are many accountability models that can provide counselors with ongoing, process-based information. Daniel Stufflebeam described and illustrated several models.[16] They all call for continuously monitoring specific objectives rather than waiting until the end of a program for outcome data to be determined and evaluated. At each program stage, inputs, processes, and outputs are established to enable counselors and others to analyze what they are doing, to estimate how well it is being done, and to introduce any needed modifications.

Gerald J. Pine noted that measuring the outcomes of counseling is essentially the same as measuring human behavior, for if counseling is successful, positive behavioral changes take place.[17] The objective measurement of behavioral change involves first selecting appropriate evaluative criteria. Some of the more common criteria that have been employed in guidance programs are (1) later success in college and at work, (2) salary in later life, (3) job satisfaction ratings, (4) fewer expressed problems, (5) realistic educational or vocational plans, (6) academic achievements, (7) increases in grade-point average, (8) improved peer relationships, (9) improved school attendance, (10) improved school attitudes, (11) improved self-concepts or self-understanding, and (12) reduction of inappropriate behavior. Most of these and other criteria set forth in the counseling literature have not yielded data that demonstrate conclusively that counseling is helpful. Pine explained this by suggesting that such criteria have not been extracted from a client's unique situation. He recommended the use of flexible criteria that encompass the diversity and complexity of human behavior. Recognition of that need is but the first step; accomplishing it is far from easy.

Ronald D. Redick compiled a list of measurement devices used in evaluating guidance programs.[18] Some thirty sources of information were identified, in addition to those presented in Buros' *Mental Measurements Yearbooks*. Among the devices that Redick

---

[16] Daniel Stufflebeam, *Education Evaluation and Decision Making* (Itasca, Ill.: F. E. Peacock, 1971).

[17] Gerald J. Pine, "Evaluating School Counseling Programs: Retrospect and Prospect," *Measurement and Evaluation in Guidance* 8 (October 1975): 136–144.

[18] Ronald D. Redick, "A Compilation of Measurement Devices Compendia," *Measurement and Evaluation in Guidance* 8 (October 1975): 193–202.

and Buros present are behavior rating scales, rating forms, cumulative records, sociometric scales, standardized tests, self-esteem inventories, school records, career development questionnaires, and personality scales. Stanley Bernknopf and his associates thought that the weakest element in counseling research has been the inadequacy of the available instrumentation, largely a result of the uniqueness of the variables under investigation.[19] Bernknopf and his associates presented a scale for assessing twenty-three guidance goals—such as self-awareness, decision-making, career development, and interpersonal relationships—and explained how scale items were selected and validated.

Careful attention must be given by counselors to any standardized measure employed in evaluating guidance programs. Reliability, validity, measurement error, and other technical considerations must be taken into account. These considerations apply equally to measures devised by counselors themselves. From a variety of viewpoints, including ethical and legal ones, counselors must strive to demonstrate the efficacy of their work. Efforts to do so are being made, but the field as a whole at present lacks specific criteria to be applied toward developing useful instruments.

ETHICAL
AND LEGAL CONSIDERATIONS

Ethics are principles or standards of conduct that are based on a commonly accepted set of values. Ethical standards are generally formulated in terms of a code of ethics. Two such codes relevant to the selection and use of tests by counselors and others are those sponsored by the American Psychological Association[20] and the American Personnel and Guidance Association.[21] These codes generally recognize the fact that counselors have ethical obligations to students, to parents, to the profession, to institutions, and to the community or to society at large. It is not easy to make ethical decisions when such obligations conflict.

Codes of ethics set forth broad guidelines for ethical decisions, but seldom are they detailed enough to apply to specific situations.

[19] Stanley Bernknopf, Duane Hartley, and William B. Ware, "Developing A Needs-Based Guidance System: A Psychometric Approach," *Measurement and Evaluation in Guidance* 8 (October 1975): 180–186.

[20] American Psychological Association, *Ethical Standards of Psychologists* (Washington, D.C.: the Association, 1973).

[21] American Personnel and Guidance Association, *Ethical Standards* (Washington, D.C.: the Association, 1974).

Counselors must make complex ethical decisions on the basis of their own internalized ethical system. In essence, an ethical system represents a hierarchy of values that permits choices to be made based on distinguished levels of right or wrong.

Standards for the educational and psychological use of tests have been developed jointly by the American Psychological Association, the American Educational Research Association, and the National Council on Measurement in Education. An abstracted version of these standards is presented in Appendix B. They urge testers to protect subjects, to make test scores available only to authorized persons, to interpret results soundly and professionally, and to view scores in the context of other relevant information about a subject. These standards provide a means of attaining a reasonable balance between finding out all that is of value about a subject and protecting a subject from undue intrusion.

Test users must be alert to the harmful consequences of test use. Robert Ebel has pointed out ways to avoid them.

1. Emphasize the use of tests to improve status and deemphasize their use to determine status.
2. Broaden the base of achievements tested to recognize and develop the wide variety of talents needed in our society.
3. Share openly with the persons directly concerned all that a test reveals about their abilities and prospects.
4. Decrease the use of tests to impose decisions on others; increase their use as a basis for better decision-making.[22]

The main factors controlling the quality of standardized tests are the integrity of their publishers and the competence of their authors, including their skill in test construction and their sensitivity to the criticism of their colleagues. Some tests on the market are below standard. Too many buyers and users of tests are relatively untrained in test theory and practice, and uniform standards of quality control, such as those applied in the manufacture and sale of drugs, are lacking. However, most people who buy tests meet certain minimum qualifications. Some publishers classify their tests into levels with reference to user qualifications, ranging from educational achievement and vocational proficiency tests through group intelligence tests and interest inventories to such clinical

---

[22] Robert L. Ebel, "The Social Consequences of Educational Testing," in *Perspectives in Educational and Psychological Measurement*, ed. Glenn H. Bracht, Kenneth D. Hopkins, and Julian C. Stanley (Englewood Cliffs, N.J.: Prentice-Hall, 1972), p. 5.

instruments as individual intelligence tests and most personality tests. They also attempt to restrict the distribution of tests in order to maintain the security of test materials and to prevent their misuse.

Another professional responsibility concerns the marketing of experimental tests by authors and publishers. Tests should not be released prematurely for general use, nor should any claim be made regarding the merits of a test in the absence of objective evidence. When a test is distributed early for research only, this condition should be specified clearly, and the distribution of the test should be restricted accordingly.

The ethics of using standardized tests also call for maintaining the confidentiality of their nature and content until the tests are administered. Obviously, if persons who are to be tested have prior knowledge of the content of a test, standardized or otherwise, the results are invalid, and no comparison with norms is proper. An exception is the standardized diagnostic test. With this type of instrument, it may be permissible, under certain circumstances, to review the test with individuals to point out their errors. If students are to be permitted to review their diagnostic test results, two or more equivalent forms of the test should be available. If retesting is required, a different equivalent form can be used, thus minimizing the effect of familiarity. We do not mean to suggest that counselors should not analyze the results of standardized achievement tests to identify students' strengths and limitations. On the contrary, this is one of the most important uses for which test results can be employed.

The question often arises of how far one may go in providing students help with a standardized test. A good rule to follow is to allow no assistance of any kind with the problems on the test. Also, it is considered good practice not to answer any question regarding the test after the students have begun to work on it. In some cases, understanding and following directions are part of the test, and examiners are forbidden to elaborate on the instructions contained in the manual.

An ethical issue that arises in connection with personality tests in particular is that of *invasion of privacy*. Insofar as some tests of emotion, motivation, or attitude are necessarily disguised, subjects may reveal certain characteristics without realizing that they are doing so. For purposes of testing effectiveness, it may be necessary to keep examinees in ignorance of the ways in which their responses may be interpreted. Nevertheless, no one should be given a test under false pretenses. Although concerns about the invasion of privacy have been expressed most commonly about personality tests, they apply to any type of test. Moreover, any observation of behavior may yield information about individuals that they would prefer to conceal. All behavioral research presents the possibility of invasion of privacy. Conflicts of values may arise that must be resolved. Students are usually willing to reveal themselves in order to obtain help with problems. Counselors do not invade privacy when they have been freely admitted. Even under these conditions, however, students should be warned that in the course of testing or interviewing, they may reveal information about themselves without realizing that they are doing so. Furthermore, when testing is conducted for institutional purposes, the examinees should be fully informed about the uses that will be made of test scores.

Whatever the purposes of testing, the protection of privacy involves two key concepts: relevance and informed consent. Information that an individual is asked to reveal must be relevant to the stated purposes of the testing. Accordingly, examiners must ascertain the validity of tests for the particular diagnostic or predictive purpose for which they are used. The concept of informed consent also requires clarification. Implications in individual cases may call for the exercise of considerable professional judgment. The examinee should be informed about the purpose of testing, the kinds of data sought, and the use that will be made of the scores. This is not to imply, however, that people should be shown the test items in advance or told how specific responses will be scored.

In the case of children, special questions arise with regard to *parental consent*. Following an interdisciplinary conference, the Russell Sage Foundation published a set of *Guidelines for the Collection, Maintenance, and Dissemination of Pupil Records*.[23] These guidelines differentiated between informed consent—given by the child, his or her parents, or both—and representational consent— given by the parents to legally elected or appointed representatives, such as a school board. While avoiding rigid prescriptions, the guidelines suggest that for aptitude and achievement tests and similar instruments, representational consent should be sufficient, whereas personality assessment, for example, should require informed consent.

No longer can tests be used without carefully considering their effects on the individuals and institutions concerned. Counselors frequently should review their goals and priorities and the possible

---

[23] Russell Sage Foundation, *Guidelines for the Collection, Maintenance, and Dissemination of Pupil Records* (New York: Russell Sage Foundation, 1970).

effects of tests on the persons concerned. Though there is at present considerable concern over the social implications of testing, even more study of the uses and misuses of tests and their values and limitations is needed. These studies should be balanced and objective and made by persons both knowledgeable about testing and aware of the social context in which tests are used.

The problem of the *confidentiality of test data* also is complex. The fundamental question is: Who shall have access to test results? Several considerations influence the answer. Among them are the security of test content, the hazards of misunderstanding test scores, and the need of various persons to know the results. Confidentiality calls for a relative rather than an absolute commitment to maintaining the privacy of information.

At one level, confidentiality involves the professional use of information. Every counselor has an obligation to handle information about students in a professional way. Records, test scores, and other kinds of information should not be released without proper consent. This precludes furnishing information to people such as potential employers and others. Whenever there is doubt about the propriety of releasing information, counselors should obtain the consent of the student and/or his or her parents.

At another level, confidentiality relates to information derived from a counseling relationship. A student has the right to expect that such information will be used only to advance his or her welfare. It is often desirable to share certain information with persons who are working with a student or who have primary concern for that student. On the other hand, students may be extremely reluctant to have such information shared, even though it may be in their best interest. The best solution is to establish this level of confidentiality with clients quite specifically before accepting confidences.

The legal status of counselors varies from state to state and from time to time. As a rule, counselors do not enjoy privileged communication, which is a legal status granted to certain kinds of relationships. Professionals who can extend privileged communication may refuse to testify in court against a client. Even though counselors do not have privileged communication in most states (twenty-five states have enacted laws, but few have been tested), they do have certain legal rights as witnesses of which they should be aware.

The issue of confidentiality of assessment records usually assumes the existence of a third person other than the examinee, his or her parents, and the examiner. The underlying principle is that such records should not be revealed to a third party without the knowledge and consent of the individual tested and/or his or her parents. When tests are administered in an institutional context, at the time of testing the individuals tested or their parents should be informed of the purposes of the test, the uses to which the results will be put, and the availability of the results to institutional personnel who have a legitimate need for them. Another problem pertains to the retention of records in institutions. On the one hand, longitudinal records on individuals can be valuable. On the other hand, the availability of old records opens the way for such misuses as incorrect inferences from obsolete data and unauthorized access to the records. To prevent such misuses, when records are retained either for legitimate longitudinal use or for acceptable research purposes, access should be subject to stringent controls.

There has been a growing awareness of the right of individual students to have *access to the findings* of their test reports. Students should also have the opportunity to comment on the contents of the report and to clarify or correct factual information. The parent's right of access to a minor child's record must also be preserved. This may present a possible conflict with a student's own right of privacy, especially in the case of older children. However, the question is not whether to communicate test results to a parent of a minor but how to do so. Parents usually have a legal right to information about their child; most often it is desirable for them to have such information.

Conversations with parents can provide counselors with a source of background data. They also provide an opportunity to enlist parental cooperation in promoting a student's welfare and development. The Department of Health, Education and Welfare's regulations governing the privacy rights of students and parents and access to educational records according to the 1974 Buckley amendment should be observed.

Publishers' *standardized tests are copyrighted material.* No part of any such test may be copied, duplicated, or reproduced in any form without the written permission of the holder of the copyright. A test represents the work of several persons over several years, as well as the expenditure of thousands of dollars. To reproduce tests or accompanying materials without the permission of the authors and/or the publisher is not only unlawful but also unethical, because it deprives those who have produced the test of the economic fruits of their labor.

Since the early 1950s, there has been increased public concern with the *rights of minorities and special interest groups,* a concern that is reflected in the enactment of civil rights legislation at both federal and state levels. As a mechanism for improving educational and vocational opportunities, testing has been a major focus of attention. Specifically, many people are concerned that cultural conditions affect the development of aptitudes, interests, motivation, and attitudes and, therefore, impact the test scores of minority students. Differences in experience and background are certainly manifested in test results. Insofar as culture affects behavior, its influence will and should be detected by test data. If all cultural differences were eliminated from a test, the validity of the test might be diminished.[24]

It is important to differentiate between factors that affect both test and criterion behavior and those that influence only the test itself. Specific effort should be made to reduce the impact of test-related factors when testing persons from culturally different backgrounds. Certain test content may also influence test scores in ways that are unrelated to criterion performance. Many test publishers now make special efforts to weed out potentially offensive, culturally restrictive, or stereotypical material. Test content is regularly reviewed to remove material that may be detrimental to the performance of minority or special-interest group members. In testing such students, it is important to avoid possible misinterpretation of test scores. An examiner may use general norms, subgroup norms based on persons with comparable backgrounds, or an individual's own previous scores, depending on the purpose of the test.

Several states enacted legislation to establish fair employment practices commissions (FEPC) prior to the development of such legal mechanisms at the federal level. Among the most pertinent federal legislation is that established by the Equal Employment Opportunity Act (Title VII of the Civil Rights Act of 1964 and its subsequent amendments) and the establishment of the Equal Employment Opportunity Commission (EEOC). When charges are filed, the EEOC investigates the complaint and, if it finds the charges to be justified, attempts to correct the situation through conferences and voluntary compliances. If these procedures fail, the EEOC may hold hearings, issue cease-and-desist orders, and, finally, bring action in the federal courts. In states having an approved FEPC, the federal commission defers to the local agency.

The Office of Federal Contract Compliance (OFCC) has the authority to monitor the use of tests for employment purposes by

---

[24] Association for Measurement and Evaluation in Guidance, "The Responsible Use of Tests," *Measurement and Evaluation in Guidance* 5 (July 1972): 388–390.

government contractors. Colleges and universities are among the institutions concerned with OFCC regulations, because they receive many research and training grants from federal sources. Both the EEOC and OFCC have drawn up essentially identical guidelines regarding the testing of employees and other selection procedures.

The Equal Employment Opportunity Act prohibits discrimination by employers, trade unions, or employment agencies on the basis of race, color, religion, sex, or national origin. Only properly conducted testing programs are acceptable under this act. The same regulations specified for tests apply as well to other formal and informal selection procedures, such as educational or occupational requirements, interviews, and application forms. When the use of a test (or other selection procedure) results in a significantly higher rejection rate for minority or other special-interest candidates than for others, its utility must be justified by evidence of predictive validity for the job in question. In outlining acceptable procedures for establishing validity, the EEOA guidelines makes explicit reference to the *Standards for Educational and Psychological Tests* (1974). In dealing with affirmative action, the guidelines note that even when selection procedures have been validated satisfactorily, if disproportionate rates result for minorities and other special-interest groups, action must be taken to reduce this discrepancy, including instituting training programs.

In recent years, the issue of *discrimination* based on sex has become a subject of national importance. Title IX of the Educational Amendments Act of 1972, which took effect in July 1975, provides that no person shall be excluded on the basis of sex from participation in or be subjected to discrimination under any educational program receiving federal assistance. Every institution that receives federal funds must: evaluate its policies and practices as to their compliance with the regulation; modify its policies and practices as necessary for compliance; take appropriate remedial steps to notify applicants for admission and/or employment; and notify students, parents, employees and all unions or professional organizations holding bargaining or professional agreements of their compliance with Title IX. Vehicles and procedures for continuing policy review are specified.

In recent years, the issue of possible sex bias in interest measurement has received special attention. The Association for Measurement and Evaluation in Guidance (AMEG) Commission on Sex Bias in Measurement has been asked by the Office for Civil Rights (OCR) to consider requirements that interest inventory scores on profiles based on other-sex norms be provided to counselees along with same-sex norms.[25] Females generally score low in comparison with male norms for scales relating to mechanical, technical, scientific, and business-contact areas and score high in comparison with male norms related to the arts and social service. Converse results are usually found for males when their scores are profiled on female norms.

The AMEG commission does not support the position that students should be informed of scores based only on same-sex norms; instead, the commission believes that knowledge of how scores differ when profiled on other-sex norms, accompanied by an explanation of why these differences occur, can be important to the student in understanding and dealing with gender differences in measured interests. On the other hand, the commission concluded that counselees do not necessarily have to take other-sex norms into consideration in career planning. Such information should be made available mainly as supporting information. Any interpretative information accompanying interest score reports should make this distinction clear.

These new *legal ramifications* make it all the more important for counselors to adhere to the precepts of appropriate test selection and usage. If those in the profession do not set standards, others are likely to move to fill the void. If counselors fail to make specific consideration of findings obtained from minority, special-interest, ethnic, or sex group members, then the ethical and legal use of tests will be mandated by authorities outside the profession. If counselors fail to take appropriate action now, testing could become an academic exercise controlled by government fiat.

ISSUES

1.   School testing programs should include the use of ability and achievement tests and other relevant measures in all grades in order to promote the individualization of the educational program afforded each child. Furthermore, such programs should be determined by test specialists and should involve components that are state-wide and national in scope.

   Yes, because:

   1. Objective appraisal data accumulated annually provide a sound basis for monitoring the educational growth of each

---

[25] Esther Diamond, Lenore Harmon, and Donald Zytowski, *Guidepost* (September 1976): 2.

child and enhance predictions made about the educational needs and probable accomplishments of children in school.

2. Teachers have limited sophistication in evaluating the achievement of students. Test data are needed to fill this void.

3. Program planning should be directed by specialists in testing, because they have expertise that others lack. Moreover, large-scale testing programs should yield findings of greater value than those of local programs, because the former provide a more comprehensive data base for interpreting an individual's performance.

No, because:
1. Teacher evaluations of student behavior cannot be ignored. Annual testing can produce redundant data. Provided that teachers are trained to evaluate their students effectively, annual testing that supplements teacher appraisal is not defensible.

2. Survey testing of children should be viewed as a periodic comparative check on the cumulative evaluations made by teachers of students' progress. Only relevant survey testing at critical transition points throughout a child's educational experience is defensible.

3. Large-scale testing programs are secondary in importance to those evaluations required by a local school that address issues of importance to the community.

Discussion:
Testing programs should bear on local needs and should recognize the crucial contributions provided by classroom teachers. Informed and selective use should be made of standardized survey tests only at critical transition points in the educational history of the individual. Participation in large-scale testing programs by local schools should be endorsed only when the data thus obtained may be used by the school to evaluate the efficacy of its curriculum compared to that of other schools. Annual participation in large-scale testing programs is counterproductive, but periodic involvement may be beneficial. We endorse the primacy of locally determined school testing programs. Furthermore, we think that limited use should be made of standardized tests; however, when such tests are employed, they should be selected wisely and with care, and the data that they yield should be employed thoroughly and appropriately.

2. *Appraisal data should be employed to establish an objective basis for determining the accountability of the school to the various publics it serves.*

Yes, because:

1. Objectivity is vital in any evaluation of accountability. Tests are the most objective data source for this purpose.
2. Regardless of subcultural differences, tests and other objective appraisal data provide a relevant index of a student's preparation for participating in and contributing to modern technological society.
3. Schools must use all appropriate resources at their disposal to demonstrate accountability to the publics that they serve.

No, because:

1. Appraisal data should not employed for purposes for which their use was not initially intended.
2. Appraisal data should help students make decisions. They may not provide an efficient means of evaluating the effectiveness of the curriculum of a given school in reflecting the needs of a local community.
3. Special circumstance may require that appraisal data be used in evaluating the effectiveness of a given educational program. However, all persons associated with such a venture should be informed clearly in advance of the purposes and objectives of such an assessment.

Discussion:

The efficacy of any educational program is difficult to establish. When employed to evaluate the accomplishments of a school, test and other objective appraisal data may contribute valuable information, provided such data are interpreted in light of the demographic characteristics and the environment of the modal student.

ANNOTATED REFERENCES

Anastasi, Anne. *Psychological Testing.* 4th ed. New York: Macmillan, 1976.

This edition merits special consideration because of Chapter 3 on the social and ethical implications of testing and the related materials presented in the Appendix. Although Anastasi writes as a psychologist who employs tests to serve others, her text easily can be related to the concerns of school counselors, teachers, administrators, and other related professionals.

Bracht, Glenn H.; Hopkins, Kenneth D.; and Stanley, Julian C., eds. *Perspectives in Educational and Psychological Measurement.* Englewood Cliffs, N.J.: Prentice-Hall, 1972.

This book of readings is a compilation of developments and discussions that complement introductory and intermediate textbooks in courses for measurement and evaluation. The readings relate to the practical problems of developing and using tests in education and psychology. Selections have been contributed by Anne Anastasi, John Dyer, Robert Ebel, Leo Goldman, David Goslin, John Lennon, and Leon Lessinger, among others.

Verheyden-Hilliard, Mary Ellen. *A Handbook for Workshops on Sex Equality Education.* Washington, D.C.: American Personnel and Guidance Association, 1976.

This handbook details experience gained by the Sex Equality in Guidance Opportunity Project staff via workshops conducted throughout the United States on sexual equality in education. The reader is provided with practical tools for conducting similar workshops locally. An extended series of appendices informs the reader about federal laws and guidelines, similar state regulations, and other data concerning the privileges and obligations of women pertaining to equality in education.

Zytowski, Donald G., ed. "Special Issue: Measurement and Evaluation in Guidance." *Measurement and Evaluation in Guidance* 8 (October 1975): 132–208.

Articles suggest means for evaluating guidance. The pieces by Lasser, Miller and Grisdale, and Pine have special references to the issues emphasized in this chapter; however, the entire issue contains much information about evaluation.

SELECTED REFERENCES

Cole, Nancy S. "On Measuring the Vocational Interests of Women." *Journal of Counseling Psychology* 20 (March 1973): 105–112.

Cook, Desmond. *A Systems Approach to the Development of Pupil Personnel Services. An Operating Manual.* Boston: Northeastern University, 1973.

Finley, Carmen J., and Berdie, Francis S. *The National Assessment Approach to Exercise Development.* Denver: National Assessment of Educational Progress, 1970.

Frisbie, David A. "Some Limitations of Expectancy Data Used with College-Level Course Placement." *Measurement and Evaluation in Guidance* 9 (January 1977): 166–171.

Green, D. R. *Racial and Ethnic Bias in Test Construction.* Monterey, Calif.: California Test Bureau/McGraw-Hill, 1973.

Harmon, Lenore W. "Sexual Bias in Interest Measurement." *Measurement and Evaluation in Guidance* 5 (January 1973): 496–501.

Kandor, Joseph R.; Kendall, David; and Suggs, Robert. "A Model for Improving Students' Test Experience Through Small Groups." *Measurement and Evaluation in Guidance* 9 (January 1977): 178–183.

Mehrens, William A. "The Consequence of Misusing Test Results." *The National Elementary Principal* 47 (1976): 62–64.

Mitchell, Anita, and Saum, J. *A Master Plan for Pupil Personnel Services.* Fullerton, Calif.: California Personnel and Guidance Association, 1972.

Popham, W. J. *Educational Evaluation.* Englewood Cliffs, N.J.: Prentice-Hall, 1975.

Stufflebeam, Daniel. *Educational Evaluation and Decision Making.* Itasca, Ill.: F. E. Peacock, 1971.

Weiss, C. H. *Evaluation Research: Methods for Assessing Program Effectiveness.* Englewood Cliffs, N.J.: Prentice-Hall, 1972.

Zytowski, Donald G., and Betz, E. L. "Measurement in Counseling Research: A Review." *Counseling Psychologist* 3, no. 1 (1972): 72–81.

Chapter 16   Trends in Assessment and Appraisal

What changes are expected to take place in assessment practices?

What changes may take place in standardized tests?

What trends can be expected in scoring services and interpretation practices?

What trends can be expected in educating counselors in assessment and appraisal?

> Behold the past, the many changes of dynasties,
> the future too you are able to foresee,
> for it will be like fashion, and it is
> impossible for the future to escape from
> the rhythm of the present.
>
> Marcus Aurelius, *circa* 160 A.D.

Marcus Aurelius's lines suggest that images of the future can be seen by examining what has been, and that any projection is derived from current practices and patterns. The hope of improving on past records is a constant motive force for all social scientists. The character and quality of assessment practices in years to come depend on decisions that are made by current theoreticians and practitioners.

Examination of the history of measurement is instructive: while the field has sometimes changed because of innovative ideas on the part of theorists, more often than not it has changed in response to social fluctuations, such as labor needs and demands during wars. Equally, it could be said that measurement innovations not only result from social change but that they, in turn, produce other changes. Change is incremental. Modifications that have been in the making for some years are more reliable bases for predictions than are trends that appear suddenly and then disappear all too quickly.

Forecasting trends in any endeavor quite often involves much wishful thinking, being based on what one wishes to happen rather than the direction that practices are actually taking. Identifying trends in assessment practices and procedures is subject to this same difficulty.

We believe that changes in assessment and appraisal practices will follow a cylical course. Therefore, we do not anticipate rapid, cataclysmic change. Sound assessment practices have a resilience that enables them to survive and endure. Time and space are powerful dimensions for generalization and projection. What *has* happened may continue to happen. What is happening *here* may happen over *there.* Our fifteen predictions, therefore, are to be viewed as projections based on current practices and promising research.

CONTINUED USE
OF STANDARDIZED TESTS

Standardized tests of ability, achievement, aptitude, interest and personality probably will continue to be relied on extensively in assessment practices. Recently, public scrutiny of standardized tests and their use has increased. This examination has produced sharp criticism and has even caused some professionals and their associations to propose abandoning tests and testing. Many would agree that most criticisms stem from the misuse of test data by counselors and those who use them for selection purposes. This is not to imply, however, that test improvements are unneeded in addition to changes by counselors and others in their use of test data for assessment purposes.

Counselors need test data in order to improve their work with students. Today, counselors in schools work with students who, as a group, exhibit wide ranges of ability and purpose. Moreover, these students and their parents seek assistance in and useful information for making educational and vocational choices. Consequently, there is an ever-present need for tests to assess abilities, interests, and aptitudes and for using these data for individual planning. We believe that comprehensive assessment is most economical, valid, and reliable when standardized test data are used in conjunction with reliable information obtained from other sources. Therefore, assessment will continue to depend to a great extent on standardized test data.

INCREASED USE
OF NON-TEST MEASURES

In the future, slowly increasing use will be made of non-test measures of behavior by counselors and other school personnel. At present, non-test measures of behavior have been relegated to the background, but growing discontent with standardized test data will bring into greater use interviews, rating scales, questionnaires, autobiographies, observation, anecdotal records, sociometrics, and other means of quantifying aspects of human behavior and drawing inferences from these estimates. Despite the great progress that has been made in testing, the variety of characteristics that can be measured by standardized instruments is far from comprehensive. Assessing a person's abilities and behavioral characteristics requires that counselors use more than testing procedures. It is true that all non-test techniques have defects that equal (and in most cases surpass) those of standardized measures of general ability, achievement, interest, personality, and aptitude, but they also have particular advantages. For example, questionnaires can reveal what a person has achieved, and interviews can uncover attitudes, ambitions, and other psychological information. Well-trained counselors, therefore, use a variety of techniques for gathering data about individuals they counsel, and they will continue to do so. Reliance on non-test measures will increase, and more efforts will be made to perfect these techniques so as to yield valid, reliable, and useful data for the use of clients, counselors, and others.

TESTS DESIGNED
FOR A SINGLE PURPOSE

Examination of current test publishing catalogs demonstrates that most nationally standardized tests are designed, advertised, sold, purchased, and used to serve multiple purposes. Many test authors might assert that their tests have been used for purposes for which they were never intended. In the future, more tests will be designed and published to serve a single purpose.

The current crop of tests is considerably improved over those in the past, especially in the relevance of their content and in the ingenuity of their authors. For example, achievement tests now being marketed seem better in assessing higher mental processes than they were in the past. Even greater improvements have taken place in the use of standardized achievement tests. Most of these tests should be administered early in the school year to serve as a guide in planning instructional activities; their results are being used more for formative than for summative evaluation purposes. Tests used this way can reveal strengths and weaknesses or unevenness of development, may lead to further, more specific, diagnostic development, and may result in more appropriate educational programming and in individual instructional and counseling services for individuals.

Associated with this trend of designing tests to serve specific purposes is the emerging development of individualized testing. Branching tests, tab tests, and applications of computer-mediated sequential testing are finding their way into practice in a growing number of situations. There are a few instances in which a short screening test is used to assign examinees to test levels. (In a way, this has been done for many years in the administration of the Stanford-Binet.) The hoped-for outcome is that each examinee takes the test that is least frustrating and most challenging, accurate, and appropriate.

This flexibility in test administration and selection causes numerous problems, including assigning students to levels, interpreting, scaling, norming, and communicating directions and interpretations. However, we believe that they are not insurmountable. A beginning has been made. The next step is to individualize by subtest and then to build different tests for different subpopulations with different needs. While many assert that these next steps cannot be taken, others suggest that they know how to do it and that the future will see the realization of their efforts.

IMPROVED DIAGNOSTIC TESTS

Diagnostic tests are designed to discover specific deficiencies in behaviors. The single total or composite score that most such tests yield is of little help to counselors, teachers, or the students they serve. Rather, the part scores or proportion of correct answers are more useful types of measures.

Currently, many of the tests used for diagnostic purposes in educational institutions are of a general type (that is, they yield a single total score as a measure of general achievement in an area). More diagnostic tests will be constructed that: (1) require responses to be made to problems approximating as closely as possible the functional; (2) are analytical and based on experimental evidence of learning difficulties and misunderstandings; (3) reveal the mental processes of the individual sufficiently to detect points of error; (4) suggest or provide specific remedial procedures for each error detected; and (5) cover a long sequence of learning sequentially. Current diagnostic tests deal almost exclusively with the more mechanical aspects of a learning sequence and neglect the higher abilities required in problem-solving. In the future, diagnostic tests will be constructed to reveal those factors that limit learning or functioning in a specific area.

INCREASED USE
OF MULTIPLE-SCORE TESTS

During the past five years, there has been an increasing number of tests that provide more than one score. This trend will continue. Currently, psychometrists disagree as to the value of multiple-score tests. Some prefer a good measure of a single dimension, given limited time for testing; others prefer several separate measurements. When separate measures are used, each score is derived from a relatively small sample of behavior and is, therefore, less accurate than single-dimensional measures. The dilemma has been stated by Lee J. Cronbach:

> Compressing behavior into one or two scores loses detailed information. But attempting to capture rich detail by using many scores, each from a small sample of behavior, gets poor information. A high school counselor would obviously prefer 10-minute tests of five abilities to a 50-minute test that samples mechanical reasoning exhaustively and tells nothing about verbal, numerical, abstract reasoning and clerical abilities. He risks getting flimsy data if he goes so far as to substitute ten 3-minute tests for the 30-minute MCT—but it is hard to define a perfect balance between breadth of coverage and precision.[1]

Cronbach also suggested that the classic psychometric ideal is an instrument with high fidelity and low band width, such as a college aptitude test. Furthermore, multiple-score tests, when profiled, are complex and overwhelm most users. But, given these philosophical and practical issues, we believe that more and more

---

[1] Lee J. Cronbach, *Essentials of Psychological Testing,* 3rd ed. (New York: Harper and Row, 1970), p. 180. Copyright, 1949 by Harper & Row, Publishers, Inc. Copyright © 1960, 1970 by Lee J. Cronbach. By permission of the publisher.

multiple-score tests will be constructed. The benefits of additional information seem to us to be preferable to incomplete pictures of the individual.

EXTENDED COMPUTER APPLICATIONS

Many test improvements have come as a direct outcome of technological progress in optical scanners and computers. Computers have made possible more complete, complex, and less costly analysis of try-out test data. The development of machine-scorable test booklets has made possible the use of item types previously regarded as impractical because of scoring problems. Moreover, computers are able to process items more quickly, more accurately, and at less cost than are other methods. These advantages are noteworthy, especially in the case of item responses that are weighted differentially or that require more complex scoring procedures.

The use of computers for test processing, scoring, and reporting makes possible the production of an almost unlimited quantity of individualized test reports to teachers, counselors, administrators, parents, and students. In fact, even now, test users are deluged with information, much of which they may not be in a position to interpret wisely to the examinees. The person who receives computer-designed test reports is in a position to consider alternatives; however, more scores may be reported at one time than can be used effectively. Future research may establish the optimal amount of information that can be processed and used by most individuals; more helpful yet, it may determine which information is most critical to an individual. In the future, computer-assisted interpretation and reporting procedures will be designed to emphasize the probable meaning of scores rather than simply present the scores themselves. Information pertinent to reasonable expectations about what persons within a given range of scores may do based on comparisons with others is likely to prove more helpful to the person than stereotyped trait descriptions.

The computer has a wide variety of psychometric applications, both practical and theoretical. Factor analysis of large test data matrices is now routine and economical. For example, Monte Carlo studies have contributed to better understanding and more practical use of test data. Moreover, large-scale psychometric research reports such as Project Talent and National Educational Assessment have been made possible by computers. To help counselors and other professionals, in the future computer applications must provide an efficient means of searching a vast body of data pertinent to decision-making. Finally, computer application provides the test user with the capacity to improve the accuracy of test data profiles. Such changes are already under way, but these applications are in their infancy. In this respect, Cronbach has stated:

> The theory of profile measurement is still undergoing development. . . . We would really like to know the person's profile of universe scores. One can estimate each point in that profile by combining all scores in the battery according to a formula. This profile, more accurate than in the profile directly observed, would not have quite the same shape as the profile in observed scores. (This improvement is too new to have been tested in practice. While the calculations are impractical when a test is hand-scored, they can easily be made a part of modern computerized scoring.)[2]

A major benefit to counselors is that computers have improved the system of reporting test scores so that their unreliability is kept in mind by those who receive and use the data. Moreover, computer-based interpretations and reports generally suggest verification of individual results by comparison with other data. Most of all, computer interpretations can do much to reinforce the idea that test scores are estimates and to urge the examinee to engage in further study and searching before making plans. Computers also make feasible more efficient standardization of tests and preparation of multiple norms. Data stored in computer memory banks on the characteristics of schools would provide a basis for selecting accurate, efficient samples on which to base comparisons. Even now, some nationally standardized batteries make routinely available the choice of such norms as national, regional, parochial, large city, and local. In the future, the possibilities of student, school, and item norms are almost unlimited.

Currently, programs such as those of the College Entrance Examination Board and the American College Testing Program, based on equations developed from applications of multivariate analysis, are being used to provide differential prediction of success in a wide variety of institutions, subjects, and circumstances. Particularly intriguing are M. R. Novick's applications of the Bayesian method of prediction.[3] This method is believed to be most suitable for

---

[2] Cronbach, *Essentials of Testing*, pp. 368–369. Copyright, 1949 by Harper & Row, Publishers, Inc. Copyright © 1960, 1970 by Lee J. Cronbach. By permission of the publisher.
[3] M. R. Novick et al., *Applications of Bayesian Methods to the Prediction of Educational Performance*, ACT Research Report no. 42 (Iowa City: The American College Testing Program, 1970).

analyzing test data and refinements in that it permits complex analysis that yields more efficient prediction than do current conventional methods. Specifically, the future use of Bayesian methodology is most promising in predicting outcome behaviors associated with career selection, training, and placement.

A final contribution of computer applications lies in their use in career decision-making. The computer-based program developed by Martin R. Katz—System of Interactive Guidance and Information (SIGI)—is particularly noteworthy.[4] Katz stated that:

> In this guidance system, the student interacts with a computer in such a way to examine and explore his own values, obtain and use relevant information, interpret predictive data, and formulate plans. This interaction helps the student to arrive at tentative career decisions and to modify them as he gains new insights and additional information. The decisions involve both educational and occupational options. Remember, however, that emphasis is not merely on the content of decisions, but on the process of decision-making. As the student progresses through SIGI, he learns to move freely within the structure of the system. In gaining control of the system, he develops competencies and masters strategies for rational behavior in the face of uncertainty—which may be the closest we can get to wisdom.[5]

SIGI, designed initially for use at community and junior colleges, has been field-tested.[6] Results present considerable evidence that it is effective in helping students understand the process of arriving at informed choices.

All these and other developments based on or assisted by computer technology give promise that measurement and assessment practices will be advanced by computer applications. However, as breathtaking as advances in computer technology applied to tests have been and probably will continue to be, it is improbable that the day will come when the computer will replace the well-prepared and experienced counselor or other professional who assists another human being. Poor counselors may be in jeopardy, and rightly so; but competent counselors have nothing to fear. Computer applications of test data are their ally, not their enemy. Competent coun-

---

[4] Martin R. Katz, "Career Decision-Making: A Computer Based System of Interactive Guidance and Information," *Proceedings of the 1973 Invitational Conference on Testing Problems* (Princeton, N.J.: Educational Testing Service, 1974), pp. 43–69.

[5] Katz, "Career Decision-Making," p. 45.

[6] W. Chapman, L. Norris, and M. R. Katz, *SIGI: Report of a Pilot Study Under Field Conditions* (Princeton, N.J.: Educational Testing Service, 1973).

selors will find their work with individuals enhanced by computer applications of measurement and assessment practices.

CONTINUED CONCERN
WITH SEX DIFFERENCES

The extent and significance of sex differences are common subjects of argument and research, much more so than they were during previous decades of development of educational and psychological measurement. The counselor must be constantly aware of the special problems of sex differences in test performances and their implications in interpreting performance in relation to vocational objectives. In particular, generalizations that apply to sex groups per se do not apply necessarily to the particular individual with whom a counselor is working.

Differences in local and general cultural requirements for the sexes may be observed in many situations despite the frequently noted reduction of restrictions for women and the increase in number of activities that are open to both sexes. Counselors must be aware of the dangers involved in accepting common generalizations of measured sex differences. Studies of such inaccurately measured characteristics as emotional responsiveness, neuroticism, dependence, and the gamut of personality characteristics do not demonstrate beyond any reasonable doubt that women, let alone every woman, possess more or less of these characteristics than do men. Even where sex differences seem to have been well established, as, for example, in manipulative skills, the counselor may find a particular individual who varies from the usual pattern. Indeed, the pattern may be reversed completely.

In the recent literature of sex differences, there have been many strained attempts to draw implications out of the findings of observed differences. It has been pointed out frequently that girls reach sexual maturity earlier than boys, but in making interpretations of these observed phenomena, there is a tendency to overlook the fact that many cultural influences tend to offset the effects of actual physical differences. Home training of a particular adolescent may produce behavior that is atypical of his or her sex. It is that particular difference with which the counselor must deal, not the average. In the future, counselors will not neglect the experimentally established differences between the sexes, but they will use them primarily as a base from which to launch their own investigations and observations of a client.

Use of separate sex norms in measurement and counseling materials is permitted only when those materials meet criteria established by the Office of Civil Rights, U.S. Department of Health, Education and Welfare, to implement Title IX (Education amendments of 1972), which became effective July 21, 1975. The criteria specify: (1) "technical information must be developed to provide a rationale for separate scales and/or separate norms by sex to demonstrate that such sex norm separation is essential to the elimination of sex bias"; and (2) "clients must receive scores on both sets of sex norms and the interpretive materials to help them see that there is no activity or occupation that is exclusively male or female."[7] In selecting testing and counseling materials, counselors will have to obtain information concerning these criteria from publishers of test and counseling materials.

INCREASED AND IMPROVED MEASURES
OF EARLY LIFE EXPERIENCES

Tools and techniques designed to assess early life experiences will increase in number and improve in quality. Comprehensive assessment materials and practices for general use with children in nursery school, kindergarten, and first grade will be improved. Young children, like adults, are amazingly diverse in their characteristics and patterns of development. Materials and methods that measure the progress of children during these important years will be designed in context. They will take into account individuals' personal and social traits or characteristics, their cognitive and intellectual development, as well as teaching and learning.

These assessment tools are based on the premise that in growing from infancy to adulthood, each person accumulates a collection of resources or strategies to be used in meeting various kinds of situations. Patterns of temperament dominant in early childhood remain dominant in persons at ages 16, 17, and 18. Such techniques will help individuals explore their temperament, take stock of their resources, and inventory and understand the strategies they have developed for coping with life situations.

---

[7] Reported in the *APGA Guidepost* 19 (July 22, 1976).

CRITERION-REFERENCED TESTS
FOR VOCATIONS

Criterion-referenced tests, now centered largely on mastery of a subject, will extend into the vocational domain. Without question, the most spectacular of recent test changes has been the development of tests that monitor, modify, and assess the effectiveness of certain types of instructional objectives.

By definition, criterion-referenced tests: (1) are built and used to assess carefully prescribed behavioral objectives; (2) are sensitive to changes brought about by interventions; and (3) permit operational classifications of success or mastery. Numerous bothersome semantic problems attend the use of the term *criterion referenced*. R. Glaser and A. J. Nitko suggest that the term *criterion-referenced test* has a different meaning from that suggested by the most prevalent uses of the terms *criterion* or *criterion tests* in the literature of educational and psychological measurement.[8] A criterion-referenced test is not the criterion-related validation mentioned in the *APGA Standards* to demonstrate correlations and prediction. Many have questioned whether the adjective *criterion-referenced* refers to the test, to its purposes, or to its interpretations. W. James Popham and T. R. Husek reported that a criterion-referenced test cannot be distinguished from norm-referenced tests by simple inspection, but that such tests are distinguished by their purpose, construction procedures, specification of information, and generalizability of test performance to domain and use.[9] Admittedly, all these distinctions are a matter of degree.

More and more research is designed to investigate aptitude-situation-treatment-outcome interactions. While the results of most such studies have not been very productive to date, much is being learned. Initial efforts to develop criterion-referenced tests may be seen in the construction, validation, and use of simulated work experiences as a basis for educational and vocational assessment and decision-making. The Program of Education and Career Exploration (PECE) in Georgia is one example of work currently under way in this area.[10] PECE was more of a guidance program than an

---

[8] R. Glaser and A. J. Nitko, "Measurement in Learning and Instruction," in *Educational Measurement*, ed. Robert L. Thorndike (Washington, D.C.: American Council on Education, 1971), pp. 625–670.

[9] W. James Popham and T. R. Husek, "Implications of Criterion-Referenced Measurement," *Journal of Educational Measurement* 6 (Spring 1969): 1–9.

[10] Gene Bottoms and Kenneth B. Matheny, *A Guide for the Development, Implementation, and Administration of Exemplary Programs and Projects in Vocational Education*, project OEG-0-9-207008 (Atlanta, Ga.: Georgia State Department of Education, 1969).

assessment program. Work simulation, however, seems to be an appropriate domain for criterion-referenced approaches to vocational assessment for use in educational and vocational planning and counseling.

CONTINUED USE OF TESTS
IN ACCOUNTABILITY PROCEDURES

Accountability is the ever-present responsibility of school personnel. As Roger T. Lennon suggested, "Accountability . . . is an idea whose time has come—again, or perhaps an idea whose time is always."[11] Simply defined, *accountability* is a set of procedures that collate information about outcomes and costs to facilitate decision-making. It involves the competent discharge of appropriate educational services by professionals. The concept goes beyond the merely perfunctory discharge of duties by educational personnel to incorporate the best possible use of skills and understandings that are appropriate, up-to-date, and acceptable to the profession. A major part of educational accountability is defining objectives, developing practices that enable these objectives to be met, assessing how well they are met, and reporting the outcome to decision-makers and the public.

For many years, most practices in education have been accepted on faith by the profession and by the public. No one knows much about productivity in education, let alone how to improve it. Universal school objectives, such as intellectual development, good citizenship, and self-actualization, are being turned into performance objectives that can be assessed and judged in terms of how well school programs have accomplished what they promised and pursued. Moreover, evidence of the outcome must be made available and reported to the public. Sound reporting practices do much to gain public support and assistance.

Most school personnel regard accountability as an important responsibility. But some object to questions being raised about productivity in education or measurement of its outcomes on the grounds that more precise, systematically collected data will be abused by decision-makers in their allocation of scarce resources. They argue that education will fare best if the enterprise is kept obscure and data about it are hard to derive. Such an argument

---

[11] Roger T. Lennon, "Accountability and Performance Contracting," invited address to the American Educational Research Association, New York City, 1971.

seem incredibly short-sighted; whatever peace such an arrangement achieved would be temporary.

Most objections are not to accountability but to some of the evaluative procedures designed to implement it. Prominent among these evaluative procedures is the use of standardized tests to assess learning or subject outcomes. The emphasis on tests for determining accountability almost inevitably contributes to the misunderstanding and misuse of standardized tests. Many teachers believe that their worth as instructors—indeed, their very job—is at stake in such measurements. Such practices run counter to the efforts that psychologists and counselors have made to convince teachers that they have nothing to fear from tests and that tests help them improve instruction. Accountability has generated more large-scale testing and has revealed a need for public understanding of what tests can and cannot do.

At present, standardized tests do little to respond to the demands for accountability of counselors and other professionals. A counselor's responsibility is to help students use their abilities and develop their uniqueness. The counselor's objectives vary at least to some degree from the classroom teacher's and are likely to be long range. However, tests that maximize individual differences both qualitatively and quantitively are at least partially appropriate, particularly when they are used for formative purposes. An important distinction is to be noted between accountability in terms of product and of process. Assessing product, such as the outcome of being in the third grade for one year, may be accomplished by a fairly straightforward input-output model. But, in assessing process, such as counselor practices, the basic questions about accountability are: What happened? What helped this individual? How did it help? When and where did it succeed (or fail)? Process accountability requires that instruments sensitive to short-range change be used for continuous monitoring of the process or procedures in order to establish cause and effect as directly as possible.

Despite these and other problems, the use of standardized tests in accountability procedures will continue and perhaps increase. Advances in teaching and in understanding the effects of instructional conditions on learning will come if the quality and nature of measures used to assess educational outcomes are improved. Counselors and others involved in accountability procedures must be sensitive to the tendency, now present and likely to increase, to equate the whole of schooling with what is currently measurable, and to describe the entire complex of activities in terms of the indices most readily available and understood. Counselors' sensitivity to this peril must be made evident in the claims and promises they make, and in the seriousness with which they undertake those educational processes not yet well-understood or the efficacy of which they can attest to theoretically but not empirically.

CONTINUED
ETHICAL AND LEGAL PROBLEMS

The collection and use of test data and information contained in student records will continue to be subject to controversy. Across the country, enormous variability exists in the use that is made of tests in schools. No one, including counselors and teachers, appears to know, for example, how much reliance can be placed on test scores in making decisions about students, estimating their capabilities in educational and vocational planning, and adapting teaching techniques to fit individual needs. Another unanswered question is who should have access to a student's record and for what purposes. This issue involves both the rights of school personnel to make use of this information and the rights of the student (and his or her parents) to be protected from indiscriminate use of the information by third parties.

In 1970, the Russell Sage Foundation released a report of a conference it had sponsored on the ethical and legal aspects of record keeping in schools.[12] The report called attention to the absence in most of the nation's schools of any clearly defined and systematically implemented policy regarding uses of information about students, the conditions under which such information is collected, and who may have access to it. The report cited examples of potential (not actual) abuse and suggested that deficiencies in record-keeping policies were a threat to individual privacy. Among recommendations presented by the guidelines were that: (1) representational consent (that given by appointed or elected representatives of the parents, such as boards of education) is sufficient for collecting and recording the results of standardized aptitude and achievement tests, while informed individual consent (the consent of individuals who fully understand what is at issue) should be required for personality testing and assessment; (2) schools should

---

[12] Russell Sage Foundation, *Guidelines for the Collection, Maintenance and Dissemination of Pupil Records* (New York: the Foundation, 1970).

establish procedures to verify the accuracy of all data maintained in students' records; (3) parents should have full access to their children's records, including the right to challenge the accuracy of the information in them; and (4) no agency or person other than school personnel who deal directly with the child should have access to data about a student without parental or student permission (except in case of a subpoena).

The principle that parents should have access to data about their child has been enacted into federal law (the Family Educational Rights and Privacy Act of 1974). The fundamental purpose of the act is to protect the privacy of individuals. Without question, the act is well-intentioned in seeking to control unlimited data collection and careless use and abuse of access to student data. However, the law appears to require disclosure to parents of all personal and confidential information collected by the school, presumably including all written judgments and recommendations. Vivian Stewart Teitelbaum and David A. Goslin suggested that if school data are subject to parental examination, special problems will arise when children reveal things about their parents that may be considered defamatory.[13]

The rights of students require clarification. Do students, under any condition, have the right to prevent their parents from knowing what is in their school records? Some rights of children may have been either overlooked or left unattended in the Privacy Act of 1974. Forcing disclosure to the parent of some kinds of information revealed in confidence by a child to a professional may be damaging to the child.

Many ethical and legal problems will undoubtedly emerge over the next few years about the use of and access to test data and record information. Some issues will not be settled until court decisions are made and precedents established. The Russell Sage guidelines urged that schools enact policies or codes for the definition, operation, maintenance, and disposition of school records. Such policies, particularly if parents, students, and school personnel are involved in their formulation and review, would do much to correct any deficiency in record-keeping practices without unduly hampering conscientious counselors or other professionals.

---

[13] Vivian Stewart Teitelbaum and David A. Goslin, "The Russell Sage Guidelines: Reactions From the Field," *Personnel and Guidance Journal* 50 (December 1974): 311–317.

INCREASED STATE-WIDE TESTING

Some states have a long history of administering state-wide assessment programs. A state-wide testing program is one in which a state educational agency selects tests, specifies target populations, and arranges for the administration, scoring, and reporting of results. In 1958, seventeen states were estimated to be conducting such programs. In 1973, Joan S. Beers reported that the overall impression one gets ". . . is that state assessment plans and programs are currently in a highly fluid state, with new developments occurring daily."[14] She classified the states and territories into three groups. The first group, consisting of seventeen states, collected information for state-wide decisions; the second group, composed of thirteen states, collected information for local decision-making; and the third group, consisting of twenty-four states, was labeled emerging because they had yet to complete a cycle of testing, analyzing, and reporting.

Most state-wide tests are funded by state and federal sources. Many state testing programs measure the influences on learning of such variables as student characteristics, school characteristics, and community characteristics. Because these tests link student performance with school and community factors in order to shed light on differences in accomplishments between groups of students, more and more states probably will develop such programs.

INCREASED USE OF ASSESSMENT
FOR SELF-UNDERSTANDING

Assessment devices—tests, inventories, questionnaires—will increasingly be designed to facilitate self-understanding and personal development. Leo Goldman, among others, has pointed out that testing emerged in response to the need for classifying individuals in order to discover and select talent and to place people in appropriate schools or jobs.[15] While tests are designed to be administered to individuals, these needs require measurement for institutional purposes. The relationship between counseling and current testing, according to Goldman, is that of a marriage that will fail. His

[14] Joan S. Beers, "State-wide Educational Measurement," *State Educational Assessment Programs*, 1973 revision (Princeton, N.J.: Educational Testing Service, 1973), p. 1.
[15] Leo Goldman, "Testing and Counseling: The Marriage That Failed," *Measurement and Evaluation in Guidance* 4 (January 1972): 213–220.

diagnosis was that the relationship has become bankrupt because tests were developed and published primarily for selection rather than for counseling. To save the marriage, he recommended that tests be designed to aid self-exploration and to prescribe remedial activities.

David Campbell, too, has pointed out that, "In the past, test scores have been treated as the property of the institution and most decisions using the scores have been made within the institutional context. The individual was a commodity to be acted upon."[16] Even as more tests and assessment techniques are coming to stress self-understanding and personal development, many complex problems still remain to be solved. Prominent among these problems are faking of answers, the influence of social desirability, the identification and quantification of intrinsic criteria that are substituted for extrinsic criteria, the interplay of affective response tendencies, the quantification of the personal patterns or styles that characterize people, and the need for longitudinal data. Nevertheless, efforts continue to produce assessment devices and techniques that explore the individual. *The Hall Occupational Inventory* is one example.[17] Still others are the card-sort technique developed by Cindy R. Dewey,[18] in which each person constructs his or her own classification system by sorting occupations according to attractive and unattractive features; John L. Holland's *Self Directed Search*,[19] a vocational counseling simulation; Kohlberg's moral dilemmas[20]; Jane Loevinger's ego-development measure[21]; and the inventory of biographical information developed by William A. Owens[22] to find out which of several possible directions a child's progress has taken.

To make self-understanding and personal development a primary rather than a secondary purpose of testing will require major changes in measurement instruments and technology. Such a

---

[16] David P. Campbell, "Interest Tests," *Proceedings of the 1973 Invitational Conference on Testing Problems* (Princeton, N.J.: Educational Testing Service, 1974), p. 9.

[17] L. G. Hall, R. B. Tarrier, and D. L. Shappell, *Counselor's Manual for the Hall Occupational Orientation Inventory*, 2nd ed. (Bensenville, Ill.: Scholastic Testing Service, 1971).

[18] Cindy R. Dewey, "Exploring Interests: A Non-Sexist Method," *Personnel and Guidance Journal* 52 (January 1974): 311–315.

[19] John L. Holland, *Professional Manual for the Self Directed Search* (Palo Alto, Calif.: Consulting Psychologists Press, 1972).

[20] See, for example, J. Rest, "New Approaches in the Assessment of Moral Judgment," in *Moral Development and Behavior Theory Research and Social Issues*, ed., T. Lickons (New York: Holt, Rinehart, and Winston, 1976), pp. 198–218, and J. Rest, D. Cooper, R. Coder, J. Masanz, and D. Anderson, "Judging the Important Issues in Moral Dilemmas: An Objective Measure of Development," *Developmental Psychology* 10, no. 4 (1974): 491–501.

[21] See, for example, Jane Loevinger, "The Meaning and Measurement of Ego Development," *American Psychologist* 21 (March 1966): 195–206; J. Loevinger and K. Wassler, *Measuring Ego Development I: Construction and Use of a Sentence Completion Test* (San Francisco: Jossey-Bass, 1970); and J. Loevinger, *Ego Development* (San Francisco: Jossey-Bass, 1976).

[22] William A. Owens, "A Quasi-actuarial Basis of Individual Assessment," *American Psychologist* 26 (November 1971): 992–999.

change is but in its infancy today. It is an exciting venture and represents a trend highly promising for the work of counselors.

INCREASED MEASUREMENT
OF ENVIRONMENTAL EFFECTS

The most important use of assessments of the environment is to provide information that will benefit individual clients and facilitate institutional change. Environmental assessment assists people in understanding the effect of the environment on them. Quantifying environmental data has been, and will continue to be, a major problem. However, some beginnings toward a solution have already been made. J. Banning and Leland Kaiser have developed an ecosystem model that focuses on individuals' interactions with their environment.[23] They presented a methodology to assess environmental conditions and to design new ones. The quality and impact of the environment are mapped, and the resulting data are used to design contexts from which help for people can be derived.

The emerging area of social ecology studies the positive and negative properties of the environment that contribute substantially to the shaping of behavior. The approach used by Moos, for example, parallels personality assessment.[24] Environments as well as people can be classified as competitive or supportive (in terms of relationships), dependent or autonomous (in terms of personal development), and loose or structured (in terms of orderliness and change). Robert Conyne and E. Harding have developed an Environmental Assessment Inventory to assess periodically and monitor a college environment.[25] The inventory contains four categories of information: (1) personal characteristics and behavior of the campus's inhabitants; (2) ecological dimensions (landscaping, weather conditions, architecture); (3) programs, policies, and procedures; and (4) psychosocial and campus climate (social climates and living situations). The 157 items in the inventory are rated on a seven-point impact scale, and the four categories are rank-ordered to provide a general impression of their relative impact. Personnel of a college

[23] J. Banning and Leland Kaiser, "An Ecological Perspective and Model for Campus Design," *Personnel and Guidance Journal* 52 (February 1974): 370–375.

[24] R. Moos, "Systems for the Assessment and Classification of Human Environments: An Overview," in *Issues in Social Ecology: Human Milieus,* ed., R. Moos and P. Insel (Palo Alto, Calif.: National Press Books, 1974).

[25] Robert K. Conyne and E. Harding, "Environmental Assessment Inventory," unpublished instrument (Bloomington, Ill.: Illinois State University, 1975).

counseling center can use the inventory data to evaluate existing programs, to develop new ones, and to facilitate their consultative efforts aimed at promoting positive interactions.[26]

These and related developments suggest that environmental assessments—long recognized as being needed—will become more sophisticated, common, and useful. Such data provide information critical to individual planning and decision-making as well as in planning changes of certain aspects of the environment.

INCREASED ATTENTION TO ASSESSMENT
IN COUNSELOR EDUCATION

Reforming and updating courses and instructional practices in assessment are needed in many counselor education programs. Emphasis on measurement and assessment practices in such programs has declined markedly during the past ten years. It may be noted that this decreasing emphasis and benign neglect in the preparation of counselors parallel the period of time in which rising criticism was being made of the misuse of test data. The reaction that prevailed in counselor education programs to the charges of test misuse and abuse seemed to be to discount the use of test data by counselors rather than to increase their competencies in testing and assessment. Needless to say, the outcome of such neglect is not promising for the future.

Currently, most counselor education programs require their master's degree students to take a single testing course, usually labeled tests and measurements. All too often, this course is designed to accommodate the needs of students in teacher education. Its primary objective, and rightly so, is that of increasing competence in constructing tests for classroom use and in the use of standardized achievement tests for classification purposes. The use of ability, aptitude, interest, and personality measures by counselors is largely ignored. Furthermore, interpretation techniques, use of non-test devices, and counselor assessment principles and practices are not attended to in such courses because of the demands of time and the areas of specialization of the students in the course. The result is that when such students finally counsel individuals in their initial counseling practicum, they are unprepared and ill-equipped to help those clients who want and need test data for any one of a variety

---

[26] Robert K. Conyne, "Environmental Assessment: Mapping for Counselor Action," *Personnel and Guidance Journal* 54 (November 1975): 150–155.

of reasons. They are unable to select tests that would provide the information needed by the client. Even when their supervisors select such tests, they are unable to interpret the results because of their inexperience and ignorance. As a result, the client is dissatisfied with the service.

In the future, counselor preparation programs will seek to remedy this deficiency by requiring course work that emphasizes testing and assessment practices. Special courses need to be designed to teach the use and interpretation of tests by counselors. Such courses will provide laboratory experience for students, enabling them to become competent in selecting, interpreting, and using commonly applied test and non-test assessment practices.

An outcome of better preparation in assessment practices for counselors is that they will know when test scores can be helpful to their clients. This does not mean that test scores are automatically of central importance in all school counseling situations, but it does mean that test scores can and will provide students and their counselors with a quick and efficient means of examining under controlled conditions certain aspects of previous and current behaviors. Better preparation means that counselors will be more competent in helping students compare their performances on set tasks with other individuals of their own age or grade. Such counselors will understand and act on the fundamental assumption that the use and interpretation of tests can be successful and helpful only when well-established personal relationships exist between counselor and student. In short, counselors in the future will be better prepared to exercise the skill, sensitivity, and maturity of judgment necessary in facilitating personal development, the ultimate goal of counseling.

ANNOTATED REFERENCES

Educational Testing Service. *Measurement for Self-Understanding and Personal Development.* Princeton, N.J.: Educational Testing Service, 1974, 78 pp.

These proceedings of the 1973 invitational conference on testing problems feature presentations by Lawrence Kohlberg, David P. Campbell, Edmund Gordon, Leo Goldman, Martin Katz, and others who built the case that measurement should be designed to facilitate self-understanding. Presenters discuss the products they have constructed.

Tyler, Ralph W., and Wolf, Richard M., eds. *Crucial Issues in Testing.* Berkeley, Calif.: McCutchan, 1974, 170 pp.

This volume, divided into seven parts, presents thirteen papers that examine specific testing issues and their implications, including the testing of minority group members, the selection of students by colleges, grouping students, criterion-referenced testing, and national educational assessment. Current concerns, trends, and growing problems are highlighted in this anthology.

Zytowski, Donald G., ed. *Contemporary Approaches to Interest Measurement*. Minneapolis: University of Minnesota Press, 1973, 251 pp.

The papers presented in this book were originally prepared and given at three workshops held in different parts of the country in order to acquaint participants with interest inventories. The book gives the basic rationale for each inventory and its fundamental characteristics. This source serves as a bridge between the person who uses an inventory and its manual. Case studies illustrate interpretation of the inventories.

SELECTED REFERENCES

Cohen, David K. "Social Accounting in Education: Reflections on Supply and Demand." *Proceedings of the 1970 Invitational Conference on Testing Problems*. Princeton, N.J.: Educational Testing Service, 1971, pp. 129–148.

Conyne, Robert K. "Environmental Assessment: Mapping for Counselor Action." *Personnel and Guidance Journal* 54 (November 1975): 150–155.

Goldman, Leo. "Testing and Counseling: The Marriage that Failed." *Measurement and Evaluation in Guidance* 4 (January 1972): 213–220.

Gooler, Dennis D. "The Development and Use of Education Indicators." *Proceedings of the 1975 ETS Invitational Conference*. Princeton, N.J.: Educational Testing Service, 1976, pp. 11–27.

Katz, Martin R. "Career Decision-Making: A Computer Based System of Interactive Guidance and Information." *Proceedings of the 1973 Invitational Conference on Testing Problems*. Princeton, N.J.: Educational Testing Service, 1974, pp. 43–69.

Kowitz, Gerald T., and Drouberger, Gladys B. "Accountability in Affective Education." *Measurement and Evaluation in Guidance* 9 (January 1977): 200–205.

Noeth, Richard J. "Converting Student Data to Counseling Information." *Measurement and Evaluation in Guidance* 9 (July 1976): 60–69.

Novick, Melvin R. "Bayesian Considerations in Educational Information Systems." *Proceedings of the 1970 Invitational Conference on Testing Problems*. Princeton, N.J.: Educational Testing Service, 1971, pp. 77–88.

Scissons, Edward H. "Computer Administration of the California Psychological Inventory." *Measurement and Evaluation in Guidance* 9 (April 1976): 22–27.

Appendix A   *Glossary of Selected Measurement Terms*

Ability   That which a person can actually do on the basis of current development and training.

Achievement   The degree or level of success attained in a certain area.

Age equivalent   The chronological age for which a specified raw score is the average raw score.

Aptitude   The capacity to acquire a proficiency with training.

Battery   A set of tests standardized on the same sample of persons in order that the results of the separate tests may be comparable; a set of tests administered at the same time to a group of people.

Capacity   Potential ability.

Coefficient of equivalence   A correlation between two forms of a given test administered at the same time.

Coefficient of stability   A correlation between two administrations of the same form of a given test separated by a significant time interval.

Coefficient of temporal equivalence   A correlation between two equivalent forms of a given test with a significant time interval interpolated between administrations of each form of the test.

Concurrent validity   An estimate of test scores' ability to match contemporary measures of real-life criterion performance.

Congruent validity   An estimate of test scores' ability to match contemporary measures obtained from other relevant tests.

Construct validity   An estimate based on a combination of logical and empirical evidence of the relationship between a test and related theory; the end product of an effective total program of test development and evaluation.

Content or curricular validity   An estimate of how well the content of a test samples the criterion about which conclusions are to be drawn.

Correlation coefficient (r)   An estimate of the degree of relationship between two variables or attributes.

Criterion   The variable, comparison with which constitutes a measure of a test's validity; the variable to be predicted by a test.

Cross validation   The process of verifying significant results obtained from the study of one group by a second analysis using data obtained from a second group sampled from the same population.

C-score   A normalized standard score of eleven units in range with a mean of 5.0 and a standard deviation of 2.0.

Decile   One of the nine points that divide a ranked distribution into ten parts, each part containing one-tenth of all cases.

Delta data-marked sensing cards   Marked-sense cards scored by computer on which examinees record their responses with an electrographic pencil.

Derived score   A score that has been converted from the units of one scale into the units of another scale.

Deviation IQ   A standard score with a mean set at 100 and a standard deviation approximating 15 or 16.

Difficulty index   The percentage of examinees in a given group answering an item in the direction keyed.

Digitek answer sheets   Answer sheets processed electronically by the Digitek Optical Test Scoring and Document Scanning System, with answers recorded on one side or both sides of the sheets with an ordinary lead pencil.

Discrimination power   Any one of several statistics used to express the extent to which a test item differentiates between high-scoring and low-scoring examinees.

Docutran answer sheets   Answer sheets scored by a high-speed electronic scanner, which reads both sides of an answer sheet at once and then transcribes the darkest pencil mark in each row of responses onto magnetic tape, from which a high speed printer records scores on report forms.

Equated scores   Derived scores that are comparable from test to test.

Equivalent forms   Two or more forms of a given test, each of which is a representative sample of the population of behaviors intended to be measured by the test; descriptive statistics should be comparable.

Factor analysis   Any one of several complex statistical procedures for analyzing the intercorrelations among a set of test items or test scores for the purpose of identifying those variables that cause the intercorrelations.

Grade equivalent   Derived score that is expressed as the grade level of those examinees for whom a given raw score was average.

Grade-o-mat answer cards   Cards on which responses are circled and later punched out before being scored by a portable IBM machine.

Hankes answer sheets   Special answer sheets designed for scoring by the high-speed electronic equipment of Testscor.

Harbor answer cards   Harcourt, Brace Optical Reading Answer Cards, a card scored by computer on which examinees mark responses with any soft-lead pencil as they would mark answers on conventional answer sheets.

IBM 805 answer sheets   Answer sheets on which responses are marked on one side or both sides with a special electrographic marking pencil and scored by an IBM 805 Test Scoring Machine.

IBM 1230 answer sheets   Sheets on which responses are marked on one side or both sides with an ordinary soft-lead pencil, *not* with a special electrographic pencil, and scored by the high-speed IBM 1230 Optical Mark Scoring Reader.

Intelligence   The capacity thought to be common to all mental behavior.

Intelligence quotient An index of the rate of mental growth up to 16 years of age, expressed as the ratio of a mental age measure to chronological age.

Interest An attitude or feeling that an object or an event is of concern to oneself.

Internal consistency analysis An analysis of data obtained from a single administration of a test; any one of several techniques for estimating consistency of responses among examinees, using knowledge of item analysis data.

Item Any individual task or question on a test.

Item analysis Any one of several methods used in test construction to examine an item empirically; the effectiveness of a test item depends on: (1) the relevance of an item with respect to its content; (2) the power of the item to distinguish among individuals differing in some characteristic; and (3) the frequency with which the keyed response to an item is made by examinees representative of a given population.

Kuder-Richardson formula Any one of several formulas developed by Kuder and Richardson for the estimation of the consistency of responses from one examinee to another.

Mean The most widely used measure of central tendency; equal to the sum of scores divided by the number of examinees.

Mental age A derived score, used on intelligence tests only, which is expressed as the age for which a given performance level is average.

MRC answer sheets Answer sheets scored by MRC's high-speed electronic scanner, which reads both sides of the answer sheet at once and transcribes the darkest pencil mark in each row onto magnetic tape, from which a high-speed printer then records scores on report forms.

NCS answer sheets Special answer sheets scored by the high-speed electronic equipment of the National Computer Systems scoring service; responses are recorded with ordinary soft-lead pencil.

Normal distribution A useful mathematical model representing the distribution expected when an infinite number of scores deviate from the mean only by chance; scores distributed symmetrically about the mean, yielding as many cases at equal distances above the mean as below the mean, with cases concentrated near the mean and decreasing in frequency as cases fall above or below the mean.

Normalized standard scores Any one of several standard scores that are based on a normalized raw score distribution.

Norms A set of specific group-relevant reference data that may be used as the basis for evaluating the performance of a given examinee.

Objective test A test for which the scoring procedure is specified in advance, thereby permitting complete agreement among different scorers.

Percentile Any one of the ninety-nine points along the scale of score values that divide a distribution into one hundred groups of equal frequency.

Personality Outward appearance; the distinguishing qualities of an individual taken as a whole being.

Pin-punch answer pads   Self-scoring answer sheets on which responses are marked by punching a hole with a pin in a sealed two-sheet answer pad; a score is determined by counting the number of holes punched in circles printed on the inside of the pad, which indicate the position of each keyed response.

Population   The total group of interest.

Power test   A maximum-performance test for which speed is not an important score determinant; items increase in difficulty.

Predictive validity   Validity for which life-related criterion measures are obtained after the test has been scored.

Proficiency   Degree of ability already acquired.

Profile   A graphic representation of the performance of an individual on a series of tests, especially the tests in an integrated battery.

Random sample   A sample drawn from a given population in such a way that every member of the population has an equal chance of being included, thus inhibiting sampling bias and enhancing the probability that the sample is representative of the population in question.

Range   The difference between the highest and the lowest scores made on a test by a particular group.

Raw score   The basic score initially obtained from scoring a test according to the directions specified by the author.

Readiness test   A test of a person's ability to engage in a new type of learning.

Reliability   The extent to which a measure is free of random error; the accuracy or precision of a measure; the consistency or stability of a test or other measuring instrument.

Scaled score   Any one of several systems of scores used to articulate different forms, editions, and/or levels of a test.

Scoreze answer sheets   Sealed packages of two sheets divided by a layer of carbon paper: the top sheet, an IBM 805 answer sheet, is marked by the examinee; the responses are imprinted on the inner side of the second sheet, premarked with the keyed responses.

Skill   Efficient performance of a mental or physical task.

Spearman-Brown prophecy formula   A formula designed to estimate the reliability that a measure exhibits if its length is changed and other factors are held constant.

Speed test   A test on which speed of response is an important determinant of the score.

Split-half (form) reliability coefficient   An estimate of the reliability of a test based on the correlation between scores on two equivalent halves of a test.

Standard   A level of performance agreed on by experts as a goal to be attained.

Standard deviation   A statistic used to express an estimate of the extent to which scores in a given distribution deviate from the mean of that distribution.

Standard error of measurement A statistic that estimates the probable deviation between an examinee's true score on a test and the score he or she actually obtained.

Standardized test An empirically developed test, designed for administration and scoring according to stated directions, involving evidence of reliability and validity and norms relevant to the population for whom the test is intended.

Standard score Any one of several derived scores based on the number of standard deviation units between a specified raw score and the mean of the distribution of raw scores.

Stanine A standard score of nine units with a mean of 5.0 and a standard deviation of approximately 2.0.

Sten A standard score of ten units with a mean of 5.0 and a standard deviation of approximately 2.0.

Stratified sample A sample in which cases are selected by the use of certain controls, such as geographical region, community size, socioeconomic status, school, grade, age, and sex.

Test A representative sample of stimuli intended to elicit responses relevant to a given population of human behaviors.

True score An error-free or perfectly reliable score; a theoretical concept never obtainable in practice.

T-score A standard score with a mean of 50 and a standard deviation of 10; also refers to a normalized standard score, the normalized T-score.

Validity The extent to which a test does the job desired of it as evaluated by rational judgment, by data from actual studies, or by both; usually, the extent to which a test predicts some specific life criterion.

Appendix B

Standards for the Use of Tests

The standards in the present volume are to varying degrees directed to all forms of use. As the use of tests moves along a continuum from the description of a single individual, in a situation allowing for corrections of erroneous interpretations, to making decisions about large numbers of people, the test user must apply more of the standards and, perhaps, apply them more rigorously. Such decisions may profoundly influence the lives of those tested, such as decisions for employment or for attendance at college, or decisions to assign a person to one treatment or opportunity rather than to another (e.g., tracking in a school system), or decisions to continue or terminate a program or to regulate its funds. The cost of error, in money and in human suffering, may be great. A test user cannot abdicate the responsibilities described in these standards by subscribing to external testing services or test suppliers.

The standards necessary for using tests for making decisions are not different from the standards necessary when tests are used simply for understanding, but the emphasis within a standard may be different. A test user should be familiar with the standards governing test use in general, and he should pay particular attention to those standards most nearly fitting his own specific type of application.

In doing so, he should realize that the standards are intended to apply, in principle, to all forms of assessment. In choosing from alternative methods of assessment, the test user should consider the differences in the case of applying these standards. . . .

G. *QUALIFICATIONS AND CONCERNS OF USERS* A test user, for the purposes of these standards, is one who chooses tests, interprets scores, or makes decisions based on test scores. He is not necessarily the person who administers the test following standard instructions or who does routine scoring. Within this definition, the basic user qualifications (an elementary knowledge of the literature relating to a particular test or test use) apply particularly when tests are used for decisions, and such uses require additional technical qualifications as well. . . .

G1.   A test user should have a general knowledge of measurement principles and of the limitations of test interpretations. (Essential)

> G1.1   A test user should know his own qualifications and how well they match the qualifications required for the uses of specific tests. (Essential)

G2.   A test user should know and understand the literature relevant to the tests he uses and the testing problems with which he deals. (Very Desirable)

G3.   One who has the responsibility for decisions about individuals or policies that are based on test results should have an understanding of psychological or educational measurement and of validation and other test research. (Essential)

> G3.1   The principal test users within an organization should make every effort to be sure that all those in the organization who are charged with responsibilities related to test use and interpretation (e.g., test administrators) have received training appropriate to those responsibilities. (Essential)
>
> G3.2   Anyone administering a test for decision-making purposes should be competent to administer that test or class of tests. If not qualified, he should seek the necessary training regardless of his educational attainments. (Essential)

G4.   Test users should seek to avoid bias in test selection, administration, and interpretation; they should try to avoid even the appearance of discriminatory practice. (Essential)

G5.   Institutional test users should establish procedures for periodic internal review of test use. (Essential)

H.   CHOICE OR DEVELOPMENT OF TEST OR METHOD

H1.   The choice or development of tests, test batteries, or other assessment procedures should be based on clearly formulated goals and hypotheses. (Essential)

> H1.2   The test user should consider the possibility that different hypotheses may be appropriate for people from different populations. (Essential)

H2.   A test user should consider more than one variable for assessment and the assessment of any given variable by more than one method. (Essential)

> H2.1   In choosing a method of assessment, a test user should consider his own degree of experience with it and also the prior experience of the test taker. (Essential)

H3.   In choosing an existing test, a test user should relate its history of research and development to his intended use of the instrument. (Essential)

H4.   In general a test user should try to choose or to develop an assessment technique in which "tester-effect" is minimized, or in which reliability of assessment across testers can be assured. (Essential)

H5.   Test scores used for selection or other administrative decisions about an individual may not be useful for individual or program evaluation and vice versa. (Desirable)

I.   ADMINISTRATION AND SCORING   A test user may delegate to someone else the actual task of administering or scoring tests, but he retains the responsibility for these activities. In particular, he has the responsibility for ascertaining the qualifications of such agents. Standards for administration apply not only to the act of testing but also to more general matters of test administration. The basic principle is standardization; when decisions are based on test scores, the decision for each individual should be based on data obtained under circumstances that are essentially alike for all.

I1.   A test user is expected to follow carefully the standardized procedures described in the manual for administering a test. (Essential)

I1.1   A test user must fully understand the administrative procedures to be followed. (Essential)

I1.3   A test user should make periodic checks on material, equipment, and procedures to maintain standardization. (Essential)

I2.   The test administrator is responsible for establishing conditions, consistent with the principle of standardization, that enable each examinee to do his best. (Essential)

I3.   A test user is responsible for accuracy in scoring, checking, coding, or recording test results. (Essential)

I3.1   When test scoring equipment is used, the test user should insist on evidence of its accuracy; when feasible, he should make spot checks against hand scoring or develop some other system of quality control. (Essential)

I4.   If specific cutting scores are to be used as a basis for decisions, a test user should have a rationale, justification, or explanation of the cutting scores adopted. (Essential)

I4.1.1   If examinees are to be selected on the basis of a set of scores that displays different regression lines for use in predicting the same criterion in different subgroups of an applicant population, cutting scores should be established with great caution to avoid unfairness to members of one or more of the subgroups. (Essential)

I5.   The test user shares with the test developer or distributor a responsibility for maintaining test security. (Essential)

I5.2   All reasonable precautions should be taken to safeguard test material. (Essential)

J.   INTERPRETATION OF SCORES

J1.   A test score should be interpreted as an estimate of performance under a given set of circumstances. It should not be interpreted as some absolute characteristic of the examinee or as something permanent and generalizable to all other circumstances. (Essential)

J1.1 A test user should consider the total context of testing in interpreting an obtained score before making any decisions (including the decision to accept the score). (Essential)

J2. Test scores should ordinarily be reported only to people who are qualified to interpret them. If scores are reported, they should be accompanied by explanations sufficient for the recipient to interpret them correctly.

J2.2 A system of reporting test results should provide interpretations. (Essential)

J3. The test user should recognize that estimates of reliability do not indicate criterion-related validity. (Essential)

J4. A test user should examine carefully the rationale and validity of computer-based interpretations of test scores. (Essential)

J5. In norm-referenced interpretations, a test user should interpret an obtained score with reference to sets of norms appropriate for the individual tested and for the intended use. (Essential)

J5.1 It is usually better to interpret scores with reference to a specified norms group in terms of percentile ranks or standard scores than to use terms like IQ or grade equivalents that may falsely imply a fully representative or national norms group. (Essential)

J5.2 Test users should avoid the use of terms such as IQ, IQ equivalent, or grade equivalent where other terms provide more meaningful interpretations of a score. (Essential)

J5.3 A test user should examine differences between characteristics of a person tested and those of the population on whom the test was developed or norms developed. His responsibility includes deciding whether the differences are so great that the test should not be used for that person. (Essential)

J6. Any content-referenced interpretation should clearly indicate the domain to which one can generalize. (Essential)

J7. The test user should consider alternative interpretations of a given score. (Essential)

J8. The test user should be able to interpret test performance relative to other measures. (Very Desirable)

J9. A test user should develop procedures for systematically eliminating from data files test-score information that has, because of the lapse of time, become obsolete. (Essential)

Appendix C   Names and Addresses of Representative Test Publishers

The American College Testing Program
P.O. Box 168
Iowa City, Iowa 52240

CTB/McGraw-Hill
Del Monte Research Park
Monterey, California 93940

Consulting Psychologist Press, Inc.
557 College Avenue
Palo Alto, California 94306

Cooperative Tests & Services Division
Addison-Wesley Testing Service
South Street
Reading, Massachusetts 01867

Educational and Industrial Testing Service
P.O. Box 7234
San Diego, California 92107

Educational Testing Service
Princeton, New Jersey 08540

Harcourt Brace Jovanovich, Inc.
757 Third Avenue
New York, New York 10017

Houghton Mifflin Company
One Beacon Street
Boston, Massachusetts 02107

Institute of Personality and Ability Testing
1602 Coronado Drive
Champaign, Illinois 61820

Ohio College Association
1945 North High Street
Columbus, Ohio 43210

Personnel Press, Inc.
20 Nassau Street
Princeton, New Jersey 08540

The Psychological Corporation
757 Third Avenue
New York, New York, 10017

Science Research Associates, Inc.
259 East Erie Street
Chicago, Illinois 60611

Sheridan Psychological Services, Inc.
P.O. Box 6101
Orange, California 92267

Stanford Press
Palo Alto, California 94301

Appendix D   Test Scoring Services

TEST SCORING SERVICE	TESTS SCORED
American College Testing Program P.O. Box 168 Iowa City, Iowa 52240	*American College Testing Program Examination*
California Test Bureau Del Monte Research Park Monterey, California 93940	*California Achievement Tests* *California Test of Basic Skills* *California Tests of Mental Maturity*
Dela Data Scoring Service P.O. Box 127 Pinole, California 94306	*Strong-Campbell Interest Inventory* *Strong Vocational Interest Blanks*

Educational Testing Service
Princeton, New Jersey 08540
  College Entrance
  Examination Board
	Achievement Tests
	Preliminary Scholastic Aptitude Test
	Scholastic Aptitude Test

National Guidance Testing Program	*School and College Ability Tests* *Sequential Tests of Educational Progress*
Harcourt Brace Jovanovich, Inc. (Psychological Corporation) Test Department 757 Third Avenue New York, New York 10017	*Academic Promise Test* *Differential Aptitude Tests* *Metropolitan Achievement Tests* *Metropolitan Readiness Tests* *Otis-Lennon Ability Tests* *Stanford Achievement Test*
Houghton Mifflin Scoring Service Box 30 Iowa City, Iowa 52240	*Henmon-Nelson Tests of Mental Ability* (revised edition) *Iowa Tests of Basic Skills* *Lorge-Thorndike Intelligence Tests* *Tests of Academic Progress*

Measurement Research Center
(MRC)
321 Market Street
Iowa City, Iowa 52240

*American College Testing
Program Examination*
Differential Aptitude Tests
*Henmon-Nelson Tests of Mental
Ability* (revised edition)
Iowa Tests of Basic Skills
*Iowa Tests of Educational
Development*
*Lorge-Thorndike Intelligence
Tests*
Metropolitan Achievement Tests
*Minnesota Vocational Interest
Inventory*
*National Merit Scholarship
Qualifying Examination*
Otis-Lennon Ability Tests
Stanford Achievement Test
*Strong-Campbell Interest
Inventory*
Strong Vocational Interest Blanks
Tests of Academic Progress

National Computer Systems, Inc.
1015 South Sixth Street
Minneapolis, Minnesota 55404

California Achievement Tests
California Psychology Inventory
*California Short-Form Tests of
Mental Maturity*
California Test of Basic Skills
*Cooperative School and College
Ability Tests*
*Edwards Personal Preference
Schedule*
*Minnesota Multiphasic
Personality Inventory*
*Minnesota Vocational Interest
Inventory*
*Sequential Tests of Educational
Progress*
*Sixteen Personality Factor
Questionnaire*
*Strong-Campbell Interest
Inventory*
Strong Vocational Interest Blanks

Ohio College Association
1945 North High Street
Columbus, Ohio 43210

*Ohio State University
Psychological Examination*

Personnel Press Scoring Service
20 Nassau Street
Princeton, New Jersey 08540

*Kuhlmann-Anderson Measure of
Academic Potential*

Science Research Associates, Inc.
Electronic Scoring Service
259 East Erie Street
Chicago, Illinois 60611

*Iowa Tests of Educational
Development
Kuder Occupational Interest
Survey, Form DD
National Merit Scholarship
Qualifying Examination
Primary Mental Abilities
SRA Achievement Series*

Testscor
2312 Snelling Avenue
Minneapolis, Minnesota 55404

*Minnesota Multiphasic
Personality Inventory
Strong-Campbell Interest
Inventory
Strong Vocational Interest Blanks*

Appendix E   Test Evaluation Form

Name of appraiser _____

Date of appraisal _____

School _____

Name of test _____

Type of test _____

Age and grade levels _____

Date of publication _____

Name and address of publisher _____

_____

_____

	Does not apply for this type of test	Sufficiently covered	Included, but poorly covered	Excessive data hides essential data	Not included
	1	2	3	4	5
A. Dissemination of Information					
1. A detailed test manual is provided.					
2. The manual is up to date.					
3. Manual copyright date and revision dates are clearly indicated.					
Comments: _____					
_____					
B. Interpretation					
1. Test manual, record forms & other accompanying material assist correct interpretation of test results.					
2. Manual states explicitly the purposes & applications for which test is recommended.					
3. Professional qualifications required for administration and interpretation are given.					
4. In revised editions, nature & extent of the revision & the comparability of data for the revised & the old test are stated explicitly.					
5. Manual presents quantitative data to support implied relationships.					

	1	2	3	4	5
6. When the term "significant" is employed, manual makes clear whether statistical or practical significance is meant.					
7. Manual clearly differentiates between an interpretation for a group as a whole and the application of such an interpretation for individuals.					
Comments: _____					
C. *Validity*					
1. Types of validity are stated clearly.					
2. Validity indices stated indicate that the test measures what it purports to measure.					
3. Criteria for validity are defined clearly.					
4. Date validation data were gathered is reported.					
5. Test scores used in validation are determined independently of criterion scores.					
6. Manual gives specific warning in regard to margins of error in interpretation.					
7. The validation samples are sufficiently described for the user to know whether the persons tested may be regarded properly as represented in the sample.					
8. Manual gives clear description of diagnostic categories.					
9. Manual reports number of cases in validation samples.					
10. Appropriate measures of central tendency, variability, & standard errors of estimate for all computations are reported for the validation samples.					
11. Differentiation is made in validity between subgroups & the total validation sample.					
12. Validity of predictions are estimated separately at different age, sex, racial & mental ability levels.					
13. Reports of validation studies describe all conditions likely to effect motivation of subjects taking the test.					
14. Manual reports all available information that will assist the user in determining what psychological attributes account for variance in test scores.					

	1	2	3	4	5
15. Manual reports correlations of the test with other previously published & generally accepted measures of the same attributes.					
Comments: _____					
_____					
D. Reliability					
1. Manual reports such evidence of reliability as would permit the reader to judge whether scores are sufficiently dependable for the recommended uses of the test.					
2. Manual notes the absence of necessary evidence of reliability.					
3. Manual cautions user against interpreting profiles or score differences if the reliability of these differences between an individual's scores is low.					
4. Results of reliability studies are quantitatively expressed.					
5. Manual reports reliability for various age, sex, racial groups and mental ability levels at which the test is given.					
6. Manual avoids any implication that reliability measures demonstrate the predictive or concurrent validity of the test.					
7. Reports of reliability, procedures, and samples are described sufficiently to judge whether the evidence applies to the persons and problems being assessed.					
D_1. *Equivalence of Forms*					
1. If two forms of a test are made available, with both forms intended for possible use with the same subjects, the correlation between forms and information as to the equivalence of scores on the two forms are reported.					
2. Manual warns user against assuming comparability when necessary evidence is not provided.					
3. When two forms of a test are correlated to determine equivalence, the time between testings is stated.					
D_2. *Internal Consistency*					
1. If the manual suggests that a score is a measure of a generalized, homogeneous trait, evidence of internal consistency is reported.					

	1	2	3	4	5

2. When a test consists of separately scored parts or sections, the correlations between the parts or sections are reported.
3. Coefficients of internal consistency are determined by the split-half methods or methods of the Kuder-Richardson type, if these methods can be applied.

D₃ *Stability*
1. Manual indicates the degree of stability expected when scores are repeated after time has elapsed.
2. Manual warns against assuming stability when such evidence is not presented.

Comments: _____

_____

E. *Administration and Scoring*
1. Directions for test administration are clearly presented.
2. Where subjective processes enter into the scoring of a test, evidence on degree of agreement between independent scoring is presented.

Comments: _____

_____

F. *Scales and Norms*
1. Scales used for reporting scores are presented so as to increase the likelihood of accurate interpretation and emphasis.
2. Standard scores are used rather than other derived scores.
3. Local norms are available along with comparative data on the national level.
4. Manual indicates amount of emphasis on local norms for accurate interpretation.
5. Norms refer to a clearly defined population.
6. Manual reports the method of population sampling.
7. Number of cases on which norms are based is reported.
8. Manual reports whether scores differ for groups differing in age, sex, amount of training, and other equally important variables.
9. Profile sheets or other appropriate means of recording and interpreting test scores are provided.

	1	2	3	4	5
10. The curve of the normalizing sample is sufficiently complete and normal so that test scores may be interpreted on the basis of normal distribution.* Comments: _____ _____ _____					

* For additional information on technical requirements regarding test construction and evaluation, see "Technical Recommendations for Psychological Tests and Diagnostic Techniques" prepared by a joint committee of the American Psychological Association, American Educational Research Association, and the National Council on Measurements Used in Education, 1974.

Index
of Names

Index
of Subjects